The Valuation of Digital Intangibles

Roberto Moro-Visconti

The Valuation
of Digital Intangibles

Technology, Marketing, and the Metaverse

Second Edition

Roberto Moro-Visconti
Catholic University
of the Sacred Heart
Milan, Italy

ISBN 978-3-031-09236-7   ISBN 978-3-031-09237-4   (eBook)
https://doi.org/10.1007/978-3-031-09237-4

This Palgrave Macmillan imprint is published by the registered company Springer Nature
Switzerland AG
The registered company address is: Gewerbestrasse 11, 6330 Cham, Switzerland

Contents

LIST OF FIGURES

LIST OF TABLES

CHAPTER 1

Introduction

An intangible is a non-monetary asset that manifests itself by its economic properties. It does not have physical substance but grants rights and economic benefits to its owner.

Intangibles are the core component of modern competitive advantage that expresses the leverage of a business over its competitors. According to Michael Porter, firms can achieve a competitive edge with a cost or differentiation advantage. Intangibles play a crucial role in both strategies, bringing cost savings (with know-how, patents, etc.) or differentiation (using brands, etc.), and fostering a structural shift in business models.

This traditional value driver has been amplified by a new generation of Internet-related intangibles, driven by the growth of the service economy and the digital explosion. The digital revolution reshapes traditional intangibles and creates new ones:

- Digital brands are indissolubly linked to their web domains;
- Know-how and patents follow product and process innovation fueled by artificial intelligence and blockchains;
- Networks become social through their digital platforms, using M-Apps to access the web;
- Technological startups ignite the creation and marketing of innovation and frontier applications, fully reengineering old-fashioned business models;

R. Moro-Visconti, *The Valuation of Digital Intangibles,* https://doi.org/10.1007/978-3-031-09237-4_1

- The information has become a worthy asset, nurtured by big data and Internet of Things sensors;
- Interoperable databases share and recombine information in real-time, adding up value;

Digital applications are to this century what oil represented for the past one: a driver of growth, wealth, and change.

The digital economy shows unprecedented opportunities but also unconventional threats, represented by cyber-crimes, monopolistic rents of tech giants, and disruption of many "analogic" jobs. Even the expression "digital" may have different meanings, since it may refer either to an IT world or—in Botanics—to *digitalis purpurea* (commonly called foxgloves), an attractive but poisonous plant.

Digital intangibles are typically embedded in catching up with traditional firms or innovative startups. The valuation framework may so conveniently start from the standard valuation approaches of the firm, and then incorporate intangibles in a more comprehensive appraisal.

In general terms, the accounting treatment of the intangibles remains controversial, and their capitalization is typically prohibited for reasons of prudence. This may bring to an underestimation of the book value of intangible-intensive firms.

Intangibles are more specific than other assets and incorporate higher information asymmetries, linked to higher risk profiles and lower collateral value. Intangible assets are usually hard to evaluate, and according to the International Valuation Standard 210, they can be appraised using:

(a) An income approach (present value of income, cash flows, or cost savings attributable to the intangible asset over its economic life);
(b) A market approach, concerning market activity (for example, transactions involving identical or similar assets);
(c) A cost approach (replacement cost of a similar asset or an asset providing comparable service potential or utility).

This book innovatively combines classic aspects of traditional intangibles (like patents or trademarks) with trendy immaterial assets and processes (like big data, IoT, artificial intelligence, blockchains, social networks, etc.). Hard-to-value intangibles are those that have the potential to create cash flows in the future but do not right now and may concern undeveloped patents or real options (to expand, abandon, suspend a business) or product and process innovation (like the impact of blockchains on digital supply chains).

Twenty-four chapters describe these complementary topics. They start from some general issues that concern the primary valuation approaches (Chapter 2), considering the value drivers embedded in digital scalability and intangible-driven growth options (Chapter 3).

The value drivers incorporated in the intangibles are the result of their characteristics, such as scalability (the ability to grow exponentially and fast) or non-rivalry (intangibles may be simultaneously used by an unlimited number of customers, with no marginal extra costs).

Technological intangibles are mainly represented by know-how (to do it), a broad concept examined in Chapter 4 that embraces industrial secrets that in most cases intentionally remain unpatented. Unlike patents, the know-how is not independently negotiable and is more difficult to enforce against third parties. At the same time, it retains some characteristics of confidentiality that with the patenting in part must be disclosed.

Patents (analyzed in Chapter 5) are the result of risky and costly R&D, and the developer will try to recover its costs (and earn a return) through the sale of products covered by the patent. Patents are typically valued for litigation or licensing purposes.

Innovative startups and FinTechs (investigated in Chapter 6) are newly formed companies with high-growth potential, which usually absorb a lot of liquidity in the early years of life, to finance development, against minimal collateralizable assets. This is unattractive for traditional banking intermediaries, usually replaced by other specialized intermediaries such as venture capital or private equity funds, or business angels and crowdfunding at earlier stages. The technological footprint implies evaluation analogies with patents, know-how, and intangibles linked to specific sectors (biomedical, internet, etc.).

A versatile intangible that has technological and web-based features is represented by software and database (examined in Chapter 7), generally understood as a sequence of computer instructions for performing functions on devices such as hardware.

Software and its sequential algorithms are the engines behind artificial intelligence (A.I.) A.I. (analyzed in Chapter 8) allows us to think and act humanly and rationally through hardware systems and software programs capable of providing performances that, to an ordinary observer, would seem to be the exclusive domain of natural (human) intelligence. The applications are more and more extensive, thanks also to the presence of big data available today and the ability of self-learning (machine learning) or instead to the synergies with the natural intelligence, which for vision, empathy, and flexibility remains irreplaceable.

Marketing intangibles are primarily represented by trademarks, illustrated in Chapter 9. Trademarks (brands) are intangibles that represent distinctive characters (with originality, truthfulness, novelty, and lawfulness as requirements) that identify a good of which they represent quality, provenience, and distinctive capacity. The surplus value that the trademark confers on a product (compared to an unmarked equivalent) is an expression of the value of this classic intangible asset, which can be exploited internally or licensed.

Digital brands represent an informatic extension of the trademarks operating on Internet platforms and connected to other intangibles such as domain names.

A peculiar intangible is represented by newspaper headings, digital media, and copyright issues (examined in Chapter 10), whose value is mainly driven by advertising revenues, increasingly digitized. Digital copyright is another extension of a classic intangible through the Internet. The virality of texts, photos, music, or videos is enhanced by trendy social networks.

Domain names (considered in Chapter 11) represent the gateway to Internet connections and access to specific websites. They may be considered the "web appendix" of trademarks, and their value depends on several parameters, such as Web traffic or search engines, and is typically calculated with "quick and dirty" algorithms freely available on the Web. The value of a web domain depends on its capacity to attract traffic, i.e., visitors, and to transform them into cash-generating customers. A more detailed appraisal should consider not only the stand-alone value of a domain name, but rather its synergies with collateral intangibles such as websites, digital brands, or M-Apps.

M(obile)-Apps (analyzed in Chapter 12) are programs used by mobile devices (smartphones, tablets, smartwatch …), now widespread, for various uses (system operation, chat, games, social networks, geolocation, e-commerce …), available for download on unique digital platforms (store). They represent the "iconic" shortcut for accessing the web.

Big data (examined in Chapter 13) consists of the computerized collection of vast amounts of data, processed with algorithms in sequential software, to be classified and stored to feed interoperable databases and decision-making processes. Data are an increasingly worthy asset, and they reduce information asymmetries.

The Internet of things (as shown in Chapter 14) is based on technologies that transform "inanimate" objects, equipped with sensors that collect and exchange data; in other words, it consists of a set of connected devices. The connectivity between objects, the network-web (as a virtual exchange platform), and the intangible, represents a driver of value creation, through product and process innovations.

IoT fuels big data and improves the informative valuation contents of the intangibles, through artificial intelligence applications nurtured by interoperable databases stored in the cloud, and validated through blockchains.

Internet companies (considered in Chapter 15) are Internet access providers for consumers. Social networks consist of social platforms on the Internet developed as free mass media, where users can present themselves to a broad audience, creating virtual communities that share the content of various kinds. The attribution of economic value for social networks is complicated, since most of the value resides in the users, in the number and quality of connections, and in the network effect that results.

A more general framework is represented by network theory, dedicated to the study of the links among interacting nodes. The Internet and the web represent a paradigmatic case of a digital network.

A puzzling challenge for evaluators is represented by blockchains (analyzed in Chapter 16), whose exponential growth is increasingly detached from controversial cryptocurrencies. The blockchain is a decentralized and distributed digital ledger. It consists of an open database with a pattern of sharable and unmodifiable data that are sequenced in chronological order. Blockchain technology can be used for e-commerce, for the recording of copyright data, or to track digital access.

The valuation shares similarities with other digital intangibles (database, Internet of Things, big data, etc.) and is primarily founded on the cost savings that derive from the use of blockchains.

Cryptocurrencies, Non-Fungible Tokens (NFT), and digital art derive from blockchain technology and are examined in Chapter 17.

Chapter 18 is dedicated to Internet 2.0. evolution, represented by the metaverse—a still unstable reality, with trendy 3D applications that bring to augmented and virtual reality.

Cloud storage is by now a dominating outsourcing solution, described in Chapter 19.

Digital platforms and virtual marketplaces are examined in Chapter 20, together with their valuation patterns.

Valuation concerns regard digital goodwill (examined in Chapter 21), still a conundrum for accountants, afraid of internally generated extra value that can be estimated but not accounted for. The economic valuation of goodwill is based on an interdisciplinary approach that synergistically considers the legal, accounting, fiscal, and strategic aspects. Goodwill (or badwill, if negative) is a residual intangible, intrinsically linked to unattributed value drivers.

The synergistic attitudes of "plastic" intangibles, easy to deform, adapt and combine, are evident whenever appraising the IP portfolio of bundled immaterial assets, as shown in Chapter 22.

ESG-driven valuation perspectives, induced by digitalization, are examined in Chapter 23.

A trendy dilemma is debated in Chapter 24, where bankability issues are addressed. The puzzle is based on a paradox: on the one hand, intangible assets have limited collateral value for lending banks when the company is in difficulty. On a complementary side, they, however, represent a fundamental element of competitive advantage primarily targeted at debt servicing through liquidity generation.

* * *

Any firm can be innovatively interpreted with network theory (examined in Chapter 15), considering them as a node that is linked to other nodes (external stakeholders, etc.) through connecting edges. This structure also applies to this book, where each chapter is connected to the others, as graphically shown in the following representation (Fig. 1.1).

* * *

Any digital comment may be sent to roberto.moro@unicatt.it or by visiting www.morovisconti.com/en.

Milan, Italy, Università Cattolica del Sacro Cuore, September, 2022.

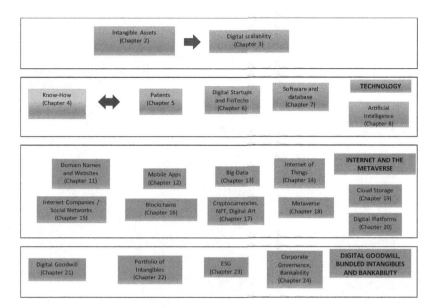

Fig. 1.1 Structure of the book

PART I

A General Valuation Approach

CHAPTER 2

The Valuation of Intangible Assets: An Introduction

2.1 PURPOSE OF THE FIRM EVALUATION

The firm evaluation represents a preliminary step for the assessment of the intangibles that it incorporates. The intangibles, consequently, incorporate the digital assets, as shown in Fig. 2.1.

The value of a company is primarily the result of a series of factors, including:

- Net assets, i.e., all the funds contributed by the partners to finance the business activity;
- Ability to generate income, i.e., the ability to produce positive income flows;
- Financial capacity.

The attitude of the net assets to produce income depends on the quality of the means of production and the entrepreneurial capacity. This last circumstance allows understanding the presence of profoundly different profit margins between companies operating in the same sector. Under ideal conditions, the subjective "value" must tend to coincide with an objective "price" at the negotiation stage.

Value is estimated from the application of one or more valuation criteria, chosen concerning the type of corporate transaction, the identity

R. Moro-Visconti, *The Valuation of Digital Intangibles*, https://doi.org/10.1007/978-3-031-09237-4_2

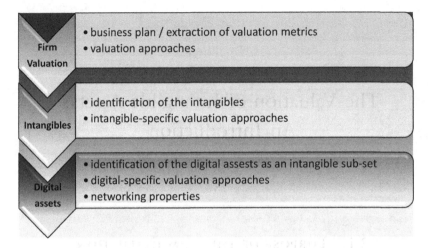

Fig. 2.1 From the valuation of the firm to the estimate of the intangibles and digital assets

of the parties involved, and the activity of the firm. It is ideally independent of the contractual strength of the parties and other subjective factors.

The price is the meeting point of expectations and benefits formulated by the supply and demand involved in the negotiation of the company. A firm can be evaluated, among other things:

1. With a view to trade (transaction purposes);

    • Purchases/sales of shareholdings (the underlying company is valued), companies or business units;
    • Extraordinary financial transactions (relating to the company/branch of business), M&A, demergers, contributions, disposals, transformations, securitization …;

2. For litigation (e.g., compute damage awards in an infringement lawsuit);
3. For arbitration or similar proceedings;
4. For bankruptcy (valuation is required by the Court to dispose of the assets properly, and pay back creditors);

5. Because of changes in the equity:

- Issue of shares (excluding pre-emptive rights; with share premium ...);
- Issue of convertible bonds;
- Issue of warrants;
- Linked to extraordinary operations (transfers, transformations, mergers, contributions, demergers, etc.);

6. With a view to the purchase of assets by the founding partners;
7. To provide guarantees;
8. For listing on the Stock Exchange (IPO);
9. For "internal" cognitive purposes (financial reporting, etc.);
10. For the evaluation of the withdrawal of the shareholder.

The main approaches for estimating the market value of companies are different and can be divided into empirical and analytical approaches.

Empirical approaches are based on the practical observation of market prices of assets that are sufficiently similar and, as such, comparable.

Analytical approaches, on the other hand, have a more solid scientific basis and a more significant tradition in the professional sphere and are based on a revenue-financial approach, to estimate what an asset is worth today based on expected future returns or an estimate of the costs incurred for its reproduction/replacement.

The main approaches to evaluating companies commonly used in practice are:

- The balance sheet-based approach, simple or complex;
- The income approach;
- The mixed capital-income approach;
- The financial approach;
- Market approaches and valuation through multiples.

The central element in determining the value of a firm is the estimate of its future ability to generate an income or financial flow capable of adequately rewarding its shareholders after debt service.

Among the approaches used by operators to identify the market value of the firm, the financial and income approaches are the most appropriate to represent the expected fair remuneration of shareholders.

While the balance sheet-based approach values tangible and intangible resources summing up the values of individual assets, the income, and financial approaches consider them as comprehensive elements able to participate in the context of the entire set of factors for the creation of value. The firm's market value is the result of the interaction of internal variables relating to its tangible and intangible assets and external variables relating to the market. The combined consideration of both makes it possible to estimate the Firm's future results and to assess its risk.

Recent valuation trends have led to the use of two approaches: the financial approach based on the estimate of discounted operating cash flows at the weighted average cost of capital (WACC) and the market approach based on the EBITDA multipliers of comparable companies. In both cases, the enterprise value (value of the firm, including debt) is estimated, and is then algebraically added to the net financial position to arrive at the residual equity value.

In the evaluation of the intangibles, "*distinctions are sometimes made between trade intangibles and marketing intangibles, between 'soft' intangibles and 'hard' intangibles, between routine and non-routine intangibles, and between other classes and categories of intangibles*" (OECD, 2017).

The choice of the correct approach and parameters depends on a bottom-up analysis of the business plan of the target firm (Moro Visconti, 2019). This helps in the estimate of trendy parameters (operating and net cash flows; economic margins, etc.) and in the functional analysis that eases the selection of comparable firms.

The functional analysis is traditionally used for transfer pricing purposes (OECD, 2017). It analyzes the functions performed (considering assets used and risks assumed) by associated firms in a transaction, providing an overview of value creation within the supply chain (Fig. 2.2). Business model and SWOT analysis influence functional analysis.

2.2   Digital Business Modeling
and Planning as a Prerequisite for Valuation

Business planning follows a typical managerial top-down approach where management-prepared forecasts and projections are conceived within the firm and occasionally compared with market returns. The increasing availability of timely big data, sometimes fueled by the Internet of Things (IoT) devices, allows receiving continuous feedbacks that can be conveniently used to refresh assumptions and forecasts, using a complementary

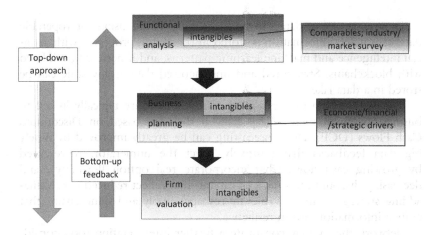

Fig. 2.2 Functional analysis, business planning, and firm valuation

bottom-up approach. Top-down and bottom-up are both strategies of information processing and knowledge ordering.

Optimal business planning using the firm's data is part of business intelligence strategies (Grossmann and Rinderle-Ma, 2015)—a procedural and technical infrastructure that collects, stores, and analyzes the data produced by a company's activities, encompassing data mining, process analysis, performance benchmarking, and descriptive analytics.

Forecasting accuracy can be substantially improved by incorporating timely empirical evidence, with a consequent reduction of both information asymmetries and the risk of facing unexpected events, concerning the magnitude of their impact. Since risk is represented by the difference between expected and real events, if occurrences are timely incorporated in expectations, this differential is minimized. This intuitive concept is well-known, but its practical implications are amplified by the unprecedented presence of big data.

Bottom-up feedbacks fed by IoT, and big data can also readdress real-time strategies, incorporating in the business model forecast value-adding real options that increase its resilience.

The passage from deterministic to stochastic scenarios may also add up further flexibility, extending the probabilistic outcomes that may undergo periodical (ideally constant) updating.

Treatment of big data can be further improved using interoperable databases where information is stored in the cloud, processed with artificial intelligence and machine learning patterns, and if necessary, validated with blockchains. Structured and unstructured data at any scale can be stored in a data lake.

Valuation criteria of the project or investment are typically linked to business planning metrics, especially if they are based on Discounted Cash Flows (DCF). DCF forecasting can be greatly improved by timely big data feedbacks that positively affect the numerator, represented by growing cash flows (that incorporate real option flexibility), and decreasing discount rates (cost of capital) that reflect reduced risk. Value-adding strategies can conveniently reshape supply and value chains that embed information-driven resilience.

Network theory may constitute a further interpretation tool, considering the interaction of nodes represented by IoT and big data, mastering digital platforms, and physical stakeholders (shareholders, managers, clients, suppliers, lenders, etc.). Artificial intelligence, database interoperability, and blockchain applications are consistent with the networking interpretation of the interaction of physical and virtual nodes.

The interaction of big data with traditional budgeting patterns creates flexible (real) options nurtured by a networked digital ecosystem, eventually bringing to augmented business planning.

Augmented reality (AR) is the real-time use of information in the form of text, graphics, audio, and other virtual enhancements integrated with real-world objects. It is this "real-world" element that differentiates AR from virtual reality (both are used in the metaverse). AR integrates and adds value to the user's interaction with the real world, versus a simulation (Gartner glossary).

Consistently with this background, this chapter deals with the analysis of big data-driven input factors on business plan forecasting, showing that if incorporates value-adding growth options, it becomes "augmented".

The flow chart of the sequential passages that start from bottom-up data and then impact on business planning, making it "augmented", is composed of these steps:

1. The empirical evidence that provides massive information is represented by the ecosystem—a network of interconnecting and interacting parts—where the firm is located. This networked ecosystem is levered by digitalization that transforms into IT data any useful

information, fostering its computational use (and so making valuation easier); the ecosystem is also consistent with personalization, for instance concerning ESG sustainability goals;

2. "Small" data, fueled by IoT or any other physical or digital source, are collected in the ecosystem, and their massive gathering makes them "big";

3. Data mastered by digital platforms and their networking properties are then stored in the cloud and fuel interoperable databases. Information is then interpreted with artificial intelligence (machine learning) algorithms and, if necessary, is validated through tailor-made blockchains. This process brings to "augmented information";

4. Augmented data are then timely incorporated in (traditional) business planning procedures (here exemplified by DCF metrics) bringing to flexible readjustments (real-time refreshing, like the "F5" in the keyboard). This constant updating ideally produces incremental cash flows that can be interpreted with real option patterns that proxy flexibility;

5. The resilience and potential increase of the cash flows also reflects in the discount factor represented in the denominator of the DCF formula; the risk is reduced as a consequence of the shrinking difference between expected and real outcomes, due to the continuous refreshing of expectations that makes them closer to the ongoing ecosystem's evidence;

6. Timely reformulation of DCF metrics (current cash flows and their discount factors) impacts prospects within the time to maturity interval, bringing to a continuous updating of deterministic expectations;

7. The abovementioned updating may well fuel a stochastic (probabilistic) scenario that adds further explanatory power to the standard deterministic outlook.

The model is graphically described in Fig. 2.3.

The methodology is consistent with the research question of this chapter, showing that business planning can become more valuable—augmented—if it incorporates big data's informative contents, validated by blockchains, and interpreted through artificial intelligence predictive and self-improving patterns.

Figure 2.3 can be further developed, as shown in Fig. 2.4, to express the added value incorporated in augmented business planning.

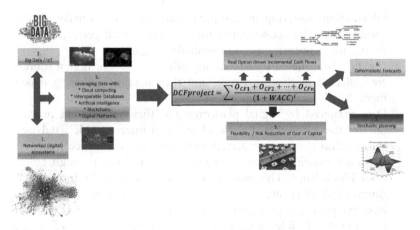

Fig. 2.3 From big data-driven forecasting to augmented business planning

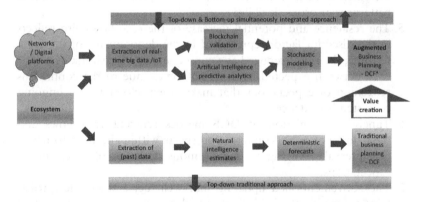

Fig. 2.4 Value creation, from traditional to augmented business planning

Interaction of top-down and bottom-up strategies can be synthesized in Fig. 2.5.

2.3   The Balance Sheet-Based Approach

The valuation of the market value according to the balance-sheet approach (Fernandez, 2001) is based on the current value of the equity contained in the last available balance sheet.

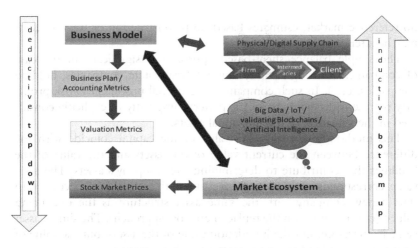

Fig. 2.5 Interaction of top-down and bottom-up strategies

There are three approaches:

- Simple balance sheet-based approach;
- Complex balance sheet-based approach grade I;
- Complex balance sheet-based approach grade II;

This approach has been traditionally used in continental Europe and less in Anglo-Saxon countries, even if globalization (and shared International Accounting Standards) are washing out the differences.

The starting point for the use of the balance sheet-based approach, both simple and complex, is represented by the shareholders' equity of the financial statements including the profit for the year net of the amounts approved for distribution.

Based on the values shown in the financial statements, an analysis of assets and liabilities must be carried out, representing non-monetary assets (technical fixed assets, inventories of goods, securities, and, depending on the approach used, intangible fixed assets) in terms of current values, to highlight implicit capital gains or losses compared to the accounting data. For assets with a significant exchange market (e.g., real estate or traded securities), the calculation of present values is generally based on the prices recorded during the most recent negotiations. When there is no reference market, estimates based on reconstruction or training costs may be alternatively used.

The simple balance sheet-based approach is significant in the case of companies with high equity content (real estate companies, holding companies, etc.). In such companies, the overall profitability/risk profile may represent the synthesis of the patterns implicitly or explicitly considered in the valuation of the individual assets.

This methodology makes the value of the capital coincide with the difference between the current value of the assets and the value of the liabilities that contribute to determining the company's assets. The asset value corresponds with the net investment that would be necessary to start a new company with the same asset structure as the one being valued (consistently with the replacement cost approach). The simple asset value is, therefore, not the liquidation value of the assets, but the value of their reconstruction from a business operating perspective.

Accounting of liabilities should never be underestimated and so their value should be consistent with their bookkeeping or lower (for prudentiality rules).

The formula is:

$$\text{Enterprise value} = \text{book equity} + \text{asset adjustments}$$
$$- \text{liability adjustments} = \text{adjusted equity} = K_1 = W_1 \qquad (2.1)$$

where asset and liability adjustments are defined as capital gains and losses net of the hypothetical tax impact.

The simple valuation considers, to estimate equity stocks, only tangible assets in addition to loans and liquidity.

The valuation provides for a detailed estimate of the assets at current replacement values, in particular:

– Assets at current repurchase value;
– Assets and liabilities based on settlement values.

The "first-grade complex balance sheet-based approach"[1] also considers intangible assets that are not accounted for but have a market value. In formula:

$$K_1 + \text{intangible assets not accounted}$$
$$\text{for but with market value} = K_2 = W_2 \qquad (2.2)$$

(e.g., bank deposits, insurance premium portfolio, shop licenses, and large-scale distribution).

Where K_1 is the value of assets determined according to the principles of the simple balance sheet-based approach.

Finally, the complex Tier II balance sheet-based approach also refers to intangible assets that are not accounted for and do not have a specific market value, bringing to the "second-grade complex balance sheet-based approach".

$$K_2 + \text{unrecognized intangible assets}$$
$$\text{without market value} = K_3 = W_3 \qquad (2.3)$$

(e.g., product portfolio, patents and industrial concessions, know-how, market shares and corporate image sales network, management, the value of human capital).

Where K_2 is the value of assets determined according to the complex-grade I balance sheet-based approach.

Intangible assets that are not accounted for and do not have a market value are:

- Strategy, concerning products and life cycle, customers, markets, market positioning, and market share achieved, orientation toward growth and partnership policies;
- Customers and market;
- Processes and innovation;
- The organization, which includes all the elements related to corporate governance;
- Human resources.

2.4 THE INCOME APPROACH

Profitability valuation can be particularly appropriate when the company has a sufficiently defined profitability trend, or the approach is deemed reliable for company projections. Or even if the degree of capitalization is not high and there is a significant intangible component.

The income approach makes it possible to estimate the market value based on profits, which the company is deemed to be able to produce in future years.

This methodology is suitable for the evaluation of cyclical companies, which have very volatile incomes, but with a tendency to compensate for overtime. In the presence of cyclical companies, normalization is a process that can identify a stable trend line, underlying the volatile trend of income flows that occur in the various periods of management. Digital firms, with a not well-established business model, are hardly cyclical, and their volatility is mostly given by their unstable nature.

The fundamental elements in an evaluation of an income approach are:

- The estimate of normalized income,
- The choice of the capitalization rate,
- The choice of the capitalization formula, based on the valuation time horizon that is adopted.

2.4.1   Estimated Normalized Income

As regards the determination of the income to be used as a basis for the valuation, reference is made to the average normalized value of income that the company is expected to produce permanently in future years.

Therefore, it is not considered as a series of future incomes, but rather as the expected average normalized value able to reflect the company's average long-term income capacity, in a time horizon consistent with the business model.

Normalized income can be derived from:

- Study of the income statement (historical and perspective);
- Analysis of the financial structure (leverage);
- Consistency between the normalized operating result and the equity evaluation process;
- Normalized income, i.e., average perspective income;
- Alternatively, the evaluator may consider operating result/EBIT, pre-tax result, net income, operating or net cash flow (if referring to a complementary financial approach).

It is essential to transform the net profit (income) into a "normalized and integrated value" capable of expressing the company's ability to generate income, through three corrective processes:

1. Normalization: this is an articulated process aimed primarily at:

    – Redistribute "extraordinary" income and expenses over time;
    – Eliminate "non-operating" income and expenses;
    – Neutralization of the effects caused by budgetary policies;

2. The integration of changes in the stock of intangible assets;
3. Neutralization of the distorting impacts of inflation (an issue since Autumn 2021 ...), to avoid fictitious losses or profits that could affect the valuation process.

The longer the extension of the evaluation scenario, the likelier the distortions.

The normalization process aims to subtract a series of income components from randomness, to bring them back to a relationship of adequate competence (accrual) with the reference period.

Extraordinary income and expenses are significant and sometimes non-recurring, components of operating income. Extraordinary income may, for example, include the realization of substantial assets on the assets side, such as real estate.

Costs include the economic consequences of exceptional events, such as restructuring costs, costs arising from the effects of natural disasters (exacerbated by the growing impact of climate change), and plant removals or relocations.

These elements must be redistributed over time to express a measure of normalized income, not burdened by components that do not present the usual manifestation. The objective of the redistribution is to replace a random size with an average value to avoid that some businesses are particularly underweighted, and others are overestimated.

The elimination of income and costs unrelated to ordinary operations must be carried out by bringing the values in the income statement to size in line with the market or practice.

As regards the neutralization of budgetary policies, reference is made to the fundamental estimates (amortization and depreciation, inventories, provisions for risks in industrial and commercial firms, fiscal policies).

The integration process is based on the observation that the dynamics of some values regarding intangible assets (adequately recorded or not in the accounts) changes across time.

The neutralization of the distortive effects of inflation makes it possible to separate real outcomes (net of inflation) from apparent and illusory nominal results since they derive from the sum of values that are not uniform in monetary terms. The most commonly used corrections are as follows:

- The adjustment of the depreciation rates of fixed technical assets at reconstruction costs, i.e., to the updated values of recent estimates;
- Adoption of the LIFO procedure in the valuation of inventories of products, semi-finished products, and raw materials;
- Determination of economic results.

2.4.2   Choice of the Capitalization Rate

The capitalization rate of normalized income represents the opportunity cost of capital employed.

This rate depends on the expected return on the risk-free securities and the risk premium that the market is expected to require for the type of investment being valued. The expected return on risk-free securities is generally identified with that on government bonds. The market return refers to all risky investments available on the market. This is consistent with the Capital Asset Pricing Model.[2]

An alternative criterion for determining the capitalization rate may be to base it on the cost of invested capital from the perspective of the potential purchaser.

In this case, the value of the company is understood as a series of future incomes that must be discounted based on the average cost of money for the purchaser. Its value, therefore, no longer depends on the degree of risk of the company.

The first approach of determining the rate of capitalization presents a theoretical-practical structure of greater importance but presupposes efficient financial markets since the entire evaluation is based on indicators that can be traced back to them.

2.4.3   Choice of the Capitalization Formula

The determination of the market value, through the discounting of income flows, occurs in many cases using the perpetual annuity formula since the company is an institution destined to last over time.

The attribution, instead, of limited duration to the production of income (from 3–5 to 8–10 years) is an assumption not verified in the business reality and tends to be arbitrary, considering the determination of the time boundary.

It is, therefore, possible to proceed with the calculation of the value of the firm, based on the average normalized value of the income flows, estimated synthetically, generated in protracted-time horizons.

Based on the chosen capitalization period, one of the two alternative formulas can be used:

- The limited capitalization:

$$W_2 = R\, a_{n\neg i} \tag{2.4}$$

- The unlimited capitalization:

$$W_1 = R/i \tag{2.5}$$

where:

W is the market value of the company;
R is the integrated normalized income;
i is the income capitalization rate;
n is the period (years) of limited capitalization.

2.5   THE MIXED CAPITAL-INCOME APPROACH

The mixed approach (Fernandez, 2019c) is based on the belief that in the long term the company's asset value is reflected in its earnings and is, therefore, based on the assumption that the use of assets, in the long run, generates an average normalized return.

For example, the mixed approach is suitable in the case of companies with significant equity holdings, which temporarily do not have a regular income capacity. In these cases, the mixed criterion can capture the value linked to the temporary ability for differential income, concerning the norm, under the hypothesis that the remuneration of the assets then returns to normal.

The market value of the company is estimated by referring to the adjusted equity, calculated using the simple or complex balance sheet-based approach, and the value of the excess revenue (goodwill)[3] that the company can produce compared to the average of the companies in the sector to which it belongs.

The mixed approach "*may incorporate different analytical values, including net book value, liabilities, goodwill, and even some specific intangibles (e.g., brands, technologies, customer lists, etc.)*". Goodwill is any future economic benefit arising from a business, an interest in a business, or from the use of a group of assets that has not been separately recognized in another asset. In general terms, the value of goodwill is the residual amount remaining after the benefits of all identifiable tangible, intangible, and monetary assets, adjusted for actual or potential liabilities, have been deducted from the value of a business. It is typically represented as the excess of the price paid in a real or hypothetical acquisition of a company over the value of the company's other identified assets and liabilities (IVS 210).[4]

This methodology allows combining the requirements of objectivity and verifiability, typical of the equity component, with those of rationality expressed by the estimate of expectations regarding the future income capacity of the company.

The integration of the equity estimate with the value of the goodwill (positive/goodwill or negative/badwill) can be particularly convenient when the profitability of the company shows deviations (positive or negative) concerning the level considered normal by the investors, expressed by the rate of remuneration.

The market value is, therefore, composed of both an equity and an income component.

In this way, the value of the company is always included in an interval that has as its lower limit the net assets at liquidation value and as its upper limit the value of the company that can be determined by the income approach.

The mixed-income approach has two different formulations:

(a) Average value;
(b) Independent (autonomous) goodwill estimate.

(a) The average value

The market value is determined as the average of the adjusted assets and the value obtained for the capitalization of income, using the perpetual capitalization formula.

$$W = \frac{1}{2}(K + R/i) = K + \frac{1}{2}(R/i - K) \qquad (2.6)$$

where:

> K is the equity expressed at replacement cost according to the balance sheet-based approach. It is an adjusted capital measure, including intangible assets and capital gains, and considering any higher market values compared to the accounting data.
> R is the normalized income expected for the future.
> i is the normalized rate of return for equity, concerning both the level of operational risk borne by the company and the level of risk deriving from the financial structure chosen.

(b) Autonomous goodwill estimate

The mixed balance sheet-based approach with an independent estimate of goodwill provides various alternatives, formulated concerning the different assumptions made for the projection and discounting of the over-returns to estimate the goodwill.

b.1. Limited capitalization of average profit

This approach considers the market value of the company as the adjusted equity plus the limited capitalization of the average profit (the difference between the expected income and the return on equity = goodwill), based on the following formula:

$$W = K + a\,n\neg i * (R - iK) \qquad (2.7)$$

where:

> i = normalized rate about the type of investment. It expresses the measure of the return considered normal, considering the levels of risk incurred by the company.

i^* = discount rate of the over-income.
n = number of years, defined and limited.

b.2. *Unlimited capitalization of average profit*

The market value is the sum of the adjusted net asset value plus good-will calculated as the perpetual annuity of the surplus profits. It assumes that the company can generate extra profits for an indefinite period, to be taken with caution considering the intrinsically ephemeral nature of goodwill, which over time inevitably tends to erode. The formulation is as follows:

$$W = K + \left[(R - iK)/i^*\right] \tag{2.8}$$

and provides for the replacement of $a_{n\neg i^*}$ with $1/i^*$.

2.6   Cash Is King: The Superiority of the Financial Approach

According to Peter Bernstein (Introduction to Rappaport and Mauboussin, 2021) "assets producing cash flows will ultimately return the owner's investment without depending on the whims of other investors. Even if those cash flows are some distance in the future, their prospects endow them with a present value. Financial markets are nothing more than arenas where investors who need cash today can obtain it by selling the present value of future cash flows to other investors willing to wait for the cash payoffs from their capital. The payment medium in this transaction is money. The crucial point: If you invest without expecting future cash flows, then you might as well collect art or play the slot machines".

The financial approach is based on the principle that the market value of the company is equal to the discounted value of the cash flows that the company can generate ("cash is king"). The determination of the cash flows is of primary importance in the application of the approach, as is the consistency of the discount rates adopted.

The doctrine (especially the Anglo-Saxon one) believes that the financial approach is the "ideal" solution for estimating the market value for limited periods. It is not possible to make reliable estimates of cash flows for longer periods. "The conceptually correct methods are those based on cash flow discounting" (Fernandez, 2019b); and also "nowadays, the cash flow discounting method is generally used because it is the only conceptually correct valuation method".

This approach is of practical importance if the individual investor or company with high cash flows (leasing companies, retail trade, public and motorway services, financial trading, project financing SPVs, etc.) are valued.

Financial evaluation can be particularly appropriate when the company's ability to generate cash flow for investors is significantly different from its ability to generate income and forecasts can be formulated with a sufficient degree of credibility and are demonstrable.

There are two criteria for determining cash flows, respectively bringing (if appropriately discounted) to the estimate of the equity or the enterprise value, as shown in Fig. 2.6. In the evaluation of CAPEX investments where the Net Present Value (NPV) is to be estimated, the two criteria can be assimilated, respectively, to the NPV_{equity} or $NPV_{project}$, where the former expresses the residual net return for the investing shareholders (as remuneration of the Equity Value), whereas the latter estimate the return for all the raised capital underwriters (shareholders + financial creditors). The Internal Rate of Return (IRR) is, mathematically, the break-even financial rate that makes the $NPV = 0$. In the income statement structure, operating cash flows can be compared to operating profit ($= EBIT$), and net cash flows to net profits.

I. The cash flow available to shareholders (free cash flow to equity—FCFE)

It is a measure of cash flow that considers the financial structure of the company (levered cash flow). It is the ultimate cash flow that remains after the payment of interest and the repayment of equity shares and after the coverage of equity expenditures necessary to maintain existing assets and to create the conditions for business growth. That is why it is also called "free" (=residually available) liquidity for the equity holders.

In M&A operations, the Free Cash Flow to the Firm (FCFF) (operating cash flow) is normally calculated, to estimate the Enterprise Value (comprehensive of financial debt). The residual Equity Value is then derived by subtracting the Net Financial Position.

The residual cash flow for the shareholders (FCFE) can be determined, starting from the net profit in Table 2.1.

Fig. 2.6 Operating
and net cash flows

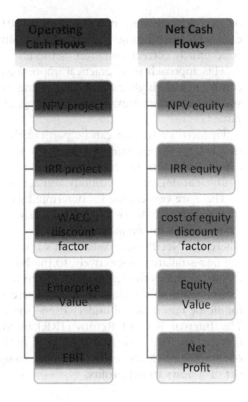

Operating Cash Flows	Net Cash Flows
NPV project	NPV equity
IRR project	IRR equity
WACC discount factor	cost of equity discount factor
Enterprise Value	Equity Value
EBIT	Net Profit

Table 2.1 Free cash flow to equity

Net profit (loss)
+ amortization/depreciation and provisions
+ divestments (−investments) in technical equipment
+ divestments (−investments) in other assets
+ decrease (−increase) in net operating working capital
+ increases (−decreases) in loans
+ equity increases (−decreases)
= Cash flows available to shareholders (Net cash flow or Free cash flow to equity—FCFE)

Alternatively to this bottom-up calculation, the net cash flow can be calculated with top-down steps, starting from the sales (monetary

Table 2.2 Free cash flow to the firm

Net operating income (EBIT)
− taxes on operating income
+ amortization/depreciation and provisions (non-monetary operating costs)
+ technical divestments (−investments)
+ divestments (−investments) in other assets
+ decrease (−increase) in operating net working capital
= **Cash flow available to shareholders and lenders (operating cash flow or free cash flow to the firm—FCFF)**

revenues) in the income statement, arriving at the operating cash flow—see II below) and eventually the net cash flow (see Table 2.2).

The discounting of the free cash flow for the shareholders takes place at a rate equal to the cost of the shareholders' equity, consistently with the representation of Fig. 2.7. This flow identifies the theoretical measure of the company's ability to distribute dividends, even if it may not coincide with the dividend paid. The dividend policy of the firm influences the Dividend Discount Model, used as a proxy for calculating the cost of equity.

II. The cash flow available to the company (Free cash flow to the firm—FCFF)

The second configuration of flows is used in the practice of Enterprise Value estimate.

It is a measure of cash flows independent of the financial structure of the company (unlevered cash flows) that is particularly suitable to evaluate companies with high levels of indebtedness, or that do not have a debt plan (as happens in most debt-free startups). If the firm is debt-free, then FCFF≈FCFE, cost of debt ≈ cost of equity ≈ WACC, operating profit ≈ net profit, raised capital ≈ equity, ROE ≈ ROI, etc.

This methodology is founded on the operating flows generated by the management of the company, based on the operating income available for the remuneration of own and third-party means net of the relative tax effect. Unlevered cash flows are typically determined with a bottom-up procedure starting from the income statement by using operating income before taxes and financial charges:

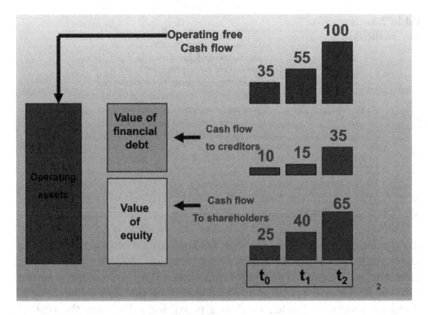

Fig. 2.7   Value of the firm and cash flows

The cash flow available to the firm is, therefore, determined as the cash flow available to shareholders, plus financial charges after tax, plus loan repayments and equity repayments, minus new borrowings and flows arising from equity increases. An example is given in Fig. 2.15.

The difference between the two approaches is, therefore, given by the different meanings of cash flows associated with debt and equity repayments. Debt service comes first, unless the firm is debt-free: in this case, as anticipated above, FCFF = FCFE.

Cash flows from operating activities are discounted to present value at the weighted average cost of capital (WACC), analyzed in formula (2.12).

This DCF metrics offers an evaluation of the whole company, independently from its financial structure (whose impact is considered later, both in the income and cash flow statement). The value of the debt must be subtracted from the value of the company to rejoin the market value of equity, obtained by discounting the residual cash flows available for the shareholders (FCFE).

The relationship between the two concepts of cash flow, consistent with Tables 2.1 and 2.2, is as follows:

cash flow available to the company (CFFF)

  = cash flow available to shareholders (CFFE)

  + financial charges (net of taxes) + loan repayments − new loans

$$(2.9)$$

An example of the Enterprise Value of the firm (value of financial debt + equity) and its partitioning between financial debtholders and eventually shareholders is illustrated in Fig. 2.7.

Cash flow estimates can be applied to any type of asset. The differential element is represented by its duration. Many assets have a defined time horizon, while others assume a perpetual time horizon such as shares. That is why firm valuation should theoretically always be unlimited, without any time constraint. In many cases, as it has been shown with the estimate of a limited capitalization of expected revenues (Sect. 2.5), it is not, but only because unlimited forecasts may prove too subjective.

Cash flows (CF) can, therefore, be estimated using a normalized projection of cash flows that it uses, alternatively:

- unlimited capitalization:

$$W_1 = \mathrm{CF}/i \qquad (2.10)$$

- limited capitalization:

$$W_2 = \mathrm{CF}\, a\, n \neg i \qquad (2.11)$$

where W_1 and W_2 represent the present value of future cash flows. Depending on the numerator of the formula, W_1 or W_2 measure either the Enterprise Value (with FCFF as the numerator) or the Equity Value (with FCFE representing the numerator).

This formulation is like that of expected revenues (see formulae [2.4] and [2.5]), simply replacing expected revenues for forecast cash flows. Theoretical accountants claim that, in the long run, the projection of cash flows should converge to that of comparable revenue returns (and so, operating cash flow $\approx$ EBIT; net cash flow $\approx$ net profit). If so, income and financial methodologies should be converging to common estimates.

The discount rate to be applied to expected operating cash flows (FCFF) is determined as the sum of the cost of equity and the cost of debt, appropriately weighted according to the leverage of the company (the ratio between financial debt and equity). This produces the Weighted Average Cost of Capital (WACC):

$$\text{WACC} = k_i(1-t)\frac{D}{D+E} + k_e\frac{E}{D+E} \qquad (2.12)$$

where:

k_i = cost of debt;
t = corporate tax rate;
D = market value of debt;
E = market value of equity;
$D + E$ = raised capital;
k_e = cost of equity.

The consistency between the numerator and the denominator in the discounted FCFF is evident since both parameters represent a mix of financial debt and equity belonging to a levered firm.

The cost of debt capital is fairly easy to determine, as it can be inferred from the financial statements of the company, representing the ratio between negative interests and average financial debt of the investigated year. The cost of equity or share capital, which represents the minimum rate of return required by investors for equity investments, is instead more complex and may use the Capital Asset Pricing Model or the Dividend Discount Model (see Sect. 2.7.1). Equity is traditionally riskier than financial debt (whose periodical remuneration and payback are contractually predetermined), and so the cost of equity > cost of debt, and also cost of equity > WACC.

Once the present value of the cash flows has been determined, the calculation of the market value (W) of the company may correspond to:

(a) the unlevered cash flow approach (to estimate the Enterprise Value):

$$W = \sum \frac{\text{CF}_0}{\text{WACC}} + TV - D \qquad (2.13)$$

(b) the levered cash flow approach (to estimate the Equity Value):

$$W = \sum \frac{CF_n}{K_e} + TV \qquad (2.14)$$

where:

$\sum CF_0 / WACC$ = present value of operating cash flows (FCFF)
$\sum CF_n / K_e$ = present value of net cash flows (FCFE)
TV = terminal (residual) value
D = initial net financial position (financial debt − liquidity)
WACC = average after-tax cost of a company's various capital sources (cost of collecting external capital), including common stock, preferred stock, bonds, and any other long-term financial debt.

What matters in formulae (2.13) and (2.14) is, once again, the consistency between the numerator and the denominator. Operating cash flows are unlevered since they are considered before debt service, and they so need to be discounted using an "operating" (unlevered) cost of capital that considers both the cost of debt and the residual cost of equity (WACC). Net cash flows are consistently discounted at the cost of equity since both the numerator and the denominator refer to the residual claims of the equity holders. Preferred equity is slightly safer than ordinary equity, as it commands a (small) premium and a priority in dividends—that is why a different cost of equity is used.

The WACC is the weighted average of the following cost of capital sources (Fig. 2.8).

Appendix 1 shows the interaction between the WACC and the other key financial ratios.

The residual (terminal) value, more comprehensively described in Sect. 2.13, is the result of discounting the value at the time n (before which the cash flows are estimated analytically, year after year). It is often the greatest component of the global value W (above all in intangible-intensive companies) and tends to zero if the time horizon of the capitalization is infinite (VR$/\infty = 0$).

The two variants (levered versus unlevered) give the same result if the overall DCF value of the firm, determined through the cash flows available to the lenders (FCFF), is deducted from the value of the net financial debts. In this case: equity value = enterprise value ± net financial position.

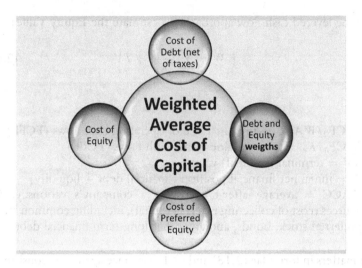

Fig. 2.8 WACC determinants

Operating cash flows (unlevered − FCFF) and net cash flows for share-holders (levered − FCFE) are determined by comparing the last two balance sheets (to consider changes in operating Net Working Capital, fixed assets/CAPEX, financial liabilities, and shareholders' equity) with the income statement of the last year, as shown in Table 2.3 that illustrates the accounting scheme of the cash flow statement.

This cash flow statement is different from the scheme proposed by the international accounting principles (see, for instance, IAS 7) since it considers both the EBITDA and the Operating Cash Flows, whose importance for firm valuation emerges from this chapter. Even if both statements—the one proposed here and the IAS 7-compliant scheme—arrive at the same net result (FCFE), they show important differences "on the road".

The net cash flow for the shareholders coincides with the free cash flow to equity (FCFE) and, therefore, with the dividends that can be ideally paid out, once it has been verified that enough internal liquidity resources remain in the firm to back its going concern perspectives. This feature, associated with the ability to raise equity from third parties and shareholders, is such as to allow the company to find adequate financial coverage for the investments deemed necessary to maintain the

Table 2.3 Cash flow statement and link with the cost of capital

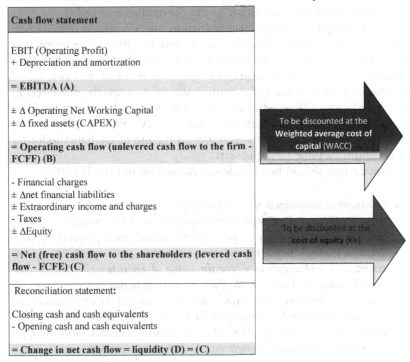

Cash flow statement
EBIT (Operating Profit) + Depreciation and amortization
= EBITDA (A)
± Δ Operating Net Working Capital ± Δ fixed assets (CAPEX)
= Operating cash flow (unlevered cash flow to the firm - FCFF) (B)
- Financial charges ± Δnet financial liabilities ± Extraordinary income and charges - Taxes ± ΔEquity
= Net (free) cash flow to the shareholders (levered cash flow - FCFE) (C)
Reconciliation statement:
Closing cash and cash equivalents - Opening cash and cash equivalents
= Change in net cash flow = liquidity (D) = (C)

To be discounted at the **Weighted average cost of capital** (WACC)

To be discounted at the **cost of equity** (Ke)

company's business continuity and remain on the market in economic conditions (minimum objectives). They should allow for the creation of incremental value in favor of the shareholders, who are the residual claimants (being, as subscribers of risky capital, the only beneficiaries of the variable net returns, which, as such, are residual and subordinate to the fixed remuneration of the other stakeholders).

The estimate of cash flows can be ideally applied to any activity.

A core differential element is service life. Many activities have a defined time horizon, while others assume a perpetual time horizon such as company shares, as anticipated.

The discounted cash flow (DCF) approach can be complemented with real options that incorporate intangible-driven flexibility in the forecasts. Real options[5] improve the flexibility of capital budgeting estimates, so fostering the NPV (higher resilience decreases the risk that is a major component of the discount factor in the denominator of DCF).

DCF is ubiquitous in financial valuation and constitutes the cornerstone of contemporary valuation theory (Singh, 2013). The robustness of the model, as well as its compatibility with the conventional two-dimensional risk-return structure of investment appraisal, makes it suited to a multitude of valuations. Accounting standards across the globe recognize the efficacy of this model and advocate its use, wherever practicable. FAS 141 and 142 of the United States and IAS 39 that relate to the accounting of intangible assets recommend the use of DCF methodology for attributing a value to such assets.

Some caveats should be considered. According to OECD (2017):

- *"Valuation techniques that estimate the discounted value of projected future cash flows derived from the exploitation of the transferred intangible or intangibles can be particularly useful when properly applied. There are many variations of these valuation techniques. In general terms, such techniques measure the value of an intangible by the estimated value of future cash flows it may generate over its expected remaining lifetime. The value can be calculated by discounting the expected future cash flows to present value. Under this approach valuation requires, among other things, defining realistic and reliable financial projections, growth rates, discount rates, the useful life of intangibles, and the tax effects of the transaction. Moreover, it entails consideration of terminal values when appropriate"* (par. 6.157).

- *"When applying valuation techniques, including valuation techniques based on projected cash flows, it is important to recognize that the estimates of value based on such techniques can be volatile. Small changes in one or another of the assumptions underlying the valuation approach or in one or more of the valuation parameters can lead to large differences in the intangible value the approach produces. A small percentage change in the discount rate, a small percentage change in the growth rates assumed in producing financial projections, or a small change in the assumptions regarding the useful life of the intangible can each have a profound effect on the ultimate valuation. Moreover, this volatility is often compounded when changes are made simultaneously to two or more valuation assumptions or parameters"* (par. 6.158).

- *"The reliability of a valuation of a transferred intangible using discounted cash flow valuation techniques is dependent on the accuracy of the projections of future cash flows or income on which the valuation is based"* (par. 6.163).

- *"The discount rate or rates used in converting a stream of projected cash flows into a present value is a critical element of a valuation approach. The discount rate considers the time value of money and the risk or uncertainty of the anticipated cash flows. As small variations in selected discount rates can generate large variations in the calculated value of intangibles using these techniques"* (par. 6.170).

- *"It should be recognized in determining and evaluating discount rates that in some instances, particularly those associated with the valuation of intangibles still in development, intangibles may be among the riskiest components"* (par. 6.172).

2.6.1 *The Capital Asset Pricing Model and the Dividend Discount Model*

The Capital Asset Pricing Model (CAPM) is possibly the most celebrated corporate finance theorem, independently elaborated in 1964–1966 by William Sharpe (a Nobel laureate in Economics), John Lintner, and Jan Mossin,[6] and based on the portfolio diversification insight (1952–1959) of Harry Markowitz, another Nobel prize laureate.

The model is used to determine a theoretically appropriate required expected rate of return of a listed security that can be conveniently added to a well-diversified portfolio.

The model considers the asset's sensitivity to non-diversifiable risk (also known as systematic risk or market—idiosyncratic—risk), often represented by the beta (β) coefficient, as well as the expected return of the market and the expected return of a theoretical risk-free asset:

$$\text{Eri} = \text{Rf} + \beta i\,(\text{ERm} - \text{Rf}) \tag{2.15}$$

where:

ERi = expected return of investment
Rf = risk-free rate of long-term Government bonds
βi = beta coefficient of the investment (i) compared to the market return $(m) = \text{cov}\,(i,\,m)/\sigma^2\ m$
(ERm − Rf) = market risk premium (excess return of the stock market index over the risk-free Government bond)

The formula of the CAPM is the equation of the Security Market Line SML), illustrated in Fig. 2.9. The efficient frontier is the set of optimal portfolios that offer the highest expected return for a defined level of risk or the lowest risk for a given level of expected return. The Minimum Variance Portfolio (MVP) that lies in the lower left part of the efficient frontier is the efficient portfolio with the lowest risk/return profile.

The SML represents the standard risk-return trade-off, considering that the portfolio diversification is completed and so only systematic risk (expressed in the horizontal axis by the beta coefficient) matters. The systematic (idiosyncratic) risk depends on country or political risk that cannot be washed away by diversification, even if international portfolio diversification furtherly reduces its amount. The equation of the SML corresponds to the CAPM formulation (2.15). In equilibrium, listed shares cannot be placed either above or under the SML, otherwise, market arbitrages are triggered, bringing the share along the SML, as shown in Fig. 2.10 (where M is the stock market portfolio, with an intrinsic beta

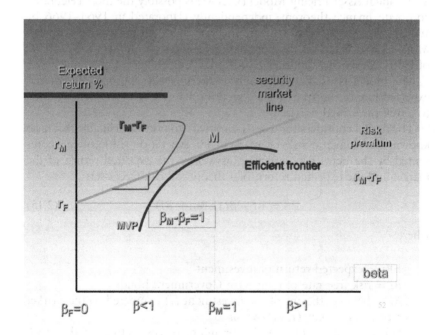

Fig. 2.9 Security market line

of 1, since cov $(m, m)/\sigma^2 m = \sigma^2 m/\sigma^2 m = 1$, showing that the average beta of the stock market index is zero). The beta coefficient of a risk-free government bond coincides with zero ($\beta_F = 0$).

The CAPM shows that the cost of equity capital is determined only by the beta coefficient that represents the asset's sensitivity towards its (domestic) stock market. Despite its failing numerous empirical tests, and the existence of more modern approaches to asset pricing and portfolio selection (such as arbitrage pricing theory), the CAPM remains popular due to its simplicity and utility in a variety of situations. In practice, the CAPM sends an important message to firm valuators, considering the trade-off between risk and return: rational investors tend to maximize returns, minimizing risk.

Whenever a firm issues capital (risky equity), it bears a cost of equity that corresponds to the return on equity for the shareholders (if transaction costs are not considered; otherwise, there is a small differential: e.g., cost of equity 10%, transaction cost 0.1%, return on equity 9.9%).

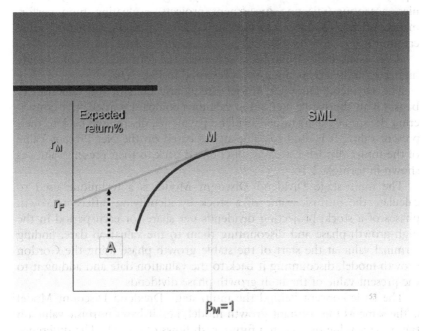

Fig. 2.10 Arbitrage equilibrium and the CAPM

Investors (potential shareholders) look for the market (and not book value) returns, comparing different investment opportunities—hence the concept of "opportunity" cost of capital. The book value of equity is an initial proxy of its market value, to be adjusted considering the current market value of the difference between assets and liabilities.

Even if CAPM assumptions rarely hold in the real world (where the rigid assumptions of the original model are inapplicable, should tax, transaction costs, risky bonds, etc., be introduced), the model still holds most of its utility, remembering that the risk-return trade-off remains valid. In corporate appraisal, extensive use of beta coefficients and the basic CAPM formulation represents a common practice to estimate the cost of capital.

Fernandez (2019a) claims that "The CAPM is an absurd model because its assumptions and its predictions/conclusions have no basis in the real world. The use of CAPM is also a source of litigation: many professors, lawyers…get nice fees because many professionals use CAPM instead of common sense to calculate the required return to equity. Users of the CAPM make many illogical errors valuing companies, accepting/rejecting investment projects, evaluating fund performance, pricing goods, and services in regulated markets, calculating value creation…".

Risky assets differ from safe assets since the former show consistently higher volatility across time, as represented in Fig. 2.11.

The Dividend Discount Model (frequently used in the valuation of banks) is an alternative method of valuing a company's stock price considering the sum of all its future dividend payments, discounted back to their present value. It is used to value stocks based on the Net Present Value of the future dividend streams, discounted back to their present value, as shown in formula 2.16.

The multi-stage Dividend Discount Model is a technique used to calculate the intrinsic value of a stock by identifying different growth phases of a stock; projecting dividends per share for each period in the high-growth phase and discounting them to the valuation date, finding terminal value at the start of the stable growth phase using the Gordon growth model, discounting it back to the valuation date and adding it to the present value of the high growth phase dividends.

The basic concept behind the multi-stage Dividend Discount Model is the same as the constant-growth model, i.e., it bases intrinsic value on the present value of expected future cash flows of a stock. The difference is that instead of assuming a constant dividend growth rate for all periods

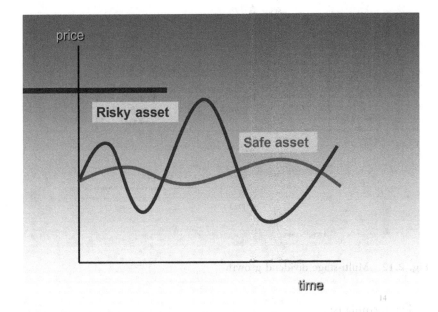

Fig. 2.11 Risky versus safe security

in the future, the present value calculation is broken down into different phases.

Figure 2.12 shows the growth rates of dividends in a three-stage timesheet. The cost of equity (a part of the denominator of the DCF formula) should ideally be decreasing across time, as initial high-growth rates coincide with the startup phase where equity risk is higher (also due to the lower level of leverage that normally characterizes this phase).

The Dividend Discount odel (DDM) (Damodaran, 1996) is a method of valuing a company's stock price based on the theory that its stock is worth the sum of all its future dividend payments, discounted back to its present value. In other words, it is used to value stocks based on the Net Present Value of future dividends. The equation most widely used is called the Gordon growth model.

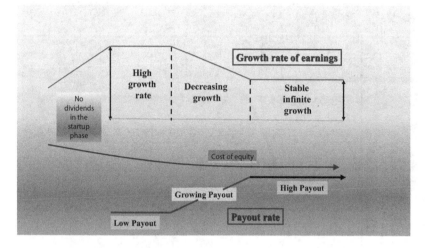

Fig. 2.12 Multi-stage dividend growth

The formula is:

$$P_0 = \frac{D_0(1+g)}{r-g} = \frac{D_1}{r-g} \qquad (2.16)$$

Next dividend

Discount rate

Growing at (growth)

where:

P_0 is the current stock price
g is the constant growth rate in perpetuity expected for the dividends.
r is the constant cost of equity capital for that company.
D_1 is the value of the next year's dividends.

This model embeds constant growth that is a theoretical oversimplification of the real world.

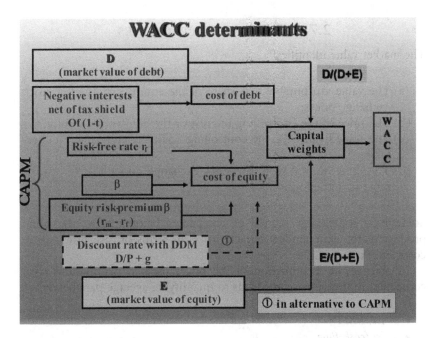

Fig. 2.13 WACC derivation

In synthesis, it may be remembered that the CAPM is often used to extrapolate a market proxy of the opportunity cost of equity, whereas the DDM is less diffused (albeit frequently used in some industries, for instance in the banking sector). Some practitioners consider as a further proxy the Return on Equity (based on the ratio between the net profit over the equity of the firm), a ratio that is much easier to figure out, even if it relies on book values that misinterpret the investor's preference for market returns.

Considering these two ways to estimate the cost of equity, the overall process of derivation of the WACC can be summarized as follows (Fig. 2.13):

2.7   EMPIRICAL APPROACHES

The market value identifies:

(a) The value attributable to a share of the equity, expressed at stock exchange prices;
(b) The price of the controlling interest or the entire share equity;
(c) The traded value for the controlling equity of comparable undertakings;
(d) The value derived from the stock exchange quotations of comparable undertakings.

Sometimes comparable trades of companies belonging to the same product sector with similar characteristics (in terms of cash flows, sales, costs, etc.) are used.

In practice, an examination of the prices used in negotiations with companies in the same sector leads to quantifying average parameters:

- *Price/EBIT*
- *Price/cash-flow*
- *Price/book-value*
- *Price/earnings*
- *Price/dividend*

These ratios seek to estimate the average rate to be applied to the company being assessed. However, there may be distorting effects of prices based on special interest rates, on a historical context, on difficulties of comparison, etc.

In financial market practice, the multiples methodology is frequently applied. Based on multiples, the company's value is derived from the market price profit referring to comparable listed companies, such as net profit, before tax or operating profit, cash flow, equity, or turnover.

The attractiveness of the multiples approach stems from its ease of use: multiples can be used to obtain quick but dirty estimates of the company's value and are useful when there are many comparable companies listed on the financial markets and the market sets correct prices for them on average.

Because of the simplicity of the calculation, these indicators are easily manipulated and susceptible to misuse, especially if they refer to companies that are not entirely similar. Since there are no identical companies in terms of entrepreneurial risk and growth rate, the assumption of multiples for the processing of the valuation can be misleading, bringing to "fake multipliers".

The use of multiples can be implemented through:

A. Use of fundamentals;
B. Use of comparable data:

    B.1. Comparable companies;
    B.2. Comparable transactions.

The first approach links multiples to the fundamentals of the company being assessed: profit growth and cash flow, dividend distribution ratio, and risk. It is equivalent to the use of cash flow discounting approaches.

Discount factors incorporate risk. According to the OECD (2017):

- "*When identifying risks in relation to an investment with specificity, it is important to distinguish between the financial risks that are linked to the funding provided for the investments and the operational risks that are linked to the operational activities for which the funding is used, such as for example the development risk when the funding is used for developing a new intangible*" (par. 6.61).
- "*Particular types of risk that may have importance in a functional analysis relating to transactions involving intangibles include:*

    (i) *risks related to development of intangibles, including the risk that costly research and development or marketing activities will prove to be unsuccessful, and considering the timing of the investment (for example, whether the investment is made at an early stage, mid-way through the development process, or at a late stage will impact the level of the underlying investment risk);*

    (ii) *the risk of product obsolescence, including the possibility that technological advances of competitors will adversely affect the value of the intangibles;*

(iii) *infringement risk, including the risk that defense of intangible rights or defense against other persons' claims of infringement may prove to be time-consuming, costly and/or unavailing;*

(iv) *product liability and similar risks related to products and services based on the intangibles;*

(v) *exploitation risks, uncertainties in relation to the returns to be generated by the intangible"* (par. 6.65).

- In some industries, products protected by intangibles can become obsolete or uncompetitive in a relatively short period in the absence of continuing development and enhancement of the intangibles. As a result, having access to updates and enhancements can be the difference between deriving a short-term advantage from the intangibles and deriving a longer-term advantage.

- The following types of risks, among others, should be considered:

  – Risks related to the future development of the intangibles. This includes an evaluation of whether the intangibles relate to commercially viable products, whether the intangibles may support commercially viable products in the future, the expected cost of required future development and testing, the likelihood that such development and testing will prove successful and similar considerations.

  – Risks related to product obsolescence and depreciation in the value of the intangibles. This includes an evaluation of the likelihood that competitors will introduce products or services in the future that would materially erode the market for products dependent on the intangibles being analyzed.

  – Risks related to the infringement of intangible rights.

  – Product liability and similar risks related to the future use of the intangibles (par. 6.128).

For the second approach, it is necessary to distinguish whether it is a valuation of comparable companies or comparable transactions.

The comparability concerns different firms but is also related to their contents. Intangible assets are however often hard to compare.

According to the OECD (2017):

- *"Unique and valuable"* intangibles are those intangibles (i) that are not comparable to intangibles used by or available to parties to *potentially comparable transactions, and (ii) whose use in business operations (e.g., manufacturing, provision of services, marketing, sales or administration) is expected to yield greater future economic benefits than would be expected in the absence of the intangible*" (par. 6.17) "*intangibles often have unique characteristics, and as a result have the potential for generating returns and creating future benefits that could differ widely. In conducting a comparability analysis with regard to a transfer of intangibles, it is, therefore, essential to consider the unique features of the intangibles*" (par. 6.116).

- "*In conducting a comparability analysis, it may be important to consider the stage of development of particular intangibles*" (par. 6.123).

In the case of comparable companies, the approach estimates multiples by observing similar companies. The problem is to determine what is meant by similar companies. In theory, the analyst should check all the variables that influence the multiple.

In practice, companies should estimate the most likely price for a non-listed company, taking as a reference some listed companies, operating in the same sector and considered homogeneous. Two companies can be defined as homogeneous when they present, for the same risk, similar characteristics, and expectations.

The calculation is:

- A company whose price is known (P_1),
- A variable closely related to its value (X_1)

the ratio $(P_1)/(X_1)$ is assumed to apply to the company to be valued, for which the size of the reference variable (X_2) is known.

Therefore:

$$(P_1)/(X_1) = (P_2)/(X_2) \qquad (2.17)$$

so that the desired value P_2 will be:

$$P_2 = X_2[(P_1)/(X_1)] \qquad (2.18)$$

According to widespread estimates, the main factors to establish whether a company is comparable are:

- Size;
- Belonging to the same sector[7];
- Financial risks (leverage);
- Historical trends and prospects for the development of results and markets;
- Geographical diversification;
- Degree of reputation and credibility;
- Management skills;
- Ability to pay dividends.

Founded on comparable transactions, the basis of valuation is information about actual negotiations (or mergers) of similar—i.e., comparable—companies.

The use of profitability parameters is usually considered to be the most representative of company dynamics.

Among the empirical criteria, the approach of the multiplier of the EBITDA (Earnings Before Interest, Taxes, Depreciation, and Amortization) is widely diffused, to which the net financial position must be added algebraically, to pass from the estimate of the enterprise value (total value of the company) to that of the equity value (value of the net assets). The formulation is as follows:

$$W = \text{average perspective EBITDA} * \text{Enterprise Value/sector EBITDA}$$
$$= \text{Enterprise Value of the company} \tag{2.19}$$

And then:

$$\text{Equity Value} = \text{Enterprise Value} \pm \text{Net Financial Position} \tag{2.20}$$

2.7.1   The Economic Value Added (EVA®)

According to the Economic Value-Added approach, the creation of value by the company is measured by the differential, if it is positive, between the company's profitability rate and the cost of the resources used to achieve it.

In a nutshell, it can be said that EVA is a performance indicator given by the difference between the return on capital employed and the cost of collecting it from equity holders and debtholders (market value of raised capital).

The value of the company is obtained by discounting the future flow of the extra values so determined and adding the initial value of the invested capital. In summary:

$$EVA = (NOPAT/I_C - WACC) * I_C \qquad (2.21)$$

where:

NOPAT = Net Operating Profit After Taxes
Return on investment = NOPAT/Invested Capital (I_C)
WACC is the weighted average cost of capital.[8]

The total value of a company according to the EVA methodology is so given by the sum of the Invested capital and the EVA that the company will be able to produce over the years:

$$\text{Company value} = \text{Net invested capital} + \text{Sum of current annual EVA values}$$
$$+ \text{ Residual value} - \text{Net financial debt} \qquad (2.22)$$

The invested capital corresponds to the sum of the net working capital and the net fixed assets. The value of the invested capital must be adjusted concerning the amounts directly inferable from the financial statements. In particular, the invested capital is the calculation of the EVA produced each year, a direct function of the return on investment, expressed as the difference between the return on investment and the cost of capital multiplied by the capital invested.

The return on capital is the operating income net of operating taxes, i.e., the sum of taxes paid, and taxes saved through deductions from financial charges (tax shield).

2.8 POTENTIAL TAX LIABILITIES

An important problem posed by the valuation of companies (through the balance sheet-based approach) is the need to estimate, on the capital gains that emerge, the potential tax burden.

The re-expression at current values of the assets and liabilities can cause (positive or negative) differences in value. These differences are only figurative, as they are neither realized nor detectable from an accounting point of view.

In theory, each positive difference in value corresponds to a tax levy, and each negative difference corresponds to a tax saving. These are, clearly, potential loads and in any case deferred, as are the potential differences in value to which they refer.

In determining the potential tax charges, it is necessary to consider any previous losses incurred by the company that can be carried forward. In this case, it will be appropriate to offset the capital gains, divided over time in proportion to the period of their possible occurrence, with the losses. Tax rules may be substantially different across countries.

2.9   Majority Premiums and Minority Discounts

The market value of a company represents the theoretical exchange value attributable to all the shares that make up the equity. Unlisted firms may consider the stock market value as a theoretical proxy, to be adjusted.

Problems arise when estimating the value of shares of various sizes. In principle, the value of a certain number of shares should be a function of two elements:

- the size of the equity shares making up the package;
- The rights which they give to the purchaser (voting rights and investment rights to receive a dividend).

The value of a package of shares is not always exactly proportional to the market value of the equity represented; therefore, the existence of majority premiums and minority discounts must be considered.

The majority shareholder has some advantages (private benefits) over the minority shareholders:

- The allocation of profits is sometimes influenced by the interests of the control group and its objectives;
- Direct and indirect remuneration (e.g., self-appointment as a director);
- Establishment of privileged channels for finding the factors of production and the remuneration of specific services;
- Notoriety;
- Other subjectively appreciable advantages.

The majority premium, i.e., the exchange value attributable to the majority package incorporates these advantages. Value is consequently more than proportional if compared to total equity value.

Majority premiums are recognized for the value of share packages that assure the control of the company, that is, the exercise of powers (with the consequent advantages) to take the fundamental decisions for the management of the company.

According to international market practices, a specular minority discount is applied to small shareholdings, often classifiable in the order of 25–35%, to which corresponds a majority premium of the same amount (so that the overall value does not vary).

The calculation of the majority premiums and of the minority discounts is influenced by the marketability of the securities, listed or not. They also depend on the voting rights: whereas ordinary shares typically have no restrictions, preferred shares are characterized by little if any voting power (in standard shareholders meetings), and so they are not influential. An example is given by takeover bids, where normally ordinary shares (whose voting right is determinant for the bidder looking for a majority) go up, and preferred shares are useless, and so show non-significant price changes.

The maximization of the majority premium—and the minority discount—is around 50%: 51% will be proportionally worth much more than 49%, while 90% will have a value just over proportional concerning 10%.

As the percentage of control increases (up to 100%), the amount of the majority premium decreases (until it disappears completely, in the case of totalitarian control). It is, therefore, possible to determine a series of intervals to identify majority bonuses and minority discounts which, being specular, represent a zero-sum game.

Valuation best practices typically identify the following benchmarks for the majority premium and, in the same way, the minority discount in Table 2.4.

2.10 The Control Approach

Once the most suitable evaluation approach has been defined, it might be appropriate to use another evaluation approach, to double-check the evaluation carried out with the main approach.

Table 2.4 Majority premiums and minority discounts

Majority share	Majority premium	Minority share	Minority discount
From 51 to 65%	From +35 to +25%	From 35 to 49%	From −25 to −35%
From 65 to 75%	From + 20 to +10%	From 25 to 35%	From −20 to −10%
From 75 to 90%	Up to +10%	From 10 to 25%	Up to −10%

The use of a control approach is applied in all cases where it is possible to estimate the market value of the company from complementary angles to arrive at a range of values, within which the market value must be positioned.

The comparison between the "main approach" and the "control" approach can lead to significant differences in absolute terms, especially if the reference values are high. It is, however, to be considered appropriate if, from a relative point of view, the deviations between the two approaches do not exceed an indicative percentage in the order of 20–25%.

2.11   THE ACCOUNTING VALUE OF INTANGIBLE ASSETS

Intangibles constitute an ongoing challenge for accountants (Giuliani & Marasca, 2011; Roslender & Fincham, 2001), and their recording is a constant dispute, with problematic consequences even on market and performance valuation, exemplified by the increasing gap—softened during recessions—between market and book values, mostly attributable to relevant but not (adequately) accounted intangibles. International homogeneous accounting treatment for intangibles is still a daunting target (Còrcoles, 2010).

Intangible value is hidden in the balance sheet by inadequate accounting, but not in the income or in the cash flow statement, where the intangible contribution to profit is detectable.

Issues relating to the valuation of intangibles are surfacing with unprecedented regularity and posit an intriguing challenge for the accounting fraternity that is entrenched in the traditional ascendancy of "reliability" over "relevance" (Singh, 2013). Digital intangibles follow this pattern, which is exacerbated by their innovative nature that makes them often riskier than "traditional" intangibles.

As the intangibles are non-monetary assets with no physical form, it is difficult to find evidence for their existence. Intangible assets may be recorded as an asset in the balance sheet if future economic benefits can be expected.

An intangible asset is identifiable when it: is separable (capable of being separated and sold, transferred, licensed, rented, or exchanged, either individually or together with a related contract) or arises from contractual or other legal rights, regardless of whether those rights are transferable or separable from the entity or other rights and obligations (IAS 38.12).

The requirement for an intangible asset to be "identifiable" is included to distinguish the asset from the (internally generated) goodwill that cannot be recorded.

Many intangibles will not be recognized in the financial statements as they fail to meet the definition of an asset or the recognition criteria. Examples include staff training, brand-building through advertising, and the development of new business processes. As no asset is recognized as a result of expenditure on such activities, it will be reported as an expense, even though it is undertaken to enhance the financial returns in subsequent accounting periods (Lennard, 2018).

Financial statements can only deal with those intangibles that meet the definition of assets and satisfy the recognition criteria, as set out in the IASB's Conceptual Framework.

Intangibles can be acquired by:

a. Separate purchase;
b. Being part of a business combination;
c. Government grant;
d. Exchange of assets, and
e. Self-creation (internal generation).

IAS 38 permits intangible assets to be recognized at fair value, measured by reference to an active market. While acknowledging that such markets may exist for assets such as "freely transferable taxi licenses, fishing licenses or production quotas" it states that "it is uncommon for an active market to exist for an intangible asset".

The lack of an active market makes it difficult to estimate the fair market value of an intangible.

According to Lev (2018):

- Most of the strategic, value-creating resources of business firms, such as patents, IT, or brands, are currently expensed, and, therefore, not recognized as assets in financial reports, thereby understating the earnings and assets of intangibles-growing firms, and overstating the earnings and assets of intangibles-declining firms;
- The fundamental inconsistency between the accounting treatment of internally generated intangibles (expensed) and that of the functionally similar acquired intangibles (capitalized) precludes a meaningful performance comparison of peer companies with different innovation strategies (internal generation vs. acquisition);
- The disclosure of intangible expenditures in financial reports is seriously deficient. Except for R&D, all other intangible expenditures are generally aggregated within large expense items, mainly the cost of sales and Selling General &Administrative expenses.

These inconsistencies severely impair the capacity to rely on the accounting data to infer the market value of the intangibles.

The accounting treatment is nevertheless a prerequisite for valuation. The issue is very complex, given that intangible assets are often not directly accounted for in the balance sheet or, in some cases, only appear in the income statement, within the operating expenses (OPEX).

In the attribution of value to intangible assets, it is necessary to consider the income capacity they generate, without which it is difficult to assign a specific value to the "intangible".

The accounting treatment and the consequent underrepresentation in the balance sheet of the real value of the intangibles often implies the necessity to appraise the growth opportunities that are naturally embedded in the intangibles.

Another accounting issue concerns the Net Present Value of growth opportunities (NPVGO) that calculates the Net Present Value of all future cash flows involved with the growth opportunities of the firm. The NPVGO is not recorded in the balance sheet and is used to determine the intrinsic value of these opportunities to determine how much of the firm's current per-share value is determined by them. The estimation of NPVGO is consistent with the appraisal of the intrinsic value of the real options linked to the intangible assets. The presence of (digital) intangibles fosters the NPVGO.

According to Damodaran (2018), the firms with intangible assets have the following characteristics:

(a) Inconsistent accounting rules that prudentially prevent capitalization of most operating expenses (OPEX)[9];
(b) Conservative financing (examined in Chapter 19) since intangibles lack any physical collateral;
(c) Extensive use of stock options to remunerate the management;
(d) The compressed life cycle of tech firms grows faster and stays mature for shorter periods (Damodaran, 2018).

2.11.1   *Intangible Assets and Capitalized Costs*

Accounting practice tends to divide intangible assets into two categories:

(a) Intangible assets in the strict sense;
(b) Intangible assets not represented by assets.

The first category includes patents, intellectual property rights (IPR), concession or rights, licenses, and trademarks; the second category includes capitalized costs, such as startup and expansion costs, bond issue discounts, study and research costs, design costs, advertising, and propaganda costs and representation costs (…).

Capitalized costs (intangible assets not represented by assets, like all elements not identifiable with certainty and not separable from the company) are not independently transferable and, therefore, do not represent straightforward intangible assets.

The valuation of intangible assets cannot fail to consider the subdivision into specific and generic (not represented by assets) intangibles: the former usually are subject to a separate estimate, which mainly uses the criterion of the cost of reproduction or the incremental income that the intangible asset guarantees.

Intangible assets are characterized by a lack of tangibility. They are made up of costs that do not exhaust their usefulness in a single period but show the economic benefits for several years. Intangible (fixed) assets include:

- Deferred charges (startup and expansion costs; development costs);
- Intangible assets (industrial patents and intellectual property rights; concessions, licenses, trademarks, and similar rights);
- Goodwill;
- Intangible assets in progress;
- Advances.

Future economic benefits arising from an intangible asset include revenues from the sale of products or services, cost savings, or other benefits arising from the use of the intangible asset by the company.

2.11.2   Valuation Drivers, Overcoming the Accounting Puzzle

The continued growth of intangible investments is the hallmark of developed economies, initiating significant changes in the business models, strategies, and performance of business firms. Accounting standard-setters, however, by and large, are oblivious to this worldwide development (Lev, 2018).

The two biggest challenges in the accounting principles are probably represented by the valuation of intangible assets and derivatives. Concerning the former, the international accounting standards (IAS, IFRS) have long adopted a strict view, and the capitalization of intangibles is admitted in very limited cases (such as development costs if they show an expected useful life). This approach privileges prudence over representativeness and may underestimate the real value of the intangibles.

Capitalized intangibles are part of the Capital Expenditure (CAPEX), whereas intangible costs recorded in the income statement are part of the monetary OPEX. Amortization is a non-monetary operating cost that reduces the balance value of the intangible CAPEX.

The two most common valuation approaches for the estimate of the enterprise value are based on the operating cash flows discounted at the WACC or on the EBITDA times a multiple of comparable firms.

The following formulation recalls the two methodologies (for simplicity, DCF does not consider any terminal value):

Enterprise Value

$$= \sum_{i=1}^{n} \frac{\text{sales} - \text{monetary OPEX} \pm \Delta \text{ Net Working Capital} \pm \Delta \text{ CAPEX}}{(1 + \text{WACC})^n}$$

$$= \frac{\text{Operating Cash Flow}}{(1 + \text{WACC})^n} \cong (\text{basic EBITDA} + \text{intangible} - \text{driven EBITDA})$$

$$* \text{ market multiplier} \tag{2.23}$$

Intangibles impact on sales (due to the scalability effect examined in Chapter 3), on monetary OPEX (cost of not-capitalized intangibles, net of the savings from synergies), and the CAPEX (capitalized intangibles less the yearly amortization).

The DCF formulation estimates the Enterprise Value of the firm discounting its Operating Cash Flow at the WACC. Since the Operating Cash flow includes both the monetary OPEX represented by the intangibles (intangible costs net of the synergies) and the intangible part of the CAPEX (incremental CAPEX due to the intangible capitalized investments net of the yearly amortization), the numerator of the DCF formula is not affected by the accounting policies of the firm.

The book value of the intangible assets is expressed by the information available from the balance sheet, income statement, and cash flow statement, following the format shown in Fig. 2.14 that comprehensively represents the different valuation approaches.

2.12   INTANGIBLE ASSETS VALUATION ACCORDING TO IVS 210

According to IVS 210 § 20.1 *"an intangible asset is a non-monetary asset that manifests itself by its economic properties. It does not have physical substance but grants rights and economic benefits to its owner"*.

§ 20.3 indicates that there are many intangible assets, but they are often considered to fall into one of the following five categories (or goodwill):

(a) *Marketing-related: marketing-related intangible assets are used primarily in the marketing or promotion of products or services. Examples include trademarks, trade names, unique trade design, and internet domain names,*

(b) *Customer-related: customer-related intangible assets include customer lists, backlog, customer contracts, and contractual and non-contractual customer relationships,*

(c) *Artistic-related: artistic-related intangible assets arising from the right to benefits such as royalties from artistic works such as plays,*

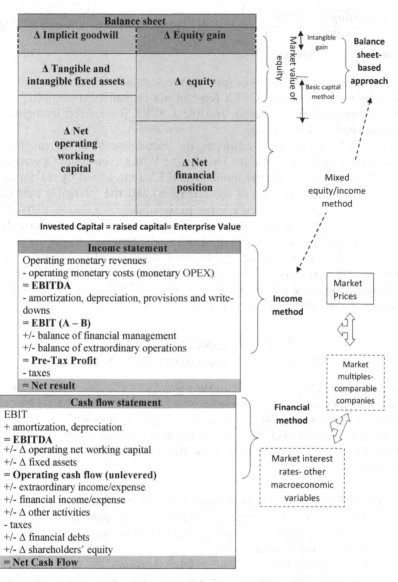

Fig. 2.14 The integrated equity—economic-financial—empirical and market valuation

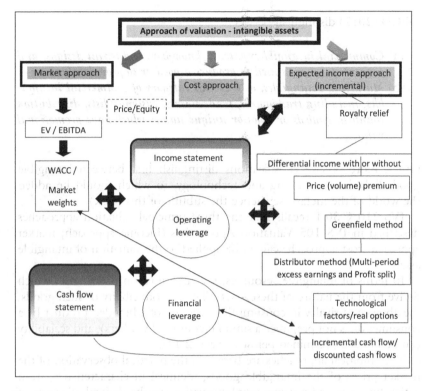

Fig. 2.15 Approaches of valuation of intangible assets

    books, films and music, and from non-contractual copyright protection,

(d) *Contract-related: contract-related intangible assets represent the value of rights that arise from contractual agreements. Examples include licensing and royalty agreements, service or supply contracts, lease agreements, permits, broadcast rights, servicing contracts, non-competition agreements and natural resource rights, and*

(e) *Technology-based: technology-related intangible assets arise from contractual or non-contractual rights to use patented technology, unpatented technology, databases, formulae, designs, software, processes, or recipes.*

OECD (2017) distinguish between:

(a) *Commercial intangibles: patents, know-how, industrial designs, and ornamental models used to produce a good or to provide a service;*
(b) *Marketing intangibles, as a special category of commercial intangibles, including trademarks, trade names, customer lists, distribution channels, symbols or logos or unique names which have promotional value.*

Other, more precise classifications distinguish first between intangible goods linked to marketing and technology, to which should be added the world of the metaverse (hence the subtitle of this book).

IVS 210 § 30.1 recalls that the three principal valuation approaches described in IVS 105 Valuation Approaches (income approach; market approach; cost approach) can all be applied to the valuation of intangible assets.

In terms of intangible resources, specific valuation issues arise, which derive from the nature of these assets. The reproducibility of such goods, the absence of rivalry in consumption (the use of a branded product by a consumer does not prejudice a simultaneous use by others), and scalability can be noticed (examined below in Sect. 2.14).

The empirical approaches are based on the practical observation of the market prices of the intangible goods, identical in characteristics, from which formulas and parameters of evaluation can be derived. The use of practical criteria is dictated by the speed of updating the value of the fixed assets in similar and homogeneous companies.

Analytical approaches, on the contrary, are more reliable because they are accepted by theory and consolidated by practice, even if they are often less intuitive.

The three principal valuation approaches described in IVS 105 Valuation Approaches (consistent with IFRS 13—Fair Value Measurement) used—individually or in a complementary way—by professional practice for the economic estimation of the value of intangible assets are (see Fig. 2.14):

1. The market approach;
2. The cost approach (reconstruction or replacement capital);
3. The (incremental) income approach.

According to the valuation practice, the appraisal of an intangible asset can be made by reference to each of the three known valuation approaches. In selecting the most appropriate approach, the expert should consider the characteristics of the intangible asset and its reproducibility, the nature of . the benefits it can generate for the owner (current or potential) and the user, and the existence or otherwise of a reference market.

Some intangibles, as trademarks (Salinas & Ambler, 2009) and patents, are particularly complex to evaluate (Moro Visconti, 2012), considering their intrinsic immaterial nature and different (complementary) approaches of evaluation, quantitative and qualitative, are traditionally used by the evaluation practice (Lagrost et al., 2010).

Valuation issues are even more complex for other intangibles, such as know-how (Moro Visconti, 2013), industrial secrets, unpatented research and development costs, goodwill, etc. ..., which are characterized by limited or absent negotiability, greater information asymmetries, and less defined legal boundaries, particularly in specific sectors (Fig. 2.15).

The valuation of intangible assets not registered or specifically protected, such as know-how, is subject to high intertemporal variability, being anchored to provisions aimed at drawing up the strategic, industrial, and financial plans applicable to the joint-stock companies. Variability is incorporated in the risk, and the information contained in the report on operations can provide valuable insights.

The breadth of the valuation interval is demarcated by upper and lower limits, in the case of (full) going concern (full business continuity) or in break-up (liquidation) scenarios, in which intangible resources traditionally lose most of their value. This happens especially if they are not independently negotiable or can be synergistically linked to other assets. In the case of discontinuity, the "organized complex of assets" that keeps together the company is eliminated.

The choice of the approaches to be used depends on the type of intangible resource and the purpose and context of the evaluation, but also on the ease with which reliable information can be found.

Of the different approaches, the complementarity in identifying—from different angles—the multi-faceted aspects of the intangible object of evaluation, suitable to allow an integrated assessment, must be grasped. For example, the relief-from-royalties is in the function of the incomes or incremental cash flows that derive from the exploitation of the intangible resource and that interact with the market surplus value or the multipliers of comparable companies. The incremental equity derives from an accumulation of differential income. The cost of reproduction estimates the future benefits and differential goodwill. The different approaches should theoretically lead to similar results, although the relief-from-royalty and reproduction cost approach sometimes tend to provide lower valuations than the differential income approach or the market comparisons.

The following sub-paragraphs contain a detailed description of the different valuation approaches (cost, income, and market) mentioned above.

2.12.1   *Cost Approach*

The cost of tangible assets is typically known or can be estimated when the asset is acquired and invoiced from the seller. The economic benefits and their occurrence may be reasonably estimated. In contrast, the cost of many intangibles is unclear, as they are not the result of a project that can be separated from the business activities.

The economic benefits that will be derived from the investment in intangibles are typically hard to estimate. Due to the intrinsic risky nature of innovation, many projects will fail and be abandoned and provide little or no benefit to the firm. This is often the case with digital projects.

The cost approach, according to IFRS 13, reflects the amount that would be required currently to replace the service capacity of an asset. Deriving fair value under this approach, therefore, requires estimating the costs of developing an equivalent intangible asset. But, as noted above, it is often difficult to estimate in advance the costs of developing an intangible. Unless these difficulties can be overcome, the cost approach would be impracticable (Lennard, 2018).

Within this framework and provided that these limitations are clear, reference to the cost may still give some useful insights for valuation.

According to the cost approach, the value of an intangible asset is determined by the sum of the capitalized costs, incurred for the realization of the (digital) intangible or to be incurred to reproduce it (restoration of rights and brand accreditation represented, in general, by advertising, promotional and distribution network investments …).

The limitation of this approach lies in the fact that it does not consider maintenance costs and the opportunity cost of time and that it does not apply to assets capable of generating income.

The main difficulties in applying this approach relate to the difficulty in finding costs incurred in the past, especially if the costs have been incurred over several years and have not been capitalized.

There are broadly two main approaches that fall under the cost approach: the replacement cost and the reproduction cost. However, intangible assets do not have a physical form that can be reproduced, and assets such as software that can be reproduced generally derive value from their function/utility rather than their exact lines of code. As such, the replacement cost is most commonly applied to the valuation of intangible assets.

Replacement cost approach assumes that a market participant would pay no more for the asset than the cost that would be incurred to replace the asset with a substitute of comparable utility or functionality. This approach requires an assessment of the replacement cost for the intangible asset new, that is *"the cost to construct, at current prices as of the date of the analysis, an intangible asset with the equivalent utility to the subject intangible, using modern materials, production standards, design, layout and quality workmanship"* (Reilly & Schweihs, 2016). The replacement cost is then adjusted for an obsolescence factor relative to the intangible asset.

2.12.2 Income/financial Approach

It is based on past and future economic benefits that can be linked to an intangible, both in terms of license revenues (royalties) and incremental revenues.

The income approach essentially converts future cash flows (or income and expenses) to a discounted present value. The calculation may be like that of value in use (a concept known since Aristoteles, Adam Smith and Karl Marx). However, to arrive at fair value, the future income must be estimated from the perspective of market participants rather than that of the entity. Therefore, applying the income approach requires an insight into how market participants would assess the benefits that will be obtained from an intangible asset (Lennard, 2018).

In the context of income approaches, intangible assets are valuable to the extent that they can incorporate a competitive advantage in the form of multi-period excess earnings. This is a pure income estimate, in which intangible assets act as Primary Income Generating Assets.

Income approaches are based on estimates of future economic benefits, for example, through discounted cash flows.

The income approaches formally include the financial ones: so the estimate of incremental cash flows or the criterion of discounted cash flows, functionally linked to the market approaches from which it derives some parameters (in fact, market) for the estimate of the value of shareholders' equity and financial debts.

The linking parameter may be represented by the EBITDA that is simultaneously an economic and financial margin, representing the difference between monetary operating revenues and costs. The EBITDA is present in both specific classifications of the income and the cash flow statements.

The main variants are:

1. **The Relief-from royalty approach**: which allows estimating the income of the intangible asset by deducting from the notional royalties that would be paid to a third party for the use of the intangible under license any direct and indirect costs of maintenance/development of the asset itself not already deducted from the notional royalty;

2. **The premium profit approach or with-and-without approach**: indirect approach of determining the economic advantage (premium price), which consists in comparing the performance of the company that disposes of the intangible asset in question with that of a similar company without such an asset;

3. **The Excess earnings approach**: to be used to estimate the value of an asset that plays a significant or primary role, based on which the notional income is obtained by calculating the income that the firm would record if it was disposed of the ownership of all the other assets to regain the right to use them through licensing or rental or rental contracts. The concepts behind the excess earnings approach were first described in 1920 in the United States Internal Revenue Services' Appeals and Revenue Memorandum (ARM) 34. Whether applied in a single-period, multi-period, or capitalized manner, the key steps in an excess earnings approach are:

   (a) Forecast the amount and timing of future revenues driven by the subject intangible asset and other supporting (i.e., contributory assets).

(b) Forecast the amount and timing of expenses that are required to generate the revenue from the subject intangible asset and related contributory asset.

(c) Adjust the expenses to exclude those related to the creation of new intangible assets. Profit margins in the excess earnings approach may be higher than profit margins for the overall business because the excess earnings approach excludes investment in new intangible assets. The Multi-period Excess earnings approach is a variation of the discounted cash flow approach. Rather than focusing on the whole entity, this approach isolates the cash flows that can be associated with a single intangible asset and estimates the fair value by discounting them to present value.

4. **The Greenfield Approach**: the value of the specific intangible is determined using cash flow projections that assume the only asset of the business at the valuation date is the specific intangible. All other tangible and intangible assets must be bought, built, or rented (see IVS 210, § 90);

5. **The Distributor approach**: a variation of the Multi-period excess earnings approach sometimes used to value customer-related intangible assets. As distributors generally only perform functions related to the distribution of products to customers rather than the development of intellectual property or manufacturing, information on profit margins earned by distributors is used to estimate the excess earnings attributable to customer-related intangible assets. The distributor approach is like the relief-from-royalty approach when a Profit split is used to estimate an appropriate royalty rate.

6. **Real options** are used to evaluate flexible investment projects with uncertain outcomes (typically patents). Real options are a fundamental characteristic of scalable investments, described in Chapter 3.

7. **Discounting of differential (incremental) income or cash flows**: this is based on quantifying and discounting the specific benefits and advantages of the intangible asset compared to "normal" situations, i.e., products for example not marked or covered by a patent. Incremental income is obtained by the difference between revenues and costs relating to the intangible asset, with discounting of the differential flows and with the exclusion of extraneous or immaterial income components;

2.12.3   Market Approach

The market approach considers the prices and other relevant information generated by market transactions involving identical or comparable assets.

Many intangible assets, however, are not traded: Lev attributes this to "contracting difficulties, negligible marginal costs and fuzzy property rights" (Lev, 2001). A market may, nevertheless, exist for mature and well-established intangibles.

As IAS 38 notes: "*an active market cannot exist for brands, newspaper mastheads, music and film publishing rights, patents or trademarks, because each such asset is unique*" (IAS 38, par. 78).

Unicity is a factor of strength but also a weakness: whereas unique intangibles (e.g., a patent) command a premium over other external assets, they are hardly comparable, making valuation more difficult.

Many intangible assets are "context-specific" and so they may have little or no value to a purchaser (Haskel & Westlake, 2017).

When applicable, this approach is based on a comparison with similar assets, in terms of income or incremental assets, or on the analysis of comparable transactions and market multipliers.

The main limitation of this approach concerns the information asymmetries structurally connected with the secrecy of intangible assets, which make the information necessary for comparisons challenging to find.

Package transactions involving multiple assets or intangibles make the valuation of stand-alone intangibles based on an empirical approach more complicated. These difficulties are even more evident considering that, as anticipated in Sect. 2.10, from an accounting point of view, according to IAS 38, there is no active market for intangible assets, which tend to be not accounted for, and their fair value seems difficult to estimate.

The main approaches are:

1. *Empirical approach*: the income attributable to the exploitation of a given intangible asset is multiplied by an expressive coefficient of the strategic strength of the asset, which depends on factors such as leadership, loyalty, market positioning, trends, marketing investments, internationality, legal protection ...;
2. *Valuation of the differential (incremental) assets*, through indicators of the market surplus value, such as the **Q of Tobin**, which relates the market value of the activities of a company to their replacement value; if the index is higher than the unit, this is due

to the presence of an implicit goodwill which can depend, among other things, on the value (not accounted for) of the intangible.

3. *Price/Book Value index*, which compares the stock market price (of a branded or other intangible listed company) to the book net assets, bringing out a surplus value (if the index is greater than 1) partly attributable to intangible assets.

2.13   INTANGIBLES WITH A DEFINED AND INDEFINITE USEFUL LIFE

The useful life of an intangible good is the period during which it can be conveniently used.

The estimate of the useful life of the intangible assets allows to discriminate between those:

1. With a defined useful life, subject to systematic amortization (as prescribed by the international accounting standard IAS 38) and an estimate of the residual useful life;
2. With an indefinite useful life, subject to impairment testing at least once a year (IAS 36).

According to OECD (2017):

- *"Many intangibles have a limited useful life. The useful life of a particular intangible can be affected by the nature and duration of the legal protections afforded to the intangible, as noted above. The useful life of some intangibles can also be affected by the rate of technological change in an industry and by the development of new and potentially improved products. It may also be the case that the useful life of particular intangibles can be extended"*.
- *"The projected useful life of particular intangibles is a question to be determined based on all of the relevant facts and circumstances. The useful life of a particular intangible can be affected by the nature and duration of the legal protections afforded the intangible. The useful life of intangibles also may be affected by the rate of technological change in the industry, and by other factors affecting competition in the relevant economic environment"*.

The determination of the residual useful life of the intangible assets is an important element in the evaluation process, in order, first, to define the time horizon. According to the evaluation practice, all the approaches of evaluation of the intangible assets require, in fact, an estimate of their residual useful life.

The useful life:

- Coincides with the period during which the intangible asset can produce cash flows;
- Requires maintenance costs, especially if the useful life is indefinite or very long;
- Must be estimated considering obsolescence and senescence.

The estimate of the residual useful life is particularly important for the bankability connected with the exploitation of the intangible asset. In synthesis:

- Useful life is the period during which the company expects to be able to use the asset. It can be determined by the quantities of units of output (or equivalent) that it is estimated can be obtained using the asset;
- Amortization is the allocation of the cost of an intangible asset over its estimated useful life using a systematic and rational approach, regardless of the results achieved during the period;
- The value to be amortized is the difference between the cost of the intangible asset, determined according to the criteria set out in principle, and, if measurable, its residual value;
- The residual value of an intangible asset is the estimated realizable value of the asset at the end of its useful life.

Future economic benefits arising from an intangible asset may include income from the sale of products or services, cost savings, or other benefits arising from the use of the asset by the company (IAS 38, par. 17).

Accounting for an intangible asset is based on its useful life. An intangible asset with a finite useful life is amortized, while an intangible asset with an indefinite useful life is not amortized (IAS 38, par. 87).

IAS 38 requires that:

(a) The useful life of an intangible asset arising from contractual or other legal rights should not exceed the period of those rights, but may be shorter depending on the period over which the asset is expected to be used by the entity; and
(b) If the rights are conveyed for a limited term that can be renewed, the useful life should include the renewal period(s) only if there is evidence to support renewal by the entity without significant cost.

Among the factors that affect the estimation of useful life, IAS 38 (paragraph 90) identifies the following:

(a) The expected use of the asset or by the group companies to which it belongs;
(b) The typical product life cycles of the asset and public information about estimates of the useful lives of assets used similarly;
(c) Technical, technological, commercial, or other obsolescence;
(d) The stability of the economic sector in which the asset operates and changes in demand in the market for the products or services generated by the asset;
(e) The actions that actual or potential competitors are expected to take;
(f) The level of maintenance expenditure necessary to obtain the future economic benefits expected from the asset;
(g) The period of control over the asset and the legal or similar limits on the use of the asset;
(h) Whether the useful life of the asset depends on the useful life of other assets.

2.14   SURPLUS INTANGIBLE ASSETS

The surplus assets indicate:

1. Ancillary capital, which expresses the current value of assets that are not relevant to the performance of operating activities, as they are not instrumental to the company's operations;
2. Components subject to an independent valuation.

These elements may include intangible assets, which have an impact both on ancillary capital and on the normalization of income.

Surplus assets are generally included in adjusted balance sheet-based approaches or mixed capital-income approaches, as an additional component that is added to the base values.

2.15   HARD-TO-VALUE INTANGIBLES

Intangibles are so peculiar and difficult to define that in many cases they become hard-to-value, especially if they are unpatented or unbranded. Comparability concerns exacerbate the issue, together with the difficulty to get input data for the appraisal.

According to OECD (2017):

- *"The term hard-to-value intangibles covers intangibles or rights in intangibles for which, at the time of their transfer between associated firms, (i) no reliable comparables exist, and (ii) at the time the transactions were entered into, the projections of future cash flows or income expected to be derived from the transferred intangible, or the assumptions used in valuing the intangible are highly uncertain, making it difficult to predict the level of ultimate success of the intangible at the time of the transfer"* (par. 6.189).
- *"Transactions involving the transfer, or the use of Hard-to-value intangibles may exhibit one or more of the following features:*
  - The intangible is only partially developed at the time of the transfer.
  - *The intangible is not expected to be exploited commercially until several years following the transaction.*
  - *The intangible is expected to be exploited in a manner that is novel at the time of the transfer and the absence of a track record of development or exploitation of similar intangibles makes projections highly uncertain"* (par. 6.190).

2.16   RESOURCE-BASED VIEW AND BALANCED SCORECARD: INTRODUCTORY REMARKS

The strategic evaluation of intangible assets is complementary to the economic-financial evaluation examined in the previous paragraphs.

In this context, the Resource-Based View (RBV) is based on the importance of the internal variables of an organization compared to the external variables. For RBV, intangible resources and human resources are the most important because they are rare and complex and, therefore, more difficult to imitate. They can, therefore, have a greater impact in terms of competitive advantage, which is the strategic basis for achieving higher performance, in terms of profitability, than the average of competitors. According to RBV, the competitive advantage derives from greater efficiency and the possession of rare and difficult to imitate resources. The company is understood as a portfolio of skills and value-added activities.

Intangible resources can, for example, coincide with knowledge, innovation, access to information, corporate identity, customer loyalty, relations with stakeholders, professionalism, and motivation of human resources.

A synthesis of the RBV is reported in Fig. 2.16.

The Balanced Scorecard (Kaplan & Norton, 1996) represents an alternative to the models for the integrated management of company resources and proposes an innovative approach for measuring company performance according to a vision that goes beyond the traditional one, limited only to the financial perspective.

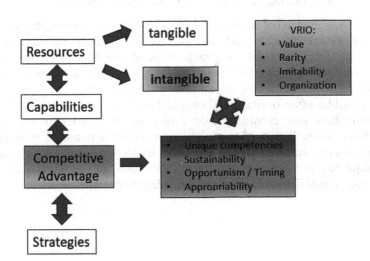

Fig. 2.16 Resource-based view

The Balanced Scorecard represents a technique for identifying and measuring the critical success factors underlying the competitive advantage obtained by the company using intangible resources.

The basic idea of the model is to indicate in a "scorecard" a summary of the fundamental financial and non-financial indicators, through which to measure the company's performance and prospects for the future.

In the conceptual framework of the model, financial performance is not the primary focus on which the company must concentrate, as this is instead the natural and consequent result of a balanced process of achieving other strategic objectives.

In the logic of the model, intangible assets have economic value to the extent that their use is aligned with the implementation of business strategies and related to the priorities set by the overall strategy of the company. The more intangible resource is needed to support the implementation of business strategies, the more important it is in the processes of generating cash flows for the company, the higher its strategic and economic value.

2.17   The Intangible Roadmap: From Patents and Trademarks to Blockchains, Big Data, and Artificial Intelligence

Due to their immaterial nature and lack of "physicality", intangible assets are often characterized by undefined boundaries and plasticity that makes them easily interchangeable, adaptable, resilient and flexible. These properties are typically exalted if the intangible has a digital dimension, as it can be used, and exchanged in real time within the web.

Intangibles often overlap, as shown in Fig. 2.17. An example is given by know-how that eventually may evolve to protected patenting, or (implicit) goodwill that expresses the non-recorded potential of trademarks, or even the information value chain recalled in Fig. 2.18. Software is ubiquitous, as it interacts with most intangibles, and algorithms are at the base of artificial intelligence (machine learning) patterns.

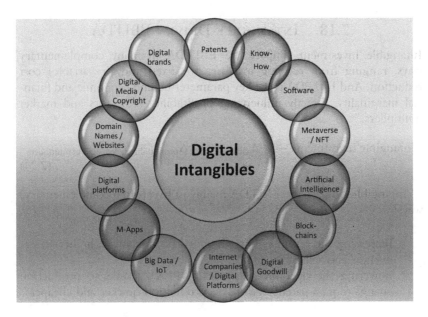

Fig. 2.17 Intangible's interaction

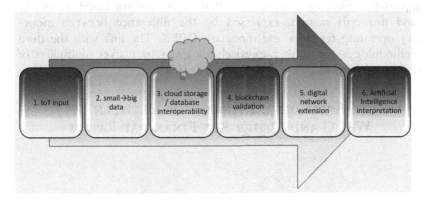

Fig. 2.18 Information value chain

2.18   INTANGIBLE-DRIVEN EBITDA

Intangible investments impact the EBITDA in many complementary ways, ranging from revenue increases to (fixed and/or variable) cost reduction. And EBITDA is the key parameter behind economic and financial marginality, directly influencing profitability indicators and market multipliers:

$$\text{Intangible Investments} \rightarrow +\Delta_{\text{EBITDA}} \rightarrow \Delta_{\text{profitability ratios/market multipliers}}$$
(2.24)

Intangibles impact the EBITDA mainly in two (often complementary) ways:

1. Increasing the revenues (e.g., branded products with higher attractiveness and selling capacity);
2. Lowering the operating expenses (OPEX), thanks to production savings (e.g., a patent that makes production quicker and cheaper).

The EBITDA's consideration is consistent with the cost and the income approach, reflecting a parameter that is an income-based economic (and financial) margin, expressed by the difference between monetary operating revenues and monetary OPEX. The link with the third methodology—the market approach—is given by market multipliers of comparable firms.

APPENDIX I: INTERACTION BETWEEN
WACC AND OTHER KEY FINANCIAL RATIOS

Ratio	Formula	Links and interactions with WACC
WACC	$$WACC = k_e \frac{E}{D_f + E} + k_d(1-t)\frac{D_f}{D_f + E}$$ where: D_f = Financial debts E = Equity K_e = Cost of equity K_d = Cost of debt t = Corporate tax rate	—
IRR$_{project}$	$$NPV_{project} = \frac{CFO_1}{1+IRR_{project}} + \frac{CFO_2}{(1+IRR_{project})^2} + \cdots + \frac{CFO_n}{(1+IRR_{project})^n} - CF_0 = 0$$ where: CFO = Operating Cash Flow CF_0 = initial investment	If WACC > IRR$_{project}$, NPV$_{project}$ < 0; then it's possible that CF$_0$ (which strongly depends on the cost of collected capital) > $\sum_{t=1}^{n}\frac{CFO_n}{(1+IRR_{project})^T}$ If WACC = IRR$_{project}$, NPV$_{project}$ = 0 and $CF_0 = \sum_{t=1}^{n}\frac{CFO_n}{(1+IRR_{project})^T}$ If WACC < IRR$_{project}$, NPV$_{project}$ > 0 and $CF_0 < \sum_{t=1}^{n}\frac{CFO_n}{(1+IRR_{project})^T}$
IRR$_{equity}$	$$NPV_{equity} = \frac{CFN_1}{1+IRR_{equity}} + \frac{CFN_2}{(1+IRR_{equity})^2} + \cdots + \frac{CFN_n}{(1+IRR_{equity})^n} - CF_0 = 0$$ where: CFN = Net Cash Flow CF_0 = Initial investment	If WACC > IRR$_{equity}$, NPV$_{equity}$ < 0; then it's possible that CF$_0$ (which strongly depends on the cost of collected capital) > $\sum_{t=1}^{n}\frac{CFN_n}{(1+IRR_{equity})^T}$ If WACC = IRR$_{equity}$, NPV$_{equity}$ = 0 and $CF_0 = \sum_{t=1}^{n}\frac{CFN_n}{(1+IRR_{equity})^T}$ If WACC < IRR$_{equity}$, NPV$_{equity}$ > 0 and $CF_0 < \sum_{t=1}^{n}\frac{CFN_n}{(1+IRR_{equity})^T}$

(continued)

(continued)

Ratio	Formula	Links and interactions with WACC
$NPV_{project}$	$NPV_{project} = \sum_{t=1}^{n} \frac{CFO_t}{(1+WACC)^t} - CF_0$ where: CFO = Operating Cash Flow t = time CF_0 = initial investment	If K_d or K_e grow, WACC increases; $NPV_{project}$ decreases If K_d or K_e reduce, WACC decreases; $NPV_{project}$ increases
NPV_{equity}	$NPV_{equity} = \sum_{t=1}^{n} \frac{CFO_t}{(1+K_e)^t} - CF_0$ where: CFN = Net Cash Flow t = time CF_0 = initial investment	If K_e grows, WACC increases and NPV_{equity} decreases. If K_e reduces, WACC decreases and NPV_{equity} increases K_d changes might influence WACC, but not NPV_{equity}
APV_{equity} (Adjusted Present Value)	NPV_{equity} + Present Value of Tax Benefit	Like NPV_{equity}, considering also the fiscal benefit of debt. Higher leverage increases APV, provided that there is a positive taxable base and that increasing probabilities of default do not prevent debt raising
Average Debt Service Cover Ratio $(ADSCR)^{10}$	$ADSCR = \frac{\sum_{t=1}^{n} \frac{CFO_t}{(D_{ft}+I_t)}}{n}$ where: CFO = Operating Cash Flow D_f = Financial Debts I = Interests t = time from 1 to n years	If K_d increases, financial charges (interests) increase too. In this case, ADSCR decreases, while WACC might increase (to the extent that riskier debt is not counterbalanced by safer equity) If K_d decreases, interests decrease too. ADSCR increases, while WACC might decrease

(continued)

(continued)

Ratio	Formula	Links and interactions with WACC
LEVERAGE	$\frac{D_f}{E}$ where: D_f = Financial Debts E = Equity	If D_f grows, K_d increases and K_e decreases. If D_f is reduced, K_d decreases and K_e increases. WACC might be unaffected
$NPV_{project}/EBITDA$	$NPV_{project}/EBITDA =$ $(\sum_{t=1}^{n} \frac{CFO_t}{(1+WACC)^t} - CF_0)/EBITDA_{AVERAGE}$	This standardized indicator expresses in relative, rather than in absolute terms, the multiplier of a project's value times the EBITDA,[11] allowing for market comparisons. If the average EBITDA grows, even CFO increases, normally at a lower rate,[12] a higher EBITDA may lower the cost of capital, with a positive impact on the WACC since the overall risk for both equity and debt holders is reduced by a higher cash generation, provided that also the CFO grows
Discounted Project Payback Period	$\sum_{t=0}^{n} \frac{CFO_t}{(1+WACC)^t} = 0$ where: CFO = Operating Cash Flow t = time from 1 to n years	If CFO decreases or WACC grows, payback period increases. If CFO grows or WACC decreases, payback period shortens
Discounted Equity Payback Period	$\sum_{t=0}^{n} \frac{CFN_t}{(1+K_e)^t} = 0$ where: CFN = Net Cash Flow t = time	If CFN decreases or K_e grows, payback period increases. If CFN grows or K_e decreases, payback period shortens. K_e is part of WACC, but it changes may have no effects on WACC, to the extent that cost of debt (K_d) symmetrically adjusts

NOTES

1. It should be remembered that these balance sheet-based approaches are diffused mainly in Continental Europe ad hardly anywhere else.
2. The CAPMs a model used in finance to assess an appropriate expected rate of return of a listed security, in proportion to its risk, to make decisions about adding assets to a well-diversified portfolio.
3. See Chapter 21.
4. https://www.ivsc.org/files/file/view/id/647.
5. See par. 7.4 and 8.10.4.
6. There seminal papers are quoted in https://www.jstor.org/stable/321 6804.
7. See for instance the Statistical Classification of Economic Activities in the European Community, commonly referred to as NACE.
8. WACC is the average after-tax cost of a company's various capital sources (cost of collecting external capital), including common stock, preferred stock, bonds, and any other long-term financial debt.
9. This topic will be addressed in Chapter 3.
10. Other cover ratio measures include Loan Life Cover Ratio, defined as: Net Present Value of Cash flow Available for Debt Service/Outstanding Debt in the period.
11. Alternatively, EBIT may be used instead of EBITDA.
12. Being EBITDA $\pm\Delta$ operating net working capital $\pm$ Δ capital expenditure = CFO, any increase in EBITDA is typically accompanied by an increase in Operating Net Working Capital (a higher inventory and a bigger credit exposure are normally linked to a growing operating economic margin) and also in capital expenditure (more investments are typically needed for an EBITDA increase). So if EBITDA grows, its positive marginality on CFO is normally lowered by an increase in Operating Net Working Capital and capital expenditure, which burns out some of the extra cash created by the EBITDA's increase.

SELECTED REFERENCES

Alonso, B. V., Garcia-Merino, J. D., & Arregui-Ayastuy, G. (2015). Motives for financial valuation of intangibles and business performance in SMEs. *Innovar*, 25(56), 113–128.
Arvidsson, S. (2011). Disclosure of non-financial information in the annual report: A management-team perspective. *Journal of Intellectual Capital*, 12(2), 277–300.
Bianchi, P., & Labory, S. (2017). The economy importance of intangible assets. London: Routledge.

Boujelben, S., & Fedhila, H. (2011). The effects of intangible investments on future OCF. *Journal of Intellectual Capital, 12*(4), 480–494.

Clausen, S., & Hirth, S. (2016). Measuring the value of intangibles. *Journal of Corporate Finance, 40,* 110–127.

Cohen, A. J. (2005). *Intangible assets: Valuation and economic benefit.* Hoboken: Wiley.

Còrcoles, Y. R. (2010). Towards the convergence of accounting treatment for intangible assets. *Intangible Capital, 6*(2), 185–201.

Damodaran, A. (1996). *The stable growth DDM: Gordon growth model.* Available at http://people.stern.nyu.edu/adamodar/pdfiles/ddm.pdf

Damodaran, A. (2018). *The dark side of valuation* (3rd ed.). Pearson FT Press PTG.

Donaldson, T. H. (1992). *The treatment of intangibles: A banker's view.* New York, NY, USA: St Martin's Press.

Dosso, M., & Vezzani, A. (2017). *Firm market valuation and intellectual property assets* (JRC Working Papers on Corporate R&D and Innovation). Seville.

Fazzini, M. (2018). *Business valuation: Theory and practice.* London: Palgrave Macmillan.

Fernandez, P. (2001). *Valuation using multiples: How do analysts reach their conclusions?* Madrid: IESE Business School.

Fernandez, P. (2019a). *CAPM: An absurd model.* Available at SSRN: https://ssrn.com/abstract=2505597

Fernandez, P. (2019b). *Valuation and common sense.* Available at https://web.iese.edu/PabloFernandez/Book_VaCS/ContentsValuation.pdf

Fernandez, P. (2019c). *Equity premium: Historical, expected, required and implied.* Available at https://ssrn.com/abstract=933070

Gamayuni, R. R. (2015). The effect of intangible assets, financial performance and financial policies on the firm value. *International Journal of Scientific & Technology Research IJSTR, 4*(1), 202–212.

Garcìa-Meca, M., Parra, I., Larràn, M., & Martinez, I. (2005). The explanatory factors of intellectual capital disclosure to financial analysts. *European Accounting Review, 14*(1), 63–94.

Garcìa-Parra, M., Simo, P., Sallan, J. M., & Mundet, J. (2009). Intangible liabilities: Beyond models of intellectual assets. *Management Decisions, 47* (5), 819–830.

Giuliani, M. (2013). Not all sunshine and roses: Discovering intellectual liabilities "in action". *Journal of Intellectual Capital, 14*(1), 127–144.

Giuliani, M., & Marasca, M. (2011). Construction and valuation of intellectual capital: A case study. *Journal of Intellectual Capital, 12*(3), 377–391.

Grossmann, W., & Rinderle-Ma, S. (2015). *Fundamentals of Business Intelligence.* Berlin: Springer Verlag.

Gruber, S. (2015). *Intangible values in financial accounting and reporting. An analysis from the perspective of financial analysts.* Wiesbaden: Springer.

Hall, R. (1993). A framework linking intangible resources and capabilities to sustainable competitive advantage. *Strategic Management Journal, 14,* 607–618.

Hand, J., & Lev, B. (2003). *Intangible assets: Values, measures and risks.* Oxford: Oxford University Press.

Haskel, J., & Westlake, S. (2017). *Capitalism without capital: The rise of the intangible economy.* Princeton: Princeton University Press.

Hilton, B. J. (2015). Intangible and valuation in the age of knowledge. *ISSS Journals, 1*(1).

Huffman, L. (1983). Operating leverage, financial leverage, and equity risk. *Journal of Banking & Finance, 7* (2), 197–212.

Jarrett, J. E. (2018). *Methods of evaluating the value of intangible assets.* University of Rhode Island: Digital Commons URI.

Jow-Ran, C., Mao-Wei, H., & Feng-Tse, T. (2005). Valuation of intellectual property: A real option approach. *Journal of Intellectual Capital, 6*(3), 339–356.

Kaplan, R., & Norton, D. (1996). *The balanced scorecard: Translating strategy into action.* Boston: Harvard Business School Press.

Koller, T., & Goedhart, M. (2015). Valuation: Measuring and managing in the value of companies. Wiley, Hoboken, New Jersey: McKinsey & Company.

Lagrost, C., Martin, D., Dubois, C., & Quazzotti, S. (2010). Intellectual property valuation: How to approach the selection of an appropriate valuation method. *Journal of Intellectual Capital, 11*(4), 481–503.

Lennard, A. (2018). *Intangibles: First thoughts.* Paper presented at IFASS Meeting, Mumbai. Available at https://www.efrag.org/Assets/Download?assetUrl=%2Fsites%2Fwebpublishing%2FMeeting%20Documents%2F1709060811163678%2F05-02%20FRC%20presentation%20on%20Intangibles%20TEG%2018-04-06.pdf&AspxAutoDetectCookieSupport=1

Lev, B. (2001). *Intangibles: Management, measurement and reporting.* Washington, DC: Brookings Institute Press.

Lev, B. (2018). *Intangibles.* New York University Stern School of Business. Available at SSRN: https://ssrn.com/abstract=3218586

Lev, B., & Gu, F. (2016). *The end of accounting and the path forward for investors and managers.* Hoboken, NJ: Wiley.

Lim, S. C., & Macias, A. J. (2014). *Intangible assets and capital structure.* Paper presented at Paris Finance meeting EUROFIDAI-AFFI, December 2016.

Madden, B. J. (2017). The purpose of the firm, valuation, and the management of intangibles. *Journal of Applied Corporate Finance, 29*(2), 76–86.

Maditinos, D., Chatzoudes, D., Tsairidis, C., & Theriou, G. (2011). The impact of intellectual capital on firms' market value and financial performance. *Journal of Intellectual Capital, 12*(1), 132–151.

Metha, A. N. D., & Madhani, P. M. (2008). Intangible assets—An introduction. *The Accounting World, 8*(9), 11–19.

Moro Visconti, R. (2012). Exclusive patents and trademarks and subsequent uneasy transaction comparability: Some transfer pricing implications. *Intertax, 40*(3), 212–219.

Moro Visconti, R. (2013). Evaluating know-how for transfer price benchmarking. *Journal of Finance and Accounting, 1*(1), 27–38.

Moro Visconti, R. (2019, June 1). *How to prepare a business plan with excel.* Available at SSRN: https://ssrn.com/abstract=2039748

OECD. (2017, July). *Transfer pricing guidelines for multinational enterprises and tax administrations.* Available at https://www.oecd.org/tax/oecd-transf erpricing-guidelines-for-multinational-enterprises-and-tax-administrations-207 69717.htm

Osinski, M., Selig, P. M., Matos, F., & Roman, D. J. (2017). Methods of evaluation of intangible assets and intellectual capital. *Journal of Intellectual Capital, 18*(3), 470–485.

Parr, R. L. (2018). *Intellectual property: Valuation, exploitation and infringement damages* (5th ed.). Hoboken, NJ: Wiley.

Pastor, D., Glova, J., Liptak, F., & Kovac, V. (2017). Intangibles and methods for their valuation in financial terms: Literature review. *Intangible Capital, 12*(2), 387–410.

Piekkola, H. (2014). Intangible investment and market valuation. *The Review of Income and Wealth, 62*(1), 28–51.

Rappaport, A., & Mauboussin, M. J. (2021). *Expectations investing.* Harvard Business School Press.

Reilly, R. F., & Schweihs, R. P. (1999). *Valuing intangible assets.* New York: McGraw-Hill.

Reilly, R. F., & Schweihs, R. P. (2016). *Guide to intangible asset valuation.* New York: Wiley.

Roslender, R., & Fincham, R. (2001). Thinking critically about intellectual capital accounting. *Accounting, Auditing & Accountability Journal, 14*(4), 383–399.

Salinas, G., & Ambler, T. (2009). A taxonomy of brand valuation practice: Methodologies and purposes. *Journal of Brand Management, 17* (1), 39–61.

Sandner, P. (2010). *The valuation of intangible assets. An exploration of patent and trademark portfolios.* Wiesbaden: Springer.

Saunders, A., & Brynjolfsson, E. (2016). Valuing information technology related intangible assets. *MIS Quarterly, 40*(1), 83.

Singh, J. P. (2013). On the intricacies of cash flow corporate valuation. *Advances in Management*, 6(3), 15–22.

Singh, S., & Kansal, M. (2011). Voluntary disclosures of intellectual capital: An empirical analysis. *Journal of Intellectual Capital*, 12(2), 301–318.

Smith, G. V., & Parr, R. L. (2000). *Valuation of intellectual property and intangible assets*. New York: Wiley.

Sullivan, P. H., Jr., & Sullivan, P. H., Sr. (2000). Valuing intangibles companies—An intellectual capital approach. *Journal of Intellectual Capital*, 1(4), 328–340.

Vetoshkina, E. Y., & Tukhvatullin, R. S. (2015). Economic efficiency estimation of intangible assets use. *Mediterranean Journal of Social Sciences*, 6(1 S3), 440.

Zambon, S., & Marzo, G. (2007). *Visualizing intangibles: Measuring and reporting in the knowledge economy*. London, UK: Routledge.

CHAPTER 3

Digital Scalability and Growth Options

3.1 INTRODUCTION

This chapter describes heterogeneous issues that represent the basic background of digital intangibles. A comprehensive understanding of these composite concepts is preliminary to any valuation approach since it helps in the identification of the main value drivers (Lòpez et al. 2017) and business model competitive forces.

Vertical and horizontal scalability is first described in Sect. 3.2, showing their links with non-rivalrous intangibles that can be endlessly replicated and consumed. Section 3.3 subsequently illustrates digital scalability that can be considered as a flexible real option (Sect. 3.4).

Scalable intangibles have a deep impact on capital and operating expenditure (CAPEX and OPEX), as described in Sect. 3.5. These are vital parameters for valuation, especially for intangibles that are intrinsically difficult to define and record in the accounts (as capitalized or income expenses).

The accounting background brings to operating leverage (Sect. 3.6) that considers the impact of revenue changes on the operating profit (EBIT), depending on the fixed versus variable cost mix. Extensions of this well-known concept to scalable (and digital) intangibles may not be trivial. Break-even analysis (illustrated in Sect. 3.7) is another classic cost accounting topic that can be adapted to intangibles. This impacts enterprise valuation (Sect. 3.8) and corporate profitability (Sect. 3.9).

© The Author(s), under exclusive license to Springer Nature Switzerland AG 2022
R. Moro-Visconti, *The Valuation of Digital Intangibles*,
https://doi.org/10.1007/978-3-031-09237-4_3

Digital extensions may conveniently consider Metcalfe's law (Sect. 3.10) which explains the exponential value of networks or Moore's law (Sect. 3.11) which considers the technological patterns.

Exponential growth (Sect. 3.12) may be ignited by factors such as geolocalization (Sect. 3.13) and bring to blitzscaling (Sect. 3.14). E-commerce and scalable Internet trading (Sect. 3.15) are based on digital platforms that represent a potentially unlimited virtual marketplace. These characteristics of digital intangibles are uneasy to exploit but much wanted for their explosive impact on economic and financial margins. Whenever properly ignited, they boost value creation.

Scalable and digital supply chains (Sect. 3.16) complementarily act in the strategic effort to boost marginality, shortening the intermediation passages and making them more flexible. Resilience to external pressures decreases risk, considered as the difference between expected and real outcomes, so improving value (e.g., reducing the denominator of discounted cash flows).

Digital transformation (Sect. 3.17) refers to the application of paperless technology to solve traditional problems, with an interaction between traditional firms and digital startups. Cross-pollination is catalyzed by Internet platforms, and digital intangibles represent the "invisible glue" behind value co-creation.

Sustainable business planning, driven by scalability patterns, is examined in Sect. 3.19, before some pandemic insights from digitalization (Sect. 3.20).

3.2   Vertical and Horizontal Scalability

Scalability represents an essential feature of any business. It indicates the ability of a process, network, or system to handle a growing amount of work, or its potential to be enlarged to accommodate growth. Scalability can be intended as the ability of a device to adapt to the changes in the environment and meet the changing needs of customers.

Scalability is also defined as the ability to handle more work as the size of the computer or application grows, scalability or scaling is widely used to indicate the ability of hardware and software to deliver greater computational power when the number of resources is increased.

So, in broader terms, scalability means flexibility, which allows to better address and achieve the specific needs of customers, which are never static. People's interests and tastes, as well as environmental conditions, change continuously over time. Scalability is therefore vital as it contributes to competitiveness, efficiency, and quality. Scalability helps the system to work gracefully without any undue delay and unproductive resource consumption while making good use of the available resources (Gupta et al., 2017).

Since scalability depends on the capability of a business to profit from the addition of (internal and/or external) resources, these latter can fall either into the "vertical" or "horizontal" category and generate two different scalability types.

Vertical scalability (scaling-up) corresponds to the ability to increase the capacity of existing hardware or software by adding more resources to the single system node. For instance, we can add processing power to a server to increase its speed. In the same way, we can scale a system vertically and expand it by providing more shared resources such as processing, main memory, storage, and network interfaces to the main node to be able to satisfy a greater number of requests per system (Gupta et al., 2017).

By contrast, horizontal scalability (scaling out) refers to adding more nodes to the same system, thus impacting and modifying the supply chain. A real case could be adding computer workstations to a network, meaning connecting multiple computers with one another to accomplish more work in less time. This method allows the system to work as a single logical unit, increasing overall efficiency (Fig. 3.1).

Westlake and Haskel (2017) identify four fundamental properties of intangible assets:

1. *Scalability*: it enables a growth in revenues accompanied by a less than proportional increase in variable costs. This has a positive impact on economic and financial margins, generating a driving force that improves the rating and bankability of intangible-intensive companies. A scalable intangible asset can be used without limits. For example, oranges (a tangible rival good) can be used to make marmalade, but only for a certain amount. In contrast, a recipe (intangible non-rival good) can be used to make marmalade without limits. Intangible assets such as a brand or an algorithm are considered the easiest to be scaled up due to network effects affecting them as well as their ability to reap incumbency advantages (e.g., Uber), as compared to tangible assets such as taxi companies.

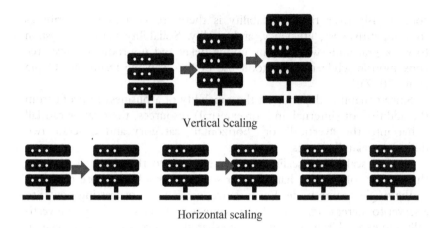

Vertical Scaling

Horizontal scaling

Fig. 3.1   Vertical and horizontal scalability

2. *Sunk Costs*: intangibles represent sunk costs in a few ways. First, businesses with a lot of intangibles, such as brands or processes innovation, often prove worthless if the firm fails. The riskiness of intangible assets stems from the non-transferability of the asset. Tangible assets like land and factories can, in theory, be sold or recycled.
3. *Spillovers*: a business that invests in a tangible asset like a new factory can usually be confident that it will get most of whatever benefits the asset produces. But intangible assets are more slippery, and value is likelier to be diverted.
4. *Synergies*: intangible assets can be particularly valuable when combined with other assets in a synergistic portfolio (Westlake & Haskel, 2017).

Scalability is intrinsically linked to the characteristics of intangible assets. Intangibles are non-rivalrous goods, i.e., non-excludable public goods that are consumed but whose supply is not depleted by consumption. When a consumer uses that digital good (e.g., a video and not a sandwich), the supply left for other people remains unchanged. Therefore, non-rivalrous goods can be consumed repeatedly without the fear of depletions of supply. The scarcity effect that impacts demand and supply is not present in this case, and non-rivalrous goods or services are scalable.

Public goods are services and products that are given to consumers by the government. Public goods are non-excludable and non-rivalrous. Whereas food is rivalrous, intangibles are not, and this characteristic allows for their multiple and scalable consumption.

There is a capacity limit in sharing a bottle of beer, but consumers can endlessly enjoy its brand.

3.3 DIGITAL SCALABILITY

Digital businesses are those which carry out transactions that are digitally mediated or involve products or services that are experienced digitally (Weill & Woerner, 2013). It is the digitalized, non-material nature of such goods and services that gives them the potential for scalability. So, the term "Digital Scalability" basically refers to the application of the scalability concept by digital companies and devices, to optimize as much as possible digital circuits and operations.

Digital business models are usually designed for rapid growth, and the recent advances in digital technologies continue to create new possibilities to scale up and reach a global scale. As described by Gander (2015) the drivers by which digital business models may attempt to gain scale are analyzed in Table 3.1.

3.4 SCALABILITY AS A REAL OPTION

Flexibility (resilience) represents a key characteristic of scalability (Baldi & Trigeorgis, 2009) and can be enhanced using real options, concerned with the right—but not the obligation—to undertake certain business initiatives. In particular, the options available can concern the expansion, the deferral, or the abandonment of a capital investment project, such as described in Table 3.2.

Real options (Ipsmiller et al., 2019) create the right, but not the obligation, to purchase the underlying asset at a defined exercise price. A case of real options application is the use of patents; in fact, patents allow their owners to choose between exclusively commercializing the patented invention sometimes during the patent term or foregoing commercialization altogether. So, real options affect the valuation of potential investments and may be incorporated in discount models as the Net Present Value,[1] in the sense that when investments or assets, like patents, are evaluated through NPV techniques, real options can be used to

Table 3.1   Scalability drivers

Scalability driver	Features	Criticalities
Learning by using	The greater the scale of a technology (or "the wider the adoption of technology"), the more its users learn about its features, strengths, and weaknesses (also using SWOT analysis)	Disseminate learning between users may be costly and may require managerial attention and resources
Networking (Network externalities)	"Scalability becomes supercharged with network effects" (Haskel & Westlake, 2018). A network is scalable if it can cope with the existing demand placed upon it but also can be flexibly expanded to meet future demand. Network externalities occur when the value obtained by using products or services increases with its greater diffusion among populations of users	Risk of contagion through the network. Examples may derive from epidemic occurrences
Scale economies	Supply-side effects of scale include economies of production and distribution. With large output quantities, the unit cost of each product or service encounter falls due to the spreading of fixed costs, advertising budgets, and research and design costs across a larger quantity of products	Conceive and maintain a generic platform; resources are required to hold non-scalable features away from the ecosystem
Information returns	Reduction in user perception of the risk of adopting a product or service following its use by others. The more widely a technology is adopted, the more it is understood	Conformity to general preferences for products and services does not necessarily imply wider adoption, as individual preferences can be different
Technological interrelatedness	The wider the adoption of technology, the greater the number of supporting technologies that are developed and become part of its infrastructure	Costly and complex to support as the number of product configurations grows with each customer

(continued)

Table 3.1   (continued)

Scalability driver	Features	Criticalities
Distributed sourcing	The way resources are decentralized across value chains and ecosystems. The distributed design enables the rapid adoption of a product or service without sacrificing performance or causing bottlenecks in the system which degrades the customer experience	congestion and consequent bottleneck due to overloading of capacity following a rapid, unanticipated, and sizeable increase in user numbers, which may result in service failure
Economies of experience	Economies in which products or services are sold by emphasizing their effects on people's lives and actions to create "memorable customers' experiences"	Additional costs and new know-how are required to switch from product to service/experience orientation. Change of customers' expectations and managers' strategies
Real options	Options available to managers range from business investment opportunities to tangible assets or financial instruments	Difficulties in estimating the exact value of real options
Blitzscaling	Specific techniques allow companies to achieve massive scale at high speed	Disrupting startups can exploit network externalities to create digital monopolies. Sharp increases in the volumes of sales are not automatically followed by economic margin improvements

Table 3.2   Real options

Real option	Main features
Option to expand	To undertake a project to expand the business operations (e.g., a sushi chain considering opening new restaurants)
Option to defer or wait	Option of deferring the business decision to the future (e.g., a sushi chain considering opening new restaurants this year or in the next year)
Option to abandon	Option to cease a project to realize its scrap value (e.g., a manufacturing company decides to sell old equipment)

make forecasts more flexible (Iazzolino & Migliano, 2015). For these reasons, real options describe the key tensions that managers face between commitment versus flexibility or between competition and cooperation (Trigeorgis & Reuer, 2017).

The ability to predict and model future and uncertain events connected with the actual economic and financial returns can be usefully codified in earn-out contractual clauses which, in purchases and sales, guarantee the seller an additional price, if certain situations occur, which are particularly uncertain at the time of the stipulation of the contract.

The real options have long been used both in the valuation of patents and in the estimation of Internet companies and social networks.

Using the real options, investment projects should be the source of a series of opportunities that management can seize when certain scenario conditions occur. Opportunities for expansion, contraction, abandonment, or postponement of the launch of an investment project give the decision-maker flexibility, the value of which must be carefully considered for the overall assessment of the project.

Figure 3.2 shows the interaction between a typical investment tree and real options.

Fig. 3.2 Investment tree and real options

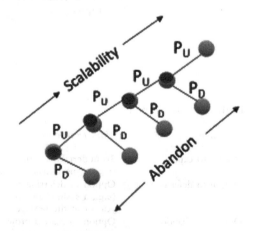

P_U = Probability up
P_D = probability down

Incorporating real options, business models become more resilient, and they improve their DCF or NPV, decreasing the risky factors in the discount rate (cost of capital) and improving the cash flows.

3.5 THE IMPACT OF SCALABLE INTANGIBLES ON CAPEX AND OPEX

Capital expenditures (CAPEX) and operating expenses (OPEX) represent two complementary categories of business expenses, deriving from the capital and operating budgets that are created by companies to support growth and adjust resources.

Capital budgets cover capital expenses, which are capitalized and appear as long-term assets on the balance sheet. CAPEX corresponds to the amounts that companies use to purchase long-term assets as major physical goods or services that will be used for more than one year. These assets may be physical (plant, equipment, property, vehicles, etc.) or represented by intangibles that are not directly expensed in the income statement. As these long-term assets depreciate over their useful lives, the depreciation for a given year shows up on the income statement as a non-monetary expense in that year. Therefore, CAPEX is subject to depreciation (with a linear methodology in constant installments over the useful life or with an impairment test, whenever applicable).

OPEX refers instead to the ordinary costs for a company to run its daily business operations (purchases; salaries; rents; sales, general, & administrative expenses; property taxes, etc.). OPEX can be divided into monetary OPEX + depreciation/amortization.

Intangibles impact directly on monetary OPEX and CAPEX (when intangible investments are capitalized, and their annual quota is amortized). Amortization is, therefore, a part of non-monetary OPEX. Only monetary OPEX affects the EBITDA. From an accounting perspective, the CAPEX is recorded (capitalized) within the assets in the balance sheet, whereas the OPEX are recorded in the operating costs within the income statement (profit & loss account).

Since the fixed or intangible asset recorded in the balance sheet is part of normal business operations, depreciation is considered in this case an operating expense.

Scalability is an intangible characteristic of the business that can quickly boost volumes of sales, up to blitzscaling.

Intangibles can, however, have a complementary impact on the business model (and consequent value creation), and they can have a joint impact on both, OPEX and CAPEX.

For what concerns OPEX, intangibles can ignite productivity gains where input costs to reach a target output are minimized. If OPEX is reduced, economic margins such as EBITDA, EBIT, pre-tax profit, or net profit improve.

Capitalization of intangible assets (into CAPEX) instead of accounting within monetary OPEX does not change Operating Cash Flows (O_{CF}) that include these items anyway since:

$$Enterprise\ Value = \sum \frac{(sales - monetary\ OPEX) = EBITDA \mp \Delta NWC \mp \Delta CAPEX}{(1 + WACC)^i}$$
$$= \sum \frac{Operating\ Cash\ Flow}{(1 + WACC)^i} \tag{3.1}$$

where ΔNWC indicates the differential Net Working Capital (concerning the previous year). As shown in Chapter 2, the operating cash flow (FCFF) is discounted using the WACC.

While DCF (expressed by $\sum O_{CF}/WACC$) is invariant to the accounting treatment of intangibles (i.e., to the fact that they are capitalized or not),[2] this is not true in the other valuation method. Should the Enterprise Value be proxied by the average EBITDA times a market multiplier of a comparable firm, then the EBITDA is influenced by the capitalization of intangibles. More precisely, capitalized intangibles (as development expenses) that become part of the CAPEX (and are never part of monetary OPEX) increase the EBITDA, and so the Enterprise Value that is estimated with market comparables.

Operating costs are divided into variable and fixed costs, to better understand the impact of scalability on operating leverage (EBIT increase due to an increase in sales).

Scalability directly boosts sales but has an impact also on the EBIT that is given not only by increased revenues but also by the presence of fixed costs in the OPEX mix. Since fixed costs are—by definition—invariant to sales, the higher their proportion within the OPEX, the better the impact on the EBIT increase due to growing scalable sales. The opposite happens when sales decrease: in that case, fixed costs are a burden.

Intangibles may have a positive impact even on CAPEX, should they contribute to improving productivity, so decreasing the amount of CAPEX needed to run the business and to generate economic and financial positive margins (EBITDA; EBIT; operating and net cash flows, etc.).

There is so a positive impact attributable to scalable intangibles improving the market value of the firm, due to the higher economic and financial marginality.

Higher operating cash flows improve the discounted cash flows (O_{CF}/WACC) and a better EBITDA boosts the economic value complemented by market multipliers.

Accounting distortions may impact the dichotomy between OPEX and CAPEX, due to the slippery qualification of the intangibles and the caution that often prevents their capitalization. There may so be, in practice, some difficulty in discriminating about the impact of intangibles on either OPEX or CAPEX, where the impact on CAPEX may be underestimated due to accounting prudentialism. This difference can, however, be overcome by evaluators, especially if they consider TOTEX = CAPEX + OPEX.

Scalable intangibles impact on the composition of raised capital (equity + financial debt):

- Any profitability gain improves, ceteris paribus, the net profit and so the equity; if dividends are paid out, then the benefit eventually accrues to the shareholders;
- Improvements in the EBITDA (that represents the contribution of the income statement to the generation of liquidity) may be used to pay back debt (so decreasing the financial leverage, expressed by the debt over equity ratio), or to fuel new investments without increasing outstanding debt or asking additional money to the shareholders. This may have a positive impact on the Weighted Average Cost of Capital (WACC) that is used to discount the Operating Cash Flow in the DCF formulation; any decrease in the WACC improves the market value of the firm, being value $\approx O_{CF}$/WACC.

Any improvement in the EBITDA backs the pecking order theory, according to which internally generated liquidity (proxied by the EBITDA) precedes the issue of risky debt and then equity. This theory presides over the formation of raised capital that is then invested in the assets (intangibles, fixed assets, net working capital, and liquidity).

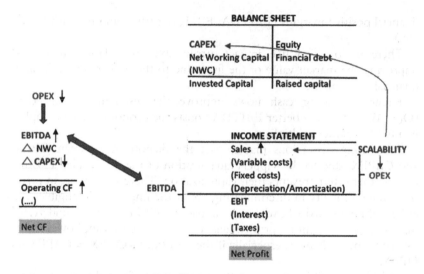

Fig. 3.3 Impact of scalable intangibles on OPEX and CAPEX

These considerations are valid not only for digital-native firms but also for traditional corporations that increasingly use new intangibles, becoming tech-enabled.

Should intangibles improve the flexibility of the supply chain where the firm is strategically positioned, then the business model may become more resilient to downturns and volatile market conditions. This reduces the difference between dreamy expectations and hard reality, so decreasing risk and the cost of collecting capital (WACC), and contributes to the reduction of the DCF formula denominator.

Figure 3.3 depicts the impact of scalable intangibles on OPEX, CAPEX, and the economic and financial margins.

3.6   The Accounting Background: Operating Leverage

Operating leverage is a measure of how revenue growth translates into growth in operating income. It is a measure of how risky, or volatile, a company's operating income is. The operating income (EBIT) is increasingly driven by the digital components that both boost revenues and save operating costs (especially variable expenses that are minimized in digital business models).

Operating leverage is the degree to which a firm or project can increase operating income by increasing its revenues. Essentially, while scalability is about volumes, operating leverage concerns economic margins (volumes * margins). For example, a business that generates sales with a high gross economic margin and low variable costs has high operating leverage. The higher the degree of operating leverage, the higher the potential danger from forecasting risk, where a relatively small error in forecasting sales can be magnified into significant errors in cash flow projections.

When a company reaches its break-even point (where the operating revenues equal the costs), then it can translate most of its incremental revenues on the EBIT if variable costs are negligible and fixed costs relevant. The opposite, however, occurs when revenues shrink: in this case, the presence of fixed costs is a burden that increases the operating losses. There is so a boomerang effect and companies with higher fixed costs are more volatile and riskier, with an impact on valuation (increasing the discount factor—the cost of capital—in the denominator of the DCF formula).

The formula is the following:

$$operating\ leverage = \frac{\Delta EBIT/EBIT}{\Delta sales/sales} \tag{3.2}$$

Operating leverage so expresses the ratio between the percentage variation in the operating income (Earnings Before Interests and Taxes, EBIT) and the percentage variation of sales.

Since the EBIT is given by sales—monetary OPEX—depreciation/amortization, operating leverage can consequently be linked to the OPEX/CAPEX classification reported in Sect. 3.5.

The elements influencing the operating leverage are:

- Sale prices;
- Volume of sales;
- Variable costs;
- Fixed costs.

We can consider a profit and loss account (income statement) where fixed and variable costs are represented separately.

---

1. **Revenues (sales)**
2. (variable costs)
3. **= Contribution margin** (1–2)
4. (fixed costs)
5. **= Operating Profit** = EBIT (3–4).

The contribution margin is the selling price per unit minus the variable cost per unit. It represents the portion of sales revenue that is not consumed by variable costs and so contributes to the coverage of fixed costs. This concept is one of the critical building blocks of break-even analysis.

The contribution margin analysis is a measure of operating leverage; it expresses how growth in sales translates to an increase in operating profits (EBIT).

The contribution margin is computed by using a management accounting version of the income statement that has been reformatted to analytically represent fixed and variable costs.

On-demand intangibles as Software as a Service (SaaS) or Platforms as a Service produce variable costs and reduce fixed costs.

The overall contribution margin is given by the product of the unitary contribution margin and the sold quantities (or the services provided). The unitary contribution margin (that expresses an economic differential, so influencing the valuation formulae) is mainly determined by the relationship between "prices and revenues" of the sold products and the "prices and costs" of the variable input factors of production.

Companies with a higher structure of fixed costs (that do not follow the variation of sold quantities, remaining unchanged—fixed) experiment with higher operating levels. If a company has only variable costs, then the operating leverage has a unitary level, and its contribution margin will coincide with the EBIT; to double the EBIT, sales will have to double, as they grow at the same pace as the variable costs and the contribution margin.

A classic dilemma is represented by the difference between a company with only fixed costs and another one with just variable costs: which one is better?

Both corner solutions have pros and cons: the former companies find it more difficult to reach a break-even point, but when they do, the marginal growth of revenues is fully translated into higher EBIT, with a scalable impact on economic marginality. Companies with higher variable costs are on the contrary, safer but less profitable when the outlook is positive, compensating for lower risk with smaller trendy returns. As anticipated, digitalization normally presupposes high startup (fixed) costs, and little variable costs. For example, the setup of a social network platform absorbs huge fixed costs (hardware, software, platform design, initial marketing expenses, etc.) but limited variable costs (that depend on the number of affiliates).

The contribution margin can be increased:

(a) With a higher profit margin, expressed by the difference between "price/revenue" vs. "price/cost";
(b) Improving the efficiency of variable factors of production;
(c) Increasing the volume of sales.

Fixed costs are the second determinant of EBIT. Costs are "fixed" if they do not vary when production changes. The cost structure and the mix of fixed vs. variable costs is a strategic option of any company but it also depends on the industry. For example, retail companies can choose from shops that are fully owned or in franchising; staff can be represented by employees or freelance workers, etc. Some sectors, however, have strategic constraints that limit the possibility of the company selecting its cost structure. For instance, in the automotive industry, fixed costs and investments are typically high, and they are difficult to reduce below certain thresholds.

Fixed costs are typically significant in the banking sector, where staff costs and IT investments matter, even if FinTech improves flexibility.[3]

Labor cost is just partially fixed, and it has extraordinary components that are linked to performance (stock options, etc.).

The degree of operating leverage (DOL) is a synthetic indicator of the operating risk, estimated by comparing the contribution margin (total revenues—total variable costs) to the EBIT (EBIT = total revenues − total variable costs − fixed costs):

$$DOL = (TR - VC) / (TR - VC - FC) = CM / EBIT \qquad (3.3)$$

where:

DOL = degree of operating leverage

TR = total revenues
VC = variable costs
FC = fixed costs
CM = contribution margin.

The higher the weight of fixed costs over total costs, the higher the degree of operating leverage.

The cost structure has a remarkable impact on the (operating) net working capital (NWC), which is given by the difference between accounts receivable, stock, and accounts payable.

Fixed costs impact the working capital, producing accounts receivable that are independent of the trend of sales. Variable costs, on the contrary, follow the dynamics of sales, with a double impact on the working capital: sales produce receivables whereas variable costs generate payables. The working capital balance depends on the rotation of the credits and debts (average days of collection and payment).

An EBITDA increase is generated by monetary revenues that grow more than monetary OPEX. This typically produces a working capital increase that absorbs liquidity. Operating cash flows are so positively affected by the EBITDA increase, less the increase in the working capital (and in CAPEX, which may grow to sustain higher revenues, so contributing to liquidity absorption).

3.7   BREAK-EVEN ANALYSIS

The break-even point or level (BEP) in economics, business—and specifically cost accounting—is the point at which total cost and total revenue are equal, i.e., "even". There is no net loss or gain, and one has "broken even", though opportunity costs have been paid and capital has received the risk-adjusted, expected return. In short, all costs that must be paid are paid, and there is neither operating profit nor loss.

The BEP represents the sales amount—in either unit (quantity) or revenue (sales) terms—that is required to cover total OPEX, consisting of both fixed and variable costs. The total profit at the break-even point is zero. It is only possible for a firm to pass the break-even point if the value of sales is higher than the variable cost per unit. This means that the selling price of the good must be higher than what the company paid for the good or its components for them to cover the initial price they paid (variable costs). Once they surpass the break-even price, the company can start making an operating profit (positive EBIT).

The break-even point is one of the most commonly used concepts of financial analysis and is not only limited to economic use but can also be used by entrepreneurs, accountants, financial planners, managers, and marketers. Break-even points can be useful to all avenues of a business, even non-digital, as it allows employees to identify required outputs and work toward meeting these.

The break-even value is not generic and will vary dependent on the individual business. Some businesses may have a higher or lower break-even point, however, each business must develop a break-even point calculation, as this will enable them to see the number of units, they need to sell to cover their variable costs. Each sale contributes to the payment of fixed costs.

The main purpose of break-even analysis is to determine the minimum output that must be exceeded for a business to profit. It is a rough indicator of the earnings impact of marketing activity. A firm can analyze ideal output levels to be knowledgeable on the number of sales and revenue that would meet and surpass the break-even point. If a business doesn't meet this level, it often becomes difficult to continue operation in a going concern.

The break-even point is one of the simplest analytical tools. Identifying a break-even point helps provide a dynamic view of the relationships between sales, costs, and operating profits. For example, expressing break-even sales as a percentage of actual sales can help managers understand when to expect to break-even (by linking the percent to when in the week or month this percent of sales might occur).

The Return on Sales (ROS) is given by the ratio EBIT/sales, and describes the operating leverage from a complementary side, as shown in Sect. 3.9.

The break-even point is a special case of Target Income Sales, where Target Income is zero (breaking even). Any sales made past the break-even point can be considered profit (after all initial costs have been paid).

Break-even analysis can provide data that can be useful to the marketing department of a business, as it provides financial goals that the business can pass on to marketers so they can try to increase sales. Finally, Break-even analysis (depicted in Figs. 3.4 and 3.5) can help businesses to cut OPEX, identifying its components. This may help the business become more effective and achieve higher returns.

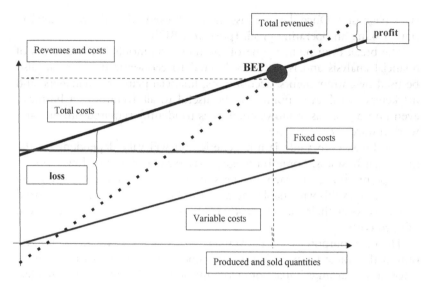

Fig. 3.4 Break-even analysis

3.8   THE IMPACT OF SCALABILITY
ON THE ENTERPRISE VALUATION

The link between scalability and liquidity is a fundamental concept to understand the cash flows that may be generated by incremental economic margins.

The key margin is represented by EBITDA which is the only parameter that simultaneously expresses both an economic and a financial marginality. EBITDA is close to EBIT—the target parameter of operating leverage—since it can be calculated from EBIT just summing up non-monetary operating costs like depreciation and amortization.

Whereas EBITDA already includes operating expenses (monetary OPEX), capital expenses (CAPEX) are reported in the cash flow statement (see the graph below) after the EBITDA and before the operating cash flow (FCFF).

CAPEX and OPEX represent two different categories of business expenses. Capital expenditures are for major purchases that will be used in the future. The life of these purchases extends beyond the current accounting period in which they were purchased. Because these costs

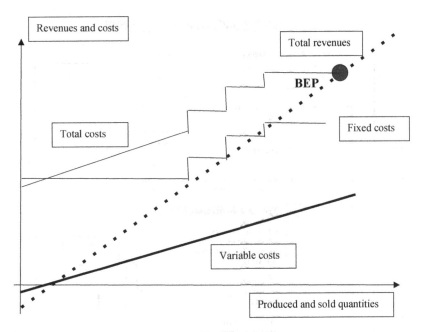

Fig. 3.5 Break-even point with growing fixed costs

can only be recovered over time through depreciation, companies ordinarily budget for long-term CAPEX purchases separately from preparing an operational yearly budget.

OPEX represents the day-to-day expenses necessary to keep the business running. These are short-term costs and are normally used up in the same accounting period in which they are purchased.

Operating leverage is a measure of how revenue growth translates into growth in operating income (EBIT). If we add up depreciation and amortization to EBIT, we get EBITDA, which is simultaneously an economic and a liquidity margin. There is so an important link between operating leverage and liquidity.

Any change in the operating leverage has an impact on liquidity (as shown in Fig. 3.6) because operating leverage is linked to EBITDA which is the first parameter of the cash flow statement.

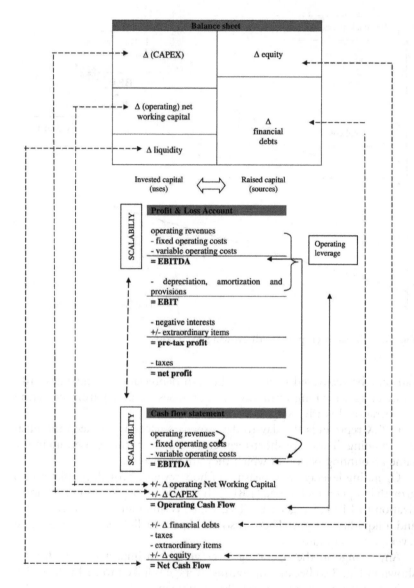

Fig. 3.6 Operating leverage and cash flows

Any sales increase has an impact on the EBITDA and the EBIT. The fixed vs. variable mix may change, influencing the operating net working capital. Normally, an increase in sales produces an increase in both receivables and stock; higher sales are typically driven by higher purchases, with a consequent increase in payables. If the economic marginality of the sales increase remains positive, then the net working capital is likely to grow, since the increase in receivables and stock exceeds the growth of payables. A higher net working capital absorbs cash and so, part of the liquidity that is generated by a higher EBIT/EBITDA is used for financing this growth. Higher sales are often fueled by an increase in CAPEX that absorbs cash.

The impact of a sales change on the net working capital can be better detected considering the aging of receivables, stock, and payables:

$$receivables/sales * 365 \qquad (3.4)$$

$$stock/production\ costs * 365 \qquad (3.5)$$

$$payables/purchases * 365 \qquad (3.6)$$

The balance (EBITDA ± Net Working Capital ± CAPEX) is represented by the Operating Cash Flow (FCFF) that is also known as unlevered (or debt-free) cash flow, as it is calculated before the debt service (debt-free companies have an operating cash flow that corresponds to the net cash flow and a raised capital equal to the equity).

3.9   CORPORATE PROFITABILITY AND SCALABILITY

Scalability has a marginal (incremental) impact not only on cash flows (starting from the EBITDA) but also on economic margins that are the core component of corporate profitability.

Corporate profitability is a core issue of financial statement analysis and corporate finance. Economic profitability derives from positive marginality where revenues exceed costs.

The return on equity (ROE) is a measure of the profitability of a business concerning the book value of shareholder equity, also known as net assets or assets minus liabilities. ROE is a measure of how well a company uses investments to generate earnings growth.

ROE is equal to net income (Rn), divided by total equity (E), expressed as a percentage:

$$ROE = \frac{Net\,Profit}{Equity} \qquad (3.7)$$

The return on invested capital (ROIC) is the ratio between the operating profit (EBIT) and the resources that back it (raised = invested capital). A high ROIC means the investment's gains compare favorably to its cost. As a performance measure, ROIC is used to evaluate the efficiency of an investment or to compare the efficiencies of several different investments. In purely economic terms, it is one way of relating profits to capital invested. The formula is the following:

$$ROIC = \frac{EBIT}{Invested\,Capital} \qquad (3.8)$$

Return on sales (ROS) is a ratio used to evaluate a company's operational efficiency; ROS is also known as a firm's operating profit margin. This measure provides insight into how much profit is being produced per € of sales. An increasing ROS indicates that a company is growing more efficiently, while a decreasing ROS could signal a looming outlook.

ROS measures the performance of a company by analyzing the percentage of total revenue that is converted into operating profits. It expresses the profitability of sales:

$$ROS = \frac{EBIT}{sales} \qquad (3.9)$$

ROE can be decomposed into four ratios that include both ROIC and ROS:

$$ROE = \frac{sales}{invested\,capital} \frac{EBIT}{sales} \frac{invested\,capital}{Equity} \frac{net\,profit}{EBIT}$$
$$= \frac{net\,profit}{equity} \qquad (3.10)$$

A further formulation of ROE is given by Modigliani and Miller's proposition II (Ross, 1988; Modigliani & Miller, 1958).

3.10   METCALFE'S LAW

Metcalfe's law concerns one of the scalability factors recalled in Table 3.1 and states that the effect of a telecommunications network is proportional to the square of the number of connected users of the system (n^2). First formulated in this form by George Gilder in 1993 and attributed to Robert Metcalfe (the inventor of Ethernet), Metcalfe's law was originally presented, c. 1980, not in terms of users, but rather of "compatible communicating devices" (for example, fax machines, telephones, etc.). Only later, with the globalization of the Internet, did this law carry over to users and networks as its original intent was to describe Ethernet purchases and connections. The law is related to economics and business management, especially with competitive companies looking to merge.

Metcalfe's law characterizes many of the network effects of communication technologies and networks such as the Internet, social networking, and the World Wide Web. Metcalfe's Law is related to the fact that the number of unique possible connections in a network of nodes can be expressed mathematically. If a network is composed of n people and each of them assigns to the network a value that is proportional to the number of other participants, then the value that all the n people assign to the network is the following:

$$n * (n - 1) = n^2 - n \tag{3.11}$$

The law has often been illustrated using the example of now old-fashioned fax machines: single fax is useless, but the value of every fax machine increases with the total number of fax machines in the network because of the total number of people with whom each user may send and receive documents increases. Likewise, in social networks,[4] the greater the number of users with the service, the more valuable the service becomes to the community.

As exemplified in Fig. 3.7, if we take two telephones, they can make only one connection, five can make 10 connections, and twelve can make 66 connections. The formula describes exponential growth. Figure 3.8 shows the exponential growth of a network following Metcalfe's law (Fig. 3.9).

The Break-even point is the following:

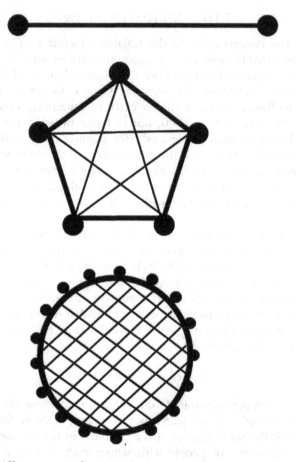

Fig. 3.7 Different types of communication networks

3.11   MOORE'S LAW AND OTHER SCALABILITY PATTERNS

Moore's law refers to the computation of the number of transistors in a dense and integrated circuit. Specifically, the computation (i.e., the price) will double about every 18 months.

Recent advancements in digital electronics are strongly linked to Moore's law: quality-adjusted microprocessor, memory capacity, sensors,

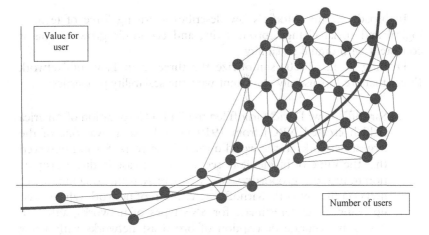

Fig. 3.8 Value for the networked user according to Metcalfe's law

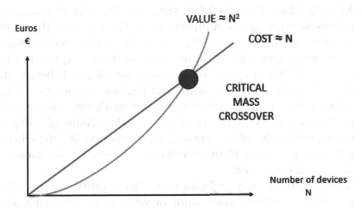

Fig. 3.9 Break-even point with Metcalfe's law

and even the number and size of pixels in digital cameras are affected by it.

Essentially, Moore's law describes an exponential growth pattern in the complexity of integrated semiconductor circuits. This concept was later revised and extended by some computer scientists and researchers to include future forms of technology.

In broader terms, Moore's law describes a driving force of techno-logical and social change, productivity, and economic growth. This is consistent with digital scalability.

Hyoung et al. (2020) summarize the three main Laws of Network Effect that are intrinsically consistent with the scalability properties:

(a) Sarnoff's Law: David Sarnoff led the Radio Corporation of America (which created NBC) from 1919 until 1970. It was one of the largest networks in the world during those years. Sarnoff observed that the value of his network seemed to increase in direct propor-tion to its size—proportional to N, where N is the total number of users on the network. Sarnoff's description of network value ended up being an underestimate for SNS types of networks, although it was an accurate description of broadcast networks with a few central nodes broadcasting to many marginal nodes (a radio or television audience).

(b) Metcalfe's Law: Metcalfe's Law states that the value of a communi-cations network grows in proportion to the square of the number of users on the network ($N2$, where N is the total number of users on the network). The formulation of this concept is attributed to Robert Metcalfe, one of the inventors of the Ethernet stan-dard. Metcalfe's Law seems to hold because the number of links between nodes on a network increase mathematically at a rate of $N2$, where N is the number of nodes. Although originally formulated to describe communication networks like the ethernet, faxing, or phones, with the arrival of the Internet, it has evolved to describe SNSs as well.

(c) Reed's Law: it was published by Reed (2001). While Reed acknowledged that "many kinds of value grow proportionally to network size" and that some grow as a proportion to the square of network size, he suggested that "group-forming networks" that allow for the formation of clusters (as described above) scale value even faster than other networks. Group-forming networks, according to Reed, increase value at a rate of $2N$, where N is the total number of nodes on the network. Reed suggested the formula of $2N$ instead of $N2$ because the number of possible groups within a network that "supports easy group communication" is much higher than 1 so that the total number of connections in the network (the network density) is not just a function of the total number of nodes (N). It is a function of the total number of nodes plus the total number of possible sub-groupings or clusters, which scales at a much faster rate with the addition of more users to the network. Since most online networks allow for the formation of clusters, they will likely behave at least somewhat as Reed's Law suggests and grow in value at a much faster rate than either Metcalfe's Law or Sarnoff's Law suggests.

Metcalfe's Law proposes that the value of a network increases geometrically with every device that's added. It explains why the telephone network and the Internet are so valuable and continue to increase in value.

Reed's Law posits that Metcalfe's Law underestimates the value of a network, especially those in which it is easy to form subgroups.

Table 3.3 (reproposed in Chapter 18) synthesizes the main properties of some of the most known network laws. Many of these laws are empirical, with a weak scientific background and controversial evidence. Technological evolution is intrinsically difficult to forecast and so differs from its expected patterns. Most of the scalability laws recalled in the following table may so look outdated or imprecise. They are, however, useful since they recall some basic principles and retain an orientation predictive power, giving a rough idea of how scalability patterns may evolve. A common denominator is represented by statistical "power laws" (according to which one quantity varies as a power of another) that are intrinsically consistent with the scalability patterns.

Here are a few examples of Reed's Law in action:

- Social Media of all kinds (Facebook, TikTok, etc.) are so valuable because everyone is the center of their subgroups, and everyone can easily add content.
- Messaging applications like Discord allow you to easily form your groups that serve as conversation hubs for games and projects.
- Open-Source software is incredibly powerful because projects can form and evolve rapidly, by opening participation from anyone who wants to contribute—building upon contributions from completely unrelated projects.
- Wikipedia became so important because content can be managed and evolved by the sphere of people who care most about certain

Table 3.3 Network scalability laws

Scalability law	formula	Features/properties
Sarnoff's law	Network Value $= n$	The value of a network seemed to increase in direct proportion to the size of the network—proportional to N, where N is the total number of users on the network
Metcalfe's law	Network Value $= n^2$	Network value increases exponentially with an increasing number of devices on the network
Reed's law	Network Value $= 2^n$	Network value increases even more than Metcalfe's as subgroups (social networks; messaging apps, etc.) become easier to form. Reed's law is consistent with multilayer network extensions
Moore's law[5]	$no = n02(yi - y0)/T2$, where $n0n0$ is the number of transistors in some reference year, $y0y0$, and $T2 = 2T2 = 2$ is the number of years taken to double this number	A doubling of real computing power has occurred every 2.3 years, on average since the birth of modern computing. Moore's Law is one of several enabling technological trends for Metaverse development. Rather than a law of physics, it is an empirical relationship linked to gains from experience in production
Henderson law		Henderson's Law also known as a variant of the "Power law" is a mathematical formula for calculating experience curves and their economic impact. It was first proposed by Bruce Henderson in 1968 while working for the Boston Consulting Group to generalize unit costs of production over time and by volume

(continued)

Table 3.3 (continued)

Scalability law	formula	Features/properties
Wright's law	$Cn = C1n-a$ where: $C1$ is the cost of the first unit of production Cn is the cost of the n-th unit of production n is the cumulative volume of production a is the elasticity of cost regarding output	Wright found that every time total aircraft production doubled, the required labor time for a new aircraft fell by 20%. This has become known as "Wright's law". Studies in other industries have yielded different percentage values (ranging from only a couple of percent up to 30%), but in most cases, the value in each industry was a constant percentage and did not vary at different scales of operation. The learning curve model posits that for each doubling of the total quantity of items produced, costs decrease by a fixed proportion. Generally, the production of any good or service shows the learning curve or experience curve effect. Each time cumulative volume doubles, value-added costs (including administration, marketing, distribution, and manufacturing) fall by a constant percentage
Kryder's law		Storage capacity growth. Kryder's Law is the assumption that magnetic disk drive density, also known as areal density, will double every thirteen months. The implication of Kryder's Law is that as areal density improves, storage will become cheaper
Butters' law		Butters' law says that the amount of data coming out of an optical fiber is doubling every nine months. Thus, the cost of transmitting a bit over an optical network decrease by half every nine months

(continued)

Table 3.3 (continued)

Scalability law	formula	Features/properties
Nielsen's law		Wired bandwidth growth
Gilder's law		the total bandwidth of communication systems triples every twelve months
Cooper's law		Wireless bandwidth growth. The number of wireless signals that can simultaneously be transmitted without interfering with each other has been doubling approximately every 30 months since the early 1900s. This steady rise of wireless capabilities also has allowed access and distribution of news, entertainment, advertising, and other information to become truly mobile
Poor's law		Network address density growth
Beckström's law		The value of a network equals the net value added to each user's transactions conducted through that network, summed over all users. This model values the network by looking from the edge of the network at all of the transactions conducted and the value added to each. It states that one way to contemplate the value the network adds to each transaction is to imagine the network being shut off and what the additional transaction costs or loss would be
Radoff's law	[Qualitative proposition]	The degree to which a network facilitates interconnections determines the extent of its emergent creativity, innovation, and wealth
Metaverse extension		3D dimension, increased networking, technological upgrade, etc. improve scalability and so value

topics. The collective value of Wikipedia increases as people maintain more content, which in turn expands the audience, resulting in people wanting to add more content to it.

- Online games with social features (multiplayer games, games featuring esports) are so sticky because each one acts as a type of social network where you join up with other people, participate in activities, and form friendships and rivalries.

Reed's Law is often mentioned when explaining the competitive dynamics of internet platforms. As the law states that a network becomes more valuable when people can easily form subgroups to collaborate, while this value increases exponentially with the number of connections, a business platform that reaches enough members can generate network effects that dominate the overall economics of the system.

Other analysts of network value functions, including Odlyzko and Tilly (2005), have argued that both Reed's Law and Metcalfe's Law overstate network value because they fail to account for the restrictive impact of human cognitive limits on network formation.

3.12   Exponential Growth

Exponential Technology can be defined as a type of technology that can double its capability or performance in each period or, conversely, halve its costs in each period.

Examples of exponential technologies include computers, networks, 3D printing, drones, robotics, and artificial intelligence. According to Ismail (2014), each exponential technology is characterized by the so-called "6 Ds" that are:

1. *Digitized*: the technology has a digital form;
2. *Deceptive*: the initial growth may seem slow and not influential;
3. *Disruptive*: the growth becomes incredibly rapid after a certain threshold;
4. *Dematerialized*: the technology loses its materiality. GPS or video cameras became smartphone apps, so they no longer need to be carried as separate entities. Location and time do not matter: there are no physical and time constraints (value of ubiquity and "any time").

5. *Demonetized*: the technology replaces other products/services previously adopted (usually more expansive), for example, *Uber* rapidly became a remarkable competitor of the traditional taxi industry;
6. *Democratic*: the technology becomes accessible (and affordable) to most of the population (Ismail, 2014) (Fig. 3.10).

The world of exponential organizations does not ensure a secure position and stable profitability in the market (as happened for *Kodak*, forced to exit the market).

Only scalable, fast-moving, and smart organizations can survive in this dynamic environment and gain exponential success.

"*An exponential organization is one whose impact (or output) is disproportionally large compared to its peers because of the use of new organizational techniques that leverage accelerating technologies*" (Ismail, 2014). This definition implies that both, a large workforce and large physical plants, are no longer essential for a company to grow. A dematerialization is taking place and the on-demand market is fast arising: exponential organizations base their activities primarily on information technologies and digital transformation.

Disruptive changes tend to occur every time that fields, which have no elements in common, do connect (as the waterpower and textile loom,

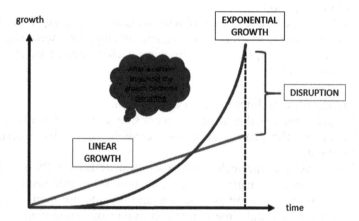

Fig. 3.10 Linear vs. exponential growth

whose combination can be considered as the premonitory factor of the Industrial Revolution). Today, due to the massive and detailed quantity of information easily accessible and supported by the strength of technology, cross-connecting innovative fields become easier, so that the most disparate connections arise, such as art and biology, economics, and chemistry. Interdisciplinary approaches add up value.

A company is traditionally characterized by linear, sequential thinking: linear operations, measures of performance, and success make the company look at the environment from a linear perspective. Nowadays, this approach is overcome by top-down and bottom-up convergence and cross-pollination, and the company has a multi-faceted vision of the competitive environment in which it operates. This increases its flexibility and favors the exploitation of real options.

Communication and interaction among people and companies have been profoundly affected by the advent of the Internet which not only reduces the traditional costs but also opens completely new advertising sources with still infinite unexplored possibilities for companies. The result of this is that the costs of distributing a product or a service have dropped almost to zero. As an example of these new advertising patterns, Google Adsense and Google Adwords were specifically created to support companies in this new era of information: the former's targets are advertisers who want to promote their products and services on the Internet, while the latter is designed for website owners who want to maximize profits and gains from their content.[6]

According again to Ismail (2014), traditional companies can only achieve arithmetic output per input, whereas "an exponential organization achieves geometric outputs per input by riding the doubling-exponential pattern of information-based technologies".

In 2006, *Amazon*, with the creation of its low-cost Cloud storage for small and medium businesses allowed companies to transform the cost of a data center, a fixed CAPEX, into a variable cost. This shows that scalability results in a reduction of CAPEX and OPEX, so boosting economic and financial margins: scalability can then be measured through explosive marginal economic increases. An example of this is provided by *Airbnb*, the company that leverages users' houses with less than 3500 employees; the company owns no physical assets, but it faced a net income of 93 million dollars in 2017 (Fig. 3.11).

Each exponential organization sets its *Massive Transformative Purpose* (MTP), which is the aspirational purpose of the company that differs

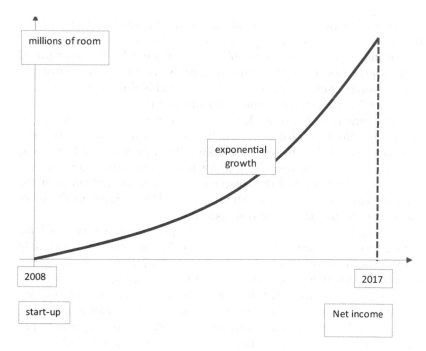

Fig. 3.11 Airbnb: an example of an exponential company

from the simple organization's mission since an MTP should be both, global and transformative. Not only is MTP a strong source of competitive advantage for the "first movers" in the industry since it is hard for competitors to replicate an aim that implies a global vision, but it also attracts new talents and retains them. An effective MTP creates a robust ecosystem around the company formed by customers, suppliers, partners, developers, and governments.

Exponential organizations tend to choose an external, updated, temporary, and highly specialized workforce: staff on demand is, in fact, a necessary characteristic that improves speed, functionality, and flexibility in a fast-changing world within a growing Internet-driven marketplace where expertise gaps need to be filled exogenously (outsourcing).

As already mentioned, Airbnb does not own the property it rents. Similarly, Uber is not the owner of any of the cars' drivers: "non-ownership, then, is the key to owning the future". These examples show that if an asset is information-based or commoditized, accessing it is better than possessing it. Leveraged assets are consistent with a non-ownership pattern that allows scalable products, lowers the marginal cost of supply, removes the assets management, and increases agility and resilience. This process needs an abundance of easily available assets and digital interfaces. However, if an asset is rare, ownership becomes the best solution: Amazon owns its warehouses and Tesla its factories.

In the last few years, the word "engagement" assumed an increasing value for any type of company: coupons, loyalty cards, and quizzes are just some of the strategies adopted to enhance the interaction with customers and, social media, supported by a large and easily accessible amount of data, play the key role in this process. Engagement not only increases customers' loyalty but also amplifies ideation, transforms an unidentified crowd into a real community, leverages marketing, enables play and learning, and provides a digital feedback loop with users.

3.13   Geolocalization and Traceability

Digital ubiquity often needs to be appropriately "grounded" in physical places where consumers live. Hence the importance of geolocalization.

Geolocalization is the attachment of geolocation to an object. Geolocation is the identification of geographic location, as of an electronic device or an animal being tracked. The concept is so both static and dynamic.

Geolocation is the identification of the real-world geographic location of an object, such as a radar source, mobile phone, or Internet-connected computer terminal. In its simplest form, it involves the generation of a set of geographic coordinates and is closely related to the use of positioning systems, but its usefulness is enhanced by the use of these coordinates to determine a meaningful location.

Geolocalization can relate to network theory since the exact positioning of different nodes represents the starting point for a more comprehensive analysis of their value-adding interactions.

Traceability is a concept that identifies the quality of having an origin or course of development that may be found or followed. Whereas the source is geolocated, its patterns follow a dynamic path that in many cases, can be located—traced—by digital devices (sensors, satellites, etc.). Geolocalized data fuel IoT and big data, populating interoperable databases typically stored in the cloud. Traceability is consistent with digital supply chains where each step needs constant monitoring.

Consequent analysis can be carried on with dedicated software, fueled by IoT and big data, and interpreted with artificial intelligence. Validation and traceability may be conducted via blockchains (see Harshini & Kumar, 2022). These concepts are so consistent with a comprehensive valuation of digital intangibles.

3.14   From Digital Scalability to Blitzscaling

As already stated, scalability indicates the ability of a business model to generate incremental demand (additional revenues) economically, i.e., without significantly increasing costs.

The concept can be interpreted, in terms of operational leverage, minimizing variable costs, typical of many technological startups: in this case, the increase in revenues creates a virtuous circle and reflects almost entirely on the EBIT.

The scalability of intangible assets allows seeing a growth in revenues accompanied by a less than proportional increase in variable costs. This has a positive impact on economic and financial margins, generating a driving force that improves the rating and bankability of intangible-intensive companies.

The sometimes-explosive effect of this phenomenon can be observed in highly successful companies (such as Amazon, Alphabet/Google, Facebook, etc.) based on digital business models, where, thanks to the scalability effect, after reaching economic break-even, the higher revenues are almost entirely transferred to operating margins (Gross Operating margin/EBITDA and EBIT).

The bankability of intangible assets is based on a paradox that although they have a lower collateral value than real estate (or even tend to zero, if they are considered intangible such as know-how or goodwill in the absence of business continuity) they have a high capacity to produce incremental economic-income flows, to be used primarily to service debt.

In this context, an application is the "Scalability of contacts" (potential customers) which allows firms to enlarge their user bases with technological devices, leveraging the growth with a synergistic combination of:

- Cloud computing and IT outsourced to remote providers;
- Smartphones and other ICT end-user devices;
- (Viral) Social media;

- M-apps as a bridging gate between the digital firm and its potential customers;
- Limited physical plant and staff with consequent minimization of tangible CAPEX and OPEX;
- Blitzscaling, i.e., adopting a specific set of practices for igniting and managing dizzying growth prioritizing speed over efficiency, and allowing firms to go from "startup" to "scaleup" (Hoffman & Yeh, 2018);
- Strong revenue growth levered by the factors above;
- Deregulation or "far-West style" lack of regulation, since new business models often precede legal prescriptions aimed at preventing abuses detrimental to consumers and competitors.

When a startup matures to the point where it reaches a killer product, a clear and sizable market, and a robust distribution channel, it can become a "scaleup"—a world-changing company that touches millions or even billions of lives. Startups evolve into scaleups by blitzscaling.

Blitzscaling is what we call both the general framework and the specific techniques allowing companies to achieve massive scale at incredible speed.

Among the risks arising from such scaling-up, startups can disrupt consolidated industries by exploiting network externalities to create digital monopolies where size is increasingly valued, often neglecting economic profitability.

Digital markets are highly contested, and margins may be low or even negative. Digital firms often try to broaden their core business with ancillary products, betting on higher spending capacity from conquered clients, eventually trying to boost profitability.

Boosting sales should be accompanied by economies of scale and experience that leverage operating profits, looking for a dreamy combination of explosive turnover and growing margins.

However, overvaluation remains a threat that characterizes firms driven by unrealistic expectations, and when reality begins to set in, the landscape of opportunities becomes much smaller for many startups.

Lack of positive economic and financial marginality eventually forces companies to break-up.

3.15   E-COMMERCE AND SCALABLE INTERNET TRADING

With the proliferation of websites, professionals sought to evaluate the features of e-commerce websites most likely to maximize Internet technology adoption, attract Internet users, turn them into cyber-buyers, encourage customer loyalty to the product, improve customer service and ultimately increase profits.

"E-commerce" refers to the activity of buying or selling products on online services or over the Internet, considering the website as a "type of store".

Nowadays, with its digital functionalities, e-commerce can greatly contribute to making a business model scalable and representing a "digital window" of the products and services of a firm which become immediately visible to web surfers.

The emergence of e-commerce has provided a more practical and effective way of delivering the benefits of digital supply chain technologies. E-commerce fosters the integration of all inter-company and intra-company functions, meaning that the three flows (physical, financial, and information flow) of the traditional supply chain could be affected and modified by e-commerce reengineering. Specifically, the impact on physical flows improves the way of product and inventory movement levels for companies. For what concerns the information flows, e-commerce optimizes the capacity of data processing, whereas, for the financial flows, it allows companies to have efficient and timely payment solutions.

3.16   SCALABLE AND DIGITAL SUPPLY CHAINS

A supply chain is a network between a company and its suppliers to produce and distribute a specific product to the final buyer. Digitalization reshapes and, typically, smooths the workings of the supply chain, making it more resilient, time-to-market, and cheaper.

Network theory is consistent with the architectural framework of the supply chain, which has gradually been modified by the widespread use of intangibles in the digital society.

Intangibles can strongly contribute to the flexibility of supply chains. What makes supply chains resilient is:

- A synergistic mix of complementary intangibles (e.g., big data and IoT that fuel patented processes and artificial intelligence applications);
- A scalable network of expanding nodes and linking edges, incorporating growth real options, and B2B or B2C relationships;
- Digital platforms as a service (cloud computing services that provide a platform allowing customers to develop, run, and manage applications without the complexity of building and maintaining the infrastructure typically associated with developing and launching an app) (Butler, 2013).

Network theory is mostly related to digital platforms, which in turn represent the linchpin of intangibles and scalability. The most powerful active platforms nowadays are Amazon, Apple, Google/Alphabet, and Facebook/Meta. They share some common characteristics and are all rooted in equally powerful technologies not predicated on physical assets. They benefit from innovative ecosystems, which emphasize core interactions between platform participants, including consumers, producers, and third-party actors (Jacobides et al., 2018).

Korpela et al. (2017) show that digital supply chain integration is becoming increasingly dynamic. Access to customer demand needs to be shared effectively, and product and service deliveries must be tracked to provide visibility in the supply chain. Business process integration is based on standards and reference architectures, which should offer end-to-end integration of product data. Companies operating in supply chains establish process and data integration through intermediating companies, whose role is to establish interoperability by mapping and integrating company-specific data for various organizations and systems. This has typically caused high integration costs, and diffusion is slow. Business to business (B2B) integration within the supply chain, refers to the electronic data exchanged over the Internet between business partners and value-added service providers.

As shown in Fig. 3.12, the key value drivers of digital supply chains include:

- Fast (just-in-time) end-to-end integration through digital enablers;
- Traceability and visibility of deliveries through smart logistics partners;

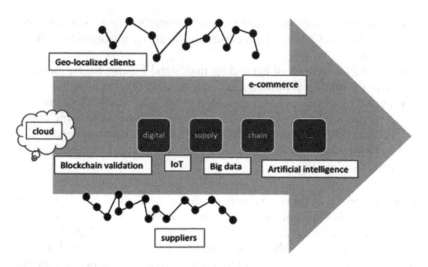

Fig. 3.12 Key-value drivers of digital supply chains

- Cost-effective cloud solutions provided by ICT partners;
- Sharing of timely information stored in the cloud;
- Standardized integration of business transactions and collaboration processes through digital platforms accessed by consortium members;
- Networking with geolocalized e-commerce customers;

According to *The Economist* (2019), digitalization will have an impact on the supply chains that steam and electricity had on manufacturing. Companies in many industries are experimenting with a variety of new technologies and methods that promise to improve how they plan, source, produce and deliver. These innovations are making supply chains smarter by increasing their predictability, transparency, and speed of delivery.

Digitalization helps predictability, using historical sales to figure out demand forecasts in today's on-demand economy. Artificial intelligence can help in the assessment of social media trends and shifts in demand, fueling real options, with an impact on the just-in-time management of the inventory.

Cognitive analytics and artificial intelligence may so deeply impact digitalized supply chains, together with blockchains. Physical delivery tools like drones may complementary help, even if they are still far from reaching mass-market potential.

Manual stick planning is increasingly replaced by digitalized big data, cutting sundry costs, and improving forecast modeling.

Many procurement tasks (vendor management, order placement, and invoice processing) can be automated, tracking in real-time delivery flows.

Outsourcing has become so widespread across countries that it needs to be digitally mastered with synergistic intangibles. Data are increasingly outside the ecosystem of the final assembler and so they need to be gathered, stored in the cloud, and processed through digital platforms linked to interoperable databases. Geolocalization, tracking, barcoding, and IoT are part of the game.

Prototyping, digital design, and 3D printers are other components of the digital supply chain, and contribute to the saving of costs and time, increasing economic and financial marginality, and reducing the risk discount rate. Discounted cash flows, traditionally used in valuation, are automatically improved.

Figure 3.13 shows the main differences between a basic (traditional) supply chain and a networked digital supply chain that incorporates trendy intangibles illustrated in the following chapters.

3.17   DIGITAL TRANSFORMATION

Digitalization is defined as the concept of "going paperless", namely as the technical process of transforming analog information or physical products into digital form. The term "digital transformation" refers, therefore to the application of digital technology as an alternative to solve traditional problems. As a result of digital solutions, new forms of innovation and creativity are conceived, while traditional methods are revised and enhanced.

Digitally born startups or similar tech businesses are not the only ones interested in adopting digital processes. Traditional businesses may be digitalized as well (e.g., a simple farmer willing to increase exponentially his/her production of tomatoes may digitalize the production activities through new systems or machines). In practice, with digitalization, traditional firms improve their key economic and financial parameters, as the EBITDA, increases, while the WACC reduces, so improving the DCF

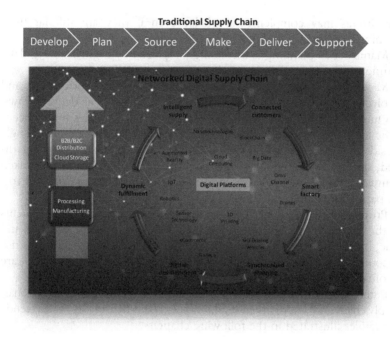

Fig. 3.13 Traditional versus digital supply chain

and the overall enterprise value (EV), expressed by the discounted ratio between the operating cash flow (FCFF) and the WACC:

$$\frac{O_{CF} \uparrow}{WACC \downarrow} \cong Enterprise\ Value \uparrow\uparrow \qquad (3.12)$$

In synthesis, digitalization brings speed and quality at a low cost, thus representing a key driver for scalability itself. Digitalization enables a business process reengineering of traditional firms which may presuppose an incremental production growth.

Figure 3.14 (recalled in Chapter 20) shows the link between digital transformation and scalability.

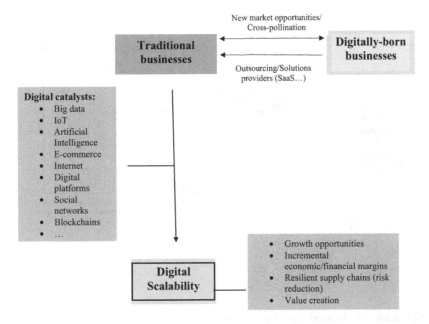

Fig. 3.14 The link between digital transformation and scalability

3.18 Networking Digital Platforms

Digital scalability is increasingly dependent on IT platforms. Spagnoletti et al. (2015, p. 364) define a digital platform as "a building block that provides an essential function to a technological system and serves as a foundation upon which complementary products, technologies, or services can be developed".

Digital platforms and supply chains are naturally linked with the networked firm (examined in Sect. 15.5) and enhance a scalability multiplier, benefitting also from Metcalfe's effect. An example is represented in Fig. 3.15. Network theory is examined in Barabàsi (2016).

Platforms are facilitators of exchange (of goods, services, and information) between different types of stakeholders that could not otherwise interact with each other. Transactions are mediated through complementary players that share a network ecosystem (Rochet & Tirole, 2003).

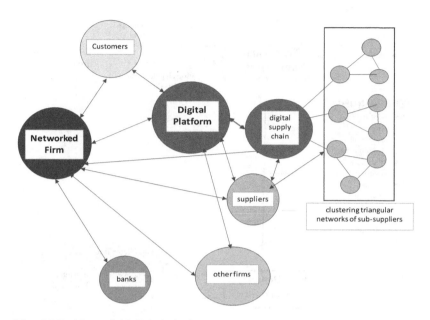

Fig. 3.15   Networked digital platforms

Digital platforms are multi-sided digital frameworks that shape the terms on which participants interact with one another. Digital platforms are also complicated mixtures of software, hardware, operations, and networks (de Reuven et al., 2018; Gawer, 2014). They provide a set of shared techniques, technologies, and interfaces to a broad set of users; social and economic interactions are mediated online, often by apps (Kenney & Zysman, 2016).

Digital platforms are complementarily defined as "software-based external platforms consisting of the extensible codebase of a software-based system that provides core functionality shared by the modules that interoperate with it and the interfaces through which they interoperate" (Tiwana et al., 2010). Software platforms represent a technological meeting ground where application developers and end-users converge (Evans et al., 2006).

Digital technologies imply homogenization of data, editability, re-programmability, distributedness, and self-referentiality (Kallinikos et al., 2013; Yoo et al., 2010). Such characteristics of digitality can lead to multiple inheritances in distributed settings, meaning there is no single owner that owns the platform core and dictates its design hierarchy (Henfridsson & Lyytinen, 2010).

Multi-sided platforms continue to disrupt long-established industries and have governance structures ranging from a very centralistic and autocratic organization to a more split approach with an empowerment on the user side (the patient). Also, the accessibility varies from a high degree of openness to detailed background checks users need to pass to participate in the platform (Schreieck et al., 2018). These characteristics may strongly impact, for instance, healthcare digital platforms.

Digital platforms have become a major mode for organizing a wide range of human activities, including economic, social, and political interactions (e.g., Kane et al., 2014; Tan et al., 2015). Platforms leverage networked technologies to facilitate economic exchange, transfer information, and connect people (Fenwick et al., 2018). Studies adopting this view focus on the technical developments and functions that form the foundation upon which complementary products and services can be developed, i.e., building on the top of the technical core that a platform owner offers and facilitates (Ceccagnoli et al., 2012; Ghazawneh & Henfridsson, 2015; Tiwana et al., 2010).

Due to their plasticity, platforms represent an ideal bridging node between complementary intangibles (e.g., big data vehiculated through mobile apps, stored in the cloud, and interpreted with artificial intelligence patterns), enhancing value co-creating patterns.

3.19   Sustainable Business Planning

Business planning is a core pillar of dynamic sustainability, as it represents a formal document that envisages long-term economic and financial perspectives. Appropriate business planning, with continuous fine-tuning, backs sustainability strategies and so fosters ESG compliance. ESG targets may well be embodied in business planning key factors, for instance envisaging:

(a) A periodical check-up of the business continuity (capacity for the firm to keep a going concern for at least the next 6–12 months);

(b) A consequential consideration of the prospective economic and financial equilibrium (capacity of the firm to generate positive economic and financial margins, respectively represented by

EBITDA, EBIT, pre-tax/net profit, or operating and net cash flows);

(c) A sensitivity analysis, conducted with a deterministic or stochastic approach that embodies stress tests, to assess the break-even point, with appropriate strategies to avoid or bypass a disaster case;

(d) A continuous reengineering and reformulation of the business plan hypotheses, exploiting bottom-up evidence from the external market and customers;

(e) A prompt reaction to equity or cashflow burnouts, should these criticalities occur.

Business planning is the fundamental prerequisite of any firm valuation, as it provides the data to be incorporated in the appraisal. Business planning is also a well-known tool for strategic formulations and execution (Lasher, 2010; Sahlman, 1997). The value of planning is driven by the possibility of evaluating alternative actions and being able to improve strategies. Before market entry, the main purpose of the evaluation is to pursue good and terminate bad business ideas (Chwolka & Raith, 2012). Planning is beneficial for performance (Brinckmann et al., 2010). Decision-making, however, remains a challenging task in the current age of forecasting (Asaduzzaman et al., 2015). As Razgaitis (2003) shows, prognosticators apply Monte Carlo Analysis to determine the likelihood and significance of a complete range of future outcomes; Real Options Analysis can then be employed to develop pricing structures, or options, for such outcomes. The forecasting effectiveness of traditional financial risk measures can be improved by integrating financial risk with an ESG risk measure that considers the ESG entropy (Ielasi et al., 2021).

Designing and creating a business model is crucial for a successful firm's operation in today's market. A business model is a factor that differentiates one firm from another—it defines the distinctions of the firm, how the firm deals with the competition, the firm's partnerships, and customer relations (Koprivnjak & Peterka, 2020). Business modeling is increasingly focused on sustainability orientation, extended value creation, systemic thinking, and stakeholder integration (Breuer et al., 2018).

Business planning follows a typical managerial top-down approach where management-prepared forecasts and projections are conceived within the firm and occasionally compared with market returns. The increasing availability of timely big data, sometimes fueled by the Internet of Things (IoT) devices, allows receiving continuous feedback that can be conveniently used to refresh assumptions and forecasts, using a complementary bottom-up approach. Top-down and bottom-up are both strategies for information processing and knowledge ordering, and they should be used in coordination.

Forecasting accuracy can be substantially improved by incorporating timely (bottom-up) empirical evidence, with a consequent reduction of both information asymmetries and the risk of facing unexpected events, concerning the magnitude of their impact. Since risk is represented by the difference between expected and real events, if occurrences are timely incorporated into expectations, this differential is minimized. This intuitive concept is well-known, but its practical implications are amplified by the unprecedented presence of big data.

Valuation criteria of the project or investment are typically linked to business planning metrics, especially if they are based on Discounted Cash Flows (DCF). DCF forecasting can be greatly improved by timely big data feedback that positively affects the numerator of the DCF formula, represented by growing cash flows (that incorporate real option flexibility), and decreasing discount rates (cost of capital) that reflect reduced risk, in the denominator. Value-adding strategies can conveniently reshape supply and value chains that embed information-driven resilience.

Network theory may constitute a further interpretation tool, considering the interaction of nodes represented by IoT and big data, mastering digital platforms, and physical stakeholders (shareholders, managers, clients, suppliers, lenders, etc.). Artificial intelligence, database interoperability, and blockchain applications are consistent with the networking interpretation of the interaction of physical and virtual nodes.

The interaction of big data with traditional budgeting patterns creates flexible (real) options nurtured by a networked digital ecosystem, eventually bringing to augmented business planning.

3.20 DIGITALIZATION BEYOND THE PANDEMICS

The coronavirus has unleashed since February, 2020 a worldwide pandemic that brings back the memories of ancestral scourges, re-proposing ancient threats like peast (the Black Death), which we considered confined to the history books. The bond between man and nature has always been conflictual and punctuated by biblical pestilences that periodically resurface, subverting an order that Sapiens claim in vain to dominate. The black swan reappears unexpectedly, an unexpected event that distorts the trajectory of our expectations, and which, in retrospect, is inappropriately rationalized and judged to be predictable.

And the pandemic spreads through a network made up of physical contiguity and social relationships, catalyzed by globalization and connected to an increasingly pervasive digital dimension. In this context, viral networks intersect with virtual platforms and networks, with an interweaving based on contradictions and connivances that are only apparently *impromptu*. The dialectic contrast between viral networks and digital platforms can also be interpreted with the myth of Plato's cave, wondering if the footprints perceived by the prisoners represent concrete reality or a mere virtual transposition.

The theory of graphs or networks (networks) elaborates mathematical models that interpret, among other things, the spread of viruses. A brief historical excursus takes us back to the story of a great discovery, intuitive and at times banal. The original problem concerns the possibility of making a route crossing all seven bridges of the city of Kant (now Kaliningrad), passing each bridge only once. The question was resolved by Euler in 1741. It identifies the origin of the theory of graphs, vertices, or nodes connected through sides, just like the bridges to be crossed. The structure of the nodes forms a network.

The applications are vast, ranging from physics to information technology (the Internet is a large virtual network), electrical engineering (transmission networks), biology (food chains), economics and finance (networks of markets and intermediaries), operations research, climatology (interrelationships between clouds, winds, temperatures) and sociology (social networks, etc.).

Among the applications, some models study viral networks and their epidemiological characteristics. The basic assumption configures two nodes (human beings) connected by a virus, through the contagion coefficient R_0, which indicates the transmissibility of an infectious disease. The parameter varies considerably (it is very high, for example, in measles) and expresses the "virality" of each node (infected patient).

In general terms, each node has mathematical properties that measure its importance: thus, for example, the Bologna railway node is the most important in Italy because it serves as an interchange and passage point for heavily trafficked routes.

The insertion of an additional node enriches the network, and this surplus value is measurable with the model of Metcalfe (the inventor of the Ethernet network) according to which the increase in value is exponential.

The issue can be understood, in opposite terms, by assuming the loss of value derived from the absence of a node. This can explain, for example, electrical blackouts that occur when a transmission node goes down, breaking the whole transmission system. In most cases, the disappearance or cancellation of a node creates significant problems, especially in physical networks, triggering domino effects and chain reactions that are not always predictable. In the epidemiological field, exactly the opposite happens. The isolation between nodes (physical persons), implemented through social distancing, eases the viral contagion. Viral networks express the mechanisms of multiplication of pathogens through networks fed by the contiguity of individuals and by life models resulting from globalization and mass socialization.

The comparative analysis between the times of spread of the Spanish flu (about a year and a half in 1918–1920) and today's Coronavirus make us understand the dimensions of the problem and the acceleration suffered in a century, also due to the demographic multiplier (almost 8 billion people, as worldometers notes every day, against 1.8–2 at that time).

Alongside viral and physical networks, there are others, more recent, such as digital networks, in which physical nodes (consumers, businesses, etc.) are connected through bridging nodes such as digital platforms.

The applications range from e-commerce sites to website domain names (such as Corona beer, which nobody drinks anymore) or to mobile apps that represent the iconic Internet access portal. The value of a node is a function of the Internet traffic flows that it can carry and mediate. The traffic of information (small data, aggregated to form big data) or commercial transactions, is detected in real time and with the gift of ubiquity (anytime, anywhere, "24/7").

Digital platforms are typical non-rival goods, being able to be used simultaneously by an unlimited number of users, with a scalable value, which grows exponentially and benefits from economies of experience, incorporating the feedback of consumers, who participate in a process of co-creation of value (think of the TripAdvisor site).

Smart working or e-learning are further examples of eco-sustainable applications based on digital platforms—unfit to supplant frontal teaching, but able to represent, in a context of lockdown, an irreplaceable surrogate.

On the basis of digital platforms, there are exchange mechanisms between node-users based on network theory. And the platforms add value to the whole network, acting as a bridge node (like an airport hub that concentrates and then routes traffic to peripheral airport nodes).

There are significant similarities and differences between viral networks and digital platforms, which can be interpreted with network theory.

Viral networks have a physicality, albeit invisible, which is lacking in the intangible-digital reality. The nodes, as anticipated, have an opposite value: in the epidemiological field, an attempt is made to destroy their interrelation, which instead takes on a digital surplus value. Alongside these antinomies, there are factors of contiguity, which occur when the real world, in its physicality as well as epidemiological, intersects—in a not always orderly way—with the virtual one. Social distancing is a positive element in the epidemiological field that we try to replace with digital social networking.

The interrelationships between physical (sometimes viral) and virtual networks can also be mathematically interpreted through innovative theories of multilayer networks, in which networks positioned on different planes (physical and/or virtual) intersect, through "bridge nodes" on several levels. And the kinetic value of networks must also be evaluated, which interprets—already and not yet—their changing becoming.

The interrelationships are also based on functional and organizational characteristics, through virtuous osmosis that aims to loosen the viral networks while strengthening the virtual ones in parallel. Thus, for example, the strengthening of smart working, in its multiple articulations.

Moreover, the digital divide does not allow a global application of digital services, penalizing technologically backward—and often over-populated—areas that are precluded from teleworking, the use of big data, artificial intelligence applications, data validation via blockchain, e-commerce based on B2B2C digital platforms, etc. Also for this reason (and due to the shortcomings of health networks), pandemics in the poorest areas are claiming more victims, as Ebola has shown. And the simulations of epidemics involving slums incorporate explosive promiscuity and poor sanitation, outclassed by other existential priorities.

But the digital barrier against pandemics affects everyone, like the search for a common vaccine, and socio-health issues take on a forced global dimension, which cannot yield to myopic localisms. Even the regional fragmentation of healthcare shows, in this area, evident limits also in our country, because viruses have no residence, regardless of local bureaucratic issues that struggle to find a coordinated synthesis.

Digital platforms are also the pivot of telemedicine applications, which facilitate the domiciliation of patients, with enormous savings and an improvement in the quality of life, decongesting hospitals, and slowing down infections.

Therefore, in hindsight, there are also useful lessons that the pandemic leaves us as a legacy.

3.21   APPENDIX—EXAMPLES OF OPERATING LEVERAGE CHANGES

	Company A	Company B
Total revenues	150	150
Total variable costs	(120)	(60)
Contribution margin	30	90
Total fixed costs	(10)	(70)
EBIT	20	20
Degree of operating leverage (DOL)	1.5	4.5

When the incidence of fixed costs grows, the economic and structural capacities of the company worsen, as it needs to sell more to reach the break-even point, since higher operating leverage increases the contribution margin. Let's consider two alternative scenarios, with the same starting figures:

(a) **Hypothesis 1** revenues decrease to 50

	Company A	Company B
Total revenues	50	50
Total variable costs	(40)	(20)
Contribution margin	10	30
Total fixed costs	(10)	(70)
EBIT	0	(40)
Degree of operating leverage (DOL)		0.75

(b) **Hypothesis 2** revenues grow to 300

	Company A	Company B
Total revenues	300	300
Total variable costs	(240)	(120)
Contribution margin	60	180
Total fixed costs	(10)	(70)
EBIT	50	110
Degree of operating leverage (DOL)	1.2	1.64

NOTES

1. Difference between the present value of cash inflows and the present value of cash outflows over a period. NPV is used in capital budgeting and investment planning to analyze the profitability of a projected investment or project. Projects with a positive NPV should always be accepted.
2. EBITDA does not consider non-monetary intangible OPEX, and CAPEX is expressed net of amortization.
3. See Chapter 6.
4. See Chapter 15.
5. See https://scipython.com/book/chapter-3-simple-plotting-with-pylab/examples/moores-law/#:~:text=Since%20the%20data%20cover%2040,T2log102.
6. https://www.reliablesoft.net/adwords-vs-adsense-what-is-the-difference-and-can-i-use-both-on-the-same-website/.

SELECTED REFERENCES

Asaduzzaman, M., Shahjahan, M., & Murase, K. (2015). Real-time decision-making forecasting using data mining and decision tree. *International Journal on Information, 18*(7), 3027–3047.

Baldi, F., & Trigeorgis, L. (2009, Fall). Assessing the value of growth option synergies from business combinations and testing for goodwill impairment: A real options perspective. *The Journal of Applied Corporate Finance, 21*(4), 115–124.

Barabàsi, A. (2016). *Network science.* Cambridge: Cambridge University Press. Available at http://networksciencebook.com/

Breuer, H., Fichter, K., Lüdeke-Freund, F., & Tiemann, I. (2018). Sustainability-oriented business model development: Principles, criteria and tools. *International Journal of Entrepreneurial Venturing, 10*(2), 256–286.

Brinckmann, J., Grichnik, D., & Kapsa, D. (2010). Should entrepreneurs plan or just storm the castle? A meta-analysis on contextual factors impacting the business planning–performance relationship in small firms. *Journal of Business Venturing, 25*(1), 24–40.

Butler, B. (2013, February 11). PaaS primer: *What is platform as a service and why does it matter?* Network World. https://www.networkworld.com/article/2163430/paas-primer-what-is-platform-as-a-service-and-why-does-itmatter-.html

Ceccagnoli, M., Forman, C., Huang, P., & Wu, D. J. (2012). Co-creation of value in a platform ecosystem: The case of enterprise software. *MIS Quarterly, 36*(1), 263–290.

Chwolka, A., & Raith, M. A. (2012). The value of business planning before start-up—A decision-theoretical perspective. *Journal of Business Venturing, 27*(3), 385–399.

Costantinides, P., Parker, G., & Henfridsson, O. (2018). *Platforms and infrastructures in the digital age.* Information Systems Research. Articles in advance (pp. 1–20).

de Reuven, M., Sørensen, C., & Basole, R. C. (2018). The digital platform: A research agenda. *Journal of Information Technology, 33*, 124–135.

Evans, D. S., Hagiu, A., & Schmalensee, R. (2006, January). *Invisible engines: How software platforms drive innovation and transform industries.* https://doi.org/10.7551/mitpress/3959.001.0001.

Fenwick, M., McCahery, J. A., & Vermeulen, E. P. M. (2018). *The end of 'corporate' governance: Hello 'platform' governance* (Lex Research Topics in Corporate Law & Economics Working Paper No. 2018-5, European Corporate Governance Institute (ECGI) - Law Working Paper No. 430/2018). Available at SSRN: https://ssrn.com/abstract=3232663

Gander, J. (2015). *Designing digital business models.* London: Kingston University.

Gawer, A. (2014). Bridging differing perspectives on technological platforms: Toward an integrative framework. *Research Policy, 43*(7), 1239–1249.

Ghazawneh, A., & Henfridsson, O. (2015). A paradigmatic analysis of digital application marketplaces. *Journal of Information Technology, 30*(3), 198–208.

Gupta, A., Christie, R., & Manjula, R. (2017). Scalability in internet of things: Features, techniques and research challenges. *International Journal of Computational Intelligence Research, 13*(7), 1617–1627. Available at http://www.ripublication.com/ijcir17/ijcirv13n7_06.pdf

Harshini Poojaa, K., & Ganesh Kumar, S. (2022). Scalability challenges and solutions in blockchain technology. In S. Smys, V. E. Balas, & R. Palanisamy

(Eds.), *Inventive computation and information technologies*. Lecture Notes in Networks and Systems, 336. Springer: Singapore.

Haskel, S., & Westlake, S. (2018). *Capitalism without capital: The rise of the intangible economy*. Princeton: Princeton University Press.

Henfridsson, O., & Lyytinen, K. (2010). The new organizing logic of digital innovation: An agenda for information systems research. *Information Systems Research, 21*, 724–735.

Hoffman, R., & Yeh, C. (2018). *Blitzscaling*. New York: Crown Publishing Group.

Hyoung, Y. J., Park, A., & Lee K. J. (2020). Why are the largest social networking services sometimes unable to sustain themselves? *Sustainability, 12*(2), 502.

Kallinikos, J., Aaltonen, A., & Marton, A. (2013). The ambivalent ontology of digital artifacts. *MIS Quarterly, 37*(2), 357–370.

Kane, G. C., Alavi, M., Labianca, G., & Borgatti, S. (2014). What's different about social media networks? A framework and research agenda. *MIS Quarterly, 38*(1), 275–304.

Koprivnjak, T., & Oberman Peterka, S. (2020). Business model as a base for building firms' competitiveness. *Sustainability, 12*, 9278.

Iazzolino, G., & Migliano, G. (2015). The valuation of a patent through the real options approach: A tutorial. *Journal of Business Valuation and Economic Loss Analysis, 10*(1), 99–116.

Ielasi, F., Capelli, P., & Russo, A. (2021). Forecasting volatility by integrating financial risk with environmental, social, and governance risk. *Corporate Social Responsibility and Environmental Management, 28*(5), 1483–1495.

Ipsmiller, E., Brouthers, K. D., & Dikova, D. (2019). 25 years of real option empirical research in management. *European Management Review, 16*, 55–68.

Ismail, S. (2014). *Exponential organizations*. New York: Singularity University Book.

Jacobides, M. G., Cernamo, C., & Gawer, A. (2018, March). Towards a theory of ecosystems. *Strategic Management Journal, 39*(8), 2255–2276.

Kenney, M., & Zysman, J. (2016, Spring). The rise of the platform economy. *Issues in Science and Technology, XXXII*(3), 61.

Korpela, K., Hallikas, J., & Dahlberg, T. (2017). Digital supply chain transformation toward blockchain integration. In *Proceedings of the 50th Hawaii International Conference on System Sciences*. Available at https://scholarspace.manoa.hawaii.edu/handle/10125/41666

Lasher, W. (2010). *The perfect business plan made simple: The best guide to writing a plan that will secure financial backing for your business*. New York: Broadway Books.

Lòpez, L., Francisco, J., & Esteves, J. (2017). *Value in a digital world: How to assess business models and measure value in a digital world*. Cham: Palgrave Macmillan.

Miller, M. H. (1988, Fall). The Modigliani-Miller propositions after thirty years. *Journal of Economic Perspectives, 2*(4), 99–120.

Modigliani, F., & Miller, M. H. (1958, June). The cost of capital, corporation finance and the theory of investment. *American Economic Review, 1*, 3.

Odlyzko, A., & Tilly, B. (2005). A refutation of Metcalfe's law and a better estimate for the value of networks and network interconnections. Minneapolis, University of Minnesota.

Razgaitis, R. (2003). *Dealmaking using real options and Monte Carlo analysis*. Hoboken: Wiley.

Reed, D. P. (2001, February). The law of the pack. *Harvard Business Review*.

Rochet, J. C., & Tirole, J. (2003). Platform competition in two-sided markets. *Journal of the European Economic Association, 1*(4), 990–1029.

Ross, S. A. (1988, Fall). Comment on the Modigliani-Miller propositions. *Journal of Economic Perspectives, 2*(4), 99–120.

Sahlman, W. A. (1997). How to write a great business plan. *Harvard Business Review, 75*(4), 98–109.

Schreieck, M., Hein, A., Wiesche, M., & Krcmar, H. (2018). The challenge of governing digital platform ecosystems. In C. Linnhoff-Popien, R. Schneider, & M. Zaddach (Eds.), *Digital marketplaces unleashed*. Berlin, Heidelberg: Springer.

Spagnoletti, P., Resca, A., & Lee, G. (2015). A design theory for digital platforms supporting online communities: A multiple case study. *Journal of Information Technology, 30*(4), 364–380.

Tan, B., Pan, S. L., Lu, X., & Huang, L. (2015). The role of IS capabilities in the development of multi-sided platforms: The digital ecosystem strategy of Alibaba.com. *Journal of the Association for Information Systems, 16*(4).

The Economist. (2019, July 13). Global supply chains. Special reports.

Tiwana, A., Konsynski, B., & Bush, A. A. (2010). Platform evolution: Coevolution of platform architecture, governance, and environmental dynamics. *Information Systems Research, 21*(4), 675–687.

Trigeorgis, L., & Reuer, J. J. (2017). Real options theory in strategic management. *Strategic Management Journal, 38*, 42–63.

Weill, P., & Woerner, S. L. (2013, March). Optimizing your digital business model. *MIT Sloan Management Review, 1*(43), 123–131.

Westlake, S., & Haskel, J. (2017). *The rise of the intangible economy: Capitalism without capital*. Princeton: Princeton University Press.

Yoo, Y., Henfridsson, O., & Lyytinen, K. (2010). The new organizing logic of digital innovation: An agenda for information systems research. *Information Systems Research, 21*, 724–735.

PART II

Technology

CHAPTER 4

The Valuation of Know-How

4.1 The Uncertain Perimeter of "Know-How", Between Organization and Technology

According to OECD (2017) *"Know-how and trade secrets are proprietary information or knowledge that assist or improve a commercial activity, but that are not registered for protection in the manner of a patent or trademark. Know-how and trade secrets generally consist of undisclosed information of an industrial, commercial or scientific nature arising from previous experience, which has practical application in the operation of an enterprise. Know-how and trade secrets may relate to manufacturing, marketing, research and development, or any other commercial activity. The value of know-how and trade secrets is often dependent on the ability of the enterprise to preserve the confidentiality of the know-how or trade secret. In certain industries, the disclosure of information necessary to obtain patent protection could assist competitors in developing alternative solutions. Accordingly, an enterprise may, for sound business reasons, choose not to register patentable know-how, which may nonetheless contribute substantially to the success of the enterprise. The confidential nature of know-how and trade secrets may be protected to some degree by (i) unfair competition or similar laws, (ii) employment contracts, and (iii) economic and technological barriers to competition"* (par. 6.20).

"There are also intangibles that are not protectable under specific intellectual property registration systems, but that are protected against

© The Author(s), under exclusive license to Springer Nature Switzerland AG 2022
R. Moro-Visconti, *The Valuation of Digital Intangibles*,
https://doi.org/10.1007/978-3-031-09237-4_4

unauthorized appropriation or imitation under unfair competition legislation or other enforceable laws, or by contract. Trade dress, trade secrets, and know-how may fall under this category of intangibles" (par. 6.38).

A trade secret is any information about a business that could give a competitive advantage to another person or business. A trade secret can include any of the following:

- Formulas, practices, processes designs;
- Instruments, patterns. Algorithms;
- commercial methods, such as distribution or sales methods;
- advertising strategies;
- lists of suppliers or clients, or consumer profiles;
- Physical devices, ideas, compilations of information.

The know-how to do it is a concept characterized by a broad perimeter of definition. The problems of application and interpretation are complex, even in the phase of drafting contracts and protection of rights, primarily in the field of technology transfer (Roberts, 2000; Teece 2008a, 2008b) or unfair competition.

"Know-how" means a wealth of non-patented practical information, resulting from experience and testing by the supplier, which is secret, substantial, and identified; in this context:

- "secret" means that the know-how, considered as a body of knowledge (Poston, 2015) or in the precise configuration and composition of its components, is not generally known or easily accessible;
- "substantial" means that the know-how includes knowledge indispensable to the buyer for the use, sale, or resale of the contract goods or services;
- "identified" means that the know-how must be described in a sufficiently comprehensive manner to make it possible to verify that it fulfills the criteria of secrecy and substantiality.

Most regulations relate know-how to products and processes and the performance of theoretical analyses, systematic studies or experiments, including experimental production, technical checks of products or processes, the construction of the necessary facilities, and the obtaining of the relevant intellectual property rights.

Know-how (savoir-faire) consists of the production and organizational method, often embodied with technological applications as part of an industrialization process, and it consists of practical knowledge of how to do something, e.g. a product. The know-how exploits a wealth of knowledge and constructive artifices acquired through entrepreneurial talent, often by way of craftsmanship and not always formally codified, not in the public domain, and therefore such as to originate exclusive information asymmetries, which often encroach on trade secrets, intrinsically characterized by requirements of novelty and not accessible to third parties.

The work leading to know-how, through technical and organizational progress, is typically carried out in teams. In the legal field, for the know-how, there are significant problems of identifiability, traceability, and identifiability (which stem from the immateriality of the *res incorporales*, inapprehensible and evanescent), as well as those of secrecy, substantiality, usefulness, and ownership. Digitalization makes know-how somewhat easier to identify and record. Digital storage typically occurs in the cloud, and could be interpreted with artificial intelligence algorithms.

The know-how, which can be considered an economic intangible asset, and which represents a relational and knowledge heritage, can include tangible and substantial activities such as formulas, instructions, and specifications, codified procedures and archetypes, technical devices, production layouts using technology, design, molds or models or intangible activities such as marketing and communication strategies, quality testing techniques, production and organizational procedures and skills. The concept of know-how is close to that of recorded patents, and somewhat precedes patenting. Know-how is also a key component of internally generated goodwill.

The know-how refers both to mass production, in which the organizational and production strategies are serially codified and standardized ("customized"), and to production by order, which represents "tailor-made clothes" in which the craftsmanship and creativity are enhanced. In any case, it is a matter of expertise and confidential internal knowledge linked to reproducible creativity of technical and/or commercial proprietary information, with an indefinite and potentially infinite useful life, which differentiates the know-how and trade secrets from patented inventions.

The extension of the concept, in its fundamental division between technical-industrial and commercial know-how (linked to marketing), is concomitant with the growing importance of innovation as a strategic driver. Insofar as patenting requires some form of disclosure, many inventions remain deliberately confined to the field of industrial secrets, where knowledge, as notorious, must be inaccessible; especially in process inventions, industrial secrecy typically offers greater guarantees, than patenting, against possible violations by third parties.

The know-how, through an orchestrated process of apprenticeship (learning by doing), involves process and product innovations, which at the strategic level can be a source of competitive advantage, understood by Porter (1998) as cost advantage and/or differentiation, in the context of competition between companies.

The voluntary cognitive dissemination of know-how is expressed in specific methods, practices, procedures, or processes, including technical assistance agreements. The know-how can be properly understood as a synergistic glue of the "organized complex of goods" that constitutes the company, as a Coasian nexus of contracts, characterized by the ability to create, transfer, assemble, integrate and economically exploit activities deriving (also) from knowledge. Its ambiguous perimeter does not always allow a clear separation concerning other intangible assets.

The know-how is the basis of R&D that can lead to the patenting of original inventions and sometimes can be associated with trademarks, considering their nature as distinctive signs that have qualitative characteristics largely based on know-how. And the know-how can be contiguous to the software or, sometimes, to the rights of use of the intellectual works.

The know-how is, in the broadest sense, the cognitive monitoring for the quality guarantee and the repair of the products, with an after-sales market, concerning also the reduction of defects, with consequent limitation of the product liability.

4.2   Galilean Replicability and Industrialization of the Experimental Scientific Method

With the invention of the Galilean scientific method, the concept of reproducibility of experiments was introduced, which is the basis of the knowledge acquired through empirical attempts, then systematized, both in scientific theories and in a technological/organizational context of functional and industrialized replicability, to make each experiment productive and successful.

The scientific method uses an inductive and deductive approach[1] and is aimed at achieving an objective—not arbitrary—knowledge of empirical reality, in a reliable, verifiable, shareable, and universally valid way. All this is based on heuristic analysis, i.e., on empirical intuition based on experience, including artisan experience, to be replicated on an industrial basis. Empirical observations, hypotheses, and deductions are used to draw replicable conclusions, through experiments inspired by know-why.

Everything is linked to the concepts of industrialization (mass production), replicability, scalability, and transferability which are of fundamental importance to fill the know-how with practical-application contents and to allow it to be exploited, shared, and negotiated.

The application of a Cartesian scientifically replicable method limits the subjectivity and irrationality of the know-how, favoring its industrialization, even if with the risk of weakening the creative vein, in favor of a replicating technicality. The know-how stems from the experience and the maieutic—Socratic—effort to bring out new industrial ideas, from the custom applied to making, inventing a method, codifying and replicating it, using the technical archetype for mass production, and the systematic organization of the business model. This process follows iterative procedures based on often unsuccessful attempts, with the progressive refinement of knowledge and skills. The know-how, understood as an engineered development of the technique, is a two-bladed scissor: deductive because it applies the first principles and inductive using the scientific method. Know-how is related to internal knowledge (Bose, 2007; Cassiman et al., 2000) that depends on the quality of human resources.

The formation of know-how is usually a slow and gradual process, based on small steps and empirical feedback often unsuccessful, with attempts and errors in constant evolution, which continuously redirect the strategies of incremental enhancement of the company.

The incremental training of know-how, even in a process of value cocreation, can be inspired by reverse engineering processes, based on a detailed examination of the operation, design, and development of an invention applied by others, to produce a similar one, improving efficiency and quality.

4.3   PROTECTION, SHARING,
AND TRANSFER OF KNOW-HOW

The protection of industrial secrets, even in the absence of patents, is possible through instruments of protection and safeguarding as an inhibitory and compensatory measure, for example against unfair competition and its inherent abuses. The vulnerability of the know-how is connected to the technological innovations that allow recording images, forms, and processes—with elements of sophistication once unknown (through photocopies, scans, films, digital photographs, recordings, computer duplications ...)—operating more and more through tools of technological piracy to unlawfully steal of data and sensitive information. There is a possibility to store data and transfer them via the web that allows a real-time migration of the wealth of the differential knowledge stolen.

The damages deriving from the subtraction of know-how are potentially significant and this imposes the adoption of particular cautions during the sharing of technologies (knowledge sharing), made necessary by increasingly interdependent value chains, where tacit knowledge becomes at least partially explicit.

In sharing know-how, strategic decisions to make or buy are marked by increasing specialization, which expands the scope of cooperation with other external parties, including business networks or technology parks. From the immateriality of the know-how comes the characteristic of an unrivaled good, in which the transfer to another subject involves the possibility of use by the assignor, with the consequent creation of a duopoly.

The technology transfer, by way of sharing through licensing contracts, or with final sales, often occurs in extraordinary operations, such as M&A, contributions or demergers of companies or their branches, asset swaps, etc.

The transfer of know-how requires its prior identifiability, at the perimeter level, and often entails the need to associate it with other tangible or intangible assets (machinery, patents, qualified personnel ...), to which it appears connected.

Key managers represent a critical aspect of know-how and the transfer of qualified personnel is the indispensable "software" governing the transfer of technologies. It must be accompanied by adequate training of new staff and, once again, the codification of procedures and knowledge, to preserve and depersonalize its use, making them fungible and interchangeable with knowledge management tools.

Contracts for the assignment or licensing of know-how may lead to unfair competition, even with criminal relevance, in the event of unlawful disclosure of industrial secrets.

The codification of tacit and routine procedures, mainly with advanced Enterprise Resource Planning management software, is an increasingly essential prerequisite for the preservation and transferability of know-how. The storage of sensitive and strategic data is increasingly using outsourcing and backup tools, such as cloud computing, with the outsourcing of security that solves some problems, but creates others, also in terms of responsibility.

The dissemination of know-how is based on the know-how of social networks, blogs, and chats, which allow exchanges of opinion and, more generally, the sharing of ideas within discussion forums. The libertarian nature of the network clashes with the entrepreneurial need to segregate knowledge, unlike what happens in academia, where free dissemination is a key principle of scientific thought, for its validation and refutability.

The diffusion of the know-how is stimulated by its frequent horizontal scalability (expanding its use in more companies with similar corporate purposes) and vertical scalability (with synergic crossings of know-how in functionally integrated companies). The extension of the value chain to more synergistically interconnected subjects and the assembly of the surplus value around shared know-how are at the origin of more refined competitive structures. This happens in an industrial district, which raises the competitive barriers to entry toward potential new competitors, preserving the incumbents' incomes. In this sense, know-how is the source of the competitive advantages, sometimes bringing to monopolistic rents (which tend to be increasingly ephemeral, as a result of increasing competitive pressure or antitrust provisions).

The implementation of a codified system of knowledge is important for large companies that repeatedly face the same problems, and that have a high turnover of staff, resulting in "skills traps".

The critical mass of continuous investment in skills is an essential strategic element, to the benefit of larger companies and/or those capable of doing systemic work. Investments in basic and applied research are based on market opportunities, the funding that can be obtained, including public funding, and the degree of legal protection.

The networking of know-how is an increasingly valuable driver for the creation of value, especially through the strategic sharing of economies of experience and scale (with minimization of fixed costs shared, first of all at the production level). This is relevant in intangible-intensive sectors intrinsically characterized by high scalability of economic margins (and the consequent financial flows).

The preservation of know-how is based on the preparation of remunerated non-competition agreements, also to limit the brain drain and, more generally, to retain the knowledge acquired within the company perimeter.

Technology transfer (Choi, 2001) refers to knowledge, technology, production methods, prototypes, patented inventions, or, more rarely, know-how on the part of governments, universities, public and private companies, research bodies, and individual inventors.

4.4   Economic and Financial Valuation

The estimate of the market value of the know-how (Choi, 2001; Kynci, 2017; Lee & van Stein, 2006) must typically be placed in an evaluation context that considers not only the company as a whole, but also its intangible resources, starting with those most contiguous to the know-how (i.e., patents and, residually, goodwill).

The exploitation of know-how stems from the value chain and the external sources of evaluation, as shown in Fig. 4.1. Transfer price benchmarking is often concerned with know-how valuation (Moro-Visconti, 2013).

Regarding intangible assets not registered or specifically protected, such as know-how, the valuation is subject to high intertemporal variability, being anchored to provisions aimed at drawing up the strategic, industrial, and financial plans.

The breadth of the evaluation interval is demarcated, in its extremes, by upper and lower limits, in the hypothesis of (full) going concern (full business continuity) or in liquidation (break-up) scenarios, in which traditionally intangible resources lose most of their value, especially if they are not independently negotiable or synergistically connected to other assets. In the hypothesis of discontinuity, the organized complex of assets that represents the firm is eliminated.

The choice of approaches depends on the intangible resource and the purpose and context of the evaluation, but also on the ease with which

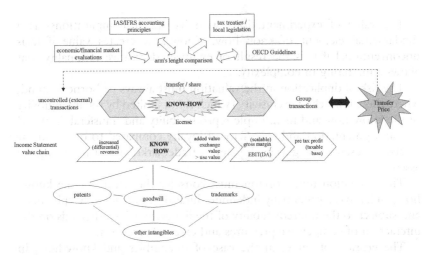

Fig. 4.1 Links between know-how, value chains, and external evaluation sources

reliable information on the market in which it is strategically positioned can be found.

Of the different approaches, the complementarity in identifying—from different angles—the multi-faceted aspects of the intangible object of evaluation, suitable to allow an integrated evaluation, must be grasped. For example:

- the relief-from-royalties is in the function of the incomes or incremental cash flows that derive from the exploitation of the know-how and that interact with the market surplus value or the multipliers of comparable companies;
- the incremental equity derives from an accumulation in the years of differential income;
- the costs of reproduction estimate the future benefits and the independent estimate of the average differential goodwill between balance sheet-based versus income approaches.

The evaluation can be carried out for different purposes, even in litigation, in case of unfair competition with appropriation, replication, and/or undue imitation and usurpation of know-how.

The value of experimentation—with its practical implications—is a fundamental element of know-how. Know-how creates value if it is unconventional if it is the result of engineered creative rationality that allows a mastering of complexity.

The risk of duplication in the valuation must always be borne in mind, where there is a lack of exclusivity (which is not limited by the intangibility of the know-how and its multiple reproducibility and transferability) and a clear segmentation and specificity of loyalty compared to other similar assets, represented by goodwill, patents, trademarks, and other intangible assets.

The evaluation time horizon must consider the nature of the know-how, which has a potentially indefinite duration but is forcibly ephemeral and subject to the unpredictability of the life cycle, which depends on the interaction of competitive pressures and external reactions.

The erosion of value, in the case of intangibles and know-how, in particular, derives from its potential obsolescence and technological decay, which eliminate its exclusive connotations, and not from a deterioration related to the use, which indeed increases the value, because of economies of experience, as well as visibility and synergistic sharing with other inventions or processes. The strategic value of the know-how must be appreciated in terms of uniqueness, specificity, non-permeability, and exclusivity, which are the basis of killer applications.

4.4.1 The Relief-from-Royalty Approach

An easily applicable empirical approach is based on the determination of the "presumed royalties" that the owner of the know-how would have required to authorize third parties to exploit it ("consent price" approach). The relief-from-royalties approach (applicable to the evaluation of many intangibles and analyzed in Chapter 2, Sect. 2.11.2) is indicated where one wants to arrive at the determination of the exchange value of the know-how.

This approach allows estimating the income of the know-how by deducting from the notional royalties that would be paid to a third party for the use of the know-how under license any direct and indirect costs of maintenance/development of the know-how itself not already deducted from the notional royalty.

The market value of know-how can be estimated as the sum of the relief-from-royalties (which the company would pay as a licensee if the know-how were not owned) discounted over a time horizon of at least 3–5 years. Hypothetical licensing (Mendi et al., 2016) is an essential element for valuation.

The concept of reasonable royalty can be relevant in the field of litigation in the quantification of damages for unlawful use of the know-how.

The presence of license agreements is appreciated by investors, because it generates not occasional revenues, and is a signal of the technological heritage and innovative capacity of the company.

4.4.2 The Incremental Income Approach

The value of know-how is proportional to its expected economic results. Therefore, the contribution of know-how in terms of price and/or volume increases (and therefore economic margin) to the profitability of the business can be measured by the differential income approach, which determines the value of the know-how as the present value of the sum of the differential income that it is likely to produce in the future.

The know-how can, therefore, be evaluated if it gives rise to differential economic benefits, which are expressed in a premium price (the price differential of the product characterized by know-how).

The number of years of discounting the income from the exploitation of the know-how depends on its life cycle (useful life). A possible variant is based on the estimate of the incremental gross operating margin that the know-how contributes to obtaining, to which a reasonable multiplier derived from negotiations of comparable intangibles is applied. The additional cash flow generated by the know-how can also be considered.

The use of the know-how acts on the economic margins expressed by the differential between revenues and operating costs as it allows both to increase revenues (with higher direct sales or with royalties receivable from licenses) and to reduce costs, producing with less labor-intensive techniques and suitable to allow savings of other costs (production, organization, energy …).

The stratification of differential incomes thanks to the know-how generates incremental equity, which expresses the differential between market value and the book value of the company. It is a suitable element to express the surplus value of know-how. The lack of symbolic recognition and capitalization of know-how costs impacts the lack of amortization and the potential undervaluation of the equity, with a book value lower than the market value.

Both the approaches considered here, and the relief-from-royalties can be reconducted, in a broad sense, to the income approaches, based on a projection of normalized future income. This income is to be discounted over a predefined (or unlimited) time horizon, consistent with the expected useful life of the know-how, at a reasonable rate, which incorporates the risk associated with the expected future manifestation of income.

4.4.3   The Estimate of the Cost Incurred (or of Reproduction)

In the absence of reliable data on expected income capacity, a possible alternative is that of the cost incurred in the past to create the know-how and to occupy in the market the positions reached by the firm at the valuation date.

The identification of a historical cost of production, based on an analytical accounting that allows to functionally separate the costs for the know-how from the others, is preparatory to the estimate of a current cost of reproduction, having the nature of investment and oriented to the expected future benefits.

A limit of this estimate derives from the unfitness, of the historical costs to measure value later, due to the change in the purchasing power. A second limit is because the value of an asset is not only due to the costs necessary to obtain it, but also mainly to its expected benefits.

A step forward is represented by the process of reproducing functionally equivalent know-how, which replaces the historical costs with the costs of reproducing the asset from scratch, i.e., the costs that would have to be incurred at the time of valuation to reconstruct the same value that the know-how reached at that time.

However, in the procedure now examined, there is still the limit of not considering the profitability of the investment and the opportunity cost deriving from the immediate non-use of the know-how. The existence of high and uncertain fixed costs related to the reconstruction of know-how represents a barrier to entry that segregates the market and distances competitors.

4.4.4   The Complex Balance Sheet-Based Approach

The balance sheet-based approaches traditionally used in continental Europe are based on the analytical valuation of individual assets and liabilities, with a comparison with their book value, to adjust the book value of equity to arrive at a market value of equity. In this approach, in the so-called "second-degree complex" variant, there are peculiar activities, such as know-how, which are not normally accounted for and do not typically have an independent market value. The capital gain should then be expressed net of potential tax liabilities, considering a tax profile that will only be applied when there is a need to move from an abstractly estimated value to a value-added price, monetarily negotiated.

4.4.5   The Mixed Capital-Income Approach, with an Independent Estimate of Goodwill

The main approach for estimating goodwill is based on the comparison between the extra yield that the company can generate for a limited period (or, more rarely, unlimited) and the normal return on capital of comparable companies, within the product sector of reference.

To the extent that the goodwill is attributable to the know-how, the approach can be used to estimate this know-how; a critical point derives from the not easy separability of the know-how from other intangible resources. The extra income due to know-how is comparable to differential income and therefore the two approaches can find useful elements of convergence or, at least, complementarity.

Figure 4.2 summarizes the valuation approaches of know-how.

4.5   PRODUCT AND PROCESS INNOVATION

Innovation is one of the key elements of a company's differentiation strategies, which allow it to become unique, acquiring a competitive advantage that can result in monopolistic rents. The innovations can be a product and/or process and are divided into main or derived: the former have an absolute degree of creativity and originality compared to the previous knowledge, while the latter has a relative character and may

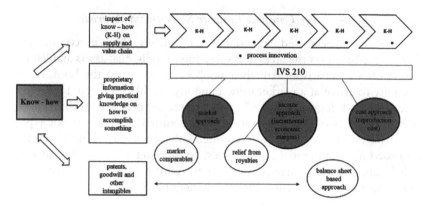

Fig. 4.2 Know-how valuation approaches

consist of progress or improvement of techniques. The derived inventions may be of:

- improvement (resolution in different and more convenient forms of technical problems previously solved in another way);
- translation (transposition of a known principle or a previous invention in a different sector and with a different result);
- combination (ingenious and original coordination of elements and means already known with a technically new and economically useful result).

Also, "chain-linked" inventions, which form patent families along the same supply chain, are essential.

There may be cases of dependent and derived inventions, of selection, improvement, combination, and translation, whereby the original patent takes on higher value as a result of other inventions that depend on it, giving rise to significant synergies. Know-how is the "glue" that keeps together sequential inventions, presiding over their smooth interaction.

Differentiation helps to create barriers to entry into the market, limiting competition and the substitutability or comparability of the company's assets. This can allow it to achieve high economic margins, even in the presence of an external demand that struggles to find satisfaction elsewhere and that may suffer the temporary monopolistic force of the leading company that may activate price-maker strategies (with a specular price-taking clientele).

At a strategic level, the differential nature of inventions, which contribute to making the company "unique", sheltering it from comparison and allowing it to avoid cost differentiation, is associated with their scalability, which allows its use—through industry and reproducibility in series—where costs are marginally decreasing as volumes increase. Low marginal costs and economies of scale are positive aspects of know-how, which are the result of often very costly initial investments and uncertain outcomes.

4.6 Know-How and Creditworthiness

The presence of know-how within the company tends to have a limited impact on the creditworthiness of the company, considering first the limited recoverable value of the know-how and its uneasy identifiability, measurability, and separability concerning other assets. This is true during crises, when business continuity may not be guaranteed, and the company may be destined to lose its synergistic value.

The residual value of the know-how changes according to its destination to minimize the effects of a crisis: if it is transferred with other healthy branches or associated with intangibles with independent collateral value (as, for example, patents, or the human capital expressed by employees) then there will be a more limited loss of value.

In situations of going concern, the know-how retains a fundamental role in facilitating the proper functioning of the company, which depends on the economic and financial flows that are needed for debt servicing.

4.7 The Impact of Artificial Intelligence and Digitalization on Know-How

Artificial Intelligence (AI) is now recognized as one of the main enablers of digital transformation in multiple industries. AI can help companies become more innovative, flexible, and adaptive than ever before, with an impact on robotics, and process automation.

With its ability to improve simulation, forecasting, and smooth proof-of-concept trials and errors, artificial intelligence can boost (human) know-how, and its industrial applications.

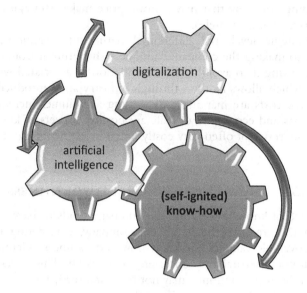

Fig. 4.3 Know-how, artificial intelligence, and digitalization

Digitalization is a further catalyst that fosters know-how through its input factors, easier to collect, store and interpret (Fig. 4.3).

NOTE

1. Inductive reasoning begins with detailed observations of the world, which moves toward more abstract generalisations and ideas. Deductive approach explores a known theory or phenomenon and tests if that theory is valid in given circumstances.

SELECTED REFERENCES

Bose, S. (2007). Valuation of intellectual capital in knowledge-based firms: The need for new methods in a changing economic paradigm. *Management Decision, 45*(9), 1484–1496.

Cassiman, B., Pèrez Castrillo, D., & Veugelers, R. (2000, August). *Endogenizing know-how flows through the nature of R&D investments* (UPF Working Paper No. 512). Available at SSRN: http://ssrn.com/abstract=248683

Choi, J. P. (2001). Technology transfer with moral hazard. *International Journal of Industrial Organization, 19*(1–2), 249–266.

Kynci, M. (2017). *Methods of valuation intangible assets with emphasis on the valuation of know-how.* Available at http://stc.fs.cvut.cz/pdf17/6598.pdf

Lee, D., & Van Den Stein, E. (2006, December). *Managing know-how* (Unit Research Paper No. 07-039). HBS Technology & Operations Management.

Mendi, P., Moner-Colonques, R., & Sempere-Monerris, J. J. (2016, June 1). Optimal know-how transfers in licensing contracts. *Journal of Economics/Zeitschrift fur Nationalokonomie, 118*(2), 121–139.

Moro-Visconti, R. (2013). Evaluating know-how for transfer price benchmarking. *Journal of Finance and Accounting, 1*(1), 27–38.

OECD. (2017, July). *Transfer pricing guidelines for multinational enterprises and tax administrations.* https://www.oecd.org/tax/oecd-transfer-pricinggu idelines-for-multinational-enterprises-and-tax-administrations-20769717.htm

Porter, M. (1998). *Competitive advantage: Creating and sustaining superior performance.* New York: Free Press.

Poston, T. (2015, December). Know how to transmit knowledge? *Nous, 50*(4), 865–878.

Roberts, J. (2000, December). From know-how to show how? Questioning the role of information and communication technologies in knowledge transfer. *Technology Analysis & Strategic Management, 12*(4), 429–443.

Teece, D. J. (2008a). *The transfer and licensing of know-how and intellectual property: Understanding the multinational enterprise in the modern world.* Singapore: World Scientific Publishing.

Teece, D. J. (2008b). *Technological know-how, organizational capabilities, and strategic management: Business strategy and enterprise development in competitive environments.* Singapore: World Scientific Publishing.

Vishwasrao, S. (2007). Royalties vs fees: How do firms pay for foreign technology? *International Journal of Industrial Organization, 25*(4), 741–759.

CHAPTER 5

Patent Valuation

5.1 Patents: Definition and Rationale

A patent is a limited monopoly that is granted for 20 years in return for the disclosure of technical information (Benty & Sherman, 2014, p. 375).

A patent is a set of exclusive rights granted by a sovereign state or inter-governmental organization to an inventor or assignee for a limited period in exchange for detailed public disclosure of an invention. An invention is a solution to a specific technological problem and is a product or a process (WIPO, 2008). The word patent originates from the Latin *patere*, which means "to lay open" (i.e., to make available for public inspection).

According to OECD (2017) *"A patent is a legal instrument that grants an exclusive right to its owner to use a given invention for a limited period within a specific geography. A patent may relate to a physical object or a process. Patentable inventions are often developed through risky and costly research and development activities. In some circumstances, however, small research and development expenditures can lead to highly valuable patentable inventions. The developer of a patent may try to recover its development costs (and earn a return) through the sale of products covered by the patent, by licensing others to use the patented invention, or by an outright sale of the patent. The exclusivity granted by a patent may, under some circumstances, allow the patent owner to earn premium returns from the use of its invention. In other cases, a patented invention may provide cost*

R. Moro-Visconti, *The Valuation of Digital Intangibles*, https://doi.org/10.1007/978-3-031-09237-4_5

161

advantages to the owner that are not available to competitors. In still other situations, patents may not provide a significant commercial advantage" (6.19).

The value of the intangibles is linked to their continuous upgrade through R&D: "In some industries, products protected by intangibles can become obsolete or uncompetitive in a relatively short period of time in the absence of continuing development and enhancement of the intangibles. As a result, having access to updates and enhancements can be the difference between deriving a short term advantage from the intangibles and deriving a longer-term advantage" (OECD, 2017, par. 6.125).

Patents are usually the result of risky and costly research and development and the developer will try to recover its costs (and earn a return) through the sale of products covered by the patent, licensing others to use the invention (often a product or process), or through the outright sale of the patent. Patents are typically preceded by internally generated know-how (see Chapter 4).

The very fact that costs are incurred mainly before patentability for inventions may have important transactional implications: patents are ripe for sale or licensing even immediately after registration, considering their finite useful life, with typically soon peaking and then declining values. The terminal value of an expiring patent is not necessarily zero if it can still be used as a distinctive, albeit no more protected, invention, during and after its phase-out. The brand associated with the expired patent (e.g., Aspirine) may still be worth it.

The protection provided by a patent is limited to 20 years, and so is shorter than the protection of copyright law or (potentially unlimited) trademark registration, but the rights are more extensive and cover most commercial uses.

Patents are granted only after a long and expensive registration process. Patent rights help firms keep unique competitiveness in the market, under the protection of the law, avoiding the copying and plagiarism of other competitors (Danchev, 2006).

Justifications and economic rationale for patents derive from:

- The natural right of inventors to the proceeds of their mental labor;
- The grant of a reward for the inventive activity that otherwise would lack proper incentives.

Patent valuation is required in many cases as:

1. M&A operations, spin-offs, demergers, joint ventures, etc.;
2. Bankruptcy;
3. Sale or license;
4. Patent conflicts and disputes;
5. Collateral for bank loans;
6. Accounting;
7. Taxation (transfer pricing; patent box, etc.).

5.2 FROM KNOW-HOW TO PATENTS

Patents represent the natural evolution of know-how.

"Know-how and trade secrets are proprietary information or knowledge that assists or improves a commercial activity, but that is not registered for protection in the manner of a patent or trademark". (OECD, Transfer Price Guidelines, § 6.5., 2017)

"Know-how is practical knowledge of how to get something done, as opposed to 'know-what' (facts), 'know-why' (science), or 'know-who' (networking). Know-how is often tacit knowledge, which means that it is difficult to transfer to another person by means of writing it down or verbalizing it. The opposite of tacit knowledge is explicit knowledge. In the context of industrial property (now generally viewed as intellectual property), know-how is a component in the transfer of unpatented proprietary technology in national and international environments, co-existing with or separate from other Intellectual Property rights such as patents, trademarks, and copyright and is an economic asset" United Nations Industrial Development Organization (1996).

Know-how (to do it) is a key and trendy factor behind competitive and comparative advantage (Hall, 1993), representing the invisible glue behind strategies of product differentiation and innovation, creating ancillary value from other factor inputs.

If overall added value may be compared to an iceberg, know-how may well represent its gravitational sunk part.

5.3 Accounting as a Prerequisite for Valuation

Accounting treatment and the consequent assessment of intangible capital are a prerequisite for financial performance appraisal and consequent bankability, combining economic margins, such as EBITDA, with debt-servicing cash flows (Metha & Madhani, 2008).

The slippery nature of intangibles and their consequent uneasy valuation boundaries represent a well-known problem, examined in Chapter 2.

According to IAS 38, the aggregate amount of research and development expenditure recognized as an expense during the period is required to be disclosed, but there are no specific requirements for disclosure of another spending on intangibles.

"The academic and professional interest in Intangible Capital is underpinned by the idea that it can be considered one of the main levers to create value" (Giuliani, 2013) and, according to Michael Porter's fundamental insights, value creation derives from the lasting competitive advantage over rival entities, embedded in continuously innovating business models, to be adequately designed and managed (Porter, 1998). Competitive edge is increasingly driven by the catalyst presence of intangibles, which represents a pivotal breakthrough, and it occurs when an organization (painfully) develops core competencies and skills that allow it to outperform its competitors, especially for what concerns customized differentiation.

Patents, often underrepresented in the balance sheet, typically constitute a significant incremental EBITDA driver, which expresses the dominant income-driven cash flow source. Intangibles, which are the invisible "glue" behind going concern and value creation, not only enhance strategic differential value but are likelier to make results more sustainable in the future, so easing proper debt service.

DCF or EBITDA calculus is currently used for the market valuation of patents. Even if academics and practitioners well know this fact, some further considerations, based on intangible driven cash generation, may add originality to the discussion of intellectual capital valuation and debt servicing. Asset-less incremental EBITDA, driven by intangibles, reinforces debt service capacity, through "economic" liquidity, which originated in the income statement.

5.4   LICENSE OR SALE?

Intangible transactions may temporarily or permanently transfer the property or the right to use the patent, being alternatively classified under a license or sale agreement. A patent can be used to protect or earn licensing revenues (Ignat, 2016).

The perimeter of a license is proportional to the value of the patent.

Even if many comparability problems are similar, some significant differences arise, and could be fiscally significant:

- (temporary) Licenses are more common within the group, where information asymmetries are minimized, and synergies shared, and on an international basis, to bypass geographical exclusivity problems—and so making transfer price arm's length comparisons applicable but more difficult to estimate;
- Definitive sales may conversely occur even outside (international) groups, especially when a small and independent company, that owns a promising patent, is aware of its intrinsic value, but lacks the economic and financial soundness to properly exploit it, especially abroad;
- Licensing may typically be riskier than selling for the owner of the patent since in many cases the royalty rate depends on unknown characteristics of the licensee (when the royalty is based on the licensee's output or sales, the rate may vary according to his or her turnover);
- Risk is asymmetrically transferred from the seller/licensor to the buyer/licensee, both in its dimension and timing, with a not negligible impact on the tax base and its repartition in different fiscal years. Albeit this parameter is difficult to estimate, it should be carefully investigated, together with its economic and fiscal impact. Risk transmission is definitive in sales (unless there are earn-out or other conditional clauses), being otherwise shared and diluted across time in license agreements.

A combination between licenses and sales is always possible, mainly when a license contract contains a put & call option, according to which after a certain period and at a stated price, the patent may be purchased by the licensee or sold by the licensor.

Legal ownership of the patent is not exclusively linked to its exploitation, not only because of possible licensing but also because of the versatility of the patent, which can be exploited with partnership agreements, risk sharing, common investments, etc., within an articulated international value chain, where it may prove difficult to estimate the value of each segment.

A license generally contains some or all the following financial provisions:

- Upfront payments;
- Ongoing pre-commercial payments;
- Patent cost reimbursement;
- Milestone payments;
- Annual minimum royalties;
- Research support;
- Sublicense income sharing;
- Manufacturing;
- Earned royalties or sales/profit sharing.

Most licenses include some form of upfront payment, variously called a license issue fee, a technology transfer fee, and technology access fee (…).

The upfront payment reflects the value of the technology at the time is being transferred. For an embryonic academic technology that lacks both market and technology validation, this initial value will be relatively low, and so will the upfront fee.

For the academic institutions, a vital element of the upfront value of the technology is the investment in legal fees that they have put into turning scientific data and publications into an intellectual property portfolio that can be licensed to a corporate partner. Academic institutions usually insist on recouping that investment upfront, in part so they can redeploy the funds into new inventions.

Newly formed startups are usually illiquid. A wise licensor will typically not seek to suck much of that expensive cash out of the company in upfront payments but will want to see those funds go into developing the technology. Instead, the licensor will generally agree to be compensated in shares of the licensee, purchased at nominal par value and characterized by upside potential.

When a large company licenses technology from a smaller, early stage company, the agreement normally includes the purchase of equity in the smaller company by the large one.

From the licensor's perspective, the validation of their technology (demonstrated by the license fees) means that the company has reached a significant value-added milestone.

Most licenses include several "pre-commercial" payments, made while the technology is still under development and before it is generating product revenues for the licensee.

Milestone payments reflect the increase in the value of the technology to the licensee as the licensee makes progress in developing the technology.

Developmental milestone payments are particularly common with life sciences inventions.

Annual minimum royalties ("AMR") refer to the payments that are made in advance, at the start of the license year. AMR typically starts low and escalates over time, following the patent's useful life.

An AMR serves as a due diligence mechanism. If the licensee has lost interest in the technology, either because it does not work or because the is no market interest, then the licensee will terminate the license and return the technology to the licensor rather than make an AMR payment.

When technology is transferred at an early stage, the licensee frequently needs the licensor to help with the development of the technology. They can then share revenues by implementing value co-creating strategies.

Exclusive licenses always give the licensee the right to sublicense the technology to third parties. Non-exclusive licenses generally don't include such a right because the licensor can still grant additional licenses to any interested third parties.

A "pass-through" is frequently found in licenses where the licensee is a large company. In such licenses, the payment obligations accepted by the licensee are equally binding on any sublicenses.

License agreements frequently include provisions for the licensor to manufacture products for the licensee. This is particularly likely in the preliminary stages of the license when the bulk of the know-how and capabilities reside with the licensor and the licensee is still starting to ramp up their skills, but it may well extend on an ongoing basis to provide for the licensor to manufacture product for commercial sale by the licensee.

Royalties on sales, named "running royalties" and "earned royalties", are payments made by the licensee once the license products have reached the marketplace. The licensor generally receives a percentage of the licensee's sales of the licensed products, usually quarterly in arrears. Such post-commercialization payments typically provide the most significant economic return to the licensor from the license if the product is successful.

The royalty base is the measurement, normally in terms of "Net Sales", of the licensee's sales of the licensed product on which the royalties will be paid.

There are two ways royalties are calculated:

1. A royalty fee based on the money value of the product's sales; or
2. A royalty fee based on the units of product sold.

A royalty based on sales is expressed as a percentage of the monetary value of product sales.

Usually, the royalty rate should be higher at higher levels of sales, rather than decreasing as sales increase. The current year's Annual Minimum Royalties will be creditable against the earned royalties due.

In some cases, the parties may agree to split the profits from the sale of licensed products rather than provide a royalty. Profit splits are often encountered in licenses by biotechnology companies of late stage products to pharmaceutical companies.

Profit-sharing license agreements require a considerably more detailed set of financial provisions to identify which costs are allowable so that the licensors will be able to audit the payments they eventually receive. Profit-sharing arrangements work best if the licensee sells a relatively small number of products, so that cost allocations are clear and transparent. This is one reason why they work well in the pharmaceutical industry.

5.5   A Comprehensive Valuation Approach

Patents may be valued with many complementary approaches (cost-based; income-based or market-based, as shown below), whose practical implications go well beyond plain appraisals, concerning proper accounting or the ability to promptly serve debt.

Intangible assets, such as patents or trademarks (Salinas & Ambler, 2009), are particularly difficult to evaluate (Moro Visconti, 2012; Oestreicher, 2011), due to their intrinsic "immaterial" nature and many different—complementary—quantitative, and qualitative evaluation approaches (Andriessen, 2004; Lagrost et al., 2010) are traditionally used within the business community; valuation issues are even more complicated for non-tradable or not deposited non-routine intangibles, such as know-how (Moro Visconti, 2013), trade secrets, and unpatented R&D (Ballester et al., 2003), goodwill, etc., characterized by limited if any marketability, higher and pervasive information asymmetries and less defined legal boundaries, especially within increasingly specific businesses.

Intangible assets may hardly be estimated on a single basis, being mostly transacted within intangible package deals. These difficulties in the market evaluation are even more evident considering that, from an accounting perspective, according to IAS 38 there is no active market for intangibles, typically undetected, and it is consequently difficult to assess their fair value.

A technology appraisal is a written analysis of its intended value, considering the methodology and data used (quoting the sources).

The main financial/market approaches used for patents' fair pricing, with an appropriate rating and ranking, are consistent with IVS 210 prescriptions (examined in Chapter 2):

1. *Cost-based approaches*, with an estimate of the "what-if" cost to reproduce or replace intangibles from scratch if there is some relationship between cost and value. This method ignores both maintenance and the opportunity cost of time (reproducing an intangible may take years, whereas its missed use is due to generating a lack of income) and is not very useful for income-generating assets, such as performing patents or trademarks. Cost-to-cost comparisons are difficult to imagine, especially if they are to be protracted over years; even if intangibles strongly depend on long cumulated costs, their perspective value may hardly be inferred from past expenses and is volatile and cost differs from the value. To the extent that costs cannot typically be capitalized, their accounting track record may (partially) be detected from past income statement recordings.

2. *Income approaches*, based on the estimate of past and future economic benefits, assessing the ability of the patent to produce licensing income (royalties, which etymologically derive from "sovereign rents") or sale of the intangible; they may include:

- Capitalization of historic profits deriving from the exploitation of the intangible;
- Discounted Cash Flow (DCF), to estimate Net Present Value (NPV), duly incorporating risk factors in the discount rate, such as technology venture capital risk; DCF may be referred to operating cash flows (FCFF), discounted at the WACC, to estimate the Enterprise Value (comprehensive of financial debt), or net cash flows (FCFE), discounted at the cost of equity, to estimate the Equity Value;
- Gross profit differential approaches; they look at the difference in sales price between an "intangible backed" product (branded, patented, with embedded know-how ...) versus a generic one; the profit differential is then forecast and discounted;
- Excess or premium profit approaches; like the gross profit, it is determined by capitalizing the additional profits generated by the business over and above those generated by similar businesses, which do not have access to the intangible asset. Excess profits can be calculated by reference to a margin differential;
- Relief-from-royalty method: based on the assumption that the owner of the intangible is "relieved" from paying a royalty to obtain its use, the process considers the hypothetic "what-if" royalty that a potential user would be willing to pay and discounts its projection; a comparable market range of "reasonable" royalties may derive from careful arm's length benchmarking.

3. *Market-based approaches*, evaluating an intangible asset by comparing it with sales of comparable/similar assets (considering their nature; using functional analysis ...). Information asymmetries often conceal the real (mostly secret) nature of the allegedly comparable transaction. A market-based variety may refer to the evaluation of the incremental equity, with indicators of the business surplus, given for example by the Tobin Q (1969), the ratio between the market value and replacement value of the same asset; a market value exceeding the replacement value may be a numerical consequence of valuable intangibles. The paradox concerning patents is that if they are valuable, it is because of their originality, scarcity, etc. that make comparisons more difficult.

The purpose of the evaluation may change according to the context and the foreseen scenario, and could be targeted at the following different values:

- Fair Market Value—The price, expressed in terms of cash equivalents, at which property would change hands between a hypothetical willing and able buyer and a hypothetical willing and able seller. This fair value is assessed acting at arm's length in an open and unrestricted market when neither is under compulsion to buy or sell and when both have a reasonable knowledge of the relevant facts[1];
- Investment Value—The value the intangible would be worth, considering the specific buyer's intended use (and so with use value higher than exchange-value);
- Intrinsic Value—The value that an investor considers, based on an evaluation of available facts, to be the "true" or "real" value that will become the market value when other investors reach the same conclusion (Pratt, 2003).
- Liquidation Value—The company may pass from a going concern to a break-up context, this being a particularly conservative scenario for intangibles, especially if not autonomously tradable. The break-up value of a patent is typically higher than that of an "informal" intangible (e.g., know-how), as it shows an autonomous market value.

Figure 5.1 synthetizes the main valuation approaches.

While income and market-based approaches may theoretically seem based on accrual or, respectively, cash flow accounting, they tend to share standard parameters, softening the difference between these two accounting procedures.

Factors affecting the value of a patent include:

- Strength/weakness of the patent (how easily are they bypassed or engineered round);
- Characteristics of the patent (what the patent protects);
- Other technology rights.

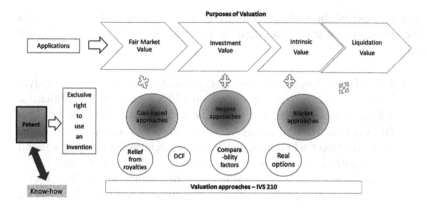

Fig. 5.1 Patent valuation approaches

Market and income valuations need to consider patent risk factors like:

- R&D risk (the risk that the technology cannot be successfully developed into a functional product);
- FDA risk (the chance that the product will not be found safe and effective by the FDA or similar authorities);
- Standards risk (the likelihood that a standard-setting body will adopt a standard that is incompatible with the product);
- Manufacturability risk (the risk that the product can't be manufactured at an acceptable cost or with enough quality);
- Marketing risk (the likelihood that the marketing launch of the product is unsuccessful);
- Competitive risk (the risk that a competitor using a different technical approach solves the same problem and reaches the market first);
- Legal risk (the risk that a competitor receives a patent that blocks others from entering the market and isn't willing to grant a license).

Valuation methodologies change over time and depend on the quality of information that typically increases over time in quantity and depth.

5.6 COST-BASED APPROACHES

The cost approach seeks to measure the future benefits of patent ownership by quantifying the amount of money that would be required to replace it and reproducing it from scratch. The starting point in this method is either the cost of reproduction of the property or its replacement cost.

The cost approach is rarely useful in the valuation of early stage technology: the cost of developing technology is seldom relevant to its value. Cost-based methodologies are frequently used for the estimate of software that in the US is often patented.

A cost-based valuation is typically divorced from the fair value of the technology.

The concept of using sunk cost to value technology is that the developer wants first to recoup their investment in developing the technology and then secure a return on that investment.

The problem with this approach is the question of whether the cost to develop a technology is relevant to its ongoing value.

Academic institutions always seek to recoup the discretionary investment they have made in securing patent rights in the license agreement. Such costs are identified separately from any other upfront cost and may be substantial if the technology has been under development for an extended period.

In licensing copyright-protected software (as it happens in the European Union) developed in an academic setting, recouping the sunk cost may be infeasible. A company interested in using the software could instead hire the researcher who wrote the code and get them to recreate it.

In corporate licensing transactions, where the licensor has made a substantial investment in developing the technology, they will want to ensure that they recoup that investment in upfront and milestone payments.

5.7 MARKET VALUATIONS AND NET PRESENT VALUE

The market approach measures the present value of future benefits by obtaining a consensus of what others in the marketplace have judged it to be. There are two requisites: an active, public market, and exchange of comparable properties. Startup technology rarely meets these valuation requisites.

Patents without established market values (e. g., no negotiated royalty rates) are often valued by comparing the number of citations the patent has received to the numbers received by other patents whose market values are established. For recently issued patents, which have not had time to accumulate citations, this procedure can be noisy or inapplicable (Falk & Train, 2016). Successful court decisions in favour of the validity of a patent typically increase its value.

Market valuations may use as preferred approaches either DCF or directly an EBITDA multiplier, inspired by (intrinsically uneasy) comparisons of intangibles. DCF theoretically stands out as the optimal method, being inspired by the golden rule according to which "cash is king".

Market evaluations frequently use a standardized EBITDA multiplied over time (from 2/3 up to 20 years) and this multiplication brings to an Enterprise Value (EV), attributable to debtholders and, residually, to equity-holders. This approach is consistent with the accounting nature of EBITDA, an economic and financial margin calculated before debt servicing.

EV/EBITDA multipliers may be connected to price/book value or Tobin Q parameters, which reflect the differential value of patents under a hypothetical cost reproduction hypothesis, so representing a precious bridge between the otherwise disconnected market and cost appraisal approaches.

As a rough calculation, the EV multiple serves as a proxy for how long it would take for the acquisition of the entire company (Enterprise Value – EV, including its financial debt) to earn enough to pay off its costs (assuming no change in EBITDA and a constantly added value contribution from the IC portfolio). Temporal mismatches between the numerator and the denominator may bias the ratio and should accordingly be minimized.

Equity may be inferred from an EBITDA multiplier, which estimates EV, and, after deduction of the market value of debt (Net Financial Position), the residual market value of equity. Whenever the residual market value of equity exceeds its book value, BV (price > book value; P/BV > 1), an implicit safety net for principal debt repayment emerges. Being EV a surrogate for the market capitalization (price), its relationship with market-to-book and Tobin q, driven by the presence of intangibles

(Chen et al., 2005; Valladares & Cuello de Oro, 2007) seems even more evident.

The stream of Operating Cash Flows—FCFF or O_{CF}—(marginally attributable to the patent's strategic contribution to the overall value) incorporates growth factors (Tan et al., 2007), whereas the weighted average cost of capital (WACC) discounting denominator embodies market risk, as recognized by debt and equity underwriters. Moreover, cash flows are a cornerstone of debt service. Qualitative issues, such as consistency, durability, depth of coverage, etc., concerning the patents, may strategically impact future EBITDA, cash flows, and consequent value. WACC may be affected by the asset substitution problem and inherent wealth transfer from debt-to-equity holders (or vice versa).

What matters is just described by differential/incremental O_{CF} or EBITDA, made possible by intangible strategic contribution, which is, however, often uneasy to isolate. Residual incremental value, not attributable to specific patent components is allocated within the goodwill.

Being O_{CF} derived from EBITDA:

$$\Delta EBITDA_{patent} \pm \Delta NWC \pm \Delta CAPEX = O_{CF} \qquad (5.1)$$

the link between key market approaches (possibly complementary, rather than alternative) is evident.

The calculation of expected benefits with Net Present Value (NPV) is given by the following formula, considering NPV accruing to equity-holders:

$$NPV_{equity} = \sum_{t=1}^{n} \frac{NCF_t}{(1 + K_e)^t} - CF_0 \qquad (5.2)$$

where:

NCF = Net Cash Flow = FCFE; t = time; K_e = Cost of equity; CF_0 = initial investment.

Proper calculation of NPV should include the other factors, incorporating in Net Cash Flows geographic limitations, restrictions, exclusivity, etc. One critical problem with NPV calculation is represented by the intrinsic difficulty of properly estimating cash flows, especially in the presence of unforeseeable events or flexibility options, particularly frequent with patents. A patent is like a real option because it allows its owner to choose between exclusively commercializing the patented invention sometime during the patent term or preceding commercialization altogether (Cotropia, 2009).

As Silberztein (2011), points out "There is currently no international consensus on the circumstances where financial valuation approaches and the Discounted Cash Flow ('DCF') may be appropriate for applying the arm's length principle", and again: "one of the main difficulties regarding the application of these approaches is that they are based on inherently uncertain projections".[2]

5.8   COMPARABILITY FACTORS

Patents are difficult to compare because there are intrinsically "unique" (if an invention is not unique, it cannot be patented!); relevant patentability requirements include novelty and non-obviousness.

Significance of market comparisons is indirectly proportional to the intrinsic value of patents; this brings to a paradoxical situation where originality and uniqueness are a distinctive core value of patents, with a consequent positive impact on its potential fiscal value, but at the same time represent a significant obstacle to its fair tax assessment. The more a patent is specific and worthy, the less it is detectable.

Possible comparability factors for patents include:

- The expected benefits from the intangible property (possibly determined through a Net Present Value calculation);
- Any limitations on the geographic area in which rights may be exercised;
- Export restrictions on goods produced by any rights transferred;
- The exclusive or non-exclusive character of any rights transferred;
- The capital investment (to construct new plants or to buy special machines), the startup expenses, and the development work required in the market;
- The possibility of sublicensing;
- The licensee's distribution network;
- Whether the licensee has the right to participate in further developments of the property by the licensor.

The market price, depending on comparability factors, may be difficult to find, especially if the intangible is unique. This is the case, especially for patents that are affected by a paradox: the more they are exclusive, the higher their value—but also the lower their comparability, etc.

Market information may derive from composite sources as:

- Internal (confidential) database;
- Published surveys and research that may establish norm standards within an industry;
- Public announcements of deals (of listed companies, etc.) and public databases (Liu et al., 2022);
- Details from litigation and required disclosure of license terms;
- State of the art;
- Word of mouth.

Deal databases may derive from the following sources (for fee):

- RoyaltySource (www.royaltysource.com);
- TechAgreements (www.techagreement.com);
- Markables (markables.com);
- RoyaltyStat (www.royaltystat.com);
- Business Valuation Resources (www.bvresources.com);
- Recap by Deloitte (www.recap.com);
- PharmaDeals (www.pharmadeals.net);
- Orbis Intellectual Property (Bureau van Dijk);
- Windhover (www.elsevierbi.com/deals).

5.9   INCOME APPROACH

The income approach focuses on the income-producing capability of the patents. The value is measured by the present worth of the net economic benefit to be received over the useful life of the patent.

The amount and the pattern of the income stream are evaluated with its duration and with the risk associated with the effective realization of the predicted income.

The income approach must properly consider the forecast profit and losses deriving from the patent.

The key differences between the classical high discount rate NPV approach and the Risk-Adjusted NPV approach are that in the latter risk is accounted for explicitly, and the discount rate used is a "cost of money" discount rate, not a risk-based discount rate.

An NPV-based valuation has the benefit that it considers trades off near-term and long-term financial terms appropriately.

Limitations of the NPV-based valuation are the following:

- Quality depends critically on the quality of the data;
- Critical data may not be available for technologies at a very early stage;
- Susceptible to the "garbage in – garbage out" issue.

Monte Carlo probabilistic approaches are another approach to accounting for risk.

Both the NPV and risk-adjusted NPV approaches require the analyst to make assumptions about all the parameters of the project—its costs, its revenues, the probability of success for each phase in the risk-adjusted NPV approach (...)—and then generate a single number that represents the analyst's best estimate of the present value of the project.

Monte Carlo approaches, by contrast, allow the analyst to put ranges around the various parameters, allowing, for cost overruns in development and the possibility, that sales may be either higher or lower than expected. The NPV is then calculated for each combination of the estimated parameters, and the results are presented as a distribution of the probability of the NPV.

Monte Carlo gives a much more sophisticated analysis of risk than NPV or risk-adjusted NPV approaches but has the limitation that data unlikely to be available for early stage academic technologies.

According to Degnan and Horton (1997), valuation methodologies are the following (Table 5.1).

Royalty rates may be estimated as follows (Table 5.2).

EBITDA is indirectly reflected in income valuation approaches, for example, those concerning royalty relief differentials or marginal economic surpluses made possible by the patent exploitation, and so it constitutes an important and precious connection between market and economic approaches. The (replacement) cost approach is not so easily linked to EBITDA, even if the projection of reconstruction costs of the portfolio of intangibles considers operating economic losses that are a core, albeit not exclusive, part of EBITDA. Revenues are missing in the

Table 5.1 License valuation

Valuation methodology	In-licensing (%)	Out-licensing (%)
Discounted cash flow	56	49
Profit sharing analysis	52	54
Return on assets	38	27
25% Rule as a starting point	24	30
Capital asset pricing model	11	10
Excess return analysis	8	7

Table 5.2 Relationship of royalty rate to magnitude of improvement

Median royalty rates	Pharma (%)	Non-pharma (%)
Revolutionary	10–15	5–10
Major improvement	5–10	3–7
Minor improvement	2–5	1–3

replacement cost method whereas key costs described for example by depreciation are not present in the EBITDA.

Being the cost method linked to accrual accounting, it may suffer from somewhat misleading historical cost convention procedures, which traditionally underestimate the accounting of the intangibles and their contribution to value creation. Accrual accounting represents an obstacle to the appraisal of the IC contribution to O_{CF} creation, even if the links pivoting around EBITDA may soften these inconveniences (Boujelben & Fedhila, 2011).

EBITDA is sometimes used as a proxy for FCFF/O_{CF}, representing a kind of price to cash flow multiple, unaffected by leverage and depreciation policies. This proxy is however misleading since O_{CF} is derived from EBITDA, considering Capital Expenditure (Capex) and Net Working Capital variations, as shown in formula (5.1). While fixed asset investments and their cashless depreciation may hardly be affected by intangibles, typically not capitalized, accounts payable included in NWC often reflect operating debt connected to costs (for R&D, advertising ...) associated with the patents.

EBITDA is a key parameter for assessing debt service capacity, so being linked even to classic capital structure concerns. To the extent that debt is properly served with positive cash inflows deriving from the EBITDA and then $FCFF/O_{CF}$, a key relationship can be established between market/income valuation models and bankability concerns.

Capacity to serve debt is often measured by EBITDA multipliers over negative interests (and by cover ratios); being EBITDA a differential and incremental economic/financial flow from operations, it should conveniently exceed negative interests at least 4–5 times, considering its contribution to the coverage of other monetary costs, such as taxes.

Being the patent appraisal so difficult, the synergistic combination of different complementary techniques is, whenever possible, recommended. Traditional financial statements do not provide relevant information for managers or investors to understand how their resources—many of which are intangible—create value in the future. Intangible statements are designed to bridge this gap by providing innovative information about how intangible resources create future value. Published intangible statements are, however, rare documents (Mouritsen et al., 2004).

Valuation approaches may be synergistically linked to operating and financial leverage since they contain key accounting and economic/financial parameters. These evaluation approaches may well be linked to the Modigliani and Miller theorems (1958) about optimal capital structure, which will be examined in Chapter 24, and to the key parameters embedded in their formulation:

- The Market approach is proxied by M&M proposition I and related cost of capital;
- Replacement cost is based on cumulated reconstruction costs and is linked to lost opportunities, whose estimate may somewhat refer to differential cumulated EBITDA and other economic/financial parameters, embedded in M&M formulations;
- The Income approach relies on EBIT/EBITDA differential contribution to value.

Coherently with IAS 38 prescriptions, DCF is the key parameter for both accounting and appraisal estimates, so representing the unifying common denominator of cost, income, or market-based approaches, which regularly need to find out their cash part. Cash is directly linked to debt service capacity, so connecting intangible value creation and its book value or a market appraisal with its financial coverage.

5.10 REAL OPTIONS

"A fairly robust economics literature exists which analogizes patents to real options. Real options create the right, but not the obligation, to purchase the underlying asset at a defined exercise price. A patent is like a real option, economists say because it allows its owner to choose between exclusively commercializing the patented invention sometime during the patent term or foregoing commercialization altogether. Economists have taken this analogy and used real options analysis to place specific values on patents" (Cotropia, 2009).

When investments or assets, like patents, are evaluated through NPV techniques, real options can be used to make forecasts more flexible (Iazzolino & Migliano, 2015).

A real option is the right—but not the obligation—to undertake certain business initiatives, such as deferring, abandoning, expanding, staging, or contracting a capital investment project. Real options describe the key tensions that managers face between commitment versus flexibility or between competition and cooperation (Trigeorgis & Reuer, 2017). Real options are intrinsically embedded in the patent's features to exploit future possibilities with a flexibility that is not captured by the standard capital budgeting metrics (to estimate the NPV, the IRR, etc.).

5.11 QUICK AND DIRTY VALUATION TECHNIQUES

It is advisable to express royalty rates in terms of Net Sales, not Net Profits. The most popular rule of thumb in licensing is the 25% rule. According to this rule, the licensor should receive 25% and the Licensee should receive 75% of the pre-tax profit from a licensed product.

In the famous Uniloc cause, the Court underlined that "the 25% rule of thumb is a fundamentally flawed tool for determining a baseline royalty rate in a hypothetical negotiation".

The rule of 25% appears broadly applicable—if a company is seeking a license to technology it must be because they believe they will derive some business benefit, either increased sales or decreased costs (Azzone & Manzini, 2008).

The main limitations of the rule are the following:

- The 25% must be apportioned over all the technologies the licensee will need to develop for a finished product;
- The licensee may resist giving 25% of their net profits if they must make a massive investment to develop and market a product.

5.12   Forecasting Patent Outcomes with Big Data and Stochastic Estimates

Prediction of future outcomes is particularly difficult. And when patents are concerned, uncertainties tend to grow, making valuation estimates hard. Imprecise forecasts bring huge differences between expectations and real outcomes, i.e., higher risk.

Both big data and stochastic estimates, especially if jointly considered, can soften these criticalities.[3]

Characteristics such as volume, velocity, variety, and veracity make big data particularly interesting for sophisticated economic and financial planning, where several variables stored in interoperable databases need to be simultaneously considered. Big data is driving better decision-making and can help to detect growth drivers. Stochastic modeling is a form of financial modeling that includes random variables to estimate how probable outcomes are within a forecast to predict different states of the world (Moro Visconti et al., 2018). Monte Carlo simulations and binomial trees are frequently used to forecast the patent's outcome, guessing different states of the world, together with their outcome probability. Estimates can be periodically refreshed using bottom-up empirical evidence, incorporated in the big data.

5.13   Medtech and Biotech Companies and the Technology Transfer Cycle

Technology transfer is the process of disseminating technology from its place of origination. It occurs among research centers, technology parks, and universities (Allen & O'Shea, 2014), from universities to businesses, from large businesses to smaller ones, from governments to businesses, across borders, both formally and informally, and both openly and surreptitiously.

Often it occurs by concerted effort to share know-how, R&D applications (pilot projects, patents, etc.), skills, knowledge, technologies, methods of manufacturing, samples of manufacturing, among governments, universities, and other institutions to ensure that scientific and technological developments are accessible to a wider range of users. Utilizers can then further develop and exploit the technology into new products, processes, applications, materials, or services.

Contractual conditions may envisage a royalty scheme or a sale of the invention. The transfer can be eased by technological brokers. Value co-creation can be enhanced by sharing the invention and joint development of its applications.

The technology transfer process often concerns Medtech or biotech companies.

Medical technology (Medtech) concerns a wide range of health-care products and is used to treat diseases or medical conditions affecting humans. Such technologies (applications of medical science) are intended to improve the quality of healthcare delivered through earlier diagnosis, less invasive treatment options, and reductions in hospital stays and rehabilitation times (Advamed, 2009). Recent advances in medical technology have focused on cost reduction. Medical technology may broadly include medical devices, information technology, biotech, and healthcare services.

Biotechnology is the use of living systems and organisms to develop or make products.

Figure 5.2 shows the technology transfer cycle.

The European Patent Office (EPO) has elaborated a tool called IPscore to evaluate patents, technologies, and research projects.

From the EPO's last annual report (http://www.epo.org/about-us/annual-reports-statistics/annual-report/2017.html), we can draw the following trends in patenting.

5.14   The Impact of Digitalization on Patents

Patents are an evolution of know-how, and they so follow the patterns synthetically described in Sect. 4.7. Artificial Intelligence (AI) is now recognized as one of the main enablers of digital transformation in

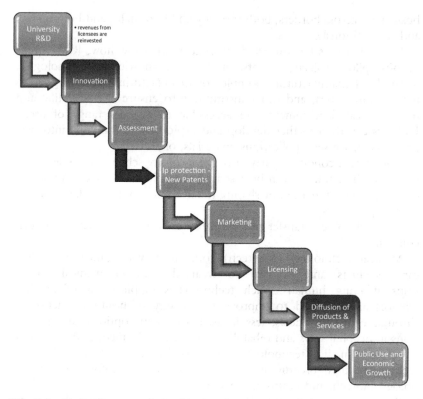

Fig. 5.2 Technology transfer cycle

multiple industries. AI can help companies become more innovative, flexible, and adaptive than ever before, with an impact on robotics, and process automation.

With its ability to improve simulation, forecasting, and smooth proof-of-concept trials and errors, artificial intelligence can boost the traditional patenting process and its industrial applications.

Digitalization smooths and catalyzes the patenting process:

1. It fosters know-how through its input factors, easier to collect, store and interpret;
2. Information, transformed into big data, is easier to collect and analyze;

3. Proof-of-concept gets easier with digital prototypes;
4. Digitalization eases knowledge transfer and sharing;
5. As-a-service instruments and platforms (Software as a Service; Platform as a Service, etc.) reduce fixed costs and improve outsourcing efficacy.

NOTES

1. International Glossary of Business valuation Terms.
2. OECD (2017) Transfer Pricing Guidelines, Chapter VI, C.4 Arm's length pricing when valuation is highly uncertain at the time of the transaction.
3. See Sect. 13.7.

SELECTED REFERENCES

Abbel, M. (2009). Mixed know-how and patent licensing agreement. In D. Campbell & R. Proksch (Eds.), *International business transactions* (pp. 5–20). The Netherlands: Kluwer Law International.

Aboody, D., & Lev, B. (2000). Information asymmetry, R&D, and insider gains. *Journal of Finance, 55*(2), 2747–2766.

Advamed (Advanced Medical Technology Association). (2009, January 7). *What is medical technology?* Code of ethics on interactions with health care professionals. https://www.advamed.org/sites/default/files/resource/112_112_code_of_ethics_0.pdf.

Allen, T. J., & O'Shea, R. P. (2014, September 18). *Building technology transfer within research universities: An entrepreneurial approach.* Cambridge: Cambridge University Press.

Al-Najjar, B., & Elgammal, M. M. (2013). Innovation and credit ratings, does it matter? UK evidence. *Applied Economics Letters, 20*(5), 428–431.

Amram, M. (2005). The challenge of valuing patents and early—Stage technologies. *Journal of Applied Corporate Finance, 17*(2), 68.

Andriessen, D. (2004). IC valuation and measurement: Classifying the state of the art. *Journal of Intellectual Capital, 5*(2), 230–242.

Azzone, G., & Manzini, R. (2008). Quick and dirty technology assessment: The case of an Italian research centre. *Technological Forecasting and Social Change, 75*, 1324–1338.

Ballester, M., Garcia-Ayuso, M., & Livnat, J. (2003). The economic value of the R&D intangible asset. *European Accounting Review, 12*(4), 605–633. Available at http://3ws-contabilidad.ua.es/trabajos/2024.pdf.

Banerjee, A., Bakshi, R., & Kumar Sanyal, M. (2017). Valuation of patent: A classification of methodologies. *Research Bullettin, 42*(4), 158–174.

Benty, L., & Sherman, B. (2014). *Intellectual property law.* Oxford: Oxford University Press.

Boujelben, S., & Fedhila, H. (2011). The effects of intangible investments on future OCF. *Journal of Intellectual Capital, 12*(4), 480–494.

Chen, M. C., Cheng, S. J., & Hwang, Y. (2005). An empirical investigation of the relationship between intellectual capital and firms' market value and financial performance. *Journal of Intellectual Capital, 6*(2), 159–176. Available at https://mpra.ub.uni-muenchen.de/92888/1/MPRA_paper_92888.pdf.

Cohen, J. A. (2005). *Intangible assets: Valuation and economic benefit.* New Jersey: Wiley.

Còrcoles, Y. R. (2010). Towards the convergence of accounting treatment for intangible assets. *Intangible Capital, 6*(2), 185–201.

Cotropia, C. A. (2009). Describing patents as real options. *Journal of Corporation Law, 34*, 1127.

Danchev, A. (2006). Social capital and sustainable behavior of the firm. *Industrial Management & Data Systems, 106*(7), 953–965.

Dawson, P. C. (2013). *Royalty rate determination.* Working paper available at http://www.econ.uconn.edu/working/A2013-03.pdf.

Degnan, A. A., & Horton, C. (1997). A survey of licensed royalties. *Les Nouvelles, XXXII*(2), 91–96.

Degryse, H., De Goeij, P., & Kappert, P. (2012). The impact of firm and industry characteristics on small firm's capital structure. *Small Business Economics, 38*(4), 431–447.

De Wit-De Vries, E., Dolfsma, W. A., Van Der Windt, H. J., & Gerkema, M. P. (2018, March). Knowledge transfer in university-industry research partnerships: A review. *The Journal of Technology Transfer, 44*(4), 1–20.

Duffy, J. F. (2005). *A minimum optimal patent term* (Paper 4). Berkeley Center for Law and Technology.

Falk, N., & Train, K. (2016). Patent valuation with forecasts of forward citations. *Journal of Business Valuation and Economic Loss Analysis, 12*(1), 101–121.

Gambardella, A. (2013, September). The economic value of patented inventions: Thoughts and some open questions. *International Journal of Industrial Organization, 31*(5), 625–633.

Giuliani, M. (2013). Not all sunshine and roses: Discovering intellectual liabilities "in action." *Journal of Intellectual Capital, 14*(1), 127–144.

Hall, R. (1993). A framework linking intangible resources and capabilities to sustainable competitive advantage. *Strategic Management Journal, 14*, 607–618.

Iazzolino, G., & Migliano, G. (2015). The valuation of a patent through the real options approach: A tutorial. *Journal of Business Valuation and Economic Loss Analysis, 10*(1), 99–116.

Ignat, V. (2016). *Modern evaluation of patents.* Paper presented at the 7th International conference on advanced concepts in mechanical engineering, IOP Conference Series: Materials Science and Engineering. 147 012069.

Jensen, M., & Meckling, W. (1976). Theory of the firm: Managerial behavior, agency costs and ownership structure. *Journal of Financial Economics, 3*(4), 305–306. Available at http://www.sfu.ca/~wainwrig/Econ400/jensenmec kling.pdf.

Jun, S., Park, S., & Jang, D. (2015). A technology valuation model using quantitative patent analysis: A case study of technology transfer in big data marketing. *Emerging Markets Finance and Trade, 51*(5), 963–974.

Kristandl, G., & Bontis, N. (2007). The impact of voluntary disclosure on cost of equity capital estimates in a temporal setting. *Journal of Intellectual Capital, 8*(4), 577–594.

Lagrost, C., Martin, D., Dubois, C., & Quazzotti, S. (2010). Intellectual property valuation: How to approach the selection of an appropriate valuation method. *Journal of Intellectual Capital, 11*(4), 481–503.

Leland, H., & Pyle, D. (1977). Informational asymmetries, financial structure, and financial intermediation. *Journal of Finance, 32*(2), 371–387.

Liu, W., Yang, Z., Cao, Y., & Huo, J. (2022). Discovering the influences of the patent innovations on the stock market. *Information Processing & Management, 59*(3).

Metha, A., & Madhani, P. M. (2008). Intangible assets—An introduction. *The Accounting World, 8*(9), 11–19.

Modigliani, F., & Miller, M. (1958). The cost of capital, corporation finance and the theory of investment. *American Economic Review, 48*(3), 261–297.

Moro Visconti, R. (2012). Exclusive patents and trademarks and subsequent uneasy transaction comparability: Some transfer implications. *Intertax, 40*(3), 212–219.

Moro Visconti, R. (2013). Evaluating know-how for transfer price benchmarking. *Journal of Finance and Accounting, 1*(1), 27–38.

Moro Visconti, R., Montesi, G., & Papiro, G. (2018). Big data-driven stochastic business planning and corporate valuation. *Corporate Ownership & Control, 15*(3), 189–204.

Mouritsen, J., Bukh, P. N., & Marr, B. (2004). Reporting on intellectual capital: Why, what and how? *Measuring Business Excellence, 8*(1), 46–54.

Myers, S. C., & Majluf, N. S. (1984). Corporate financing and investment decisions when firms have information that investors do not have. *Journal of Financial Economics, 13*(2), 187–221. Available at http://www.nber.org/pap ers/w1396.pdf?new_window=1.

OECD. (2017, July). *Transfer pricing guidelines for multinational enterprises and tax administrations.* https://www.oecd.org/tax/oecd-transfer-pricinggu idelines-for-multinational-enterprises-and-tax-administrations-20769717.htm.

Oestreicher, A. (2011). Valuation issues in transfer pricing of intangibles: Comments on the scoping of an OECD project. *Intertax, 39*(3), 126–131.

Parchomovsky, G., & Wagner, R. P. (2004). *Patent portfolios* (Paper 51). University of Pennsylvania law school, scholarship at Penn Law.

Porter, M. E. (1998). *Competitive advantage: Creating and sustaining superior performance.* New York: The Free Press.

Pratt, S. P. (2003). *Business valuation body of knowledge: Exam review and professional reference.* Wiley.

Salinas, G., & Ambler, T. (2009). A taxonomy of brand valuation practice: Methodologies and purposes. *Journal of Brand Management, 17*(1), 39–61.

Silberztein, C. (2011). Transfer pricing aspects of intangibles: The OECD project. *Transfer Pricing International Journal, 8*, 4.

Smith, C. W., & Warner, J. (1979). On financial contracting: An analysis of bond covenants. *Journal of Financial Economics, 7*(2), 117–161.

Tan, H. P., Plowman, D., & Hancock, P. (2007). Intellectual capital and financial returns of companies. *Journal of Intellectual Capital, 8*(1), 76–95.

Thoma, G. (2015, January). The value of patent and trademark pairs. In *Academy of management proceedings* (Vol. 2015, No. 1, p. 12373). Briarcliff Manor, NY 10510: Academy of Management.

Tobin, J. (1969). A general equilibrium approach to monetary theory. *Journal of Money Credit and Banking, 1*(1), 15–29.

Trigeorgis, T., & Reuer, J. J. (2017). Real options theory in strategic management. *Strategic Management Journal, 38*, 42–63.

United Nations Industrial Development Organization. (1996). *Manual on technology transfer negotiation.* Vienna, Austria: United Nations Industrial Development Organization. Available at http://www.wipo.int/cgi-bin/koha/opa cdetail.pl?bib=12398.

Valladares Soler, L. E., & Cuello De Oro, C. D. J. (2007). Evaluating the scope of IC in firms' value. *Journal of Intellectual Capital, 8*(3), 470–493.

Vanacker, T. R., & Manigart, S. (2010). Pecking order and debt capacity considerations for high-growth companies seeking financing. *Small Business Economics, 35*(1), 53–69.

Wipo. (2008). *Wipo intellectual property handbook: Policy, law and use.* Fields of intellectual property protection WIPO, chap 2.

Wu, X., & Yeung, C. K. A. (2012). Firm growth and capital structure persistence. *Journal of Banking & Finance, 36*(12), 3427–3443.

CHAPTER 6

The Valuation of Digital Startups and Fintechs

6.1 RISK CAPITAL FOR GROWTH: THE ROLE OF VENTURE CAPITAL, PRIVATE EQUITY, AND BUSINESS ANGELS

The terms "venture capital" and "private equity" are generally used to describe the provision of equity capital flowing from specialized intermediaries to unlisted companies with high growth and development potential. The basic assumption of this activity remains the acquisition of shareholdings in startup companies in a long-term perspective, to obtain a capital gain on the sale of the shareholding. Technological startups frequently go digital; in other cases, they could adopt significant digital tools.

In general, private equity refers to all operations carried out during the companies' life cycle stages after the initial one, while venture capital refers to those investments carried out in companies' early stages of life. In this sense, a typical example is represented by technological startups.

The capital invested can be allocated to various projects, such as the development of new products, the expansion of working capital, and the strengthening of the financial structure of a startup. Private equity can be used to solve problems related to the ownership structure of a startup (diluting the founding shareholders) or its restructuring. It is the

R. Moro-Visconti, *The Valuation of Digital Intangibles*, https://doi.org/10.1007/978-3-031-09237-4_6

most appropriate tool for management buyouts (MBOs) and management buy-ins. Venture capital investment offers several advantages for target companies.

First, specialized intermediaries offer companies the opportunity to exploit their expertise in the field of financial support to companies aimed at creating value over time. This means that the startup will be able to use the capital made available for a relatively long period, enough to carry out its projects (strategies, company acquisitions, new product development, company reorganizations, etc.).

The support of the institutional investor is not limited to the mere provision of risk capital but often provides the startup with its managerial knowledge to achieve the project. The institutional investor can take advantage of a vast experience based on diversified entrepreneurial realities, on sectoral knowledge matured for similar investments, and usually has specific expertise to which the startup can have recourse.

As far as intermediaries are concerned, there are now two major types of risk capital investors:

- Venture capital and private equity companies;
- Personal venture capitalists, more commonly known as "business angels", often being part of a club deal of "family and friends".

The former are generally borne by banks, insurance companies, pension funds, or large companies (corporate venture capital) and are specialized by the investment sector. Business angels, on the other hand, are informal investors with significant personal assets, who acquire shares of small–medium firms with high growth potential. Business angels favor a personal relationship with the entrepreneur they finance and deal mainly with startups or early development.

Private equity is a financing instrument through which an investor provides new capital to a target startup, generally not listed on the stock exchange, which has promising growth potential, thanks to the support of management with the sharing of strategies and the contribution of additional financial resources.

The investor intends to disinvest in the medium term, realizing a capital gain from the sale of the shareholding. Private equity funds are investment vehicles that operate as venture capital (high-risk innovative startups) or through leveraged buyouts (LBOs), mainly with debt acquisitions. Crowdfunding platforms are increasingly popular in the seed phase.

The growing attention to private equity derives from a combination of factors, including the returns of funds, often higher than those of the stock market (public equities), and the weak correlation with the market, with a significant diversification of risk if the investment in private equity funds is included in an equity and bond portfolio represented by listed securities.

In countries where private equity has had less of an impact so far, such as continental Europe and Japan, investors access private equity preferably through funds of funds, with an intermediate investment that diversifies the funds but leads to an increase in fees.

Governance issues have a cascade effect on the fund's portfolio companies, which are investment objectives compliant with the characteristics suitable for these types of investors. These concerns include the dilution of the shareholding structure (reference shareholders who enjoy private benefits of control), the presence of independent directors, and the voluntary production of quality information and standards for the protection of corporate democracy and minorities.

The members of the fund (limited partners) allocate capital to the fund, and the resources are called up by the fund managers (the general partners of the management company) and invested when equity is called. When an investment is liquidated, the general partners share the proceeds among the members. Institutional investors (pension funds, investment funds, hedge funds, funds of funds, ...) prefer private equity funds with advanced corporate governance, capable of mitigating conflicts of interest between stakeholders, protecting minority shareholders like them, and reducing agency costs, which are traditionally high in private equity funds.

Within this institutional framework, some market considerations emerge about the investment prospects.

The Gartner Hype-Cycle model represents the five phases of the life cycle of a technological application:

1. The trigger for innovative activity;
2. Peak of inflationary expectations;
3. Disillusionment;
4. (Ascending) curve of the Enlightenment;
5. Plateau of productivity.

6.2   Types of Investments, Intermediaries, and Bankability

Financial intermediaries and institutional investors involved in startups are often different from those who traditionally assist conventional firms. This is the result of a series of factors including, first, the young age of these companies, which have no (payback) history and therefore no previous performance score, which is an important element of creditworthiness.

Another distinctive feature of startups is the nature and composition of their assets, often represented by high-tech investments that take years to produce revenues and are characterized by a high level of risk, with modest collateral value. It is not surprising that traditional banking intermediaries are far from a world they are not familiar with and that is not fully compliant with their characteristics.

The startup's ability to repay debts emerges only in the mid-term, once the initial phase is over, and the startup passes unscathed the so-called "valley of death" (a phase in which the startup runs out of its initial capital, entering into a context of cash and equity burn out, without having yet activated a sustainable revenue model). Many young companies do not survive the test of commercial viability.

Investments in startups, which are intrinsically risky, do not allow the lender who underwrites standard debt to take up an upside profit-sharing option that is typical of either shareholder (direct underwriters of risk capital) or quasi-equity underwriters (as convertible bonds or cum warrants).

The impact on bankability is typically significant, to the extent that only specialized intermediaries such as venture capital or private equity funds tend to assist startups that only after having reached consolidation can access the traditional credit. There are different types of investments that institutional investors can make, depending on the different phases of the startup's life cycle. Each stage of a startup's life corresponds to different needs, which must be considered by the institutional investor. The interventions of specialized intermediaries can be grouped and classified into three main categories: startup financing, financing for expansion and development, and financing for change.

Venture capital deals with the first category, while private equity deals with the other two. The types of investment depend on the performance of the target startup, which often records negative results in the early

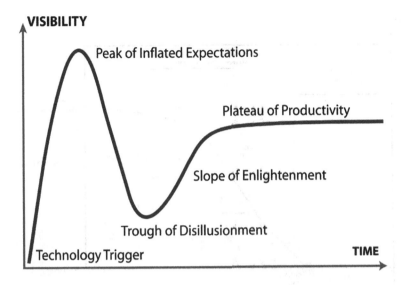

Fig. 6.1 The Gartner Hype-Cycle model

years, and then recovers and grows in the medium term (if it successfully survives Darwinian selection). Investment record is reflected in the performance of venture capital or private equity[1] funds, which may follow a yield curve (in terms of Internal Rate of Return that start negative and may reach break-even after some years) known as the J curve (Fig. 6.2).

6.2.1   Startup Loans and Venture Capital Activities

Within this category of interventions, it is possible to distinguish different types of actions that a venture capitalist may decide to take.

The request for intervention is generally made through the presentation of a business plan to several institutional investors, by an entrepreneur intending to start a new business, develop a new product, a new service, or a new technology (Moro Visconti, 2019). What the entrepreneur needs most is not only the amount of capital made available by the institutional investor but, above all, the contribution he can make in terms of entrepreneurial ability and competence in defining a successful strategy.

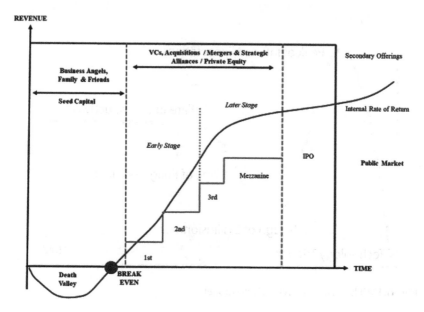

Fig. 6.2 Startup financing cycle

It is possible to analyze the various types of intervention that the venture capitalist can implement, depending on the development of the new business reality:

1. *Seed financing* or financing the idea of *business* if the investor intervenes in the early stages of conception and testing of new products, which exist only at the level of the concept. The skills that the investor must have are not only managerial but also technical and scientific, i.e., aimed at the practical transformation of the idea into a working business. The risk associated with this type of investment is high. However, with a high risk of failure, the expected return is a multiple of the initial investment.
2. *Research and development financing*: funds are granted to finance the development of a new product both in a new startup and in a startup that is already established.
3. *Startup financing* is granted to complete the development of the product and the initial *marketing*, to pass market testing (albeit

at the level of the prototype). The companies financed are in the organizational phase, since the conditions for the development of a startup already exist, even though they have not yet put their products on the market. The problems are still technical, and the characteristics of the intermediaries are essentially the same as in the previous cases.

4. *First-stage financing* is finally granted to companies that have used their initial capital to test the prototype on the market and need funds to start large-scale production and then sale.

6.2.2   Financing for Expansion and Development: The Role of Private Equity and Bridge Financing

Expansion financing or development capital interventions historically represent the most important activity of private equity. These are all the interventions that the institutional investor makes when the target startup is faced with problems concerning its development. The tools that a startup can use for this purpose are mainly:

- Increasing or diversifying production capacity;
- The acquisition of other companies or business units;
- The integration with other business realities.

It is possible to identify a series of different interventions, related to the stage of development of the startup:

1. *Second-stage financing* is represented by the working capital for the initial expansion of a startup that produces and sells its products, which has increasing receivables and goods ready in stock;
2. *Third-stage financing* occurs when the private equity grants funds for the expansion of startups that have already reached the break-even point and whose turnover is growing. These funds are used to finance the purchase of additional machinery and plant, market research, or the development of an existing product to improve it;
3. *Bridge financing*, or transition financing, is granted to a startup that intends to be listed on the stock exchange. This investment can be defined as the intervention in risk capital representing a bridge financing between the startup with closed capital and the future

listed startup. Bridge financing is often structured to be repaid by the proceeds of the IPO but it can be a restructuring of the positions of the major shareholders through secondary transactions if there are investors who want to reduce or liquidate their shareholdings.

In all the cases analyzed above, the intervention of the intermediary is more complex than that of the startup phase. The institutional investor will have to negotiate with a higher number of shareholders, who may have divergent interests. Furthermore, the startup to be financed already has its track record, which leads the investor to a detailed preliminary analysis.

6.2.3   Financing of Change and Modification of Ownership Structures: Replacement Capital, Buyout, Venture Purchase, and Turnaround Financing

Change processes may be financed with replacement capital or other forms of intervention. The reasons are different, even if they generally lead to a substantial change in the ownership structure. Companies that undergo this type of financing often find themselves in a stalemate, with a consequent need for rethinking their structure.

The first cause is related to the situation where there is a change in the equity composition of the target startup, and in which, one or more shareholders want to leave the business.

If only minority shareholders want to exit, there is a replacement capital situation, normally with no problems related to the change in the strategy of the startup.

The situation is different if the majority of shareholders want to leave the startup. There can be different situations leading to this solution, even if the intervention of the institutional investor is always aimed at financially supporting the new entrepreneurial group in the purchase of the target startup, thus favoring the change of the ownership structure.

The transaction is part of the more general category of buyouts.

We can talk about management buyout if it is a management group within the startup to take control of the startup or management buy-in if it is an external group to take over. If the institutional investor favors the involvement of employees of the startup itself, this is referred to as a workers' buyout.

There may be a venture purchase of quoted shares and occurs to guarantee the possibility of delisting. In this situation, the investor buys, through a takeover bid, directly on the market the securities available to allow delisting and uses her managerial knowledge to restructure the startup.

Finally, there may be a need for restructuring in the event of a corporate crisis, which often requires a change in the composition of the corporate structure. The operation that the institutional investor operates in these cases is called turnaround financing and is often the only way to save loss-making companies in need of a relaunch.

6.2.4   Scaleup Valuation

The scaleup phase naturally follows the startup period and its Darwinian selection.

The scaleup valuation patterns are somewhat in between a startup and a traditional (mature) firm, as shown in Fig. 6.3.

The transition from a debt-free to a levered startup typically occurs beyond the early stage period and rotates around the composition of the

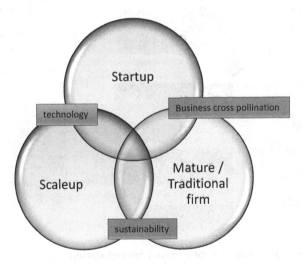

Fig. 6.3   Startups, scaleups, and mature firms

raised capital. What mostly matters for such a composition is the debt-to-equity ratio (financial leverage), as a function of the asset subdivision, as shown in Fig. 6.4.

The introduction of (financial) debt changes the valuation parameters. Startups are normally debt-free since they have little if any collateral value of their assets and they produce negative cash flows, especially in the first years of their existence. Consequently:

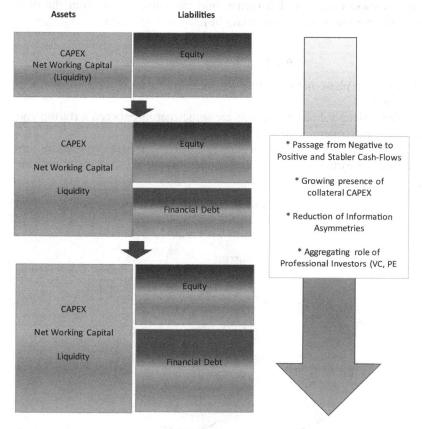

Fig. 6.4 Evolution from a debt-free to a levered startup

- in the balance sheet raised capital (funds) tend to coincide with equity;
- in the income statement, EBIT is similar to the net result (considering that interest rates are non-existent, and taxes also, due to a negative tax base);
- in the cash flow statement, the operating cash flow tends to coincide with the net cash flow;
- In the absence of the cost of debt, the cost of capital (WACC) coincides with the cost of equity.

When a (levered) scaleup is under evaluation, equity and enterprise values diverge, and so do EBIT versus net result, or operating versus net cash flows. This impacts the valuation metrics and results.

6.3   The Investment Process

After analyzing the general characteristics of private equity and venture capital activities and the different methods of intervention by institutional investors, it is worth focusing on the phases through which the investment process is structured.

The first phase consists of identifying the target startup.

At the end of this activity, when the most interesting investment opportunities have been identified, the intermediaries will have to evaluate in-depth the profile of the target startup.

At this point, we come to one of the most delicate stages of the entire process, which consists of the most thorough evaluation of the startup and the structure of the operation. In addition to the general characteristics of the entrepreneur, other factors are being considered, including the market position of the startup and its potential location, the potential growth in value of the startup, its technological capabilities, and the possibilities of divestment of the shareholding.

If this analysis leads the investor to make a favorable decision, the investor will be concerned with structuring the operation, in terms of time and method of execution.

This will be followed by a phase of negotiation aimed at defining the price, in which the decisions regarding the timing of disbursement of the loan and the methods of payment will be crucial, ranging from a capital increase to the purchase of shares from the old partners.

Once the participation has been acquired, the investor will have to monitor the operation, constantly following the trend of the investee startup, to be able to detect and resolve any problems in time. In this phase the investor can directly contribute to the management of the target startup, appointing her managers.

The last stage is the most critical and consists of the divestment, whose outcome determines the profit or loss for the institutional investor (Fig. 6.5).

Investing funds typically have predetermined exit schedules, following the fund's contractual agreements.

The divestment operation is generally planned, in its manner and timing, at the time of the initial investment, although often the initial project undergoes inevitable changes, always concerning the objective of the investor who is to maximize their ROIC compared to the WACC (creating value if ROIC > WACC) (Fig. 6.6).

a. *The value chain in risk capital intermediation in the presence of information asymmetries and debt constraints*

Technological startups or those with a core business in other innovative sectors and with interesting growth prospects are unlikely to obtain the financial resources necessary for the implementation of the business plan, up to the achievement of the financial break-even. This happens because

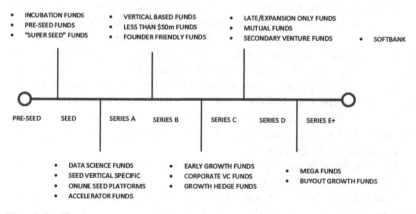

Fig. 6.5 The investment process

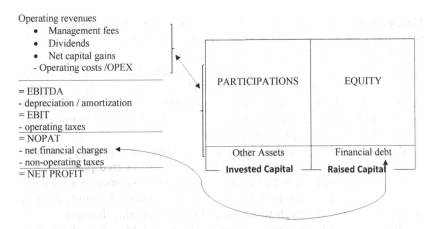

Fig. 6.6 Economic and financial performance of a venture capital

they can offer limited guarantees, with no significant assets collateralized and being the payback of loans distant and uncertain.

Hence the need to look for alternative financial resources, which share the business risks in a noncontingent time perspective and are aligned with the development cycle of the business model. The value chain in risk capital intermediation is based on the tendency to overcome traditional information asymmetries between historical and potential shareholders (venture capital or private equity funds; …).

Conflicts of interest between existing and future shareholders following a capital increase have been addressed in the Myers and Majluf model (1984), according to which:

1. The managers of each startup have a more in-depth knowledge of current earnings and investment opportunities than external investors;
2. Managers act in the interest of existing shareholders.

The existence of information asymmetries and the tendency to favor existing shareholders means that managers who develop profitable investment initiatives are unable to channel good news to new shareholders, who are suspicious and fear underwriting new capital at a high price, with a consequent unfair transfer of wealth from new to old shareholders.

Managers, on the other hand, have an incentive to communicate the good news, otherwise, it would be difficult to raise stock prices (which are linked to stock options and other incentives).

Only time could say if the news communicated by the management is true or false. If in doubt, the potential new shareholders will accept to underwrite the new shares only at a discounted price compared to a hypothetical equilibrium value in the absence of informative asymmetries, unless full disclosure is given by managers.

Managers understand these problems and, in some cases, prefer not to undertake new investments—even if they are considered profitable—if such investments can only be financed through the issuance of additional equity. If the capital increase takes place at an excessive discount, there is an unfair transfer of wealth from the old to the new shareholders.

The paradoxical consequence of the Myers and Majluf model is that if investment projects cannot be financed through self-financing and/or debt issuance, then there is a disincentive for the management and historical shareholders to undertake profitable new investment projects. There is under-investment that does not allow for creating value (Myers & Majluf, 1984).

Venture capitalists are intermediaries who perform this function, especially in capital rationing contexts where bank credit or alternative means of financing is limited or excessively expensive.

Capital rationing phenomena occur with greater frequency and intensity in a negative market situation, in which interest rates are low (to encourage economic recovery, taking advantage of the low bargaining power of workers, as not to feed inflationary spirals with the price-wage race). In the presence of the credit crunch phenomena, the low-interest rate differentials between lending and borrowing, associated with an increase in the riskiness of loans (induced by the low-growth economic cycle), represent a disincentive for banks to grant loans. Loans become unprofitable and characterized by potential non-performing loans that may affect their capital adequacy.

b. *Prospective evaluation of the target startup (venture-backed) and peculiarities of the cash flows of the startups*

According to ISAE 3400,[2] prospective financial information is based on assumptions about events that may occur in the future and possible actions by an entity. Following this reasoning, the prospective evaluation of the target startup turns out to be a fundamental step in the screening of the venture capitalist's investment possibilities, aimed at a strong increase in the expected value of the investee startup.

Expected capital gains must be:

- Discounted at a rate that considers an adequate risk premium and incorporates the lack of marketability discount, typical of unlisted companies;
- Suitable to include a possible terminal value of the investment, to be discounted to re-express it in current currency.

The longer the initiative is in an early stage phase, the longer the cycle of the business model is extended.

The expected remuneration of the target startup must be sufficiently high to ensure an adequate return for the venture capitalist, considering the possibility of failure of the investment, which in many cases involves a full write-off of the holding.

Most companies in the first years of life generate negative financial flows, due to significant startup costs and consequent cash disbursement that anticipates revenues.

There are some characteristics of intangible-intensive startups:

- Monetary operating revenues tend to be modest or even non-existent for an extended period (especially if investments are high and reach a threshold of profitability only in the medium or long term);
- Monetary operating costs tend to be high, despite the use of outsourcing (which is limited to making them more flexible), and because of leasing fees;
- The low level of indebtedness means that EBITDA is substantially in line with the operating loss, typical of the startup phases and destined to last for several years;
- The greater propensity of stakeholders (directors, managers, employees, etc.) to be paid through stock options decreases monetary operating costs and increases—with a time dilution—risk capital;

- The presence of high fixed costs (which tend to increase as entry barriers go up) is accompanied by variable costs that are usually limited (once the break-even is reached) there is liquidity generation;
- Taxes (operating and non-operating) tend to be low or zero, in the presence of negative taxable income (which generates a possibility of carrying forward losses to subsequent years);
- The cash flow is negative, even significantly;
- Trade receivables follow the trend of operating revenues and are modest or non-existent;
- The warehouse is virtual and therefore does not absorb financial resources;
- Suppliers follow the trend of operating costs;
- Operating Net Working Capital tends to be negative and represents a source of funding;
- The change in fixed assets tends to be positive and significant for new investments (expressed in terms of CAPEX);
- The operating cash flow is usually negative and is financed by working capital and risky capital;
- Financial debts are negligible since the risk profile is high; their size is associated with (limited) cash outflows for financial charges;
- The residual cash flows attributable to the shareholders are normally negative, and shareholders often need to recapitalize the startup until the financial break-even is reached.

Performance in private equity investing[3] is traditionally measured via (i) the internal rate of return (IRR) which captures a fund's time-adjusted return and (ii) multiples of invested capital which captures return on invested capital (ROIC).

IRR reflects the performance of a private equity fund by considering the size and timing of its cash flows (capital calls and distributions) and its net asset value at the time of the calculation. Internal Rate of Return for the shareholders (IRR_{equity}) expresses the rate that makes the Net Present Value equal to zero:

$$IRR_{equity} = NPV_{equity} = \sum_{t=1}^{n} \frac{N_{CF}}{(1+r)^n} - C_0 = 0 \qquad (6.1)$$

where:

N_{CF} = Net cash inflow during the period t;

C_0 = initial investment costs;

r = discount rate;

t = number of periods.

The IRR considers the equity dimension, since the startup is borne debt-free. The Multiple on Invested Capital (MOIC) allows for measuring the value generated by an investment. MOIC is a gross return traditionally calculated before fees and carry:

$$MOIC = \frac{Realized\ Value + Unrealized\ Value}{Total\ Amount\ Invested} \qquad (6.2)$$

MOIC expresses a multiple of the initial investment; a ratio of 1.8 means that an initial investment of 100 has generated a final payoff of 180.

Table 6.1 shows the cash flow generated by *startups*, with the most significant items shown in bold.

Table 6.1
Determination of operating and net cash flows in startups

Net monetary operating revenues
net monetary operating costs
(excluding depreciation and amortization)
operating taxes
= *Cash flow of the operating area*
+/− Δ trade receivables
+/− Δ stock
+/− Δ suppliers and other current payables
= change in operating net working capital
+/−Δ of assets
net of amortization and depreciation
= *Net operating cash flow*
(unlevered or debt-free cash flow)
− financial charges net of financial income
+/− Δ net financial liabilities
+/− Δ shareholders' equity
Cash flow available to shareholders
(levered cash flow)

6.4   THE IPEV VALUATION GUIDELINES

The International Private Equity and Venture Capital Valuation (IPEV) Guidelines[4] set out recommendations, intended to represent current best practices, on the valuation of Private Capital Investments.

The Valuation Guidelines are applicable across the whole range of Alternative Funds (seed and startup venture capital, buyouts, growth/development capital, infrastructure, credit, etc., collectively referred to as Private Capital Funds) and financial instruments commonly held by such Funds. They provide a basis for valuing Investments by other entities, including Fund-of-Funds, in these Private Capital Funds.

Furthermore, the Valuation Guidelines have been prepared with the goal that Fair Value measurements derived when using these guidelines are compliant with both International Financial Reporting Standards (IFRS) and the United States Generally Accepted Accounting Principles (US GAAP).

According to the EVCA Guidelines,[5] Fair Value is the price that would be received to sell an asset in an Orderly Transaction between Market Participants at the Measurement Date. It is the amount for which an asset could be exchanged between knowledgeable, willing parties in an arm's length transaction. A Fair Value measurement assumes that a hypothetical transaction to sell an asset takes place in Principal Market or its absence, the Most Advantageous Market for the asset. For actively traded (quoted) Investments, available market prices will be the exclusive basis for the measurement of Fair Value for identical instruments.

For Unquoted Investments, the measurement of Fair Value requires the Valuer to assume the Investment is realized or sold at the Measurement Date whether the instrument or the Investee Startup is prepared for sale or whether its shareholders intend to sell soon. Some Funds invest in multiple securities or tranches of the same Investee Startup. If a Market Participant would be expected to transact all positions in the same underlying Investee Startup simultaneously, for example, separate Investments made in series A, series B, and series C, then Fair Value would be estimated for the aggregate Investment in the Investee Startup. If a Market Participant would be expected to transact separately, for example, purchasing series A independent from series B and series C, or if Debt Investments are purchased independent of equity, then Fair Value would be more appropriately determined for each financial instrument.

Fair Value must be estimated using consistent Valuation Techniques from Measurement Date to Measurement Date unless there is a change in market conditions or Investment-specific factors, which would modify how a Market Participant would determine value. The use of consistent Valuation Techniques for Investments with similar characteristics, industries, and/or geographies would be expected.

In selecting the appropriate Valuation Technique, the Valuer should use one or more of the following Valuation Techniques as of each Measurement Date, considering Market Participant assumptions as to how Value would be determined:

A. Market Approach

- Multiples
- Industry Valuation Benchmarks
- Available Market Prices

B. Income Approach

- Discounted Cash Flows
- Replacement Cost Approach
- Net Assets

The Price of a Recent Investment, if resulting from an orderly transaction, generally represents the Fair Value as of the transaction date. At subsequent Measurement Dates, the Price of a Recent Investment may be an appropriate starting point for estimating the Fair Value. However, adequate consideration must be given to the current facts and circumstances, including, but not limited to, changes in the market or changes in the performance of the Investee Startup.

Inputs to Valuation Techniques should be calibrated to the Price of a Recent Investment, to the extent appropriate. These approaches are fully consistent with those examined in Chapter 2.

6.4.1 An Estimate of the Fair Value in Investee Companies

The valuation of target companies presupposes a startup valuation. The evaluation methodology should be referred to as the type of startup being evaluated. In most cases in which the evaluation refers to industrial, commercial, or service companies, the evaluation methodologies—even if different, depending on the type of startup—will be those typically adopted for such companies.

The general considerations made on balance sheet-based, income, mixed (capital-income), market (empirical) approaches[6] are fully applicable to non-financial companies, with adaptations that presuppose a preliminary analysis of:

- The different *business models* applicable from time to time, with repercussions on value drivers, the value chain, strategic, and market aspects (...);
- The financial statements (balance sheet, income statement, and cash flow statement);
- The presence of accounting parameters relevant to the valuation, such as EBIT, EBITDA, the Net Financial Position, etc.

In the evaluation of the target startup, especially when estimating the enterprise value, it is necessary to adequately consider the changes in the financial structure induced by the entry of private equity funds. Leveraged buyouts are frequent, through which the fund finances part of its investment making the target startup indebted. Debt sustainability, subject to the startup's ability to generate adequate cash flows and the level of market interest rates, has a decisive impact in determining the overall risk level of the startup, which in turn influences its value.

In private equity buyouts, debt is typically reshaped by type and maturity to make it compatible with the new business plans formulated with the contribution of the fund and is usually characterized by a strategic orientation more oriented towards the creation of value assisted by an extension of debt maturities.

Among the various approaches to estimating the fair value, the following matter:

- Price of recent investments, including those made by others (a reasonable estimate of fair value, the validity of which erodes rapidly over time);
- Income multiples (appropriate, sustainable, and equitable, usually applicable to consolidated businesses): P/E; EV/EBIT; EV/ EBITDA ...;

- Adjusted balance sheet-based approach, suitable for holding companies, or real estate companies (...) whose value is linked more to Net Assets than to profits or expected cash flows;
- Discounted cash flows, including terminal value;
- Sector benchmarks, whenever applicable (e.g., rate of occupancy of hotel rooms; the price per hospital bed; the price per subscriber to cable TV ...);
- Market prices, if the subsidiary is eventually listed.

If the fair value is challenging to estimate, the best estimate is often represented by the fair value referred to in the previous report, adjusted, if necessary, by applying the impairment test.

6.4.2   An Estimate of the Fair Value of Investments in Portfolio Companies

The valuation of the investment portfolio is the most critical aspect and the fundamental prerequisite for a valuation of the private equity fund. This valuation must refer first to the existing holdings in the portfolio and must not prudently consider possible future investments and the ability to expand the portfolio, which relates to purely potential goodwill.

In the estimate, the entire investee startup and its underlying business must first be evaluated, and then the fund's investment in that startup must be evaluated accordingly.

The estimate of the periodic performance of private equity funds is essential to establish portfolio benchmarks, the fair remuneration of asset managers, and to analyze the degree of efficiency and sophistication of investors concerning unlisted companies.

Once the individual investee companies have been evaluated, the investments in these companies are estimated using a procedure that can be summarized as follows:

a) The starting point is the gross equity value of the investee startup, adjusted to consider the surplus assets and estimated by applying the approaches described above;
b) The pro-rata share of this Equity Value, based on the fund's percentage shareholding in the startup; the percentage is adjusted

to consider the minority discount or majority premium[7]; the net Equity Value is estimated.

If the target is to value a loan (bridge financing or mezzanine loan) instead of a shareholding, the market value of this financial loan must be estimated.

According to the valuation guidelines, in private equity, the value is usually crystallized by the sale or listing of the entire investment portfolio, rather than by the sale of individual holdings. The market value of the fund is determined by estimating the adjusted Enterprise Value of each startup, using the most appropriate valuation approaches, and then arriving at an estimate of the fair value of all the investments.

6.5   Startup Evaluation with Binomial Trees

The valuation of *startup* portfolios can be carried out with binomial trees (grids), frequently used in decision-making processes under uncertainty and in Monte Carlo simulations. Suppose, for example, that a venture capital decides to invest in three *startups* at the same time, underwriting capital for 100 in each startup and with an exit after 2 years. The three *startups* have a different risk profiles:

- The S1 *startup* has an expected variance in value, on an annual basis, of 20% (defensive investment);
- The S2 *startup* has an expected variance in value, on an annual basis, of 40% (risky investment);
- The S3 *startup* has an expected variance in value, on an annual basis, of 60% (highly speculative investment).

The payoff (expected results) is as follows (Fig. 6.7)[8].

The total *payoff* is the following (Table 6.2).

The total Net Present Value of the three projects, which are considered not mutually exclusive (since venture capital can take over all of them), nor with synergistic effects between them (which is possible, especially if the sectors and business models intersect), is positive if the rate at which they are discounted is less than 13.93%. This rate represents the watershed, which expresses the break-even point at which the Net

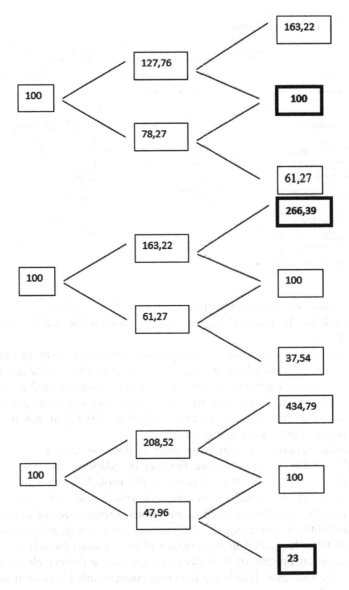

Fig. 6.7 Representation of the payoff

Table 6.2 Payoff calculation

	investment year 0	year 1	exit year 2	capital gain (loss)	Value i = 5%	actual i=10%	i=20%	net i=30%	IRR
Start up S1	-100	0	100	0	-9,30	-17,36	-30,56	-40,83	0,0%
Start up S2	-100	0	266,39	166,39	141,62	120,16	84,99	57,63	63,2%
Start up S3	-100	0	23	-77	-79,14	-80,99	-84,03	-86,39	(*)
Total investment portfolio	-300	0	389,39	89,39	53,19	21,81	-29,59	-69,59	
interest 5% Total Net Present Value					53,19				
interest 10% Total Net Present Value						21,81			
Internal Rate of Return (NVP = 0)									13,93%
interest 20% Total Net Present Value							-29,59		
interest 30% Total Net Present Value								-69,59	

(*) individually not calculable because it is negative

Present Value of the project portfolio is zero, calculated through the iterative search for the Internal Rate of Return (which is the rate that makes the NPV = 0).

Venture capital must make a comparison between its cost of raising financial resources (weighted average cost of capital, which coincides with the cost of equity capital if the venture capital has not resorted to debt) and the return that the investments offer. In all cases where the expected return is lower than the cost of capital (IRR < WACC), it will not be convenient to undertake the investment.

Binomial networks (traditionally used as decision trees or to determine the pricing of options) are flexible: by adapting the parameters of the expected variance of the value and the probability that the value increases (upside potential) or decreases (downside risk), it is possible to estimate, with basically unlimited ramifications, a wide range of scenarios. The possibility of correcting the estimates along the way, refining them based on what happened in the portion of time passed (which declines a chronological process of time decay), represents a further element to improve the forecasts. Timely big data may conveniently be introduced in the model.[9]

6.6 THE VENTURE CAPITAL METHOD

To identify the current value of a startup, before an investment is made (pre-money valuation), the Valuation Capital Method can be applied. This valuation approach was first described by Bill Sahlman in the late 1980s.

The basic keywords used in this valuation approach are:

- Harvest year: the time (year) that the investor plans to exit the startup;
- Pre-money Valuation: the value of the startup before any investment has been made;
- Post-money Valuation: the value of the startup after the investment has been made;

The formula for post-money valuation is[10]:

Post-Money Valuation = Pre-Money Valuation + Investment Amount

(6.3)

The Venture Capital Method is organized into a 2-step process:

1. The terminal value of the business in the harvest year is derived
2. The (desired) ROIC and the investment amount are used to derive the pre-money valuation. The return on investment can be estimated by determining what return an investor could expect from that investment with the specific level of risk attached.

In calculating the terminal value, the following inputs are required:

- Projected revenue in the harvest year;
- Projected (or industry average) profit margin in the harvest year;
- Industry P/E ratio.

The formula is as follows:

Terminal Value = projected revenue * projected margin * P/E

Terminal Value = earnings * P/E

(6.4)

In the same way, when calculating the pre-money valuation, the *inputs* needed are:

- Required Return on Investment Capital (ROIC)
- Investment amount
- The formula is as follows:

Pre-Money Valuation = Terminal value /ROIC − Investment amount

(6.5)

The advantages of the Venture Capital Valuation Method are linked to its simplicity in understanding and implementation.

However, besides the industry average P/E ratio, many of the required *inputs* are based on not-so-reliable assumptions. It follows that, if one feeds the model with wrong assumptions, a wrong value will be derived.

6.7   BREAK-UP VALUE OF VENTURE-BACKED COMPANIES

Most venture-backed investments are directed towards companies that are unable to take off and that will not only never reach the stock exchange listing, which is the primary exit approach for the intermediary but are typically tricky to demobilize. When they are, the disposal of the investment typically takes place at a significant discount compared to the investments made by the venture capitalist.

This may be the case for companies in which a private equity fund has an interest, although in this case the target startup is typically at a more advanced stage of its life cycle and is generally more likely to contain losses in value, thanks to a more stable and well-established business model. If going concern is irreparably compromised and no more shareholders are willing to recapitalize the startup, which is typically affected by cash and equity burn outs, different prospects open up. Scenarios range from a liquidation, with disposal of attractive business units or sale of individual assets, to insolvency, if the market value of the assets realized is not sufficient to meet the liabilities (typical event of equity burnout, in which the shareholders' equity has zeroed or even become negative). The break-up value of the assets represents the lower limit in the valuations and is related to the possibility of selling them to third parties.

Venture-backed companies are typically represented by a composition of assets in which intangibles (that represent the present value of growth opportunities) have a predominant weight.

The existence of intangible assets, especially if they are not included in the balance sheet, limits the startup's capacity for indebtedness because of the difficulty of establishing a guaranteed title on them and their uncertain or sometimes non-existent market value.

The idea that the capacity for indebtedness increases in the presence of tangible assets with collateral value on which a guarantee can be provided is confirmed by numerous studies.

The fact that venture-backed startups have a portfolio of assets with a book value and—a fortiori—a market value represented essentially by intangibles sharply limits their ability to borrow but at the same time minimizes conflicts of interest between shareholders and third-party creditors, which are typical of situations of insolvency or prodromal to a state of crisis (Moro Visconti, 2015).

The transition from a going concern scenario to a break-up context implies the disappearance of the startup's income expectations. It only considers the market value of the individual assets (including the intangibles) that make up the startup. The market value is usually well below the operating value and sometimes even below the book value (as is the case for intangibles without market value): using a concept introduced by Adam Smith, we can speak in this case of the prevalence of the exchange value over the value in use of the individual asset. The presence in the startup of highly specialized activities (firm-specific) increases the difference between the value in use and exchange and, while it makes these activities more challenging to sell, it reduces agency costs between shareholders and creditors, since the former will have greater difficulties in making substitutions with other activities, making it more challenging—but less necessary—to collateralize them (Smith & Warner, 1979).

The market value of an intangible (as well as a tangible asset) depends, to a large extent, on the existence of a large and well-established secondary market for the goods being traded. The secondary market is reduced by the more specific the intangible is, even though it is usually more value-added (Titman & Wessels, 1988).

Internally generated goodwill (not accounted for, as the startup has not paid a sum in this regard) of the venture capitalist is incorporated in the value of the investment in the venture-backed startup. In the case of badwill related to a startup in crisis, it emerges the need to write-off the investment, with a significant impact on the shareholders' equity of the intermediary. Equity can be eroded substantially, especially if the write-off is significant compared to a portfolio of investments in other assets unable to offset the loss of some initiatives with the gains of others.

6.8   STOCK EXCHANGE LISTING
AND OTHER EXIT PROCEDURES

The listing of the venture-backed startup on the stock exchange is the traditional way for the venture capitalist to exit the investment. This option represents a mighty goal for any startupper, eager to become a Unicorn entrepreneur.

The fact that this intermediary typically represents a minority facilitates the sale of the share package, on the occasion of the Initial Public Offering and/or subsequently and does not help to signal to the market any feeling of distrust since the market knows in advance the nature and mission of the intermediary.

If the startup to be listed has a value that is strongly influenced by the permanence of some key managers (typically historical shareholders of the startup), it may require them to have a lock-up period. This constraint is not imposed on the intermediary, for the reasons mentioned above and for the disappearance of its strategic role (the financial resources are guaranteed by the stock market and the advisory service of the intermediary may continue, if necessary, through external consultancy). The stock market, when the time windows that allow divestments—usually fractioned—are opened to key managers bound by lock-up clauses, questions their behavior (often reacting negatively to their exit, knowing that they have privileged information).

The exit of some shareholders and, more generally, the purchases and sales, are significantly influenced by the degree of liquidity of the stock, which is expressed in the ability to allow significant purchases or sales without having a significant impact on the price. In an illiquid market, which characterizes thin stocks and is typical of technological companies, strongly growing and with recent history, the price typically moves against the shareholder who carries out the transaction.

The intermediary plays an active role in assisting the startup in the listing process, not only because it is involved in the success of the operation but because of its privileged relations with the financial community and with the intermediary that takes care of the IPO. With the quotation on the stock exchange (going public), the structure of the stakeholders is divided, and the process of fragmentation involves the passage from concentrated shareholders to a more intense fragmentation. This transition can preserve some reference shareholders, expression of a majority (individually or—more frequently, especially as the size increases—through coalitions of shareholders through syndicate agreements). A public company model may apply, in which many small shareholders live together, none of whom can exert a significant influence on the startup (in this context, the power of management is growing, and this can lead to a loss of value, counterbalanced by the value of the contestability of control).

The majority premium inherent in the controlling shareholding is gradually eroded with the splitting up of the equity until it tends to zero in a public company. Stock exchange listing creates intrinsic value not only by allowing the intermediary shareholder (or other shareholders, subject to any lock-up constraints) to sell all or part of their holding but—above all—by facilitating the search for a counterparty, to the point of making it anonymous and, in a liquid market, free of implicit costs.

With the listing, the so-called lack of marketability discount, which consists of the depreciation usually applied to unlisted companies, is eliminated. As a result, unlisted companies have traditionally been granted a discount resulting from the lack of marketability discount.

Empirical evidence allows identifying a range of variations of the discount for lack of marketability (Novak, 2016).

6.9 Valuation of the Investment Portfolio with a Net Asset Value

The valuation of venture capital or private equity fund must be based on the book value of equity, to which the market value of the investments must be added, and the book value of the investments subtracted.

The market value of investments is based on their Net Asset Value and any capital gain over their book value must be expressed, where appropriate (where the participation exemption is not applicable …), net of potential tax charges. In formulae:

$$
\begin{aligned}
\text{Net Asset Value} = \text{NAV} &= \text{Market Value of the Fund} \\
&= \text{Book Value of the Fund} \\
&+ (\text{market value} - \text{book value of the investments}) \\
&\quad (1 - \text{tax rate}) \qquad (6.6)
\end{aligned}
$$

The valuation of equity investments at fair value, applying international accounting standards (IAS/IFRS), should decrease the difference between the market and the book value of equity investments and the book value of shareholders' equity will already reflect the market value of the venture capital or private equity fund.

In the case of the valuation of venture capital or private equity funds, the following aspects should be considered:

- The value of each subsidiary must be estimated by discounting it at the cost of capital that incorporates the systematic risk of the most similar stock index (Nasdaq, Numtel, ...), increased by a firm-specific risk premium, as to include the lack of marketability, the volatility of economic and financial flows (higher in startups ...);
- The valuation of the shareholding must sometimes consider the size of the package, which may be subject to a minority discount (i.e., less frequently—a specular majority premium) in the absence of co-sale options, non-participation in syndicate agreements, etc.;
- The financial flexibility of the intermediary, which may or may not intervene in the event of cash or equity burnout of the investee startup, with the possibility of retaining at least part of its value (post-equity recapitalization burnout involves a reshuffling of the shareholding structure, in the event of failure by all shareholders to exercise the option right);
- There may be a synergistic value of the investment portfolio (if it relates to vertically integrated companies operating in contiguous segments of the value chain ...), such that the market value of that portfolio is higher than the sum of the NAVs per share of each holding. This synergistic value expresses goodwill not accounted for but considered in the estimate of the market value;
- The holding of a stake can generate management consulting services, placement fees, intermediation, which must be independently evaluated;
- The intermediary has its intrinsic value linked to its portfolio of holdings but is dependent on its reputation (which is an asset of primary importance for any financial intermediary).

6.10 Fintech Valuation

Technological startups include companies operating in the Financial Technology segment (FinTech), providing services and financial products with ICT technologies that reformulate business models, making use of innovative software and algorithms, value chains based on interactive computer platforms, artificial intelligence, and big data.

Financial services, which focus on the transmission of information on digital platforms, rely on innovative activities concerning the processing of data and their interpretation in real-time with automated descriptive, prescriptive, and predictive technologies. As anticipated, digitalization is intrinsically embedded in the business model of FinTechs.

The main areas of activity are:

- Financial technologies applied to blockchains and distributed ledger technology based on data archives, whose records are public on a computer network and without the need for a central register;
- Crypto and digital money;
- Peer-to-peer loans (P2P);
- Smart contracts (using the blockchain) that automatically execute contracts between buyers and sellers;
- Open banking is supported by blockchain applications that create a service through a connected network of financial institutions and third-party providers.
- IT security, through or decentralized storage of data, and anti-fraud systems;
- Applications in the insurance field (InsurTech) or regulation (RegTech).

6.10.1 Business Models

FinTech is an elastic business that can concentrate on market niches and specific customer segments, leveraging an innovative use of (big) data, and proposing new disruptive products and services.

Osterwalder et al. (2005, p. 12) identify nine common business model elements: value proposition, target customer, distribution channel, relationship, value configuration, core competency, partner network, cost structure, and revenue model.

FinTechs can complementarily be a:

a) A catalyzer/upgrader (digital enabler) of traditional business models, bringing to efficiency gains and pollinating the activity of ordinary banks or other financial intermediaries; FinTech providers use technology to disrupt these services by offering consumers a more compelling offering such as enhanced capabilities, convenience, or lower prices and fees (EY, 2019).

b) A pioneer of innovative products and services, normally through a B2B channel. An invented service is one that did not exist before but is now possible by technology and alternative business models, such as peer-to-peer lending and mobile-phone payments. Some invented services fill niches in the market, and others have the potential to redefine and transform entire financial subsectors (EY, 2019).

Innovation may for instance concern:

- Digital platform economy: handling of third parties: improving existing processes—coopetition as a new business model;
- Open architectures and cloud: open vision—biometric and geolocalization to improve security standards;
- Change management—new legacies;
- Frictionless processes for client onboarding.

Table 6.3 synthesizes the FinTechs main typologies and business models (see also Das, 2019; Tanda & Schena, 2019).

The appraisal methodology may conveniently start from a strategic interpretation of the business model (that derives from accounting data) to extract the key evaluation parameters to insert into the model, as shown in Fig. 6.8.

FinTechs cooperate with banks (Dorfleitner & Hornuf, 2019). Cooperation is primarily geared to the integration or use of a FinTech application (product-related cooperation).

An interpretation of the business model of each FinTech can be given using the SWOT analysis.

A further issue to be considered in the strategic analysis of the business model is the patentability of the algorithm that is behind FinTech's

Table 6.3 FinTech typologies and business models

Typology	Business model
Financing solutions	Pure equity crowdfunding (retail); club deals; funding from institutional investors
Blockchain	The blockchain is a decentralized and distributed digital ledger that corresponds to an open database with a pattern of sharable and unmodifiable data that are sequenced in chronological order. The main applications are cryptocurrencies; banking and payments; cyber-security; supply chain management; forecasting; networking and IoT; insurance; private transport and ride-sharing; cloud storage; charity; voting; healthcare; crowdfunding
Payment systems and processing (PayTech)	Credit cards; mobile payments through apps; virtual POS; online wallet; money transfers. Payment innovations throughout the year have been largely all about mobile e-wallets and contactless payments. PayTech firms also focused on ensuring the security of transactions leveraging artificial intelligence and machine learning technologies Global consumers have grown less reliant on cash, enhancing the growth profile of mobile payments firms
P2P loans	Peer-to-peer (P2P) lending is the practice of lending money to individuals or businesses through online services that match lenders with borrowers. Peer-to-peer lending companies often offer their services online and attempt to operate with lower overhead and provide their services more cheaply than traditional financial institutions
Open Banking	In October 2015, the European Parliament adopted a revised Payment Services Directive, known as PSD2. The new rules included aims to promote the development of neo-banks or challenger banks' use of innovative online and mobile payments through open banking

(continued)

Table 6.3   (continued)

Typology	Business model
Big Dataand Analytics	Big data analytics is the often-complex process of examining large and varied data sets, or big data, to uncover information—such as hidden patterns, unknown correlations, market trends, and customer preferences—that can help organizations make informed business decisions. Big data based on payment transaction data provides insight into customer retention, identification of criminal activities, or future customer behavior
Insurtech	Insurtech refers to the use of technology innovations designed to squeeze out savings and efficiency from the current insurance industry model
RegTech	Regulatory technology, in short, RegTech, is a new technology that uses information technology to enhance regulatory processes. With its main application in the Financial sector, it is expanding into any regulated business with an appeal to the Consumer Goods Industry. Regtech, post-financial crisis—with MiFiD II, Basel III, and GDPR—may have been the initial external driver to ensure full compliance, and this has ensured a dramatic rise in technological solutions, and is crucial in increasing efficiency, for example, by reducing gap-analysis time
SupTech	Use of innovative technology (big data, artificial intelligence, blockchains, etc.) by supervisory agencies to support supervision. Suptech will help authorities to become more data-driven (Di Castri et al., 2019)
Micro-FinTech	FinTech applications to microfinance activities (microcredit; microdeposits; microinsurance; micro-consulting). M-banking boosts volumes and fosters marginality gains (Moro Visconti, 2019)

(continued)

Table 6.3 (continued)

Typology	Business model
Banking-as-a-Service	End-to-end process ensuring the overall execution of a financial service provided over the web
Artificial Intelligence	AI will transform nearly every aspect of the financial service industry. Automated wealth management, customer verification, and open banking all provide opportunities for AI solution providers
PropTech	Property technology, short called Proptech, sometimes also called Real estate technology, is a term that encompasses the application of information technology and platform economics to real estate markets

An analysis of the business model may conveniently consider:
1. The revenue model;
2. The strategic goals;
3. The growth drivers;
4. The expected investments;
5. The market trends.

Fig. 6.8 Evaluation methodology

formulation. Software applications may be protected by patent law (in the US) or copyright law (in the EU).

The potential of FinTechs (in terms of products and services offered, strategic goals, etc.) concerns:

1. Problem-solving capacity (disruptive solutions to existing problems);
2. Total Addressable/Available Market;
3. New applications/Products / Services enabled by technology;

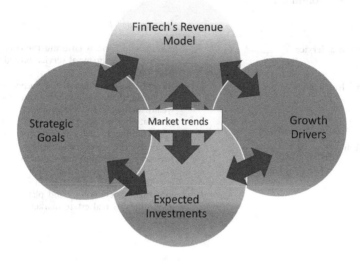

Fig. 6.9 Business model and value drivers

4. Lower Distribution/Intermediation and Operational costs (efficiency gains);
5. Revenue Model (market traction);
6. Cross-selling opportunities.

6.10.2   Valuation Metrics

The evaluation criteria of a FinTech typically follow the (actual and prospective) business model of the target company.

The technological value driver seems, at least in this historical phase, prevalent in the banking/financial activity, as shown in Fig. 6.10. A preliminary consideration may, however, indicate that the business model is slightly more "bank-centric" than the evaluation criteria.

The reasons for this divergence are manifold: banks are capital- and labor-intensive institutions and are strictly supervised (not only since they are financial institutions but also because they collect deposits and are so regulated by Central Bank authorities).

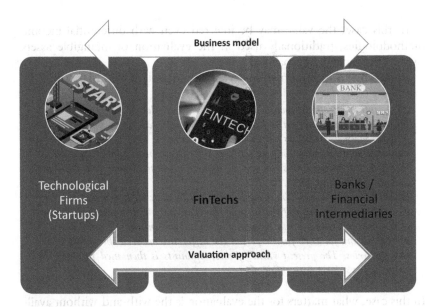

Fig. 6.10 Business model and valuation approach of FinTechs

FinTechs are quite different, although they share with banks a common underlying framework.

Banking and financial activities (Damodaran, 2009) follow peculiar valuation patterns that often concentrate on parameters like adjusted equity or dividends. These parameters are, however, not particularly meaningful with FinTechs since they are not capital-intensive firms, and their capacity to pay-out dividends is absent in the startup phase.

If the FinTech activity is developed within a banking group by a captive company, its strategic meaning may be that of a catalyzer of (traditional) banking activity. In this case, what mostly matters is not the value of FinTech as a stand-alone reality, but rather its contribution to the incremental marginality of the (traditional) banking group to which it belongs. FinTechs naturally tend to cooperate with banks, as in most cases they represent their customers. (Product-related) cooperation is primarily geared to the integration or use of a FinTech application cooperation (Brandl & Hornuf, 2017).

In this case, the value may be inferred even with differential income methodologies, traditionally used in the evaluation of intangible assets (within the income approaches).

According to the International Valuation Standard IVS 210, § 80:

80. Premium Profit Method or With-and-Without Method
80.1 The premium profit method, sometimes referred to as the with-and-without method, indicates the value of an intangible asset by comparing two scenarios: one in which the business uses the subject intangible asset and one in which the business does not use the subject intangible asset (but all other factors are kept constant). (...)
80.2 The comparison of the two scenarios can be done in two ways:
a) calculating the value of the business under each scenario with the difference in the business values being the value of the subject intangible asset, and
b) calculating for each future period the difference between the profits in the two scenarios. The present value of those amounts is then used to reach the value of the subject intangible asset.

In this case, what matters for the evaluation is the with-and-without availability of the FinTech business that can be considered as the "intangible" asset indicated in IVS 210.

Demyanova (2018) considers several methodologies that, in most cases, are hardly applicable to FinTechs. For example, the liquidation value or book value method is not consistent with the innovative nature of startups that become valueless if wound up and derive most of their potential value from intangible assets. The Berkus method appears too undetermined, and real options may be embedded in the estimate of future cash flows with multiple scenarios. A synthesis is reported in Table 6.4.

As shown in Chapter 2, in an equity valuation theory and practice, there are generally two valuation approaches—discounted cash flows (DCF) and comparables.

A comparison of the primary evaluation criteria in traditional (non-financial) firms, high-tech firms (startups), and banks/financial intermediaries is reported in Table 6.5.

Table 6.5. is complementary to Table 6.4.

The valuation issues of FinTech companies must be adapted to often young companies, given the novelty of the sector, which have all the prerogatives of *startups* (in terms of expected growth, survival rate,

Table 6.4 Comparison of the main evaluation approaches of traditional firms, technological startups, and banks

Traditional firm	Technological startup (IPEV, 2018; other methods)	Bank (Financial intermediary)
Balance sheet-based (Fernandez, 2001)	Venture Capital method	Expected dividends per share/Dividend Discount Models
Income	Binomial trees	Adjusted book value of equity (to proxy Market value)
Mixed capital-income Financial (DCF)	Net Asset Value	Excess Return Models
Market multiples (comparable firms) (IPEV, 2018)		

Table 6.5 FinTech valuation approaches

Method	Description
Liquidation value	Break-up value of tangible assets
Book value	Accounting value of tangible assets
Discounted Cash Flows	Discount of Operating Cash Flows to get Enterprise Value or Net Cash Flows to get Equity Value
First Chicago	Situation-specific business valuation approach used by venture capital and private equity investors for early stage companies. This model combines elements of market-oriented and fundamental analytical methods
Payne scoring	Weighted average value compared to similar firms
Berkus	Considers five key success factors: (1) Basic value, (2) Technology, (3) Execution, (4) Strategic relationships in its core market, and (5) Production, and consequent sales
Real options	An economically valuable right to make or else abandon some choice that is available to the managers of a company, often concerning business projects or investment opportunities

volatility, etc..), with valuation methodologies that must consider first the underlying business model.

Among the main evaluation methodologies of FinTech companies, the following are first relevant:

1. Relief-from-royalty approach;
2. Multi-period excess earnings;
3. Incremental cash flows, embedded in the DCF.

Startup failures are so common that they cannot refrain from influencing valuation, for instance, increasing the risk embedded in the discount rate of expected cash flows.

Failures have common features among the different startups but are industry-specific. And the financial sector has its own rules.

Among the reasons that may cause the default of Fintech startups, the following are worth mentioning[11]:

- **Underfunding.**
- **Choosing an inexperienced Venture Capital.**
- **Overlooking compliance.** Regulatory complexity is often underestimated.
- **Thinking a fintech startup is the same as any other tech startup.** Psychological behaviors around money, credit, savings, and payments are different from those concerning IT, biotechnologies, etc.
- **Competing solely on cost.** Banks have massive (traditional) scale advantages.
- *Going digital, Fintechs may re-engineer traditional business models but the task is uneasy and risky.*
- **Overconfidence.** Creating a new market is no easy task. Many Fintechs think that their business model is so innovative that they have no competitors. Whenever there is competition, geographical segmentation may represent a weak barrier, due to increasing financial globalization. Innovation may become increasingly challenging in a crowded and over-competitive market.
- **Underestimation of the length of the sales cycle.** Financial institutions are notoriously slow purchasers of anything new.
- **Missing sales strategy.** Fintech startups are often the brainchild of software experts that have limited sales and marketing skills.
- **Lack of understanding of the financial market.** Fintech startups pursuing a B2C business model often overestimate the extent to which consumers will (1) change their behavior and (2) pay for a new product or service in addition to all of the things they already pay for. While a B2B model may be a better path for some fintech

startups, some fail by not understanding that they're a vendor—not a partner—which may require a completely different set of skills and capabilities from those they already have.

6.11 UNICORNS

In the venture capital industry, a unicorn refers to any tech startup founded after 2003 and reaching a 1 billion-dollar market value, as determined by private or public investment. Since the term was coined in 2013 by the founder of Cowboy Ventures, Aileen Lee, the number of unicorns has increased manifold.

According to the *Economist* (2019), 156 unicorns exist worldwide, with the top five being:

- Uber, with a valuation of $68 billion;
- Didi Chuxing, with a valuation of $56 billion;
- Xiomi, with a valuation of $46 billion;
- Meituan Dianping, with a valuation of $30 billion, and
- Airbnb, with a valuation of $29.3 billion.

What most characterizes these innovative businesses has to do with their being data providers and innovation disruptors, given their internet-focused business models. Digital data are to this century what oil was to the last one: a driver of growth and change.

Digital information is unlike any previous resource; it is extracted, refined, valued, bought, and sold in different ways. The potential for digital scalability in the unicorn businesses is confirmed by their ability to provide customers with the same products and services as traditional companies while cutting on physical plant, staff, and other expenses thanks to the online digital platforms put in place.

For example, Uber came into the market as a ride-sharing app and it became the best known and most valuable startup because it owns the biggest pool of data about supply (drivers) and demand (passengers) for personal transportation. Uber's business model is based on a digital platform that makes it possible for people to simply tap their smartphone and have a cab arrive at their location in the minimum possible time. According to this innovative B2C mechanism, Uber customers would eventually be both the passenger booking a cab, as well as the driver (not an official taxi driver) offering the lift.

Today there is a "new regime of company formation" (Kenney & Zysman, 2019). The design and manufacture of unicorns have become gradually industrialized, and many of the ingredients needed are available on tap as online services. Smartphones let companies distribute what they offer at home and abroad, social media allow them to market it, and cloud computing lets them ramp up as demand grows.

If from one side unicorns are a paradigm representing the dream for any startup, on the other side there is still some concern about their reliability.

While the production of unicorns gathered pace and slickness, their disposal did not keep up. The rate at which venture-backed companies make public offerings has slowed.

New forms of regulation came out after the dot-com bubble burst, which gave protection to investors and increased the number of shareholders beyond which startups must disclose financial information, thus making going public much riskier.[12]

And there was no significant shortage of private capital willing, indeed eager, to help with that. As Komisar, a venture capitalist at Kleiner Perkins said: "Silicon Valley's lust for scaling … is more a result of the desires of capital than the needs of innovation".[13]

Several factors have come together to bring this period of reticence to an end. For example, a lot of venture capital funds were started around 2010, and they mostly have a ten-year term; investors now want to cash out.

Several public listings in 2018 showed that markets have a bigger appetite for tech shares. And the window of opportunity may soon close, meaning that a global downturn would both limit investors' appetite and severely test some of the unicorns' business models. Much the same might happen if several IPOs failed to live up to their hype. So again, the incentives are to go big and go quick. To get a sense of the going, *The Economist* (2019) has examined a panel of a dozen former and current internet-focused unicorns in Silicon Valley and elsewhere. This one includes most of the larger prospects and covers a range of industries. Uber and Lyft are in transport, Spotify in music-streaming, WeWork in real estate, Meituan, and Pinduoduo in Chinese e-commerce.

Given they offer the same opportunity as their precursors but through more innovative and efficient means, these businesses, which are now only a subset of their market, may hope to dominate soon. Apart from the issues described above, what they lack, are profits. Today, according to Gao et al. (2013) 84% of companies pursuing IPOs have no profits, while ten years ago, this proportion was just 33%. *If all this dearly bought growth has not supplied profits, what will happen?* The answers for the unicorns could be more growth, more spending by existing customers, and higher margins. However, the first is not necessarily that plausible.

Among the companies that disclosed the number of customers they have in America, growth slowed to 9% in 2018. Moreover, few of the firms sit behind barriers to entry as strong as those that protected Alibaba, Facebook, and Google. They can lose customers as well as gain them. Lots of property companies can rent out office space, as WeWork does. Spotify customers can get music from Apple, too. Drivers often toggle between Lyft and Uber apps; so, do passengers. There are already several big Chinese e-commerce firms to choose from.

None of these considerations necessarily mean unicorn startups are bad businesses. But they do make them look like pricey ones.

Another growing concern is that innovation produced by some unicorns does not leave society better off as it is intended to. There are real benefits, but critics point to real downsides, such as increased congestion and other environmental costs, a weakening of public transport systems, and the precarious lives of the workers who make these platforms function.

6.12 Key Person Discounts

A further characteristic of young firms is that they are typically highly dependent on the founder/owner and a few other key people until the firm gets sufficiently stable and large.

The impact of key person losses on the value can be significant, especially if the replacement is challenging.

According to Damodaran (2018), the key person discount can be estimated as follows:

$$\text{key person discount} = \frac{\left(\text{Value of Firms}_{\text{status quo}} - \text{Value of firm}_{\text{key person lost}}\right)}{\text{Value of Firm}_{\text{status quo}}} \quad (6.7)$$

A fair estimation of the discount is in practice extremely difficult, and often the loss of key people is a major threat to business continuity, with a strong impact on value.

NOTES

1. Following the IPEV Valuation Guidelines (privateequityvaluation.com).
2. See http://www.ifac.org/system/files/downloads/b013-2010-iaasb-han dbook-isae-3400.pdf.
3. See https://www.insead.edu/sites/default/files/assets/dept/centres/ gpei/docs/Measuring_PE_Fund-BN-EN-1-02-2019-for_GPEI_website. pdf.
4. IPEV Guidelines, http://www.privateequityvaluation.com/Portals/0/ Documents/Guidelines/IPEV%20Valuation%20Guidelines%20-%20Dece mber%202018.pdf?ver=2018-12-21-085233-863.
5. https://www.investeurope.eu/uploadedFiles/Home/Toolbox/Industry_ Standards/evca_international_valuation_guidelines_2009.pdf.
6. See Chapter 2.
7. See paragraph 2.8.
8. See also Fig. 3.2.
9. See paragraph 13.7.
10. An Excel application can be found in https://docs.google.com/spread sheets/d/1B-ivgVc5VtXjlbrmA_Fn3r4a8JLidtS6CKCnwQGUnAs/edit# gid=35.
11. See https://www.forbes.com/sites/ronshevlin/2019/07/29/why-fin tech-startups-fail/#30c33e6a6440.
12. Sarbanes–Oxley Act and JOBS Act of 2012.
13. https://pdfs.semanticscholar.org/3087/addf40b7ed3215423ca6286f0c4 c0a7cad23.pdf.

SELECTED REFERENCES

Achleitner, A. K. (2005). First Chicago method: Alternative approach to valuing innovative startups in the context of venture capital financing rounds. *Betriebswirtschaftliche Forschung Und Praxis (BFuP), 57* (4), 333–347.

Aggarwal, R., Bhagat, S., & Rangan, S. (2009). The impact of fundamentals on IPO valuation. *Financial Management, 38*(2), 253–284.

Batista de Oliveira, F., & Perez Zotes, L. (2018). Valuation methodologies for business startups: A bibliographical study and survey. *Brazilian Journal of Operations & Production Management, 15*(1), 96–111.

Bednar, R., Tariskova, N., & Zagorsek, B. (2018). Startup revenue model failures. *Montenegrin Journal of Economics, 14*(4), 141–157.

Braun, R. (2009). Risk of private equity fund-of fund investments—A detailed cash flow-based approach. *SSRN Electronic Journal.*

Brandl, B., & Hornuf, L. (2017, September 13). *Where did fintechs come from, and where do they go? The transformation of the financial industry in Germany after digitalization.* Available at SSRN: https://ssrn.com/abstract=3036555.

Burger, E. S. C., & Kohn, A. (2017). Exploring differences in early-stage startup valuation across countries. In *Academy of management proceedings* (Vol. 2017, No. 1, p. 13639). Briarcliff Manor, NY: Academy of Management.

Charsios, G., Moutafidis, K., & Foroglou, G. (2016). *Valuation model for Internet-of-Things (IoT) startups* (Conference Paper).

Damodaran, A. (2009, April). *Valuing financial service firms.* Working paper, New Yok University.

Damodaran, A. (2018). *The dark side of valuation* (3rd ed.). Pearson FT Press PTG.

Das, S. R. (2019) The future of fintech. *Financial Management, 48,* 981–1007.

Davila, A., Foster, G., & Gupta, M. (2003). Venture capital financing and the growth of startup firms. *Journal of Business Venture, 18*(6), 689–708.

Demyanova, E. A. (2018). The topical issues of valuation of companies under the conditions of fintech. *Strategic Decisions and Risk Management,* (1), 88–103.

Di Castri, S., Hohl, S., Kulenkampff, A., & Prenio, J. (2019). The SupTech Generations. *FSI Insights on policy implementation, 19.*

Diller, C., Herger, I., & Wulff, M. (2009). The private equity J-curve: Cash flow considerations from primary and secondary points of view. *Investing in private equity.* Available at https://www.capdyn.com/Customer-Content/www/news/PDFs/the-private-equity-j-curve_private-equity-mathematics_apr-09__2_.pdf.

Dorfleitner, G., & Hornuf, L. (2019). FinTech business Models. In *FinTech and data privacy in Germany.* Springer Nature.

Economist. (2017, May). *Fuel of the future, data is giving rise to a new economy.* Available at https://www.economist.com/briefing/2017/05/06/datais-giving-rise-to-a-new-economy.

Economist. (2019, April). Herd instincts—The wave of unicorn IPOs reveals silicon valley's groupthink. Available at https://www.economist.com/briefing/2019/04/17/the-wave-of-unicorn-ipos-reveals-silicon-valleys-groupthink.

EY. (2019). *Global FinTech Adoption Index 2019.* Available at https://www.ey.com/en_gl/ey-global-fintech-adoption-index.

Fenn, J. (2007). *Understanding Gartner's hype cycles.* Available at https://www.gartner.com/en/documents/509085.

Fernandez, P. (2001). *Company valuation methods.* Available at SSRN: https://ssrn.com/abstract=274973.

Festela, G., Wuermseherb, M., & Cattaneo, G. (2013). Valuation of early stage high-tech startup companies. *International Journal of Business, 18*(3), 216.

Gao, X., Ritter, J. R., & Zhu, Z. (2013, December). Where have all the IPOs gone? *Journal of Financial and Quantitative Analysis, 48*(6), 1663–1692.

Havard, E. (2018). *Internet startups' profit dilemma: A theoretical paper on using two-sided markets theory as a framework in a valuation setting.* Master's thesis in business administration, The Arctic University of Norway.

Hering, T., Olbrich, M., & Steinrucke, M. (2006). Valuation of startup internet companies. *International Journal of Technology Management, 33*(44), 406–419.

Hoffman, R., & Yeh, C. (2018). *Blitzscaling: The lightning-fast path to building massively valuable companies.* Amazon's top 20 Business and Leadership Book. New York: Crown Publishing Group.

IPEV. (2018). *Valuation guidelines.* privateequityvaluation.com.

Jensen, M., & Meckling, W. (1976). Theory of the firm: Managerial behavior, agency costs and ownership structure. *Journal of Financial Economics, 3*(4), 305–360.

Jogekar, N. (2009). Marketing R&D, and startup valuation. *IEEE Transaction on Engineering Management, 56*(2), 229–242.

Kenney, M., & Zysman, J. (2019). Unicorns, Cheshire cats, and the new dilemmas of entrepreneurial finance. *Venture Capital, 21*(1), 35–50.

Kohn, A. (2017). The determinants of startup valuation in the venture capital context: A systematic review and avenues for future research. *Springer link, 68*(1), 3–36.

Koller, T., & Goedhart, M. (2015). *Valuation: Measuring and managing the value of companies.* McKinsey & Company.

Krishna, A., Agrawal, A., & Choudhary, A. (2016). Predicting the outcome of startups: Less failure, more success. *Paper presented at IEEE 16th International Conference on Data Mining workshops (ICDMW).*

Linton, J. (2016). Towards a better understanding of the university ground that underlies tech startups and other small businesses. *Paper presented at ICSB World Conference Proceedings*, Washington, US.

Melegati, J., Wang, X., & Kon, F. (2019, February). A model of requirements engineering in software startups. *Information and Software Technology, 109*, 92–107.

Miloud, T., Cabrol, M., & Aspelund, A. (2012). Startup valuation by venture capitalists: An empirical study. *Venture Capital, 14*(2–3), 151–174.

Moro Visconti, R. (2019). *How to prepare a business plan with excel* (working paper). Available at https://www.researchgate.net/publication/255728204_How_to_Prepare_a_Business_Plan_with_Excel.

Moro Visconti, R. (2015). Leveraging value with intangibles: More guarantees with less collateral? *Corporate Ownership & Control, 13*(1), 241–252.

Available at http://www.virtusinterpress.org/IMG/pdf/COC_Volume_13_Issue_1_Autumn_2015_Continued_2_.pdf.

Myers, S. C., & Majluf, N. S. (1984). Corporate financing and investment decisions when firms have information that investors do not have. *Journal of Financial Economics, 13*, 187–221.

Nasser, S. (2016). *Valuation for startups—9 methods explained.* ICT Strategic Consulting.

Novak, N. P. (2016, Winter). Measuring the discounts for lack of marketability for noncontrolling nonmarketable ownership interests. *Gift and Estate Tax Valuation Insights.* Available at www.willamette.com.

Osterwalder, A., Pigneur, Y., & Tucci, C. L. (2005). Clarifying business models: Origins, present, and future of the concept. *Communications of the Association for Information Systems, 16*(1).

Polimenis, V. (2018). *Valuation issues with early equity finance.* Hephaestus Research Repository, NUP Academic Publications, School of Economic Sciences and Business.

Rohm, P., & Kuckertz, A. (2018, May). A world of difference? The impact of corporate venture capitalists' investment motivation on startup. *Journal of Business Economics, 88*, 531–557.

Sahlman, W. A. (1997). How to write a great business plan. *Harvard Business Review, 75*(4), 98.

Sassi, R. (2016). *An improved valuation method for startups in the social-media industry.* RUN Nova School of Business and Economics (NSBE).

Sepideh. (2019). *The venture capital method—Basic startup valuation.* Porsud.

Shimizu, T. (2017). Intellectual properties and debt for startups. In T. Kono (Eds.), *Security interests in intellectual property (perspectives in law, business and innovation)* (pp. 39–50). Singapore: Springer.

Smith, A., & Rawnet, M. D. (2015). *How can businesses achieve digital scalability?* Freshbusinessthinking.com.

Smith, C. W., & Warner, J. (1979). On financial contracting: An analysis of bond covenants. *Journal of Financial Economics, 7* (2), 117–161.

Sokol, M. (2018). What drives the magic of startups? *People & Strategy, 41*(3), 4–5.

Tanda, A., & Schena, C. (2019). *FinTech, BigTech and Banks: Digitalisation and its impact on banking business models.* Cham: Palgrave Macmillan.

Titman, S., & Wessels, R. (1988, March). The determinants of capital structure choice. *Journal of Finance, 43*(1), 1–19.

Trichkova, R., & Kanaryan, N. (2015). *Startups valuation: Approaches and methods.* Paper presented at 1st Balkan Valuation conference "Best valuation practices", pp. 19–21, Sofia, Bulgaria.

Venture Valuation. (2019). *Valuation methods.* Available at https://www.venturevaluation.com/en/methodology/valuation-methods.

CHAPTER 7

The Valuation of Software and Database

7.1 Definition and Main Features

In general terms, the software is a sequence of computer instructions, written in a programming language (C, Visual Basic, ...), to obtain a certain result and to perform functions in an electronic device. These instructions form the source code, transformed through a compiler into an object code, which the CPU (Central Processor Unit) can process. In other words, the software is represented by information (data) and rules (programs) to manage the given data. This information can, therefore, be represented by one or more programs, or by one or more data, or by a combination of the two. The software is a basic feature of digitalization.

The source code of the proprietary software is usually not distributed and is considered a trade secret, following know-how valuation patterns.[1] In this context, there is proprietary software, as opposed to open-source software (free software), in which the source code is made public by the authors, allowing independent programmers to make changes and extensions.

Software represents a fundamental element in computer science, which deals with the processing of information through automated procedures, using algorithms, i.e., formal procedures that solve problems (procedural, computational, etc.), interpreting the computability through a finite number of steps. Algorithms, usually based on mathematical concepts,

© The Author(s), under exclusive license to Springer Nature Switzerland AG 2022
R. Moro-Visconti, *The Valuation of Digital Intangibles*,
https://doi.org/10.1007/978-3-031-09237-4_7

are thus a key aspect in the programming phase of software development which uses IT languages then executed by a computer.

The theoretical concept of software, not without ambiguity (because of its constantly evolving technical characteristics), turns out to be instrumental to its legal framework. According to a first definition, provided by the World Intellectual Property Organization (WIPO) in 1984, the software is "the expression of an organized and structured set of instructions in any form or on any medium capable, directly or indirectly, of having a function or task performed or of obtaining a specific result by means of an electronic information processing system".

In the English language "software" is born in contrast to the term "hardware" and from the composition of the words "soft" and "ware".

According to their different characteristics, the software can be classified according to:

- The functions it fulfills (accounting, document consultation, documents video-writings, spreadsheets, payroll management, databases, graphics, etc.);
- The degree of openness of the license (free use or ownership);
- The installation in hardware or portability equipment, with Internet evolutions which have opened the space to cloud computing. Remote storage allows to backup data and process information remotely (Data as a Service—DaaS), or to use programs always from remote, outside the physical computer or the local LAN (software as a service), through an external cloud provider using mass storage in outsourcing;
- The operating system on which they can be used (DOS, Unix, Mac OS, Linux, Windows, Android, iOS, ...);
- The type of interface which uses them (single PCs or networked, textual or graphical);
- The criticality of the processes they govern.

The term "suite" refers to software structured in different programs/modules, usually configurable separately but forming part of a single IT solution (such as, for example, office automation application packages or antivirus).

The realization of software is a complex activity articulated in several phases, starting from a basic platform of programs (e.g., Java) on which applications and customizations are developed, within an environment of execution, and for this reason, the software is generally associated with an engineering product, but differing mainly for its formability according to the need.

7.2   Accounting and Fiscal Aspects

The accounting aspects related to the recording of the software in the financial statements play an important role in its economic evaluation, for the estimate of the damages due to counterfeiting, which may include the accounting of the counterfeiter for the estimate of his marginality. In a broad sense, accounting evaluates the impact:

- On revenues, costs, and differential economic margins (EBITDA; EBIT; pre-tax profit ...);
- On provisions for assets (of profit reserves ...);
- On incoming, outgoing operating (FCFF), and net cash flows (FCFE).

The accounting discipline, dictated by the national accounting principles or by the international accounting principles (IAS/IFRS), is increasingly adopting the new valuation standards, providing for the alignment of the book values recorded in the balance sheet and based on the fair value cost.

Accounting standards distinguish software, based on its intrinsic characteristics, in:

a. Basic software: consisting of the set of instructions required for the computer operation (hardware);
b. Application software: the set of instructions enabling the use of basic software functions to meet specific user requirements.

Since the basic software is closely related to the hardware, this one is treated as a core component of a tangible asset. Costs incurred for the internal production of "unprotected" application software can either be charged to the income statement in the period in which they are incurred (being part of the OPEX) or can be recognized under "other" intangible assets (CAPEX), linked to programs that can be used for a certain number of years within the company and have the characteristics specified below. Capitalized costs include direct and indirect costs that relate to the development of the software. Indirect costs attributable to the project, such as rents, depreciation and amortization, supervisory personnel costs, and other similar items, are excluded.

Capitalization of costs (CAPEX) begins only after the company is reasonably certain of the completion and suitability for the expected use of the new software. This moment may vary depending on the nature of the project.

The amortization of the cost of the unprotected software is made within its foreseeable period of use. The software is typically improved with incremental investments.

As far as fiscal aspects are concerned, a distinction is made between software entered under intellectual property or licenses of assets: concerning tax amortization, only a limited number of financial years are recognized for the former, while for the latter the tax amortization follows the duration of the license agreement.

The tax aspects are relevant for transfer price problems, within international corporate groups, for instance, when the software is concentrated in foreign royalty companies, which charge the fees back to other group companies for the license of the same.

7.3   LEGAL PROTECTION
OF SOFTWARE: INTRODUCTORY REMARKS

Regarding the possible forms of protection, the software, given its nature, could be qualified both as an industrial invention, thus enjoying patent protection, as well as intellectual work, with the consequent traceability to the protection of copyright. In the past, the protection of software using copyright or patent has been the subject of a wide doctrinal and jurisprudential debate.

There are still differences between the United States and the European Union.

The choice of copyright for the protection of computer programs has been, since the 1960s, strongly advocated by the manufacturers of hardware, since in those days the software was supplied with it and in source format so that the user could adapt it to his needs. It is only with the birth, in the 1970s, of companies producing only software that it acquires its independence and therefore requires a legal effort for better protection.

The aspect of the originality of software is of decisive importance for those who produce and develop such products, especially if third parties market products with similar characteristics and content.

7.4 ECONOMIC AND FINANCIAL VALUATION

The software is classified as an intangible asset and, therefore, its valuation is based on the IVS 210 valuation principles normally applicable to intangible assets (examined in Chapter 2), to be adapted to the case.

The economic evaluation of the software can be applied in cases of contractual/extra-judicial nature or for disputes, relating to counterfeiting or unfair competition.

The evaluation of the software must be carried out with an interdisciplinary approach, which considers different aspects together, appreciating its impact from an economic and financial point of view.

The main approaches to evaluating software will be summarized below. In the following paragraphs, a specific analysis will be dedicated to software as well as to the development companies (software houses).

The distinction between proprietary and open-source software has an impact on the valuation, given that only the proprietary closed code model allows a remuneration based on the exploitation by the user.

The open-source code is not however entirely devoid of potential remuneration, which is based on nonproprietary licensing models or on value co-creation mechanisms in which external developers contribute to improving the software, which can then serve as a basic IT platform for the sale of other related products (e.g., Mobile Apps) to support-oriented buyers.

The evaluation is typically limited to software only, as a separate legal entity, even if in some cases it is associated with other activities—primarily immaterial—which have characteristics of contiguity and affinity with the software.

These complementary assets can represent a synergistic portfolio of intellectual property, expressing an entire company—as an organized complex of assets—or an organic branch. Among the intangibles closest to software, there are, first, patents (to the point that the software is considered patentable in some systems) or trademarks with which software can be associated. If the software is not yet completed, its nature is similar,

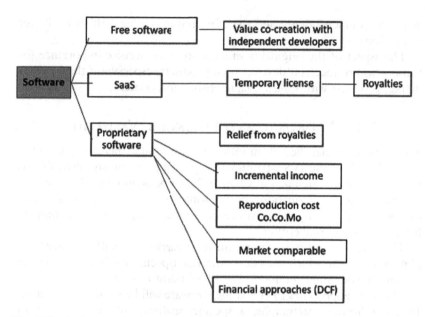

Fig. 7.1 Software valuation approaches

first from an economic point of view and always from an evaluative point of view, with the know-how and industrial secrets.

The main approaches—used individually or in a complementary way—of professional practice for estimating the value of intangible resources have already been described in Chapter 2.

The choice of the approaches depends on the type of intangible and the purposes and context of the evaluation, but on the ease with which reliable and significant information can be found on the resource and on the market in which it is strategically positioned.

Figure 7.1 shows the main valuation approaches.

7.4.1   Software House Revenue Model

Software houses are companies specialized in the production of software and applications (operating systems, office automation, design systems, video games, ...), both for computers and for other devices (tablets, smartphones, machinery, ...).

Among the most famous software houses, there are, for example, Adobe Systems, Apple, IBM, Microsoft, Oracle, Symantec, ...

The software houses can be distinguished according to the type of product developed (commercial customized, on-demand, individual components, hosting providers, ...) and according to the activity carried out (specific products on order or products in series ready-to-use).

Revenues from software houses mainly refer to the sale of software or its licensing, as well as those related to maintenance and periodic customer service contracts (theoretically constant and less volatile).

The license is the contract of use by which the owner of the proprietary software (closed source), defines the legal regime of circulation and limitations in its use and transfer. In the case of free software (open-source), there is no fee for its use. A recent trend followed by some large companies (such as Adobe Systems, for example) is to direct their revenue model more toward temporary (renewable) licensing of program packages rather than to the sale of individual software for perpetual use. In many cases, the software is freely available and is distributed free of charge (freeware) or in shared mode (shareware), with downloads from the Internet.

Many applications (mobile apps installed on the user's device) for smartphones or tablets are free of charge and find their economic rationale in the fact that they allow the user to channel quickly and intuitively toward the use of paid services of e-commerce (App stores) or linked to advertising banners or other revenue models. In many cases, apps are not developed by specialized software houses, but by individual inventors, who sell them or make them available, even for free, on the web, with viral interactions often associated with social networks.

The evaluation of a single (stand-alone) software, generally to be pursued through the approaches of appraisal of intangible resources, tends to differ from the evaluation of software houses, for which it is possible to apply the canonical approaches of evaluation of companies, considering the specificity of their revenue model.

An intrinsic characteristic of the software—and many other intangible resources—is its scalability.[2] Its fruition, mainly linked to a download from the web (free or paid or with other indirect remuneration approaches, for example, linked to the fruition of editorial contents or linked to other media), entails, for the owner of the rights, the incurrence of fixed costs associated with negligible variable costs (deriving from each incremental fruition of the software, by new users).

Scalability means that the software house that sells proprietary software, once it has reached an economic break-even point in which revenues equal fixed costs incurred, at that point has additional and incremental revenues, in fact, unrelated to costs that have already been incurred, with significant profiles of economic marginality.

This is not the case for firms that provide software customization services, adapting their platforms to the personalized needs of users, charging customers for man-hours (body rental), in the absence of the scalability requirements described above. For these reasons, proprietary software houses are typically more profitable than "body-renting" firms, as they incorporate scalability options that are counterbalanced by little variable costs (that are, instead, important in the "body rental" business).

Replication of software licenses is almost costless for the producer (little if any variable costs add up to the initial investment). Hence the direct impact of revenues on the EBIT, and the consequent scalability of the business model.

7.4.2   Applicability of Empirical and Analytical Evaluation Approaches to Software

The applicability to the software of the different evaluation approaches illustrated in Chapter 2 requires an adaptation that ackwnowledges its intrinsic characteristics, considering the revenue model previously described, if necessary, in a stand-alone perspective, in which the software is considered extractable by the company and distinctly appraisable.

The evaluation can be carried out for different purposes, even in litigation, in case of unfair competition with appropriation, replication, and/or undue imitation and usurpation of software, in violation of the right of exclusivity.

In this context, the traditional legal concepts based on the emerging damage and, in a perspective, on the loss of profit, are used, projecting the prospective market shares and their contraction, considering the failure to recover the investments made.

The erosion of value derives from its obsolescence and technological upgrades, which eliminate exclusive connotations. The strategic value of software should be appreciated in terms of uniqueness, specificity, non-permeability, and exclusivity, which must be associated with flexible versatility, even in terms of applications to multiple sectors, with customized adaptations.

The main valuation approaches are:

A. *The relief-from-royalties approach*

The market value of software can be estimated as the sum of the relief-from-royalties (which the company would pay as a licensee if the software were not owned) discounted over a given period.

The concept of *reasonable royalty* can be relevant in the field of litigation in the quantification of damages from counterfeiting. It is also a proxy for valuation in standard (non-litigation) cases.

In the evaluation of a company with software, the presence of license contracts is particularly appreciated by investors, because it generates revenues that are not occasional and constitutes a signal of the technological equity and the innovative capacity of the company.

The exploitation of the software is alternatively linked to the payment of periodic royalties, one-off amounts, use on consumption (pay per use), periodic maintenance, technical support, updates, etc. Revenues from maintenance, updating, services, etc., in many cases, tend to exceed those related to the product license. This must be considered in the economic estimate, even in the case of counterfeiting.

B. *The incremental income approach*

The value of software depends on its expected economic and financial margin. Therefore, if a going concern is considered, the contribution of software in terms of price and/or volume increases (and therefore of economic margin) to the profitability of the business can be measured through the differential income approach. The value of the software corresponds to the present value of the sum of the differential income that it will presumably produce in the future. The software can, therefore, be evaluated considering its contribution to tangible differential economic benefits and potential future benefits, which are expressed at a premium price.

The number of years of exploitation of the software depends on its life cycle (useful life). A possible variant is based on the estimate of the incremental gross operating margin or other partial economic margins that the software allows obtaining, to which a suitable multiplier is applied, derived from negotiations of comparable software. In addition to or as an alternative to the incremental income, the additional (operating or net) cash flow generated by the software can be considered.

The use of the software acts on the economic margins expressed by the differential between revenues and operating costs since it ideally allows both to increase revenues (with greater direct sales or with royalties from licenses) and to reduce costs, producing with less labor-intensive techniques and savings of other costs (production, organizational, energy, …). The stratification of differential income thanks to the software generates incremental equity, which expresses the differential between the market value and the book value of the company; it is a suitable element to express the surplus value of software.

Both the approaches considered here, including the relief from royalties, can be traced, in a broad sense, to the income approaches. They are based on a projection of normalized future incomes, to be discounted in a predefined (or unlimited) time horizon, consistent with the expected useful life of the software, at a reasonable rate. Such a rate incorporates the risk connected to the expected future manifestation of the income, in terms of both an and quantum.

C. *The estimate of the cost incurred (or of reproduction)*

In the absence of available data on income capacity, a possible alternative is that of the cost incurred in the past to create the software and to occupy in the market the positions reached by the same software at the valuation date. It is, therefore, necessary to identify the most significant costs incurred, considering the percentage of sales:

– Research and development costs;
– Costs for raw materials;
– Hours worked;
– Other accessory charges.

The identification of a historical cost of production, based on analytical accounting that allows the functional separation of the costs for the software from the others, is preliminary to the estimate of a current cost of reproduction, having the nature of investment and being oriented to the future economic returns.

A step forward is constituted by the cost of reproduction of a functionally equivalent software that substitutes to the historical costs for the costs of reproduction ex novo, i.e., the costs that it would be necessary to sustain at the moment of the evaluation to rebuild the same value that the software has reached that very moment.

In this procedure, there is still the limit of not considering the return on investment and the opportunity cost resulting from the immediate failure to use the software. Reproduction costs can potentially be expressed in terms of emerging damage and loss of profit for lost revenues.

The existence of high and uncertain fixed costs connected to the reconstruction of the software represents an entry barrier, which segregates the market and distances competitors.

Among all the intangibles, the software is possibly the most versatile, as it is ubiquitous and indispensable for any application.

Figure 7.2 synthetizes the links of software with the other intangibles and its pivoting role, like that of a digital hub (main link) within a network.

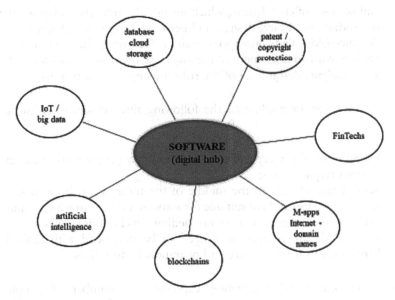

Fig. 7.2 Software as a digital hub

7.4.3   CO.CO.MO Method and Putnam Model

COnstructive COst MOdel (CO.CO.MO.) is a mathematical model created by Barry Boehm (initially in 1981 and later implemented; see Boehm et al., 2005) to estimate some basic parameters (such as delivery time and man-months) necessary for software development. The model is based on the study of sixty projects (with different lines of code and programming languages) of a Californian automation and software development company. CO.CO.MO. is considered a static and analytical model; static because the input and output variables are well-defined and fixed, analytical because it can be used not necessarily to a project in its entirety but also to its parts. There are three different versions of the model, which differ in the precision with which the different values are estimated:

- Basic—the estimate is made starting from the size of the software to be developed calculated in KNCSS.
- Intermediate—it calculates the software development effort as a function of the size of the program, always expressed in KNCSS, and on a set of cost drivers, which include the subjective assignment of product, hardware, design, and personal attributes evaluations;
- Advanced/detailed—incorporates all the features of the intermediate version, with an assessment of the impact of the various costs for each step (analysis, design, ...) of the software engineering process.

CO.CO.MO. can be applied to the following three classes of software projects:

- Organic: small projects, where teams of a few people work on a set of strict requirements;
- Semi-detached—are in the middle of the three types (both in size and complexity) and are suitable for software projects in which teams with average experience work on medium-level requirements.
- Embedded—are projects that need to be developed with limited hardware and with software and operational constraints.

The CO.CO.MO. basic equation expresses the number of people required for the development of software as a ratio between the effort applied person/month (depending on the estimate of lines of code for the project) and the development time in months, based on empirical coefficients, different according to the class of project (abovementioned).

The Putnam model is an empirical software effort estimation model. The original paper by Putnam (1978) is a pioneering work in the field of software process modeling. As a group, empirical models work by collecting software project data (for example, effort and size) and fitting a curve to the data. Future effort estimates are made by providing size and calculating the associated effort using the equation which fits the original data (usually with some error).

The Putnam model describes the time and effort required to finish a software project of a specified size. SLIM (Software Lifecycle Management) is the name given by Putnam to the proprietary suite of tools his company QSM, Inc. has developed based on his model. It is one of the earliest of these types of models developed and is among the most widely used. Closely related software parametric models are Constructive Cost Model (COCOMO), shown above, Parametric Review of Information for Costing and Evaluation—Software (PRICE-S), and Software Evaluation and Estimation of Resources—Software Estimating Model (SEER-SEM).

This estimating method is sensitive to uncertainty in both size and process productivity. Putnam advocates obtaining process productivity by calibration:

$$Process\ Productivity = \frac{Size}{\frac{Effort^{1/3}}{B}Time^{4/3}} \tag{7.1}$$

Putnam makes a sharp distinction between "conventional productivity": size/effort and process productivity.

One of the main pros of this model is its simplicity. Most software houses, regardless of their maturity level, can easily collect the size, effort, and duration (time) for past projects. Process Productivity, being exponential, is typically converted to a linear productivity index. Firms can use it to track their productivity changes to apply in future effort estimates.

7.5   OPEN-SOURCE SOFTWARE

Open-source software is open-source meaning that its source code is left to the availability of any developers, with a free circulation of information about the programs, freely modifiable.

The Debian Free Software Guidelines[3] represent a set of ten principles for defining the concept of free software (published under the terms of a free software license, which grants its use, study, modification, and redistribution), as opposed to proprietary software:

1. Free Redistribution
   Licensing a Debian component may not restrict anyone from selling or transferring software as a component of an aggregate software distribution of programs from different sources. The license may not require royalties or other payments for sale.
2. Source Code
   The program must include the source code. In addition, it must be possible to distribute it both as source code and in compiled form.
3. Derivatives
   The license must allow modifications and derivative works and must allow their distribution under the same terms as the license of the original software.
4. Integrity of the author's source code
   The license may restrict the distribution of modified source code only if it allows the distribution of patch files together with the source code to modify the program during compilation. The license must explicitly allow the distribution of software compiled with modified source code. The license may require that the derivative works have a different name or version number from the original software. This should be a compromise between the possibility of modifying the code and the right of authors to be recognized as such.
5. No discrimination against persons or groups
6. No discrimination in the fields of employment
   The license may not restrict the use of the program in a specific field of use. For example, it may not restrict commercial use or genetic research.
7. Distribution of the license

The rights applied to the program must apply to anyone receiving the program without the need to use additional third-party licenses.

8. The license may not be specific to Debian
   The rights applied to the program cannot depend on whether it is part of a Debian system. If the program is extracted from Debian and used or distributed without Debian but subject to the terms of the license, all parties should have the same rights as those who receive it with the Debian system.

9. The license must not contaminate other software
   The license may not restrict other software that is distributed with the licensed software. For example, the license cannot require that all other programs distributed with the same medium be free software.

10. Examples of licenses
    The GNU General Public License, BSD, and Artistic are examples of licenses that are considered free.

Open-source software evaluation issues are peculiar, considering that traditional parameters, such as the expected royalties, are not applicable. Customizations and applications can be an alternative source of remuneration, even as support or additional services or advertising agreements, within strategies of co-creation of value. Knowledge sharing can lead to incremental or cumulative value and the open-source paradigm is an expression of a shared model of exploitation of intellectual property rights.

Open-source software can be part of a freemium strategy, a pricing strategy by which a product or service is provided free of charge, but money (premium) is charged for additional services.

7.6   Software as a Service (SaaS)

Software as a service (SaaS) is an outsourced software distribution model in which a third-party provider hosts applications made available to customers over the Internet. SaaS is one of the three main categories of cloud computing, alongside Infrastructure as a Service (IaaS) and Platform as a Service (PaaS). SaaS is closely related to the Application Service Provider (ASP) and on-demand computing software delivery models.[4]

Software as a service has grown to be a significant segment of many software product markets. SaaS vendors, which charge customers based on use and continuously improve the quality of their products, have put competitive pressure on traditional perpetual software vendors, which charge a licensing fee and periodically upgrade the quality of their software (Guo & Ma, 2018).

SaaS has the potential to provide substantial opportunities for organizations to improve their information technology without cost and management concerns (Safari et al., 2015).

SaaS represents an opportunity for trendy software houses to expand traditional business models, outreaching new clients with digital (cloud) scalability.

7.7   Definition and Characteristics of Databases

In computer science, the term database means a set of data, homogeneous in content and format, stored in a computer and interrogated via terminal using the access keys provided. The data is "that which is immediately present to the knowledge, before any form of processing".[5]

The most similar intangible asset to the database is the software, which consists of information used by computer systems, stored on a computer medium (hardware, as a physical component of a computer system), and represented by one or more programs.

The database is incorporated in hardware (physical or more and more frequently in the cloud) and is fed and interrogated with specific software. The connection between these types of intangible assets, which are highly complementary, is important for their legal framework and economic development.

Users interface with databases through so-called query languages (search or query queries, insertion, deletion, updating, etc.) and thanks to special dedicated software applications (DBMS).

The databases may have various structures (computer architectures), including the following:

1. Hierarchical (represented by a tree);
2. Reticular (represented by a graph);

3. Relational (currently the most widespread, representable through tables and relations between them);
4. Object-oriented (extension to databases of the "object-oriented" paradigm, typical of object-oriented programming);
5. Semantic (representable with a relational graph).

In the field of database use/administration, any operation on the database by the user/administrator on DBMS can be obtained through an appropriate language through a DBMS manager with a graphical interface or a command-line interface.

The server is the part of the DBMS that provides the services of the use of the database to other programs and other computers, according to the client/server mode. The server stores data receives client requests and processes appropriate responses. Big databases exploit economies of scale and experience, minimizing ESG concerns, especially if they are linked to renewables.

7.8 LEGAL PROTECTION

The problem of creating databases populated by progressively accumulated and ordered information, together with access to it, is intertwined with copyright protection and with software, within an international framework.

According to the provisions of the European Dir. 96/9/EC, there is a double track of protection for databases: on the one hand, there is a reference to copyright, so that "databases which, because of the choice or the arrangement of the material, constitute a creation of the author's intellectual property are protected as such by copyright"; this protection under copyright "does not extend to their content and does not affect existing rights on such content".

According to Recital 15, "the criteria to be applied to determine whether a database is protected by copyright should be limited to the fact that the choice or arrangement of the content of the database constitutes an intellectual creation, which is the author's own; that this protection concerns the structure of the database" and "no criteria other than originality, in the sense of intellectual creation, should be applied to determine whether or not a database is protected by copyright, and in particular no assessment of the quality or esthetic value of the database should be made".

A very important aspect concerns the protection of privacy, especially considering databases that collect sensitive data (such as health data, bank details, etc.). In this context, they detect cybersecurity issues related to improper access or blockages of databases and the inherent liability profiles of different subjects, with civil and/or criminal profiles.

7.9   ACCOUNTING AND FISCAL ASPECTS OF THE DATABASE

The accounting aspects connected with the bookkeeping of the database in the financial statements play an important role in the economic evaluation, in the context of the estimates of damages due to counterfeiting, which may include, in a mirror-like way, the accounts of the counterfeiter and the related economic marginality (excess of revenues over costs, associated with the typical problem of the relief of fixed costs for the counterfeiter). In a broad sense, accounting records the impact on:

- Revenues, costs, and differential economic margins (EBITDA, EBIT, ...);
- Capital provisions (following the allocation of the net income in the equity);
- Operating (FCFF) or (FCFE) net cash flows (and consequently, DCF).

The accounting and tax aspects of the software have already been dealt with in Sect 7.2, to which reference should be made.

The analogic extension to the database must be carried out with caution, proceeding first to a technical and commercial framework to identify the real nature of the intangible classified as a database.

The tax aspects are relevant for any transfer price problems, within international corporate groups, when the databases are, for example, concentrated in foreign royalty companies, which charge the fees back to other companies in the group for the license related to their exploitation.

7.10   INFORMATION VALUE CHAIN, DATA MINING AND INTERACTION WITH NETWORKS, BIG DATA, AND THE INTERNET OF THINGS

The value chain relating to the information supply chain is based on a series of steps and processes (organizational, managerial, etc.), individually represented by consequential links, which can be expressed at the IT level through algorithms. Each link in the chain represents a point of connection with the previous and subsequent steps, with incremental added value taking on economic and legal significance (at the contractual level and, if necessary, in the case of litigation). What is important is the synergistic contribution of the individual links to the composition of a unitary chain. The logical-sequential steps (relevant from a legal point of view) for the databases are as follows:

1. Data collection;
2. Organization of the data;
3. Data processing;
4. Analysis of the results;
5. Archiving (storage, basically in the cloud) and indexing;
6. Usability and sharing.

Data collection is the first—fundamental—link in the value chain and takes place by attracting, often in a complementary way, to different sources, among which the following ones are collected:

- Digital platforms (for the intermediate interchange of data, transactions, etc.);
- Sensors/Internet of Things (IoT);
- (Social) networks;
- New media;
- Wireless protocols;
- Encrypted and tracked internet access.

The next steps (organization, processing, analysis, archiving, sharing) take place through increasingly automated algorithms in a sequential perspective, also through automatisms driven by artificial intelligence.

The organization of the data is based on:

– Classification;
– Coupling/correlation;
– Connectivity.

Data processing, on the other hand, is based on:

– Computational methods;
– Calculation tools.

Archiving is increasingly based on cloud storage technologies in remote archives (with delicate legal issues, such as data retention, access restrictions, real-time usability, privacy protection, etc.).

The use of the information that populates the databases is in perspective, increasingly relevant for procedures:

– Strategic planning and management;
– Descriptive, prescriptive, and predictive analyses;
– Performance monitoring;
– Functional analysis;
– Support in experimental analysis;
– Production optimization.

The progressive increase in the size of the data that populate the databases (big data) is linked to the need for analysis of a single set of data, to extract additional information compared to that which could be obtained by analyzing small series, with the same total amount of data.

In this context, databases exploit data mining, a set of techniques and methodologies that have as their object the extraction of knowledge, starting from large quantities of data (through automatic or semi-automatic methods), and the scientific, industrial, or operational use of this knowledge. Data mining is often preceded by harmonization of the same data, especially if derived from heterogeneous and unstructured sources, through data fusion processes.

Data analysis technologies are becoming part of many aspects of everyday life (sensors, biometrics, domotics, communications, ...). The

Internet of Things (IoT) interacts with databases, especially in the phase of feeding information flows. It is based on a family of innovative technologies (chips, wired and wireless sensors, tags, QR codes, radio frequency RFID identifications, etc.), which connect inanimate objects (gadgets, ...) in smart devices always connected to the web (such as mobile phones), to collect, exchange and process data in real-time.

The innovative paradigms that govern the IoT move around networks that connect sensors and actuators with the Internet.

The examination of the information value chain, subdivided into its fundamental components, is important in the legal sphere, to understand the problems of causal links, and the responsibility, from a contractual point of view or in litigation.

7.11   Economic Valuation of Database and Links with Cloud Computing

The value of a database cannot always be estimated considering it as an independent "legal asset" (in this case, the declination of software) since it is within a wider context that it finds a complete framework.

The database can, therefore, be estimated within a portfolio of intangible resources and be linked to patents or trademarks and logos (think, for example, of the value of the Bloomberg brand in the field of economic and financial information).

Cloud computing is an outsourcing delivery of computing services—including servers, storage, databases, networking, software, analytics, and intelligence—over the Internet ("the cloud") to offer faster innovation, flexible resources, and economies of scale. The user typically pays only for cloud services you use, helping lower operating costs, run infrastructure more efficiently, and scale up as business needs change (https://micros oft.com/).

Current trends show that enterprises are increasingly embracing multi-cloud solutions, rising their cloud spending (https://www.flexera.com/blog/cloud/cloud-computing-trends-2021-state-of-the-cloud-report/).

The main features of cloud computing are synthesized in Fig. 7.3.

Numerous industries are implementing cloud computing as part of their business processes. Valuation patterns may so be concerned not only with public or private cloud but also with their impact on traditional businesses.

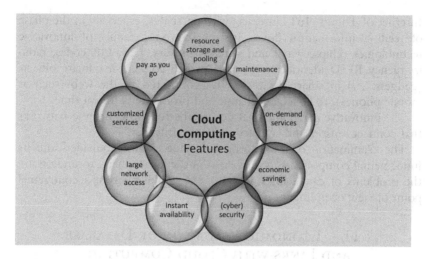

Fig. 7.3   Features of cloud computing

As-a-Service models represent a primary outsourcing option for end-users and may be synthesized in Fig. 7.4. They may also include Infrastructure as a Service (IaaS).

Cloud computing can be represented as a digital node that masters a virtual ecosystem, as shown in Fig. 7.5.

For the economic evaluation of the databases, first, the most well-known approaches of estimating the value of the intangibles used by the applicative practice can be the starting point, appropriately adapted. The approaches are those foreseen by IVS 210.

7.11.1   The Cost Approach

According to this approach, the value can be obtained by estimating the costs incurred for the realization of the software or to be incurred for its reproduction.

Still, in the context of the cost approach, the already mentioned "CO.CO.MO" approach applies. As anticipated in Chapter 2 and elsewhere, the most frequent application of the cost approach concerns the software, and, analogically, the database estimate.

The cost approach has a significant semantic value for the estimation process but does not always allow to sort out a precise correlation between

Fig. 7.4 As-a-Service models

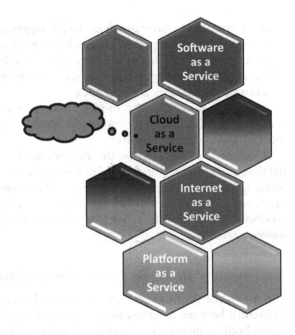

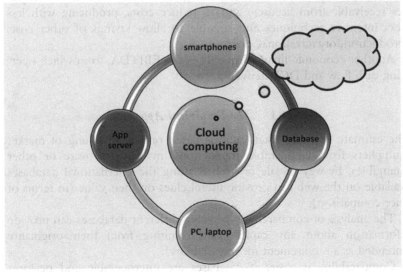

Fig. 7.5 Cloud computing ecosystem

costs incurred and potential value, which depends essentially on other variables (such as the expected marginality at an economic-financial level). The costs incurred by individual developers, insofar as they are comparable, represent a reference point for the analysis of the break-even point between operating costs and revenues.

A trended historical cost model evaluates recent software through a cost accounting system, considering historical costs of development indexed to incorporate inflation.

A variant is represented by the Putnam model (1978) that describes the time and effort required to finish a software project of a specified size, bringing to SLIM (Software Lifecycle Management). The non-linear mathematical model estimates the cost of the software combining a productivity index with a workforce build-up index to estimate the software efficiency.

7.11.2   The Income-Financial Approach

The use of the database acts on the economic margins expressed by the differential between revenues and operating costs (EBIT) in that it ideally allows both to increase revenues (with greater direct sales or with royalties receivable from licenses) and to reduce costs, producing with less labor-intensive techniques and suitable to allow savings of other costs (production, organizational, energy, …).

Another economic-financial margin is the EBITDA, from which operating cash flow and DCF derive.

7.11.3   The Empirical Approach

The estimate of the market value is based on the screening of market multipliers from comparable transactions involving software or other intangibles, by way of sale or license, using the international databases available on the web can provide useful clues on their value (in terms of price comparison).

The analysis of comparability between different databases can provide information about any capital gain resulting from their originality (intended as a requirement for patentability).

Comparability is easier if databases are interoperable and perform similar tasks.

7.11.4   New Assessment Scenarios and Monetization Strategies

In addition to the traditional approaches highlighted above, there are peculiarities, typical of databases, which affect their use, with consequences on the evaluation. This refers, for example, to ways of co-creating value between database owners and users, when the latter do not just draw on information sources, helping to feed the databases with feedback, information, data sharing, etc.

Value co-creation does not always go hand in hand with its sharing, due to the presence of asymmetries in the database business model, which often does not appropriately reward users for their function as data providers. Privacy issues related to the use of personal data are very delicate, and the individuals directly concerned are not always fully aware of this issue (see the example of social networks that steal personal data even without the users' knowledge).

An element that can increase the value of databases relates to their interoperability, which allows different databases to communicate with each other, implementing a sharing of digital information, appropriately harmonized. In this context, they detect data fusion procedures, typical of the value chain that rotates around big data.

Databases are increasingly used as a source of information for economic and financial planning (business planning) and in this context, information data become a real asset (an intangible asset with its intrinsic value), which can be the subject of a sale, license, or sharing, showing economic exploitation that can be used in comparable transactions.

The strategies of monetization of the databases can be declined in the following cases:

1. Use of data for internal purposes, maintaining ownership and exclusive use;
2. Use to facilitate entry into new businesses, through product differentiation;
3. Exclusive or shared licenses to third parties, with subscriptions or pay-per-use services over multi-year time frames;
4. Interchange and sharing of data (also with commercial partners);
5. Sale of premium products associated with the exclusive use of data (data vending; through digital platforms);
6. Free provision of data (with advertising or other income);
7. Selective use of data for vertical advertising purposes (profiled advertising).

NOTES

1. See Chapter 4.
2. See Chapter 3.
3. https://people.debian.org/~bap/dfsg-faq.html.
4. https://searchcloudcomputing.techtarget.com/definition/Software-as-a-Service.
5. EU General Data Protection Regulation.

SELECTED REFERENCES

Amran, M. (2005, Spring). The challenges of valuing patents and early-stage technologies. *Journal of Applied Corporate Finance, 17*(2), 68–81.

Azura, Z. N., Suhaimi, I., & Mohd, N. M. (2015). *A survey of value-based factors in software development*. American Scientific Publishers, Ingenta Connect.

Ben-Menachem, M. (2007, Fall). Accounting software assets: A valuation model for software. *Journal of Information Systems, 21*(2), 117–132.

Bernaroch, M., & Appari, A. (2010). Financial pricing of software development risk factors. *IEEE Software, 27*(5). IEEE Computer Society.

Boehm, B., & Valerdi, R. (2008). Achievements and challenges in COCO-MObased software resource estimation. *IEEE Software, 25*(5). IEEE Computer Society.

Boehm, B., Valerdi, R., Lane, J. A., & Winsor Brown, A. (2005, April 20). COCOMO suite methodology and evolution. *The Journal of Defense Software Engineering, 18*(4).

Brown, W., & Boehm, B. (2010). Software cost estimation in the incremental commitment model. *Systems Research Forum, 4*(1), 45–55.

Contractor, F. J. (2001). *Valuation of intangible assets in global operations*. British Library Cataloguing, Permanent Paper Standard issued by the National Information Standards Organization.

Cusumano, M. A. (2008). The changing software business: Moving from products to services. *Computer, 41*(1), 20.

Degenne, A., & Forsè, M. (2006). *Introducing social networks*. London: Sage.

De Groot, J., Nugroho, A., Back, T., & Visser, J. (2012). What is the value of your software? In *MDT'12 Proceedings of the Third International Workshop on Managing Technical Debt* (pp. 37–44). Leiden, The Netherlands: LIACS Leiden University.

Denne, M., & Cleland-Huang, J. (2004). *Software by numbers*. Upper Saddle River, NJ: Prentice Hall.

Dhillon, S., & Mahmoud, Q. H. (2015). An evaluation framework for crossplatform mobile application development tools. *Software: Practice and Experience, 45*(10), 1331–1357.

Du, W. L., Capretz, L. F., Nassif, A. B., & Ho, D. (2013). A hybrid intelligent model for software cost estimation. *Journal of Computer Science, 9,* 1506–1513.

Erdogmus, H., Favaro, J., & Halling, M. (2008). Valuation of software initiatives under uncertainty: Concepts, issues, and techniques. In *Value-based software engineering* (pp. 39–66). Heidelberg: Springer.

Garcia, J., & De Magdaleno, M. I. A. (2013). *Valuation of open-source software: How do you put a value on free?* (Vol. 3, No. 1). Revista de Gestao, Financas e Contabilidade.

Guo, Z., & Ma, D. (2018). A model of competition between perpetual software and software as a service. *MIS Quarterly, 42*(1), 101–120.

Head, S. J., & Nelson, J. B. (2012). *Data rights valuation in software acquisitions.* Alexandria, VA: Center for Naval Analyses.

Jiang, B., Chan, P., & Mukhopadhyay, T. (2007) *Software licensing: Pay-per-use versus perpetual.* SSRN.

Kalaiselvi, S. (2009). *Financial performance in software industry.* New Delhi, India: Discovery Publishing House Pvt Ltd. Vellalar College for Women.

King, K. (2007, January). A case study in the valuation of a database. *Journal of Database Marketing & Customer Strategy Management, 14*(2), 110–119.

Puntambekar, A. A. (2009). *Software engineering.* Pune, India: Technical Publications.

Putnam, L. H. (1978). A general empirical solution to the Macro software sizing and estimating problem. *IEEE Transactions on Software Engineering, SE-4*(4), 345–361.

Ramzan, M., Anwar, S., & Shahid, A. A. (2009). Need to redefine "value" and case for a new "software valuation" technique: An analytical study. In *Proceedings of International Conference on Computer Engineering and Applications.*

Reilly, R. F., & Scwihs, R. P. (2014). *Guide to intangibles asset valuation.* New York, NY: AICPA American Institute of Certified Public Accountants Inc.

Safari, F., Safari, N., & Hasanzadeh, A. (2015). The adoption of software as a service (SaaS): Ranking the determinants. *Journal of Enterprise Information Management, 28*(3), 400–422.

Saunders, A., & Brynjolfsson, E. (2015). Valuing IT—Related intangible assets. *MIS Quarterly, 40*(1), 83–110.

Tansey, B., & Stroulia, E. (2007). *Valuating software service development: Integrating COCOMO II and real options theory.* Paper presented at 2008 1st International Workshop on the Economics of Software and Computation. IEEE Xplore.

Thurman, C. J. (2018). *Application of the cost approach to value internally developed computer software*. Available at http://www.willamette.com/insights_jou rnal/18/summer_2018_4.pdf.

Tockey, S. (2014) Aspects of software valuation. In *Economics-driven software architecture*. Science Direct.

Ullrich, C. (2013). Valuation of IT investments using real options theory. *Business & Information Systems Engineering*, 5(5), 331–341.

CHAPTER 8

The Valuation of Artificial Intelligence

8.1 Introduction

Artificial intelligence (Anzai, 2012; Ertel, 2018; Li and Du, 2017; Mariusz, 2016; Müller and Bostrom, 2016; Nilsson, 1980; Parag and Prachi, 2015; Pedersen, 2016; Short and Adams, 2017; Skansi, 2018; Stein, 2020; Stuart and Norvig, 2016) is a broad and varied concept, based on processes and reasoning of thought and behavioral dynamics, faithful to human performances and tending toward rationality. Russell and Norvig (2016) recall complementary definitions, according to which artificial intelligence consists in designing computers and machines that think and act as human beings (even though limited to specific predefined applications, such as decision making, problem-solving, and learning). Artificial intelligence consists, therefore in the study of mental faculties through computational models making possible actions such as learning, reasoning, and action, to design intelligent agents. These agents must be able to act humanely and to this end must be able to communicate with human beings through processes defined by the Turing test:

a. Natural language processing (NLP), for language communication;
b. Representation of knowledge to store it;
c. Automatic reasoning to use stored knowledge to answer questions and draw new conclusions;

d. Dynamic learning (machine learning) to adapt to new circumstances or to extrapolate new paths;
e. Computer vision to perceive objects; and
f. Robotics to manipulate objects and move around.

To pass the Turing test (a method of inquiry for determining whether or not a computer is capable of thinking like a human being), the computer needs a computer vision to frame the objects and robotic capabilities to manipulate and move them.

One of the biggest criticalities of artificial intelligence concerns its flexibility and resilience: differently from the plasticity inherent in human intelligence, artificial intelligence cannot easily reinvent new strategies or patterns with collateral thinking, etc. Cooperation with other devices and humans can also be limited. Another issue is represented by empathy: artificial intelligence is hardly able to "cook the ingredients of emotions", incorporating them in an algorithm, or establish social ties. When computers can read emotions by analyzing data, including facial expressions, gestures, tone of voice, force of keystrokes, and more to determine a person's emotional state and then react to it, we call this artificial emotional intelligence. This ability will allow humans and machines to interact in a much more natural way and is very similar to how human-to-human interaction works.

Harari (2015) writes about the "cognitive revolution" occurring roughly 70,000 years ago when Homo sapiens supplanted the rival Neanderthals and other species of the genus Homo, developed language skills, and structured societies. His books also examine the possible consequences of a futuristic biotechnological world in which intelligent biological organisms are surpassed by their own creations. This can be represented, for instance, by artificial intelligence. According to Harari, we will soon have the power to re-engineer our bodies and brains, whether it is with genetic engineering or by directly connecting brains to computers, or by creating completely non-organic entities, artificial intelligence which is not based at all on the organic body and the organic brain. And these technologies are developing at break-neck speed.

A still largely unanswered question concerns self-learning (a key feature of artificial intelligence) and its capacity to improve flexibility or to increase the scope. Artificial intelligence is a basic component of the digitalization process. Artificial intelligence raises growing freedom concerns, as it is increasingly used by illiberal regimes to control citizens, limiting their liberty.

8.2   THE FUNDAMENTALS OF ARTIFICIAL INTELLIGENCE

Artificial intelligence is a discipline that over the years has made an important contribution to the progress of whole computer science. It has been influenced by numerous disciplines including philosophy, neurology, mathematics, psychology, cybernetics, and cognitive sciences.

Artificial intelligence is not to be considered a single intangible asset, but rather a product and process innovation, intersecting with typical intangible assets such as software, patents and know-how, other intangible internet-driven (M-App, etc.), and input data derived from big data or sensors IoT.

The pervasiveness of artificial intelligence and its applicability to wider solutions and business models represents a strong element of innovation, which can operate within a portfolio of intangible resources, enhancing their characteristics and potential.

Artificial intelligence studies the theoretical foundations, methodologies, and techniques which allow the design of hardware systems and software program systems capable of providing the computer with performances that, to an ordinary observer, would seem to be the exclusive competence of natural (human) intelligence.

The purpose of artificial intelligence is not to replicate this intelligence, an objective which for some is even inadmissible, but rather to reproduce or emulate certain functions of it. There is no reason why certain (but not all) performances of human intelligence—for example, the ability to solve problems through inferential processes—should not be provided by a machine. In the case of emulation, intelligent performance is achieved by using the machine's mechanisms, to provide performance that is qualitatively equivalent and quantitatively superior to human performance.

One of the fundamental contributions that artificial intelligence has given to computer science has been to have placed the accent on the notion of the problem, positioning it side by side with those of algorithms and data, studying and highlighting the various modalities for its modeling.

Augmented reality begins to become nowadays public knowledge thanks to the introduction of Google Glass which, through a small display positioned above the eye, fills the field of view with data and information on the surrounding environment of the wearer. However, even before conquering the entire mobile sector (smartphones, laptops, tablets, glasses, and viewers combined with special software or applications), it took its first steps in much more technical and specific areas, such as military, scientific research, and medicine.

The first examples of augmented reality, not by chance, have been introduced in the field of military aeronautics in the form of head-up displays (HUD). This technology was later adopted by civil aviation. Both Augmented and Virtual Reality represent a cornerstone of the metaverse.

8.3   APPLICATIONS AND BUSINESS MODELS

Artificial Intelligence firms can be divided into:

1. Infrastructure: firms that run in the back office and provide computational services to others.
2. Application: Firms active in the B2B and B2C segments. In the B2B space, they may offer SaaS-based subscription services. These companies generally develop applications for specific use-cases defined by their clients.

Table 8.1 shows some examples of the application of artificial intelligence in the field of business solutions. The applications of artificial intelligence systems are innumerable, and their complete cataloging is very difficult because of the quantity and heterogeneity of the sectors involved, and due to constant evolution.

An important aspect of artificial intelligence is represented by the ability to formulate forecasts, which play a fundamental role in decision-making. A reduction in the cost of forecasts impacts the increase in the value of the data. Better accuracy reduces risk (the denominator of the DCF formulation), improving value.

Artificial intelligence relates to big data usually stored in the cloud that provides essential real-time input data, which is then processed through algorithms for different purposes.

Figure 8.1 shows the links between artificial intelligence and its main business models.

Table 8.1 Examples of the application of artificial intelligence in the field of business solutions

Technology	Definition	Example of solution
Computer vision—Image recognition	Acquisition, processing, analysis, and understanding of images and objects	Video analysis integrated with cameras for video surveillance systems. Analysis of consumer behavior in shops. Scan and diagnosis of X-rays. Photo tagging of friends
Audio processing	Identification, recognition, and analysis of sounds and languages	Integrated language recognition in call centers
Sensor processing	Processing and analysis of information from camera sensors and microphones	In the agricultural sector, sensors in the fields can be integrated with software that can communicate information about temperature, humidity, etc
Natural language processing	Understanding and formulation of spoken and written languages	Personal assistants on mobile devices
Knowledge representation	Representation and communication of knowledge to facilitate forecasting and decision-making	Knowledge-based tools that correlate content with related topics across the web
Inference engines	Identification of answers from basic knowledge such as business rules	Automatic approval for financing concessions; issuing of visas; decisions on credits
Expert systems	Emulation of human problem-solving and decision-making skills by reasoning with the information available in the basic knowledge	Medical diagnostics and legal research can be improved through the ability of an expert system to use millions of pieces of data, summarizing the information to be presented to the user
Augmented reality—3D applications	Enrichment of human sensory perception with additional data in digital format	Head-up display (HUD): Overlay display for pilots
Machine learning	Changing the decision-making process based on experience	Software tools and personal assistants can learn from users (email classification, calendar updates, etc.) to increase productivity

(continued)

Table 8.1 (continued)

Technology	Definition	Example of solution
Web search engines	A web search engine or Internet search engine is a software system that is designed to carry out web searches (Internet search)	The system learns how to rank pages through a complex learning algorithm
Email spam detector	Email spam, also known as junk email, is unsolicited messages sent in bulk by email. There are different approaches to spam detection. These approaches include blacklisting, detecting bulk emails, scanning message headings, gray-listing, and content-based filtering	The machine learning system operates by classifying the mails and moving the unwanted emails to a spam folder. This is again achieved by a spam classifier running in the back-end of a mail application
Virtual personal assistant	Intelligent digital personal assistants on the platforms. they help to find relevant information when requested using voice. Artificial Intelligence is critical in these applications, as they gather data on the user's request and utilize that data to perceive speech in a better manner and serve the user with answers that are customized to his inclination	Virtual assistants can provide a wide variety of services: * Provide information such as weather, facts set the alarm, make to-do lists, and shopping lists * Play music from streaming services; * Read audiobooks; * Play videos, TV shows, or movies on televisions, * Conversational commerce; and * Complement and/or replace customer service with humans
Robotic vehicles	Proposing driverless solutions	Self-driving cars where artificial intelligence improves driving patterns

8.4 Legal Aspects: Introductory Notes

The radical changes brought in by artificial intelligence and machine learning inevitably impact regulatory and social practices. One of the most complicated aspects concerns the legal personality of intelligent

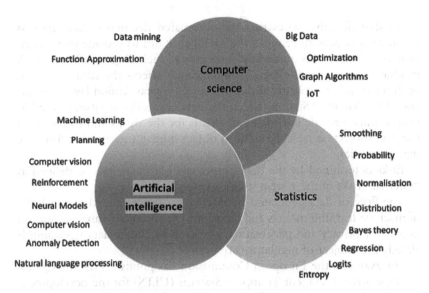

Fig. 8.1 Artificial intelligence and business models

systems. Specifically, the risks associated with the development of artificial intelligence methodologies and technologies include "cause-driven" and "data-driven" risks.

Risks "determined by causality" refer to how questions relating to the attribution of human responsibility are decided. Risk is based on the attribution of the factual consequences of a subjective condition, fault or malice, to a human being, identified through the application of the principle of causality.

The limit of natural causality to phenomena related to algorithmic decision-making processes of machine learning lies in the fact that the decisions that the machine adopts or the acts it performs can become increasingly distant from any logic implemented by the human being in the software code.

A useful normative reference, in addition to the provisions of the General Regulation on the subject of protection of personal data (GDPR), in the EU Directive 680 of 27 April 2016, on the subject of protection of natural persons concerning the processing of personal data by the competent authorities for prevention, investigation, detection, and prosecution of crimes or execution of criminal sanctions. In particular, Article

11 of that directive states that the automated decision-making process about natural persons requires the Member States to provide that a decision based solely on automated processing, including profiling, which produces adverse legal effects or significantly affects the data subject, is prohibited unless explicitly authorized by European Union law or by the law of the Member State to which the data controller is subject. In addition, it must provide adequate safeguards for the rights and freedoms of the data subject, at least the right to obtain human intervention from the data controller.

Risks determined by the data—especially big data—can be defined as "internal" risks of the system itself.

The flow of data generated by intelligent devices and the availability of machine learning models and algorithms for predictive analysis are risk factors for privacy and personal data protection. Smart data streaming is already the subject of regulatory attention.

For example, the European Commission has published its Strategy on Co-Operative Intelligent Transport Systems (CITS) for the development of an intelligent transport infrastructure that allows vehicles to communicate with each other and with a centralized traffic management system, as well as with other transport systems agents. The potential risk of misuse of data is evident, as the intelligent infrastructure can identify each vehicle in real-time along its route, know its destination, and report the driver's behavior and any possible infringement of traffic rules.

If a self-driving car led by artificial intelligence applications causes an accident, who is responsible? Legal solutions to questions like this are a prerequisite for the large-scale implementation of artificial intelligence.

8.5   Valuation Metrics

The valuation of artificial intelligence must consider that:

a. Standard firms, based on traditional business models, use some artificial intelligence tools to expand their business or improve efficiency targets;
b. Born-digital firms are built around artificial intelligence and other related intangibles.

These two typologies of firm interact, sharing an evolving marketplace where innovative companies propose new solutions often as an unconventional answers to well-known problems. Traditional firms, on their side, provide unmet demand, market potential, and hints for customer upgrades.

A valuation metric for traditional firms may consider the "with or without" methodology illustrated in Chap. 2, showing the incremental EBITDA given by artificial intelligence (in the form of higher revenues deriving from new market opportunities and lower monetary OPEX consequential to efficiency gains).

Figure 8.2 shows the link between the main artificial intelligence business models and the valuation approaches.

The assessment metrics of the business models connected to the artificial intelligence must first consider their nature: such models can be the basis of entrepreneurial realities for which the artificial intelligence constitutes the primary mission (prevailing social object) or a mere accessory activity.

In the first case, the objective is to estimate the overall value of companies that are mainly focused on artificial intelligence, while in the second case, the estimate is limited to identifying, where possible, the differential (incremental) value made possible by traditional business models by the introduction of artificial intelligence, to stimulate product or, more frequently, process innovation.

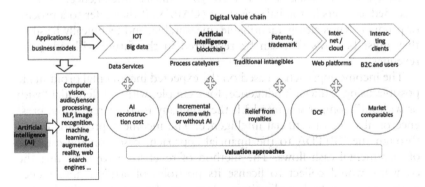

Fig. 8.2 Application of artificial intelligence, digital value chains, and valuation approaches

The incremental economic and financial marginality induced by artificial intelligence directly influences the evaluation parameters and must consider the possibility that these parameters can be subject to (digital) scalability, with a multiplying impact on the evaluation. First, it is possible to refer to the economies of scale and experience (linked to learning curves that are inherent to artificial intelligence) that allow cost savings and increases in revenues, thus expanding the economic marginality and with it, the cash flows produced (EBITDA impacts on operating cash flows and on DCF metrics).

Scalability[1] is typical of unrivaled intangible assets (i.e., assets that can be used simultaneously by several parties) and allows operating revenues to be increased while minimizing variable extra costs, thus giving the business model plasticity that enhances its key value drivers.

The use of traditional methods of valuation of intangible assets (cost, income, or market approach, following IVS 210 prescriptions) can be adapted, especially when the valuation of artificial intelligence is part of a synergistic portfolio of intangible assets. They may be linked, for example, to big data or IoT sensors as input data, to databases in the archiving phase, to the software and development algorithms, etc. Software is the one that has the greatest affinity with artificial intelligence, which in many ways represents an advanced declination of it. In the use of the reconstruction or replacement cost approach, the accounting aspects ease the search for clues on the costs sustained for investments in artificial intelligence.

Development costs, also related to artificial intelligence, can be recorded as assets in the balance sheet (CAPEX) if they refer to a process or product that is clearly identifiable, measurable, and technically feasible; they must be costs that can be recovered in the future with adequate revenues.

The income approach is based on the expected incremental profit made possible using artificial intelligence, for example, with a differential "with or without" comparison in which the company is compared in the presence or absence of artificial intelligence. The income approach is linked through the EBITDA to the financial approach, based on the estimate of incremental cash flows. The method of relief from royalties that the company would collect to license its portfolio of artificial intelligence applications can find applications, always in the sphere of the income approaches.

Both for the companies that base their mission on artificial intelligence and for the others that use it as a complement to more traditional business models, it is considered appropriate to use a valuation methodology that converges on these two approaches:

a. Thediscounted cash flow (DCF); and
b. Themarket method of the EBITDA multipliers.

Both approaches lead to the estimation of the enterprise value, intended as the total market value of a company (shareholders' equity and debt).

To estimate the equity value only, the evaluator must subtract the (typically negative) net financial position from the enterprise value, meaning the algebraic sum of financial receivables, cash and cash equivalents, and financial payables.

Business models introducing artificial intelligence have a positive impact on incremental revenues or a reduction in costs, with a consequent improvement in economic and financial marginality, showing greater efficiency.

Always from an incremental point of view, the impact on economic marginality can be examined through the so-called with or without technique, which compares situations in which artificial intelligence has been introduced, concerning pre-existing scenarios.

Excess returns are related to the applicability of real options (of expansion or development), linked to the concept of augmented reality. Artificial intelligence increases the scope of existing technologies and opens new markets.

The real options are connected to the use of big data giving real-time information on the underlying reality, allowing precisely to exercise strategic options (development, expansion, temporary suspension, abandonment, deferral, etc.). The valuation approach based on the combined use of real options and big data is bottom-up in that it uses empirical evidence of the underlying reality to reformulate and update (in real-time, thanks to big data) the business plans to which the valuation parameters are linked.

In the evaluation, the distinction between companies providing artificial intelligence services as their core business is compared to companies (much more numerous) that just use single applications to integrate their strategies. Only in the first case, the surplus value of the artificial intelligence constitutes the principal asset of the enterprise, while in the second case, the autonomous identification of the artificial intelligence applications is more complex and can follow the "with or without" differential methodologies.

In this context, artificial intelligence interacts with big data (as cited above) and impacts information asymmetries, which affect corporate governance and bankability issues (also in terms of rating).

8.6   The Financial Method

The financial method is based on the principle that the market value of a company is equal to the discounted value of the cash flows that it will be able to generate.

Operating cash flows (unlevered – FCFF) and net cash flows for shareholders (levered – FCFE) are determined by comparing the last two balance sheets (to make changes in operating net working capital, fixed assets, financial liabilities, employee severance indemnities, and shareholders' equity available) with the income statement for the last year.

The cash flows to be used can be the operating cash flow (FCFF) or the net cash flow for the shareholders (FCFE). Cash flows from operating activities (FCFF) are discounted to present value at the weighted average cost of capital (WACC). This flow configuration offers an evaluation of the whole company, independent of its financial structure.

Net cash flows (FCFE) are discounted to present value at the cost of equity (K_e).

Once the present value of the cash flows has been determined, the calculation of the economic value (W) may correspond:

a. to the unlevered cash flow (FCFF) method:

$$W = \sum \frac{CF_0}{WACC} + VR - NFP \qquad (8.1)$$

b. to the levered (FCFE) cash flow method:

$$W = \sum \frac{CF_n}{K_e} + TV \qquad (8.2)$$

where:

- $\sum CF_0 / WACC$ = present value of operating (debt-free) cash flows (FCFF);

- $\sum CF_n / K_e$ = present value of net cash flows (FCFE);
- TV = terminal value; and
- NFP = net financial position (cash + financial receivables – financial payables).

The residual value, if subject to appreciation, is the result of discounting the value attributed to the capital of the company operating at the time n (before which the cash flows were estimated analytically). IT is often a significant component of the overall value W and tends to zero if the time horizon of capitalization is infinite (VR/$\infty \to 0$).

The terminal value (TV) corresponds to:

$$TV = [F_m/(i - g)] * (1 + i)^{-(n+1)} \qquad (8.3)$$

where:

- F_m = the average flow that the company expects to obtain in the explicit planning period (the flow relative to the last year of the explicit forecast is often used);
- i = the discount rate of the flows;
- g = expected growth rate in the period following the explicit planning period; and
- n = number of years of explicit planning.

If the evaluator opts for a perpetual capitalization horizon, the terminal value formula corresponds to:

$$TV = [F_m * (1 + g)]/(i-g) \qquad (8.4)$$

8.7 THE EMPIRICAL METHOD OF MARKET MULTIPLES

In addition to the analytical approaches described above, synthetic approaches, based on indicators and market multiples, allow the estimate of the value based on the observation of specific parameters, found in similar companies listed on regulated markets. These parameters are taken as reference for the entire sector to which they belong, which considers the peculiarities of artificial intelligence and the comparability of the business models of the companies that adopt it.

Comparability profiles can be hampered by increasingly unique business models, even if the growing spread of databases accelerates and stimulates the digital dissemination of information, allowing for increasingly sophisticated and capillary databases.

Among the empirical criteria, the approach of the multiplier of the EBITDA is widely diffused, to which the net financial position must be added algebraically, to pass from the estimate of the enterprise value (total value of the company) to that of the equity value (value of the net assets), according to the following formula:

$$W = p * m \pm \text{NFP} \qquad (8.5)$$

where:

- W = market value;
- p = income parameter;
- m = multiplier; and
- NFP = net financial position.

Valuations based on the application of multiples derived from stock market prices require the identification of a sample of comparable firms. EBITDA, expressed as the difference between operating revenues (sales revenues, changes in inventories of finished products, and other operating revenues) and operating costs gross of amortization/depreciation and provisions, is often used as the basic parameter of (monetary) operating profitability.

In the market negotiations of companies operating in the services sector, reference is increasingly made to the company's ability to generate operational profitability in its typical business; this applies to companies competing in growing or highly competitive markets.

The functional link between the financial approach and the multiples approach is provided, once again, by the EBITDA, which is the basis of both the operating cash flow and the application of market multipliers.

8.8 FORECASTING RATIONAL EXPECTED OUTCOMES: SALES PREDICTION

In artificial intelligence, economics, game theory, or decision theory, a rational agent (software, person, machine, firm, etc.) has clear-cut preferences, models uncertainty through expected values of variables, and always chooses to act with the optimal expected outcome.

The rational agent acts with the best outcome after considering past and current input data.

The rational agent is a theoretical entity based on a realistic evolutionary model, and prefers advantageous outcomes that maximize its performance targets, and will seek to achieve them in a (machine) learning scenario.

Intelligent agents interact with the environment through sensors and actuators.

The relationship between artificial intelligence and standard valuation approaches is two-sided: whereas artificial intelligence follows the same valuation criteria that concern standard firms and their intangibles, the basic features of artificial intelligence can help to improve forecasts—one of the critical points of any appraisal. Forecasts may concern episodic or sequential task environments in a static or dynamic environment whose evolution can be deterministic or stochastic (following probabilistic patterns that artificial intelligence can model and autonomously refine).

Artificial intelligence can so nurture future patterns that follow rational outcomes with autonomous learning; milestones and occurrences can be detected in real-time and automatically included in a self-learning software that continuously improves. The tendency is to embed artificial intelligence in valuation methodologies.

AI-driven sales prediction, with its temporal granularity, is a key part of the planning process, as the revenue model is the basis for the forecast of cash flows. Tsoumakas (2019) shows that food sales prediction is concerned with estimating future sales of companies in the food industry. Accurate short-term sales prediction allows companies to minimize stocked and expired products inside stores and at the same time avoid missing sales.

AI is so fully consistent with the research scope of this chapter since it impacts predictive analytics. AI can ideally automize the value creation process, making it self-fulfilling and automatically increasing its potential with self-learning patterns that boost scalability and real options. The reality is, however, harder than these ideal targets, and AI setup needs careful tailor-made configuration, still characterized by limited applications. Digitalization is a prerequisite for the usability of (preferably, numerical) big data.

AI fosters data analytics that impacts cash flow forecasting, as shown in Table 8.2 which represents just an example of the possible AI applications.

Table 8.2   Impact of data analytics on cash flow forecasting

Artificial Intelligence-Driven Data Analytics	*Discounted Cash Flow Forecasting*
Artificial Intelligence can improve the following processes, and in particular predictive analytics	Cash flow forecasts are nurtured by data analysis, a process of inspecting, cleansing, transforming, and modeling data to discover useful information, informing conclusions, and supporting decision-making
• Descriptive Analytics illustrates what happened in the past and is widely used in traditional business planning	
• Diagnostic Analytics helps to understand why something happened in the past	
• Predictive Analytics uses data mining to predict what is most likely to happen in the future	
• Prescriptive Analytics recommends actions to affect those outcomes	
Customer analytics	Client profiling eases cash flow forecasting, responses to unexpected positive or negative events (incorporating real options), experience sharing to foster value co-creation, and viral networking through social media. Customer analytics mainly impacts revenues, easing their prediction and leveraging the scalability of the business model that becomes more reactive and timelier
• Client profiling	
• Client experience / feedbacks	
• Market segmentation	
• Social Network analysis	
• Brand awareness	
• Marketing mix optimization	

(continued)

Table 8.2 (continued)

Artificial Intelligence-Driven Data Analytics	Discounted Cash Flow Forecasting
Supply Chain analytics • Demand forecasting • Optimization of inventory • Pricing • Scheduling • Transportation and Storage • Human capital/Workforce analytics	Optimization of the supply chain improves demand forecasting and stock turnover, providing useful insights for reactive pricing Operating costs can be reduced, improving the efficiency and efficacy of used resources, and so productivity. Lower Operating expenditure (OPEX) increases the EBITDA, and optimizes Net Working Capital Management, with a positive impact on the Operating Cash Flows
Risk analytics • Market risk • Operational risk • Credit scoring • Macroeconomic risk (interest rates, currency rates, country, and political risk, inflation, GDP forecasts, etc.)	Improved forecasting of future events reduces risk, incorporated in the denominator of DCF metrics

NOTE

1. See Chap. 3.

SELECTED REFERENCES

Anzai, Y. (2012). *Pattern recognition and machine learning*. Amsterdam: Elsevier.

Ertel, W. (2018). *Introduction to artificial intelligence*. London: Springer.

Harari, Y. N. (2015). *Sapiens: A brief history of humankind*. Vintage Publishing.

Li, D., & Du, Y. (2017). *Artificial intelligence with uncertainty*. London: CRC Press.

Mariusz, F. (2016). *Introduction to artificial intelligence*. Cham: Springer.

Müller, V. C., & Bostrom, N. (2016). Future progress in artificial intelligence: A survey of expert opinion. In V. Müller (Ed.), *Fundamental issues of artificial intelligence*. Synthese Library (Studies in epistemology, logic, methodology, and philosophy of science, Vol. 376). Cham: Springer.

Nilsson, N. J. (1980). *Principles of artificial intelligence*. San Francisco: Morgan Kaufmann Publishers, Inc.

Parag, K., & Prachi, J. (2015). *Artificial intelligence: Building intelligent systems.* Delhi: PHI Learning.

Pedersen, M. (2016). *Artificial intelligence for long-term investing.* SSRN. https://ssrn.com/abstract=2740218 or https://doi.org/10.2139/ssrn.274 0218

Russel, S., & Norvig, P. (2016). *Artificial intelligence: A modern approach.* Pearson: Upper Saddle River.

Short, T., & Adams, T. (2017). *Procedural generation in game design.* New York: CRC Press.

Skansi, S. (2018). *Introduction to deep learning: From logical calculus to artificial intelligence.* Cham: Springer.

Stein, S. S. (2020). *Blockchain, artificial intelligence and financial services.* Future of Business and Finance. Cham: Springer.

Stuart, R., & Norvig, P. (2016). *Artificial intelligence: A modern approach (Global edition).* Harlow: Pearson.

Tsoumakas, G. (2019). A survey of machine learning techniques for food sales prediction. *Artificial Intelligence Review, 52,* 441–447.

PART III

Marketing

CHAPTER 9

The Valuation of Trademarks and Digital Branding

9.1 THE TRADEMARK'S DIFFERENTIAL STRATEGIC VALUE

The trademark,[1] in law terms, indicates any sign susceptible to be graphically represented, specifically words (including the name of a person), drawings, letters, numbers, sounds, the shape of a product or its packaging, combinations or color tones, as long as it is suitable to distinguish the goods or the services of a company from those of others.

According to OECD (2017):

- *"a trademark is a unique name, symbol, logo or picture that the owner may use to distinguish its products and services from those of other entities. Proprietary rights in trademarks are confirmed through a registration system. The registered owner of a trademark may exclude others from using the trademark in a manner that would create confusion in the marketplace. A trademark registration may continue indefinitely if the trademark is continuously used and the registration appropriately renewed. Trademarks may be established for goods or services and may apply to a single product or service, or a line of products or services. Trademarks are perhaps most familiar at the consumer market level, but they are likely to be encountered at all market levels"* (par. 6.21);

© The Author(s), under exclusive license to Springer Nature Switzerland AG 2022
R. Moro-Visconti, *The Valuation of Digital Intangibles*,
https://doi.org/10.1007/978-3-031-09237-4_9

- *"A trade name (often but not always the name of an enterprise) may have the same force of market penetration as a trademark and may indeed be registered in some specific form as a trademark"* (par. 6.22);
- *"The term "brand" is sometimes used interchangeably with the terms "trademark" and "trade name." In other contexts, a brand is thought of as a trademark or trade name imbued with social and commercial significance. A brand may, in fact, represent a combination of intangibles and/or other items, including among others, trademarks, trade names, customer relationships, reputational characteristics, and goodwill. It may sometimes be difficult or impossible to segregate or separately transfer the various items contributing to brand value. A brand may consist of a single intangible, or a collection of intangibles"* (par. 6.23).

Trademarks are the core component of marketing intangibles. According to OECD (Glossary), a marketing intangible "relates to marketing activities, aids in the commercial exploitation of a product or service and/or has an important promotional value for the product concerned. Depending on the context, marketing intangibles may include, for example, trademarks, trade names, customer lists, customer relationships, and proprietary market and customer data that is used or aids in marketing and selling goods or services to customers".

A trademark is typically registered.

Most countries offer some form of trademark protection whose registration is stored in the national or regional Trademark Register. The World Intellectual Property administers two treaties that comply with the System of International Registration of Marks: the Madrid Agreement concerning the International Registration of Marks and the Madrid Protocol.[2] Citizens who live in a country that adhered to either or both the agreements, belong to the Madrid Union and are therefore allowed to register with the trademark office of a single country and simultaneously receive international protection in as many other Madrid Union countries the applicant prefers (as of April 2014, 91 countries were members of the Union).

There are different types of trademarks. Concerning the breadth of the product portfolio to which they refer, trademarks are:

- Mono-brand: adopted for one or a few products, and therefore evoking specific functional characteristics of the product to which it relates;
- Family-brand: referring to many products, they recall non-specific features (given that they differ for every product of the "family"), such as emotional situations or abstract values. Then there are the umbrella brands, in which the leading brand is associated with the specific product (e.g., Alfa Romeo—Giulietta).

According to the distance from the corporate identity, we can identify a:

- Corporate brand: adopted both for the products and for recalling the image of the company and its distinctive competencies (usually the company brand itself);
- Furtive brand: distant from the corporate identity, traceable only to specific products.

There are hybrid forms:

- Brand endorsed: incorporates two brands that belong to two different typologies among those mentioned above.
- Individual brand: different brands for each product.

The "de facto" trademark (brand) differs from the registered trademark:

- the latter enjoys reinforced protection for its certain date due to the registration process at the Patents and Trademarks Office;
- the former must prove both its reputation and its extensive pre-use.

The registration lasts ten years starting from the date of filing of the application, except in the case of renunciation of the holder, and at the expiry date, it can be renewed each time for a further ten years. In practice, in the valuation, it is assumed that trademarks never expire.

The trademark is closely related to the domain names.[3]

The economic valuation of the brands is widely applied in cases of contractual/out-of-court circumstances, typically concerning hypotheses of counterfeiting or even for fiscal matters (primarily for transfer pricing issues).

The economic valuation is used in the event of:

- Quantification of the actual economic damage in counterfeit trademark actions or acts of unfair competition (servile imitation, dumping, misleading advertising, denigration, boycotting, parasitic competition, etc.);
- The estimate of the appropriate royalty rates to be negotiated in the licensing agreements (brand licensing) or franchising or other brand extension methods;
- Determination of the appropriate rent of the company that owns the brand;
- Impairment test (in the financial statements valuation, applying the international accounting principles);
- Conferment of a trademark (with or without a company);
- Merger or demerger exchange in the presence of trademarks;
- Brand managers, directors, and sales agent's performance evaluation, for rewards and bonuses;
- Liquidation of the company and sale of the brand;
- Sale and leaseback of brands;
- Assessment of the adequacy of documents for consideration concerning trademarks, to verify the enforceability of the bankruptcy revocation clause and the preferential bankruptcy (in the case of undersold marks...);
- Value of the assets (trademarks) of distressed firms;
- Transfer/assignment of the trademark;
- A tax estimate of the normal (fair) value;
- Pledge, mortgage, and usufruct on brands.

The classification of the trademark within the company or of an autonomous branch allows, if necessary, to appreciate the synergies with other activities, not always recorded (recorded or internally generated goodwill, etc.).

The brand, estimated from an economic point of view with an adequate evaluation metric, can be adopted to assess:

- A distinctive function of identification, certification, and attestation of the product origin source, aimed at avoiding confusion (danger of deception with other products and risk of association among different signs) and at allowing consumers a conscious selection of products and services;

- A qualitative guarantee function, intended as a customer's expectation of the consistent quality of the products distinguished with the same brand (maintenance of identical merchandise characteristics over time), stimulating brand loyalty and customer satisfaction. The brand can significantly reduce the risk embodied in purchasing decisions;
- An evocative or advertising function, following the ever-increasing attitude of the distinctive sign and the specialty that emanates from it to be endowed with an intrinsic power of appeal and notoriety—bringing out the brand awareness of consumers—and to become a client's collector.

The evaluation of the brand must be carried out with an interdisciplinary approach, which considers various aspects together, appreciating its impact from an economic–financial perspective. The profiles that must be considered are:

- Legal (analysis of the intensity of the degree of protection offered by the registration of the trademark in the various cases ...);
- Behavioral and strategic/marketing (differential surplus value of the brand, a key element to guide consumers' choices, ...).
- Economic, accounting (evaluation of the brand in the financial statements and the costs of advertising that support it ...), and fiscal (impact of taxation in the event of a transfer of the trademark; taxation of royalties;...).

The development of the strategic value of the brand can allow a company to achieve significant competitive advantages. The brand, when known, represents a substantial component of the overall value of a company.

The positive aspects that can derive from the strategic value of the brand include, first, the following:

- Symbol of product differentiation;
- Adaptability to market changes (less vulnerability to competition marketing actions; less sensitivity to a market crisis);
- Internationality;

- Leadership;
- Celebrity (status symbol);
- Legal protection against counterfeits;
- Customer loyalty and brand awareness;
- Bargaining power about distribution;
- Ability to increase market shares;
- Market attractiveness.

A weak brand has the following negative aspects:

- Weak distinctive power;
- Low differentiation;
- Limited reactivity to changes in competitive market scenarios (vulnerability to competition marketing actions; higher sensitivity to market crises; …);
- Geographically limited distribution;
- Low legal protection;
- Modest consumer retention;
- Low attractiveness of the market segment in which the company operates.

It is very common to incur types of trademark evaluation within a portfolio of intellectual properties, in which brands synergistically coexist with patents, know-how, goodwill, copyright, or other intangible assets, sometimes within dedicated companies (royalty companies).

Even if trademarks are classified as marketing intangibles (see OECD, 2017), they frequently overlap with technological or Internet intangibles (e.g., brands linked to know-how or web domains).

9.2   Trademark Accounting

The accounting aspects connected to the registration of the brands have an increasingly important role in the evaluation. This is also the case in the estimate of counterfeit damage, which can include the counterfeiter's accounting. In a broad sense, bookkeeping detects the impact:

- On revenues, costs, and differential economic margins (EBITDA, EBIT, pre-tax profit …);

- On equity allocations (of profit reserves ...);
- On operating (FCFF) and net (FCFE) cash flows.

The accounting discipline in different countries is becoming more and more in line with the new valuation standards, envisaging the alignment of the accounting values in the financial statements and based on the fair value.

Trademarks must be classified under intangible assets, within a broader category. The identification of the original historical cost—and any revaluations and devaluations—can be deduced from the explanatory notes of the financial statements, in which it is mandatory to specify the analytical movements of fixed assets, including capitalized intangibles.

The cost of intangible assets, whose use is limited in time, must be systematically amortized in each financial year concerning their residual possibility of utilization (IAS 38). Trademarks, however, tend to have an indefinite useful life.

The depreciation calculated in this way must be entered in the income statement as amortization of trademarks.

The devaluations of trademarks must be entered in the income statement and recorded, as for depreciation, as a direct reduction of the value of the fixed assets in the balance sheet. Devaluations must be made explicit in the explanatory notes of the financial statements.

The registration in the balance sheet of the brands with very low values is frequent—only the registration and accessory costs are considered—and they are treated as expenses directly in the income statement, based on a prudential criterion that does not give any visibility to the brand in the balance sheet, in contradiction with its nature and function.

Prudence typically prevails over concrete representation, and this is an obstacle when looking for clues for valuation. In other words, the real value of trademarks is often disguised in the accounts, and has to be reconstructed from other complementary sources.

9.2.1 Trademarks and International Accounting Standards: Impairment Test and Inapplicability of the Fair Value

The international accounting standards normally require the use, instead of the historical cost, of the fair value, defined by IAS 39 (now replaced by IFRS 13) as the consideration for which an asset could be exchanged, or a liability extinguished, in a free transaction between knowledgeable and independent parties. This is the evaluation method that can be defined as market or current, as defined by the EU directives "fair value". Here too there are similarities with the tax concept of normal (fair) value.

IAS 38, about intangible assets, explicitly excludes the possibility of applying fair value for brands, due to the uniqueness of this asset and, therefore, its difficult comparability with similar elements.

Intangible assets with an indefinite useful life, such as trademarks, are no longer eligible for the systematic amortization and must be annual—at each balance sheet reporting date—subject to the impairment test. It consists of a periodic review of the intangible value recorded in the balance sheet, applying valuation approaches based on the discounting of future cash flows and/or market-based approaches. Indefinite life appraisal eliminates the problem of estimating the terminal value of the brand, but leaves open queries about its maintenance value. Digitalization, even here, matters, and a brand with no digital dimension (and a corresponding website and domain name) is increasingly worthless.

9.3   The Evaluation Standard ISO 10668

The standard 10668 was published by the International Organization for Standardization (ISO) in Autumn of 2010. It identifies a methodology for assessing the economic value of brands, defining the objectives, approaches, evaluation methods, and selection methods, and identification of the starting data, to be used in the evaluation process, to guide the evaluator, reducing the margins of discretion and proposing a sort of evaluation protocol. ISO 10668 is fully consistent with the IVS 210 principles (examined in Chapter 2).

ISO 10668 is aligned with the existing valuation standards, the IAS/IFRS accounting standards, but includes the valuation aspects that are not solely economic and financial, but linked to legal and behavioral aspects, which are an integral part of the brand value judgment.

The valuation principles ISO 10668 apply to the valuation of trademarks in those situations in which it is necessary to have a fair value, comparable to the brand selling price.

The standard ISO 10668 defines the analyses and the steps necessary for the evaluation of the brands, which can have a legal, behavioral, or financial nature. The three steps are essential to evaluate existing brands, new brands, and the definition of the impact of brand extension strategies.

The second aspect for the evaluation of brands, based on the standard ISO 10668, is behavioral analysis, which allows the assessor to gain a complete opinion on customer behavior and the value perceived by the distribution network and by customers in markets where the brand is widespread, with particular reference to its positioning concerning its competitors.

9.4 Economic, Financial, and Accounting Analysis

To conduct a complete analysis of the brand, the first requirement is to define its meaning and extension from the property rights and/or licensing agreements or grant the use of the brand to third parties in the countries concerned. Each accounting source, typically recorded as OPEX in the income statement (advertising expenses; yearly cost of registration, etc.) is a precious source of information for appraisal. CAPEX recording is rarer (see Chapter 3 for a distinction).

The analysis of the variegated rights associated with the brand is accompanied by a survey of the trademarks associated with it, concerning intellectual property rights, to be included in the definition of a trademark and consequently to be considered in the assessment judgment.

After defining the perimeter of the assessment from the legal point of view and considering the rights and behavioral perspectives, the third step involves the economic and financial evaluation of the brand, through the evaluation approaches to be used either as the main method or in a complementary manner.

9.5 Valuation Approaches

The three different approaches proposed by the standard ISO 10668 (consistently with IVS 210) are based on the:

- Income Approach that allows a trademark to be valued based on the current value of its ability to generate future income, over its useful life. The assessment is based on the specific knowledge of the expected income or cash flows, of the royalties, from the forecast growth of the markets in which the brand is widespread, considering the specific market risk.

- Market Approach that defines the value of the specific trademark referring to the values expressed by verifiable transactions on the market that have involved brands with similar characteristics. The comparability of transactions is the fundamental requirement for the reliability of the valuation and must consider both factors linked to the brand and factors related to the market context.
- Cost Approach which recognizes the value of the brand as the sum of the costs incurred for building it. This methodology assumes that an investor, to acquire a brand, only considers the replacement costs.

The identification of the approach to be used as the primary valuation method must be consistent with the valuation purposes, considering the possibility of using observable assumptions.

Among the different approaches, the evaluator should carefully consider the complementarity in identifying—from different angles—the multi-faceted aspects of the trademark.

The relief from royalties are based on the income or incremental cash flows that derive from the exploitation of the trademark and that interact with the market surplus value or the multipliers of comparable companies. The incremental equity derives from an accumulation of differential income over the years. The cost of reproduction assesses the future benefits the independent estimate of the differential (incremental) goodwill has an average between equity and income approaches.[4]

The different approaches should theoretically lead to similar results, even if the relief from royalties and the reproduction cost sometimes tend to provide lower valuations concerning the differential income method or market comparisons.

The main approaches for estimating the market value of brands are the empirical and analytical approaches.

The empirical approaches, as the Market Approach and the Cost Approach, are based on the observation of the market prices of trademarks, identical in terms of characteristics, from which formulas and parameters derive. The use of "quick and dirty" criteria is dictated by the speed of updating the value of fixed assets in similar companies.

Analytical approaches, such as the Income Approach, on the other hand, are of higher professional reliability, as accepted by the theory and consolidated by practice, although they are less intuitive.

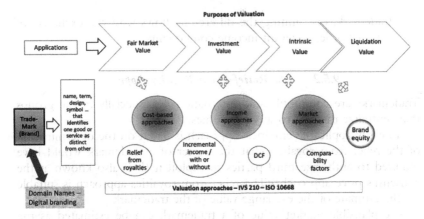

Fig. 9.1 Trademarks and their valuation approaches

The assessment is strongly influenced by the scenario concerning the company (in the case of business continuity or liquidation or insolvency); in the second case, the estimate must be aimed at identifying the recoverable value.

Figure 9.1 synthetizes the main valuation approaches for trademarks, consistently with IVS 210 and ISO 10668.

9.5.1 Income Approach

The income approach is the most widely used valuation tool and is mainly based on the following methodologies:

- Discounting of income or cash flows deriving from the exploitation of the trademark: according to this approach, the value is given by the sum of the discounted income deriving from the exploitation of the resource itself (in terms of royalties, expected turnover, …);
- Discounting of the relief from royalties, which the company would pay to a licensee if the trademark were not owned;
- Discounting of income or differential cash flows (incremental): it is based on quantifying and discounting the benefits and specific advantages of the trademark concerning normal situations, namely products not covered by branding. Incremental income is obtained by the difference between the revenues and costs relating to the

trademark, discounting the differential flows with the exclusion of external or less relevant income components.

9.5.2   The Relief-From-Royalty Approach

Trademarks are commonly sold internationally, especially in the groups that centralize them in royalty companies.[5]

An easily applicable empirical approach is based on the determination of the relief from royalties that the owner of a trademark would have required to authorize third parties to exploit it (it is also known as the consensus price approach). The relief-from-royalties approach is suitable for the estimate of the exchange value of the trademark.

The plausible market value of a trademark can be estimated as the discounted sum of the relief -from-royalties (which the company would pay as a licensee if the trademark were not owned) discounted along a time horizon of at least 3–5 years and in any case not longer than the contractual deadline.

The concept of reasonable royalty can be relevant in the context of litigation in the quantification of the damage for unlawful use of the trademark.

The general principles of transfer pricing have last been revised by OECD (2017) which define royalties as "payments of any kind received as consideration for the use of, or the right to use intellectual property, as copyright, patent, trademark, design or model, plan, secret formula or process".

These normative and interpretative sources identify the guiding criteria to establish what the normal (fair) value should be in the operations, referring to the general criterion of prices determined under the regime of free competition (arm's length) and therefore responding to a correct economic logic.

Percentages can fluctuate between the minimum and maximum values and reference must be made to the type of market in which the company operates. In exceptional cases, relating to famous brands, especially in particular merchandise sectors (high fashion, etc.), the percentages can be higher.[6]

9.5.3   The Incremental Income Approach

The higher the expected operating result associated with a trademark, the greater the resource itself.

Therefore, the contribution of a trademark to business profitability can be measured through the differential income approach. The value of the trademark so corresponds to the current value of the cumulated expected differential income. The brand can, therefore, be assessed as a source of differential economic benefit and future utility, expressed in a premium price, (price differential of the product with a strong market recognition).

The failed or symbolic capitalization of the costs associated with the brand impacts in terms of non-depreciation and the undervaluation of the equity, with a book value lower than the market value.

The incremental income approach can be used in the estimation of the trademark's counterfeit damage, to quantify the lost profit of the owner or the specular counterfeiter's profit and his illicit enrichment (unjust enrichment, gain-based), based on a reasonable royalty, which leads to the alleged royalties mentioned above. The estimate of the compensation for damages (restitution damage) in the form of compensation can be equitably conducted using the legal concepts of the emerging damage and loss of future earnings. Incremental income is consistent with the with-or-without approach: which is the differential/incremental revenue deriving from the free use of the (digital) brand? Which is the comparison between an unbranded vs. a branded product?

The unfair appropriation of differential results qualifies the damage perpetrated by the infringer, whose occasional or repeated nature and purpose must be assessed.

9.5.4   Market Approach

The estimate of the market value is based on the screening of transactions involving trademarks, for sale or license, using the international databases currently available on the web that can provide useful clues about their value, even from a fiscal comparison, to estimate the normal (fair) value of international transactions between independent counterparties for transfer pricing. Several private databases contain useful information for market transactions; these M&A operations are, however, typically private, and that is why sources are so precious but somewhat ... misleading.

The market approach is consistent with the principle established by IFRS 13 according to which the fair value must be determined by adopting the assumptions that market operators would use in determining the price of the brand, presuming that market operators act to satisfy their economic interest in the best manner.

The comparative analysis is based on the Price/Book Value ratio, which compares the stock market price (of a listed company) to the equity, producing a capital gain (if the ratio is higher than 1) in part attributable to the trademark. What pertains to patents (if they are valuable, it means that they are hardly comparable) often works even with trademarks, whose originality is, however, somewhat softened. Really worthy (digital) brands are hard to compare, and that is why they incorporate a competitive advantage.

9.5.5   Cost Approach

In the absence of available data on the income capacity, a possible alternative is that of the cost incurred in the past to create the trademark and to occupy in the market the positions reached by the same at the valuation date. It is, therefore, a question of identifying the most significant costs incurred, considering (as a percentage of sales):

- Advertising and marketing costs;
- Research and development costs;
- Charges related to the deposit and concession of the trademark (legal advice, application, publication, concession fees, etc.);

A limitation of this procedure derives from the known inadequacy of the historical costs in estimating values since the purchasing power of money (even in times of high inflation, as it occurs since Autumn 2021) and the economic conditions change over time. An even stronger limitation is given by the fact that the value of an asset is not only due to the costs necessary to obtain it but to the future benefits that can be obtained from it. How much would it cost to reproduce a (digital) brand from scratch? Nice question, providing some (limited) clue for appraisal.

A step forward compared to the previous approach is given by the reproduction cost of a functionally equivalent trademark, which replaces historical costs with the costs of reproducing the good from scratch, meaning the costs that would incur at the time of the assessment to reconstruct the same value that the trademark has reached at that exact time.

9.6   OTHER INTERNATIONAL EVALUATION STANDARDS

Several international institutions, in their standard-setter activity, issue operational and interpretative guidelines to assess trademarks; the principles ISO 10668 are supported by other valuation standards, like those issued by the Appraisal Foundation. In June 2012, the Foundation emitted the discussion draft valuation advisory n. 2 (The Valuation of Customer-Related Assets), related to the valuation of assets linked to marketing and consumers, in the context of financial statement valuations.

The International Evaluation Standard Council has issued the Technical Information paper n. 3 (The Valuation of Intangible Assets), which includes, in the sphere of intangible assets, trademarks.

Regarding international taxation and, specifically, transfer pricing, OECD (2017) Guidelines (and their forward updates) are relevant.

Several empirical approaches describe branding models, to estimate the economic value of the market: for instance, the Brand Asset Valuator (developed by the consulting company Young and Rubicam) or the Interbrand approach.

For prospective assessments (business plans, etc.), not necessarily linked to the expected value of the brands, the ISAE 3400[7] principle is relevant.

There are other methods of evaluation for brands:

1. **Interbrand[8] empirical method**: the revenues attributable to the brand are multiplied by an expressive coefficient of the strategic strength of the brand, which depends on factors such as leadership, loyalty, market, trends, marketing investments, internationality, legal protection, ... Interbrand publishes a yearly report about the best global brands;
2. **Financial brand equity**: aimed at evaluating the brand in monetary terms and consisting in the enhancement of a set of assets and liabilities linked to the brand, which increase (or decrease) the value of a product.

9.7   BRAND EQUITY

The brand heritage or value (brand equity) is an intangible resource that is based on the knowledge of a brand by a given market and its consequent enhancement. Brand equity is consistent with the cumulated capital advantage of a successful brand that produces excess economic and financial margins (higher EBITDA, etc.) that are eventually recorded in the reserves within the equity, unless distributed as dividends.

Brand equity expresses the value of the brand, from a financial (financial-based) or marketing (image asset) point of view in operating conditions, summarizing its strength in the reference market.

The main determinants of brand equity are the following:

- Brand image and resonance;
- Brand preference;
- Brand positioning and relationship between market share and price;
- Brand experience;
- Distinctive features and recognition (brand awareness);
- Brand personality, perceived quality, and ability to earn higher prices (premium price);
- Brand loyalty and brand trust area;
- Brand awareness (brand knowledge) and retention rate of acquired customers;
- Penetration rate and ability to attract new customers;
- Brand associations, as a link between the consumer's mind and the brand itself;
- Diffusion, reliability, and differentiation;
- Consumer satisfaction.

From the consumer-based perspective, the brand value corresponds to the capital accumulated by the brand thanks to the cumulative marketing investments.

9.8   BRAND VALUATION IN BUSINESS
CRISES AND RESIDUAL CREDITWORTHINESS

Brands are born and prosper within healthy companies, with an osmotic flow in which the brands and the company that hosts them grow together, synergistically strengthening their mutual value. Internal and external growth finds its appropriate financial coverage in self-financing or recourse to debt, typically through banking channels, or residually through equity underwriting.

Debt is hardly manageable in a crisis, and under normal conditions is guaranteed with a physiological service that originates from the company's ability to generate adequate cash flows first to repay creditors and eventually shareholders, following an absolute priority rule. The guarantees can be cash flow based, which is based on the capacity to financially serve the debt, or asset-based, with specific guarantees on single collateralizable assets.

The role of brands, in this context, is ambivalent and in some ways contradictory: on the one hand, brands, along with other intangible resources, represent a precious and essential element for value creation, through incremental and differential cash flows (object of appreciation, to estimate the value of the brands with DCF metrics), thus corroborating the cash flow based strategies. On the other hand, brands retain an autonomous collateral value typically modest, especially in the startup phase, when they have not yet adequately developed their potential, or in a context of crisis, suffering the contagion of a sick company.

And the brands, like the other intangibles, are a typical source of information asymmetry, suffering from an ontological accounting underestimation and assuming an uncertain determination value, especially from external sources. This can lead to an inevitable reluctance of the third-party financiers, not always inclined to renounce collateral guarantees which, like the 2008 financial crisis teaches, are valid only on paper, that is when they are not needed.

When a company enters a state of (reversible) crisis, the trademarks included in it suffer an inevitable contagion. Differences may sometimes arise between the value of the trademark and that of the company to which it belongs, expressed by the oxymoron "the strong brand—the weak company" or by other combinations. Their contradictory nature typically leads to convergences in the medium term (the trademark can revive the company, thanks to rebranding strategies, or the danger of being infected by the depreciation of the company could destroy the brand itself).

The solutions for a turnaround of the company, sharply reduced and set free from debts and structural costs that have proved unsustainable, typically pass through the revival of the brands, together with the core assets that have survived significant depreciation in terms of functionality and value.

The strategies of maintaining business continuity through continuation arrangements with strategic suppliers, typically protect the brands, preserving them within a reorganized corporate vehicle, or, frequently, allocating them to crisis-free newcos.

The refreshing of the brands in situations of corporate crisis is important, especially in the presence of the strong brand—weak company paradox, which will be examined in the next paragraph. The renewal and the use of the trademark may face difficulties during crises, where typically the trademark is sold with public evidence, to protect creditors, avoiding discrimination.

9.9   THE "STRONG BRAND - WEAK COMPANY" PARADOX

The brand, when known, represents a significant component of the overall value of a company. In many cases, there is a difference between the real quality of the branded product and the perceived quality. This implies an overvaluation or an underestimation of the brand, determined by a set of contributing factors, characterized by a temporary nature, and linked to a fashion effect or market opacity. This may cause a sub-optimization of the quality-price ratio or difficulties in communicating the product's value.

Due to globalization, the brand may assume a value higher than the entire company, which—consequently—has a value that without this asset would become negative, highlighting a bad will. The growing competitiveness gap between countries may contribute to explaining this phenomenon, and appears relevant, in terms of labor costs, confronting Western countries with emerging economies.

This has favored the outsourcing of non-strategic production factors and has made the company more flexible and competitive, allowing it to concentrate on higher value-added activities (research and development of new products and markets, process innovation, design excellence, optimization of the logistic and commercial network), suitable to represent a barrier to entry for external competitors.

In this context, the brand is the hallmark of the overall quality of the product, divided into individual components that are produced in different countries (depending on their complexity and the incidence of labor) and then assembled and marketed as a finished product.

Counterfeiting is difficult to contrast in jurisdictions that have only recently been provided with laws protecting intellectual property; however, without these legal innovations is discouraged.

We are witnessing a negative effect produced by companies with a consolidated brand: they destroy value since they insist on doing everything at home or, assigning part of the production to a third party in an induced surrounding, without significant savings in the cost of production. This is to save the costs of quality control that delocalization and disarticulation of production entails. There may be, however, opportunities to enter the new markets where the goods are produced. These are emerging markets, with increasing spending capacities and new rich attitudes of hundreds of millions of people coming out of ancestral conditions of poverty and autarky, who are looking for exotic products, which represent a status symbol typical of consumerism (Table 9.1).

Brand development depends on:

- Characteristics of the market (emerging or mature; localized or global; niche or mass; ...);
- Availability of adequate resources to invest in development (critical mass of financial resources, which favor medium-large companies or small companies allied in industrial districts or synergistic segments in the value chain, with subcontractors, ...);
- Dissemination of value, to adequately remunerate all stakeholders in a balanced manner;
- Transparency in corporate information, aimed at mitigating the information asymmetries between the company and the lenders (shareholders or banks) and reducing the cost of raising capital (WACC, representing the denominator of DCF);
- Adaptation to administrative, productive, financial quality standards (strengthening of internal audit, quality of ISO or Vision procedures, obtaining and maintaining a good rating, ...);
- Creation of an independent royalty company,[9] dedicated to the development and exploitation of the brand (and other intangibles synergistic with the brand, for example, patents), so enabling an independent evaluation of the brand.

When a company goes into crisis, the value of the brand shrinks, even if there is a decrease in value that may be less than proportional

Table 9.1 The "strong brand—weak company" paradox

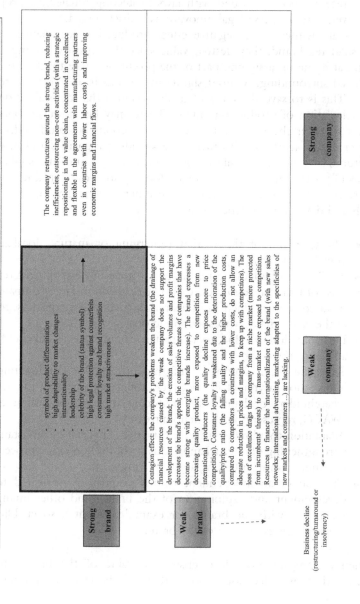

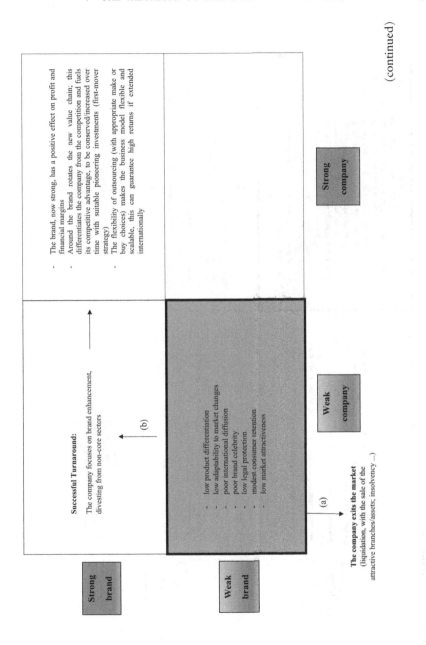

Strong brand

Successful Turnaround:

The company focuses on brand enhancement, divesting from non-core sectors

(b)

- The brand, now strong, has a positive effect on profit and financial margins
- Around the brand rotates the new value chain; this differentiates the company from the competition and fuels its competitive advantage, to be conserved/increased over time with suitable pioneering investments (first-mover strategy)
- The flexibility of outsourcing (with appropriate make or buy choices) makes the business model flexible and scalable, this can guarantee high returns if extended internationally

Weak brand

- low product differentiation
- low adaptability to market changes
- poor international diffusion
- poor brand celebrity
- low legal protection
- modest consumer retention
- low market attractiveness

(a)

The company exits the market
(liquidation, with the sale of the attractive branches/assets; insolvency …)

Weak company   **Strong company**

(continued)

Table 9.1 (continued)

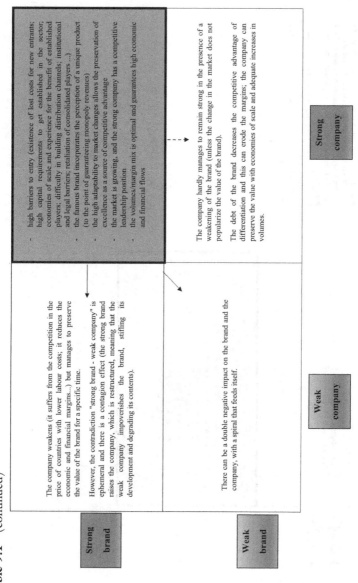

	Strong company	Weak company
Strong brand	high barriers to entry (existence of lost costs for new entrants; high capital requirements to get established in the sector; economies of scale and experience for the benefit of established players; difficulty in building distribution channels, institutional and legal barriers; retaliation of consolidated players ...) – the famous brand incorporates the perception of a unique product (to the point of guaranteeing monopoly revenues) – the high adaptability to market changes allows the preservation of excellence as a source of competitive advantage – the market is growing, and the strong company has a competitive leadership position – the volumes/margin mix is optimal and guarantees high economic and financial flows	The company weakens (it suffers from the competition in the price of countries with lower labour costs; it reduces the economic and financial margins...) but manages to preserve the value of the brand for a specific time. However, the contradiction "strong brand - weak company" is ephemeral and there is a contagion effect (the strong brand raises the company, which is restructured, meaning that the weak company impoverishes the brand, stifling its development and degrading its contents).
Weak brand	The company hardly manages to remain strong in the presence of a weakening of the brand (unless the change in the market does not popularize the value of the brand). The debt of the brand decreases the competitive advantage of differentiation and this can erode the margins; the company can preserve the value with economies of scale and adequate increases in volumes.	There can be a double negative impact on the brand and the company, with a spiral that feeds itself.

The strength of the company allows adequate investments in the brand, which represents and incorporates its success and distinctive features, a source of competitive advantage by differentiation.

The strong company - weak brand combination is typical of not yet consolidated but growing and with good prospects realities.
Growth is synonymous with product success and perception of their quality and can generate the resources needed to strengthen the brand.

If the growing company fails to develop the brand and absorbs financial resources, it can weaken without being able to differentiate, losing the potential competitive advantage.

Strong brand

Weak brand

Strong brand

Weak brand

than that of the entire company. This occurs with the paradox "the strong brand—weak companies", with an impact on bankability. Opposite considerations, of course, should be made if the trademark was and remains weak. The weakness of the brand is not necessarily associated with a negative performance of the company and can have a limited impact on the rating, especially if it is linked to the belonging to a sector that is not very visible to consumers (e.g., manufacturing of work in progress that may end up in unbranded products).

The preservation of the residual value, even if reduced, can conveniently take place by enucleating the healthy branch of the company (including the trademark, the customer portfolio, and the connected assets/liabilities) and subsequent sale.

These circumstances affect the rating of both the company in crisis and the going concern company that acquires the brand.

Dorfleitner et al. (2019) observe the differences between the market and the most valuable global brands in terms of financial performance: the tight gap that used to separate the market from the investments in valuable brands is increasingly expanding in the last decade, proving that the latter investments follow an independent path. Not only do valuable brands "perform better during bearish market conditions" and crises but "the extent of the outperformance is much larger during market turmoil (bear periods) than during normal periods".

Brands, characterized by a huge size, respected reputation and name, and predominantly non-cyclical demand, show better performances. Four industries have been identified as the most influencing ones in the generally positive trend of valuable brands: business services, retail, sporting goods, and technology. These sectors exploit digitalization, e-commerce, and technological progress in the offering of their goods and services to customers.

Strong trademarks especially during market turmoil, represent an incredible source of competitive advantage that steers companies through bearish markets.

The most valuable brands' portfolios create value for the shareholders, since "brand value estimates are significantly positively related to prices and returns and only incremental to accounting variables".

Amazon whose brand value increased by 19% per annum between 2000 and 2018 and Apple which faced an increase of 21% in the same period (Interbrand) confirm the importance that building a strong brand has for a firm evaluation (the total brand value increased from 912 billion

USD in 2000 to 1.872 billion USD in 2018 with an average of 14 billion USD per company).

9.10   Logos

The logo (an abbreviation of logotype) is the part of the brand that represents the typographical exposure of the name of a company or a product, an icon, an image, the color, the handwriting, or the graphic mode with which it is composed, which can be more or less characterized. In other words, it is an emblem, of a graphic type with a precise indication and lettering.

Different types of logos can be used simultaneously within the brand and its evaluation:

- Logotype: it is the graphic sign whose referent is a phonetic expression; it is a pronounceable written mark. In typography, the logotype is a unique character, in which several letters are fused;
- Pictogram: consists of a stylized drawing or symbol in one or more colors, characterized by simplicity, recognizability, immediacy, and conventionally taken as a signal (e.g., in signs, in road signals, in computer icons, etc.). It is an iconic sign whose referent is an object or a class of objects, an aspect or an action that the object can express;
- Diagram: it is a symbolic and graphically elaborated representation of quickly accessible; it consists of a non-iconic sign, or any case with a low degree of iconicity and can, therefore, have no reference to reality.

The logo assumes fundamental importance in the evaluation of Mobile Apps, in which the icon constitutes an essential distinctive character, in a crowded competitive landscape, characterized by graphic emblems that tend to be confused, because of the reduced dimensions of the smartphones screens. And M-Apps represent the virtual digital passage from the physical to the Internet world. No Internet, no party, even for celebrated trademarks.

9.11   DIGITAL BRANDING

Personalized marketing represents an innovation of the undifferentiated mass-market experiences, based on a targeted segmentation of consumer preferences, using their data. This enables the creation of new business opportunities deriving from the crossing of offers of personalized goods and services that address sophisticated demand.

Business models follow new paradigms that have a profound impact on the value chain (for producers, service providers, intermediaries, and consumers), with significant legal consequences.

Many companies have long decided to invest in Customer Relationship Management (CRM), to develop long-term relationships with consumers. With the advent of big data, these companies are trying to exploit new opportunities, developing new data analysis systems already in their possession and integrating new information from these data sources into their CRM system.

Social networks and other community platforms have become fundamental tools for most companies, regardless of the sector and the organizational dimension.

In this perspective, digital tools are becoming increasingly important not only as places of expression and sharing on the web but as effective vehicles for information, brand development, marketing, and business.

The development of new and high-performance data analysis tools should bring a long-term increase in efficiency and opportunities, for example, through the collection and analysis of detailed information on consumers, to develop a personalized digital marketing system.

Based on the chronology of the user's activities, preferences, and interactions with the brands, it is possible to propose promotional messages, tailored to each consumer.

In this context, social networks and Communications Service Providers (CSP) play an important role.

Communication service providers can retain consumers by focusing primarily on their overall experience.

The experience of consumers is a primary factor, given that the functionality of the network, coverage, speed, and costs have a significant impact on the perception of service quality by users. The experience analysis of the users of communication services represents a problem related to big data.

Mehta and Kaushik (2015) evidence that before "the introduction of the web the relationship between brands and consumers has mostly been one way. Brand Marketing has undergone a sea change, and the Internet has proved a catalyst in bringing the changes forward and magnifying their scale. With growing competition in the marketplace, firms are engaged in a constant search for better ways of communicating the various features of their products/services and of marketing them effectively. Many factors like more educated and demanding customers, shorter product lifecycles, and growing competition have added to the problems facing firms. Intent on acquiring new customers while retaining the old, firms turned to brand. (...) Digital marketing consists of search engine optimization, permission-based email marketing, SMS, and online coupons. Internet advertising has recaptured the imagination of marketers, who see enormous potential to raise the profile of their brands through engagement vehicles such as paid search and online video. One-way marketers are trying to reach consumers is with Multi-Channel digital marketing".

9.12 THE IMPACT OF ADVERTISING PLATFORMS ON BRANDS

Advertisements are an efficient tool to attract the public: when walking in the streets in the traffic of the city, people are captivated by advertising panels on the buildings or the metro's walls. Similarly, when navigating on the Internet, surfers are faced with marketing insertions, advertising announcements, and texts, displays ads, and rich media (videos, images) in the form of a banner, i.e., "a heading or advertisement appearing on a web page in the form of a bar, column, or box".[10]

Google, the leader among the search engine options, responded to the current necessity of companies to be visible online by developing two ad hoc advertising platforms, that not only strongly contributed to its success, but provided a digital marketing tool and an effective solution for businesses campaigns:

- Adwords, created for advertisers who want to promote their products and services on the Internet;
- Adsense, designed for website owners who want to maximize profits and gains from their content.

The former allows advertisers (in possess of a registered account) to choose the budget for the ads and where to position them, with the advantage concerning traditional marketing forms that they will be charged only when someone clicks on the ad, this explains the "pay per click" (PPC) principle. The platform allows the user to select for which keywords the ads are shown, to set locations, days, and times and even to target users that are physically located in a particular area, promoting the local marketing.

Adsense, on the contrary, is mostly adopted by webmasters or blog owners, since it enables them to gain a portion of what the Adwords advertiser pays when someone clicks on an ad that is shown on their website (Chris, 2019).

The two programs offered by Google *"work hand-in-hand with one another to form one of the largest online ad services in the world"* (Kirk, 2016) and are certainly among the first choices for online editors. However, some alternatives are emerging.

The most similar service is provided by Media.net, but also Propeller Ads, specialized in monetizing websites that include entertainment, videos/movies, games, and Revcontent, adopted by some of the largest websites in the world like Forbes and Pc World, are valid alternatives (Servando, 2019).[11]

Social media, including Facebook and Instagram, are advertising providers since they allow companies to "engage with the most relevant on-target audiences based on their interests, background and social circles".

> Amazon, unlike Facebook and Google has actual records of what people buy and not just the things their habits suggest they might buy. It is a gold mine of information that no one else can offer.

All these services provided by different companies share the aim to enhance the brand awareness of companies through the increase of traffic in a website and the engagement of targeted customers encouraged to interact with the brand.[12]

Brand awareness improves brand recognition and customer loyalty, with a positive impact on valuation. Internet presence makes the trademark more valuable, even if its real value is more ephemeral, since the digital churn rate of volubile clients is typically higher.

9.13 FashionTech and Digital Clothing

Fashion—a source of looking better/attractive—is a form of self-expression and autonomy at a particular period and place and in a specific context, of clothing, footwear, lifestyle, accessories, makeup, hairstyle, and body posture. Fashion is also an expression of culture, art, and creativity, allowing people to display their unique tastes and styling. Fashion is also an expression of culture (Kaiser, 2018), art, and creativity, allowing people to display their unique tastes and styling. Fashion is a source of looking better/more attractive. Fashion is, possibly, the industry that is iconically the closest to trademark valuation and exploitation.

Valuation patterns are inspired by changing intrinsically volatile business models, following timely "fashionable" attitudes, taste, spending power, and other trendy patterns. Competition among fashion firms is driven by a Differentiated Value Proposition that makes products or services stand out against the competition. The incremental perceived value is continuously compared by potential customers that use digital "display windows" to confront different products. The Differentiated Value Proposition is incorporated in the brand (trademark) of each fashion firm—that is why branding (and its cumulated value expressed by the brand equity) is so important in the industry.

Fashion technology describes innovative technologies in material procurement and fashion design, and their applicability in fashion manufacturing, transportation, and retail. In simple terms, fashion technology creates contemporary tools for the fashion industry to improve the way we produce and consume fashion. Modern tools such as the use of Artificial Intelligence in fashion design, 3D printers instead of sewing machines, lab-made leather alternatives instead of animal leather, body scanners instead of measuring tape, augmented reality, virtual reality for retail, and much more.[13]

The interaction of technology with material consistency (physical form) is illustrated in Fig. 9.2.

Digital Fashion represents a section of FashionTech and consists of the visual representation of clothing built using computer technologies and 3D software.

Digital clothing exists only in the digital space. This FashionTech trend is nowadays more realistic than previous digital clothing attempts. Customers purchase a piece of digital clothing (which could be an NFT as well), and the clothing is then overlaid with their image.

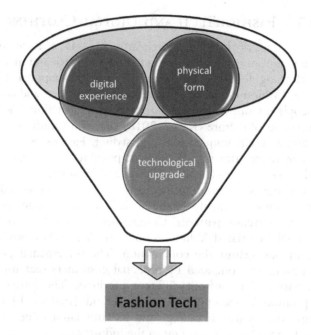

Fig. 9.2 From physical consistency and digital technology to FashionTech

FashionTech also affects brand valuation. From the consumer-based perspective, the brand value corresponds to the capital accumulated by the brand thanks to the cumulative marketing investments.

Digital fashion is the interplay between digital technology, dematerialization, metaverse consumers interacting through social networks, and couture, as shown in Fig. 9.3.

Any firm appraisal follows a comprehensive understanding of its underlying business model. Since firms evolve and their valuation is forward-looking, any trendy pattern is worth considering. The transition from "traditional" fashion models to FashionTech and eventually "smart" fashion is synthetically described in Fig. 9.4.

Re-engineered supply chains, ignited by innovation and trendy consumer habits, bring a reduction of fixed costs that are sensitive to sunk costs and lack of flexibility. Scalability improves and OPEX reduction produces higher EBITDA. This value-generating process improves both

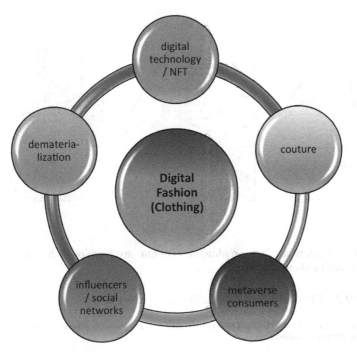

Fig. 9.3 Digital fashion

operating cash flows and EBITDA-driven market multipliers, as shown in Table 9.2.

9.14 DIGITALIZATION AND SPORTS BRANDS

The brands represent the emblem of professional and amateur sports clubs. In the first case, there is a more intense formalization (presence of normally registered trademarks), which is associated with the exploitation of the image represented by the trademark and its digital extensions (domain names, website, mobile apps, etc.). Sports clubs leverage their name with sponsorships, merchandising, customer/fan loyalty, and a growing presence on media channels. Sports brands have incredible popularity, albeit still largely unexploited. Their digital dimension is, consistently, mostly underdeveloped, as the industry is typically "conservative".

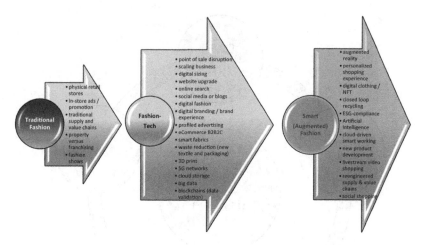

Fig. 9.4 Evolution from traditional fashion to FashionTech and smart (augmented) fashion

Table 9.2 EBITDA gains from traditional to smart fashion

From traditional to smart Fashion through FashionTech	Discounted Cash Flows	Market multipliers
Higher monetary revenues*		
Lower fixed monetary costs *		
Lower variable monetary costs*		
Higher EBITDA		
	Lower CAPEX*	Higher multipliers@
	Lower Operating Net Working Capital#	
	Higher Operating Cash Flow	
	Lower Cost of Capital§	
	Improved Discounted Cash Flows (≈ Enterprise Value)	Higher Enterprise Value

* scalability/productivity gains # shorter supply chain exposure § if the business is less risky; more resilient … @fast-growing firms with higher EBITDA are compared to high-ranking peers

The application of international best practices and integrated assessment standards, such as ISO 10668 or IVS 210, must be adapted to the present case, in which the trade-off "the strong brand—weak company" typically coexists.

In amateur sports clubs, the evaluation metrics are formally the same, albeit in the presence of brands that are not always registered and endowed with an actual and potential value commensurate with their more limited characteristics and dimensions. Amateur sports clubs and associations are exempt from paying taxes on government trademark concessions.

Sports clubs are, to all intents and purposes, companies that exploit their name through sponsorship, sale of advertising space, merchandising, customer/fan loyalty, etc. In this context, the brand and its enhancement take on a central role.

In the specific case of sports clubs, the brands take on a particular significance, expressing the emblem of the identity of the customer—the fan with his team.

Ex art. 8, paragraph 3, of the Italian Code of Intellectual Property, the signs used in the field sports (if known) can be registered (or used) as a trademark.

Brands and corporate valuation are inspired by the revenue model of the target firm. In the specific sports industry, the main revenue drivers are reported in Fig. 9.5.

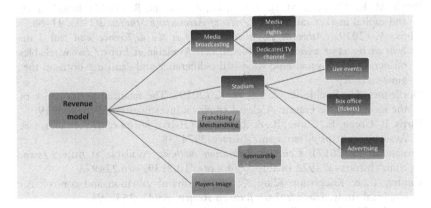

Fig. 9.5 Sports revenue drivers

NOTES

1. "Trademarks" and "brands" are considered synonyms, although they are a bit different. A trademark is a mark that legally represents something, usually a business, by their goods or services. A brand name is the name that a business chooses for one of their products. A brand identifies a specific product or name of a company.
2. Guide to the International registration of marks under the Madrid Agreement and the Madrid Protocol, 2018. Available at https://www.wipo.int/madrid/en/guide/.
3. See Chapter 11.
4. See Sect. 2.4.
5. See Chapter 18.
6. See Sect. 5.10.
7. International standard on assurance engagement 3400. Available at http://www.ifac.org/system/files/downloads/b013-2010-iaasb-handbook-isae-3400.pdf.
8. https://www.interbrand.com/.
9. See Chapter 18.
10. Oxford dictionary.
11. Available at https://stream-seo.com/best-google-adsense-alternatives/.
12. www.support.google.com.
13. https://thevou.com/fashion/what-is-fashion-technology/.

SELECTED REFERENCES

Batyh, M. E., Clement, M. B., Foster, G., & Kasznik, R. (1998). Brand values and capital market valuation. *Review of Accounting Studies, 3*(1–2), 41–68.

Chris, A. (2019). *Adwords vs Adsense—What is the difference and can I use both on the same website?* Reliablesoft.net. Available at https://www.reliablesoft.net/adwords-vs-adsense-what-is-the-difference-and-can-i-use-both-on-the-same-website/

Dorfleitner, G., Roeble, F., & Lesser, K. (2019). The financial performance of the most valuable brands: A global empirical investigation. *Heliyon, 5*, 19.

Farris, P., Gregg, E., Chinn, B., & Razuri, M. (2016). *Brand equity: An overview.* Available at https://ssrn.com/abstract=2974738

Fernandez, P. (2017). *Company valuation methods.* Available at https://ssrn.com/abstract=274973 or https://doi.org/10.2139/ssrn.274973

Gunter, T., & Kriegbaum Kling, C. (2001). Brand valuation and control: An empirical study. *Schmalenbach Business Review, 53*(4), 263–294.

Ishan, K. M., & Noordin, N. (2015). Capitalising on income approach as trademark valuation for entrepreneurs. *Social Sciences & Humanities, 23*(S), 147–160.

Kaiser, S. B. (2018). *Fashion and cultural studies*. Bloomsbury Visual Arts: New York.

Kirk. (2016). *An overview of Google's advertising platforms*. Kearney events. Available at http://www.kearneyevents.com/an-overview-of-googles-advertisingplatforms/

Kubjatkova, A., Kolenčík, J., & Kliestik, T. (2020). Trademark evaluation of the selected company in the aspect of globalization. In *SHS Web of Conferences* (74, p. 01020). Available at https://doi.org/10.1051/shsconf/202074 01020

Lafrance, M. (2009). *Understanding trademark law*. Newark: LexisNexis.

Macìas Rendon, W., & Rodriguez Morales, K. (2013). Brand valuation: A review of interbrand and brand capability value models. *International Journal of Management Research and Business Strategy, 2*(1), 121. Available at www.ijmrbs.com/ijmrbsadmin/upload/IJMRBS_50e5542908c65.pdf

Mehta, R., & Kaushik, N. (2015). A study of emerging trends in brand engagement through digital marketing. *Journal of Marketing & Communication, 11*(2), 39–45.

OECD. (2017). *Transfer pricing guidelines for multinational enterprises and tax administrations*.

Paugam, L., Philippe, H., & Harfouche, R. (2016). *Brand valuation*. New York: Routledge.

Salinas, G. (2009). *The international brand valuation manual*. Hoboken: Wiley.

Sandner, P. G., & Block, J. (2011). The Market value of R&D, patents and trademarks. *Research Policy, 40*(7), 969.

Schilling, M. A. (2010). Protecting innovation (Chap. 9). In *Strategic management of technological innovation*. New Delhi: McGraw-Hill.

Servando, S. (2019). *10 best Google Adsense alternatives*. Stream SEO. Available at https://stream-seo.com/best-google-adsense-alternatives/

Simon, C. J., & Sullivan, M. W. (1993). The measurement and determinant of brand equity: A financial approach. *Marketing Science, 12*(1), 28–52.

CHAPTER 10

The Valuation of Newspaper Headings, Digital Media, and Copyright

10.1 THE CHARACTERISTICS OF NEWSPAPER HEADINGS

Press regulations do not contain a precise definition of newspaper heading, just as there are no references in the legal and tax rules, as well as in the national accounting principles, regarding their treatment. This applies even to online newspapers.

The journalistic or editorial heading is a periodical publication (daily, weekly, fortnightly, monthly, bi-monthly, quarterly, half-yearly, …) or aperiodic, registered by law, even for media different from the paper (radio, TV, etc.), which conveys information or news. The term head derives from the fact that, historically, the title of a publication has always been placed at the head of the page, identifying the editorial product referring to it.

Newspaper headings an their valuation issues (Alavi & Azmi, 2019; Armando, 2019; Das, 2016; Graf et al., 2007; International Valuations Standards Council, 2016; Kao et al., 2019; Lynn, 2019; Maurer, 2018; Torres Vargas & Morales Lopez, 2014) are included in a company's intangible assets. Specific intangible assets can be defined and described according to their characteristics such as their ownership, function, market position, and image.

No specific reference will be made here to radio or television headings, whose merchandise and valuation characteristics are only in part like

© The Author(s), under exclusive license to Springer Nature Switzerland AG 2022
R. Moro-Visconti, *The Valuation of Digital Intangibles*,
https://doi.org/10.1007/978-3-031-09237-4_10

those of the other headings, with which they share, above all, journalistic content, covering the information sector in various ways.

Press laws are laws about licensing for books and freedom of expression in all typography products, particularly newspapers. They apply to press releases, that is any "written, audio-taped, or video-taped matter about a book, event, person, or program, presented by its promoters or principals to the media for editorial comment and free coverage".[1]

Each country presents its regulations concerning the media and press releases; transparency, in terms of authorship, is a common trait. Italian Law, for example, focuses on the relevant data necessary to identify all the subjects involved in the publication, from the name and the domicile of the editor to the identity of the person who printed it. In the United States, more relevance is placed on the legal definition of the freedom of the press, "the right to publish and disseminate information, thoughts, and opinions without restraint or censorship", as guaranteed under the First Amendment of the US Constitution.

From an appraisal and jurisprudential point of view, the concept of the head can give rise to different interpretations, regarding its possible legal protection. Indeed, the head seems to be mostly attributable to the identifying title of the heading and the logo that distinguishes it, rather than the newspaper.

The accounting and tax classification of the newspaper headings reflects the absence of specific indications (except for the international accounting standard IAS 38). IAS 38 prescribes the accounting treatment for all intangible assets that are not specifically covered elsewhere in IFRS.

10.2   Accounting Issues and Tax Treatment

A brief examination of the accounting aspects and the recording in the balance sheet of relevant items such as the headings (sales revenues, advertising costs, operating losses, etc.) are preparatory to the identification of the assessment parameters.

According to the international accounting standard IAS 38 (referring to intangible assets):

- Considering that it is difficult that an active market for editorial headings emerges, they cannot be recognized at fair value, but only at cost;

- Being intangible assets with an indefinite useful life, editorial headings must not be amortized, but subject to an impairment test, at least once a year;
- If internally generated, the editorial headings cannot be evaluated and accounted for as intangible assets;
- Subsequent expenses for editorial headings (both purchased and generated internally) are always charged to the income statement for the year in which they incur.

IAS 38 disciplines the case of a revalued class of assets that contain an asset that does not have an active market, and when assets must stop being revalued because of a lack of an active market. The definition of an active market does include the need for publicly available prices. This contrasts with IFRS 10, which does not include this definition. Under IAS 38, if there is an asset without an active market then the asset should be held at cost less amortization and impairment. If the assets cannot be revalued because there is not an active market, then the amount carried should be the last revalued amount that was referenced to an active market less any subsequent amortization and impairment.

This creates a potential issue for publishing companies where IAS 38 states that newspaper headings cannot have an active market due to their uniqueness. Titles are frequently bought and sold using a sales price based on a multiple of the current year's profits. Which multiple is used depends on the industry and/or geographical area where the title is published. This creates an estimation for the fair value of the title but, because there is no open market, this value may be capped if it would otherwise create or increase the badwill. Once recognized such titles are not permitted to be revalued.[2]

The intangible asset classes provided for by IAS 38 include journalistic headings and the rights to use publishing titles.

The accounting of advertising revenues is relevant, as part of the algorithm for estimating the market value of the heading.

The sale of headings can lead to taxation of the transferor, if capital gains arise, usually taxable in installments, if the sale price exceeds the tax-relevant value (typically, the cost), which does not even appear in the assets of the balance sheet, as it is completely depreciated. In practice, unlikely capital gains are offset by typically higher previous tax losses.

10.3   VALUATION APPROACHES

The accounting treatment of intangible assets is a prerequisite for their valuation. The issue is complex, given that intangible assets (which lack any physical substance, as recalled by IAS 38) are not directly accounted for in the balance sheet or, in some cases, only appear in the income statement, under costs.

According to the Italian accounting principle OIC 24[3] (§ 4.), "intangible fixed assets are assets usually characterized by the lack of tangibility. They are made up of costs which do not exhaust their usefulness in a single period but show the economic benefits over several years". According to the same principle, newspaper headings, as well as trademarks and similar rights, can be recorded as an asset under intangible assets, both if generated internally and if acquired from third parties, while according to IAS 38 they must be recorded under intangible assets only if they are acquired from third parties (as a result of a business combination).

According to the IVS 210,[4] when "valuing an intangible asset, it is critical to thoroughly understand specifically what needs to be valued". Customer data typically has a different value from customer contracts and customer relationships. The purpose of the valuation is critical in determining what intangible assets need to be valued and how they are defined.

Each publishing company is unique but the valuation approaches adopted by buyers are standardized and the ultimate value of a publishing company can be finally determined through the consideration of some variables: when the buyer establishes the purchase price with the seller a valuation approach (consistent with IVS 210) must be selected:

- **Income approach**: adopted for validating a purchase price, it focuses on the net present value of discounted future cash flows (DCF). Thus, the buyer can verify if the future cash flows confirm the purchase price and are aware of the necessary additional capital investments. Based on past and future economic benefits that can be linked to the heading, both license revenues (royalties) and incremental revenues are considered.
  "Under the income approach, the value of an intangible asset is determined by reference to the present value of income, cash flows or cost

savings attributable to the intangible asset over its economic life" (IVS 210).

- **Market approach**: adopted to provide a guideline or range to support the value of a publishing company, this approach can be based on comparable sales transactions of private or publicly traded companies like the company being sold with regards to revenue size and product focus. As an alternative, the market approach can focus on a profitability multiple, usually EBITDA: the greater the EBITDA, the higher the potential value.

"Under the market approach, the value of an intangible asset is determined by reference to market activity (for example, transactions involving identical or similar assets)" (IVS 210).

The main limitation of this approach concerns the information asymmetries structurally connected with the secrecy of intangible assets, which make the information necessary for comparisons challenging to find. Moreover, according to IAS 38, there is no active market for intangible assets, which tend to be not accounted for, and their fair value seems difficult to estimate. These limitations apply even to headings.

Cost approach: according to this approach, the value of an intangible asset is determined by the sum of its capitalized costs, incurred for the realization of the intangible or to be incurred to reproduce it. The limitation of this approach lies in the fact that it does not consider maintenance costs and the opportunity cost of time and that does not apply to assets capable of generating income. The main difficulty consists in finding costs incurred in the past, especially if they have been incurred over several years and have not been capitalized.

The valuation approaches for newspaper headings fall within the ones used in the estimation of intangibles with an indefinite useful life and, in particular, those that have greater affinities with the headings: brands, as distinctive signs, copyright, and technology in terms of contents, patents, and software, especially for the online media.

The editorial heading is an intangible asset with a potentially indefinite useful life (as well as the trademarks, but not the patents) and is abstractly separable from the company in which it is inserted, an event that postulates independent negotiability, similar to that of a brand (and with similar criticalities).

For the estimation of the likely market value of the newspaper headings, the (empirical) formula based on multipliers, proposed by appraisal practitioners (normally used in the Italian valuation practice), is the following:

Market value of the heading $= a *$ turnover(subscriptions and sales) $+$ $b *$ revenues from advertising $- c *$ operating losses

$$(10.1)$$

where:

> $a =$ multiplier of the turnover (usually equal to 1);
> $b =$ multiplier of the advertising revenues (usually included in the range from 1 to 2);
> $c =$ multiplier of the operating losses (usually included in the range from 3 to 5).

In this context, Guatri and Bini (2009) point out that "an (...) example of the application of empirical multipliers in a complex formula is the valuation of newspaper headings and periodicals in publishing companies. The identification of the specific intangible asset heading has various explanations. First of all, with particular reference to newspapers and political or economic–political periodicals, it is based on the assumption that the value of a heading is not a simple economic fact, being linked to the influence factor, i.e., to its capacity to influence the public opinion, especially in the political and social fields. Secondly, it is based on the idea that the assertion, and therefore the spread at a certain level (beyond the break-even point) of a heading, requires important investments and above all initial losses. In this perspective, it is a substantial reconstruction cost of the heading, up to the level of success achieved". A consistent methodology is shared by Zanda et al. (2013).

The algorithm reported in formula (10.1) is an expression of a market valuation approach that expresses the implicit multiples, which do not make specific and explicit reference to actual multiples derived from real market prices (deal prices), which would be misleading, if not supported by frequent and effectively comparable transactions.

Newspapers are typically unprofitable businesses, and advertising revenues together with subscriptions and direct sales through newsstands are unlikely to cover huge running costs fully. Newspapers give their owner some private benefits, including political power, the capacity to address public opinion, and notoriety. That is why so many tycoons end up owning newspapers.

As part of the algorithm reported in formula (10.1), advertising revenues have been the prevailing revenue source for many decades, even though the international media advertising market has been characterized since the end of the 1990s, by strong contractions, only minimally attributable to the recessionary crisis that started in 2008. There is an ongoing paradigm shift in the advertising business model, from paper to digital.

The interest in advertising for online headings currently does not seem to fully compensate for the fall in advertising in the traditional segments (which continue to be based on particular advertisements, such as small announcements, obituaries, notifications of sentences, notices of public tenders, etc.). The free web is, in many cases, a formidable competitor. Concerning the items included in the estimation algorithm or, more broadly, in the other valuation principles, it should be noted that their nature is to be understood as a perspective rather than a historical-retrospective aspect; this postulates the reference to long-term business plans, drafted considering the international auditing standards, such as ISAE 3400.[5]

In the context of these business plans, the forecasts regarding the operational management (and its economic margins, in terms of EBITDA, EBIT, etc.), contained in the prospective economic accounts, are particularly relevant.

The time frame is consistent with the theoretically, indeterminate useful life of the heading, which moreover tends to lose a good part of its significance and reliability as it extends beyond more contingent forecasts, normally confined to 2–3 years.

Again, concerning the items that characterize the algorithm of formula (10.1) (turnover, advertising revenue, and net operating margin, typically at a loss), the level of variability associated with each item must be verified—case by case and along with the schedule of the projections. Operating margins must be achieved by subtracting the operating costs, the subdivision of the revenues, and fixed and variable costs from the turnover and the other operating revenues.

The variability of the operating revenues (influenced by loyal readers, by advertising revenue in the presence of a guaranteed minimum, etc.) must be verified considering the related costs (first of all the labor cost, made flexible using precarious contracts, particularly widespread in the sector, or from outsourcing of articles and pieces with external signatures).

The empirical approach does not conflict with the meta-standards provided by ISO 10668 for trademarks[6] but represents a coherent variation since the revenue approach incorporates the three algorithm parameters (turnover, advertising revenue, and operating losses).

The income approach (and its connection with the financial approach) is also relevant regarding the differential income (incremental) which may hopefully derive from the use of the heading compared to others. This approach is in tune with the competitive advantage proposed by Porter (1998) due to differentiation strategies, such that the publication on a premium heading ensures an otherwise non-existent surplus value, which must be recognized in the valuation.

The link between the empirical approach enclosed in the algorithm and the opportunity cost approach is less direct, but still worth considering. The question about the time and the cost of reconstructing a heading is not separated from the empirical observation of operating costs that produce net losses, after having discounted the subscription and advertising revenues.

According to a complementary perspective, in a complementary way, among the factors that influence the application of the market multipliers, the following are relevant:

- The seniority of the title (stability concerning the market and reader loyalty);
- Competition (position of the heading for those that can be homogeneously compared);
- Dissemination (printed copies and copies sold, subscriptions; local or national Circulation; print or digital distribution, etc.);
- Sale price (not particularly significant for daily newspapers and non-existent for free press);
- Editing (degree of notoriety and authority of journalists, collaborators, and management);

- Advertising attractiveness (type and number of ads);
- Future potential (market opportunities, also based on online technological prospects);
- Profitability (expressed by the operating result, typically at the operating level).

Advertising is intended as the mass communication form used by companies to create consensus around their image or to achieve their marketing objectives. The main feature of advertising communication is to spread paid messages through the mass media, with pre-packaged standard formats and, especially in online advertising, increasingly personalized ads.

From a legal point of view, each country has its directives related to advertisements: according to the Advertising Association of the UK "advertising is a means of communication with the users of a product or service. Advertisements are messages paid for by those who send them and are intended to inform or influence people who receive them".[7]

Another important aspect in the valuation of newspaper headings is represented by the human capital employed by the editorial staff, with an impact on revenues from sales/subscriptions, which can be influenced in some way by the appreciation that readers can show toward some signatures.

The sales network is a parameter that can influence the assessment, given the widespread distribution of the headings.

10.3.1 The Contextualization of the Assessment, Depending on the Type of Heading

The calculation algorithm of formula (10.1) must be concretely adapted to the case under assessment, in a market context characterized by a strong discontinuity of business models.

The type of heading is relevant (daily newspaper, general or specialized magazine, linked to trade associations or as house organ, etc.), its diffusion (national or local), with the segmentation of readers (community, especially in the virtual field with social media) and a consequent degree of loyalty that can be statistically detected with historical data on sales (by subscription or at newsstands or with web accesses).

There are numerous exceptional cases; for example, the valuation of a political newspaper is, at least partially, different from that of a common newspaper. In particular, the political nature, that strongly characterizes the heading, could entail, for the shareholders, benefits of a pecuniary nature and not (in terms of reputation or other), known in the literature as private benefits of the control, which could be the subject of specific appraisal, even at the level of surplus assets.[8] Journalistic headings, especially those of a political nature, can enjoy public contributions, which in any case have diminished in recent years.

In the following paragraphs, references will be made to new media, including online headings. They are characterized by strategic and product-related features that make them profoundly different from traditional media, especially if they are paper-based. The relevant aspects of new media include:

- The speed (immediacy) of distance communication;
- The geographical and potential demographic scope;
- The unlimited potential of memory (which contrasts with the physical limits of newspapers and printed magazines);
- The interactivity and participation of users, who can become key players from passive readers;
- Hyper-targeting and selectivity (increasingly targeted and profiled identification of contents, recipients, etc.);
- The lack of space–time limits.

10.3.2   The Valuation Paradox "Strong Heading, Weak Publishing Company"

Many newspaper headings are characterized by a glorious past and an uncertain future, due to the epochal changes in business models, which further compress an operating margin that is already structurally negative, as evidenced by the algorithm illustrated in formula (10.1), which explicitly mentions the operational losses.

Despite the losses of readers and diffusion, the evocative charm of historical newspapers resists, more than it could seem rationally logic.

The valuation may so follow the estimative oxymoron "strong heading". Estimates of the value of newspaper headings that do not perform as they should, while retaining their theoretical capacity, can, for example, be carried out starting from a more conservative base value, to which to add elements of potential enhancement, upon the occurrence of certain milestones, incorporated within more conservative business plan variants.

And the additional valuation can be appropriately shared between sellers and buyers through earn-out contractual clauses, especially where the former retains, at least in part, managerial responsibilities.

10.4 THE ONLINE HEADINGS

Electronic printing is a popular online editorial product that has a heading, and a regular periodicity and that collects, comments, and criticizes news addressed to the public.

Online headings can be combined with the printed edition (as is the case for the main newspapers and magazines) or available exclusively on the web; subscriptions can be finalized in one of the two modes (with discounts for the possibility of using, with a customized download, only for the online version, more relevant for foreign subscribers, not affected by any geographical segmentation if they access the World Wide Web) or both.

The business model of online headings, even at the level of the value chain, is profoundly different from that—much more traditional—of paper headings and this affects a leaner supply chain that lacks the physicality of some suppliers (paper and ink; typography; distribution chain typically through newsstands, with return management) and with completely different space–time characteristics (online headings are accessible anywhere and anytime, with a digital proximity 24/7).

The business model is influenced by scalability for physical newspaper headings; this term indicates the possibility of increasing the circulation (purely virtual) instantaneously and without limits, even geographically, with almost zero additional costs.

Accessibility is usually segmented and can be completely free, after registration (an event that allows a user profiling, used, to the limits of legality, to then resell its marketing content) or for a fee (usually, with an introductory section open to anyone and a dedicated section, containing the entire articles, accessible for a fee).

The editorial contents originally consisted of an online transposition of the paper model (with a copy and paste saved in PDF or another protected file of the printed version). Today they are characterized by multimedia hyper-textuality and interactivity (search by keywords, links with other sites, content sharing with social media and other viral modes, presence of photos, music and videos, etc.) that until a few years ago were completely unthinkable. The technological innovations propose increasingly sophisticated solutions because they are profiled for new IT tools (in addition to fixed PCs and laptops, smartphones, and tablets, now increasingly widespread). In editorial headings, the diffusion of color, with chromatic modalities, in terms of pixels and other resolutions, which only partially appear in the printed paper (especially in newspapers), is relevant.

Thanks to the interactive community, made technologically possible by the web, the reader-user becomes the protagonist.

As Thurman and Fletcher (2018) point out, "newspapers and TV news broadcasts can be perceived as sub-genres of the news genre and the integration of the web medium and the traditional newspaper genre defines a genre for online newspapers". The profiling of the headings, also from a graphic point of view, is becoming part of a multimedia context, in which smartphones and tablets make a now unavoidable use of mobile apps that connect, in a quick, simple, and intuitive way, with appealing logos, the touchscreen keyboard to the heading and its contents.

Earlier research on the design or use of online newspapers has so far mostly relied on experimental design and surveys: research on the design of online newspapers may concern e.g., location of information, content features, and interactive functions. "*Content refers to themes and topics, whereas form refers to observable physical and linguistic features. Functionality refers to capabilities available through the new media*" (Ihlström & Lundberg, 2004).

The considerations summarized here are related to the vast world of online media, describing their characteristics, destined to affect the parameters for evaluating the headings.

Then there is the issue, for a long-time discussed by practitioners, of the applicability of the rules relating to paper printing to online headings. On the web, some realities that are perfectly like the printed press, and a mere structural difference, deriving from the tool used for dissemination (the web instead of the paper) cannot prevent the applicability of the rules on printing to websites. It is not possible to derive general applicability of the rules on the press to websites that have a purely voluntary nature, such as forums (virtual discussion sites) or blogs. Authors are becoming increasingly powerful, and their right to get appropriate remuneration from publisher grows. Publishers and digital platforms, on their own, are transferring to content creators part of their oligopolistic power. Big data, including journalistic content, increasingly matter, and they need fair remuneration for their use.

The valuation of online headings can fall within the scope of estimating the value of websites and internet domains.[9]

10.5   THE VALUATION OF THEMATIC CHANNELS

Alongside the traditional editorial headings, now widely available online, in recent years the so-called thematic channels have emerged, both on television and the web, referring to the in-depth study of topics related to certain realities, including political ones.

The traditional approaches of assessing journalistic headings, which consider multipliers of turnover, advertising, and operating results, seem challenging to apply to thematic channels, since there are generally no substantial advertising revenues nor from sales/subscriptions, as is typically the case for newspapers headings or other websites, also in the hypothesis of pay-per-view (for example, satellite channels, ...).

It may so be necessary to use a method that bypasses the standard capital, economic and financial parameters, to refer to alternative market parameters, used in valuations of companies in the sector; among these the following are relevant:

- The number of unique visitors (identified by the sum of persistent cookies);
- The number of pages viewed per month;
- The number of registered members on the website.

In the absence of external subsidies and other revenues (from sales/subscriptions and advertising), in a stand-alone hypothesis, the revenue model of the thematic channels must be based on business models focused on advertising revenues. The model needs to adapt to new scenarios, understanding the inputs coming from the market, first advertising, without distorting the characteristics of the site, whose value derives from its identity. The profiling of unique users, even at the level of segmentation of their characteristics, can enhance their specificity, avoiding a generalization of identity profiles, suitable for the mass-market but not for niche sites.

The advertising revenue of a website substantially derives from banners and pop-ups, which can be inserted through specific contracts with operators, or through the Google Adsense service, the advertising platform that works together with Google Adwords. The former is created for advertisers who want to promote their products and services on the Internet, the latter is designed for website owners who want to maximize profits and gains from their content.[10]

In general, advertising revenues are variable and depend on the number of visitors to the pages and the clicks on the banner/pop-up, or they can be fixed, in the case of ad hoc contracts stipulated directly with advertisers or with advertising concessionaires.

10.6   THE PROSPECTS OF THE MEDIA SECTOR, FROM PAPER TO DIGITAL

Among the numerous market media, the most relevant are:

1. Free television;
2. Pay television;
3. Radio;
4. Newspapers;
5. Periodicals.

Even though these traditional tools are consolidated, the market trend is clearly in favor of the growing digitalization of the use of publishing its products.

The evidence in recent years enables us to point out that the digital market of headings no longer represents a mere online transposition of the printed version. This new market is characterized by its contents, at a technological level and with an impact on the reader's usability (link multimedia, photo galleries, videos, links with social networks, apps, etc.), which require significant investments. This is reflected in the profile of advertising sales, increasingly oriented toward new interactive paradigms, to segment and profile customers, personalizing advertising.

The headings restyling (in graphics, content, layout, etc.) and the gradual transmigration to online channels, keeping the traditional paper products where possible, aim to face the challenges of a rapidly evolving market, still looking for stabilization of strategic models. The fall in sales in paper-based media markets is partially offset by a constant growth in the online market, which struggles to generate revenues and needs more effective modeling.

Moreover, the future of books and printed media is characterized by a truly competitive technology, being easy to transport, difficult to deteriorate, with high-resolution pagination, without battery problems, etc. Therefore, thinking that e-books will take over is, at least, premature; these considerations apply to newspapers and magazines.

A further element concerns the competition between the leaders of digital information, represented by the platforms of the main search engines or social networks, and the printed and/or online headings. Traditional printing firms complain about indiscriminate passages on social media of news and data on readers without carriage fees and with limited traffic flow from social media to the original newspaper headings, which do not remunerate the latter.

Fake news involves distortions of information that reduce the credibility of the media, causing reputational damage with economic implications (loss of advertising revenue, reduction of subscribers and occasional readers, etc.). Fake news exacerbates information asymmetries, and destroys value for all the stakeholders involved in the media supply & value chain. Blockchains, with their validation properties, may soften the issue.

In general, the proliferation of innovative business models is not yet accompanied by stable and consolidated revenue models, with the risk of arbitrage or unfair competition from some operators that can abuse their dominant position on key variables, such as Web traffic flow and personalized user information.

10.6.1   *Legal Protection of Editorial Headings and Copyright: Some Introductory Notes*

Communication and information constitute an increasingly important moment in social relations and commercial activity. Hence the importance of the distinctive sign is expressed by the heading.

Unlike the title of a specific work, a periodical work belongs to entrepreneurial products, with seriality characteristics.

The title of a work, when it identifies the work itself, cannot be reproduced on top of another work without the consent of the author. It is prohibited and considered unfair competition, an act of reproduction or imitation over other works of the same species, of the emblems, the dispositions of signs or printing characters, and any other particular shape and color in the external aspect of the work, when reproduction or imitation may create confusion of work or author.

The risk that the audience may confuse the works arises when the average reader of two newspapers can reconnect equality or similarity of a formal aspect (heading) to the uniqueness of the publisher. The genres to which the publications belong and therefore the contents offered, and the method of presentation to the public (typographical characters, the position of titles on the cover, subtitles, colors, etc., …) are relevant concerning the categories of readers to which they are responding, and beyond the analysis of the words used in the titles.

Online headings imply profiles related to the protection of intellectual property on the web. A matter of practical interest is represented by the habits of publishing materials of third parties (articles, photos, files, texts, etc.) taken from other sources (newspapers, books, other Internet sites) covered by Copyright that can easily be copied, pasted and uploaded with digital devices.

Starting from the mid-nineties, the first editorial products started to be sold together with newspapers and magazines, mainly books and disks, as collateral goods. Dissemination and profitability were the main objectives. The strategies applied included brand extension, but also distribution strategies since books began to be sold on newsstands.

Within this framework, we can consider, even as a benchmark for other countries, the Digital Services Act (DSA)—a legislative proposal by the European Commission to modernize the e-Commerce Directive regarding illegal content, transparent advertising, and disinformation.

10.7   DIGITAL PUBLISHING

The term digital publishing consists of the publishing phenomenon in which the entire editorial process and access to the contents are implemented using information technology. Digital publishing covers different fields of action, from the elaboration of print content to the widespread dissemination via the Internet of digital contents.

Digital publishing has undergone several changes, from its first hybrid appearances in the second half of the twentieth century to its exponential diffusion through the World Wide Web. It currently involves professional fields of commerce and learning, entertainment, information, and free dissemination of knowledge.

Digital publishing is referred to as both the creation of content implemented by computerized means and electronic publishing to indicate the use of content through an electronic device. Through a site (which is also a bookshop) it is possible to access the catalog and possibly some digital parts of the product which remains usable mainly offline.

Being a relatively recent phenomenon, different definitions of the term digital publishing can be provided. These definitions, on the one hand, represent the evolutionary process that still concerns it today and on the other, clarify its various fields of action, from pre-press processing to actual content in digital form.

The term pre-press refers to the digital product processing phase that occurs for traditional paper distribution. In some cases, the product is combined with a website that plays the role of a static showcase. The most accurate term is digital press, which is the use of the computer to produce digital contents, which always has a printed version that is considered the main one and is faithfully reproduced.

It is possible to manage the creation of products and access digital content on the Internet, by downloading the contents from the Web. The end-user is interactive: he/she can register, and download the catalog, parts of the product, or the entire digital content. So, all the elements that characterize the entire digital cycle begin to be found, implementing complete digital management of the access and dissemination of the contents, including services such as e-commerce, the search interface, and other features allowed to the user. The context of online sales is increasingly favorable and there is greater interest in improving it.

Examples of materials that are fast emerging in the world of digital publishing include:

- Newsletters;
- Journals and blogs;
- Advertisements;
- Company reports;
- Catalogs;
- Books, magazines, and other periodicals;
- Massive libraries, resource materials, and databases;
- Scrapbooks.

Firms facing digitalization respond to the mutating environment with the adoption of these unconventional tools and the development of new products, which results in newly emerging business models.

Recently, publishers started to spread online versions of their newspapers. Despite early attempts at electronic dissemination of text and graphics (e.g., Teletext), the first fully web-based newspaper, The Palo Alto Weekly, appeared in 1994. This initiated an explosion of online newspapers (in the United States, for instance, there were already at least 1.296 online editions in 2002) (Ihlström & Lundberg, 2004).

Another relevant piece of evidence is The Independent, a general-interest UK national newspaper that, present in the British newsstands since 1986, went digital-only in 2016, becoming the first national newspaper brand to publish online-only. The results of the research conducted by Thurman and Fletcher (2018) proved that the mobile-only readers grew by a significant 31% since the title went online-only, and this increase more than made up for the loss of print-only readers.

Despite the increase in net monthly readership (expressed in time spent reading), a dramatic drop in the attention received by The Independent[11] from its British audience after it stopped printing. Considering that the growth in mobile-only readers at The Independent is actually lower than the average (143%) for other similar newspaper brands (all of which retained print editions) and that this rise in mobile-only readers is mainly part of a general trend, international visibility and consensus from the overseas audience was the primary advantage that going online ensured to the newspaper, respecting the global ambitions of the management.

"In the process of designing online newspapers, publishers seek to identify good ways to use web technology for establishing their online editions. Today, there is a demand from both academics and practitioners for more knowledge about how to design the online newspapers to become as recognizable and familiar as the printed ones" (Ihlström & Lundberg, 2004). The subsequent effect is the loss of readers of the printed versions and the traditional newspaper consultation in general, as the research study carried out by Opara and Nse (2017) confirms: the rate of consultation of newspapers by the students of The Federal University of Technology (Owerri) is declining as only 33% use the library daily and "most of the students use the newspapers because of information on scholarship offers and job advertisements", exclusively.

As Thurman and Fletcher (2018) underline, newspapers cover a much deeper position that entails an irreplaceable responsibility, they "perform valuable democratic functions, including informing the public and, directly or indirectly, encouraging civic and political participation. It is difficult to see how these outcomes can be achieved to the same degree if reading continues to be replaced by glancing and other low-intensity news consumption practices".

10.7.1 Forms of Digital Publishing

"Adobe is arguably the company that put digital publishing on the map by making it an accessible technology for the masses". Many other tools allow publishing works beyond the *PDF* format: digital technology includes websites, blogs, and social networking platforms, but also games, apps, videos, CDs, and downloadable materials, and even a simple text message is a form of digital publication marketing (Wolfe, 2019). Digital publishing is completely upsetting the industry, as Gutemberg did with his printed Bible edition, in 1455.

10.8 BANKABILITY OF THE NEWSPAPER HEADINGS

The bankability issues are particularly sensitive. This is relevant especially for the profiles of the negative profitability, with a consequent need for periodically refinancing the company, with direct commitments of the partners.

The reduction of fixed costs due to the use of digital technologies responds to a downward trend in newspaper sales that must be offset and contrasted with innovative revenue models. The stability of expected revenues can be guaranteed with long-term advertising contracts and a well-established readership base.

The extension to structured and diversified media companies is more articulated: the newspaper or periodicals' heading is inserted within a more articulated portfolio, in which the heading can synergistically interact with other products and services.

In this context, a consolidated group valuation, in which the heading assumes complementary importance concerning other more performing assets, is relevant.

10.8.1   Copyright and Artistic-Related (Creative) Intangible Assets

Copyright is a form of intellectual property that grants the creator of an original creative work an exclusive legal right to determine whether and under what conditions this original work may be copied and used by others, usually for a limited term of years.[12] Copyright protects the form of expression of an idea, not the idea itself.

Article 2 (viii) of the Convention Establishing the World Intellectual Property Organization (WIPO) states that Intellectual Property Rights (IPR) relate to: "...literary, artistic and scientific works; performances of performing artists, phonograms, and broadcasts; inventions in all fields of human endeavor; scientific discoveries; industrial designs; trademarks, service marks, and commercial names and designations; protection against unfair competition; and all other rights resulting from intellectual activity in the industrial, scientific, literary or artistic fields".[13]

According to Gilbert (2009), the copyright benefits from a specific bundle of legal rights that provides the author/creator the right to authorize or prohibit the uses of the copyrighted work. Generally, the author of the original work owns the copyright, even though there are exceptions to this rule. Copyrights can be sold or transferred by assignment or by licensing. From a valuation perspective, copyright-related intangible assets have similar economic and legal characteristics to other types of commercial intellectual property. The author has the right:

- To reproduce all or part of the work;
- To make new (derivative) versions;
- To distribute copies by selling, renting, leasing, or lending them;
- To perform (that is, to recite, dance, or act) the work publicly;
- To display the work publicly, directly, or employing film, TV, slides, or other devices or processes.

Copyrights are typically transmitted with assignments (unconditionally) and licenses.

Copyright valuation approaches typically follow the IVS 210 methodologies:

1. Market approaches (royalty rate; peruse compensation) are commonly used in a copyright valuation analysis. There is an active market concerning the fee simple sale of copyrights;

2. Income approach (incremental/differential income; profit split; residual income, etc.);
3. Cost approach (less used).

Copyright assets typically have little intrinsic value, unless they become viral (through social networks or other media platforms). Value can be extracted with direct exploitation, sale, or licensing.

Digitalization is deeply reshaping the copyright industry. As an example, the digital world has turned millions of people into active photographers. The photographs that we capture are our creations and, without any action on our part, are intellectual property that belongs to us. What is the monetary value of our IPR in these photographs? Very little, if anything. There is the potential for monetary value if we choose to exploit these photographs to obtain some economic benefit (Smith & Yossifov, 2013).

Whereas the intrinsic value of IPRs is typically negligible, copyrighted material may in some cases produce some economic benefit for its owner if it is marketable.

Evaluation of IPRs may be conducted using the market, income, or cost approach illustrated by IVS 210 and examined in Chapter 2. The cost approach has limited validity unless it is linked to the economic and financial exploitation of the IPR. Royalties are an important form of remuneration, even in their hypothetical form (relief from royalties). An assessment of the reasonable royalties that would be payable under a license agreement is a useful benchmark for valuation.

A synthesis of the valuation approaches is represented in Fig. 10.1.

The useful life of a copyright is typically long. In general, the copyright lasts for the duration of the author's life plus 70 years. If the work is done anonymously or under a pseudonym, the period extends for 95 years beyond the publication of the work or 120 years from the creation of the work, whichever is shorter.[14] The copyrighted duration may so be considered almost unlimited, even if exploitation rights granted by publishers are often consistently shorter.

Artistic-related intangibles represent a heterogeneous category that includes plays, ballets, books, magazines, newspapers, other literary works, musical works such as compositions, song lyrics, and advertising jingles, pictures, photographs, video, and audio–visual material, including motion pictures, music videos, television programs, broadcast rights, etc.

Most of the artistic-related intangibles are protected by copyright.

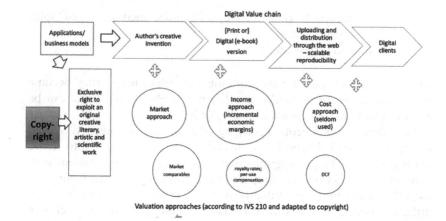

Fig. 10.1   Copyright valuation approaches

Copyright is a form of intellectual property that grants the creator of an original creative work an exclusive legal right to determine whether and under what conditions this original work may be copied and used by others, usually for a limited term of years.[15]

Artistic intangibles are increasingly digitized, through thematic or general websites (see for instance YouTube), where videos, music, etc. are uploaded and shared. These sites are mainly accessed for free and their revenue model is mostly based on advertising.

Valuation is mostly based on royalty projections. The period is long: typically, the public law duration of a copyright expires 50–100 years after the creator dies, depending on the jurisdiction. This extension influences valuation approaches and assimilates these creative intangibles to perpetual trademarks or other intangibles with infinite life. In these cases, any terminal value approaches zero (being TV $/ \infty \rightarrow 0$) and so is not considered in the formulation.

Even artwork does not have a determinable useful life, and its potential value may so be considered perpetual.

Artwork, especially if first-class, represents pieces that are held for capital appreciation purposes as a store of wealth. Artwork may not produce any periodical return, if it is not merchandised or made visible to a paying public, even digitally through the web. Consistently with IAS 16, artwork can be accounted for using a:

1. Cost model, under which you hold your assets at cost less depreciation less impairment loss; or
2. Revaluation model, under which you hold your assets at fair value at the date of revaluation less subsequent depreciation less subsequent impairment loss.

Creative assets (as the other intangibles) do not autonomously produce any interest rate and may yield a royalty stream or a potential royalty that can be used as a clue to estimate their value. Digitization of artistic-related intangibles, whenever possible (e.g., the transformation of a paper book into a digital edition) increases potential fruition and, in some cases, scalable value.

Copyright authorship entitles to monopolistic rents (since the creative work is protected) with consequent pricing power and protected profitability.

10.8.2   Digital Media and Video Games

Video games are an electronic game that involves interaction with a user interface to generate visual feedback for a player. The typologies range from action games to adventure, role-playing, strategy, or sports games. Digitalization and web channels of fruition are embedded in most business models, making the whole industry intrinsically scalable. Video games are the most powerful industry behind the metaverse development.

Video gaming may bring addiction or compulsive gambling, with ESG consequences that may impact valuation.

The analysis of the innovative business model of video game firms is a prerequisite for its appraisal and embeds scalability options. The evaluation depends on the prioritizing identification of the crucial value drivers. The evaluation metrics are mainly based on expected cash flow and market comparisons.

Nowadays, video game developers record every virtual action performed by their players. As each player can remain in the game for years, this results in an exceptionally rich dataset that can be used to understand and predict player behavior. This information may serve to identify the most valuable players and foresee the amount of money they will spend on in-app purchases during their lifetime. This is crucial in free-to-play games, where up to 50% of the revenue is generated by just around 2% of the players, the so-called whales (Chen et al., 2018).

Lifetime value (LTV), also called customer lifetime value or lifetime customer value, is an estimate first introduced in the context of marketing, used to determine the expected revenue customers will generate over their entire relationship with a service. LTV has been used in a variety of fields—including video games—and is a useful measure for deciding on future investment, personalized player retention strategies, and marketing and promotion plans. The fundamental elements in historical LTV computations originally come from RFM (recency, frequency, monetary value) models, which group customers based on recency, frequency, and monetary value—namely, on how recently and how often they purchased and how much they spent. The basic assumption of RFM models is that users with more recent purchases, who purchase more often or who spend larger amounts of money are more likely to purchase again in the future.

Marketing strategies can greatly vary. For instance, a publisher can either bundle a game and add-on (functional item) or offer the add-on separately through microtransactions (Vu et al., 2020).

NOTES

1. Business dictionary at http://www.businessdictionary.com/definition/press-release.html.
2. https://www.iasplus.com/en/binary/dttpubs/publish.pdf.
3. Available at http://www.fondazioneoic.eu/wp-content/uploads/2011/02/2019-01-OIC-24-Immobilizzazioni-immateriali.pdf.
4. Available at https://www.ivsc.org/files/file/view/id/647.
5. The examination of prospective financial information. Available at http://www.ifac.org/system/files/downloads/b013-2010-iaasb-handbook-isae-3400.pdf.
6. See Sect. 9.3.
7. According to the Italian Legislation, advertisement can be defined as "any form of message that is disseminated, in any way, in the exercise of a commercial, industrial, craft or professional activity in order to promote the transfer of movable or immovable property, the provision of works or services or the establishment or the transfer of rights and obligations to them" (Article 2 of Legislative Decree 145/2007).
8. See Sect. 2.13.
9. See Chapter 11.
10. https://www.reliablesoft.net/adwords-vs-adsense-what-is-the-difference-and-can-i-use-both-on-the-same-website/.
11. Available at https://www.independent.co.uk/.
12. https://www.lexico.com/en/definition/copyright.

13. www.wipo.int/treaties/en/convention/trtdocs_wo029.html#P50_1504.
14. https://www.fool.com/knowledge-center/how-to-calculate-the-annual-amortization-of-copyri.aspx.
15. https://en.oxforddictionaries.com/definition/copyright.

SELECTED REFERENCES

Alavi, R., & Azmi, I. M. A. G. (2019). The copyright reward system and content owners in the creative industry: A study of the Malaysian film and TV industry. *The Journal of the World Intellectual Property, 22*(3–4), 129–145.

Armando, S. (2019). The other side of the coin: Editors vs writers in professional journals. *Journal of Human Behavior in the Social Environment, 29*(3), 430–434.

Chen, P. P., Guitart, A., Fernandez del Rio, A., & Perianez, A. (2018). Customer lifetime value in video games using deep learning and parametric models. *IEEE International Conference on Big Data*, 2134–2140.

Das, S. (2016). *Magazine publishing innovation: Two case studies on managing creativity.* Department of Journalism & Publishing, London College of Communication, University of the Arts London, London SE1 6SB, UK.

Gilbert, K. A. (2009, Autumn). The valuation of copyright-related intangible assets. *Intellectual Property Valuation Insights.*

Graf, C., Wager, E., Bowman, A., Fiack, S., Scott-Lichter, D., & Robinson, A. (2007). Best practice guidelines on publication ethics: A publisher's perspective. *International Journal of Clinical Practice, 61*(152), 1–26. PMCID: PMC1804120.

Guatri, L., & Bini, M. (2009). *Nuovo trattato sulla valutazione delle aziende.* EGEA editore.

Ihlstrom, C., & Lundberg, J. (2004). A genre perspective on online newspaper from page design. *Journal of Web Engineering, 3*(1), 50–74.

International Valuations Standards Council. (2016). *IVS 210, Intangible assets.*

Kao, G., Chiang, X., & Foulsham, T. (2019). Reading behavior and the effect of embedded selfies in role-playing e-books: An eye-tracking investigation. *Computers & Education, 136*(1), 99–112.

Lynn, E. (2019). *Successful publishing of research: An editor's view.*

Maurer, S. M. (2018). Digital publishing: Three futures (and how to get there). *Cardozo Arts & Entertainment Law Journal, 36,* 675.

Opara, G., & Nse, J. (2017). Trend of newspaper consultation by students of Federal university of technology. *The Information Technologist, an International Journal of Information and Communication Technology, 14*(1), 165–172.

Porter, M. E. (1998). *Competitive advantage: Creating and sustaining superior performance.* New York: The Free Press.

Smith, G. V., & Yossifov, V. (2013). *Monetization of copyright assets by creative enterprises.* World Intellectual Property Organization.

Thurman, N., & Fletcher, R. (2018). Are newspapers heading toward post-print obscurity? A case study of the Independent's transition to online-only. *Digital Journalism, 6*(8), 1003–1017.

Torres Vargas, G. A., & Morales Lopez, V. (2014). *A business model for electronic books.*

Vu, D., Zhao, X., & Stecke, K. (2020). *Pay-to-win in video games: Microtransactions and fairness concerns.* Available at https://ssrn.com/abstract=3658537

Wolfe, L. (2019). *Digital marketing defined: The definition of digital publishing extends far beyond the mighty PDF.* Available at https://www.thebalancecareers.com/digital-marketing-defined-3515308

Zanda, G., Lacchini, M., & Onesti, T. (2013). *La valutazione delle aziende.* Torino: Giappichelli.

Internet and the Metaverse

CHAPTER 11

Domain Name and Website Valuation

11.1 INTRODUCTION

A domain name is a group of alphanumeric symbols that compose a name, followed by an extension defined by the Registration Authority of a specific country or an organization. The domain name is directly associated with a DNS,[1] which is a system that allows converting a domain name (easier to remember) to an IP address.

Domain names are the gateway to websites. A website is a collection of related web pages typically identified with a common domain name and published on at least one web server. All publicly available websites collectively form the world wide web. The valuation of domain names can take place autonomously or jointly. Websites cannot exist without access domains, whereas domain names can be an empty shell, with little if any content.

According to Pokorná and Večerková (2013), every computer connected to the Internet has its definite Internet Protocol (IP) address formed of a combination of numbers, today four numbers lying between 0 and 255 and separated by periods, thus from 0.0.0.0 to 255.255.255.255. This creates the possibility of using around four billion possible IP addresses.

For practical use in ordinary life or during business activity, the IP address constructed in this way is impractical. It is not possible to expect Internet users to remember these numerical combinations; it is utterly

© The Author(s), under exclusive license to Springer Nature   349
Switzerland AG 2022
R. Moro-Visconti, *The Valuation of Digital Intangibles*,
https://doi.org/10.1007/978-3-031-09237-4_11

useless for promoting and offering goods and services or for identifying the entrepreneurs who provide them. Therefore, the idea has gradually come about to replace numbers with a different designation that would be closer to users. The Domain Name System (DNS) thus emerged in 1984—a hierarchically arranged system of names that removed numerical series on technical network addresses. When the network user requests a domain name, his request is transferred from the user's server to the name server, where a technical IP address can be registered, which the domain name replaces. Whereas the domain name with the same TLD can only be assigned once, the option exists of registering the same name, which contains a differing TLD.

Domain names serve to identify Internet resources, such as computers, networks, and services, with a text-based label that is easier to memorize than the numerical addresses used in the Internet protocols. A domain name may represent entire collections of such resources or individual instances. Individual Internet host computers use domain names as host identifiers, also called hostnames. The term host-name is used for the leaf labels in the domain name system, usually without further subordinate domain namespace. Hostnames appear as a component in Uniform Resource Locators (URLs) for Internet resources such as websites.

Domain names are used as simple identification labels to indicate ownership or control of a resource. Such examples are the realm identifiers used in the Session Initiation Protocol (SIP), the Domain Keys used to verify DNS domains in email systems, and in many other Uniform Resource Identifiers (URIs).

An important function of domain names is to provide easily recognizable and storable names to numerically addressed Internet resources. This abstraction allows any resource to be moved to a different physical location in the address topology of the network, globally or locally in an intranet. Such a move usually requires changing the IP address of a resource and the corresponding translation of this IP address to and from its domain name.

Domain names are used to establish a unique identity. Organizations can choose a domain name that corresponds to their name, helping Internet users to reach them easily. Research on brand name classification (Arora et al., 2015) shows that brands make extensive use of the promoter's name and place of origin (39.7% of all brand names coded), compounding (34.1%), abbreviations (18.2%), and blending (7.9%). Brand name transliteration in multiple socio-linguistically different markets represents another issue for global brands.

A generic domain is a name that defines a general category, rather than a specific or personal instance, for example, the name of an industry, rather than a company name. Some examples of generic names are books.com, music.com, and travel.info. Companies have created brands based on generic names, and such generic domain names may be valuable.

Domain names are often referred to as domains and domain name registrants are frequently referred to as domain owners, although domain name registration with a registrar does not confer any legal ownership of the domain name, only an exclusive right of use for a duration of time. The use of domain names in commerce may subject them to trademark law.

Internet domains are classified by the Internet Assigned Numbers Authority (IANA, www.iana.org) in two distinct types:

1. ccTLD (country code top-level domains) that are used by countries, for example, in Italy .it, Europe .eu, France .fr, Germany .de., etc. (see www.icann.org);
2. gTLDs (generic top-level domains) that are used for commercial organizations, for example, .com, .gov, and .edu.

There are also the second-level domains, which consist of the part before the top-level internet domain. The number of levels is counted from right to left (for example maps.google.com, google is the second-level domain).

Afterward, there are the third-level domains composed from the far left (in the previous example the word "maps." is a subdomain). The maximum number of subdomains is 127 and each label can be 63 characters long, the complete domain name cannot exceed 255 characters.[2]

Among the third-level domains, there are www2 or www3 used to identify alternative servers that are used to reduce the traffic on the main server.

The evaluation of domain names has already been investigated in the literature (Dieterle & Bergmann, 2014; Lindenthal, 2014; Meystedt, 2015; Tang et al., 2014). This chapter considers:

1. evaluation issues within a general appraisal framework of intangibles, going beyond "quick and dirty" algorithms;

2. domain names and their related websites either as a stand-alone asset or within a synergistic portfolio of web intangibles that include digital trademarks and M-apps.

11.2   INPUT PARAMETERS FOR VALUATION

The domain name appraisal (Alberti et al., 2017; Andriessen, 2004; Anson & Suchy, 2005; Ballester et al., 2003; Boujelben & Fedhila, 2011; Cavallari & Moro Visconti, 2016; Hackett, 2002; Lagrost et al., 2010; Solum, 2013) can have different strategic targets such as:

- willingness to buy or sell domains in the market;
- assessment of the fair royalty rate for licensing;
- determination of fair value for forensic purposes (litigations and dispute resolution).

Whereas domain names may be sold as a stand-alone asset, especially if they are just copyrighted without any specific content (being their websites empty), websites incorporate the domain name and are so negotiated together with their IP addresses. Intermediation of websites as an asset is less common since their contents (e-commerce products and/or services; advertising-driven revenues linked to data, etc.) are typically sold or licensed together with the website (Iparraguirre, 2016; Rocha, 2012).

The valuation of domain names is complex and is based on several parameters (internal or publicly available from the Web) that derive from the key value drivers described in the following paragraphs.

The value of a web domain depends on its capacity to attract traffic, i.e., visitors, and to transform them into cash-generating customers.

Domain names and especially websites represent the virtual "shop window" of selling agents that want to promote their products or services. For that reason, domain names are increasingly used and recalled in business cards, packaging labels, addresses, letterheads, etc. The domain name is just the gateway to the website and so its intrinsic value is just a small, albeit essential, part of the whole web value chain.

11.3   CHARACTERISTICS OF SELLABLE DOMAIN NAMES

Characteristics of sellable domain include:

1. Good Top-Level Domain

Though there are hundreds of domain extensions to end domain names with, most users prefer .com. It is certainly possible to sell a domain name with an alternative TLD, but it is possible to get a much higher amount if it is a .com. In many cases, a regional TLD like .ca or .us can ask for high figures, but it will be harder to attain because the pool of potential buyers will be significantly smaller.

Organizations might prefer to register a .org domain, and companies targeting very specific geographical regions might want to register a local domain (e.g., .it; .co.uk; .cn, etc.). Apart from these cases, a .com domain is always the best option. This extension is the most popular around the around, and it is already stuck in people's minds. Visitors coming to the website via search engines or organic links will pay attention mostly to the name and not to the URL. The next time they want to visit the site it is very likely that they will just type its name followed by a .com.

2. Short Length

Short domains are mostly already registered and challenging to find, so the shorter the domain is, the higher its asking price can be.

3. Capacity to Pass the Radio Test

Domain names were invented to make it easier for people to access websites, so the domain must be easily understandable. Does the domain sound good? Will people know how to spell it after hearing it? Is it easy to remember? Any confusion that the domain causes will negatively impact how much others are willing to shell out.

4. Correct Spelling

A valuable domain needs to be spelled properly. No one is going to have their sights set on sportsdawkter.com. The same can be said about using 4 instead of four, u instead of you, or other spelling variations. That is not to say that it is not possible to sell alternate spellings at all, just that the asking price will be much lower. The least desirable thing is visitors misspelling the domain and ending up somewhere else. Avoid unusual foreign words, words that have complex pronunciation, strange combinations of letters, and anything else that might cause someone to misspell the address.

5. Meaningful Keywords

In-demand keywords with good SEO will increase the value of the domain. There must be a balance here, though; more keywords do not equal more money. People would not want hockeybasketballsoccerdoctor.com as much as sportsdoctor.com. The importance of domain name keywords has changed dramatically over time as search engine algorithms have evolved. While there certainly are benefits of having targeted words in the domain, they are not as important as they once were for SEO.[3]Domain names can attract interested web surfers by their wording. Google Trends will help determine whether interest in the domain's keywords is rising or declining, as well as compare how it stacks up against similar keywords. Having a descriptive domain name will give visitors an idea of what the site is about even before they enter it. If related keywords are present in the domain, it might help the search engine rankings.

6. Easy to remember

Many Internet users do not use bookmarks. They just memorize the domains of their favorite websites and type them whenever they want to visit one. Guess what, if the domain is complex and not easy to remember you will lose these visitors along the way.

7. Brandable

A brandable domain will have a nice pronunciation, an interesting combination of letters, or simply an appealing visual effect. Sometimes they will not be descriptive, but they can be equally efficient. Brandable domains will make the visitors associate the name with the website and its content (Notice that brandable domains can be descriptive at the same time, but that is not always the case).

8. Domains that do not contain hyphens or numbers

Domain names containing hyphens and numbers are cheaper for a reason. They suffer the same problem of domains not using a .com extension or with complex spelling.

Google AdWords' Keyword Planner tool shows how popular keywords are and how much advertisers are paying for that traffic.

A price index for Internet domain names is analyzed in Lindenthal (2014).

11.4   ACCOUNTING DATA

Accounting data can represent a useful informative set for domain and website valuation. According to Sic 32 (interpretation of IAS principles) "firms may bare internal costs for the development and the functioning of their website, both for internal and for external use".

A website for external use may serve for the promotion and advertising of products and services, the supply of e-services, and the sale of products and services.

A website for internal use may serve as a piece of archive information on the firm, details of clients, and a store of valuable information. Sic states that the development phases may be described as follows:

a. Planning—the definition of objectives and technical features, the evaluation of the various, possible alternatives, and the choice of the most suitable.
b. Definition of application software and infrastructural aspects— includes obtaining a domain, acquiring and developing operative hardware and software, installment of developed applications, and verification under solicit.
c. Development of design—refers to the graphical aspect of web pages.
d. Development of contents—includes creation, purchase, preparation, and upload of information (both textual and graphical) on the website before completing it.

Information can be stored in different databases that result and are all accessible on the website, or they are codified directly in web pages. After the website has been developed, the operative phase begins, during which the firm maintains and improves applications, infrastructure, graphic design, and contents of the website. When accounting for internal costs for the development and performance of the website for internal or external use, problems consists in determining:

a. if the website is an internally generated intangible asset that is subject to IAS 38 rules;
b. the correct accounting rules for these expenses.

IAS 38 defines criteria for the accounting of intangible assets that are not specifically dealt with by other International accounting principles. It is also used for advertising expenses, employee training, plant costs, and research and development costs.

All internal costs related to the development and functioning of an entity's website must be accounted for in conformity with IAS 38. The nature of each of these activities (e.g., the training of employees and the maintenance of the website) and the phase of development must be assessed to determine the most appropriate accounting principle.

Traditional financial statements do not provide relevant information for managers or investors to understand how their resources—many of which are intangible—create value in the future. Intellectual capital statements are designed to bridge this gap by providing innovative information about how intangible resources create future value. Published intellectual capital statements are rare documents (Mouritsen et al., 2004).

11.5   WEB SEARCH ENGINE RANKING

A web search engine is a software system that is designed to search for information on the web. Promoting a website on search engines is done either through Search Engine Optimization (SEO) (Beel et al., 2010)[4]; or through Search Engine Marketing (SEM) (Sherman, 2006).

SEO includes all activities implemented to improve the ranking of a website on search engines in keyword matching considered more strategic.

Search engine optimization is the process of affecting the visibility of a website or a web page in a web search engine's unpaid result. In general, the earlier (or higher ranked on the search results page), and more frequently a site appears in the search results list, the more visitors it will receive from the search engine's users, and these visitors can be converted into customers.

Search Engine Marketing refers to a set of web marketing activities carried out to increase the visibility of a website on search engines and manage Pay per Click campaigns (Toscano, 2009).

Among the techniques used to improve ranking on search engines, there is the promotion of a website to get external links and structuring to meet the criteria required by the search engines. Web Search Engines, especially Google, creating the "page rank" (Sullivan, 2007)[5] mainly consider:

- The number of known pages;
- The number of pages that contain a link to the site;
- The relevance of the pages that contain the link (Brin & Page, 1998).

Each method for evaluating websites pays attention to the "page rank" of an internet site but also analyzes many other variables to analyze the reason why a site is top-ranked in the search engines. Several internet sites are placed at the top thanks to advertising.

The evaluation depends on real visits. Visits (or sessions) measure the number of times individuals request a page on the firm's server. The first request counts as a visit. Subsequent requests from the same individual do not count as visits unless they occur after a specified timeout period (usually set at 30 minutes).

11.6 INTERNET TRAFFIC AND ADVERTISING IMPACT ON THE EVALUATION

Internet traffic is the flow of data across the Web. To the extent that traffic turns out into contacts that can be monetized (through the sale of e-commerce goods or the supply of services or web advertising), it becomes a key parameter for the evaluation of domain names, websites, and other web intangibles.

Internet traffic can be evaluated with sophisticated algorithms and can be divided into different categories (Kemmis, 2018)[6]:

1. Direct Traffic
Direct traffic is one of the most common sources of visits to websites. Direct traffic is defined as visits with no referring website. Direct access (direct traffic) to a website occurs when a visitor arrives directly on a website, without having clicked on a link on another site. Direct traffic can come from different sources:

- If a visitor knows the URL and enters it directly into his/her browser's address bar;
- If a visitor has bookmarked the site or saved it as a favorite in his/her browser;
- If a visitor clicks on a link contained in an email (the URL has been shared by a third person).

When a visitor follows a link from one website to another, the site of origin is considered the referrer. These sites can be search engines, social media, blogs, or other websites that have a link to other websites for visitors to follow. Direct traffic categorizes visits that do not come from a referring URL. Often, these visitors manually enter the URL of the website or have it bookmarked. In many cases, direct traffic can be due to internal employees logging onto the company's webpage or current customers going to the login screen.

2. Organic Traffic

Organic traffic is defined as visitors coming from a search engine, such as Google or Bing. Paid search ads are not counted in this category. In HubSpot and Google Analytics, paid search traffic or PPC is marked in a separate category. Organic traffic deals directly with SEO. The better the ranking for competitive keywords, the more organic traffic will result. Websites that blog consistently will see a steady increase in organic search traffic and improved positioning in the search results. As a marketer, it is important to look at keywords and identify new ranking opportunities each month. These should guide the blogging efforts.

Direct traffic is so different from referred traffic, with implications on the appraisal of domain names versus internet search engines, etc.

Web traffic information may include visitors, visitor base, subscribers, subscriber base, and/or web traffic. Web traffic information may include the number, type, demographics, language, income, attributes of the visitors and/or subscribers; most requested entry and exit pages; top path (way visitors navigate the site); type, number, quality, attributes of the referrers and backlinks; search engine listings; reach, rank, page views, ranking on a search engine; and/or web traffic logs.

Web traffic characteristics may include the average, maximum, minimum, growth rates, trends, and ratios of search engine rankings; search engine listing; keyword saturation; incoming paid traffic; organic paid traffic; page views per visitor; visitor duration; page duration; a page busy time and/or a website's busy time. Web traffic characteristics in some cases may be computed by a third-party web traffic site or software program.

In analyzing online advertising, it is important to consider the method of calculating the cost of advertising on websites. The main models by which online advertising is paid for and sold are:

- «Cost Per Thousand» (CPT); is the cost an advertiser pays for one thousand views/impressions of an advertisement. The "cost per thousand advertising impressions" metric (CPM) is calculated by dividing the cost of an advertising placement by the number of impressions (expressed in thousands) that it generates. CPM is useful for comparing the relative efficiency of various advertising opportunities or media and in evaluating the overall costs of advertising campaigns (Farris et al., 2010);
- «Cost Per Click» (CPC), or «Pay Per Click» is a specific type of cost per action program where advertisers pay for each time a user clicks on an ad or link. An advertiser can use several tracking systems, including "cost per click", "pay per click" or "cost per thousand". The cost per click and pay per click systems require the advertiser to pay the website publisher a negotiated fee each time a user clicks on the advertiser's promotional materials and visits the advertiser's website (Wittlake, 2016);
- «Cost Per Visitor», (CPV), an online advertising model based on where advertisers pay for the delivery of a targeted visitor to the advertiser's website;
- «Cost Per View», (CPV): you pay only when a viewer watches the video, while traditional display ads charge you for impressions;
- «Cost Per Impression», (CPI): refers to the cost of traditional advertising or internet marketing, or email advertising campaigns, where advertisers pay each time an ad is displayed. CPI is the cost or expense incurred for each potential customer who views the advertisement(s), while CPM refers to the cost or expense incurred for every thousand potential customers who view the advertisement;
- «Cost Per Action», (CPA), an online advertising payment model where payment is based solely on qualifying actions such as sales or registrations;
- «Banner advertising». It consists of placing a graphical banner advertisement on a webpage. The role of this banner is to catch the eye of incoming traffic to the page, enticing readers to click the advertisement. This form of monetization is implemented by both affiliate programs and advertising networks. Banners originally just referred to advertisements of 468 × 60 pixels, but the term is now widely used to refer to all sizes of display advertising on the internet.[7]

Website monetization is the process of converting existing traffic being sent to a website into revenue. The most popular ways of monetizing a website are by implementing pay per click (PPC) and cost per impression (CPI/CPM) advertising. Various ad networks facilitate a webmaster in placing advertisements on pages of the website to benefit from the traffic the site is experiencing.

To evaluate a website, it is so important to assess profitability in terms of advertising returns because this allows calculating the cash flows related to the number of visitors and their appreciation of the contents of the site. In such cases, care is taken not to overly consider these elements because they do not consider all aspects related to the value of a site, the fame, the brand, etc.

The capacity of websites to generate revenues through advertising depends on the calculation method used to track users who view and click on ads.

Alexa's traffic estimates and ranks are based on the browsing behavior of people in the global data panel (which is a sample of all internet users), considering a rolling 3-month period. Traffic ranks are daily updated.[8]

Sites ranking is based on a combined measure of Unique Visitors and page views. Unique Visitors are determined by the number of unique "Alexa" users who visit a site on a given day. Page views are the total number of Alexa-users URL requests for a site.

The site with the highest combination of unique visitors and page views is ranked #1.

Alexa's Traffic Ranks are for top-level domains only, and not for sub-pages or subdomains unless Alexa can automatically identify them. This underestimates the ranking (and the consequent value) of a website with sub-pages and subdomains.

The bounce rate is an Internet marketing term used in web traffic analysis, that represents the percentage of visitors who enter the site and then leave ("bounce"), rather than continuing to view other pages within the same site. Bounce rate is a measure of the effectiveness of a website in encouraging visitors to continue with their visit. It is expressed as a percentage and represents the proportion of visits that end on the first page of the website that the visitor sees. Bounce rates can be used to help determine the effectiveness or performance of an entry page at generating the interest of visitors.

11.7 WEB ANALYTICS

Web analytics is the measurement, collection, analysis, and reporting of web data for purposes of understanding, and optimizing web usage (WAA Standards Committee, 2008). Web analytics is not just a process for measuring web traffic but can be used as a tool for business and market research, and to assess and improve the effectiveness of a website.

There are various terms used to describe the science of recording and interpreting website statistics. Web metrics, web analytics, web stats, and site stats are examples.

Data analytics have been extracted using, for example, Google Analytics, a freemium web service that tracks and reports website traffic. Google launched the service in November 2005, after acquiring Urchin. Google Analytics is currently the most widely used web analytics internet service.

Dark traffic (http://www.wolfgangdigital.com/blog/dark-traffic-find/) is effective traffic that Google Analytics either cannot attribute or incorrectly attributes. It comes in many different shapes and forms, like in-App searches, image searches, or carrying out secure searches. These kinds of search activities do not share information with Google Analytics which does not know how to attribute them.

11.8 RANKING PARAMETERS

The strategic value of a particularly attractive domain can lead to a price particularly high and well above its hypothetical intrinsic value (e.g., pizza. com[9]).

To get an assessment, specialized websites make "quick and dirty" real-time estimations,[10] which can be used as a guide for more detailed evaluations.

The most known sites are sitevaluecheck.com, stimasito.com, valuem yweb.com, urlappraisal.net, valoredominio.com, valuate.com.

These ratings are indicative instruments to make comparisons with comparable sites as several visits or market niches.

The parameters can be considered from the following sources:

- DMOZ is the largest, most comprehensive human-edited directory on the Web. It is constructed and maintained by a passionate, global community of volunteer editors. It was historically known as the Open Directory Project;

- Alexa ranking; Alexa Internet, Inc. is a subsidiary company of Ama zon.com which provides commercial web traffic data;
- Google ranking;
- Quantcast (www.quantcast.com), specializes in audience measurement and real-time advertising;
- Compete (www.compete.com), provides daily estimates of the share of consumer attention garnered by the top Internet sites and the velocity of change of this attention.

There are various methods of website valuation that have been patented by Google. For example, the method of "valuation website" of Glassman and Arvelo[11] allows automatically to evaluate an entire website, based on a series of variables. This process considers the information and the features that can be observed on a website, such as operative elements, contents, feeds, marketing elements, and the website's classification.

Operating elements include information on the process and functioning of the internet website. They include, for example, the programming code of the website, the software used, or web applications. The information considers negative aspects of the website, problems in programming, bugs, malfunctioning, viruses, trojans, and spyware.

Another important detail is the type of server—dedicated, shared, rented—owned by a website. Time for reply, download and upload speed, and reputation of services are other key elements, along with the average, the minimum and maximum number of visitors, trends, growth rate, presence in search engines, number of page views, number of registered users and other parameters.

Another application is the "Domain appraisal algorithm", an algorithm for the evaluation of the website, analyzing the domain name semantic. This method enables to give a value to the domain based on the etymology of the domain name. This method may involve various phases, including the user inserting the domain name in an interface; the system then analyses and searches for similar keywords using semantic research.[12]

The process is composed of several steps:

1. Precision evaluation: distinct keywords, length, dictionary search;
2. Popularity evaluation: search engine result metrics, word searches;
3. Presence evaluation: domain age, website ranking by service;
4. Pattern evaluation: premium characters noun/verb, vowel/consonant;

5. Pay per click (PPC) evaluation: maximum pay per click, the number of ads returned.

11.9   DOMAIN AUCTIONS

According to Meystedt (2015), several factors are considered when auction specialists estimate the value of a domain name. Some of these factors include:

1. Traffic.
2. Advertising costs.
3. The age of the domain name.
4. The extension (.com, .org etc.).
5. The length (brevity) of the name.
6. Comparable sales.
7. Advertiser competition in the category.
8. Industry growth.
9. Overall marketability.

11.10   OTHER VALUATION PARAMETERS

To achieve a more complete evaluation of a website, additional parameters may be considered. You can first make questions about the current revenue of the site, about the value of the industry sector to refer to (it is a risky sector or a steady one? Large companies are focusing on this market niche?), and about the keywords on this site.

Internet domains have an intrinsic value, proved by the fact that exist real auction websites. One of the most important is www.sedo.com.

A domain name is typically not worth itself as a stand-alone asset if it is not associated with any known product or service. Domains may be appraised separately from other IT assets, especially if they have popular naming without any specific link to a website.

In this case, the monetization value is potential, depending on the domain exploitation along the IT value chain.

11.11   VALUATION WITH "QUICK AND DIRTY" ALGORITHMS

Many websites provide free of charge "quick and dirty" evaluations of web domain names, based on standardized algorithms. Examples can be found in:

- https://www.freevaluator.com/appraise/expert-domain-appraisals
- http://thedigitalelevator.com/domain-name-value/.

Some free appraisal sites include:

- http://www.urlappraisal.net/
- https://www.freevaluator.com/
- https://www.estibot.com/
- https://www.register.it/domains/appraisal.html?lang=en.

According to Meystedt (2015), domain valuation tools use a mixture of criteria to determine value, including:

1. The search volume of a particular keyword in Google or other search engines;
2. The pay per click rate that advertisers are paying for the keyword in Google;
3. The length of the domain name;
4. The extension of the domain name (.com, .net etc.);
5. The age of the domain name;
6. Past sales of the name in question;
7. Comparable sales of other domains in the same category.

The 3Cs appraisal model from GreatDomains.com was the first to describe factors for domain appraisal. Using a matrix, the criteria of characters (number of characters), commerce (commercial potential), and .com (value relevance of the TLD) determine the value of a domain (Dieterle & Bergmann, 2014).

Appraisals like these are determined automatically based on SEO-related factors like keywords, the number of searches, Alexa rank, monthly searches, and cost per click.

According to http://worthmysite.net/page/about/, Key Performance Indicators (KPIs) for the evaluation of web domains and websites are based on:

- website traffic estimator with a daily unique view (which is maybe the most important factor). Estimated daily unique visitor count is trying to be estimated with several sources like Alexa, Compete, Google Ad Planner, etc. ... Unique user count is a common way of measuring the popularity of a website and is often used by potential advertisers or investors;
- appraisal daily page view;
- estimated daily advertisement income (which will help to indicate the logical price of the domain). Daily Advertisement Revenue calculation is based on AdSense income. Today most webmasters use Google AdSense. Our estimation is trying to emulate for a better AdSense usage if this website uses 3 AdSense ads on all pages. It is not easy to calculate for different keywords because AdSense can show an Ad not related only to the page content, AdSense can choose a specific ad for a visitor;
- Alexa rank. Alexa is one of the most common website trackers. It measures site traffic and compares all other website traffic. It helps webmasters and advertisers to see the true marketing potential of the website. Unfortunately, it does not give always correct values because of manipulations. But it is still the most trustable tracker. And without Alexa rank values, it is hard to estimate a domain's worth;
- domain Google Page Rank. Google Page Rank is one of the most determining factors for website quality today. And getting a high Page-Rank value is not an easy task. It requires lots of quality work. So, the Google Page-rank value is an important factor for site price worth calculation. PageRank affects the number of pages of a website that gets indexed by Google. So basically, to have more visitors with getting more pages indexed it is necessary to increase Page Rank;
- search engines: Google, Yahoo, and Bing index status. The more pages that search engines index, the better. Search engines access websites to crawl site content and index some of the pages to their databases. They may not index all the pages, mostly index pages with quality and unique content. So Indexing is one of the hardest factors

for big websites, so search engine visibility is very important in calculating the website value. In the presence of lots of indexed pages, the website can be visited by more visitors;

- domain age (which is an important ranking factor for search engines). Domain age is an important SEO factor for search engine rankings because search engines use it for calculating trust and authority. Another thing is that spammers register and drop domains quickly, so spamming sites usually have newly registered domain names. But the indexing of the site is more important from domain age;
- social media visibility, share count of the website on social media shows that it has quality content (Facebook, Twitter, Google+);
- backlink count (backlinks mean that links count that point to the website from other websites and it is like a popularity rating for the website. Google, Yahoo, Bing, Alexa, and total external backlink count. Low but quality backlinks are better than high but poor-quality backlinks. So, this value has a lower impact on our site price calculation algorithm. Backlinks are very related to Google Page Rank, so we believe that Page-Rank value is more important than backlink count).

These are the key value drivers that matter for the appraisal. Search volume is related to Internet traffic that represents the flow of data across the Web. The monetization process is the following (Fig. 11.1).

Domain names are only a part of this monetization process. Paying clients that use the website for their purchases (e-Commerce, etc.) or generating advertising revenue models do so not only because they are attracted by the domain name but—mostly—because they are looking for a (branded) product or service. The domain is just the IT gateway to a larger environment (the website and its contents).

11.12   Market Approach

Valuation multiples are widely used for comparative appraisal of company assets, for an evaluation of Internet companies with multiples (Ho et al., 2011), consistently with IVS 210.

A widespread valuation method for domain name evaluation is the use of earnings multiples (see for instance flippa.com), such as P/E multiples as well as EV/EBITDA and EV/Sales (revenues).[13]

Enterprise-Value-to-Sales is a valuation measure that compares the enterprise value of a company to its sales, giving investors an idea of how much it costs to buy the company's sales. Generally, the lower the EV/sales, the more attractive or undervalued the company is believed to be.

Enterprise value (EV), or firm value is an economic measure reflecting the market value of a business. It is a sum of claims by creditors (secured and unsecured) and shareholders (preferred and common).

Sales represent the upper part of the income statement and are widely used in valuation metrics, especially for scalable businesses (such as domain names and IT-related activities) where the cost component is not particularly relevant.

In the internet business world, investors have increasingly gravitated around the multiple-based methodology because of its simplicity and robustness in the face of scant financial or comparable data.

Sales (revenues) have pros and cons in business evaluations: while they are hardly subjective, they may be unable to express the economic marginality (i.e., revenues net of costs) that is embedded in parameters such as EBIT or EBITDA, which are typically used in appraisals. Being domain names a scalable business where variable costs are minimized, gross sales are typically used, irrespectively of marginality. This method is so widely utilized in this industry.

According to this method, a domain name may be evaluated through the following formula:

$$\text{Domain name value} = P * M \qquad (11.1)$$

where:

P = parameter (i.e., revenues ...);
M = multiple.

The revenue multiple helps in determining a ratio of the value of the business to the revenue it generates (Sharma & Prashar, 2013).

Revenue multiples for domain names evaluation strictly depend on several factors, such as:

- Related intangibles to the domain name (websites, app, trademark ...);
- The complexity of the hardware architecture and software structure;
- Annual incomes;
- The rarity of the domain names;
- Number of directly generated sessions;
- Site ranking (Alexa, etc.);
- Website contents;
- Social network correlations;
- Number of page views/users;
- Traffic growth over the years;
- Website popularity;
- Opportunities/potentialities /scalability.

Considering the present case, in addition to these aspects, there are further factors to be considered in the estimation, particularly concerning:

- The singularity of the context;
- Geographical scalability.

According to flippa.com,[14] other approaches to determining the value of a site include:

- Comparable Sales. A comparison is found by searching for related sites in the niche that are as close to the site's age, traffic, and revenue as possible. The closer the numbers are for a comparable site, the higher the relevance the site has in the evaluation;
- Traffic Value Appraisal Method, specifically for sites that have yet to be monetized but have traffic, is determined by researching the top key phrase or phrases that drive most of the traffic to a domain name. Then find the Cost Per Click value of the keywords;
- Reverse Engineering Cost, with a formula that calculates the price to build a site from scratch to match the site being sold.

A synthesis of the domain name valuation approaches is reported in Fig. 11.2.

Fig. 11.1 The Internet traffic monetization process

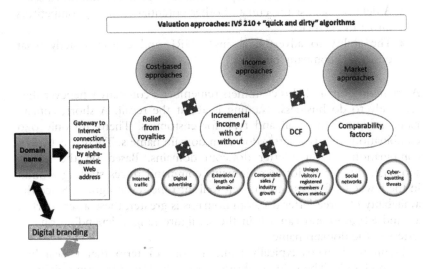

Fig. 11.2 Domain name valuation approaches

11.13 PREMIUM DOMAIN NAMES

A premium (memorable) domain name is a trophy asset that is already owned by a person or registry. It corresponds, essentially, to a keyword that attracts Internet traffic. Its cost can be significantly more than a typical domain purchase due to its perceived higher value. The higher price will apply to the initial acquisition of the domain, but it will renew at the regular renewal price for whichever domain extension it uses.

A domain becomes premium when it is considered more valuable than the average domain. Domains are considered premium for many reasons including length, keywords, and brand-ability.[15]

According to Meystedt (2015), a category-defining domain name can offer significant advantages for companies operating on the Internet, such as:

- Instant trust and credibility in the eyes of prospective consumers.
- Authority status in an industry.
- The ability to rank higher on search engines with proper development.
- The ability to use existing type-in traffic to generate additional sales.
- A defense against the entry of other potential entrants/competitors into a marketplace.
- The ability to advertise a single URL and convey exactly what business a company operates.

A premium domain helps customers remember a company whenever they are ready to do business. Naming is about the recall. A short, concise name is simple to recall and type for customers. There are only 676 combinations of a two-letter dot. com domain name s. There are 17,576 combinations of three-letter dot.com domains. Based on the supply shortage, two-letter dot.com domains command prices starting around in the lower six figures and can sell well into the seven figures. Since the availability of three-letter dot.com domains is greater, these assets start at around $10,000 and can sell in the six-figure range, depending on the letters in the domain name.

Premium domains typically name a word or term that is searched often in Google. The volume of searches can be found by using different domain tools available on the Internet. If a word or phrase is searched often in Google, there will be more advertisers competing for the eyeballs related to these searches. The exact matching domain name for these highly searched phrases will have value.

If a domain name has many visitors, a business can turn these people into profitable leads and sales. Several premium domain names have a high traffic count, and this increases the potential value of the asset. Premium domain-based traffic represents a value driver for innovative business models.

11.14 THE VALUATION
OF STAND-ALONE DOMAIN NAMES

Wu et al. (2009), show that traditional estimation methods, such as the discounted cash flow method, etc., ignore some crucial non-financial factors that influence the domain value, for instance, creativity. The model is based on semantic theory and content analysis and the model combines the traditional method with the modification process forming a two-stage model.

Once the appropriate valuation method is selected, its general principles are to be applied to the specific domain.

The first parameters to be considered are:

- the domain name;
- the amount of monthly gross income earned in foreign currency, expenditure on advertising and hosting;
- the number of months has produced a steady gain like the current one;
- the kind of website (static, dynamic, e-commerce, flash, web portal, blog, ...);
- the number of unique visitors (number of distinct individuals requesting pages from the website during a given period, regardless of how often they visit);
- the number of views per month (number of times a page is viewed);
- the number of registered members, the volume, and the uniqueness of the content.

To figure out the domain's value, valuators ultimately need to understand who the potential buyers are. What industry are they in? Is a website important for their business? How relevant is the domain? A domain is only as valuable as someone is willing to pay for it, so knowing what related domains are priced at, how sought after the domain is, and how much to reasonably expect a buyer to pay will help you arrive at the right number.

One way to get an idea of the current valuations of web properties is to use a multiple of Trailing Twelve Month (TTM) revenues that the site has generated. According to http://www.stuntdubl.com/2006/02/20/ website-valuation, mainstream web properties are selling at the following median multiples[16]:

$$e\text{-Commerce sites}: 3 \times TTM \qquad (11.2)$$

$$\text{Content sites}: 6 \times TTM \qquad (11.3)$$

$(12 \times (\text{Net Income Average})) + 12 \times (\text{Unique Visitor Average} \times \text{Unique Visitor value})) \times 1$plus the content value $=$ High Value for Website

$(9 \times (\text{Net Income Average})) + 9 \times (\text{Unique Visitor Average} \times \text{Unique Visitor value})) \times 1$plus the content value $=$ Low Value for Website * Unique visitor value $= 1/2$ the value of the top fifteen bid placements on Overture for relevant keyword.[17]

Domain names are typically evaluated assuming that they are correctly registered and that registration is continuously renewed. In the early days of the Internet when a domain name expired it was already available for other people to register it. Nowadays, the process is more complex; the Internet Corporation for Assigned Names and Numbers (ICANN) created what is called the "Grace Period" to protect the registrants. Once a domain expires it enters the "Auto-Renew Grace Period". This period usually lasts 30 days and the owner of the domain can renew anytime during that time frame. Should the owner fail to renew the domain it will enter the Redemption period.

The registrar becomes the owner of the domain during this period, and it will try to sell the domain through auctions or retain it in the case it generates PPC revenues. Finally, if the domain is not sold through an auction and if it is not generating revenues the registrar will release it.[18]

If the domain registration is periodically renewed, then the domain can be evaluated as an intangible asset with infinite life (see IAS 38 for a distinction between definite and infinite life in the accounting of intangibles). In such a case, the terminal value tends to zero $(TV/\infty \to 0)$ and so is not considered in the valuation.

11.14.1   Domains and (Web) Trademarks

Choosing the right domain name is a prerequisite for building a sound web brand.

The three dimensions of domain names—semantic, invented and non-word names—show significant differences in frequency. Practitioners may consider using newly defined categories, such as semantically related acronyms, in creating distinctive brand names. The use of sound symbolic names for brands is also investigated.

The value of a brand can be estimated with brand equity metrics.

Forrester (2016) analyzes the changing use of trademarks in the Domain Name System, from the introduction of new generic Top-Level Domains and their impacts on trademark rights.

11.14.2   Domains and Social Networks

The main social networks may have a strong impact on the evaluation they contribute to making the contents of the website viral. The most important are Facebook, Twitter, My Space, Google Plus, and Linkedin (www. ebizmba.com/articles/social-networking-websites). Socials increase the Web traffic and can carry it to specific domains. Through web marketing, many strategies can be put in:

- *Benchmarking online* (the study of several scenarios);
- *Online branding* (increasing brand reputation through the internet);
- *E-commerce* (commerce of products B2B or B2C);
- *E-learning* (employees' online training);
- *Online customer support.*

For what concerns Social Networks, it should be checked in any valuation if the domain name and its related website have a:

- Facebook/LinkedIn page;
- Google Plus account;
- Twitter account;
- YouTube channel;
- Instagram profile.

11.15   CYBERSQUATTING, TYPO-SQUATTING, AND DOMAIN TROLLS

Domain names bear cases of misuse, including phishing, spam, hit and traffic stealing, and online scams, among others (Spaulding et al., 2016).

Cybersquatting is the phenomenon of registering domain names corresponding to trademarks or names of other people. It has two typical goals: the realization of gain on the domain transfer to anyone who has a real interest and unfair competition, such as diverting the customers of the competitor on other sites or other products.

Cyber-squatters sometimes register "variants" of popular trademarked names, a practice that is known as "typo-squatting". As a first step toward this misuse, the registration of a legitimately looking domain is often required. For that, domain typo-squatting provides a great avenue for cybercriminals to conduct their crimes (Spaulding et al., 2016).

"Domain name trolls" is a generic term for people or businesses that strategically register desirable domain names, which they do not intend to use for legitimate purposes. This is known as "domain squatting" or "cybersquatting".[19] These could be:

- Another business' name or slogan which has not yet been registered as a domain name by the business itself;
- An existing domain name that is in use, but about to expire;
- A variant of a current business domain name—for example, differently spelled, misspelled, or separating words differently, e.g., using hyphens or dots;
- Breaking news—for example, the name of a new venture or brand announced by a major corporation.

They can:

- Sell the domain name to the most likely party (such as the business whose name or slogan it is) for a profit;
- Sell it to a competitor or someone else who might use it to harm the business, such as a disgruntled customer;
- Otherwise misuse the name—e.g., by using the site to show advertisements or sell their products, setting it to redirect to another site, or even infecting users' computers with malware when they mistakenly visit.

Another strategy is as follows: Internet domain name registrations are for a fixed period. If the owner of a domain name does not re-register the name with an internet registrar before the domain's expiration date, then the domain name can be purchased by anybody else after it expires.[20]

Being the value of domain names is intrinsically linked to Internet traffic and openness, it tends to zero in the dark or deep web, is not indexed by search engines, and requires specific software, configurations, or authorization to access.

Malware may use unregistered domains or manipulated domain names to be spread across the Web.

11.16   INTERNET PROTOCOL ADDRESSES

The evaluation of IP addresses (Folorunso, 2012; Hussein, 2016; Huston, 2013) falls within the broader scope of estimating intangible assets. We will therefore proceed to summarize the main metrics for the valuation of intangibles and then focus, in particular, on those specifically referable to the present case.

The evaluation of IP addresses, aimed at establishing their fair market value, also follows the economic laws of supply and demand. To this end, the above considerations on the "relay" between IPv4 and IPv6 apply, concerning the enhancement of IPv4 addresses, of which the supervening scarcity must be considered, which inevitably leads to an increase in value, in a market not yet fully IPv6 ready.

As part of the approaches illustrated before, it is appropriate to make some preliminary considerations, to exclude methodologies that are difficult to apply to the present case.

The cost approach already rarely used (except in the software enhancement, with the so-called Co.Co.Mo. method), seems difficult to propose here, because the market value of the addresses does not seem to a very fleeting way, linked to the "cost" of their creation, also considering their original free distribution.

The income-financial approach already seems more relevant to the present case, even if it is not easy to estimate the economic and financial benefits associated with the use of the IP address. This is not due to the absence of an ontological assumption (not being able to deny the indispensability of IP addresses for even basic use of the Internet), but rather due to the difficulty, under the practical level, of finding income or differential (incremental) cash flows. Once again, these flows undeniably exist, even if their relevance, on the evaluation level, is diluted by their indispensability, in the sense that, being essential, it is difficult to evaluate the surplus value related to their use (if they are not used, no comparison holds). These reserves automatically reverberate on the "with or without" market approach, because the "without" hypothesis does not seem realistically prefigurable. Even the use of differential assets discounts the same perplexities, as well as the reference to the Price/Book Value, in the presence of companies, holders of IP addresses, typically unlisted.

The number of possible approaches, after this brutal skimming, tapers to include a few but significant cases. Among these, first, the market comparison with similar transactions is relevant.

The market comparison is facilitated by two fundamental elements:

1. The easy comparability of IP addresses (of course, within the same category—IPv4 or IPv6);
2. The existence of a large, liquid, and therefore significant reference market, with an international projection.

The evaluation also raises questions that cannot be solved immediately. The first is represented by the fact that IP addresses are not owned by the user, and therefore—according to some—have no intrinsic value. Not infrequent are the cases of users who grab addresses with purely speculative intentions, far from the canonical purposes of a mere means of accessing the Internet.

If participation on the Internet has, as is undeniable, a monetary value (despite being the Internet—the largest communication network in the world—a "common good", which some consider constitutionally guaranteed), this also occurs, analogically, in head to IP addresses. The latter value, however, changes according to the roles and objectives of the surfer on the Web and the governance of the network—a complex and still controversial issue.

The addresses can also be used by multiple users and have their intrinsic scalability, connected to the intensity and "monetary value" (where measurable) of such use.

As a complement to the sale on the secondary market (which developed after the exhaustion of the addresses provided free of charge until 2015 by ARIN), there may be a multi-year monetization of IPv4 with a lease, with yields even higher than 15% on a yearly.

The price of IPv4 ranges from 15 to 20 dollars per address but is growing rapidly, due to the scarcity effect, and is continuously updated also by online auction platforms. The most recent prices are, in a consistent sense,

/17 and larger	/18 to /22	/23 and /24
$30 USD per IP	$28 USD per IP	$30 USD per IP

As reported by <https://auctions.ipv4.global/>, prices range from $35 to $40. Brenac's statistics (<https://www.brenac.eu/en/ipv4-price-statistics/>) show price ranges, growing, on average above $20 per address.

11.17   CONCLUSION

Domain names represent the gateway to Internet connections and access to specific websites. They can be appraised as a stand-alone IP asset or within a portfolio of web intangibles that includes websites, digital brands, M-Apps, and other related devices.

Internet traffic stands out as the main value driver, even if the contacts that it generates need to be properly monetized, following increasingly sophisticated business and revenue models. Revenue models depend either on web advertising or on e-commerce sales, with data sales representing a niche activity. Revenue and business models are the key substrates for any valuation that should consider the peculiar nature of increasingly sophisticated businesses, where benchmarking is often uneasy.

Several valuation models have been thoroughly described, considering the peculiar nature of domain names but its analogic reference to the broader category of IP assets. While "quick and dirty" algorithms freely available on the Web may provide instant appraisals, more professional valuations are typically needed.

Domain name disputes, due to cybersquatting or other causes, are growing and may be solved with professional mediation.

New research questions should address the impact of Internet traffic on domain names more comprehensively, considering not only traffic data with algorithms but also the impact on the IT value chain, where domain names form a synergistic portfolio with websites, digital brands, and M-Apps.

Whereas the link between domain names and websites is strong and thoroughly investigated, the connection between domains, and M-Apps (where the former depend on naming and the latter are represented by logos) is still under-examined and so needs further scrutiny from both academics and practitioners.

NOTES

1. DNSSEC: DNS Security Extensions Securing the Domain Name System, at http://www.dnssec.net/.
2. Internet Assigned Numbers Authority (IANA), at www.iana.org/dom ains/root/db.
3. Hover (2015), How important are keywords in a domain name for SEO? 2015. Available at https://www.hover.com/blog/how-important-are-key words-in-a-domain-name/.
4. Available at www.sciplore.org/publications/2010-ASEO-preprint.pdf.
5. Available at https://searchengineland.com/what-is-google-pagerank-a-guide-for-searchers-webmasters-11068.
6. Available at https://www.smartbugmedia.com/blog/what-is-the-differ ence-between-direct-and-organic-search-traffic-sources?utm_medium=soc ial&utm_source=email.
7. Online advertising glossary.
8. https://www.alexa.com/.
9. BBC, US man gets $2.6 m for domain name, 2008.
10. See Sect. 11.11.
11. https://patents.google.com/patent/US8214272B2/en.
12. www.google.com/patents/US20110208800.
13. See Sect. 2.6.
14. See, for instance, http://wpcurve.com/what-is-my-website-worth/.
15. www.hover.com/blog/premium-domain-names.
16. www.ventureplan.com/web.valuations.html.
17. www.buysellwebsite.com.
18. https://www.dailyblogtips.com/how-expired-domains-work/.
19. https://business.yell.com/knowledge/what-are-domain-name-trolls/.
20. BBC, Renew or lose, 2003, http://news.bbc.co.uk/2/hi/programmes/ working_lunch/3239639.stm.

SELECTED REFERENCES

Alberti, A. M., Casaroli, M. A. F., Sighi, D., & Da Rosa, Righi R. (2017). Naming and name resolution in the future internet: Introducing the NovaGe-nesis approach. *Future Generation Computer Systems, 67*, 163–179.

Andriessen, D. (2004). Intellectual capital valuation and measurement: Classifying the state of the art. *Journal of Intellectual Capital, 5*(2), 230–242.

Anson, W., & Suchy, D. (2005). *Fundamentals of intellectual property valuation: A primer for identifying and determining value*. Chicago: American Bar Association.

Arora, S., Kalro, A. D., & Sharma, D. (2015). A comprehensive framework of brand name classification. *Journal of Brand Management, 22*(2), 79–116.

Ballester, M., Garcia-Ayuso, M., & Livnat, J. (2003). The economic value of the R&D intangible asset. *European Accounting Review, 12*(4), 605–633.

Beel, J., Gipp, B., & Wilde, E. (2010). Academic search engine optimization (ASEO): Optimizing scholarly literature for Google Scholar & Co. *Journal of Scholarly Publishing*. Available at www.sciplore.org/publications/2010-ASEO-preprint.pdf

Boujelben, S., & Fedhila, H. (2011). The effects of intangible investments on future OCF. *Journal of Intellectual Capital, 12*(4), 480–494.

Brin, S., & Page, L. (1998). *The anatomy of a large-scale hypertextual web search engine*. Stanford. http://Infolab.Stanford.Edu/Pub/Papers/Google.Pdf

Cavallari, M., & Moro Visconti, R. (2016). A service-value approach to mobile application valuation. In T. Borangiu, M. Dragoicea, & H. Novoa (Eds.), *Exploring services science presented at 17th International Conference, IESS, Bucharest, Romania*. Switzerland: Springer International Publishing.

Dieterle, S., & Bergmann, R. (2014). A hybrid CBR-ANN Approach to the appraisal of internet domain names. *Lecture Notes in Computer Science, 8765*, 95–109.

Farris, P., Neil, W., Bendle, T., Pfeifer, P. E., & Reibstein, J. (2010). *Marketing metrics: The definitive guide to measuring marketing performance*. Upper Saddle River, NJ: Pearson Education.

Folorunso, S. O. (2012). Evaluating Internet protocol version 6 (Ipv6) against version 4 (Ipv4). *Computing, Information Systems & Development Informatics, 3*(5).

Forrester, H. A. (2016). *The evolution of domain names and their impacts on trademark rights, global governance of intellectual property in the 21st century* (pp. 151–172). Available at https://link.springer.com/book/10.1007/978-3-319-31177-7

Hackett, L. P. (2002). Valuing internet domain names: Considerations and market factors. *Australian Property Journal, 37*(4), 273–275.

Ho, C. T. B., Liao, C. K., & Kim, H. T. (2011). Valuing internet companies: A Dea-based multiple valuation approach. *Journal of the Operational Research Society, 62*, 2097–2106.

Hussein, S. K. (2016). Performance evaluation of mobile Internet protocol version 6. *International Journal of Management, Information Technology and Engineering, 4*(3), 35–52.

Huston, G. (2013). Valuing IP addresses. *The ISP Column*. Available at https:// www.dotnxdomain.net/ispcol/2013-09/valuation.pdf

Iparraguirre, J. B. C. (2016). *Evaluation and economic valorization of websites using the technical evaluation and economic valorization methodology*. Available at http://Ieeexplore.Ieee.Org/Abstract/Document/7556061/Authors?Ctx= Authors

Kemmis, A. (2018). *The difference between direct and organic search traffic sources*. SmartBug. Available at https://www.smartbugmedia.com/blog/ what-is-the-difference-between-direct-and-organic-search-traffic-sources?utm_ medium=social&utm_source=email

Lagrost, C., Martin, D., Dubois, C., & Quazzotti, S. (2010). Intellectual property valuation: How to approach the selection of an appropriate valutation method. *Journal of Intellectual Capital, 11*(4), 481–503. https://doi.org/ 10.1108/14691931011085641

Lindenthal, T. (2014). Valuable words: The price dynamics of internet domain names. *Journal of the Association for Information Science and Technology, 65*(5), 869–881.

Meystedt, A. (2015). What is my URL worth? Placing a value on premium domain names. *Valuation Strategies, 10*, 12.

Mouritsen, J., Bukh, P. N., & Marr, B. (2004). Reporting on intellectual capital: Why, what and how? *Measuring Business Excellence, 8*(1), 46–54.

Pokorna, J., & Vecerkova, E. (2013). Trade name and trademark versus domain. *Acta Universitatics Agriculturae Et Silviculturae Mendelianae Brunensis, 61*, 1069–1076.

Rocha, A. (2012). Framework for a global quality evaluation of a website. *Online Information Review, 36*(3), 374.

Sharma, M., & Prashar, E. (2013). A conceptual framework for relative valuation. *The Journal of Private Equity, 16*(3), 29.

Sherman, C. (2006). *The state of search engine marketing*. Search Engine Land.

Solum, L. B. (2013). *Models of internet governance* (Illinois Public Law Research Paper No. 07–25). University of Illinois, Law & Economics Research No LE08-027. Available at SSRN. https://ssrn.com/abstract=1136825

Spaulding, J., Upadhyaya, S., & Mohaisen, A. (2016). The landscape of domain name typosquatting: Techniques and countermeasures. In *Proceedings, Presented at 11th International Conference on Availability, Reliability and Security (ARES 7784584)* (pp. 284–289).

Sullivan, D. (2007). *What is google pagerank? A guide for searchers & webmasters*. Search Engine Land. Available at https://searchengineland.com/whatis-goo gle-pagerank-a-guide-for-searchers-webmasters-11068

Tang, J. H., Hsu, M. C., Hu, T. Y., & Huang, H. H. (2014). A general domain name appraisal model. *Journal of Internet Technology, 15*(3), 427–431.

Toscano, L. (2009). *SEO strategy*. Trento: Uni Service.

WAA Standards Committee. (2008). *Web analytics definitions*. Washington, DC: Web Analytics Association.

Wittlake, E. (2016). *How account-based advertising really works*. B2B Digital Marketing. Available at http://b2bdigital.net/2016/04/20/how-accountba sed-advertising-really-works/

Wu, Z. G., Zhu, G. H., Huang, R., & Xia, B. (2009). Domain name valuation model based on semantic theory and content analysis. In *Proceedings Presented at Asia-Pacific Conference on Information Processing (APCIP 2,5197179)* (pp. 237–240).

CHAPTER 12

The Valuation of Mobile Apps

12.1 Definition and Types

M-Apps, (a shortening of the term "Mobile Application Software") represent a computer program (software) designed to run on mobile devices such as smartphones, tablet computers, phablets, smartwatches, or other mobiles, such as notebooks (with specific extensions). Each app is associated with a logo that represents the touchscreen gateway to the app. A logo is a graphical label even more difficult to conceive than a domain name, due to its stricter constraints (no different extensions, predefined measure). The relationship between M-Apps logos and domain names is still under-investigated: they both convey internet traffic but in a different (complementary) way.

M-Apps are increasingly popular and by now represent the trendiest software device. Investigations about their valuation paradigms are so increasingly common. Even if M-Apps belong to the broad category of Intellectual Property (IP) assets, their underlying business model is so innovative and different from traditional intangibles (such as patents, brands, etc.) that standard appraisal patterns, normally used for IP, may only be used as a starting point for the valuation.

From a legal point of view, M-Apps is a piece of software. M-Apps are to be included within the software system since they are embedded in hardware devices (albeit different from PCs), to perform some defined tasks, linked to the Web.

R. Moro-Visconti, *The Valuation of Digital Intangibles*, https://doi.org/10.1007/978-3-031-09237-4_12

According to Cavallari and Moro Visconti (2016), some apps are free while others must be bought. Usually, they are downloaded from the platform to a target device, but sometimes they can be downloaded to laptops or desktop computers. For apps with a price, a percentage, 20–30%, goes to the distribution provider (such as iTunes), and the rest goes to the producer of the app.

The same app can, therefore, cost a different price depending on the mobile platform.

Public demand and the availability of developer tools drove rapid expansion into other categories, such as those handled by desktop application software packages. As with other software, the explosion in the number and variety of apps made discovery a challenge, which in turn led to the creation of a wide range of review, recommendation, and curation sources, including blogs, magazines, and dedicated online app-discovery services.

Platforms (stores) represent a key value driver in the industry, becoming pivotal nodes (hubs) within the networks that link different stakeholders, such as users and developers.

The sale of Apps through stores represents a classic e-commerce transaction. When platforms become dominant, they represent industry standards (as happened with MS Windows) and generate scalable returns, since their fixed costs can easily reach a break-even point: Returns are then complemented by negligible variable costs, associated with incremental users.

Apps can be sold for free (freemium = free + premium) or paid. Some 90% of the apps downloaded tend to be freemium. Revenue streams for freemium app providers follow different patterns and are mainly represented by subsequent premium services (e.g., a free app that introduces paying services). Even paid apps earn much of their revenues from accessories (online advertising; B2B or B2C e-commerce; customer web profile to be sold, etc.).

Paid apps are normally cheap (from 0.99 $ up to a few $) and their revenue model relies on high volumes of customers and users.

Since the app market is becoming increasingly crowded, with millions of apps competing, their added value is growing as the industry is becoming saturated and mature. For instance, popular weather forecast apps find it increasingly difficult to differentiate from others, and they tend to be all freemium.

A growing number of apps use geolocalization with Geographic Information Systems (GIS), to improve the quality of GPS services and to geo-tag social network users.

Some companies offer M-Apps as an alternative method to deliver content (media) with certain advantages over an official website. Platforms (stores) represent a key value driver in the industry, becoming central nodes (hubs) within the networks that link different stakeholders, such as users and developers. The sale of M-Apps through stores represents a typical e-commerce transaction. When platforms become dominant, they represent industry standards (as happened with MS Windows) and generate scalable returns, since their fixed costs can easily reach a break-even point, being complemented by negligible variable costs, associated with additional users.

M-Apps can be sold for free (freemium = free + premium) or paid. Some 90% of the M-Apps downloaded tend to be freemium. Revenue streams for freemium app providers follow different patterns and are mainly represented by following premium services (e.g., a free app that introduces paying services).

Multi-homing M-Apps supply several platforms, such as Apple's iOS and Google's Android operating systems.

The term mobile application (more commonly abbreviated to app) refers to a program (software), structured to run from a smartphone, tablet, phablet, smartwatch, and other mobile devices. The main operating systems for mobile devices (where apps are run) are:

1. ANDROID: it is the most popular operating system in the world, used by Samsung;
2. WINDOWS: The second operating system which is mainly used by Nokia;
3. IOS: used by Apple smartphones (iPhone) and tablets (iPad);
4. other: custom minor operating systems.

Some apps are already pre-installed on the mobile device (system app), while others are available on the internet (web app) or downloadable from special sites (native app), called platforms (store), which are indexed by special algorithms, among which the most popular are:

- App Store (Apple);
- Google Play (Android);
- Windows Phone Store.

The sale of apps through distribution through stores is a typical case of e(lectronic)-commerce, which includes transactions carried out exclusively through an electronic channel. Apps are part of the mobile computing trend, which is much more dynamic and interactive than less innovative contexts of use. The evolution and maturation of the app market lead to increasing fragmentation, which often hampers standardization, thus damaging developers and users.

Apps can be free (freemium = free + premium), directing the user to paid applications, or directly paid; about 90% of downloaded apps are free.

Paid apps are generally low priced (even in the order of € 0.99) and base their revenue model on high volume expectations and accessory services (online advertising; B2B or B2C e-commerce; user profiling with big data to be marketed, etc.). These ancillary services are even more vital for free apps, which often act as a loss leader product to attract users to paid services.

The app market is constantly increasing, as are the preferences of end-users, which are influenced by the pricing and advertising strategies of the different platforms. The object of the purchase from the stores is the license to use the apps, while the copyright remains with the developer.

Apps can be used in a variety of ways, for example:

- Social networks (Facebook, Twitter, Instagram ...);
- Chat and ICT (WhatsApp; Skype ...);
- Games/entertainment;
- Educational;
- Traffic information (Google Map);
- Tools (calculator, currency converter, translator ...);
- Utilities (hotel reservations, flights, trains, type Bookings.com, Expedia, AirBnB, taxis with platforms like Uber; information and comments on hotels and restaurants, like TripAdvisor ...);
- e-commerce (eBay, Amazon ...);
- Home banking and trading;
- Music videos (iTunes, YouTube ...);

– Image management;
– Personal care services (biomedical, diagnostic, etc.) with M-health apps.

More and more apps are using geolocation, to increase the quality of GPS services and the use of social networks.

App ideas may be divided into four groups[1]:

- Outstanding new app ideas;
- Concepts that combine one existing solution with another one or with a fresh idea;
- Businesses that want to build an exact analog of the existing app;
- Companies that need an app for their business.

12.2   DIGITAL VALUE CHAINS: FROM DEVELOPMENT TO DISSEMINATION OF APPS

As mentioned above, the developer of an app generally does not coincide with the distributor (the store).

Developing apps for mobile devices requires considering the technical specifications of the various devices. Smartphones have less powerful processors than personal computers, are battery-powered, and have GPS and micro-camera, with increasingly higher definitions. The spread of increasingly capillary wi-fi networks, associated with SIM cards receiving the signal in uncovered areas, allows wider and faster use of smartphones related to apps, with connections that do not consider the constraints of space and time (everywhere and always, 24/7).

The spread of apps has an impact on information asymmetries, strongly reducing their impact and generating added value for users. On the other hand, digitization and computerization, even using the apps, destroy largely obsolete business models (think of travel agencies, newsagents, bookstores, music stores, etc.).

An essential part of the development process is the design of the graphical interface, which must be easy and intuitive because the apps are intended for a different audience, not necessarily computer experts; the development of the apps must consider the operating system of the mobile device.

There are over 20 million app developers in the world (from large IT operators to simple individuals, passing through software houses from small to medium/medium-large), of which about 25% work on the cloud. The principle of the cloud is the use of large data centers (owned by the giants of IT), which virtualize the machines, replacing the physical media (personal or business computers and servers).

The development of a traditional app follows a precise path: the developer works in the development environment, then goes to the test phase, then to pre-production, and finally to final production. The development of new apps is closely related to the end-user demand, which influences their diffusion.

The value chain (from development to dissemination) of apps is shown in Fig. 12.1.

The cost of developing an app varies according to complexity (e.g., address book management or 3D games); the revenue is usually divided between the distributor and the manufacturer/developer of the app according to variable measures, depending on different factors (distribution, distributor, number of downloads into operating income …).

App development creates new markets, stimulating the spending power of users entering new markets.

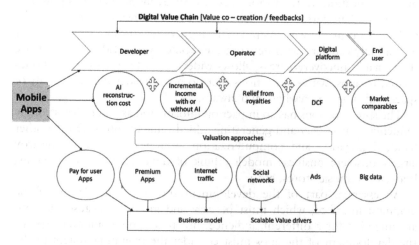

Fig. 12.1 M-Apps, digital value chains, valuation approaches, and business models

The versatile development of multi-homing apps (i.e., adaptable to different operating systems) increases their value and usability, as well as their profitability for developers.

Mobile advertising is strategic for apps, to the benefit of developers and distribution platforms.

In this context, apps incorporating probabilistic algorithms for estimating market trends are detected, as part of increasingly focused marketing strategies.

The advertising revenues of an app derive essentially from banners and pop-ups, which can be inserted through special contracts with operators.

In general, advertising revenues are variable and depend on the number of visitors to the pages and the clicks on the banner/pop-up, or they can be fixed, in the case of ad hoc contracts stipulated directly with advertisers or advertising dealers.

The progressive consolidation of the app market means that until a few years ago it was unthinkable to be crowded, with the consequent growing difficulty for developers to create real added value that did not exist before and to find free marketing spaces. This influences the evaluation profiles of the apps.

Apps play an important role in the IoT, as these new devices revolve around applications interacting with each other.

12.3 ACCOUNTING AND FISCAL ASPECTS: AN INTRODUCTION

The accounting of M-apps (application software) in financial statements plays a significant role in their economic valuation. The accounting rules for the recording of intangible assets, dictated by the international accounting principles (IAS/IFRS), are overtime becoming increasingly compliant with the new valuation standards, providing for the alignment to the fair value of the book values recorded in the financial statements. The analysis of the accounting aspects shows, for evaluation purposes, the parameters (historical or, even better, perspective) then used in the estimate (costs incurred; economic or financial margins; applicable royalties, etc.).

Concerning the tax aspects of apps, a distinction should be made between developers (often individuals) and distributors (usually computer giants that master operating systems). Moreover, application problems arise about income or indirect taxes. The Western countries' tax system adopts the worldwide taxation principle, according to which income produced anywhere by a person resident in the national territory is subject to taxation in his country of origin.

While for developers the concept of residence is less complex, for the service of selling apps, as well as in e-commerce in general, there has long been a problem (currently unresolved) of identification of the state of residence of companies.

The identification of the type of income of developers is influenced by the store used, as there are differences, for example between Apple and Amazon, which act as real intermediaries, or Google Play.

E-commerce taxation remains a controversial global issue, due to territoriality issues that arise from the dichotomy between the fiscal residence of increasingly concentrated players and that of the more ubiquitous customers.

12.4   THE BUSINESS PLAN AND THE PESTLE AND SWOT ANALYSIS

A business plan is a formal accounting statement that numerically describes a set of business goals, the reasons why they are believed attainable, and the strategic plan and managerial steps for reaching those goals. Hypotheses and visionary ideas of game-changers must be transformed into numbers and need to be backed by reasonable and verifiable assumptions about future events and milestones (Moro Visconti, 2019).

Budgeting lies at the foundation of every perspective economic and financial plan, not only for startups. Budget types include[2]:

- Sales/revenue budget;
- Production budget;
- Cash flow budget;
- Marketing budget;
- Project budget;
- Expenditure budget.

The accounting backbone of any business plan—with its consequent Excel formulation—is first represented by the interactive matching of the three basic balance sheet documents:

1. The balance sheet, with a representation of assets, liabilities, and differential net equity;
2. The income statement, with a coherent matching of revenues and costs;
3. The cash flow statement, showing the quantity (and quality) of liquidity created or absorbed.

An appropriate combination of the balance sheet and the income statement, as shown in Chapter 2, produces the cash flow statement.

M-App developers need to start from an expected income statement with a horizon of some 3 years, building around it a pro forma balance sheet for the same period, and obtaining a cash flow statement.

Basic parameters (EBITDA, EBIT, pre-tax result; operating and net cash flows, net financial position, equity, leverage, etc.) need then to be extracted and analyzed, as an input to the valuation approaches.

Real options incorporating different scenarios and digital scalability may be conveniently incorporated in the sensitivity analysis of the model.

The business model, propaedeutic to the fairness opinion of the expected value, must consider the interactions with end customers, and their capacity to co-create scalable value. Even the relationship with the operator that runs the digital platform (store) needs to be properly considered.

All these hypotheses must be estimated in the business plan.

The strategic analysis may be conveniently conducted with PESTLE and especially SWOT analysis.

PESTLE and SWOT analyses provide a systematic and comprehensive reflection of the external and internal operational environment. They can so be widely used in forecasting and business planning and may be combined with big data.

PEST(LE) considerations, being essentially external, somewhat tend to precede SWOT analyses: while the former shape the analytical framework of the investment, the latter resume environmental analysis (scanning the business environment for Threats and Opportunities), with a subsequent internal focus on organizational issues (Strengths and Weaknesses) (Table 12.1).

According to The App Solution,[3] the main features of SWOT analysis applied to M-Apps are:

Table 12.1   PESTLE and SWOT determinants

Variable	Definition
PESTLE	Strategic methodology comprehensively uses Political, Economic, Social, Technological, Legal, and Environmental trendy analysis for reviewing the macro environment, with its external forces that impact the ability to plan
SWOT	The structured planning method is used to evaluate the Strengths, Weaknesses, Opportunities, and Threats involved in a project, to consider if the objective (i.e., building and running a hospital) is attainable and, if so, how. Opportunities may be considered as real options

a. Strengths

First, think about all characteristics of the app idea or the business that requires an app. Part of this list will hopefully be a strength. Also, try to look at competitors. If any players in the market have the same characteristics that are to be defined as strength, for your business it becomes a necessity, not a strength.

Find answers to these questions:

1. What advantages does your idea or business have?
2. What unique selling proposition do you have?
3. What does your app do better than anyone else?
4. Are there any unique resources you can draw upon?
5. What is the final goal that you define as a sale?

b. Weaknesses

At this step, you are to be realistic and brave enough to face the truth. There is no limitation for perfection. That means that you can always find weaknesses to improve. Compare your weak sides to your competitors' ones and try to analyze how they deal with the same challenges. These questions are here to help you:

1. What improvements could you bring?
2. What should you abandon?
3. What do your users consider as a weakness?
4. What characteristics of your product do negatively affect your sales?

c. Opportunities

Catch a clue for this stage. Look at your strength and think about how you can turn them into new opportunities. Also, analyze your weaknesses carefully and consider how you can improve them for new opportunities.

You can find new opportunities everywhere. Follow up on trends and technologies in your local market and international one. Don't forget about government police monitoring and observing your potential user's lifestyle and behavior patterns.

You might need this questionnaire:

1. What trends and technologies can you implement?
2. What weaknesses of your competitors can you use?
3. What opportunities can you get when scaling your idea?

d. Threats

Both for threats and opportunities it might be useful to implement the PEST tool. It helps to analyze your business environment for political, economic, social–cultural, and technical changes. It gives a big picture for further planning.

Here are the questions that would help you to identify your threats:

1. What are the difficulties to face?
2. How do competitors overcome threats?
3. How do quality standards influence your mobile app or idea?
4. Will the mobile app be ready for changing technologies?
5. Are there going to be funding problems?

An example of SWOT analysis is represented in Fig. 12.2.

12.5   Economic Valuation

The evaluation of the M-apps (Avinadav et al., 2015; Bresnahan et al., 2014; Gunwoong & Raghu, 2014; Hao et al., 2013) should be based on methodological criteria partially different from those traditionally used in the evaluation of companies or individual assets (Fernandez, 2001; International Private Equity and Venture Capital Valuation Guidelines IPEV, 2018; Jarrett, 2018).

The value of apps can hardly be estimated, considering it as a legal asset (in this case, software) in its own right, as it is only within a wider context that the M-apps find a complete framework. The usefulness of an app and its added value (as a facilitator of business models and a catalyst that can ideally be assimilated to enzymes) must be estimated within the

Strengths	Weaknesses
• Internet Traffic • Virality • Visitors • Value • Visibility • Technology	• Crowded and competitive market • Difficulty to get distinguished • Technological drawbacks
Opportunities	**Threats**
• Digital scalability • Monetization • Simplified Search	• The predominance of platforms in value sharing • Competing Apps • Negative SEO

Fig. 12.2 SWOT analysis and M-Apps

value chain of which the app is a fundamental, though not exclusive, link. This chain goes far beyond the company's boundaries, involving several firms connected in a network, along an interactive supply chain.

From a methodological point of view, where possible, an overall assessment of the value chain that rotates around the app could be made, subdividing it according to the different stakeholders that preside over the individual segments (app developer—inventor; platform provider; users, etc.). At a later stage, the distribution of the value attributable to each segment can be estimated autonomously, to the point of valuing the app by the inventor, holder of the right of use, or the algorithms and formulas underlying the app itself.

In this context, the functional analysis of the value chain, which is the basis of the key value drivers, is a starting point for any appraisal.

The functional analysis concerns the activity carried out by each person involved in the value chain, with particular reference to the structure, the tangible and intangible assets used, the human resources employed, as well as the production cycle, the contracts in place, the strategies adopted, and the various risks assumed (unsold risk, credit risk, exchange rate risk … etc.).

The links between the app owner and the platform webmasters (Android, Apple, etc.) must be examined from a legal point of view. The analysis should consider the criteria of revenue sharing (distribution of revenues) and the resulting economic marginality (excess of revenues over costs) and financial marginality (excess of monetary revenues over expenditures), as well as the possible extension to apps of the typical copyright of the software, the presence or absence of which may affect the economic valuation.

The valuation models must consider, in addition to the unitary marginality (deriving from the use of the app for every single connection), the overall volumes of use, to achieve an improvement that multiplies the volumes of exchange on the web activated by the app by the unitary margins. These margins can change depending on the degree of use (simple contact, use of the app for B2B or B2C transactions) and are characterized by increasing profiles of scalability, which indicates, as shown in Chapter 3, the ability of a business model to generate incremental demand (additional revenue) economically, i.e., without significantly increasing costs.

The concept can be interpreted, in terms of operating leverage (i.e., the translation of incremental revenues into operating income/EBIT),[4] by minimizing variable costs, typical of many technological startups. In this case, the increase in revenues creates a virtuous circle and is reflected almost entirely in the EBIT.

Scalability is particularly important when evaluating apps, since their use generates increasing revenues, with almost zero cost increases. An example is given by the costs incurred to produce and market an app and its expected revenues: when revenues reach costs, at a break-even level, a process of positive income and financial marginality begins, in which the incremental costs to support higher revenues are typically very low. The impact on marginality to such an extent can be very significant; this explains the success of some apps (e.g., Uber).

The fact that the app ultimately corresponds to the software must consider that:

1. It is application software that does not typically require in-house customization (to which are connected the costs of body rental of computer developers, which compress the economic-financial marginality);
2. An app is a peculiar software, which must have characteristics of immediacy, practicality, and ease of use, enclosed in a captivating

app icon (logo), which absorbs some distinctive functions and identification typical of the brand, as well as represents a potential reserve
of value.

The icon of the app plays a crucial role, especially considering its
use through smartphones with small screens and increasingly secondary
screens, where the positioning of the app (like the ranking in the pages
of search engines) is crucial in encouraging its concrete and frequent use.

The high competition in the crowded world of apps and the relatively
low entry barriers for new developers (who, moreover, must be equipped
with increasingly innovative content, to achieve a differential advantage)
tend to compress the economic marginality. This is relevant considering
the ephemeral nature of the apps, whose value is always the subject of
challenge from new inventors.

The value chain finds its pillar in the underlying business model, to
which the app is ontologically addressed; in other words, the value triggered by the app, depends on its ability to solve or simplify concrete
problems intuitively (renting a taxi or a hotel or a bed and breakfast;
checking traffic in real-time, etc.), creating new business models that must
produce a perceived and widespread utility.

The value created in the new business model through the app can then
be divided between those who have contributed to its production. The
examination of the complex legal problems can never be separated from
an economic and functional analysis of the business model to which the
app is oriented, without which any consideration would be emptied of
content. For the economic evaluation of apps, therefore, the best-known
methods for estimating the value of the intangibles used by the application
practice can be used as a starting point, appropriately adapted to the case
in question.

12.5.1   The Cost Approach

According to this approach, consistent with IVS 210 standards, the value
of an app can be obtained by estimating the costs incurred for the realization of the intangible resource or to be incurred for its reproduction:
the value is determined by the sum of the capitalized costs, incurred for
its realization or to be incurred to reproduce it.

Within the scope of the cost approach, the so-called CO.CO.MO. (COnstructive COst MOdel)[5] is used to estimate some basic parameters (such as delivery time and man-months) necessary for software development.

The cost approach has a semantic value at the level of the estimation process, but it does not always allow a precise correlation between costs incurred and potential value, which depends essentially on other variables (such as the economic-financial expected marginality). The costs incurred by individual developers, if comparable, represent a reference point for the analysis of the break-even point between operating costs and revenues, pointing out the competitive barriers to entry into the market.

12.5.2 The Income-Financial Approach

The use of apps is alternatively linked to the payment of periodic royalties, one-off amount, use on consumption (pay per use), periodic maintenance, technical support, updates, etc. Revenues from maintenance, updating, etc. services in many cases tend to exceed those related to the license of the product.

A possible variant is based on the estimation of the incremental gross operating margin or other economic margins (differential EBITDA, EBIT, pre-tax profit ...) that the app allows obtaining. A reasonable multiplier derived from negotiations of comparable intangibles is then applied. The additional cash flow generated by the app can also be considered.

The use of the app impacts the economic margins expressed by the difference between revenues and operating costs as it ideally allows both to increase revenues (with higher direct sales or with royalties receivable from licenses) and to reduce costs, producing with less labor-intensive techniques and allowing savings of other costs (production, organizational, energy, etc.).

This approach is in line with the competitive advantage proposed by Porter (1998) thanks to strategies of differentiation, such that particular use or a high diffusion of an app ensures an otherwise non-existent extra profit, which must be recognized in the evaluation.

The time horizon of the discounting of DCF or other valuation metrics must consider the expected useful life of the app, which depends on the persistence of its estimated competitive advantage. Estimating this horizon is one of the most critical parameters, considering the volatility of the reference markets and the relative business models, in a context that is not yet mature, in which constant innovation implies elements of discontinuity that cannot easily be estimated.

12.5.3   *The Empirical Approach*

The estimate of the market value is based on the screening of comparable transactions involving intangible resources, by way of sale or license, using the international databases now available on the web that can provide useful clues on their value (in terms of price comparison).

The analysis of comparability between different apps can provide information about any capital gain resulting from originality.

Still, within the empirical approach, a further method of valorization could concern, in partial analogy with the estimate of the value of the Internet sites, their diffusion (number of downloads), or the web traffic (number of clicks and/or visits) generated.

12.6   CRITICALITIES OF THE VALUATION ASSESSMENT

The evaluation of the apps briefly outlined above involves countless profiles of criticality and uncertainty.

Reference has already been made to the issue of the valuation horizon to be used for the projection of expected income or cash flows.

The instability and lack of predictability of the revenue model can lead to different evaluation scenarios. Hence the possibility of estimating apps through wide ranges of values, linked to specific milestones and legally classifiable through earn-out clauses.

The difference in estimates is based on probabilistic scenarios that follow binomial models.

In the evaluation, the value chain pivots on the app and follows logical-sequential steps (from the app to e-commerce, for example) that correspond to functions operated by developers, platforms, etc., within an interactive supply chain. In this context, the value of each player increases the overall value of the supply chain, to the benefit of all the stakeholders rotating around it.

Apps are evaluated differently depending on whether they are developed internally (captive) to promote their products (e.g., newspaper apps) or for external goods or services. In the first case, they represent a virtual shop, which typically does not have an independent valorization concerning the goods or services it promotes.

The value of the app can be estimated, if necessary, from an incremental or differential point of view (how much would the good or service be worth in the absence of the app?), where it is possible to identify it, even legally, from the company to which it refers. In the second case, the independent assessment of the app is justified by the fact that the owner of the app is not the same as the owner of the goods or services to which it relates.

Contractual agreements, if present, could be a clue in the assessment of the M-app's value.

The evolution of the sector, which is still in the adjustment phase, will make it possible to refine evaluation methods that today still lack consolidated benchmarks.

12.7   Financing App Developers

Mobile Apps are built around a value chain in which the key players are their digital hosting platforms and users.

In this area, bank credit issues concern only developers, given that oligopolistic hosting platforms are the responsibility of large IT groups and user-consumers do not need credit to access Apps, which are often free of charge or, in any case, with pricing models that are typically negligible.

In this context, credit rating metrics are important, and rating systems must adapt to the industry specificities and the often-small size of developers. The taxonomy of developers is essential in this field, given that they belong to software houses or refer to individual freelances, even if not established as a company.

The co-creation of value that arises from the synergic and constant interaction between developers and consumers has an impact on the expected economic and financial flows, which are positive for bankability, as well as the issues of scalability. Developers can be included in technological startups, for which the specific considerations first regarding the types of intermediaries that deal with them.

The business models linked to the use of Apps and their role as a portal to specific products and services, i.e., advertising revenues, contribute to defining the revenue model that must be evaluated, in terms of prospective sustainability, in a crowded and competitive context.

NOTES

1. https://theappsolutions.com/blog/marketing/swot-for-mobile-app/.
2. http://en.wikipedia.org/wiki/Budget#Budget_types.
3. https://theappsolutions.com/blog/marketing/swot-for-mobile-app/.
4. See Chapter 3.
5. See Sect. 7.4.3.

SELECTED REFERENCES

Avinadav, T., Chermong, T., & Perlman, Y. (2015). Consignment contract for mobile apps between a single retailer and competitive developers with different risk attitudes. *European Journal of Operational Research, 246*, 949–957.

Bresnahan, T. F, Orsini, J., & Yin, P. L. (2014, February 13). *Platform choice by mobile app developers*. Available at http://siepr.stanford.edu/system/files/sha red/pubs/papers/seminarseries/multihoming-boy.pdf

Cavallari, M., & Moro Visconti, R. (2016). A service-value approach to mobile application valuation. In T. Borangiu, M. Dragoicea, & H. Novoa (Eds.), *Exploring services science presented at 17th international conference, IESS, Bucharest, Romania.*Switzerland, Geneva: Springer International publishing.

Fernandez, P. (2001). Valuation using multiples: How do analysts reach their conclusions? Madrid: IESE Business school.

Gunwoong, L., & Raghu, T. S. (2014). Determinants of mobile apps' success: Evidence from the app store market. *Journal of Management Information Systems, 31*(2), 133–170.

Hao, L., Guo, H., & Easley, R. (2013). *A mobile platform's monetizing strategy for advertising under agency pricing for app sales*. Available at http://misrc. umn.edu/workshops/2013/fall/hao.pdf

International Private Equity and Venture Capital Valuation Guidelines IPEV. (2018).

International valuation standard 210.

Jarrett, J. E. (2018). *Methods of evaluating the value of intangible assets*. The University of Rhode Island—Digital Commons URI.

Moro Visconti, R. (2019). *How to prepare a business plan with excel*. Working paper, June 1st, available at SSRN https://ssrn.com/abstract=2039748

Porter, M. E. (1998). *Competitive advantage: Creating and sustaining superior performance*. New York, NY: The Free Press.

CHAPTER 13

Big Data Valuation

13.1 INTRODUCTION

The term big data is used to describe a data collection so extensive in volume, speed, and variety as to require specific technologies and analytical methods for the extraction of value.

Big data represents the interrelation of data potentially coming from heterogeneous sources, thus including not only structured data, such as databases but also unstructured data, such as images, emails, GPS data, and information taken from social networks (Snijders et al., 2012).

Big data are increasingly becoming a strategic factor in production, market competition, and growth, considering the continuous evolution of business models and markets in the modern era (Zillner et al., 2014). The progressive increase in the size of the datasets is linked to the need for analysis of a single set of data to extract additional information compared to that which could be obtained by analyzing small series, with the same total amount of data.

Data mining is the set of techniques and methodologies having as their object the knowledge, coming from large amounts of data (through automatic or semi-automatic methods), and the scientific, industrial, or operational use of this knowledge (Xintong et al., 2014).

Data analysis technologies are being integrated into many aspects of everyday life (sensors, biometrics, home automation, communications, healthcare, etc.).

© The Author(s), under exclusive license to Springer Nature Switzerland AG 2022
R. Moro-Visconti, *The Valuation of Digital Intangibles,*
https://doi.org/10.1007/978-3-031-09237-4_13

Firms have seen the emergence of the professional figure of the data scientist, the person who analyzes the data to provide useful information to management, to make decisions and strategies to be undertaken.

The analysis of big data requires, first, the management, acquisition, organization, storage, and processing of data; second, it is necessary to identify the data to be extracted and the methods of this operation.

Finally, the process requires the ability to communicate (storytelling), with different forms of representation, what the extracted data suggest.

A privileged channel for the collection of big data is represented by the information released, voluntarily or not, by users who surf the Internet.

The information requested with personal data, often related to the possibility of using free apps (e.g., antivirus, online reservations, etc.), is collected and transmitted on databases for commercial purposes, and then sold to third parties. This usually happens without the user's knowledge and is not always in compliance with the protection of his data, taking advantage of the extraterritoriality of many servers, which hampers the imposition and enforcement of rules to protect privacy.

13.2   BIG DATA 10Vs

The spread of portable devices (smartphones, tablets, i-watch ...) is continuously increasing, and most transactions are online. The actions, activities, and behaviors of individuals are now measurable by data that can be combined with other data and analyzed by special tools. Thanks to technological sensors and biometric identification, it is possible to arrive at a collection of increasingly representative quantitative data on the inhabitants of the world.

The development of data and technology has brought out the sector known as the Internet of Things, which indicates a family of innovative technologies, whose purpose is to make any type of object, even without a digital vocation, a device connected to the Internet, which can enjoy all the features that have objects born to use the web (Mignemi, 2014).

The features of big data are expressed in Table 13.1, with the so-called 10 v, which refers to volume, velocity, variety, veracity, validity, variability, virality, visualization, viscosity, and value.

For big data analysis, the initial idea is to put together different volumes of data and identify a pattern in their aggregation using intelligent software, to identify the correct conclusions (where possible, capable of generating economic value). The primary aggregation of data can

Table 13.1 The big data 10Vs and their impact on forecasting

Big data features	Impact on the forecast
Volume	Large amounts of data significantly increase the depth, accuracy, and quality of available information. Using big data for budgeting and reporting purposes may allow for more accurate estimates. Differences between forecasts and actual data are reduced, as is the risk (inversely proportional to the Value for Money ratio), strengthening the supply chain. Relationships between different stakeholders are likely to improve
Velocity	Data is accumulated in real-time and quickly. The speed of the data increases when the system (represented, for example, by the databases) improves, thanks to artificial intelligence and the learning of the machine. Speed, like volume, can reduce the gap between forecast data and actual data
Variety	Empirical samples, together with big data, analyze a variety of structured, semi-structured, and unstructured data to match forecasts with actual results, predict risk models, and provide more in-depth and effective analysis. Variety increases the understanding of stakeholders' needs
Veracity	One of the key parameters in investments is the reliability of the data. Increased variety and speed can hamper the ability to filter data before analyzing it and making decisions, amplifying the problem of data truthfulness, which can help reduce opportunistic behavior and conflicts of interest
Validity	Integrity, associated with truthfulness, can be defined as the validity, accuracy, reliability, timeliness, and consistency of data
Variability	The variability of the data increases their informative value and should be correlated with other parameters, such as speed and variety. When variability is considered and readily reflected in updated business models, the risk is reduced
Virality	Measures the rate of data dissemination (speed of sharing) across the network. Increases the involvement of different stakeholders
Visualization	The connection between the display of information and visual analysis through an IT system and technological representations could help users to better understand the data. The synthesis reproduced by data visualization tools is a key element in transforming the information revealed by big data processing, including only by specialists, into user-accessible knowledge
Viscosity	It characterizes the resistance to navigating the data set or the complexity of data processing. It is a common feature of complex data in many industries

(continued)

Table 13.1 (continued)

Big data features	Impact on the forecast
Value	The monetizable value is the synthesis of the features of big data, considering data as a resource to be exploited to produce innovation and new information-sensitive products and services (Walker, 2015)

be recursively analyzed. The opportunities are manifold and range from increasing productivity, reducing costs, and improving communication with consumers, to improving the accuracy of forecasts.

The combination of information and communication technologies can increase efficiency, reducing costs and human error.

Being able to discover unexpected correlations, the analysis of big data is an important driver of innovation, applicable to the fields of experimentation and creativity, with the possibility of creating new business models, products, and services for interactive stakeholders.

Information is, in general, generated by the combination of:

– Data generated by machines: sensors, audio/video applications, data services, questionnaires, and statistics (…);
– User-generated data: social networks, correspondence, publications, images, blogs (…);
– Commercial data: transactions, personal data, customer relationship management (…).

Unstructured data must be extracted automatically from these sources and processed and organized into analyzable data sets.

13.3   BIG DATA REGULATION

Given their importance and potential, as well as the privacy concerns that they raise, big data has gradually become the recipient of a tremendous amount of attention from industry groups and policymakers alike. Big data are driving a trend toward behavioral optimization and personalized law, in which legal decisions and rules are optimized for best outcomes and where the law is tailored to individual consumers based on analysis of past data.

Looking at the broad legal context, in the United States, there are no specific laws that currently regulate big data. Rather, companies seeking to participate in big data operations must ensure that their proposed activities comply with privacy laws that apply to the data involved in their operations, as well as the companies' privacy policies and all applicable contractual requirements.

For example, financial institutions wishing to use non-public personal information (NPI) in connection with data processing operations will need to ensure that they comply with the Gramm Leach-Biley Act (GLBA). In the same way, entities subject to the Health Insurance Portability and Accountability Act (HIPAA) will need to ensure that their use of Protected Health Information (PHI) complies with the requirements of HIPAA. Moreover, to minimize some of the risks that may be associated with the use of big data, companies often elect to anonymize or de-identify the data before conducting analyses or sharing the information with third parties. Anonymization of data can be an effective mechanism for allowing a company to manipulate, analyze, and study data without needing to be concerned about privacy considerations.

Unlike the United States, the EU has regulated the treatment of big data. In fact, in May 2018, a new *General Data Protection Regulation* (GDPR) replaced *Directive 95/46*, consolidating, and innovating data protection rules. GDPR will govern the way data is stored and protected, and it is intended to give citizens back more control of the data held about them.

13.4   THE VALUE CHAIN

The value chain related to big data is based on a series of progressive steps. Each link in the chain represents a connection with the previous and subsequent stages, with incremental added value that is of economic and legal importance (at the contractual level and, where appropriate, in the case of litigation).

The above value chain can be graphically represented as follows (Fig. 13.1):

Data collection is the first—fundamental—link in the value chain and is done by drawing, often in a complementary way, from different sources like:

Fig. 13.1 Big data value chain

- Digital platforms (for the intermediate interchange of data, transactions, etc.);
- Sensors/Internet of Things (IoT);
- (Social) networks;
- New media;
- Wireless protocols;
- Encrypted and tracked Internet access.

The next steps (organization, processing, analysis, archiving) take place through increasingly automated algorithms from a sequential perspective.

Each of these functions has a significant impact on the creation of economic value, with legal consequences to be assessed on a case by case basis (in contractual, judicial, etc.).

At the IT level, the various links in the value chain follow sequential calculation algorithms that regulate the information flows with specific software. Several studies consider big data and its valuation issues (Athanassakos, 2007; Barnicle, 2015; Buckley, 2017; Chen & Zhang, 2014; Chen & Lui, 2014; Dakova et al., 2018; Devins et al., 2007; Dimitrov, 2016; Gani, 2014; Hartmann et al., 2016; Internet society, 2015; Klosek, 2014; La Torre et al., 2018; Louveaux, 2016; Lugmayr & Scheib, 2016; Moro Visconti, 2017; Moro Visconti et al., 2017; Moro Visconti et al., 2018; Muhtaroglu et al., 2013; Najjar & Kettinger, 2013; Nasser & Tariq, 2015; Oguntimilehin & Ademola, 2014; Stander, 2015; Sunghae et al., 2015; Thierer, 2015; Torrace & West, 2017; Vom Lehn, 2016; Warren et al., 2015; Yuncheng et al., 2016).

13.5   DATA-DRIVEN INFORMATION
AND THE IMPACT ON KNOW-HOW

As already noted, data are increasingly at the heart of new strategies that determine the approach to the most advanced business models, increasingly data-driven, that is, guided by the input data that are collected and that, if promptly analyzed, can give information necessary to implement profitable strategic actions, even from a marketing perspective, and increase productivity.

This approach has a significant impact on the company's digital know-how.

The know-how exploits a wealth of knowledge based on the power of data acquired through entrepreneurial talent, often by way of craftsmanship and not always formally codified, not in the public domain, and therefore such as to originate exclusive information asymmetries, which often infringe trade secrets, characterized by requirements of novelty and not accessible to third parties.

The know-how is closely linked to knowledge management, the set of methods and software tools that allow to identify and capitalize on business knowledge, especially to organize and disseminate them. Even knowledge is closely related to big data and its analysis (AaaS—Analytics-as-a-Service).

In the field of new digital technologies, the development and integration of knowledge is therefore increasingly a process of innovation in the value chain.

13.6   THE DARK SIDE OF THE WEB: CRITICALITIES
OF THE NEW INFORMATION PARADIGMS
AND IMPACT ON THE ECONOMIC VALUE

The development of technological innovation fueled by big data is accompanied by the emergence of opportunities, unthinkable until a few years ago, inevitably accompanied by critical issues relating to the new information paradigms, still largely unexplored.

The analysis of big data is first based on their correlation, even random, obtained by coupling and processing heterogeneous data with appropriate algorithms. The much more refined and penetrating analysis of the causality of the data goes beyond the perimeter in which the big data are formed and crossed. The correlations identified by the algorithms are not always completely logical, being a set of tools and computerized formulas, which are limited to mechanistically coupling the connections between the data.

The consequences of this correlation, which does not include causality, are significant, both from a theoretical and a practical point of view. In this context, two aspects concern the inference of the scientific method and the causal link in the legal sphere.

Scientific methods are based on cause–effect relationships which, if verified and generalized, can lead to the development of explanatory models of phenomena that allow the large-scale application of technologies and process and product innovations, with significant practical repercussions, in terms of increased productivity and value creation.

The causal link is, moreover, with some adaptations, a concept theoretically well-known in the legal sphere.

The absence of an interpretation of the causal link in raw big data reduces their applicability in the scientific field, with consequent repercussions in the economic field (lack of value creation) and in the legal field (difficulty or impossibility of interpreting the relations between data).

Data analysis remains the basis for decision-making, but the power to make decisions cannot be fully delegated to algorithms, even if they include self-learning computer techniques that rely on artificial intelligence patterns.

The standardization, control, and certification of algorithms should help to increase the protection of their conscious use, which, however, cannot be dissociated—to be truly useful—from an in-depth hermeneutical analysis.

The proponents of big data, although aware of these limits, rely on the circumstance that the amount of data that can be processed is so significant that it can solve the lack of a causal interpretation, simply by increasing the observed sample and then mapping a large number of possible correlations. Correlation is a necessary but not enough condition and the interdisciplinary interpretation of causality (from the scientific-technological, sociological, economic, legal, etc.) represents an essential step for a conscious use of data.

The analysis of the juridical problems arises from empirical observation of the processes of creation, aggregation, and analysis of the big data, briefly described above, which must be accompanied by reflections on the consequences of the use of data.

Big data imply a drastic reduction of information asymmetries which can create enormous potential added value while threatening the privacy of subjects or surreptitiously depriving them of a share in the added value that they contribute to generate.

The protection of privacy and anonymity and the request for greater transparency are critical issues as well as the implementation of increasingly secure IT architectures. Legal regulation is in pursuit of a reality that currently surpasses largely inadequate prescriptions.

The numerous purposes of the use of big data, often based on sensitive personal data, should be adequately protected and standardized at the international level. Regulations should consider the now global extension of the data supply chain, to avoid convenient locations of servers and clouds in countries that are less attentive to sensitive situations, such as taxation profiles or the security and protection of people.

The evaluation of data involves problems in estimating the incremental applications made possible by big data. It is appropriate to focus on the added value that data bring to other intangibles (trademarks, patented inventions, product and process innovations, digital know-how, etc.), within a synergistic portfolio of Intellectual Property. It is an incremental value, often inseparably associated with one or more intangibles, compared to a context in which big data are not used. For example, the incremental value of a trademark or patent can be estimated, if it is associated with big data. This method of valuation is typical of intangible assets (e.g., unbranded products compared to branded ones).

The incremental valuation profiles of big data are recorded in negotiations, in terms of royalties to be paid for their use.

13.7   Big Data and Augmented Business Planning with Real Options and Stochastic Projections

The drafting of a business plan is a prerequisite for the evaluation, as it evidences key parameters like expected cash flows or economic margins. Both estimates may be biased by inaccurate forecasts, leading to substantial differences between expectations and actual results (Fig. 13.2).

An innovative process methodology could consider the interaction between the following methods/parameters:

Fig. 13.2 Impact of big data and stochastic models on business plans and business valuation

1. Cross-section data integrated with time series analysis;
2. Stochastic development of forecast time series;
3. Big data as input for both cross-section data and time series analysis;
4. Real options for big data and stochastic projections.

The development of business plans and economic projections is based on the interaction of accounting data from the projected income statements, combined with pro forma balance sheets, to arrive at a prospective cash flow statement.

The company valuation is based on complementary methods to estimate the enterprise value (including debt) or the equity value (residual value for the shareholders).

Business models, which are intrinsically dependent on data, are increasingly connected with digital information, provided by big data. Forecasting models use historical and transactional data patterns to predict market trends, risks, and opportunities.

The information and knowledge extracted from big data are determined for the development of the business in several (complementary) ways: the speed allows a mark-to-market update and a renewal of the forecasts, which adapt flexibly to changing market conditions, while the volume of data makes the estimates more accurate and less volatile.

Big data improve the features of crucial planning and evaluation parameters:

- Operating revenues are the primary driver leading to EBITDA, after considering fixed and variable (monetary) operating costs. While fixed costs do not depend on the volume of revenues, variable costs represent a percentage of sales, which can be estimated using stochastic models, fueled by big data;
- digital scalability is fueled by big data, and it enhances economic marginality;

- Supply chain management (smart logistics): big data helps optimize logistics and warehousing; they foster coordination with suppliers, shortening the supply chain and making it less sensitive to external shocks; this has a positive impact on operating leverage and economic and financial margins such as EBITDA;
- EBITDA can be interpreted as the algebraic sum of revenues and monetary OPEX[1]; big data can improve the revenue model and its related costs;
- Operating cash flows (O_{CF}) derive from the combination of EBITDA, net working capital (NWC), and the change in fixed assets (CAPEX—capital expenditure), available from the projected balance sheets. Big data can improve the analysis and forecasting of economic and financial margins and their related assets and liabilities;
- The WACC is another parameter that considers the weighted cost of capital raised; big data can help to identify and improve its forecast, estimating its evolution with constantly updated inputs and considering together the internal parameters (debt and capital) with expected interest rates or the cost of equity;
- The net financial position (NFP) corresponds to the algebraic difference between financial receivables, cash, cash equivalents, and financial payables. The net financial position is added algebraically to the enterprise value to arrive at the equity value. Big data can facilitate the forecast of the estimated net financial position, correlating it with the evolution of CAPEX and Net working capital (in turn correlated with sales revenues).

The valuation of big data considers its impact on economic and financial marginality. Data typically have an incremental value on the key valuation parameters.

IVS 210 and its cost, income, or market approaches apply to big data appraisal. The value of data can be appraised considering, for instance, the cost of reproducing them (building up a database), the rental possibilities (and their related royalties), or even the market value of comparable data. Data can be self-produced or purchased, being an increasingly valuable asset. Value co-creation connects data generators along a digitized supply chain.

Figure 13.3 shows how useful information can be extracted from big data and accounting data.

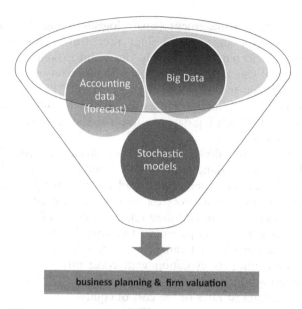

Fig. 13.3 The extraction of information values from big data and accounting data

While cross-section data are about observing the determinants of a variable at some point in time, time-series data observe their dynamics.

The economic data sets are presented in various forms. The main types of data sets are cross-sectional data, time-series, and panel data.

Cross-sectional data consists of micro or macroeconomic units taken at a specific date, while time-series refers to information related to one or more variables over time.

Data panels correlate cross-sectional data with time series. The use of time series for forecasting purposes is an essential component of management, planning, and decision-making. Following the big data trend, large amounts of time-series data from heterogeneous sources are available in an increasing number of applications.

The interactions between cross-section data and time series analysis, fed by big data in a stochastic evolution model, are illustrated in Fig. 13.4.

Economic and financial information can be linked to big data, given its size and impact on the value chain.

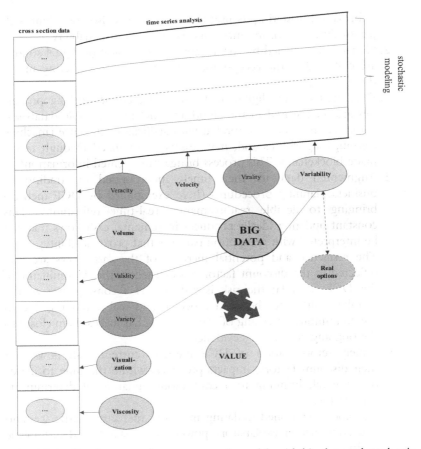

Fig. 13.4 Development of revenue growth models with big data and stochastic processes

The flow chart of the sequential passages that start from bottom-up data and then impact business planning, making it "augmented", is composed of these steps:

1. The empirical evidence that provides massive information is represented by the ecosystem—a network of interconnecting and interacting parts—where the firm is located. This networked ecosystem is levered by digitalization that transforms into IT data any useful

information, fostering its use; the ecosystem is also consistent with personalization, for instance concerning ESG sustainability goals;

2. "Small" data, fueled by IoT or any other physical or digital source, are collected in the ecosystem, and their massive gathering makes them "big";

3. Data mastered by digital platforms and their networking properties are then stored in the cloud and fuel interoperable databases. Information is then interpreted with artificial intelligence (machine learning) algorithms and, if necessary, is validated through tailor-made blockchains. This process brings "augmented information";

4. Augmented data are then timely incorporated in (traditional) business planning procedures (here exemplified by DCF metrics) bringing to flexible readjustments (real-time refreshing). This constant updating ideally produces incremental cash flows that can be interpreted with real option patterns that proxy flexibility;

5. The resilience and potential increase of the cash flows are also reflected in the discount factor represented in the denominator of the DCF formula; the risk is reduced as a consequence of the shrinking difference between expected and real outcomes, due to the continuous refreshing of expectations that makes them closer to the ongoing ecosystem's evidence;

6. Timely reformulation of DCF metrics (current cash flows and their discount factors) impacts prospects within the time to maturity interval, bringing to a continuous updating of deterministic expectations;

7. The abovementioned updating may well fuel a stochastic scenario that adds further explanatory power to the standard deterministic outlook.

The model is graphically described in Fig. 13.5.

The methodology is consistent with the research question of this chapter, showing that business planning can become more valuable—augmented—if it incorporates big data's informative contents, validated by blockchains, and interpreted through artificial intelligence predictive patterns.

Figure 13.5 can be further developed, as shown in Fig. 13.6, to express the added value incorporated in augmented business planning.

The interaction of top-down and bottom-up strategies can be synthesized in Fig. 13.7.

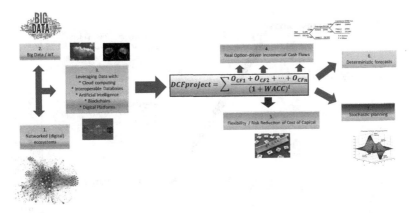

Fig. 13.5 From big data-driven forecasting to augmented business planning

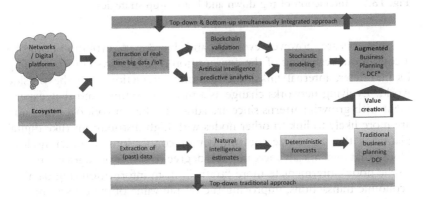

Fig. 13.6 Value creation, from traditional to augmented business planning

13.8 Networking Ecosystems

The networked ecosystem is the external source of information and represents the competitive environment where the firm is positioned. The standard ecosystem, inspected with the lens of network theory, can be rearranged including a pivoting node represented by the digital platform. This brings to an incremental (differential) value that positively affects the DCF, increasing the numerator, and softening the risk component embedded in the denominator.

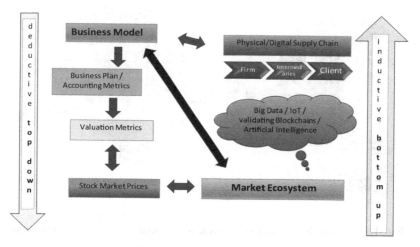

Fig. 13.7 Interaction of top-down and bottom-up strategies

Networks are, however, evolving, and their kinetic evolution brings to a continuous reshaping of the composition of the ecosystem, concerning its perimeter, internal links, and osmotic interaction with the outside world. Evolving networks change as a function of time, and they experiment with growth patterns since are added to the network over time and are more likely to link to other nodes with high distributions (like digital platforms that maximize the number of connections to other nodes). Nodes that dynamically increase their degree (number of edges connected to the node) intermediate more "traffic", from information (big data) to economic transactions, improving the overall value of the ecosystem.

The informative contents of the nodes depend on their features that continuously change over time and may be recalled in Table 13.2.

A comprehensive picture of the evolving network ecosystem is shown in Fig. 13.8.

The strategic drivers that impact the DCF formulation are recalled in Table 13.3.

The network interacts with business planning through digital and physical connections, and transactions. The sequential impact is dynamic and subject to continuous adjustments, due also to the feedback that fuels value co-creation, reshaping the supply and value chain. A representation is reported in Fig. 13.9.

Table 13.2   Network (node) features and impact on the business planning

Network (node/edge) property	Explanation	Impact on business planning/DCF
Network (un)directed links	A network is called directed (or digraph) if all its links are asymmetric, and cause–effect relationships are only one-way; it is called undirected if all its links are symmetric (one-to-one)	Most links within the network ecosystem are undirected. They have a greater potential impact on value
Node degree	Number of links to other nodes	The higher, the bigger the "intensity" of the network and its potential value. The digital platform is a catalyzing node
Edge—Physical links	Pairs of nodes can be physically connected by a tangible link	Physical links coexist with digital ones, and their synergic impact can generate value
Edge—Physical interactions	Connection determined by a physical force	Physical interaction among physical (and digital) links impacts the supply chain
Edge—(intangible) connections	Information or other immaterial links	Digital connections complement physical ones
The geographic closeness between nodes	The geographic closeness between nodes	Physical proximity is an added value
Social connections (friendship, collaboration, family ties, etc.)	Social connections (friendship, collaboration, family ties, etc.)	Social ties ease information spreading and transactions, generating value
Functional linking (actions that activate other activities)	Functional linking (actions that activate other activities)	Bridging nodes favor value-adding indirect links

Dynamic network analysis may give an innovative interpretation of how the relationships among different nodes evolve. Nodes may be represented, for instance, by key business planning analytics (expected sales, economic and financial margins, etc.), whose evolution could be mathematically mapped with network theory.

13.9   Big Data and Bankability

The use of big data, of information deriving from the Internet of Things and artificial intelligence, is still limited in the traditional banking field,

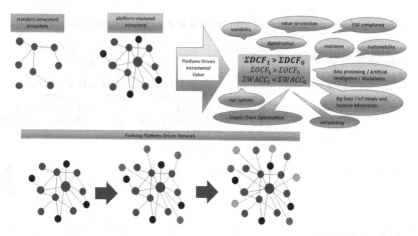

Fig. 13.8 Platform-driven evolving networks

being confined to FinTech experiments and simulations. However, there is an enormous potential for big data in corroborating increasingly accurate, updated, and expressive information sets, capable of capturing details and trends with a capacity for collection and processing unknown until a few years ago.

Data have always existed, but what distinguishes big data are their features, highlighted in Table 13.1. In this context, data have become an increasingly essential asset that companies form and collect internally or purchase from external databases.

The rating processes are gradually being refined to include performance data that can be entered in real-time in the algorithms of calculation, helping to make more effective forecasts. This involves a reduction in information asymmetries and helps to minimize the differences between forecasts and empirical findings, with a consequent reduction in risk, which is reflected in the lower WACC, with a consequent improvement of DCF.

The distinction between different types of data is relevant, given that the numerical data are those intrinsically most suitable for popular databases linked to the algorithms for calculating the rating. They detect qualitative or other data (words to be interpreted semantically; figures or sounds).

Table 13.3 Impact of the strategic drivers on the discounted cash flows

Strategic driver	Impact on the discounted cash flows
Scalability	A scalable firm can improve profit margins while sales volume increases. This positively affects the EBITDA and the operating and net cash flow
Value co-creation	The joint creation of value by the firm and the customer with her feedback positively impacts economic and financial marginality, also improving customer loyalty, and reducing the churn rate
Digitalization	The process of converting information into a digital format increases the value of data making them accountable and manageable
Resilience	It expresses the toughness or elasticity of a system, and its capacity to recover quickly from difficulties. Resilient cash flows mitigate risk incorporated in the discount factor
ESG compliance	Environmental, social, and governance (ESG) criteria are a set of standards for a company's operations that socially conscious investors use to screen potential investments. Their impact on DCF is mixed (Cornell & Damodaran, 2020; Moro Visconti, 2020)
Sustainability	Economic sustainability complements the social and environmental dimensions and consists of the ability of an economy to support a defined level of economic production indefinitely. Sustainable business models incorporate resilience and scalability, with a positive impact on DCF
Data processing/Artificial Intelligence/Blockchains	Data processing and archiving in the cloud, together with artificial intelligence interpretation and blockchain validation, improve the value of information and may positively affect DCF

(continued)

Table 13.3 (continued)

Strategic driver	Impact on the discounted cash flows
Big Data/IoT	Big data and IoT nurture the business planning input factors with massive and timely information, improving the expected cash flows, and reducing their riskiness
Networking	Networking, especially if mastered by digital platforms, is a scalability catalyzer that impacts DCF
Supply chain optimization	Digital supply chains reduce intermediation costs, and improve resilience, with positive effects on cash flows
Real options	Real options increase the resilience and scalability of forecasted cash flows

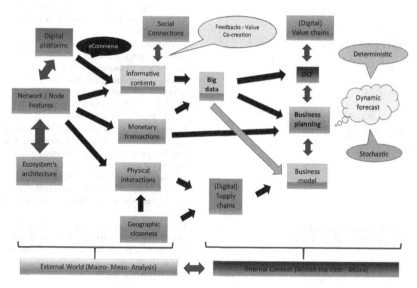

Fig. 13.9 From interacting networks to business model and planning

NOTE

1. See Sect. 3.5

SELECTED REFERENCES

Athanassakos, G. (2007). Valuing internet ventures. *Journal of Business Valuation and Economic Loss Analysis, 2*(1), 1–17.

Barnicle, A. (2015). *Mergers, acquisitions and combining data*. Big Data and the Law.

Buckley, M. (2017). *EU welcoming big data legislation*. Financial services, Cisco blogs.

Chen, C. L. P., & Zhang, C. (2014). Data-intensive applications, challenges, techniques and technologies: A survey on Big data. *Information Sciences, 275,* 314–347.

Chen, M. S. M., & Lui, Y. (2014). Big data: A survey. *Journal of Mobile Networks and Applications, 19*(2), 171–209.

Cornell, B., & Damodaran, A. (2020, March 20). *Valuing ESG: Doing good or sounding good?* NYU Stern School of Business. Available at SSRN: https://ssrn.com/abstract=3557432

Dakova, J., Chiu, Y., & Antunes, P. (2018). *A pluralistic approach to information valuation*. Paper presented at 22nd Pacific Asia Conference on Information Systems (PACIS), Yokohama, Japan.

Devins, C., Felin, T., Kauffman, S., & Koppl, R. (2007). The law and big data. *Cornell Journal of Law and Public Policy, 27*(2), 357.

Dimitrov, D. V. (2016). Medical internet of things and big data in healthcare. *Health Informatics Research, 22,* 156.

Gani, A. (2014). Big data survey, technologies, opportunities and challenges. *The Scientific World Journal, 2014,* 18. Article ID 712826.

Hartmann, P. M., Zaki, N. F., & Neely, A. (2016). Capturing value from bigdata—A taxonomy of data-driven business models used by start-up firms. *International Journal of Operations & Production Management, 36*(19), 1382–1406.

Internet Society. (2015). *The internet of things: An overview*. Available at https://www.internetsociety.org

Klosek, J. (2014). *Regulation of big data in the United States*. New York, NY: Goodwin Proctor LLP.

La Torre, M., Botes, V. L., Dumay, J., Rea, A.M., & Odendaal, E. (2018). The fall and rise of intellectual capital accounting: New prospects form the big data revolution. *Meditari Accountancy Research, 26*(3), 381–399. https://www.scopus.com/record/display.uri?eid=2-s2.0-85058090349&origin=inward&txGid=3619118fae282625b93b47da87effa69

Louveaux, S. (2016). *Big data and the new EU data protection regulation: The role of big data in healthcare.* London: European Data Protection Supervision EDPS.

Lugmayr, A. B. S., & Scheib, C. (2016). *A comprehensive survey on big data research and its implications: What is really 'new' in big data?—It's cognitive big data!* Paper 248 presented at PACIS.

Mignemi, M. L. (2014). Business analytics contro la complessità di Big Data e Internet of Things. *Harvard Business Review, 11,* 52.

Moro Visconti, R. (2017). Public private partnership, big data networks and mitigation of information asymmetries. *Corporate Ownership & Control, 14*(4–1), 205–215.

Moro Visconti, R. (2020). *The interaction of big data, flexible options, and networked ecosystems in augmented business planning.* Available at https://www.researchgate.net/publication/346442792_THE_INTERACTION_OF_BIG_DATA_FLEXIBLE_OPTIONS_AND_NETWORKED_ECOSYS TEMS_IN_AUGMENTED_BUSINESS_PLANNING

Moro Visconti, R., LaRocca, A., & Marconi, M. (2017). Big data-driven value chains and digital platforms: From value co-creation to monetization. In A. K. Somami & G. Deka (Eds.), *Bigdata analytics: Tools, technology for effective planning.* Boca Raton: CRC Press.

Moro Visconti, R., Montesi, G., & Papiro, G. (2018). Big data-driven stochastic business planning and corporate valuation. *Corporate Ownership & Control, 15*(3–1), 189–204. Available at https://doi.org/10.22495/cocv15i3c1p4

Muhtaroglu, F., Pembe, C., Demir, S., Obali, M., & Girgin, C. (2013, October 6–9). *Business model canvas perspective on big data applications.* Paper presented at IEEE International Conference on Big Data, Santa Clara, CA. https://doi.org/10.1109/bigdata.2013.6691684

Najjar, M. S., & Kettinger, W. J. (2013). Data monetization: Lessons from a retailer's journey. *MIS Quarterly Executive, 12*(4), 213–225.

Nasser, T., & Tariq, R. S. (2015). Big data challenges. *Journal of Computer Engineering & Information Technology, 4*(3), 1–10.

Oguntimilehin, A., & Ademola, E. O. (2014). A review of big data management, benefits and challenges. *Journal of Emerging Trends in Computing and Information Sciences, 5*(6), 433–438.

Snijders, C., Matzat, U., & Reips, U. D. (2012). Big data: Big gaps of knowledge in the field of internet science. *International Journal of Internet Science, 7*(1), 1–5.

Stander, J. B. (2015). *The modern asset: Big data and information valuation.* M.sc. thesis, Stellenbosch University.

Sunghae, J., Sangsung, P., & Dongsik, J. (2015). A technology valuation model using quantitative patent analysis: A case study of technology transfer in bigdata marketing. *Emerging Markets Finance and Trade, 51*(5), 963–974.

Thierer, A. D. (2015). *The internet and wearable technology: Addressing privacy and security concerns without derailing innovation.* Available at http://ssrn.com/abstract=2494382

Torrace, A. W, & West, J. D. (2017). All patents great and small: A big data network approach to valuation. *Virginia Journal of Law and Technology, 20*(3), 466–504. https://jevinwest.org/papers/Torrance2017Virgin iaLaw.pdf

Vom Lehn, D. (2016). Data, now bigger and better! *Consumption Markets & Culture Journal, 21*(1), 101–103.

Walker, R. (2015). *From big data to big profits.* Oxford: Oxford University Press.

Warren, J. D., Moffitt, C., & Byrnes, P. (2015). How big data will change accounting. *American Accounting Association, Accounting Horizons, 29*(2), 397–407.

Xintong, G., Hongzhi, W., Song, Y., & Hong, G. (2014, December). Brief survey of crowdsourcing for data mining. *Expert Systems with Applications, 41*(17), 7987–7994.

Yuncheng, S., Bing, G., Yan, S., Xuliang, D., Xiangqian, D., & Hong, Z. (2016). A pricing model for big personal data. *Tsinghua Science and Technology, 21*(5), 482–490.

Zillner, S., Rusitschka, S., & Skubacz, M. (2014). Big data story: Demystifying big data with special focus on and examples from industrial sectors, *Whitepaper, Siemens AG.* https://www.bibsonomy.org/bibtex/2ec1ca5231e8 8bd230216bfe5c4cb6a7f/bigfp7

CHAPTER 14

Internet of Things Valuation

14.1 Internet of Things and New Intangible Assets

The Internet of Things (IoT) is based on a family of innovative technologies (chips, wired and wireless sensors, tags, QR codes and barcodes, radio frequency Rfid identifications, GPS, etc.), which connect objects (gadgets ...)—in and of itself inanimate—in smart devices always connected to the web (such as mobile phones), to collect, exchange, and process data in real-time. The IoT is the extension of the Internet to the world of physical objects and places, which through the web are delocalized and made potentially usable anywhere, acquiring an electronic identity and an active role linking to the network sensors that interface with the physical world.

Protocols, interchangeable computing platforms, and enabling technologies permit to rotate around the IoT, and allow combining functions of hardware, software, data, and services to obtain new products in which the physical component is intimately connected with the intangible.

Intangibles connected to objects through the Internet acquire a potentially high added value, depending on the new economic exploitation prospects deriving from the network. The connectivity between objects, the network-web (as a virtual exchange platform), and the intangible, represents a lever of value creation especially if the intangible resources interact with each other within a synergistic portfolio of Intellectual Property (IP).

The consequences of these epochal changes in the functionalities and potential of the intangible have legal significance and require innovation in the forms of protection that must conform to new paradigms and business models.

The value of the network, which acts as a transmission chain of the links, can be estimated from the surplus value it gives to the intangible or directly, considering it as an autonomous platform for data exchange.

The main areas of operation and sectors affected by the IoT chain concern first and foremost:

- Home automation;
- Robotics;
- Avionics;
- Automotive industry;
- Biomedical;
- Industrial monitoring;
- Environmental intelligence;
- Telemetry;
- Wireless sensor networks;
- Surveillance;
- Detection of adverse events;
- Smart grid, smart metering, and cyber-security;
- Smart home and smart city;
- Embedded systems;
- Telematics;
- Internet of Plants.

The value of classic intangible assets (trademarks, patents, software, know-how, etc.) increasingly depends on whether they are digitized and connected to the Internet, as a privileged platform for the exchange and use of information in real-time. Innovative business models are increasingly oriented to enhance the differential (incremental) value expressed by intangible assets to pursue a strategic competitive advantage. The versatility that the intangible can acquire if linked to other immaterial assets through connectivity to the Internet is a source of added value and can allow a product and geographical scalability, able to cover new products and markets.

New intangibles, like IoT, increasingly integrated within an IP port-folio (often shared between companies, with cross-licensing or network agreements), tend to be designed from the beginning to be constantly interconnected. The exchange of information of the devices, mediated through the Internet, reduces the information asymmetries (with all the legal consequences of the case) and allows various applications, such as, for example, the collection of statistical data (which can become big data for their volume) to support increasingly targeted and personal-ized marketing initiatives. In other circumstances, the sensors applied to objects allow a variety of applications, often patented (e.g., home automa-tion, with remote control of appliances or other appliances). IoT inputs are typically represented by small data that, once gathered in massive amounts, become "big".

The exchange between producers and users of goods and services, through mobile apps, with assessments and reviews in real-time, allows undertaking shared paths, until recently unthinkable, from which new business paradigms emerge, based on the co-creation of value.

14.2 Internet of Things, Networks, and Big Data: A Synergistic Interaction

The innovative paradigms governing the IoT rotate around networks that connect sensors and actuators with the Internet.

Figure 14.1. shows the different phases of the IoT, starting from the sensors connected to computerized systems and the Internet, with cloud storage, and then collected, classified, and applied on a large scale, using big data:

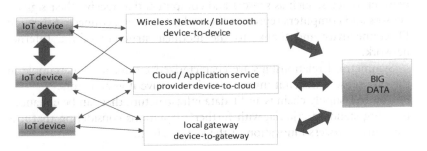

Fig. 14.1 The phases of the IoT

The connected (smart) devices can communicate with each other (device to device) through a wireless network, connected to the Internet, or directly via Bluetooth. When different devices interact in clusters, innovation can grow significantly.

Devices can communicate and exchange data (device to cloud) through existing cloud services with appropriate apps (application service providers).

Smartphones or other Internet-connected devices can be used as doors (portals) to access cloud services and exchange data between IoT (device to gateway). Big data can record information to IoT devices—actuators.

The articulation of the IoT along the process chain starts with sensors connected to serial computers (which amplify the capacity to receive vast amounts of data) via the Internet and often wirelessly. Data transmission can follow encrypted paths and protocols, where cybersecurity strategies are pursued, especially for sensitive applications (in the medical or financial field, for security aspects, etc.).

The extraction of data from the remote cloud that stores information follows data mining and processing patterns typical of big data, i.e., the set of techniques and methodologies that have as their object the extraction of knowledge from large amounts of data (through automatic or semi-automatic methods), and the scientific, industrial, or operational use of this knowledge. The data mining of heterogeneous information, conducted through the interoperability of different databases, is suitable to generate significant increases in value.

The different passages briefly illustrated above can be interpreted through the theory of networks,[1] given that the IoT networks are connected things.

Network theory deals with symmetrical or asymmetrical relationships between objects, such as sensors and computers that receive their signals. Sensors and computers represent the nodes (vertices), connected through IT connectivity and thanks to the modular structure of the Internet network.

Symmetrical relationships are characterized by duality, for example in the case sensors transmit information but receive it as actuators.

The IoT supply chain is an IT data infrastructure that can be enhanced by using standard criteria, with further adaptations considering that it is a product/process innovation of the supply chain.

The synergistic interaction of products and processes through networks that guarantee connectivity is a source of added value for the IP portfolio incorporated into the IoT chain.

Figures 14.2 and 14.3 show the interactions with big data and artificial intelligence, bringing to smart data that represent a valuable asset.

The individual elements of the IoT supply chain network are to be considered as links in a value chain. Some rings of the chain may be of strategic importance, if they take on exclusive characteristics, with a bargaining power that can lead to monopolistic rents (typical of certain patents). In the digital field, interoperability between the individual links in the supply chain and convergent standard protocols reduce the areas of exclusivity and allow wide-ranging applications, which increase the versatility—and therefore the value—of the same links (or nodes in the network).

The creation of incremental value is associated with its diffusion and sharing, as a co-creation strategy (regarding the B2C interrelations between producer and consumer), in an evolutionary context in which the value of information increasingly matters. The IoT should, therefore, be considered as a highly innovative process, which incorporates coordinated and connected intangibles, giving them a systemic added value.

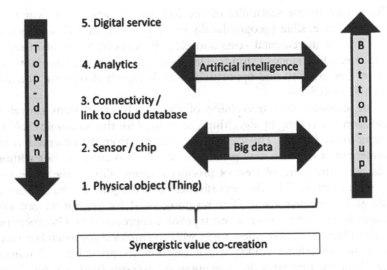

Fig. 14.2 Iot, big data, and artificial intelligence

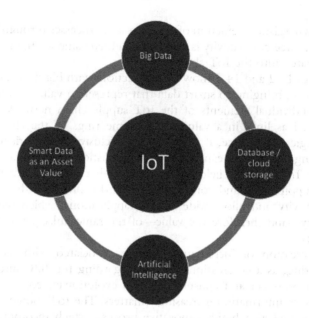

Fig. 14.3 From IoT to smart data

This is due to the scalability of the IoT model, which makes it replicable and extensible (geographically or by-product, in different sectors) with limited incremental costs and clear benefits in terms of increased economic and financial margins. The resulting Schumpeterian innovation creates new markets and opportunities while rapidly destroying outdated business models.

The computerized traceability of the supply chain steps can allow detection and coding by algorithms, to be used for the economic exploitation of the IoT chain. The legal problems derive from the observation and hermeneutics of these new paradigms of value co-creation, not without risks from the point of view of product responsibility or the protection of privacy (stressed by the pervasiveness and ubiquity of the sensors, as well as by sensitive data). The resulting need for regulation can take various forms, with a more or less repressive approach. The US experience tends to favor a creative orientation, with an empirical approach borrowed from the underlying reality, which captures its proactive and innovative elements, pragmatically containing its excesses (with self-regulatory strategies, shared best practices, social pressures, and public opinion, awareness-raising, transparency, etc.).

This occurs in an increasingly globalized context, in which different legal systems interact in real-time, laboriously in search of common and shared rules delimiting the unfair competition created by elusive locations in tax heavens.

14.3 INTERNET-RELATED PRODUCT AND PROCESS INNOVATION AND B2B AND B2C SOLUTIONS

Technological innovation consists of *"the deliberate activity of companies and institutions to introduce new products and services, as well as new methods of producing, distributing and using them"* (Porter, 1990).

The Schumpeterian distinction between product innovation (creation of new goods or services) and process innovation (new methods of production or distribution) applies even to IoT-related businesses. Both types of innovation, incremental or radical, are intimately linked to intangible assets (in particular, know-how, software, and patents). IoT is part of the process of connecting physical data to the Web.

Product innovation enables new goods or services to be brought to market and thus has a direct impact on revenues, while process innovation (e.g., with B2B or B2C solutions in e-commerce) makes more efficient use of existing products or services with cost savings. Both act on the revenue-cost differential and therefore foster the economic and financial marginality of the company or the business networks that exploit the innovation induced, for example using IoT.

The product-revenue and process-price paradigm should not be referred to as single intangibles: there are evident intersections between products and processes and consequent synergies that intersect innovations involving a portfolio of intangibles. Think of new products, for example in the IT or digital field (smartphones geolocated in real-time), which allow changing processes (B2C sales, etc.), with a synergistic added value that involves a chain of coordinated intangibles.

In this context, the role of the IoT plays a major role, in that it allows the development of new products and markets, and with them to propose operational solutions, within a digitized supply chain, which profoundly innovates processes and business models, reformulating their paradigms.

The supply chain networks connected to the IoT are primarily informative (transmission and progress of orders ...) for wholesale B2B or retail

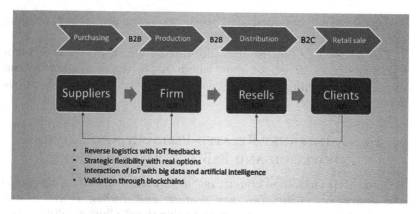

Fig. 14.4 IoT-driven supply chain

B2C. In these networks, a multiplicity of virtual stakeholders interact, in ecosystems characterized by volatile contractual boundaries.

The IoT-driven supply chain is represented in Fig. 14.4.

14.4   VALUATION OF THE PORTFOLIO OF INTERNET-RELATED INTANGIBLES

The capital gain generated by the IoT has a significant impact on the economic valuation of intangibles related to objects originally inanimate. Many authors examine the valuation issues (Abdel-Basset et al., 2018; Athanassakos, 2007; Cao et al., 2013; Cowls & Schroeder, 2015; Dimitrov, 2016; Higson & Briginshaw, 2000; Ho & Hou, 2015; Kossecki, 2011; Rose, 2011).

The information flows from sensor-objects to computerized systems and the return flows to the actuator objects can be measured and mapped with algorithms that detect their qualitative and quantitative characteristics.

Qualitative surveys depend on an estimation of the processing capacity of the data and on the surplus value of interpretation of the same, made possible by an analysis of big data going beyond a mere random correlation (obtained by statistically coupling heterogeneous data, processed by supercomputers), identifying elements of interaction and linking them with causality patterns. The applications of causality links in the legal field or even in the scientific one, through the replicability of the Galilean method, are well-known. Knowing that the information inferable from more than one sensor is correlated (perhaps randomly) is a first step in analyzing its unidirectional or bi-univocal causal link, to bring out a relevant hermeneutic value.

The instability of constantly evolving business models accentuates their risk profiles, to be considered in the evaluation process.

The characteristics of the IoT chain are so different from those of traditional intangibles that they require an adaptation of the canonical evaluation criteria.

IVS 210 approaches apply to IoT valuation.

The cost approach, often of little relevance for traditional intangibles, is even less representative of the value for the IoT chain, limiting itself to providing, at most, indications about the number of investments required, intended as a barrier to entry to protect incumbents against potential competitors.

The economic-income/financial approach is based, at least in part, on a comparison between branded or unbranded products or products with or without patent cover, to estimate in a differential (incremental) way the added value of the branded or patented asset. In the case of the IoT supply chain, this comparison must consider that inanimate sensor-objects (compared to unbranded or unpatented goods) have a value often tending to zero, with a consequently added value of connectivity which represents almost the entire value.

Trademarks, patents, copyrights (etc.) are often at the origin of the company's ability to charge sales prices that incorporate a premium compared to competing products/services meeting the same needs but offered by companies that do not have intangibles.

In the IoT world, the granting of exploitation rights and the resulting royalties are still not widespread, although there is ample room for growth, especially about big data and their personalized marketing applications. Given the novelty of the IoT chain, the available cases, to be used in an analogical way as benchmarking, are still limited.

Note

1. See Chapter 15.

Selected References

Abdel-Basset, M., Manogaran, G., & Mohamed, M. (2018). Internet of things (IoT) and its impact on supply chain: A framework for building smart, secure and efficient systems. *Future Generation Computer Systems, 86*, 614–628.

Athanassakos, G. (2007). Valuing internet ventures. *Journal of Business Valuation and Economic Loss Analysis, 2*(1), 1–7.

Cao, E. L., Lai, K. K., & Fu, Y. (2013). *A real option analysis framework for the valuation of internet-based companies*. Available at http://ieeexplore.ieee.org/abstract/document/6961158/authors

Cowls, J., & Schroeder, R. (2015). Causation, correlation and big data in social science research. *Policy & Internet, 7*(14), 447–472.

Dimitrov, D. V. (2016). Medical internet of things and big data in healthcare. *Health Informatics Research, 22*, 156.

Higson, C., & Briginshaw, J. (2000). Valuing internet business. *Business Strategy Review, 11*(1), 10–20.

Ho, C. H., & Hou, K. C. (2015). Exploring the attractive factors of app icons. *Transactions on Internet and Information Systems, 9*(6), 2251–2270. Available at www.internetsociety.org

Kossecki, P. (2011). *Valuation and value creation of internet companies—Social network services*. Working paper, The Lodz Filmschool.

Porter, M. (1990). The competitive advantage of nations. *Harvard Business Review, 68*(2), 73–93.

Rose, C. (2011). Internet valuations and economic sustainability. *Journal of Business & Economics Research, 9*, 5.

CHAPTER 15

The Valuation of Internet Companies, Videoconferences, and Social Networks

15.1 INTERNET COMPANIES AND VIDEOCONFERENCES

Internet companies represent a composite group of companies, including Internet Service Providers (ISP), which provide users with access to the web and email. Information technology platforms are becoming more and more popular, with functionalities such as e-commerce or mobile apps.

The ISP, as far as web access is concerned, are the nodes of the Internet's computer network. The Internet is one of the most significant examples of the network.

ISP perform various types of services in the information society, such as:

- Editorial services (content/information providers);
- Activities of content providers and competitive intelligence systems which interact with B2B transactions;
- Storage and domiciliation services (hosting);
- Connection and transmission services (conduit or connectivity providers);
- Search and indexing services (search engine).

At the level of the value chain, various segments can be distinguished, for example, at the systemic and infrastructural level, by backbone service providers or access service providers. The various business models have an

R. Moro-Visconti, *The Valuation of Digital Intangibles*, https://doi.org/10.1007/978-3-031-09237-4_15

435

impact on revenue models and consequently on valuation methodologies, to be considered (for each ISP) or at a systemic level, in which the overall value created is distributed among the stakeholders involved in the virtual value chain.

The valuation of Internet companies, to be adapted to the specificities deriving from the ISP business models, can follow traditional methods such as those based on the Enterprise Value/EBITDA multipliers of comparable transactions, considering business parameters such as:

- The contractual terms that bind the customers, with the remaining duration of the contracts and the renewal percentages, through the churn analysis (abandonment rate);
- The resulting rate of retention/loyalty of customers;
- Average Revenue per User (ARPU), based on total revenue about the number of active subscribers;
- Monthly Recurring Revenue, which is the sum of the value generated by customers (ARPU * number of customers).

According to Athanassakos (2007), Internet venture valuations are not subject to different valuation standards and rules, even though one needs to expand on the traditional valuation approach to make it applicable to Internet valuations. Traditional valuation methods (such as the discounted cash flows approach) understate value twice; first, when risk changes over time, and second when flexibility matters to an investment decision.

As a result, when analysts use traditional valuation approaches to value Internet companies, they may arrive at estimates of low P/E ratios vis-à-vis observed multiples. The observed high P/E ratios[1] may make most investors turn away from such investments, although the high P/E ratios may be justified based on the option of great riches in the future and the lower risk associated with Internet ventures and future cash flows with a successful progression through early phases.

An analysis of the networks is propaedeutic to the estimate of the ISP.

A videoconference is a set of interactive telecommunication technologies which allow two or more locations to interact via two-way video and audio transmissions simultaneously. It has also been called visual collaboration and is a type of groupware". Videoconferencing started to be very popular since the Covid-19 pandemic eruption, in February 2020. By now, it represents a cornerstone of smart working.

Videoconferencing is a digital network application: digital as it relies on electronic technology, applied to a network where the videoconferencing platform (e.g., MS Teams, Zoom, GoToMeeting, Google Meet, Cisco Webex, Skype, etc.) is a (hub) node that connects in real-time other nodes (the conference participants).

Digitalization is evolving, making it possible to share in real-time texts, messages, voice, videos, files, etc.

Many videoconference suppliers apply a freemium strategy (free/costless option with limited resources + monthly subscription with advanced features). The valuation of videoconference devices and providers should adequately consider their digital features, starting from their ubiquitous service (24/7), up to the networking properties of connected ecosystems that corroborate social networking ties.

15.2 NETWORKS

Networks have an invasive presence in everyday people's life: think of the interconnections related to the exchange of emails or messages, the use of social networks, telephone calls, transport, money transfers, epidemics, food chains and ecosystems, electricity grids, etc. In all these cases, the networks and their properties are used.

Disorderly or random modes of interaction connect individuals or things, with relevant consequences from a legal point of view. Some recent network applications with no hierarchical structure concern blockchains.

A network represents, in its most elementary formulation, a set of points (vertices or nodes) connected by lines (sides or edges).

Figure 15.1 illustrates a network with various types of nodes, central or peripheral. The central nodes have a greater number of connections (not only with the other nodes but as a bridge between one node and another) and are consequently the most valuable.

The concept applies to social networks that connect various individuals. The Internet is an example of a virtual network, just as other networks are found in physics, biology, or social sciences. A grade identifies the number of lines (sides) associated with each node. The centrality of the nodes and the increasing number of degrees associated with them are proportional to their value. The most connected nodes (hubs) act as pivots and

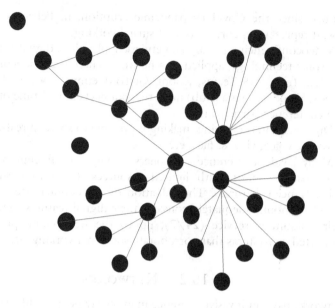

Fig. 15.1 Example of a network

have a more relevant value which depends on the relationship that other peripheral nodes have with them.

Networks can be egocentric if they revolve around an individual; then there are affiliate networks based on a common belonging to groups or communities which nurture lasting social relationships and collective networks (system of social groups connected by common bonds). The performance of a team depends on the interaction among its members.

The theory of networks was born from the theory of graphs, in the field of topological geometry following the problem of the Konigsberg bridges: in 1736 the mathematician Leonhard Euler wondered if it was possible to follow a pedestrian path crossing each bridge only once and then returning to the starting point. The question and the (negative) answer were not of great importance, except for the fact that they gave rise to the random topological theory of graphs. Graphs express an architecture of nodes obtained by connecting various points between them (Fig. 15.2).

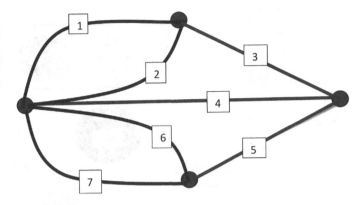

Fig. 15.2 The Konigsberg bridges and the graph theory

What is most relevant, in the interpretation of the connections between different nodes, is not so much their distance, as the characteristics of the interrelations, starting with the intensity. An example is given by the nodes deriving from an exchange of emails between several subjects: the distance between the computers sending and receiving email messages is completely irrelevant, while the influence of the subjects and the nature of their interrelationships matters. Networks try to explain how isolated elements can be transformed into groups and communities through models of interaction (such as computer platforms on the Internet).

Practical applications for the interpretation of interconnected systems are extremely relevant and to some extent still unexplored. These applications concern the legal field: for example, synallagmatic or contractual relations or corporate governance issues involving a network of stakeholders. They detect, in full adherence with the networks, the business networks or the industrial districts where specialized clustered firms cooperate.

The competitive advantage is based more and more on strategic networks and relational rents between companies, following an integrated supply chain where each company presides over a link in the overall value chain. The supply chain is a comprehensive intangible resource, whose value must be shared among its constituent companies, according to their contribution and the resulting margins.

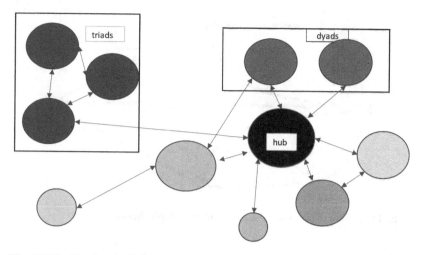

Fig. 15.3 Dyads, triads, and hubs

Networks can connect various sensors within the Internet of Things. The interchange point is represented by cloud platforms and databases which collect data, classify them, and send them to users.

Bilateral links give rise to a dyad, trilateral links to a triad. Some nodes are central to the others and are of greater importance, acting as hubs (Fig. 15.3).

There are various possible combinations within the triads, considering the monodirectional flows (from one node to the other two), bidirectional or multi-directional (in which all three nodes interact with each other), as illustrated in Fig. 15.4. The distinction is relevant and allows each node to be given a weight, in terms of economic importance.

15.3   Network Theory: An Introduction

Network theory and the related scalability issues are examined in Albert and Barabási, 2002; Bianconi and Barabási, 2001; Caldarelli and Catanzaro, 2011; Cook, 2012; Degenne and Forsè, 2006; Erdös and Rényi, 1959; Gneiser et al., 2012; Heidemann et al., 2012; Hoffman and Yeh, 2018; Jackson, 2008; Karapanos et al., 2016; Martin et al., 2009; Moro Visconti et al., 2017; Newman, 2010; Odlyzko and Tilly, 2005; Oh et al.,

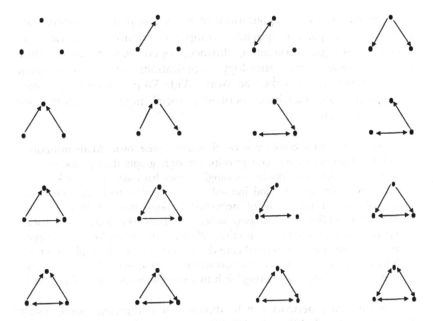

Fig. 15.4 Combinations and interactions between triads

2015; Van Steen, 2010. Network theory is the study of graphs as a representation of either symmetric or asymmetric relations between discrete objects. In computer science and network science, network theory is a part of graph theory: a network can be defined as a graph in which nodes and/or edges have attributes (e.g., names).

An interdependent network is a system of coupled networks where nodes of one or more networks depend on nodes from other networks. Such dependencies are enhanced by developments in modern technology. Dependencies may lead to cascading failures between the networks and a relatively small failure can lead to a catastrophic breakdown of the system. Blackouts are a demonstration of the critical role played by the dependencies between networks.

Networks represent a fundamental characteristic of complex systems whose connected structure may give an innovative interpretation of the interactions among (linked) stakeholders.

Network theory has applications in many disciplines including statistical physics, particle physics, computer science, electrical engineering, biology, economics, finance, operations research, climatology, ecology, and sociology. Applications of network theory include logistical networks, the World Wide Web, Internet, gene regulatory networks, metabolic networks, social networks, epistemological networks, etc.

> Today many fields consider network science their own. Mathematicians rightly claim ownership and priority through graph theory; the exploration of social networks by sociologists goes back decades; physics lent the universality concept and infused many analytical tools that are now unavoidable in the study of networks; biology invested hundreds of millions of dollars into mapping subcellular networks; computer science offered an algorithmic perspective, allowing us to explore very large networks; engineering invested considerable efforts into the exploration of infrastructural networks. It is remarkable how these many disparate pieces managed to fit together, giving birth to a new discipline. (Barabási, 2016)

The links of a network can be directed or undirected. Some systems have directed links, like the WWW, whose uniform resource locators (URL) point from one web document to the other, or phone calls, where one person calls the other. Other systems have undirected links, like transmission lines on the power grid, on which the electric current can flow in both directions. A network is called directed (or digraph) if all its links are asymmetric, and cause–effect relationships are only one-way; it is called undirected if all its links are symmetric (one-to-one). Some networks simultaneously have directed and undirected links. For example, in the metabolic network, some reactions are reversible (i.e., bidirectional or undirected) and others are irreversible, taking place in only one direction (directed) (Barabási, 2016).

Most relationships in corporate governance are bidirectional and so undirected.

A key property of each node is its degree, representing the number of links it has to other nodes. The degree is an important parameter even in corporate governance, as it identifies the connections among stakeholders and their intensity.

A complete description of a network requires keeping track of its links. The simplest way to achieve this is to provide a complete list of the links. For example, the network of Fig. 15.5 is uniquely described by listing its four links: {(1, 2), (1, 3), (2, 3), (2, 4)}. For mathematical purposes, a network is represented through its adjacency matrix (Horn & Johnson, 2012; Ketoviki and Mahoney, 2017). Any square matrix can be interpreted as a network.

The adjacency matrix of a directed network of N nodes has N rows and N columns, its elements being:

a. Adjacency matrix

$$A_{ij} = \begin{matrix} A_{11} & A_{12} & A_{13} & A_{14} \\ A_{21} & A_{22} & A_{23} & A_{24} \\ A_{31} & A_{32} & A_{33} & A_{34} \\ A_{41} & A_{42} & A_{43} & A_{44} \end{matrix}$$

b. Undirected network

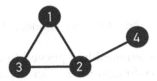

c. Directed network

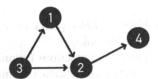

$$A_{ij} = \begin{matrix} 0 & 1 & 1 & 0 \\ 1 & 0 & 1 & 1 \\ 1 & 1 & 0 & 0 \\ 0 & 1 & 0 & 0 \end{matrix}$$

$$A_{ij} = \begin{matrix} 0 & 0 & 1 & 0 \\ 1 & 0 & 1 & 0 \\ 0 & 0 & 0 & 0 \\ 0 & 1 & 0 & 0 \end{matrix}$$

Fig. 15.5 (Un)directed networks

- $A_{ij} = 1$ if there is a link between node j and node I;
- $A_{ij} = 0$ if nodes i and j are not connected.

Figure 15.5 shows the pattern of undirected or directed networks, considering four nodes that are linked. In the example, node 2 is the pass-through node, acting as a hub. The adjacency matrix of the network is reported after the graphical representation.

Figure 15.5 shows:

a. The labeling of the elements of the adjacency matrix;
b. The adjacency matrix of an undirected network. Figure 15.5 shows that the degree of a node (in this case node 2) can be expressed as the sum over the appropriate column or the row of the adjacency matrix. It shows a few basic network characteristics, like the total number of links, L, and average degree, ‹k›, expressed in terms of the elements of the adjacency matrix;
c. The same as in (b) but for a directed network.

Edges among nodes (i.e., stakeholders) represent (Estrada & Knight, 2015):

- Physical links (pairs of nodes can be physically connected by a tangible link);
- Physical interactions (connection determined by a physical force);
- Ethereal (intangible) connections (information or other immaterial links);
- Geographic closeness between nodes;
- Social connections (friendship, collaboration, family ties, etc.);
- Functional linking (actions that activate other activities).

Nodes may not be directly linked by an edge but still have some bridging relationships, through a walk (trail) among distinct edges. A path is a sequence of edges that connect nodes. Network connectivity (Estrada & Knight, 2015, Chapter 2) links two nodes. If the connection is not circular, we have a tree or a forest (union of trees). The ramification of connections is consistent with a representation of many firm interactions.

Matrix algebra (Bapat, 2011) is useful in the design of the connecting patterns that can be quantified.

Physical distance plays a key role in determining the interactions between the components of physical systems. In networks, distance is a challenging concept. What is the distance between two web pages, or between two individuals who do not know each other? The physical distance is not relevant here: two web pages could be sitting on computers on opposite sides of the globe, yet, have a link to each other. At the same time, two individuals that live in the same building may not know each other.

In networks, physical distance is replaced by path length. A path is a route that runs along with the links of the network. A path's length represents the number of links the path contains.

In network science, paths play a central role. In corporate governance, they represent the interactions between stakeholders. Whereas traditional relationships among stakeholders typically occur through physical interaction, whenever these relationships can be expressed in terms of networking, they follow the path length rule.

The shortest path between nodes i and j is the path with the fewest number of links. The shortest path is called the distance between nodes i and j, and is denoted by d_{ij}, or simply d. We can have multiple shortest paths of the same length d between a pair of nodes. The shortest path never contains loops or intersects itself.

In an undirected network $d_{ij} = d_{ji}$, i.e. the distance between node i and j is the same as the distance between node i and j. In a directed network often $d_{ij} \neq d_{ji}$.

Even the shortest path can be important, considering (digital or traditional) supply and value chains where each passage (or node) is presided by interacting stakeholders, who share marginal economic returns (and bear corresponding costs), so co-creating value.

In an undirected network, nodes i and j are connected if there is a path between them. They are disconnected if such a path does not exist. A network is connected if all pairs of nodes in the network are connected. Connections are relevant for corporate governance as they make interactions among stakeholders possible. Disconnections may happen in case of failures or other value-destroying occurrences.

The clustering coefficient captures the degree to which the neighbors of a given node link to each other. Clusters are relevant for interfirm coordination when companies cooperate within an industrial district, joint ventures, or other forms of cooperative competition—coopetition

(Bengtsson & Kock, 2000). The degree of a node contains no information about the relationship between a node's neighbors. Do they all know each other, or are they perhaps isolated from each other? The answer is provided by the local clustering coefficient that measures the density of links in the node's immediate neighborhood.

Links between the nodes are often placed randomly. A random network consists of N nodes where each node pair relates to probability p. The evolution of random networks illustrates their dynamic process. In corporate governance, most networks are intentionally built among selected stakeholders and so they are not casual, even if some random components typically coexist. Real networks are not random and there is typically an order behind most complex systems. The random network model is neutral. As it lacks hubs, it does not develop structural correlations either.

Networks can alternatively be scale-free; whereas a random network follows a Poisson distribution, like a bell curve, and most nodes have the same number of links and are not highly connected, in a network with a power-law degree distribution most nodes have only a few links. These numerous small nodes are held together by a few highly connected hubs. Once hubs are present, they change the way we navigate the network. The difference is reported in the comparison in Figs. 15.6 and 15.7.

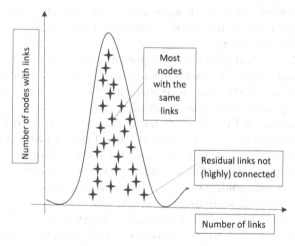

Fig. 15.6 Poisson network (Erdos–Renyi random graph) scale-free (power-law) networks

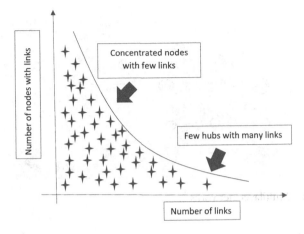

Fig. 15.7 Scale-free (power-law) network

The study of degree distribution is particularly suited to the analysis of complex networks (Estrada & Knight, 2015).

Scale-free networks are consistent with corporate governance patterns and with the presence of hubs represented by pivoting stakeholders (large creditors; managers; key shareholders, etc.). Once the hubs are present, they fundamentally change the system's behavior.

Networks can be interpreted in both static and dynamic terms that represent their evolution and may be used for predictive purposes. Evolving networks can predict the growth rate of a node which may depend on its age.

Multilayer networks are networks with multiple kinds of relations with multiplex or multidimensional configurations (Bianconi, 2018; Lee et al., 2015; Tomasini, 2015). In a multiplex network, the same set of nodes is connected via more than one type of link, so enhancing scalability.

In most real-world systems an individual network is one component within a much larger complex multi-level network (is part of a network of networks). Most real-world network systems continuously interact with other networks (Kennet et al., 2015).

There is a wide range of systems in the real world where components cannot function independently so these components interact with others through different channels of connectivity and dependencies. Complex Networks theory is, in fact, the formal tool for describing and analyzing

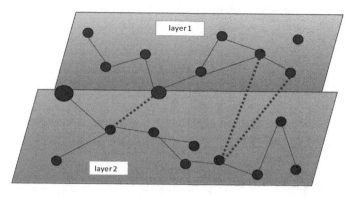

Fig. 15.8 Multilayer networks

fields as disparate as sociology (social networks, acquaintances or collaborations between individuals), biology (metabolic and protein networks,
neural networks) or technology (phone call networks, computers in
telecommunication networks) (Boccaletti et al., 2015).

Many real-world networks do interact with and depend on other
networks via dependency connectivities, forming "networks of networks".
The interdependence between networks has been found to largely
increase the vulnerability of interacting systems, when a node in one
network fails, it usually causes dependent nodes in other networks to fail,
which, in turn, may cause further damage to the first network and result
in a cascade of failures with sometimes catastrophic consequences (Liu
et al., 2014).

Figure 15.8 shows an example of a multilayer network where two
layers are superimposed and shows two common nodes and three joining
edges. Connections increase the overall value of this network of networks
(even following Metcalfe's law) and so its digital scalability. Conversely,
connecting nodes and edges augment the contagion risk and percolation
of negative externalities.

15.4   Social Networks and Social Media

Social networks are networks in which the summits (pivoting nodes) are
represented by individuals or groups of people, and the sides constitute the bonds and forms of social interaction (by way of friendship,
professional relationship, exchange of goods and services or money, mode

of communication or otherwise) between individuals. Populous social networks have scalable properties.

A social network consists of any group of individuals connected by different social ties analyzed by sociometric (social network analysis). A social network service, commonly called a social network, is an Internet service, typically usable through browsers or mobile applications, for the management of social relationships and that allows communication and sharing for textual and multimedia media.

The services of this type, born at the end of the '90s and popular since then, allow users to create their profile, organize a list of contacts, publish their stream of updates, and access that of others.

Social networks are based on some basic propositions, among which they detect homophilia (people with similar characteristics tend to be connected) and the mutual influence of connected people, either individually or within organizations. Connection modalities are both a cause and a consequence of human behavior, characterized by contractual obligations and interactive feedback. Other characteristics of the networks are the ubiquity and speed with which relations are established, potentially anywhere, between anyone, and at any time; therefore, the space–time barriers that commonly accompany human relations not mediated by Internet platforms can be eliminated.

The services can be distinguished according to the type of relationships to which they are oriented, for example, those friendly, working, or public, or according to the format of communications that provide, such as short texts, images, or music. Their use is often offered free of charge, as suppliers are remunerated by online advertising advertisers.

To become part of an online social network, adherents need to build their profile, starting from information such as email addresses up to their interests and passions, past work experiences, and references (information necessary for the profile "work"). At this point friends can be invited to join your network, which in turn can do the same, so that they expand the circle of contacts with friends of friends and so on, to include the entire population of the world. It is, therefore, possible to create thematic communities according to one's passions or business areas, aggregating other users and establishing contacts of friendship or business.

The concept of social networks intersects and overlaps with that of social media, defined by Kaplan and Haenlein (2010) as "a group of web-based applications built on the paradigms (technological and ideo-logical) of web 2.0 allowing the exchange and creation of user-generated content".

According to Kaplan and Haenlein, there are six types of social media:

1. Blogs and microblogs (e.g., Twitter);
2. Social networking sites (e.g., Facebook);
3. Virtual worlds of play (e.g., World of Warcraft);
4. Virtual social worlds (e.g., SecondLife);
5. Collaborative projects (e.g., Wikipedia);
6. Content communities (communities sharing multimedia material, e.g., YouTube).

In addition to these types, chats (e.g., WhatsApp) and messaging services (e.g., Facebook Messenger) are widespread and are now considered social networks too.

The research on social networks is largely dedicated to examining how different links interact with each other.

Social networks represent a key feature of the Internet ecosystem, and they interact with the main digital models and products, representing the spokesman of the customers' feelings and feedback. Social virality magne-tizes and clusters the mood of the internauts/customers, addressing their volatile choices. Client profiling and customized advertising represent a basic revenue source for most social networks. The scalability proper-ties described in Chapter 33 are fully applicable to this interconnected ecosystem.

Social networks represent a public platform whose freedom is limited by censorship (due to authoritarian regimes, or decency purposes). Content moderation and tech-regulation of speech online (e.g., under the Twitter model) is a controversial issue, with implications on busi-ness modeling, revenue streams, and subsequent valuation. Moderation on many media platforms is increasingly heavy-handed and capricious, showing that nobody monopolizes wisdom.

Algorithms (open source or private) incorporate these restrictions, representing the invisible engine behind the social media workings.

As anticipated, the primary way social media companies make money is through selling advertising. The concept of selling advertising while

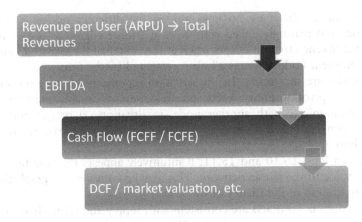

Fig. 15.9 Impact of ARPU on the valuation metrics

offering a free service is not new and has been readapted to social media business models. Television, newspapers, and traditional media companies have been doing this long before.

The average revenue per user (ARPU) is one of the most important metrics for large social media companies, as shown in paragraph 15.12. The ARPU (together with other metrics) impacts the main valuation parameters, as shown in Fig. 15.9.

15.5 THE FIRM AS A COASIAN NEXUS (NETWORK) OF CONTRACTS

A networked interpretation of the theory of the firm may represent an important starting point for any evaluation approach.

The firm can be considered as a nexus of contracts both internally, so justifying in a Coasian way its very existence, and externally, should agreements with third parties be considered, within a broader framework. These contracts may well include intangible assets.

This interpretation is fully consistent with the network theory since nexuses are the links among different nodes (here represented by composite stakeholders, in a multilayer framework).

Consider an initial situation where there is no firm. Each node represented by a circle can have different links with the others. Figure 15.10 shows an increasingly linked framework where the network (a) is initially empty (since there are no links among the different nodes) and then becomes increasingly linked with more and more edges (b → c → d).

A different situation occurs when at the center of the crossroad among the different nodes there is a hub represented by the firm.

Nodes are increasing. In the situation represented by (e) the hub is the only pivoting entity: each stakeholder must pass through the hub to communicate with another node; in situation (f) or (g) nodes are (increasingly) linked among them, without necessarily passing through the hub.

From Figs. 15.10 and 15.11, it intuitively appears that the hub/firm adds value to the whole network. This may be considered a graph-theory interpretation of the theory of the firm.

Nexuses of contracts are consistent with supply and value chains where stakeholders interact to co-create shared value.

External nexuses of contracts typically involve synergic stakeholders, linked to the firm with pass-through contracts or other cooperation agreements. While stakeholders always include shareholders, they typically go beyond, being represented by debtholders, clients, suppliers, workers, and

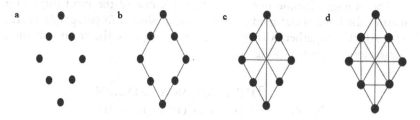

Fig. 15.10   Network (without a firm)

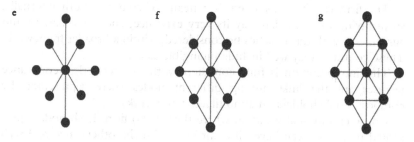

Fig. 15.11   Network with a hub firm

public authorities, up to the civil society surrounding the company and interested in its well-being.

Vertical integration represents a well-known form of networked cooperation, within the make it or buy strategic decision, that stands out as one of the basic elements of the theory of the firm, as illustrated by Williamson (1979), Holmstrom and Tirole (1989), and Hart (1995, part I). In microeconomics, vertical integration describes a management control system where companies within a vertical supply chain are controlled by a common owner. The specialization of each firm within the vertical value chain allows a synergic combination of products and services, cementing upstream buyers with downstream suppliers.

The value chain is consistent with the networking stakeholders that rotate around it.

The Coasian rationale behind the ontological existence of the firm, considered as a nexus of contracts, may tentatively be extended to a wider framework, where the firm is analyzed within its broader legal web; the internal nexus of contracts may so be expanded to consider external legal agreements. The firm is the glue that brings together many heterogeneous stakeholders.

The Coasian theory of the firm is linked to transaction economics. Ketokivi and Mahoney (2017) make some key questions about the issue: "Which components should a manufacturing firm make in-house, which should it co-produce, and which should it outsource? Who should sit on the firm's board of directors? What is the right balance between debt and equity financing? These questions may appear different on the surface, but they are all variations on the same theme: how should a complex contractual relationship be governed to avoid waste and create transaction value? Transaction Cost Economics is one of the most established theories to address this fundamental question".

The concept of node centrality (Estrada & Knight, 2015, Chapter 14) is used in the determination of the most critical nodes in a network, acting as hubs. Their characteristics include the ability to communicate directly with other nodes, their closeness to other nodes, and their indispensability to act as a communicator between different parts of a network. Usefulness—up to indispensability—of central nodes is fully consistent with the Coasian nature of the firm as a nexus (network) of contracts and ties among composite stakeholders.

Degree centrality measures the ability of a node to communicate directly with others, this being a founding characteristic of the firm. Firms have a closeness centrality, having the shortest path distance with other nodes represented by surrounding stakeholders. Furthermore, firms are characterized by their betweenness centrality, being a key communication node between other pairs of nodes. Closeness to other nodes is critical even in terms of higher influence.

Communities in networks (Estrada & Knight, 2015, Chapter 21) represent an explanation of the organization of nodes in complex networks. Communities are groups of nodes more densely connected among themselves than with the rest of the nodes of the network. Communities may be represented by social networks and could be magnetized by hub nodes represented by the firm that clusters stakeholders with its gravitational centrality.

The firm is seen as a contract among a multitude of parties (Holmstrom & Tirole, 1989) and this vision is consistent with an interaction of networked stakeholders.

15.6   Social Networks Diffusion

In recent years there has been a continuous growth in the spread of the Internet, social networks, and the use of smartphones, both nationally and globally.

The most used social networks are (https://buffer.com/library/social-media-sites/):

1. Facebook – 2.9 billion MAUs
2. YouTube – 2.2 billion MAUs
3. WhatsApp – 2 billion MAUs
4. Instagram – 2 billion MAUs
5. WeChat – 1.26 billion MAUs
6. TikTok – 1 billion MAUs
7. Sina Weibo – 573 million MAUs
8. QQ – 538.91 million MAUs
9. Telegram – 550 million MAUs

Average MAU is the sum of each month's active users/12 (Number of months in a year). Average DAU is the sum of each day's active users. These two parameters impact the revenue generated from ads.

15.7 MISINFORMATION IN THE AGE OF THE INTERNET: FAKE NEWS AND THE RIGHT TO BE FORGOTTEN

Social networks can be powerful value drivers, but they may, in an increasing number of circumstances, contribute to value destruction levered by the virality of the web. Examples may be given by cyber-crimes that fuel fake news or violate the privacy of web surfers, who may claim the right to be forgotten.

Fake news, also known as junk news or pseudo-news, is a type of yellow journalism or propaganda that consists of deliberate disinformation or hoaxes spread via traditional news media (print and broadcast) or online social media (Tufekci, 2018). The false information is often caused by reporters paying sources for stories, an unethical practice called checkbook journalism. Digital news has brought back and increased the usage of fake news, and the news then reverberates as misinformation on social media but occasionally finds its way to the mainstream media as well (Himma-Kadakas, 2017).

The right to be forgotten reflects the claim of an individual to have certain data deleted so that third persons can no longer trace them. The right to be forgotten leads to allowing individuals to have information, videos, or photographs about themselves deleted from certain Internet records so that they cannot be found by search engines (Weber, 2011).

The right to be forgotten addresses an urgent problem in the digital age: it is hard to escape your past on the Internet now that every photo, status update, and tweet lives forever in the cloud (Rosen, 2012).

The right is nothing more than a way to give (back) individuals control over their data and make the consent regime more effective (Ausloos, 2012). The problem is exacerbated by artificial intelligence: whereas humans forget, machines remember (Villaronga et al., 2018).

15.8 SHARING ECONOMY AND VALUE CO-CREATION

The sharing economy is based on common access to resources, going beyond the traditional concept of ownership. Resources are typically shared through computer platforms that act as a meeting point for communities, including virtual ones that meet and exchange information mainly through social networks.

The types of sharing economy are related to the car-sharing or sharing of other means of transport, houses, food, social shopping, up to co-working or crowdfunding.

The co-creation of value represents a new paradigm according to which the corporate value is shared with the customer with whom forms of continuous interaction and exchange of information are established, including social networks and B2C e-commerce platforms. Think for example of sites (such as TripAdvisor) that require experiential feedback from users. In this case, there is a value chain between the supplier and the user of a service.

The existence of a reciprocal relationship is evident in contracts in which there are corresponding obligations, consistent with value co-creation patterns.

Business models based on intangible resources, such as those at the base of social networks, tend to have marked scalability characteristics, due to economies of scale and experience (the latter fed by computerized self-learning processes, typical of machine learning or artificial intelligence). Increases in sales revenues are largely translated into higher operating margins (such as EBITDA or operating income), which are the basis of traditional methods of evaluating companies (bringing to DCF or market comparables).

15.9   PERSONALIZED MARKETING, SOCIAL NETWORKS, AND DIGITAL BRANDING

Social networks and other participatory platforms have become fundamental tools for all types of companies, regardless of sector and organizational size.

Social networks allow website owners to make a profit mainly by providing third parties with user information, which feeds the knowledge base free of charge, and by targeted advertising where companies address users based on the sites they visit, links opened, media stay, the information they enter themselves.

Personalized marketing represents an innovation in the experiences of uniform and undifferentiated mass market, based on an increasingly targeted segmentation of consumer preferences, including through the use of their data, to create new business opportunities arising from the intersection of offers of goods and services more and more personalized with an increasingly sophisticated demand.

Based on the chronology and geolocation of the user's activities, preferences, and interactions with the various brands, firms can propose personalized promotional messages, tailored to each consumer that is unaware of the tracking of her or his habits.

Business models follow new paradigms that have a profound impact on the value chain (for producers, service providers, intermediaries, and consumers), with significant consequences of a legal nature.

In this perspective, digital tools are becoming increasingly important not only as places of expression and sharing on the web but as effective vehicles of information, brand development, marketing, and business.

Communication service providers can build consumer loyalty by focusing primarily on their overall experience.

Consumer experience is, in fact, a primary factor, given that network functionality, coverage, speed, and cost have a significant impact on users' perceptions of the quality of the service.

15.10   Social Network Valuation

Social networks are, in the broadest sense, part of the wider sector of Internet companies, from which they borrow general characteristics and valuation models.

Some believe that while the traditional methods of evaluating companies and intangibles do not apply to all social networks, on the other hand, there is no universally recognized criterion for their appraisal.

Traditional methods can be applied to social networks if there are adaptations that capture their salient features. The valuation methods of the most famous social networks listed (such as Facebook) do not seem different from the traditional ones.

Social networks considered firms can therefore be evaluated with traditional or specific methods. A synthesis between the two approaches can be conveniently sought by analyzing how specific parameters, for example, the average advertising revenue per user (examined below), can influence traditional parameters such as profit margins (EBITDA or EBIT, etc.) or finance (operating or net cash flows).

Social networks are associated with mobile apps that contain several features. Internet traffic can be routed in both directions, from social media to apps and vice versa. Valuation issues depend on the degree of complementarity between social and apps, contractual relationships, value co-creation modalities, and other parameters, to be evaluated on a case by case basis.

A fundamental parameter for the valuation remains anchored in the analysis of the projection of revenues over time, associated with the overall profitability of the company.

The valuation of a network grows according to Metcalfe's law (see Chapter 3).

15.11   VALUATION WITH TRADITIONAL METHODOLOGIES

The valuation of social networks should so be addressed using traditional methods (especially discounted cash flows), but taking care to adapt these models to Internet companies, which are characterized by innovative business models, higher value of intangibles and significant growth rates, able to compress the life cycle of the company, especially in its early stages.

Under the financial method, the value of a business is equal to the sum of its discounted future cash flows (DCF). The cash flows can be the operating or the net cash flow for the shareholders; this depends on whether the objective is to evaluate the Enterprise Value (value of the entire company, including debt) or, residually, the Equity Value (value of shareholders' equity). Cash flows from operations are discounted to present value at the weighted average cost of capital (WACC). This flow configuration offers a valuation of the whole company, independent of its financial structure. The value of the company (enterprise value) must be subtracted from the value of the debt to rejoin the value obtained through the net cash flows for the shareholders (equity value). Net cash flows are discounted to present value at the cost of equity (Ke).

Another traditionally used method is represented by the relationship between Enterprise Value and EBITDA, which expresses an estimated multiplier.

The Enterprise Value indicates, as shown above, the market value of the entire company, given by the sum of the shareholders' equity and the net financial position. EBITDA is a margin that expresses at the same time an economic flow but a financial flow, highlighting the liquidity that is created (sometimes absorbed) by the current economic management. The differential income expressed by Gross Operating Profit can therefore be understood as the incremental operating cash flow (gross of the impact of financial and extraordinary operations and taxes) deriving from the exploitation of the intangible.

15.12 SPECIFIC VALUATION METHODOLOGIES

Traditional valuation methods can be usefully supported by specific methodologies that interpret and describe the metrics and parameters typical of social networks. The complementarity between traditional and specific methods can be found and used by estimating traditional parameters (such as EBITDA or operating cash flows) through specific metrics, such as average advertising revenues per customer.

Facilitation of the use of specific valuation metrics lies in the fact that it is possible to extrapolate from the Internet real-time traffic data and other information.

The difficulty in properly evaluating social networks is because their value depends on hard-to-value intangibles and on the number and loyalty of users who use this service. Social media rating metrics (web blogs; consumer ratings) have a significant impact on the rating of companies, higher than other more conventional metrics (Google searches, web traffic).

Many popular social networks are listed, so expressing a benchmark for market value. From the time of acquisition of the social networks, it is possible to deduce the valorizations attributed by the parties.

The most common approaches for the valuation of social networks refer to the number of users or, considering their business model, advertising clicks.

Average Revenue per User (ARPU) is an acronym used in TLCs to attribute average revenue (advertising) to each user through voice or data traffic. Some social networks (such as Facebook) report ARPU for a given year (broken down by geographical area) in their financial statements. The ARPU is normally calculated every month. A complementary indicator is the Daily Active Users.

The Social Return on Investment (SROI) is useful and is based on the social impact of the investment, arriving at an unconventional estimate of the value for stakeholders.

Some authors have proposed more sophisticated models for estimating the value of users (Customer Lifetime Value—CLV), which consider the future flows generated by each user and the retention rate (loyalty).

The CLV can be defined as the current value of all cash flows generated by each user, dividing all consumers, present, and future, into different groups, so that each of these represents the time when the user has made or will make entry into the social network.

The valuation metrics should be adapted to target companies. The most well-known indicators are the following:

- Number of fans/fan pages;
- Engagement (involvement/sharing, comments, likes, etc.);
- Impression (display of a web page or banner by an Internet user);
- Number of followers, re-tweets, and mentions (for business models like Twitter);
- Retention rate of existing customers;
- Conversion rate, measured as the number of visitors to a social site that becomes a buyer or subscriber of a good or service (purchase of e-commerce products; registration as a subscriber of service, etc.).

Since Facebook's acquisition of WhatsApp in February 2014, at a record $19 billion, WhatsApp's value per user is approximately $42. In 2012, Facebook acquired Instagram for a value of about $30 per user.

On the web, it is easy to find updated valuations of the main social networks, usually based on market capitalization or transactions that took place recently.

An alternative method is that of so-called impressions, which refers to the measurement of online advertising exposure. In particular, the value of a social network can be inferred based on the cost per thousand impressions (CPM), multiplied by the number of users and advertisements (banners). The problem with this methodology lies in the difficulty of estimating a cost per objective impression.

On the web, it is possible to find various sites specialized in quick but dirty valuations, based on a few parameters; the reliability of these estimates is relevant only for guidance.

The specific methodologies can usefully consider the relationships and interactions between social and mobile apps, in terms of traffic on the Internet. Internet traffic can be assessed based on sophisticated algorithms and is mainly divided into two categories:

1. Direct traffic, by people who go to the site by typing directly the address in the browser;
2. Organic traffic from a search engine.

15.13 Valuation With Real Options

The valuation of social networks involves high profiles of uncertainty that are reflected in the difficulty of estimating cash flows. The cash flows of investment are usually estimated ex-ante, without introducing rigid mechanisms for calculating the Net Present Value evolutionary assumptions that can adjust the estimates across time.

The real options allow for the inclusion of elements of flexibility in the estimation model, incorporating the reactions of the market, so difficult to predict. In this way, there are options for deferral, temporary suspension, abandonment, contraction, or—in a more optimistic sense—expansion or development, which make patented inventions elastic, increasing their potential value.

The ability to predict future events connected with the economic and financial return can be usefully codified in earn-out contractual clauses which, in purchases and sales, guarantee the seller an additional price, if certain situations occur, which are particularly uncertain at the time of the stipulation of the contract.

The real options have long been used both in the valuation of patents and in the estimation of Internet companies and social networks.

Using the real options, investment projects should be the source of a series of opportunities that management can seize when certain scenario conditions occur.

Opportunities for expansion, contraction, abandonment, or postponement of the launch of an investment project give the decision-maker flexibility, the value of which must be carefully considered for the overall assessment of the project.

The discounted cash flow method leads to an undervaluation of the value of the investment as a result of the failure to consider its strategic value.

The NPV does not consider the fact that the manager deals with real activities, and is, therefore able to respond to changes in the market. Strategic choices enable to benefit from the positive evolution of the scenario and to intervene to limit the negative consequences of an unfavorable evolution of the variables that affect the value of the project. The investment projects therefore incorporate real options, which can be exercised by management at the most appropriate time.

NOTE

1. The price-to-earnings ratio (P/E ratio) is the ratio for valuing a company that measures its current share price relative to its per-share earnings.

SELECTED REFERENCES

Albert, R., & Barabási, A. (2002). Statistical mechanics of complex networks. *Reviews of Modern Physics, 74*(1), 47–97.

Athanassakos, G. (2007). Valuing Internet ventures. *Journal of Business Valuation and Economic Loss Analysis, 2*(1). https://www.degruyter.com/view/j/jbvela. 2007.2.1/jbvela.2007.2.1.1005/jbvela.2007.2.1.1005.xml

Ausloos, J. (2012). The right to be forgotten—Worth remembering? *Computer Law & Security Review, 28*(2), 143–152.

Bapat, R. B. (2011). *Graphs and matrices*. Berlin: Springer.

Barabási, A. (2016). *Network science*. Cambridge: Cambridge University Press. Available at http://networksciencebook.com/

Bengtsson, M. A., & Kock, S. (2000, September). "Coopetition" in business networks—To cooperate and compete simultaneously. *Industrial Marketing Management, 29*(5), 411–426.

Bianconi, G. (2018). *Multilayer networks*. Oxford: Oxford University Press.

Bianconi, G., & Barabási, A. (2001). Competition and multiscaling in evolving networks. *Europhysics Letters, 54*, 436–442.

Boccaletti, S., Herrero, R. C., Benito, R. M., & Romance, M. (2015, January). Editorial on "Multiplex networks: Structure, dynamics and applications". *Chaos Solitons & Fractals, 72*, 1–106.

Caldarelli, G., & Catanzaro, M. (2011). *Networks: A very short introduction*. Oxford: Oxford University Press.

Cook, V. J. (2012). *What's Facebook really worth?* (Working Paper). Freeman School of Business, Tulane University.

Degenne, A., & Forsè, M. (2006). *Introducing social networks*. London: Sage.

Erdös, P. A., & Rényi. (1959). On random graphs I. *Publicationes Mathematicae, 6*, 290–297.

Estrada, E., & Knight, P. A. (2015). *A first course in network theory*. Oxford: Oxford University Press.

Gneiser, M., Heidemann, J., Klier, M., Landherr, A., & Probst, F. (2012). Valuation of online social networks taking into account users' interconnectedness. *Information Systems and e-Business Management, 10*, 61–84.

Hart, O. (1995). Corporate governance: Some theory and implications. *The Economic Journal, 105*, 678–698.

Heidemann, J., Klier, M., & Probst, F. (2012). Online social networks: A survey of a global phenomenon. *Computer Networks, 56*, 3866–3878.

Himma-Kadakas, M. (2017). Alternative facts and fake news entering journalistic content production cycle. *Cosmopolitan Civil Societies: An Interdisciplinary Journal, 9*(2), 25–41.

Hoffman, R., & Yeh, C. (2018). *Blitzscaling*. New York, NY: Currency.

Holmstrom, B. R., & Tirole, J. (1989). The theory of the firm. In R. Schmalensee & R. Willig (Eds.), *Handbook of industrial organization* (Vol. 1, 1st ed., Chapter 2, pp. 61–133). Amsterdam: Elsevier.

Horn, R. A., & Johnson, C. R. (2012). *Matrix analysis*. Cambridge, UK: Cambridge University Press.

Jackson, M. O. (2008). *Social and economic networks*. Princeton: Princeton University Press.

Kaplan, A. M., & Haenlein, M. (2010). Users of the world, unite! The challenges and opportunities of social media. *Business Horizons, 53*, 59–68.

Karapanos, E., Teixeira, P., & Gouveia, R. (2016). Need fulfillment and experiences on social media: A case on Facebook and WhatsApp. *Computers in Human Behavior, 55*, 888–897.

Kennet, D. Y., Perc, M., & Boccaletti, S. (2015). Networks of networks—An introduction. *Chaos, Solitons & Fractals, 80*, 1–6.

Ketokivi, M., & Mahoney, J. T. (2017). Transaction cost economics as a theory of supply chain efficiency. *Productions & Operations Management, 29*(4, April 2020), 1011–1031.

Lee, K. M., Min, B., & Goh, K. I. (2015). Towards real-world complexity: An introduction to multiplex networks. *European Physical Journal B, 88*(2), 1–20.

Liu, Y., Kliman-Silver, C., Bell, R., Krishnamurty, B., & Mislove, A. (2014, October 1–2). *Measurement and analysis of online social networks and auctions*. Paper presented at the 2nd ACM conference on Online Social Networks, Dublin, Ireland, pp. 139–150.

Moro Visconti, R., Larocca, A., & Marconi, M. (2017). Big data-driven value chains and digital platforms: From value co-creation to monetization. In A. K. Somani & G. Deka (Eds.), *Big data analytics: Tools, technology for effective planning*. Boca Raton: CRC Press.

Newman, M. E. J. (2010). *Networks. An introduction*. Oxford: Oxford University Press.

Odlyzko, A., & Tilly, B. (2005). *A refutation of Metcalfe's law and a better estimate for the value of networks and network interconnections*. Minneapolis: Digital Technology Center, University of Minnesota.

Oh, J., Koh, B., & Raghunathan, S. (2015). Value appropriation between the platform provider and app developers in mobile mediated networks. *Journal of Information Technology, 3*(3), 245–259.

Rosen, J. (2012, February 13). The right to be forgotten. *Stanford Law Review Online, 64*, 88.

Tomasini, M. (2015). *An introduction to multilayer networks biocomplex laboratory*. Florida Institute of Technology. https://www.researchgate.net/pro file/Marcello_Tomasini/publication/321546271_An_Introduction_to_Multil ayer_Networks/links/5a26fe48aca2727dd8839dee/An-Introductionto-Mul tilayer-Networks.pdf

Tufekci, Z. (2018, January 16). It's the (democracy-poisoning) golden age of free speech. *Wired*.

Van Steen, M. (2010). *Graph theory and complex networks. An introduction*. Maarten Van Steen.

Villaronga, E. F., Kieseberg, P., & Li, T. (2018). Humans forget, machines remember: Artificial intelligence and the right to be forgotten. *Computer Law & Security Review, 34*, 304–313.

Von Martin, G., Heidemann, J., Klier, M., & Weiá, C. (2009). *Valuation of online social networks—An economic model and its application using the case of Xing.Com*. Available at https://epub.uniregensburg.de/25618/1/Valuat ion_of_Online_Social_Networks.pdf

Weber, R. H. (2011). The right to be forgotten. More than a Pandoraìs Box. *Journal of Intellectual property, Information technology and E-commerce Law*, 120 par 1.

Williamson, O. (1979, October). Transaction-cost economics: The governance of contractual relations. *Journal of Law and Economics, 22*(2), 233–261.

CHAPTER 16

Blockchain Valuation: Internet of Value and Smart Transactions

16.1 Blockchains: Definition and Main Features

A blockchain[1] is a consequential list (chain) of blocks (records) that are linked using cryptography. Each block contains a cryptographic hash of the previous block, a timestamp, and transaction data (generally represented as a Merkle tree root hash[2]).

Blockchain could be regarded as a public ledger technology in which all committed transactions are stored in a chain of blocks. This chain continuously grows when new blocks are added to it. Blockchain technology has characteristics such as decentralization, persistence, anonymity, verifiability, and auditability. It can be then used to ensure authenticity, reliability, and integrity of data and business activities. Blockchain can work in a decentralized environment thanks to the integration of technologies such as cryptographic hash, digital signature (based on asymmetric cryptography), and distributed consensus mechanisms. With blockchain technology, a transaction can take place in a decentralized manner. As a result, blockchain can reduce notable costs, producing efficiency gains[3] (Fig. 16.1).

Blockchain formation is represented in Fig. 16.2. The main chain (black) consists of the most extended series of blocks from the first block (green) to the current block. Orphan blocks (blue) exist outside of the main chain.

R. Moro-Visconti, *The Valuation of Digital Intangibles*,
https://doi.org/10.1007/978-3-031-09237-4_16

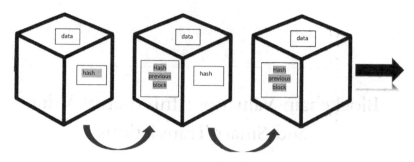

Fig. 16.1   Blockchain as a sequential chain of data

Fig. 16.2   Blockchain
formation

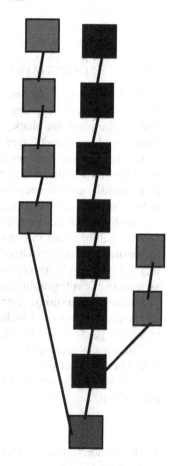

A blockchain belongs to the distributed ledger (database) technologies and represents a process where many subjects share IT data to make a virtual database available to a community of users. In most cases, this database is public, and the community is open, although there are examples of private implementations where each participant has a copy of the data.

A blockchain is mainly an open and distributed ledger that can memorize encrypted digital transactions (peer-to-peer) between two counterparts in a secure way that is verifiable and permanent. Electronic money transfers made from one person to another through an intermediary are typically referred to as P2P payment applications. P2P payments can be directly sent and received via mobile device or any computer with access to the Internet, offering an alternative to traditional payment methods involving banks or other financial institutions. The cryptocurrency payment system is also used to fuel Non-Fungible Tokens and the metaverse.

Once recorded, the data within a block cannot be retroactively altered without modifying the subsequent blocks. Due to the nature of the protocol and the validation scheme, this would require the consensus of most of the network participants (Norman et al., 2018) and is practically unfeasible being the participants many, exponentially growing and hardly interrelated.

In summary, a blockchain has the following key characteristics[4]:

1. Decentralization. In conventional centralized transaction systems, each transaction needs to be validated through the central trusted agency (e.g., the central bank) with fixed cost and performance bottlenecks at the primary servers. A transaction in the blockchain network can instead be conducted between any two peers (P2P) without the authentication by the central agency. In this manner, blockchain significantly reduces server costs (including the development and the operation costs) and mitigates the performance bottlenecks at the central server.

2. Persistency. Since each of the transactions spreading across the network needs to be confirmed and recorded in blocks distributed in the whole network, it is nearly impossible to tamper. Furthermore, each broadcasted block would need to be validated by other nodes and transactions would be checked. In this way, any falsification could be detected easily.

3. Anonymity. Each user can interact with the blockchain network with a generated address. In addition to this, a user could create many addresses to avoid identity exposure. There is no longer a central party recording users' private information. This mechanism preserves the privacy of the transactions in the blockchain.

4. Auditability. Since each of the transactions on the blockchain is validated and recorded with a timestamp, users can easily verify and trace the previous records by accessing any node in the distributed network. In a bitcoin blockchain, each transaction could be traced to previous transactions iteratively. This improves the traceability and the transparency of the data stored in the blockchain.

5. Trust. Confidence is shifted away from human actors toward a cryptographic system, with incentives for participating actors.

16.2   DISRUPTING TRADITIONAL BUSINESS MODELS

Numerous industries are implementing blockchain as part of their business processes. Valuation patterns may thus be concerned not only with public or private blockchains (see Sect. 16.4) but also with their impact on traditional businesses.

The employment of blockchain technologies and the possibility to apply them in different situations enables many industrial applications through increased efficiency and security, enhanced traceability and transparency, and reduced costs (Al-Jaroodi & Mohamed, 2019).

Blockchain technology has been initially used for controversial cryptocurrencies like bitcoins and FinTech applications and later in many other industries and supply chains (Blossey et al., 2019) such as:

- Energy (Fan et al., 2017; Sawa, 2019);
- IoT electric business model (Andoni et al., 2019; Veuger, 2018);
- Property transfer[5] (intangibles, real estate property, registered movable property ...);
- Industry/manufacturing;
- Logistics and transports (tracking of goods, etc.);
- Automotive (shipment of vehicles with frictionless information among connected systems; tracking of original spare parts; car-sharing; retention of the clients, etc.)[6];
- Food supply chain (Chen, 2022; Mao et al., 2018);

- E-commerce;
- Stock markets (asset pricing; appraisal of shareholders, etc.). With blockchain technology, it is possible to automate and secure the entire process of selling, buying, and trading stocks;
- Healthcare (for track record; clinical trials; personalized medicine; pharmaceutical supply chains; prescription drug management; health records management, etc.)[7];
- Contemporary art (Lotti, 2016);
- Insurance (InsurTech);
- FinTech (validation of payments; P2P lending and crowdfunding, etc.);
- RegTech;
- Microfinance (assisting with smart contracts several microfinancing bodies without the need for mediators or central authorities);
- E-governance (transparency and accessibility of government information; information sharing, etc.);
- Crowdsourcing (decentralized and secured petition systems);
- Smart cities (Xie et al., 2019).

The list above is far from being exhaustive and represents just an example of some applications of this versatile technology.

Since payments can be completed without any bank or intermediary, a blockchain can be used in various financial services such as digital assets, remittances, and online payments. Additionally, blockchain is becoming one of the most promising technologies for the next generation of Internet interaction systems such as smart contracts,[8] public services, the Internet of Things (IoT), reputation systems, and security services.[9]

Blockchains go well beyond the cryptocurrencies (like Bitcoins) that made them famous. Cryptocurrencies can fuel money laundering and other malpractices, given that their market is opaque, irrespective of any regulation, and subject to speculative bubbles. Cryptocurrencies should so be regulated by Central Banks or, where not possible, prohibited. This, however, does not prejudice other useful applications of blockchain technology.

These many applications contribute to the valuation patterns, describing possible business models: the broader, the higher the potential value of a blockchain that can enable and forge new products, and processes.

For example, in the manufacturing industry blockchains are used to manage and control (audit) supply chains. Blockchains will also be used for Industry 4.0 (industrial automation) and IoT.

The Internet of Things (IoT) has been connecting an extraordinarily large number of devices to the Internet. Current solutions are mostly based on cloud computing infrastructures, which necessitate high-end servers and high-speed networks to provide services related to storage and computation. However, a cloud-enabled IoT framework manifests several significant disadvantages, such as high cloud server maintenance costs, a weakness for supporting time-critical IoT applications, security and trust issues, etc., which impede its wide adoption. Therefore, it is essential for research communities to solve these problems associated with the cloud-enabled IoT frameworks and to develop new methods for IoT decentralization. Recently, blockchain is perceived as a promising technique to solve problems and design new decentralization frameworks for IoT.[10]

There are innovative blockchain solutions for 3D printing where the widespread development of printed components (concerning, for instance, the rapid delivery of spare parts), creates a new challenge when differentiating between originals, copies, and counterfeits.

The current technological evolution will concern an extension of blockchain applications to many other sectors.

16.3   Internet of Value

Innovation is a critical element in a company's differentiation strategy that contributes to achieving Porter's competitive advantage and leads to monopolistic rents.

With the Internet of Value, a value transaction can happen instantly, at the same speed at which we share words, images, and videos online. The potential of the Internet of Value extends well beyond money. The Internet of Value will enable to exchange any asset that is of value to someone, including stocks, votes, frequent flyer points, securities, intellectual property, music, scientific discoveries, and more.[11]

Until now, selling, buying, or exchanging these assets always required an intermediary like a bank, a physical or digital marketplace, a credit card company, or a third-party service. Blockchain technology allows assets to be transferred from one party to another without any intermediation.

The transfer is immediately validated, completed, and will be recorded permanently.

Blockchain contributes to a new generation of web patterns (Internet of Value) consisting of a digital network built on open standards.

Corporate use of blockchains contributes to product and process innovation with a positive impact on the supply chain (Dujak & Sajter, 2019; Korpela et al., 2017; Saberi et al., 2018) thanks to the exploitation of big data.

Blockchain can generate a value increase in digital platforms (B2B, B2C ...) through its secured transactions, facilitating e-commerce.

The sharing economy economic model is often defined as a peer-to-peer (P2P) based activity of the acquiring part, providing or sharing access to goods and services that are facilitated by a community-based online platform. Information is exchanged through (virtual) communities that exchange data mainly through digital platforms linked to social networks.

Monopolies dominate the current sharing economy, and markets like this are vulnerable to disruption. The emergence of blockchain cuts out middlemen so savvy startups can create headaches for the likes of Uber and Airbnb.[12]

As per the intangible capital, one area that seems particularly promising for blockchain is represented by value co-creation and open innovation.

There are meaningful correlations between blockchains and FinTech applications or artificial intelligence that influences the workings of blockchains and payment systems thanks to its machine learning patterns.

16.4   THE LEGAL NATURE OF PUBLIC OR PRIVATE BLOCKCHAINS AS A PREREQUISITE FOR VALUATION

The legal nature of the blockchain is essential for its valuation. There are three main kinds of blockchain:

1. Public;
2. Private;
3. Consortium.

There are so different types of blockchains: some are open and public while others are private and only accessible to specific users. This blockchained structure is consistent with De.Fi—Decentralized Finance, exploited using FinTechs and their applications.

A public blockchain is an open network. Anyone can download the protocol and read, write or participate in the network. A public blockchain is distributed and decentralized.

Transactions are recorded as blocks and linked together to form a chain. Each new block must be timestamped and validated by all the computers connected to the network, known as nodes before it is written into the blockchain.

All transactions are public, and all nodes have the same importance (and value). Therefore, a public blockchain cannot be modified: once verified, data cannot be altered. The best-known public blockchains used for cryptocurrency are Bitcoin and Ethereum: open-source, smart contract blockchains.

A private blockchain is a controlled ledger governed by a single entity that can be accessed only by specific users. A new user requires permission to read, write, or audit the blockchain. There can be different levels of access restrictions and information can be encrypted to protect commercial confidentiality. Private blockchains allow organizations to employ distributed ledger technology without making the data public. However, this implies the lack of a defining feature of blockchains: decentralization. Some critics claim that private blockchains are not blockchains at all, but only centralized databases using distributed ledger technology. Private blockchains appear to be faster, more efficient, and more cost-effective than public blockchains, which require a lot of time and energy to validate transactions.[13]

A blockchain does not represent a firm but a semi-public good (being public or private) that is shared among different stakeholders that co-create value by constructing and implementing a sequential pattern of codes. As a result, the evaluation of a blockchain is very different from that of a firm or a physical asset (Fig. 16.3).

Public blockchains are non-marketable, meaning that it is difficult to assess their potential value; they may have a symbolic value emerging from the public savings that they enable; the real value accrues to each user.

A firm may own a private blockchain, and valuation patterns may follow its innovative revenue model. Revenues deriving from new businesses are hard to assess since they lack historical performance records and do not follow traditional patterns. Profit streams can derive from subscriptions, pay-per-use income, performance-based fees (cashing in part of the

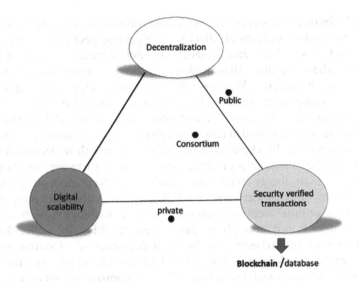

Fig. 16.3 Public, private, and consortium blockchain

savings of the blockchain users), or extraction of validated big data (sold outside for vertical advertising; e-commerce applications, etc.).

Public blockchains lack ultimate private ownership and may be harder to evaluate. They represent the only fully decentralized model.

Semi-public blockchains may somewhat resemble consortiums. A consortium is an association of two or more individuals, companies, organizations, or governments (or any combination of these entities) that participate in a shared activity or pool their resources to achieve a common goal. This may be consistent with blockchains, joint ventures, company networks, and value co-creation paradigms, representing an innovative business model. Different stakeholders may join in setting up coopetition, by merging cooperation and competition. Coopetition is used when companies that are, otherwise, competitors, collaborate in a consortium on areas non-strategic to their core businesses. They prefer to reduce their costs in these non-strategic areas and compete in other areas where they can differentiate better. The value of consortium membership is typically derived from the private rents that any participants can extract from it, being the consortium a non-profit alliance.

The business model of the blockchain influences its peculiar corporate governance issues (Yermack, 2017). Their peer-to-peer (P2P) interactions may link stakeholders and in general do not coincide with the ordinary stakeholders of a firm (shareholders; debtholders; employees; managers; suppliers, clients, etc.). Whereas value co-creation is typical of digital businesses, sharing of co-created value tends to work differently. For example, social networks are based on shared information (personal data) that platforms can monetize unilaterally, through the tacit and unaware consent of the participants. Blockchains work differently, and their decentralization prevents the abuses of a pivoting platform since there are no dominant players able to distort competition, exploiting information asymmetries.

"Consortium blockchains differ from their public counterparts in that they require access permissions: the bare availability of an Internet connection is not enough to gain access to this sort of blockchain. Consortium blockchains can be semi-decentralized. Control over a consortium blockchain is not granted to a single entity, but rather to a group of approved individuals. With a consortium blockchain, the consensus process is likely to differ from that of a public blockchain. (…) Thus, consortium blockchains have the security features that are inherent to public blockchains while allowing for a greater degree of control over the network."[14]

Each stakeholder has an interest in the decentralized blockchain and gets monetary or non-monetary remuneration from her or his participation. Stakeholders are like the participants of a consortium (so with no economic gain target) and may share the services and information that the blockchain offers or could be remunerated with crypto-assets[15] (digital virtual units mainly represented by tokens or cryptocurrencies).

What matters is the capital gain or value-added that each participant could achieve in terms of incremental income from using the blockchain. It is in practice difficult to evaluate a blockchain per se, since, as stated above, it is neither a firm nor an asset but a good that is sharable among its participants.

Federated blockchains operate under multiple authorities instead of a single trusted node. Authority nodes are pre-selected from the adherents to the network.

16.5   Economic and Financial Valuation

The appraisal of a blockchain (Alabi, 2017; Cong & He, 2018; Goorha, 2018; Lui, 2016) must start from its legal nature: public blockchains differ from private or consortium blockchains. Wondering who is the real ultimate owner of a blockchain is an useful question for valuation. The business model, with emphasis on the revenue model (where do profits come from?), is another prerequisite for valuation. Industry applications—exemplified in Sect. 16.2—may give valuable hints for an estimate.

The ideal scenario would be that of incorporating the prospects of the blockchain into a traditional accounting system (pro forma balance sheet interacting with forecast income statements to get expected cash flow statements). However, this is hardly possible, and so instead of considering the blockchain, the evaluation should autonomously be based on users' economic and financial savings (in terms of lower costs, higher availability, speed of data, etc.). The traditional cost-centric approach must be replaced by a value-focused perspective (Zhang & Wen, 2016).

The valuation of a blockchain can be analogically assimilated to that of a database or to the appraisal of big data that fuels the blockchain with information that becomes secured (so increasing its value). A blockchain is a peculiar database with no stable center of gravity since its equilibrium is pushed forward each time that a block is added.

The extension of a networked blockchain adds up value, in analogy with Metcalfe's law.[16]

Since the blockchain incorporates information, it is naturally linked to (big) data and related to the data sourcing IoT that can be extrapolated and used, as a by-product, for further value-adding strategies.

The collateral value of blockchains depends in most cases on their complementary applications rather than on their very existence.

Blockchains merge product and process innovation, creating a validation process that increases the value of data.

The object of the appraisal may concern either the blockchain as an asset (belonging to identified shareholders and incorporated in a firm) or the value that the blockchain brings to an external user.

16.5.1   Accounting of Intellectual Property as a Prerequisite for Valuation

Blockchains are difficult to define, and their intrinsic nature can hardly be described and treated following standard accounting or legal patterns. For this reason, the principles synthesized in the next sub-paragraphs cannot be easily extended to blockchains that are merely different from standard intangibles. The analogy with traditional intangibles (Pastor et al., 2017) and digital processes (databases, process innovation applied to supply chains, big data, digital networks, fintech applications, etc.) may anyway represent a useful starting point for the appraisal of blockchains.

It is well-known that intangibles have an undefined nature which makes them difficult to evaluate.

IAS 38 (Para. 12) defines an intangible asset as "an identifiable non-monetary asset without physical substance". Identifiability (being the asset separable or arising from contractual or other legal rights), control (power to obtain benefits from the asset), and expected future economic benefits are the three critical attributes of intangibles that are non-monetary assets without physical substance. Whatever is not identifiable is allocated in (residual) goodwill, an Arabian phoenix for accountants.

According to Michael Porter's fundamental insights, value creation derives from a lasting competitive advantage over rival entities, embedded in continuously innovating business models that must be properly designed and managed. Competitive edge is increasingly driven by the catalyst presence of intangibles, which represents a pivotal breakthrough, and it occurs when an organization (painfully) develops core competencies and skills that allow it to outperform its competitors, especially for what concerns customized differentiation.

Intangible value is hidden in the balance sheet by inadequate accounting, but not in the income or in the cash flow statement, where the incremental contribution to profit is detectable.

Intangibles often overlooked in the balance sheet are so a typical incremental driver of EBITDA which expresses the dominant income-driven cash flow source, representing an economic and financial margin traditionally used in valuations (within the DCF metrics or with market multipliers, as reported in Chapter 2). Being the invisible "glue" behind going concern and value creation, the EBITDA not only enhances strategic differential value but also leads to more sustainable results in the future, easing proper debt service (cash flow internally generated through a positive EBITDA is used to pay-back bank loans).

What may be reflected in the balance sheet is hardly a blockchain per se, unless its "owners" (whenever existing) find a way to record its asset value. In most cases, participants in blockchains can use their membership costs as an estimation of the marginal value of their affiliation. Faster and more reliable data are the natural output of blockchains that can be captured and exploited by adherents. This is what primarily needs to be recorded in their accounts. The CAPEX and OPEX dilemma, analyzed in Chapter 3, also relates to blockchains: few capitalized investments are recorded within the CAPEX in the fixed assets, whereas most of the blockchain expenses are included within the OPEX in the income statement. What really matters for valuation is, once again, TOTEX = CAPEX + OPEX.

DCF or EBITDA calculation is currently used for the market valuation of intangibles; although this is standard knowledge and practice, some further considerations based on intangible-driven cash generation may help to further develop the discussion of valuation patterns.

IAS 38 (§ 12) defines an intangible asset as "an identifiable non-monetary asset without physical substance". The definition requires an intangible asset to be identifiable to distinguish it from goodwill. An asset is identifiable if either:

(a) It is separable from the entity and can be sold, transferred, licensed, rented, or exchanged. This can occur individually or together with a related contract or identifiable asset or liability, regardless of whether the entity intends to do so or not;

(b) It arises from contractual or other legal rights, irrespective of whether those rights are transferable or separable from the entity or other rights and obligations.

From this taxonomy, it is evident that the identification of blockchains is difficult—if not impossible—since they are unlikely to be separated among their adherents. If the blockchain is private, then its property rights may be better identifiable, and it can be related to its owning firm or legal entity.

Intangible assets may be carried at a revalued amount (based on fair value) less any subsequent amortization and impairment losses only if fair value can be determined in an active market [§ 75]. Such active markets are expected to be uncommon for intangible assets [§ 78]. According to IFRS 13, Appendix A, an "active market" is "a market in which transactions for the asset or liability take place with sufficient frequency and volume to provide pricing information on an ongoing basis". And an active market for blockchains is an illusion.

Since blockchains tend not to have a fixed expiring date, their evaluation patterns may consider them as intangibles with an indefinite useful life. The contribution of a blockchain to value can be measured considering either incremental revenues (due to the blockchain's exploitation that fosters sales, opening new markets, etc.) or lower OPEX (any use of the blockchain can reduce operating costs, making the supply chain more resilient and efficient).

16.5.2   General Valuation Methodologies

The classification of the leading financial/market valuation approaches is consistent with international accounting principles; according to IFRS 13:62 and IVS 210, three widely used valuation techniques are:

- Market approach—uses prices and other relevant information generated by market transactions involving identical or comparable (similar) assets, liabilities, or a group of assets and liabilities (e.g., a business);
- Cost approach—reflects the amount that would be required to currently replace the service capacity of an asset (current replacement cost);
- Income approach—converts future amounts (cash flows or income and expenses) to a single current (discounted) price, reflecting prevailing market expectations about those future amounts.

These general approaches should consider the peculiar nature of blockchains. For example:

- The market approach seems still hard to use since there is no active market for private or consortium blockchains; even public blockchains are uneasy to compare due to their peculiarities (targets

and aims of public utility; effective adherents; geographical segmentation and territoriality, etc.);
- The cost approach may give some useful insights (how much would it cost to create a similar blockchain from scratch?) but again it seems difficult to link it to the appraisal;
- The income approach that considers future earnings/cash flows is theoretically suitable even if it is difficult to sort out the basic accounting data behind it. It should be mentioned that traditional appraisal parameters for intangibles, like royalties, are hardly compatible with blockchains where using fees may be applicable;
- In some cases, a single valuation technique will be appropriate, whereas, in other states of the world, multiple valuation techniques will be recommended [IFRS 13:63].

The income approach is based on the incremental income (deriving mainly from cost savings) linked to the use of a blockchain. The benefits should consider time savings or lower collateral costs since the "blockchained" data is more reliable.

Digital scalability applied to blockchains may improve economic and financial margins even through sales increases.

A complimentary valuation pattern might consider the appraisal techniques traditionally used for databases (that represent the most similar intangible). The value of a database can be extracted from its use by different users, again with value co-creation patterns that rotate around the blockchain and include feedback, data sharing, etc.

Blockchain evaluation is highly uncertain because cash flows are difficult to estimate.

The cost approach might consider the savings for the users, in terms of lower costs, higher speed and reliability of data, etc. Further considerations will be made in Table 16.1. As anticipated, the blockchain can ease the production of higher revenues or the minimization of OPEX, so improving the operating cash flow (FCFF) margin, as a consequence of a higher EBITDA.

16.5.3   Financial Evaluation

A comprehensive model for the evaluation of intangibles considers their economic (incremental) marginality as a starting point to assess their capacity to generate liquidity. Coherently with IAS 38 prescriptions, DCF

Table 16.1 Impact of blockchains on economic and financial marginality

Economic/financial marginality	Standard company	Blockchain extension
Revenues	These parameters depend on the traditional business model of the firm, without the impact of the blockchain applications	• New business models and opportunities (real options for expansion and development
− Fixed monetary costs − Variable monetary costs		• Validation of data can decrease costs and speed up processes, with time savings
= **EBITDA**		• Economic and financial marginality grows because of higher revenues and lower costs
± Δ Operating Net Working Capital (NWC)		• Blockchains may shorten the supply chain, making payments more straightforward and quicker, so reducing the accounts receivable and payable. Even the stock might be decreased
± Δ Net Investments ± Δ Capex)		• Blockchains may reduce some fixed investments, with a positive consequence on some fixed costs and depreciation
= **Operating Cash Flow**		• Liquidity may increase because of the higher EBITDA and lower NWC and Capex

is the key parameter for both accounting and appraisal estimates, representing the unifying common denominator of cost, income, or market-based approaches which regularly all need to find out their monetary value.

A synthesis of the market, cost, and income approach may be found in a financial appraisal methodology (consistent with a more general evaluation of a firm) where the estimate is based on the capacity to generate liquidity, remembering that "cash is king".[17]

Market valuations may use as preferred approaches either DCF or directly an EBITDA multiplier, deriving from multiple comparisons of intangibles. DCF theoretically stands out as the optimal method, being inspired by the golden rule according to which cash is king.

DCF is ubiquitous in financial valuation and is the cornerstone of contemporary valuation theory (Singh, 2013). The reliability of the model, as well as its compatibility with the conventional two-dimensional risk-return structure of investment appraisal, adapts it to a multitude of asset/liability valuations. Accounting standards across the globe recognize the efficacy of this model and advocate its use wherever practicable. FAS 141 and 142 of the United States and IAS 39, related to the accounting of intangible assets, recommend the use of the DCF method to evaluate such assets.

Market valuations frequently use a standardized EBITDA multiplied over time (from 2/3 up to 15 or more times/years, in exceptional cases) and this (apparently) simple multiplication brings an Enterprise Value (EV), to be divided between debtholders and equity-holders. This approach is consistent with the accounting nature of EBITDA, which is calculated before debt servicing.

EV/EBITDA multipliers can be connected to price/book value or Tobin q parameters which reflect the differential value of intangibles under a hypothetical cost reproduction hypothesis. They are a precious bridge between the otherwise disconnected market and cost appraisal approaches.

As a rough calculation, the EV multiple indicates how long it would take for the complete acquisition of the entire company (including its financial debt) to earn enough to pay off its costs (assuming no change in EBITDA and a constantly added value contribution from the intangible portfolio). Temporal mismatches between the numerator and the denominator may bias the ratio and should be minimized accordingly. The estimate of the Enterprise Value can be conducted also discounting FCFF with the WACC.

Equity and debt value may be jointly inferred from an EBITDA multiplier which estimates EV and, after deduction of the market value of debt, the residual market value of equity.

Debt and equity underwriters recognize that the stream of growing Operating Cash Flows (FCFF/O_{CF}) (marginally attributable to the intangible strategic contribution to the overall value) incorporates growth factors, whereas the weighted average cost of capital (WACC) discounting denominator embodies market risk elements. Moreover, cash flows are a cornerstone of debt service. Qualitative issues such as consistency, durability, depth of coverage, etc., concerning the intangible assets, may strategically impact future EBITDA, cash flows, and consequent value. WACC may be affected by the asset substitution problem and inherent wealth transfer from debt- to equity-holders (or vice versa). The blockchain can ideally impact both the numerator (higher EBITDA and consequently, better FCFF) and the denominator (lower risk, represented by a minimized WACC), so fostering the overall valuation.

Should the valuation consider an intangible-driven marginal contribution to the overall company's value, what matters is just the differential/incremental O_{CF} or EBITDA made possible by the strategic contribution of the blockchain, although often uneasy to isolate. Additional value, not attributable to specific intangible components, is allocated as goodwill.

Since O_{CF} is derived from EBITDA, the link between market approaches and DCF is evident. This finding is significant, and it has an essential impact on valuation.

Calculation of expected benefits with Net Present Value (NPV) is given by the following formula, considering NPV accruing to equity-holders:

$$NPV_{equity} = \sum_{t=1}^{n} \frac{CFN_t}{(1 + K_e)^t} - CF_0 \tag{16.1}$$

where:

CFN = Net Cash Flow/FCFE;
t = time;
K_e = Cost of equity;
CF_0 = initial investment.

A more detailed calculation of NPV should include even the other factors, incorporating in Net Cash Flows/FCFE geographic limitations, restrictions, exclusivity, etc.

The synthesis between the two methodologies is represented by the calculation of FCFF/Operating Cash Flows that reflect the impact of scalability. Liquidity is calculated by comparing changes in balance sheet figures/numbers with the current income statement. Blockchains are expected to improve the EBITDA through higher revenues and lower costs, as anticipated.

16.5.4   *"With or Without" Incremental Valuation*

The incremental evaluation can be useful to external users of the blockchain that incorporate its functions in their (traditional) business model or use its certified data.

The "with or without" methodology is currently used to evaluate intangibles (consistently with IVS 210) and estimates the fair value of an asset by comparing the value of the business inclusive of the asset to the possible value of the same business excluding the asset.

Blockchains may impact both revenues and costs. Their economic and financial (incremental) marginality are represented in Table 16.1.

Operating cash flows (FCFF) eventually bring to net cash flows (FCFE), as shown in Table 2.1.

EBITDA and Operating Cash flow are the cornerstones of the two primary evaluation criteria. The "with or without" approach considers the impact of the blockchain on both (higher) revenues and (lower) costs, as seen above, when the blockchain-driven firm is compared to a similar company that does not use any blockchain. Comparisons are, once again, typically market-driven, and precious sources can be retrieved from specific databases of M&A transactions.

16.6   CONCLUSION

The evaluation of blockchains should start with their legal status. Blockchains may have an independent appraisal as soon as they are private or belong to a consortium. Public blockchains are a fully decentralized public good whose value might be estimated indirectly, considering the benefits for its external users (mainly in terms of cost savings, time savings, and increased reliability of [big] data).

Another requirement for valuation is the uneasy estimate of the revenue model of the blockchain. How can the blockchain cash in its services? Is there any subscription or pay-per-use mechanism? Which is the incremental value of verified (big) data? These are the (apparently) simple questions that any evaluator should ask before starting his job. Applications of blockchains to many different industries and products, well beyond the controversial cryptocurrencies, can help create value from innovation.

Disintermediation with decentralization and enhanced scalability of re-engineered supply chains is a natural by-product of blockchains.

Finally, blockchains can be ideally linked to artificial intelligence, providing validated data to machine learning patterns.

NOTES

1. https://www.economist.com/briefing/2015/10/31/the-great-chain-of-being-sure-about-things.
2. In cryptography and computer science, a hash tree or Merkle tree is a tree in which every leaf node is labelled with the hash of a data block and every non-leaf node is labelled with the cryptographic hash of the labels of its child nodes. Hash trees allow efficient and secure verification of the contents of large data structures. A Merkle tree is recursively defined as a binary tree of hash lists where the parent node is the hash of its children, and the leaf nodes are hashes of the original data blocks (https://en.wikipedia.org/wiki/Merkle_tree).
3. https://www.henrylab.net/wp-content/uploads/2017/10/blockchain.pdf.
4. https://www.henrylab.net/wp-content/uploads/2017/10/blockchain.pdf.
5. Real estate blockchain applications can help in recording, tracking, transferring of land titles, property deeds and even ensure that all the documents are accurate and verifiable. Blockchain offers a distinct method to reduce the need for paper-based record keeping and speed up the transactions, thus assisting the stakeholders to improve the efficiency and help in the reduction of transaction costs at all sides of the transaction (https://medium.com/coinmonks/blockchain-as-a-business-model-ed4de3c91763).
6. https://medium.com/swlh/blockchain-in-automotive-dea04e51a079.
7. Healthcare institutions are presently suffering from an inability to share data securely across platforms. Blockchain technology could allow hospitals, payers, patients and other parties in the healthcare value chain

to share access to their networks compromising on the data security and integrity (https://medium.com/coinmonks/blockchain-as-a-business-model-ed4de3c91763).

8. A smart contract is a computer protocol intended to digitally facilitate, verify, or enforce the negotiation or performance of a contract.

9. https://www.henrylab.net/wp-content/uploads/2017/10/blockchain.pdf.

10. https://www.journals.elsevier.com/future-generation-computer-systems/call-for-papers/special-issue-on-blockchain-and-decentralization-for-internerne.

11. https://ripple.com/insights/the-internet-of-value-what-it-means-and-how-it-benefits-everyone/.

12. https://coincentral.com/sharing-economy-companies-are-set-to-be-disrupted-by-blockchain/.

13. See https://www.intheblack.com/articles/2018/09/05/difference-between-private-public-blockchain.

14. https://www.mycryptopedia.com/consortium-blockchain-explained/.

15. See https://www.ey.com/Publication/vwLUAssets/EY-IFRS-Accounting-for-crypto-assets/$File/EY-IFRS-Accounting-for-crypto-assets.pdf.

16. See Sect. 3.8.

17. "Cash is king" is a slang term reflecting the belief that money (cash) is more valuable than any other form of investment tool (https://www.investopedia.com/terms/c/cash-is-king.asp).

SELECTED REFERENCES

Alabi, K. (2017). Digital blockchain networks appear to be following Metcalfe's law. *Electronic Commerce Research and Applications, 24*, 23–29.

Al-Jaroodi, J., & Mohamed, N. (2019). *Blockchain in industries: A survey.* https://www.researchgate.net/publication/331600305_Blockchain_in_Industries_A_Survey

Andoni et al. (2019). Blockchain technology in the energy sector: A systematic review of challenges and opportunities. *Renewable and Sustainable Energy Reviews, 100*, 143–174. https://www.sciencedirect.com/science/article/pii/S1364032118307184

Blossey, G., Eisenhardt, J., & Hahn, G. (2019). *Blockchain technology in supply chain management: An application perspective.* Proceedings of the 52nd Hawaii International Conference on System Sciences. http://hdl.handle.net/10125/60124

Chen, Z. (2022). *The applications of Blockchain in food supply chain management.* Doctoral thesis, University of Southampton, pp. 341.

Cong, L. W., & He, Z. (2018). *Blockchain disruption and smart contracts* (NBER Working Paper No. 24399), April.

Dujak, D., & Sajter, D. (2019). *Blockchain applications in supply chain.* Berlin: Springer Verlag.

Fan, T., He, W., Nie, E., & Chen, S. (2017). *A study of pricing and trading model of blockchain & big data-based energy internet electricity.* Paper presented at IOP Conference Series, Earth and Environmental Science.

Goorha, P. (2018). The return of 'The nature of the firm': The role of the blockchain. *Journal of the British Blockchain Association, 1*(1), 1–5.

Korpela, K., Hallikas, J., & Dahlber, T. (2017). *Digital supply chain transformation toward blockchain integration.* Paper presented at the 50th Hawaii International Conference on System Sciences, 4182.

Lotti, L. (2016). Contemporary art, capitalization and the blockchain: On the autonomy and automation of art's value. *Finance and Society, 2*(2), 96.

Lui, P. T. (2016). *Medical record system using blockchain, big data and tokenization.* Paper presented at the Information and Communications Security: 18th International Conference, pp. 254–261.

Mao, D., Wang, F., Hao, Z., & Li, H. (2018). Credit Evaluation system based on blockchain for multiple stakeholders in the food supply chain. *International Journal of Environmental Research and Public Health, 15*(8), 1627.

Norman, M. D., Karavas, Y. G., & Reed, H. (2018). *The emergence of trust and value in public blockchain networks.* https://www.researchgate.net/publication/325552991_The_Emergence_of_Trust_and_Value_in_Public_Blockchain_Networks

Pastor, D., Glova, J., Liptak, F., & Kovac, V. (2017). Intangibles and methods for their valuation in financial terms in literature review. *Intangible Capital, 13*(2). http://www.intangiblecapital.org/index.php/ic/article/view/752/627

Saberi, S., Kouhizadeh, M., Sarkis, J., & Shen, L. (2018). Blockchain technology and its relationships to sustainable supply chain management. *International Journal of Production Researching, 57*(7), 2117–2135.

Sawa, T. (2019). Blockchain technology outline and its application to field of power and energy system. *IEEJ Transactions on Power and Energy, 138*(7), 537–540. (B. Denki Gakkai Ronbunshi, Trans.). https://doi.org/10.1541/ieejpes.138.537, https://onlinelibrary.wiley.com/doi/abs/10.1002/eej.23167?af=R

Singh, J. P. (2013). On the intricacies of cash flow corporate valuation. *Advances in Management, 6*(3), 15–22.

Veuger, J. (2018). Trust in a viable real estate economy with disruption and blockchain. *Facilities, 36*(1–2), 103–112.

Xie, J., et al. (2019). A survey of blockchain technology applied to smart cities: Research issues and challenges. *IEEE Communications Surveys & Tutorials, 21*(3), 2794–2830.

Yermack, D. (2017). Corporate governance and blockchains. *Review of Finance, 21*(1), 7–31.

Zhang, Y., & Wen, J. (2016). The IoT electric business model: Using blockchain technology for the internet of things. *Peer-to Peer Network Applications, 10,* 983–994.

CHAPTER 17

Cryptocurrencies, Non-fungible Tokens, and Digital Art Valuation

17.1 CRYPTOCURRENCIES

A cryptocurrency is a digital or virtual currency that is secured by cryptography, which makes it nearly impossible to counterfeit or double-spend. Many cryptocurrencies are decentralized networks based on blockchain technology—a distributed ledger enforced by a disparate network of computers. A defining feature of cryptocurrencies is that they are generally not issued by any central authority, rendering them theoretically immune to government interference or manipulation (https://www.investopedia.com/terms/c/cryptocurrency.asp). This leads to De.Fi. – Decentralized Finance, an ecosystem that is mapped by peculiar distributed networks where there are no pivoting nodes (hubs).

Cryptocurrency is a recent phenomenon that is receiving significant attention. On the one hand, it is based on fundamentally new technology, the potential of which is not fully understood. On the other hand, at least in the current form, it fulfills similar functions as other, more traditional assets (Liu & Tsyvinski, 2021).

Digital currency can either be centralized (with the central control point of the money supply, for instance, ruled by a Central Bank as it happens with fiat money) or—more frequently—decentralized, where supply control is regulated by the consensus and verified by a network of users, normally through Decentralised Finance (De.Fi.) that, as anticipated in Chapter 16, are ruled by blockchains. Despite the growing

R. Moro-Visconti, *The Valuation of Digital Intangibles*, https://doi.org/10.1007/978-3-031-09237-4_17

Fig. 17.1 Digitalization, scalability, and cryptocurrencies

adoption of decentralized exchanges, not much is yet known about their market quality. To shed light on this issue, Barbon and Ranaldo (2021) compare decentralized blockchain-based venues (DEX) to centralized crypto exchanges (CEX) by assessing two key aspects of market quality: price efficiency and market liquidity. The cryptocurrency market is extremely volatile, as shown by its spectacular collapse since Autumn 2021, preceded by a sharp increase.

Digitalization is a fundamental prerequisite behind scalability, and they both represent a basic feature of cryptocurrencies, as shown in Fig. 17.1.

Cryptocurrencies represent the monetary component of many digital networks (from basic blockchains to the metaverse) that otherwise would not be liquid. The absence of liquidity dries up a market, making it unattractive.

17.2   Non-Fungible Tokens

Non-fungible tokens (NFTs) are cryptographic assets on a blockchain with unique identification codes and metadata that distinguish them from each other. Unlike cryptocurrencies, they cannot be traded or exchanged at equivalency. This differs from fungible tokens like cryptocurrencies, which are identical to each other and, therefore, can serve as a medium for commercial transactions (Forbes, 2022).

An NFT is a digital asset that represents real-world objects like art, music, in-game items, and videos—new underlying physical assets are likely to be included in this list. They are bought and sold online, frequently with cryptocurrency, and they are generally encoded with the same underlying software as many virtual currencies.

The links among cryptocurrencies, NFTs, and blockchains are depicted in Fig. 17.2, and can be reshaped forming different combinations, due to the intrinsic plasticity of digital intangibles. Even the difference between

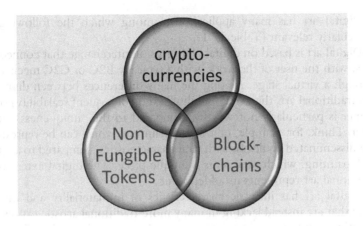

Fig. 17.2 Cryptocurrencies, NFTs, and blockchains

fungible cryptocurrencies and intrinsically non-fungible NFTs is softened by their osmotic connections.

17.3 Digital Art

Digital art (also called computer art) identifies a work or an artistic practice that uses digital technology as part of the creative process or exhibition presentation. Electronic art has a broader meaning than digital art, as it involves many interrelationships between art and technology.

Crypto art (cryptographic art) is a category of art related to blockchain technology and concerns digital artworks published directly on a blockchain in the form of non-fungible tokens (NFTs), which makes it possible to own, transfer, and sell artwork in a cryptographically secure and verifiable manner. NFTs make digital art tradable, contributing to the creation of a new market, and representing an opportunity for otherwise neglected artists.

Neologisms such as video art, computer art, cybernetic art, virtual reality, multimedia art, digital art, and interactive art—nowadays preferably united in the broader and more ductile definition of electronic art—have been spreading for several decades in the language of artists, critics, and the public. Digital art traditionally identifies works of contemporary art, although there may be digitalization, even with creative reinterpretations, of works of classical art.

Digital art has many applications, among which the following are particularly relevant (Table 17.1).

Digital art is based on digital platforms of interchange that connect the artist with the user of the work, with a typically B2C or C2C mechanism, through a virtual stage. Among the many differences between digital art and traditional art, the "viral usability" (and consequent scalability) of the former is particularly noteworthy, compared to the "uniqueness" of the latter. Think, for example, of a digital painting, which can be reproduced and disseminated endlessly, with viral characteristics, compared to a "physical" painting, which represents a unique piece. The digital extension of traditional art represents its added value.

Digital art has intrinsic characteristics of immateriality and intangibility that are instead lacking in many more traditional artistic expressions (painting, sculpture, etc.), represented by physical goods. There are, however, artistic expressions, such as music, which overlap these two sets, originating from "physical" scores but assuming a diffusion over the air that, since the time of Napster, uses the Internet and immaterial modes of fruition (MP3 files or other).

The uniqueness of some "pieces", expression of traditional art is reflected intrinsically in the rarity and value; this is counterbalanced by the usability of digital art that, thanks to the support on which it is built, is intrinsically usable through the web. Even in traditional works of art, uniqueness is not, however, an exclusive element, since for many prints or serigraphic reproductions there is usually a print run, certified by the author, which increases the usability to tens or sometimes hundreds of copies (art multiples or numbered series). The higher the number of existing multiples, the lower the value, following the property of supply and demand, intersected by an equilibrium price.

The immaterial goods have, as a rule, characteristics of non-rivalry, being able to be used even simultaneously by a large number of subjects, as shown in Chapters 2 and 3. On the other hand, "physical" artistic goods have a more limited number of users, not only because they belong to a single owner, but also because of the constraints of usability in a physical presence, lacking the aforementioned characteristics of virality and scalability that are typical of the digital world (always, everywhere, potentially for everyone, especially in the absence of premium applications).

Among the many intersections between "physical" and "digital" art, there is no shortage of transpositions of traditional artistic assets onto

Table 17.1 Digital art—taxonomy

Application/type description	Description
Digital photography	Procedure for the acquisition of static images, projected through an optical system, on a light-sensitive electronic device (sensor), with subsequent conversion into digital format and storage on a memory medium
Digital imaging	The creation of a visual representation of an object, through image acquisition, processing, compression, storage, printing, and representation
Digital publishing	The term digital publishing refers to the publishing phenomenon in which content, the entire publishing process, and access to content are implemented with the help of information technology. Digital publishing covers various fields of action, from the processing of printed content to the widespread distribution of digital content via the Internet
Electronic literature	Electronic literature, also known as digital literature, e-literature, or eLiterature, is a particular cross-sectoral phenomenon, ascribable to different fields, primarily literary, which through the use of innovative creative methodologies and the means offered by technological evolution, including computers, the web, and ICT (information and communication technologies), produces innovative literary works
Electronic poetry	Artistic experimentation that integrates poetic text and new media art (video art, digital art, net.art, installations, etc.). It can be distinguished in two major areas, often intertwined in research: video poetry, and computer poetry, which integrates the use of digital technologies
Internet art	Contemporary artistic discipline aimed at creating works of art with, for, and on the Internet
Electronic music	Music produced or modified through the use of electronic instrumentation
Pixel art	A type of computer graphics and a form of digital art. Pixel art is when the creator of an image can freely manipulate each pixel of the image
New media art	Artistic compositions designed and reproduced with new media technologies (visual art; computer graphics; digital art; interactive art; sound art; cyborg art, etc.)[1]
Digital museums	Enable virtual tours of museums. Using the mouse and keyboard, clicking on the hotspots inserted in the environments, and navigating the interactive maps, the visit is deepened with contextual elements: photos, videos, and texts, and the route is freely chosen by the visitor

(continued)

Table 17.1   (continued)

Application/type description	Description
Collections[2]/digital databases	Databases uploaded and saved on digital media allow the online archiving and consultation of collections from digital museums or other archives

digital format: thus, the reproduction of a painting or a sculpture, the performance of a musical score reproduced via the web, etc.

Another issue that has always been a concern for traditional artists is represented by plagiarism or theft of works of art. Digitization, on the one hand, increases this risk, making it much easier to acquire, manipulate, and disseminate the artistic creations of others, but on the other hand, it has IT tools, based primarily on the blockchain, which validate sources and information, protecting digital works from the start.

All these features, and more, affect the evaluation metrics. The increasing valorization of the contents published on the web, also based on the long-standing tug-of-war that pits the digital platforms of big tech against newspapers or the variegated world of authors, lies in the wake of these issues and grasps their evolutionary aspects, marking the difficult revenge of contents against communication platforms, with a view to a fairer sharing of advertising revenues and subscriptions for premium services.

The preservation of digital works of art is of particular importance, also for value durability.

17.4   TIMESTAMPS

The problem of literary or artistic plagiarism, or other forms of copyright infringement, has been known since ancient times.

In this context, the well-known claims on the subject of the prior art are also relevant.

The Temporal Mark is part of this application and consists of a service that allows associating date and time certain and legally valid to a computer document, thus allowing to associate a temporal validation opposable to third parties.

The Temporal Marking service can also be used on files that are not digitally signed, guaranteeing a certain and legally valid temporal location.

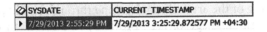

17.5 EVALUATION APPROACHES

The boundaries of digital art are particularly blurred and constantly evolving, under the propulsive thrust of technological innovation that opens the door to new forms of creation, experimentation, and dissemination of creativity. The legal protection of digital art and its classification as an intangible "asset" can be a valid aid to valuation, even if it suffers from the same uncertainties mentioned above.

In the writer's opinion, any attempt at valuation should follow a methodological approach in line with the sequence of reasoning and frameworks proposed here:

1. Classification of the artistic work being evaluated and its inclusion within a taxonomy, where existing (also for comparability with similar works);
2. Identification of legal issues regarding prior art, ownership, right of economic exploitation, etc.
3. Accounting of the work by the author;
4. Examination of royalty, sale, or other contracts relating to the work, if any;
5. Analogical reference to other types of intangible assets or rights being evaluated (copyright; software; blockchains; digital logos or trademarks; mobile apps; social networks; digital platforms, etc.);
6. Use of valuation approaches (cost, income, or market) traditionally used for the valuation of intangible assets.

The economic valuation of digital art is based on methodological approaches that differ, in part, from those used for traditional art, incorporating elements already illustrated such as (greater) usability, dematerialization, and reproducibility.

In more general terms, artistic works, like other activities based on the use and exploitation of culture, are difficult to evaluate, partly because the economic metrics derived from their exploitation and comparability with "similar" works are often inconvenient.

The framing of the artwork can be done through an "Expertise", used, in the technical language of art historians, to indicate an official document, which contains the technical characteristics of a work of art and certifies its authenticity, age, dating, and state of preservation. As a whole, it can be defined as the identity document of a work of art containing a description (as complete as possible) of the work's history, based also on any laboratory analysis, if deemed necessary. The expertise, therefore, consists of a detailed report for the evaluation of the originality and the historical-artistic framework of the work under examination, whatever the nature of the asset, i.e., a painting, a piece of furniture, or another figurative work. The expertise does not indicate the commercial value of the work, and may conveniently use blockchain technology to validate information.

The valuation techniques of works of art, even digital, follow the appraisal purposes (auction valuation, insurance, for hereditary purposes, to constitute a pledge or corollary on a loan, for inclusion in the budget, for judicial appraisals in case of civil or criminal litigation, etc.).

The valuation of a work of art must consider the author (emerging or already known), which suggests a range of indicative value, based on market comparisons for other works by the same author. Title of the work, date of creation, the technique of execution, dimensions of the work (not always easy to determine in the digital sphere), certifications of authenticity are relevant elements, as well as the origin (belonging to illustrious collections or families, though balanced by the short history of digital art), personal or collective exhibitions (mainly through the web channel, beyond the "physical" exhibition of traditional works of art). Also noteworthy is the presence of a catalog raisonné of the artist's works (facilitated by increasing digitization, which makes it possible to archive and search, mainly online, data and information). The traditional impact on the price and value of the state of preservation of work takes on different connotations in the digital sphere, given that digitization preserves the work from wear and tear and "physical" consumption, while leaving it exposed to technological obsolescence and the emergence of new standards, which could hinder its preservation and use (think of analog works or digital formats that are no longer supported).

The distinction between the primary market (first sale) and the secondary market (subsequent resale, even through auction houses) is also relevant for digital art, even if it is balanced by the possibility of collective fruition that increases the diffusion but reduces the exclusivity of the buyer.

In particular cases, the so-called resale right can also be the object of evaluation. This case occurs in secondary markets, whose liquidity represents an important parameter for the appraisal of the overall value chain (a more liquid secondary market positively affects the liquidity of the primary market—people are more eager to buy if they know that they can resell).

The interaction between digital art and intangible assets (exemplified in Fig. 17.3) allows extending the traditional paradigms of evaluation of works of art, using innovative methodologies and tools of creation, dissemination, and use of the same. However, the problem of valuing works of art, including digital works, without a market remains unsolved. The absence of a market would seem to suggest non-existence in terms of value, if not in terms of future potential.

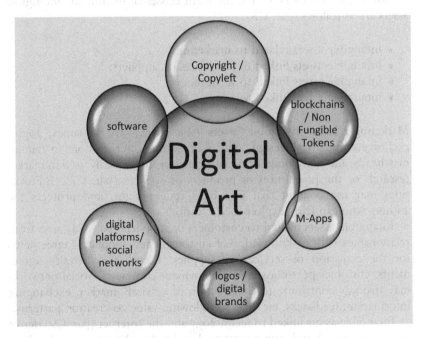

Fig. 17.3 Interaction between digital art and intangible assets

The International Valuation Standards (IVS) 210, examined in Chapter 2, is entirely dedicated to intangible assets.

According to IVS 210, an intangible asset may be identifiable or unidentifiable (par. C3). An asset is identifiable if:

(a) it is separable, i.e., it can be separated or spun off from the business and sold, transferred, licensed, leased, or exchanged, either individually or in connection with a contract or identifiable assets or liabilities, regardless of whether the business intends to do so; or

(b) arises from contractual rights or other legal titles, regardless of whether such rights are transferable or separable from the business or other rights and obligations.

Goodwill is generally defined as any non-independently identifiable intangible asset associated with a business or group of businesses (par. C4).

Also according to IVS 210, the main classes of identifiable intangible assets are as follows (par. C5):

- intangible assets related to marketing;
- intangible assets linked to customers or suppliers;
- intangible assets linked to technology;
- intangible assets linked to art.

Marketing-related intangible assets (trademarks, trade names, logos, exclusive commercial design, digital branding, Internet domain names, mastheads, and non-competition agreements) are primarily used in market research or the promotion of products or services (par. C7). Editorial titles may use content that is subject to copyright, and protects the authors who can fairly exploit their creations.

Intangible assets related to customers or suppliers (par. C8) arise from relationships with or knowledge of customers and suppliers (agreements for the provision of services or supplies, licensing or royalty agreements, customer portfolios, and employment contracts). Social networks may strongly contribute to the creation of a "viral" market, exchanging information, feedbacks, etc. and so following value co-creation patterns.

Intangible assets linked to technology and the Internet (par. C9) derive from contractual and non-contractual rights for the use of technology (patents, databases, formulas, designs, industrial drawings, ornamental models, software, know-how, procedures, or recipes). Databases (also related to the digital archiving of works of art) fall within the taxonomy provided for by art. 2 of the l.d.a.[3]

Art-related intangible assets (par. C10) arise from the right to benefits such as royalties for works of art, including plays, books, films, and music, and non-contractual copyright protection.

The main methods (approaches) used—singly or in a complementary manner—by valuation standards for the economic estimation of the value of intangible assets are as follows:

1. market method;
2. cost method (of reconstruction or replacement);
3. expected income method (incremental).

According to the PIVs (par. III.5.5), used in the Italian best practices and fully consistent with the IVS 210 standard, the valuation of an intangible asset can be carried out by referring to each of the above three known valuation methods. To select the most appropriate method, the expert should consider the characteristics of the intangible asset, and in particular its reproducibility, the nature of the benefits it is capable of generating for the owner (current or potential, considering the resale right), and the user, and the existence or otherwise of a reference market.

The breadth of the possible valuation range is marked, in its extremes, by upper and lower limits, in hypotheses of (full) going concern (full business continuity) or in break-up liquidation scenarios, in which intangible resources traditionally lose most of their value, especially if not independently negotiable or synergistically linked to other assets; in hypotheses of discontinuity, the "organized complex of assets" that frames the firm is completely lost. The different gradations of value also reflect the possibilities of growth and, with them, the possible scenarios to which to associate the estimates.

The choice of methods to be used, within the scope of those mentioned above or further variants, depends on the type of intangible resource and the purpose and context of the valuation, but also on the ease with which reliable and significant information can be found on the resource and the market in which it is strategically positioned.

17.6   VALUATION OF INTANGIBLE ASSETS

This valuation paragraph synthetically reproposes the contents of Chapters 2 and 3, with some adaptation to the current case.

Art is a tangible asset (a painting, sculpture, etc.) with intangible features (as it produces emotions, inspiration, imitation, empathy, aesthetics, beauty, etc.). Digital art dematerializes its underlying features but its "emotions" could be similar. This is why the valuation of intangible assets is consistent with digital art. Art consists of tangible (or digital-intangible) assets that in principle, like gold or diamonds, do not and will never produce a flow of cash to their owners—no dividends, interest rates, or other liquid inflows.

But art can be exploited—an art craft can occasionally be rented, sold with a capital gain, produce monetary royalties, etc. And digitalization extends usability well beyond the formal owners of digital art.

This somewhat paradoxical framework is essential for the understanding of how art and its digital extension can be estimated.

17.6.1   Cost Approach

The main method of this approach is to determine the costs incurred to create the intangible asset (usable for intangibles in the process of formation) or to be incurred for its reproduction: according to this method, the value of an intangible asset is determined by the sum of the capitalized costs incurred to create the intangible or to be incurred to reproduce it (restoration of rights and brand accreditation represented, in general, by advertising, promotional and distribution network investments ...).

The limitation of this approach lies in the fact that it does not consider maintenance costs and the opportunity cost of time and that does not apply to assets capable of generating income.

The main difficulties in applying this approach relate to the difficulty in identifying costs incurred in the past, especially if the expenses have been incurred over several years and have not been capitalized.

17.6.2   Income/Financial Approach

This is based on the past and future economic benefits that can be linked to an intangible, either in terms of licensing revenues (royalties) or incremental income.

In the context of the income approach, intangible assets have value insofar as they can incorporate a competitive advantage in the form of multi-period excess earnings. This is a purely income-based estimate, in which intangible assets act as Primary Income Generating Assets. Income methods are based on estimates of future economic benefits, for example through discounted cash flows. Income methods also include financial methods.

The main methods related to this approach (uneasy to apply to digital art, but anyway worth trying) are the following:

1. discounting of income or cash flows (FCFF or FCFE) deriving from the exploitation of the intangible asset: according to this method, the value of an intangible asset is given by the sum of the discounted income deriving from the exploitation of the same (in terms of royalties, turnover ...);

2. Excess Earning criterion (differential/incremental income), to be used for estimating the value of an asset that plays a significant or, in any event, primary role, based on which the imputed income is obtained by calculating the income that the company would record if it were to free itself of the ownership of all the other assets to reacquire the right to use them through licensing, rental or hire contracts;

3. criterion of implicit income (return on) in the market value, which is based on the relationship between value and cash flows that the asset can generate, based on its residual useful life and an appropriate rate of return.

4. discounting of differential (incremental) income or FCFF/FCFE cash flows: this is based on the quantification and discounting of the specific benefits and advantages of the intangible asset compared with "normal" situations, i.e., products that are, for example, not branded or not covered by patents. The incremental income is obtained by the difference between the revenues and costs relating to the intangible asset, with discounting of the differential flows and exclusion of extraneous or insignificant income components;

5. discounting of losses deriving from the disposal of the intangible asset: this is based on the assumption that the loss of availability of an intangible asset is likely to lead to a reduction in turnover (legally comparable to "loss of profit");

6. real options, used to evaluate flexible investment projects with uncertain outcomes.

17.6.3   Market Approach

This is based on comparison with similar assets, in terms of income or incremental assets, or on the analysis of comparable transactions and market multipliers. The digital art market is almost new, and for that reason its track record is limited and the prices are very volatile (as we can see considering speculative NFTs with a questionable underlying artistic creation).

The main limitation of this approach concerns the information asymmetries structurally linked to the secrecy of intangible assets, which make the information necessary for comparisons difficult to find, and sort out.

Transactions of packages comprising several assets or several intangibles make the valuation of stand-alone intangibles based on an empirical method more complicated. These difficulties are even more evident considering that, from an accounting point of view, according to IAS 38, there is no active market for intangibles, which tend not to be accounted for, and their fair value is difficult to estimate.

The main methods relating to this approach are as follows:

1. the Relief-from-Royalties method (the so-called relief-from-royalties method) makes it possible to estimate the income of the intangible asset by deducting from the notional royalties that would be paid to a third party for the licensed use of the work any direct and indirect maintenance/development costs not already included in this notional royalty; royalties are, however, uncommon in the digital art exploitation;

2. the With or Without criterion is an indirect method of determining the economic advantage (premium price), which consists in comparing the performance (incremental) of the company that has the intangible asset in question with that of a similar company without this asset; this criterion also uses a differential/incremental approach; again, any analogical application to digital art of this standard principle is uneasy;

3. empirical method: the income attributable to the exploitation of a given intangible asset is multiplied by a coefficient expressing the

strategic strength of the asset, which depends on factors such as leadership, loyalty, market positioning, trends, marketing investments, internationality, legal protection; the added value of digital art needs to be considered when using this approach;

4. valuation of differential (incremental) assets, through indicators of market surplus value such as Tobin's Q, which relates the market value of a company's assets to their replacement/replacement value; if the index is higher than unity, this is due to the presence of implicit goodwill that may depend, among other things, on the value (unrecognized) of the intangible asset; again, this approach is uneasy to apply to digital art, to be considered as an incremental asset, consistently with the with/without approach (which is the value of a collection with or without the digital art piece?);

5. Price/Book Value index, which relates the stock market price (market capitalization of a listed company that owns digital art goods) to the book equity, bringing out a surplus value (if the index is greater than 1) largely attributable to intangible assets.

17.7 INTERACTIVE ART (PARTICIPATORY OR RELATIONAL) AND VALUE CO-CREATION

Interactive art involves the viewer by giving her or him an active role in the contemplation of the work; it is a dynamic art form that responds to the audience and/or the environment. Unlike traditional art forms in which viewer interaction is mostly a mental event—of the order of reception—interactive art allows for different types of navigation, assembly, or participation in the artwork. Interactive art goes far beyond purely psychological activity. Interactive art installations are generally computerized and use sensors, which measure events such as temperature, movement, proximity, and weather phenomena that the author has programmed to elicit particular responses or reactions. In interactive works, the audience and the machine work or play together in a dialogue that produces a unique work of art in real-time.

A declination of interactive art is a participatory art, which uses an approach to art-making that directly involves the audience in the creative process, empowering them to become co-authors, editors, and observers of the work itself. In some expressions, participatory art borders on tribal or traditional art.

Interactivity, inherent in the technological (digital) characteristics of artistic expression, encourages behaviors inspired by the co-creation of value between the inventor and the users, who participate in artistic creation with interactive strategies of value-based pricing based on consumer choices (pay-what-you-want; pay-as-you-wish). Value co-creation is, in this field, a core paradigm; to the extent that users/customers contribute to this value creation process, they deserve fair remuneration (profit sharing; discounts, etc.).

17.8   COPYRIGHT FRAMEWORK AND EVALUATION

According to the Italian law on copyright—l.d.a.—of April 22, 1941, n. 633, copyright—right to copy—protects "the intellectual works of a creative nature that belong to literature, music, figurative arts, architecture, theater and film, whatever the mode or form of expression" (art. 1). This taxonomy, with some adaptation, may be useful even outside Italy, adapting civil or common law principleas of other countries.

Article 2575 of the Italian Civil Code (which, once again, represents an example for other countries) states that: "intellectual works of a creative nature belonging to the sciences, literature, music, figurative arts, architecture, theater, and cinematography, whatever the mode or form of expression, form the subject matter of copyright".

At a general level (art. 1 l.d.a.) the creative works belonging to literature, music, figurative arts, architecture, theater and cinematography, computer programs, and databases are protected.

Copyright extends to a very varied and heterogeneous set of works or creations, creating problems with the taxonomy of typified works (from art. 2 of the l.d.a.) or, a fortiori, of non-typified creations; the following typified works are included in the protection:

1. literary, dramatic, scientific, educational, religious works, whether in written or oral form;
2. Musical works and compositions, with or without words, dramatic-musical works, and musical variations constituting original works;
3. the choreographic and pantomime works, of which the trace is fixed in writing or otherwise;
4. works of sculpture, painting, drawing, engraving, and similar figurative arts, including set design;
5. the drawings and works of architecture;

6. works of cinematographic art, silent or sound, (...);
7. photographic works and those expressed by a process similar to that of photography (...);
8. computer programs [software, editor's note] (...);
9. databases (...), understood as collections of works, data, or other independent elements systematically or methodically arranged and individually accessible by electronic means or otherwise;
10. works of industrial design which in themselves have creative character and artistic value.

Then there are the non-typed creations:

1. critical editions and restoration;
2. sporting events;
3. advertising creations;
4. the fantasy character;
5. the television format;
6. museums;
7. multimedia works;
8. websites;
9. other cases (maps; floral arrangements; party symbols; collages; genetic engineering products; perfumes; sports commentaries; decoupage cards; public installations; SMS collections; embroidery; art historical itineraries, etc.).

Bently and Sherman (2014) propose a complementary taxonomy of copyright, in which they note:

1. literary works;
2. dramatic works;
3. musical works;
4. films;
5. the recording of sound;
6. broadcasts;
7. printed editions;

8. other related rights: of performers of a work; related to a database; technological protection measures in the digital environment; software; broadcasting; management of information rights; public lending right; resale right.

The varied perimeter of the works (simple; composite; collective; derivative) covered by copyright protection also entails economic problems, preparatory to the estimation of value. We refer, first of all, to the analysis of business models and the identification of the value creation levers connected to the exploitation of the work.

Copyright is an intangible asset, and its intangibility makes it easy to overlap with other assets (tangible or intangible) with which it can interact synergistically. Think, for example, of software fed by big data and the Internet of Things, with information flows that then flow into artificial intelligence applications, sometimes validated through blockchain, stored in the cloud, or interoperable databases.

17.8.1   *Exploitation and Copyright Protection*

There are two cases of copyright exploitation (economic external use): the case in which the right is directly exploited by the author or the case in which it is transferred and therefore exploited by a third-party purchaser, even in a secondary market.

The transfer of copyright is regulated by the l.d.a., which establishes that the author of the work has the exclusive right to use it economically; in particular, copyright can be divided into three parts:

1. right of publicity;
2. right of use;
3. right of paternity.

The l.d.a. lists a series of patrimonial rights:

– the right of reproduction in several copies of the work (art. 13);
– the right of transcription of the oral work (art. 14);
– the right of performance, representation, or recitation in public (articles 15 and 15 bis);

- the right of processing, translation, and publication of collected works (art. 18);
- the right of rental and lending (art. 18 bis).

Only the first and second rights mentioned above can be assigned, as in these cases they are patrimonial rights. The right of paternity, on the other hand, is a non-transferable personal right.

The rights granted to authors, in addition to those recognized by the Berne Convention, are:

- Distribution right (art. 6): the right to authorize the availability to the public of the original work or its copies through sale or other transfer of ownership;
- rental right (art. 7): the right to authorize the rental for the profit of the original work or its copies. It exclusively concerns three types of works: computer programs (except when the program is not the essential object of the rental), cinematographic works (unless the rental for profit has caused such a widespread reproduction of the work as to substantially compromise the exclusive right of reproduction), and works contained in phonograms;
- the right of communication to the public (art. 8): the right to authorize any form of communication to the public, by wire or over the air, in such a way that "any person may freely access it from a place or at a time of his or her choosing", thus including on-demand services and interactive communication through the Internet.

Directive 2019/790, which was approved by the European Parliament on March 26, 2019, and by the Council of the European Union on April 15, 2019, aims to ensure adequate remuneration for content producers (and copyright holders) and to extend copyright rules to online content as well. The impact on copyright enhancement, also considering developments in digital applications, is potentially significant.

The patrimonial protection of copyright is a prerequisite for its economic use and subsequent valuation. The author is granted a patrimonial right, consequent to the moral right of unpublishing, which allows him to multiply the copies of the work, with copyright.

The patrimonial right guarantees the author the exclusivity of multiplying the copies of the work. According to art. 12, paragraph 2, of the copyright law, the author "also has the exclusive right to use the work economically in any form and manner, original or derivative".

The right of reproduction includes all the ways of multiplying the original work into copies and that of representation, execution, and public performance. The work can be diffused at a distance, in the context of communication with the public. Note, even in this area, the potential of digital technologies.

In addition to exclusivity, the author has the right to compensation for certain uses of the work.

The right of economic use must be able to provide an economic benefit to the author, including any form of exploitation of the work, even without economic advantage.

The basis of copyright is the interest in remunerating creative work and investments, including entrepreneurial ones.

The protection of copyright and its consequent economic remuneration is based on various arguments of a juridical nature, which can be applied economically. In this regard, Bently and Sherman get inspired by the natural rights connected to the author's intellectual productions, to which it is considered fair to recognize a property right.

It follows, as a matter of fairness, that the author's effort should be protected through a reward represented by an exclusive right. The incentive for the author also has a public interest purpose, representing a stimulus to creativity and also a compensation for the costs incurred for the creation and production of a work which, in many cases, can be easily copied or manipulated, especially with modern digital technologies (think of serial duplication or photoshopping).

Among the interests protected at the basis of the author's patrimonial rights, the interest in remunerating the creative work and the entrepreneurial investments necessary for the production and diffusion of works of culture and entertainment is of particular importance.

Among the patrimonial rights recognized by the l.d.a. there are.

- the right to publish the work (publication coincides with the first form of economic use);
- the right to reproduce copies in any way;
- the right to represent the work in public;
- the right to disseminate the work using a remote broadcasting medium, including satellite and cable;
- the right of distribution;

- the right to translate; the right to process;
- the right to hire and lend from libraries.

The rights of economic utilization are exclusive to the author, are all independent of each other (and therefore can lead to an incremental evaluation, in the presence of several rights economically endowed with autonomous or synergic valorization), and their economic exploitation is carried out according to agreements, contracts, and licenses.

The valuation of copyright can be carried out based on the three approaches outlined above. The cost approach has limited validity if not linked to the economic exploitation of copyright.

Royalties represent an important benchmark for the financial approach, even in hypothetical form (relief from royalties).

The useful life of copyright is typically extended; in general, rights last for the author's lifetime and 50/70 years after his death (depending on the law), or even longer in the case of anonymous or pseudonymous works.

The (long) duration of copyright, for valuation purposes, could therefore be considered almost perpetual (without application of the terminal value), even if in general the right of exploitation granted by the authors (in publishing contracts, etc..) often has a more limited duration than what is abstractly provided for by law.

For copyright valuation, the recent European Directive 2019/790 is also relevant, which provides (among other things) some innovations on the subject of remuneration of so-called content creators.

A summary of digital art valuation methodologies is reported in Fig. 17.4.

17.8.2   From Copyright to Copyleft and Creative Commons

In addition to copyright, there is a model of copyright management based on copyright permission, a system of licenses through which the author (as the original holder of rights on the work) indicates to the users of the work that it can be used, disseminated, and often modified freely while respecting some essential conditions. Copyleft (copyright permission) can be applied to a multitude of works, ranging from software to literary works, from videos to musical works, and from databases to photographs.

The economic evaluation is sensitive to the passage from copyright to copyleft; in the second case, the author's monetization is less, even if

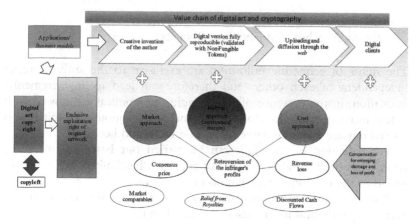

Fig. 17.4   Digital art evaluation methodologies

the work can assume a much greater diffusion, generating non-economic benefits for the author (prestige; notoriety; visibility, even viral, etc.), which can then be subject to economic exploitation with new products or creations of authors who can become influencers.

Creative Commons licenses provide a simple and standardized way to communicate which copyright of the work is reserved and which others are renounced, to the benefit of users. Copyright is consequently relaxed and does not cover all rights but only some.

17.9   REPRODUCIBILITY OF WORKS, REAL OPTIONS, AND DIGITAL SCALABILITY

The digital platforms operating on the Web allow digitized art to implement a diffusion and a related immediate and global usability, with characteristics of "virality".

The issue of reproducibility of copyrighted works has a clear impact on their economic exploitation, on which the valuation, also in terms of price of consent, depends.

Reproducibility is facilitated by a typical feature of intangible goods, represented by non-rivalry in consumption. The concept has traditionally been developed regarding public and private goods, exclusive or shareable. Rivalry in consumption is typical of private physical goods (e.g., a sandwich, which can be consumed by only one person, precluding enjoyment by others). Intangible goods—and typically those subject to copyright (e.g., a film, a song, etc.)—can instead be enjoyed simultaneously and shared by a potentially unlimited number of users, without being "consumed" by anyone. In the digital environment, reproducibility is further facilitated by the immediacy and ubiquity of the Internet.

In addition to this feature, there are others connected with the versatility of intangible assets (whose intangible nature makes them flexible and adaptable to multiple uses, regardless of "physical" problems that hinder their transportability and fungibility) or digital applications (think of a song or a film broadcast on the Internet). The synergic interaction of these characteristics affects the scalability of copyright-protected assets; this concept means the ability of a business model (also fed by intangible assets) to manage growing volumes (of sales, etc.) quickly and with reduced or even non-existent incremental costs. In the face of the greater revenues connected to scalability and the ontological invariance of fixed costs, a limited increase in variable costs emerges, with a consequent increase in economic and financial margins, which have a positive impact on valuation.

Think of accessing a website at the same time to watch a film: The circumstance that the number of connected users can grow exponentially in real-time (if the film becomes viral) does not presuppose, as a rule, an appreciable increase in costs for the owner or host of the site, even by way of the web platform, aggregator site of news and other content or snippet. This is not the case, however, for the production of rival physical assets, which involves additional time and cost.

The transition from analog to digital involves a very significant potential increase in the usability of the work and its consequent economic exploitation. The effects on established business models can be disruptive, as occurred, for example, in the record industry with mass peer-to-peer systems such as Napster, at the end of the 90s of last century.

The driving force behind scalability is represented not only by the aforementioned characteristics of digitization of intangible assets but also by the presence of computer platforms on the Internet (linked to interoperable servers and databases with access through websites) where it is possible to share and simultaneously enjoy movies, songs, texts, images, etc., that is, works that, in a broad sense, are attributable to copyright protection.

A further catalyst is represented by social networks, which feed Internet traffic, promoting the virality of digital content. Artificial intelligence applications can also act as catalysts for the exploitation of copyrighted goods, with application scenarios yet to be discovered. Further support can be provided by the validation of information (for example on the authorship of a work of art) through blockchains.

From this area descend valuation issues that can conveniently exploit features of digital scalability to apply real options.

Real options, unlike the best-known financial options, allow to include in the model of estimation of prospective cash flows (traditionally used in the evaluation of companies) elements of flexibility and resilience, incorporating into it the reactions of the market, often difficult to predict. In this way, it is possible to have options (also linked to the right of resale of works of art) of deferment, temporary suspension, abandonment, contraction, or—in a more optimistic sense—expansion or development, which give elasticity and adaptability to patented inventions, increasing their potential value.

The ability to foresee and model future and uncertain events related to the actual economic and financial return deriving from the exploitation of the intangible asset (typically, a patent, but also a scalable asset protected by copyright) can be usefully codified in contractual earn-out clauses which, in sales, ensure the seller an additional price, if certain events occur, which are particularly aleatory and uncertain at the time of contract signing. This makes it possible to overcome delicate situations of deadlock, in which the seller is not willing to give up extra earnings (to the extent that the merits are attributable to him) and the buyer to recognize them without the presumable verifiability of the positive events associated with them being ascertained. Useful links can be established between earn-outs and real options, by contractually codifying the economic aspects of possible and uncertain events, also in the context of transactions in which the aim is to limit the uncertainty of the initial price, linking it to future increases subject to the achievement of pre-established milestones.

17.9.1   The Secondary Market

Secondary markets make primary markets more liquid and more valuable. The primary market refers to the market where securities or goods (art

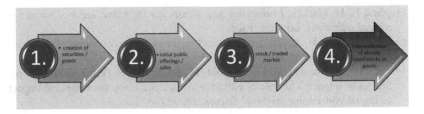

Fig. 17.5 Primary and secondary digital art market

products, etc.) are created, while the secondary market is one in which they are traded among investors.

Without both primary and secondary markets, the overall capital markets would be much harder to deal with and much less profitable. Figure 17.5 shows the sequential flow-chart of a primary and secondary market.

These standard features can be applied to this peculiar case, where cryptocurrencies are "minted" and then circulate. Something similar happens with NFTs or with digital art (that can be represented by NFTs or different forms).

NOTES

1. See Catricalà (2015).
2. See Hughes (2012), Marsh et al. (2016).
3. Italian law on copyright—l.d.a.—of April 22, 1941, n. 633.

SELECTED REFERENCES

Barbon, A., & Ranaldo, A. (2021). *On the quality of cryptocurrency markets: Centralized versus decentralized exchanges.* Available at https://www.res earchgate.net/publication/357047036_On_The_Quality_Of_Cryptocurr ency_Markets_Centralized_Versus_Decentralized_Exchanges

Bently, L., & Sherman, B. (2014). *Intellectual property law.* Oxford: Oxford University Press.

Catricalà, V. (2015). *Media art: Towards a new definition of arts in the age of technology.* Available at https://www.academia.edu/11185472/Media_Art_Tow ards_a_New_Definition_of_Arts_in_the_Age_of_Technology

Forbes (2022). *What is an NFT? Non-fungible tokens explained.* Available at https://www.forbes.com/advisor/investing/nft-non-fungible-token/

Hughes, L. H. (2012). *Evaluating and measuring the value, use and impact of digital collections*. London: Facet.

Liu, Y., & Tsyvinski, A. (2021). Risks and returns of cryptocurrency. *The Review of Financial Studies, 34*(6), 2689–2727.

Marsh, D. E., Punzalan, R. L., Leopold, R., Butler, B., & Petrozzi, M. (2016). Stories of impact: The role of narrative in understanding the value and impact of digital collections. *Archival Science, 16*, 327–372.

CHAPTER 18

Metaverse: A Digital Network Valuation

18.1   THE METAVERSE

A metaverse is a network of 3D virtual worlds focused on social connection; a set of virtual spaces where an individual can create and explore with other people who are not in the same physical space. It is a powered iteration on the web, designed to bring the digital and physical realms together. Several definitions are reported in https://metaverseroadmap. org/inputs4.html#glossary.

"The Metaverse is the post-reality universe, a perpetual and persistent multiuser environment merging physical reality with digital virtuality. It is based on the convergence of technologies that enable multisensory interactions with virtual environments, digital objects, and people such as virtual reality (VR) and augmented reality (AR). Hence, the Metaverse is an interconnected web of social, networked immersive environments in persistent multiuser platforms" (Mystiakidis, 2022).

The term "metaverse" has its origins in the notorious 1992 science fiction novel Snow Crash as a portmanteau of "meta" (in Greek μετα = beyond/transcending) + "universe".

The metaverse is a shared digital and online space that is inhabited by digital twins (avatars) of people, places, and things that interact in real-time, incorporating 3D graphics. Users are expected to be identified by their avatars who will interact in real-time with each other across multiple

© The Author(s), under exclusive license to Springer Nature Switzerland AG 2022
R. Moro-Visconti, *The Valuation of Digital Intangibles,*
https://doi.org/10.1007/978-3-031-09237-4_18

virtual locations. In addition, they will be able to purchase or build virtual items and environments, such as NFTs.

Regarded as the next iteration of the Internet, the metaverse is where the physical and digital worlds come together. As an evolution of social technologies, the metaverse allows digital representations of people, avatars, to interact with each other in a variety of settings. Whether it be at work, in an office, going to concerts or sports events, or even trying on clothes, the metaverse provides a space for endless, interconnected virtual communities using virtual reality (VR) headsets, augmented reality (AR) glasses, smartphone apps, or other devices (Johnson, 2022).

From a social perspective, the development of more immersive virtual experiences is helping people to build communities based on shared values, and to express themselves in more authentic ways. Meanwhile, COVID-19 accelerated the digitization of our lives and normalized more persistent and multi-purpose online engagement and communication. It is this combination of technological, social, and economic drivers that are resulting in explosive interest in the metaverse (JP Morgan, 2022).

Metaverse seamlessly integrates the real world with the virtual world and allows avatars to carry out rich activities including creation, display, entertainment, social networking, and trading (Yang et al., 2022). Metaverses have existed for decades in the form of multiplayer online games. But we may soon enter an age of immersive experience hardly distinguishable from our real world—fostering new modes of interaction for gamers and non-gamers alike (https://www.ft.com/partnercontent/crypto-com/nfts-the-metaverse-economy.html).

The metaverse aims to create a shared virtual space that connects all virtual worlds via the Internet, where users, represented as digital avatars, can communicate, and collaborate as if they are in the physical world (Cheng et al., 2022).

According to Gartner's research (2022) metaverse will require a host of technologies and combinatorial innovations to create a persistent and immersive digital environment. Product leaders across industries must invest selectively and not overspend in the short term, as a complete metaverse will take at least eight years to develop.

The three-step supply and value chain patterns from the physical world to the metaverse (synthesized in Fig. 18.1) pass through the Internet[1] and follow a technological upgrade whose eventual outcome is still uncertain.

In the future, the metaverse is likely to fully incorporate the earlier-stage Internet dimension.

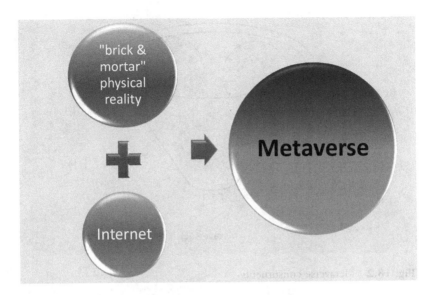

Fig. 18.1 From physical reality to the Internet and metaverse

This Chapter starts from the evidence that physical reality can be partially mapped with network theory, showing the edging links between connected nodes, and their spatial and intertemporal dynamic interaction. The Internet is a network of networks representing a global system of interconnected computer networks. The metaverse is a network of 3D virtual worlds focused on social connection. There is so an evident Ariadne's thread between these ecosystems, interpreted with multilayer network theory that examines the connectivity and interdependency between nodes positioned in the physical world, the web, or the metaverse.

The metaverse is an Internet evolution that is oriented toward shared activities (mainly through social networking) with an exponential rise in creativeness, unleashed by a decentralized ecosystem, and integrated technologies, as shown in Fig. 18.2.

This pioneering Chapter illustrates a new research avenue, analyzing the application of some of the most evident properties of network theory to the case, showing for instance how replica (corresponding) nodes can link through an avatar (an "augmented/virtual" replica node) the physical world with the metaverse. Consistently with this framework, the main

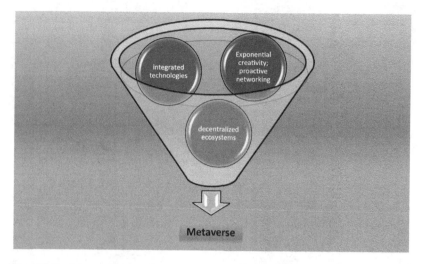

Fig. 18.2   Metaverse constituents

research question of this Chapter is to investigate the potential market value of metaverse ecosystems, using a with-and-without approach, the scalable network approach, or multilayer network metrics.

18.2   Scale-Free Networks and the Metaverse Topology

Network theory (see Barabási, 2016; Bapat, 2011; Beckström, 2008; Bianconi & Barabási, 2001; Caldarelli & Catanzaro, 2011; Domenico et al., 2013; Erdös & Rényi, 1959; Estrada & Knight, 2015; Gander, 2015; Garcia et al., 2008; Gawer, 2014; Gneiser et al., 2012; Gupta et al., 2017; Hoffman & Yeh, 2018; Ismail, 2014; Jackson, 2008; Jacobides et al., 2018; Kane et al., 2014; Kenney & Zysman, 2016; Korpela et al., 2017; Lòpez et al., 2017; Moro Visconti, 2019; Murray, 2020; Newman, 2010; Park & Kim, 2022; Pesce, 2021; Reuven et al., 2018; Spagno-letti et al., 2015; Tiwana et al., 2010; Tsekeris, 2017; Van Steen, 2010; Wang & Zhou, 2017; Williams & Smith, 2004) is the study of graphs as a representation of either symmetric or asymmetric relations between discrete objects. Patients, for instance, are a key albeit under-investigated stakeholder and smart technologies applied to public healthcare represent a trendy innovation that reshapes the value-driving metaverse proposition.

The World Wide Web is a network whose nodes are documents, and the links are the uniform resource locators (URLs) that allow to "surf" with a click from one web document to the other (Barabási, 2016). This is consistent with the metaverse scale-up.

A scale-free network is a decentralized network whose degree distribution follows a power law and is characterized by the presence of large hubs. Decentralization is consistent with the web, blockchains, and the metaverse. In other words, the metaverse is a "democratic" network characterized by the absence of dominating (hub) nodes, and consistent with blockchain-driven decentralized finance (De.Fi.).

A scale-free network looks like the air-traffic network, whose nodes are airports and links are the direct flights between them. Most airports are tiny, with only a few flights. Yet, we have a few very large airports, like Chicago or Los Angeles, that act as major hubs, connecting many smaller airports.

Once hubs are present, they change the way we navigate the network. For example, if we travel from Boston to Los Angeles by car, we must drive through many cities. On the airplane network, however, we can reach most destinations via a single hub, like Chicago (Barabási, 2016).

Scale-free networks have a very heterogeneous distribution of degrees, and their dynamical behavior is dominated by the hub nodes having a degree order of magnitude larger than the average.

The topology of the metaverse influences its dynamics, workings, and wealth distribution. According to Radoff (2021), the metaverse, consistently with the Internet, is more like a scale-free network than a "hub and spoke" architecture, where every network node connects to a central authority that is responsible for controlling access and managing any of the exchanges.

In scale-free networks (e.g., the Internet, open-source software, smart contract blockchains, etc.), the central node acts more like a facilitator than an authority, and where nodes are then free to connect.

The Barabási and Albert (2002) model is an algorithm for generating random scale-free networks using a preferential attachment mechanism. Several natural and human-made systems, including the Internet, the world wide web, citation networks, and some social networks are thought to be approximately scale-free and certainly contain few nodes (called hubs) with an unusually high degree as compared to the other nodes of the network. The Barabási & Albert model tries to explain the existence of such nodes in real networks.

18.3   Scalability and the Network Effect

Scalability (https://hpc-wiki.info/hpc/Scaling_tutorial) indicates the ability of a process, network, or system to handle a growing amount of work. Scalability fosters economic marginality, especially in intangible-driven businesses—such as the Internet or the metaverse—where variable costs are typically negligible. Massive volumes may offset low margins, producing economic gains. Digitalization is defined as the concept of "going paperless", the technical process of transforming analog information or physical products into digital form. Digital scalability operates in a web context, where networked agents interact to generate co-created value, as shown in Chapter 3.

Economic and financial margins (EBITDA, etc.) that represent a primary parameter for valuation (as shown in Chapter 2) are boosted by cost savings and scalable increases in expected revenues. Digitalized intangibles synergistically interact through networked platforms that reshape traditional supply chains. Link (edge) overlaps and replica nodes foster these synergies.

Hyoung et al. (2020) summarize the three main Laws of Network Effect that are intrinsically consistent with the scalability properties:

(a) Sarnoff's Law: David Sarnoff led the Radio Corporation of America (which created NBC) from 1919 until 1970. It was one of the largest networks in the world during those years. Sarnoff observed that the value of his network seemed to increase in direct proportion to its size—proportional to N, where N is the total number of users on the network. Sarnoff's description of network value ended up being an underestimate for SNS types of networks, although it was an accurate description of broadcast networks with a few central nodes broadcasting to many marginal nodes (a radio or television audience).

(b) Metcalfe's Law: Metcalfe's Law states that the value of a communications network grows in proportion to the square of the number of users on the network (N^2, where N is the total number of users on the network). The formulation of this concept is attributed to Robert Metcalfe, one of the inventors of the Ethernet standard. Metcalfe's Law seems to hold because the number of links between nodes on a network increase mathematically at a rate of N^2, where N is the number of nodes. Although originally formulated to describe communication networks like the ethernet, faxing, or phones, with the arrival of the Internet, it has evolved to describe SNSs as well.

(c) Reed's Law: it was published by Reed (2001). While Reed acknowledged that "many kinds of value grow proportionally to network size" and that some grow as a proportion to the square of network size, he suggested that "group-forming networks" that allow for the formation of clusters (as described above) scale value even faster than other networks. Group-forming networks, according to Reed, increase value at a rate of $2N$, where N is the total number of nodes on the network. Reed suggested the formula of $2N$ instead of N^2 because the number of possible groups within a network that "supports easy group communication" is much higher than 1 so that the total number of connections in the network (the network density) is not just a function of the total number of nodes (N). It is a function of the total number of nodes plus the total number of possible sub-groupings or clusters, which scales at a much faster rate with the addition of more users to the network. Since most online networks allow for the formation of clusters, they will likely behave at least somewhat as Reed's Law suggests and grow in value at a much faster rate than either Metcalfe's Law or Sarnoff's Law suggests.

Metcalfe's Law, illustrated in Chapter 3, proposes that the value of a network increases geometrically with every device that's added. It explains why the telephone network and the Internet are so valuable and continue to increase in value.

Reed's Law posits that Metcalfe's Law underestimates the value of a network, especially those in which it is easy to form subgroups.

Table 18.1 (already analyzed in Chapter 3) synthesizes the main properties of some of the most known network laws. Many of these laws are empirical, with a weak scientific background and controversial evidence. Technological evolution is intrinsically difficult to forecast and so differs from its expected patterns. Most of the scalability laws recalled in the following table may so look outdated or imprecise. They are, however, useful since they recall some basic principles and retain an orientation predictive power, giving a rough idea of how scalability patterns may evolve. A common denominator is represented by statistical "power laws" (according to which one quantity varies as a power of another) that are intrinsically consistent with the scalability patterns.

Here are a few examples of Reed's Law in action:

- Social Media of all kinds (Facebook, TikTok, etc.) are so valuable because everyone is the center of their subgroups, and everyone can easily add content.
- Messaging applications like Discord allow you to easily form your groups that serve as conversation hubs for games and projects.
- Open-Source software is incredibly powerful because projects can form and evolve rapidly, by opening participation from anyone who wants to contribute—building upon contributions from completely unrelated projects.
- Wikipedia became so important because content can be managed and evolved by the sphere of people who care most about certain topics. The collective value of Wikipedia increases as people maintain more content, which in turn expands the audience, resulting in people wanting to add more content to it.
- Online games with social features (multiplayer games, games featuring esports) are so sticky because each one acts as a type of social network where you join up with other people, participate in activities, and form friendships and rivalries.

Reed's Law is often mentioned when explaining the competitive dynamics of Internet platforms. As the law states that a network becomes more valuable when people can easily form subgroups to collaborate, while this value increases exponentially with the number of connections, a business platform that reaches enough members can generate network effects that dominate the overall economics of the system.

Other analysts of network value functions, including Odlyzko and Tilly (2005), have argued that both Reed's Law and Metcalfe's Law overstate network value because they fail to account for the restrictive impact of human cognitive limits on network formation.

Table 18.1 Network Scalability laws

Scalability law	Formula	Features/properties
Sarnoff's law	Network value $= n$	The value of a network seemed to increase in direct proportion to the size of the network—proportional to N, where N is the total number of users on the network
Metcalfe's law	Network value $= n^2$	Network value increases exponentially with an increasing number of devices on the network
Reed's law	Network value $= 2^n$	Network value increases even more than Metcalfe's as subgroups (social networks; messaging apps, etc.) become easier to form. Reed's law is consistent with multilayer network extensions
Moore's law[2]	$n_0 = n_0 2(y_i - y_0)/T_2$, where $n_0 n_0$ is the number of transistors in some reference year, $y_0 y_0$, and $T_2 = 2T_2 = 2$ is the number of years taken to double this number	A doubling of real computing power has occurred every 2.3 years, on average since the birth of modern computing. Moore's Law is one of several enabling technological trends for Metaverse development. Rather than a law of physics, it is an empirical relationship linked to gains from experience in production

(continued)

Table 18.1 (continued)

Scalability law	Formula	Features/properties
Henderson law		Henderson's Law also known as a variant of the "Power-law" is a mathematical formula for calculating experience curves and their economic impact. It was first proposed by Bruce Henderson in 1968 while working for the Boston Consulting Group to generalize unit costs of production over time and by volume
Wright's law	$C_n = C_1 n^{-a}$ where: C_1 is the cost of the first unit of production C_n is the cost of the n-th unit of production n is the cumulative volume of production a is the elasticity of cost regarding output	Wright found that every time total aircraft production doubled, the required labor time for a new aircraft fell by 20%. This has become known as "Wright's law". Studies in other industries have yielded different percentage values (ranging from only a couple of percent up to 30%), but in most cases, the value in each industry was a constant percentage and did not vary at different scales of operation. The learning curve model posits that for each doubling of the total quantity of items produced, costs decrease by a fixed proportion. Generally, the production of any good or service shows the learning curve or experience curve effect. Each time cumulative volume doubles, value-added costs (including administration, marketing, distribution, and manufacturing) fall by a constant percentage
Kryder's law		Storage capacity growth. Kryder's Law is the assumption that magnetic disk drive density, also known as areal density, will double every thirteen months. Kryder's Law implies that as areal density improves, storage will become cheaper

Scalability law	Formula	Features/properties
Butters' law		Butters' law says that the amount of data coming out of an optical fiber is doubling every nine months. Thus, the cost of transmitting a bit over an optical network decrease by half every nine months
Nielsen's law		Wired bandwidth growth
Gilder's law		the total bandwidth of communication systems triples every twelve months
Cooper's law		Wireless bandwidth growth. The number of wireless signals that can simultaneously be transmitted without interfering with each other has been doubling approximately every 30 months since the early 1900s. This steady rise of wireless capabilities also has allowed access and distribution of news, entertainment, advertising, and other information to become truly mobile
Poor's law		Network address density growth
Beckström's law		The value of a network equals the net value added to each user's transactions conducted through that network, summed over all users. This model values the network by looking from the edge of the network at all of the transactions conducted and the value added to each. It states that one way to contemplate the value the network adds to each transaction is to imagine the network being shut off and what the additional transaction costs or loss would be
Radoff's law	[qualitative proposition]	The degree to which a network facilitates interconnections determines the extent of its emergent creativity, innovation, and wealth
Metaverse extension		3D dimension, increased networking, technological upgrade, etc. improve scalability and so value

18.4   MULTILAYER NETWORKS

Multilayer networks are networks with multiple kinds of relations with multiplex or multidimensional configurations (Bianconi, 2018; Lee et al., 2015). In a multiplex network, the same set of nodes is connected via more than one type of link, enhancing scalability.

The world is more complex than conventional economic models traditionally assume. Many real-world complex systems are accordingly best modeled by multiplex (multidimensional) networks of interacting layers (Lee et al., 2015). These interconnected systems are very sophisticated and may explain better the applications in the field of social network analysis, economics, operations management, finance, etc., being consistent with corporate governance concerns.

Multilayer networks are an extension of the traditional networks and are fully consistent with the framing and research aim of this Chapter. Multilayer networks are intrinsically fit for leveraging the scalability features already examined, since they host bridging (replica) nodes, digital networks, or firms that are simultaneously present in several layers. These properties have deep, albeit non-investigated, governance consequences for all the stakeholders involved in the supply & value chains.

Complex multidimensional networks host multiple kinds of relations (multiplex, multilayer, multi-level, multi-relational, interconnected, interdependent, etc.), and may yield valuable insight into many interdisciplinary fields. These networks of networks may affect social networks that involve different types of connections, networks of airports connected by different air carriers, multiple infrastructures of a country that are mutually connected, etc.

Nodes that simultaneously belong to different layers (networks) can be represented mathematically by adjacency tensors with inter-layer edges that connect each network to the other. These links enhance the overall value of the network of networks, boosting Metcalfe's formulation.

Whereas the sophisticated mathematics that explains these relations (see Bianconi, 2018) goes far beyond this preliminary Chapter, some economic implications may be worth considering.

In most real-world systems an individual network is one component within a much larger complex multi-level network (is part of a network of networks). Most real-world network systems continuously interact with other networks (Kenett & Havlin, 2015). This may well be the case in interacting metaverses.

There is a wide range of systems in the real world where components cannot function independently so these components interact with others through different channels of connectivity and dependencies. Complex Networks theory is, in fact, the formal tool for describing and analyzing fields as disparate as sociology (social networks, acquaintances, or collaborations between individuals), biology (metabolic and protein networks, neural networks), or technology (phone call networks, computers in telecommunication networks) (Boccaletti et al., 2014).

The inter-layer edges (links) between the different nodes go beyond every single layer and connect two (or more) adjacent layers, resulting in a network of networks with multiple subsystems and connectivity properties. If the links between the nodes increase (both in the same layer and thanks to an inter-layer connection), there is a corresponding value growth of the systemic network of networks that might be estimated with Metcalfe's law. Figure 18.3 shows a simplified example of how multilayer networks interact.

Figure 18.3 shows at first sight that inter-network bridging edges (that link node in country A with country B, product 1, and product 2) add value to the whole network ecosystem. This incremental value may be tentatively estimated (with a differential without/with approach) by comparing unrelated networks with linked ones. An economic interpretation of multiplex networks is—to the author's best knowledge—still

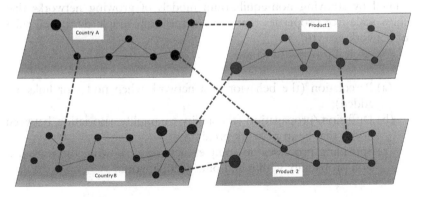

Fig. 18.3 Multilayer networks

underexplored and may be generalized (including further interacting layers in a dynamic ecosystem), giving an innovative explanation of the interactions between e-supply and e-value chains. As anticipated, digital platforms may once again act as the virtual linking edge among the networks. Digitalization is a powerful catalyzer of interconnectivity, adding value to the whole ecosystem, here represented by adjacent metaverses. Interconnectivity could, once again, be estimated using a with-or-without approach (described by IVS 210 and analyzed in Chapter 2), if we compare interconnected versus disconnected layers, showing the added (incremental) value of the former.

A multilayer network—of which multiplex and interdependent networks are peculiar cases—is a network made up of multiple layers, each of which represents a given operation mode, social circle, or temporal instance.

In a multiplex network, each type of interaction between the nodes is described by a single layer network and the different layers of networks describe the different modes of interaction.

Multilayer networks show connectivity links between the nodes of each layer that bring interdependency links.

A key feature of any network is represented by its dynamic properties: a network is hardly ever static, and this is never the case on the Internet-metaverse dimension. Many networks expand and grow by increasing their number of nodes and links over time, following dynamic rules. Examples include the Internet and social online networks this evidence is described by non-equilibrium dynamics important information can be gained by studying non-equilibrium models of growing networks that show scale-free properties that can emerge from simple dynamical rules of network growth.

Dynamical processes include:

(a) Percolation (the behavior of a network when nodes or links are added);
(b) Diffusion/propagation (the ability to amplify association between nodes that lie in network proximity);
(c) Spreading processes on complex networks, showing the transmission probability within and outside a network.

The interplay between the "random versus orderly" structure and the dynamics of multilayer networks contributes to explaining their essential features.

Relevant information from multilayer network data sets cannot be found by considering networks in isolation. Connectedness allows for the possibility of diffusing information and hyper-navigating the network. A further characteristic is represented by communicability—the number of paths that connect the node to the rest of the nodes within the network. Once again, connectedness, navigability, and communicability add value.

Precious informative sets are represented by big data that are gathered in cloud databases. The digital nature of data softens interoperability concerns, easing information dissemination and exploitation, and opening the door to much-wanted common standards.

This contributes to explaining why interconnected (multilayer) networks are worth more than isolated networks. The implications for metaverse networks that are ontologically connected are evident, albeit hardly investigated.

A further feature is represented by navigability—the possibility of exploring large parts of the network by following its paths through connectedness. This concept can be associated with supply chains and shows which are the iterative patterns from the real world to the metaverse, passing through the Internet.

18.5 SLIDING DOORS: NETWORK-BRIDGING MULTI-SIDED PLATFORMS

Multilayer networks are consistent with multi-sided platforms—a service or product that connects two or more participant groups, playing a kind of intermediation role. Digital platforms, especially if multi-sided, are an access facilitator to both the web and the metaverse, thanks to their network effects and their virtual/digital nature. Platforms can be IoT-driven (Degrande et al., 2018), and they can incorporate big data or other digitized information, typically stored in cloud, processed with artificial intelligence and consisting of big data validated, if necessary, by blockchains.

The multi-sided platform is a bridging node between two counterparts that are put in contact through the intermediating platform to which each part is affiliated. The platform earns a commission from its mediation or,

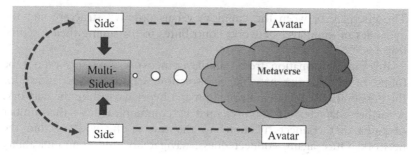

Fig. 18.4 Multi-sided platforms bridging to the metaverse

sometimes, a subscription. The platform may be extended to the metaverse, so representing a portal to this new ecosystem, as exemplified in Fig. 18.4.

The multi-sided platform business model is adopted by some of the most valuable startups in the world, such as PayPal, Uber, Alibaba, eBay, YouTube, and Facebook/Meta (Pereira, 2021).

To be useful for all the participant groups and, therefore, a profitable business, the multi-sided platforms must attract users. The more users, the more valuable the business (https://businessmodelanalyst.com/multisided-platform-business-model/), following a scalable model.

18.6   From the Internet to the Metaverse

The metaverse can be interpreted as a collection of different virtual worlds built on the blockchain by FANGAM firms (an outdated acronym indicating Facebook/Meta, Amazon, Netflix, Google/Alphabet, and Microsoft) or other BigTechs. Segmentation matters and is profitable, at least in the short/medium term since it brings tailor-made ecosystems that reproduce exclusive environments. There is a diverse range of online networks, and dedicated environments allow for better experiences that produce greater engagement.

The metaverse building features are illustrated in Fig. 18.5.

There is no one single technology underpinning the metaverse, as it relies on several complementary devices and IT instruments (pooled intangibles, mastered by digitalization).

Broadly, the technologies that will make it up will include blockchain, cryptocurrencies, virtual and augmented reality, artificial intelligence (a

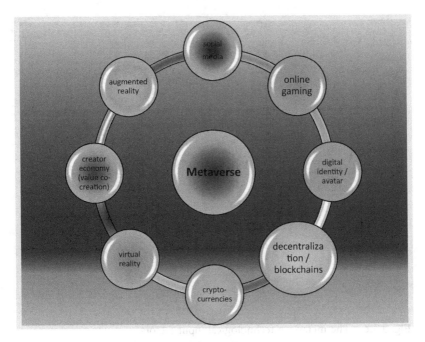

Fig. 18.5 The metaverse building features

key to unlock the metaverse), brain-computer interfaces, and the Internet of Things. Blockchain cryptocurrencies are consistent with Decentralized Finance (De.Fi.). De.Fi. disintermediates the payment system and is driven by FinTechs.

Blockchain technology provides a decentralized and transparent solution for digital proof of ownership, governance, accessibility, digital collectability, transfer of value, and interoperability among complementary databases. Cryptocurrencies enable users to transfer value while they work and socialize in the 3D digital world.

Complex and interdependent technologies are the core constituents of the metaverse ecosystems, as shown in Fig. 18.6.

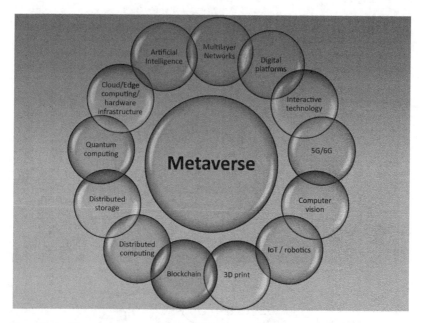

Fig. 18.6 The metaverse technological input factors

18.7   SYNCHRONIZING THE PHYSICAL AND VIRTUAL: THE AVATAR BRIDGING NODE

In computing, an avatar is a graphical representation of a user or the user's character or persona. It may take either a two-dimensional form as an icon in Internet forums and other online communities (where it is also known as a profile picture) or a three-dimensional form, as in games or virtual worlds. Another use of the avatar has emerged with the widespread use of social media platforms. There is a practice in social media sites: uploading avatars in place of the real profile image. In network science, the avatar (digital twin) is a bridging node between the physical world (the original archetype) and its 3D virtual dimension, connecting adjacent layers (again, the physical world, and the metaverse, passing through the Web).

Avatars—a sort of virtual second life—can so be considered the main bridging node connecting the real world to the metaverse (through the web), as shown in Fig. 18.7.

Fig. 18.7 The avatar value chain

Even if avatars are traditionally linked to "light" applications (e.g., video games or social entertainment), they are increasingly used in more significant practices. For instance, digital twins are used in telemedicine (to show up the 3D image of a patient in front of a doctor).

A digital twin is a digital representation of real-world entities—an object, system, or process—that is synchronized with the real world. With sensors that relay information and two-way Internet of Things (IoT) object connections, this technology can synchronize the digital environment with the physical world and vice versa. Any change in the material world is reflected in the digital representation (the twin) and feedback gets sent in the other direction. These intrinsic properties make digital twins one of the fundamental building blocks of the metaverse. In technical training programs, technicians can already use applications to operate 3D representations of complex systems (https://hellofuture.orange.com/en/journey-through-the-metaverse-digital-twins-are-synchronizing-the-physical-and-virtual).

Even if the original node in the real world (represented by a physical person) is different from Her digital avatar, they may tentatively be considered, as a necessary simplification in this study, substantially coincident.

Thanks to augmented (and virtual) reality, an avatar can be identified, copied, measured, increasing Her value, if compared to the original.

According to Cozzo et al. (2016) "In Multiplex Networks a set of agents might interact in different ways, i.e., through different means. Since a subset of agents is present at the same time in different networks of interactions (layers), these layers become interconnected". These agents are represented, in our case, by bridging avatars and other players (digital platforms, etc.).

18.8   A Holistic Ecosystem: From Physical Reality to the Internet and the Metaverse

The metaverse and the physical world interact in both directions, generating value-enhancing synergies.

According to Wang et al. (2022) "MetaEnterprises and MetaCities can be regarded as the mapping of real enterprises and cities in the virtual cyberspace. They are virtual enterprises and cities running parallel to real enterprises and cities, which can realize the description of real enterprises and cities. Corresponding to the human, material, organizations, scenarios, and other elements in real enterprises and cities, there are various virtual elements such as virtual humans, virtual objects, virtual organizations, and virtual scenarios in MetaEnterprises and MetaCities. These virtual elements in MetaEnterprises and MetaCities can be used to analyze and evaluate the decision-making scenarios with a computational experiments approach to realize the prediction of real enterprises and cities. Through the interaction and feedback between MetaEnterprises/MetaCities and real enterprises/cities, we can realize the prescription of decision-making in real enterprises and cities, to effectively improve the efficiency and effect of various decisions in real enterprises and cities".

The three-step pattern from the physical reality to the metaverse can be illustrated in Fig. 18.8. which represents an upgrade of Fig. 18.1.

Any consideration about the potential market value of the metaverse would be considered science fiction since the underlying concept is uneasy to define and impossible to measure.

An estimate of the value of the metaverse is, however, important because investors need market traction to drive their efforts, envisaging potential returns out of their expenditures.

The metaverses are spaces where you can not only admire places, monuments, and works of art but also conclude business. The metaverses represent worlds in which commercial exchanges are becoming increasingly important together with the market value of the companies that produce supporting technology. According to a Bloomberg Intelligence

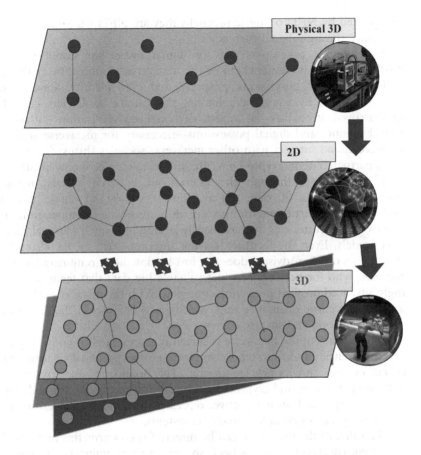

Fig. 18.8 From physical reality to the internet and the metaverse

report, the market value of companies operating in metaverses is expected to reach $ 800 billion by the middle of this decade and $ 2.5 trillion by 2030.

Inside the metaverse, on the other hand, commercial exchanges take place on two floors. On the one hand, there is the presence of shops that act as a showcase and traditional e-commerce, while allowing a more immersive experience in which the customer chooses a product that exists in the real world and pays for it with fiat currency. At the same time, in the metaverse, there are properties, goods, and other values that are represented by NFTs or, more precisely, they are NFTs whose exchanges take place through digital currencies.

Non-fungible tokens—records of digital ownership stored in the blockchain—will be the linchpin of the metaverse economy, by enabling authentication of possessions, property, and even identity. Since each NFT is secured by a cryptographic key that cannot be deleted, copied, or destroyed, it enables the robust, decentralized verification—of one's virtual identity and digital possessions—necessary for metaverse society to succeed and interact with other metaverse societies (https://www.ft.com/partnercontent/crypto-com/nfts-the-metaverse-economy.html).

The metaverse, through the interactions between avatars, makes possible strategies of value co-creation in which the single virtual nodes actively participate in this creation, receiving remuneration in tokens/cryptocurrencies that are usually lacking in many traditional business models. Even the feedback on the Internet (such as, for example, the reviews on TripAdvisor) does not involve any direct remuneration for the user, who for her part provides valuable big data that feeds increasingly advanced profiled marketing strategies. With the metaverse, there is a customer-centric qualitative leap, which places the user at the center of value co-creation and sharing of new value.

The currency of the metaverse is currently represented by controversial cryptocurrencies, linked to blockchain technologies potentially harbingers of tax evasion and money laundering. The boundaries and exchanges between fiat money and cryptocurrencies are still confused, although full convertibility could, in perspective, represent an important milestone in the convergence of complementary ecosystems.

The value of the metaverse can be direct, if it concerns this integrated ecosystem (declined, as it has been shown, in many interrelated dimensions), or transferred to the real world and the Internet, which expands the range of goods and services exchanged, also in terms of usability, generating a differential/incremental surplus value.

The new paradigms of value co-creation rely, in many cases, on social networks and behavioral models inspired by the sharing economy, facilitated by the plasticity and resilience of the digital and virtual world.

The growing sensitivity toward development paths inspired by sustainability and ESG metrics must be confronted, first, with the energy-intensive trends of blockchains.

The pioneering investments in the metaverse are based on prospects of economic returns in the medium–long term, which in turn depend on the revenue model incorporated in the business models and disruptive strategies, with a highly innovative and discontinuous scope. These investments are made above all by Big Tech (starting with FAANG—Facebook, Amazon, Apple, Netflix, and Google), intent on creating new lifestyles and entertainment, in the hope that they will become market standards, guaranteeing promoters the role of first movers and standard settlers, from which oligopolistic rents can derive (where barriers to entry are created for new competitors).

In the logic of the metaverse (a reality that is still predominantly conceptual, with no well-defined contents), the experiential experience and the contents shared between the virtual players will assume preponderant content in the co-creation of shared value. In perspective, the content will be able to count more than the technological infrastructure, destined to become a commodity (this trend is already visible in the world of digital media).

18.9 The Metaverse Monetization

Metaverse business models fuel value creation and monetization strategies, based on subscriptions (membership/affiliation fixed/transaction fees), advertising (Jooyoung, 2021), purchase of content, services, or products, intermediation of big data, etc. Third-party applications improve the supply of products and services, adding value to the ecosystem. Customer segmentation shapes the perimeter of each metaverse ecosystem. The (social) network effect improves customer relationships. Platform hubs catalyze interactions between users, advertisers, and content developers. Monetization is an essential passage before economic appraisal (no money, no value), and it shows which are the economic/financial parameters used in the evaluation process (e.g., EBITDA, EBIT, pre-tax profit, FCFF/operating profit, FCFE/net profit, DCF, Enterprise and Equity Value, etc.).

The target of the metaverse, similarly to what happens in any new market, is to meet and create consumer demand with innovative products and services. Market-based products and services respond to signals from the customers and create new opportunities, stimulating the demand. The link with the "brick & mortar" reality, consistently with the research

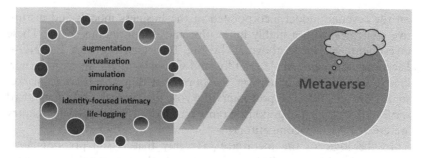

Fig. 18.9 From the physical reality to the metaverse

thread of this study, makes this "reality extension" likelier and, possibly, more useful, improving the monetization process (Fig. 18.9).

A lifelog is a personal record of one's daily life in a varying amount of detail, for a variety of purposes.

Value creation derives not only from additional revenues (consistent with the creation of new markets in the virtual world, products, and services) but also from cost savings deriving from the metaverse (e.g., savings with a 3D medical visit, if compared to a "physical" one).

Monetization, as anticipated, normally takes place with cryptocurrencies or stablecoins—that are represented by cryptocurrencies where the price is designed to be pegged to a cryptocurrency, fiat money, or exchange-traded commodities (such as precious metals or industrial metals). This is an important limit to the fungibility of the metaverse and may be softened with full convertibility between cryptocurrencies and fiat money and/or commodities.

A further element of valuation is represented by the customer acquisition cost (CAC) which describes how much a firm must spend to get a new customer, exploiting web analytics, powered by the metaverse, artificial intelligence, and other innovative technologies. Consistently with CAC, the customer lifetime value (CLV) represents the amount earned from each customer during the customer's "lifetime", and considering the:

- Average customer life span—how long the individual remains a customer.
- Rate of customer retention: The percentage of customers who buy again.
- Profit margin per customer: Expressed as a percentage, this may consider CAC as well as other expenditures such as the overall cost of goods sold, which includes production and marketing costs, and how much it costs to run the company.
- The average amount each person spends over a lifetime as a customer—add up what each customer spends over their lifetime and divide it by the number of customers.
- Average gross margin per customer.

A summary of the value propositions deriving from the innovative business model is shown in Table 18.2.

Consistently with the methodology of this study, the potential value of each metaverse ecosystem may be tentatively appraised with at least two complementary approaches that are based on the mentioned monetization strategies:

1. With-and-without approach (comparing a hypothetical value with or without the metaverse, so showing its incremental/differential contribution in value creation);
2. Mathematical modeling consistent with multilayer networks;
3. Network effect laws.

The with-and-without methodology is traditionally used in the evaluation of intangibles (as shown in Chapter 2) and is so consistent with the intrinsic features of the metaverse. For instance, the International Valuation Standard (IVS) 210 considers this method within the income approach methods (§ 60.5), then shows its application criteria:

Table 18.2 The metaverse: business models and value creation

Business model/application	Value leverage, revenue model, and monetization strategies
e-commerce platform/ online shopping	Through the proposed new intermediary platform, consumers can look and feel the brand and experience the functions of the product in the virtual world, thereby enhancing the purchasing experience. In addition, sellers can create innovative content through the metaverse and design a concept space to secure brand awareness and loyal customers (Jeong et al., 2022). Virtual commerce applies immersive technology such as augmented reality and virtual reality into e-commerce to shift consumer perception from 2D product catalogs to 3D immersive virtual spaces (Shen et al., 2021)
Social media	People with homophily and similar digital affiliation interact in the metaverse, expanding their traditional virtual links
Digital business assets	Enabling interaction, play, debate, study, and business activities provide enhanced immersive experiences and customer engagement
Reality simulation	The virtual world can simulate the physical environment with Brain-Computer Interface and other tools. Simulations have practical applications in medicine, job training, prototypes, etc
3D clothing	With a 3D scanner, it is possible to fit a 3D virtual version of the cloth on the 3D virtual version. Presentation of the product in the metaverse with offline delivery to the customer. Sale of virtual products (e.g., the "Gucci Garden Experience" event on the Roblox platform for all)

Business model/application	Value leverage, revenue model, and monetization strategies
Metaverse platforms	Sale of cryptocurrency that can be spent on the platform, advertising agreements, license agreements, and royalties on the sales of products on the platform. Retention of customers to minimize churn rate is a key marketing strategy. Multi-sided platforms are upgraded in the metaverse, reducing search and transaction costs, and improving audience and participation
Content creators/developers	Metaverse developers create comprehensively engaging and immersive worlds (interactive games, platforms, or experiences, allowing storytelling without boundaries), contributing to value creation. Users can deepen and extend social interactions digitally through dedicated communities. Revenues include Peer-to-peer; developers (content creators) directly earn revenue from sales. Users/gamers can earn through play or participation in platform governance. Royalties emerge on secondary trades of NFTs to creators
Real Estate/land/digital parcel rentals	Sale of "finished" properties and both virtual plots of land. The user, in turn, can monetize the investment through renting and other forms of management. Sale of professional services (architecture, design, etc.) necessary or useful for the construction of the virtual property. Sale of waste materials following the demolition of virtual properties. A complimentary business is represented by Digital parcel rentals. All metaverse parcels are contiguous to others at a fixed location—within a finite geographical boundary (adjacency of land). This creates a scarcity effect, due to the limited amount of property supply, which enables property value to fall or rise, following universal laws of supply and demand

(continued)

Table 18.2 (continued)

Business model/application	Value leverage, revenue model, and monetization strategies
Sale of NFT artworks	Direct or auction-based sale of unique "computer codes" linked to digital-only works or digital representations of physical works with or without transfer of the relative copyright. NFT unlock the exploitation of new digital economy products (e.g., digital art), bringing marketability to non-exploited and illiquid assets. NFTs enable the growth of societies within immersive virtual worlds. NFT allow for "tokenization" of virtual assets
(Other) digital assets/hyper-tokenization	Digital assets can be exchanged through the metaverse and transferred through portability. Hyper-tokenization through NFTs
Cryptovoxel (Vox)	Cryptovoxels is a virtual world and metaverse, powered by the Ethereum blockchain. Players can buy land and build stores and art galleries. Editing tools, avatars, and text chat are built-in
Digital/profiled advertising	Sale of experiential marketing services in which the customer can experiment with a product and submit indications for its further development
Gaming/gambling	Gaming empowers individuals and communities to interact, create content and digital products, and then social interaction through play, events, entertainment, education, and commercial engagement. Sale of the cryptocurrency needed to purchase the characters and accessories to participate in the game. Play-to-earn revenue model that awards rewards to users based on their participation in the game. These rewards are in cryptocurrency that users reinvest in the game itself, guaranteeing liquidity to the system. Subscription revenues from affiliated players. Sale of game characters in the form of NFT

Business model/application	Value leverage, revenue model, and monetization strategies
Online KTV (karaoke)	People can interact online and virtually meet for KTV in the metaverse
Crypto/digital wallets	Main payment infrastructure, beyond traditional payments (e.g., credit/debit cards). A digital wallet, also known as an e-wallet, is an electronic device, online service, or software program that allows one party to make electronic transactions with another party bartering digital currency units for goods and services
Immersive infotainment experiences	Immersion is the experience where people are so focused on the designed environment that they forget about reality. The business consists of the sale of the devices necessary to take advantage of the gaming experience or participation in virtual events (3D viewers, headphones, gloves, etc.)
Augmented data analytics	Big data collection, cloud storage, and exploitation can be enhanced by the metaverse
The bridge between digital and physical merchandise	NFT owners receive physical products that match their NFTs. Any commodity or artifact that can be virtualized (e.g., is not consumed, like fossil fuels, food, water, education, healthcare, etc.) can be tokenized in current and near-future virtual realms, which could become metaverses
Decentralized autonomous organization (DAO)—Realistic workspaces	Each company can work in its own space inside the Metaverse, making it a decentralization concept. Virtual offices allow users to engage in a 3D space that mimics a real office environment
Decentralized jobs/workplaces	Workers in any country, for example, may be able to get jobs "abroad" (in the metaverse) without having to emigrate. Videoconference (e.g., Teams) avatars are in the pipeline

(continued)

Table 18.2 (continued)

Business model/application	Value leverage, revenue model, and monetization strategies
Decentralized Finance (De.Fi.)	Emerging financial technology based on secure distributed ledgers similar to those used by cryptocurrencies. The system removes the control banks and institutions have on money, financial products, and financial services. Centralized decentralized finance (CeDeFi) represents the offering of decentralized financial products and services, such as peer-to-peer lending, by centralized financial companies, e.g., exchanges or banks. Similarly, centralized decentralized anything (CeDeX) represents the offering of any type of decentralized products and services, for example, digital collectible trading applications, by centralized companies, e.g., issuers of digital collectibles and NFTs
Education	The metaverse can provide a more intense and immersive way to take field trips anywhere in the world and anywhere in history
Healthcare 4.0	The Health Metaverse framework mainly focuses on multimodal medical information standards, medical and social data fusion, telemedicine and online health management, and medical artificial intelligence. It also provides invaluable innovative drive-in medical education, surgical procedures, and connection between service providers and patients (Chen & Zhang, 2022). Virtual reality (VR) is a potentially significant component of the health 4.0 vision (Liu et al., 2022)

Business model/application	Value leverage, revenue model, and monetization strategies
Virtual world navigation	
Online agent	The avatar becomes an online agent, becoming a traveling avatar (travatar)—capable of traveling between different but interoperable 3D virtual spaces
Mirror world	A literal representation of the real world in digital form. It attempts to map (or mirror) real-world structures, like geography, or the stock market, in 2D or 3D form. GIS systems are often 2D mirror worlds. Google Earth is an example of a 3D mirror world. (Def: Avi Bar-Ze'ev)

With-And-Without Method

60.22. The with-and-without method indicates the value of an intangible asset by comparing two scenarios: one in which the business uses the subject intangible asset and one in which the business does not use the subject intangible asset (but all other factors are kept constant).

60.23. The comparison of the two scenarios can be done in two ways:

(a) calculating the value of the business under each scenario with the difference in the business values being the value of the subject intangible asset, and

(b) calculating, for each future period, the difference between the profits in the two scenarios. The present value of those amounts is then used to reach the value of the subject intangible asset.

60.24. In theory, either method should reach a similar value for the intangible asset provided the valuer considers not only the impact on the entity's profit, but additional factors such as differences between the two scenarios in working

(a) capital needs and capital expenditures.

60.25. The with-and-without method is frequently used in the valuation of non-competition agreements but may be appropriate in the valuation of other intangible assets in certain circumstances.

60.26. The key steps in applying the with-and-without method are to:

(a) prepare projections of revenue, expenses, capital expenditures, and working capital needs for the business assuming the use of all of the assets of the business including the subject intangible asset. These are the cash flows in the "with" scenario,

(b) use an appropriate discount rate to present value of the future cash flows in the "with" scenario, and/or calculate the value of the business in the "with" scenario,

(c) prepare projections of revenue, expenses, capital expenditures, and working capital needs for the business assuming the use of all of the assets of the business except the subject intangible asset. These are the cash flows in the "without" scenario,

(d) use an appropriate discount rate for the business, present value of the future cash flows in the "with" scenario, and/or calculate the value of the business in the "with" scenario,

(e) deduct the present value of cash flows or the value of the business in the "without" scenario from the present value of cash flows or value of the business in the "with" scenario, and

(f) if appropriate for the purpose of the valuation (see pars. 110.1–110.4), calculate and add the TAB for the subject intangible asset.

60.27. As an additional step, the difference between the two scenarios may need to be probability-weighted. For example, when valuing a non-competition agreement, the individual or business subject to the agreement may choose

not to compete, even if the agreement were not in place.

60.28. The differences in value between the two scenarios should be reflected solely in the cash flow projections rather than by using different discount rates in the two scenarios.

The mathematical modeling that interprets the metaverse ecosystem with multilayer network analysis will be examined in paragraph 10. The incremental (marginal) value of an added network, represented in this case by a metaverse ecosystem, can be economically appraised by the with-and-without approach, and mathematically evaluated using (multilayer) network theory. The Network Effect Laws illustrated in Sect. 18.3 are complementary to these approaches, as shown in Fig. 18.10.

To the author's best knowledge, this joint approach has never been used in network valuation.

Every network can be expressed mathematically in the form of an adjacency matrix. In these matrices, the rows and columns are assigned to the nodes in the network and the presence of an edge is symbolized by a numerical value.

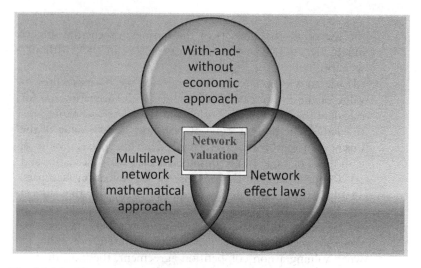

Fig. 18.10   Network valuation approaches

The matrix representation is fully consistent with:

(a) The with-and-without approach (each "with" is represented by the introduction of a new node and edging link; "without" represents node absence, deletion, or isolation);
(b) Network effect laws that are enhanced by new nodes and edges;
(c) Multilayer networks, where interconnections are mapped with adjacency matrices.

The with-and-without approach is also consistent with the differential analysis (confrontation) between networks without and then with inter-links (that depend on avatars or other linking nodes or edges). Digital links are intrinsically flexible and favor immediate linking through the web or the metaverse.

18.10   Value Co-Creation and Economic Marginality

The valuation approaches indicated above are fully consistent with value co-creation patterns (Akaka et al., 2012; Beirão, et al., 2017; Blaschke et al., 2019; Ceccagnoli et al., 2012; Galvagno & Dalli, 2014; Moro Visconti et al., 2017) that exploit the network governance properties of digital platforms and, in perspective, their metaverse extension.

Value co-creation impacts economic marginality and its monetary outcomes, as ideally shown in Table 18.3.

Whereas the corporate players (metaverse enablers, platforms, etc.) have an economic, financial, and equity impact, users (represented by households and their avatars) typically enjoy the non-monetary value and some monetary savings (if they "monetize" their participation in the metaverse, the data and feedback they share, etc.).

18.11   Metaverse Evaluation with Multilayer Network Analysis

Metaverse evaluation is still a frontier research issue. Each single metaverse ecosystem, ideally corresponding to a closed network (with well-defined boundaries) may be evaluated, even in economic terms, considering it as a static single entity. This is just the first step for appraisal that needs to be complemented (and complicated) introducing dynamic interactions, and interrelations with other networks (both within and outside the metaverse).

Interrelations incorporate economic synergies, for instance, if a node (individual) in the physical world is complemented by her avatar in the metaverse—their joint value, albeit difficult to assess, is certainly higher than their straightforward sum $(2+2>4)$.

Communities intersect several multilayer networks and are driven by centripetal forces, magnetized by consensus clustering and pairwise homophily that reduce the intrinsic entropy of scale-free networks.

Porous borders make networks intrinsically unstable and more difficult to appraise, but also increasingly valuable. Interchangeable networks add value, allowing consumers to surf through adjacent metaverses, where segmentation is minimized (BigTechs may be unwilling to carry on interoperable strategies, but in the long run everybody should gain from a larger and more open metaverse market, mastered by shared standards).

Scalability is a further feature that encompasses the physical world—Internet—metaverse value chain (Fig. 18.11).

Multilayer network analysis is a powerful tool for the evaluation of a metaverse (considering every single layer-finite ecosystem, wherever possible). The mathematical properties of the network and its multilayer

Table 18.3 Value co-creation and economic-financial impact

	Metaverse enabler (BigTech …)	Metaverse platform	Metaverse user
Economic impact			
revenues	Product/services sale	B2B2C intermediation fees	Revenues from data sharing
– Monetary OPEX	Running costs	Platform costs	Fees/purchasing costs, running expenses …
= EBITDA			
– Non-monetary OPEX	Depreciation, amortization		Depreciation of technological investments
= EBIT			
EBITDA/revenues	Monetary profitability ratio		
EBIT/revenues = Return on Sales	Operating profitability ratio		
Financial impact			
EBITDA	Higher EBITDA improves monetary (financial) margins		Cash outflows (for metaverse fruition) net of co-creation gains/savings
	Higher EBITDA improves FCFF		
	Higher FCFF improves FCFE		
Operating Cash Flows FCFF			
Net Cash flows FCFE			
Equity impact			

	Metaverse enabler (BigTech ...)	Metaverse platform	Metaverse user
Book value of equity	Product/services sale, improving retained earnings and so book value of equity Higher book value of equity and goodwill improve market value of equity Economic/financial marginality improves CAPEX Depreciation, amortization Higher equity improves rating and bankability		Revenues from data sharing
Market value of equity			Fees/purchasing costs, running expenses ...
Investment capacity			Depreciation of technological investments
Goodwill/brand equity			
Rating (debt service capacity)			
Non-monetary impact			
Reputation, visibility, standing	Corporate image improvement, with an impact on goodwill and revenues		Customer satisfaction, loyalty reinforcement, use value ...
...			

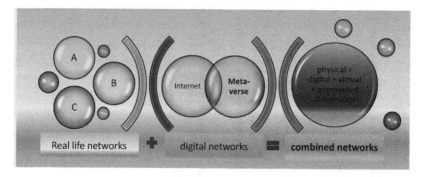

Fig. 18.11   Network interrelations, from the real life to the metaverse

extensions preside over the evaluation patterns that should conveniently consider:

(a) The architecture of the metaverse network (scale-free, etc.);
(b) The number of its nodes and edges;
(c) The intensity of the edging relationships;
(d) The hyperlink with other (multilayer) networks (real life, Internet, other metaverses);
(e) The dynamic evolution of both the networks and their interactions.

The monetization of the edging relationships within and outside the metaverse stands out as the final valuation target.

18.12   Concluding Remarks

Network theory, with its multilayer extensions, is well suited to represent a cornerstone in the interpretation of the evolutionary path from real life to the metaverse. This explanation is also consistent with the attempt to give a rough estimate of the potential economic value of metaverse layers.

Interactivity represents the degree to which a person can make choices within an environment. These choices, when present, are based on the rules and behaviors of the environment and should ideally mesh with our desires/intentions/expectations. Network theory describes interactivity which is a cornerstone of value co-creation patterns.

The metaverse can be roughly interpreted as a digital (virtual/augmented) social network, confirming its consistency with network theory—by now a well-established discipline, albeit still under-exploited in its economic applications. The network is bidirectional (undirected), as it communicates with the real world, enhancing overall value.

The evolution of the metaverses is still largely unknown and uneasy to conceive, even if dynamic processes are immanent and represent a critical feature, shaping community structures, and degree correlations and distributions (the node degree is the number of edges adjacent to the node).

The segregation of the metaverse from the real life and the bridging Internet is far from representing a real threat in this still pioneering phase, even if it may represent a concern in the future. Node or edging deletion is the primary cause of isolation, a state of the world that typically destroys value (erasing the synergies between the real life and the metaverse). This occurrence is well-known in network theory (see Ben-Naim & Krapivsky, 2007) and should be carefully examined, to anticipate and possibly fix unwanted consequences (e.g., digital identity theft, when the avatar is detached from the originating individual). In most networks, some nodes are likely to disappear. If the network continues to grow, its scale-free nature can persist (Barabási, 2016, p. 220).

An interdisciplinary examination of the metaverse monetization process is, to the author's best knowledge, still missing but most wanted—as it may justify the huge investments poured in the metaverse, sooner or later awaiting fair payback. The valuation approach exemplified in figure combines traditional economic and mathematical approaches, providing a rationale for consistent appraisal metrics.

When considering the adjacency matrices that describe related networks and their multilayer extensions, two parameters are crucial: "augmented" nodes (resulting from the interaction of physical and virtual layers) and "augmented" edges (linking more nodes and accommodating for higher traffic of worthy information/big data, and monetary transactions through blockchain cryptocurrencies).

This chapter does not consider controversial aspects that concern the metaverse and may affect its market value. For instance, a digital image (avatar) theft or misuse has already emerged as a critical issue (that may be softened by preventive blockchain intervention to validate the avatar).

Another issue relates to the territoriality of virtual operations (Where do they effectively take place? Which are the competent authorities?).

Metaverse is a persistent and immersive digital environment of independent, yet interconnected networks that will use yet to be determining protocols for communications. It enables lasting decentralized, collaborative, interoperable digital content that intersects with the physical world's real-time, spatially oriented, and indexed content (Verma & Nguyen, 2022).

This preliminary study considers the value chain relationship that starts from real-life networks and arrives at metaverse networks, passing through the Internet (that, sooner or later, is expected to "merge" with the metaverse).

As most complex ecosystems are composed of interacting elements, networks are ubiquitous and are linked among themselves through replica nodes like avatars. Multi-slice networks describe time-dependent interactions that represent an intrinsic feature of naturally evolving temporal social networks. Metaverse interactions are continuously updated in real-time, being consistent with this dynamic framework that instantaneously incorporates socio-pattern data.

Networks are a powerful common denominator of all these states of the real or digital world, so represent a clue for joint interpretation. Since these networks operate on different layers, multilayer networking applications need to be considered. While the investigation area is fascinating, the evaluation issues are complicated by several factors, starting from the novelty of still unstable metaverses to the mathematical intricacies of multilayer networks.

Adjacency matrices represent a powerful tool to estimate the potential value of each metaverse subset, being consistent with the with-and-without approach, the network effect laws, and the multilayer network interpretation. Network theory interpretations are also consistent with combinatorial innovation where different intangible assets and processes (AI, blockchains, big data, decentralized P2P networks, etc.) synergistically interact. Full interoperability of the different metaverses, as it happens for the Internet, is an additional value-enhancing goal.

Further scrutiny is needed for a more comprehensive dynamic evaluation that inspires and justifies the huge investments that Big Techs are pouring into the metaverse. A better comprehension of the mathematical and appraisal properties of these extended networks, from the real life to the metaverse, can ease the understanding of value co-creation patterns, systemic failures, and shock resilience (even to targeted cyber-attacks), improving the overall efficiency, to the benefit of all the real and virtual stakeholders.

Incoming metaverse ecosystems raise sustainability concerns that need to be adequately known and foreseen to attract impact investors before their standards become consolidated and ubiquitous. Artificial intelligence and blockchains that validate the big data and provide the background for a cryptocurrency-driven payment system represent the engine behind 3D virtual platforms where physical individuals are replaced by their avatars (digital twins). A compelling target for future sustainability is to address accessibility, diversity, inclusion, and equity issues in the metaverse before they become fully ingrained in a system that may get harder to manage and control. The metaverse opens unknown dimensions of sustainability, and Environmental, Social, and Governance (ESG) parameters, albeit imperfect, can lead to their interpretation. BigTechs, currently representing the largest investors in the metaverse, are characterized by ESG scores that are better than those of traditional firms in polluting industries. This could probably lead to a more sustainable metaverse ecosystem, due to replacing larger sectors of the real economy with less polluting ones. Whereas the impact of the digital footprint, mostly represented by energy-eating cryptocurrencies, can be softened by the technological upgrade (big datalakes with in-cloud storage, exploiting economies of scale and experience), the strongest ESG issues lie somewhat in between the social and governance component: access to the metaverse can be hardened by authoritarian regimes that control and censor avatars, or ludopathies may be exacerbated by 3D dependence, further detaching addicted surfers from the real world.

NOTES

1. While the terms WWW and Internet are often used interchangeably in the media, they refer to different systems. The WWW is an information network, whose nodes are documents and links are URLs. In contrast the Internet is an infrastructure network, whose nodes are computers called routers and whose links correspond to physical connections, like copper and optical cables or wireless links (Barabási, 2016, p. 127).
2. See https://scipython.com/book/chapter-3-simple-plotting-with-pylab/examples/moores-law/#:~:text=Since%20the%20data%20cover%2040,T2l og102.

SELECTED REFERENCES

Akaka, M. A., Vargo, S. L., & Lusch, R. F. (2012). An exploration of networks in value co-creation: A service-ecosystems view. *Review of Marketing Research, 9*, 13–50.

Bapat, R. B. (2011). *Graphs and Matrices*. Berlin: Springer.

Barabási, A. (2016). *Network science*. Cambridge: Cambridge University Press.

Barabási, A., & Albert, R. (2002). Statistical mechanics of complex networks. *Reviews of Modern Physics, 74*(1), 47–97.

Beckström, R. (2008). *The economics of networks and cybersecurity*. Available at https://www.slideshare.net/RodBeckstrom/economics-of-networks-beckst rom-national-cybersecurity-center-department-of-homeland-security

Beirão, G., Patrício, L., & Fisk, R. P. (2017). Value co-creation in service ecosystems. *Journal of Service Management, 28*(2), 227–249.

Ben-Naim, E., & Krapivsky, P. L. (2007). Addition–deletion networks. *Journal of Physics A: Mathematical and Theoretical, 40*(30), 8607.

Bianconi, G. (2018). *Multilayer networks*. Oxford: Oxford University Press.

Bianconi, G., & Barabási, A. (2001). Competition and multiscaling in evolving networks. *Europhysics Letters, 54*, 436–442.

Blaschke, M., Uwe, R., Kazem, H., & Aier, S. (2019). Design principles for digital value co-creation networks: A service-dominant logic perspective. *Electronic Markets, 29*(3), 443–447.

Boccaletti, S., Bianconi, G., Criado, R., Del Genio, CI., Gómez-Gardeñes, J., Romance, M., Sendiña-Nadal, I., Wang, Z., & Zanin, M. (2014, November 1). The structure and dynamics of multilayer networks. *Physics Report, 544*(1), 1–122.

Caldarelli G., & Catanzaro M. (2011). *Networks: A very short introduction*. Oxford: Oxford University Press.

Ceccagnoli, M., Forman, C., Huang, P., & Wu, D. J. (2012). Co-creation of value in a platform ecosystem: The case of enterprise software. *MIS Quarterly, 36*(1), 263–290.

Chen, D., & Zhang, R. (2022). *Exploring research trends of emerging technologies in health metaverse: A bibliometric analysis*. Available at https://ssrn.com/abs tract=3998068

Cheng, R., Wu, N., Chen, S., & Han, B. (2022). *Will metaverse be NextG Internet? Vision, hype, and reality*. Available at https://arxiv.org/abs/2201. 12894

Cozzo, E., Ferraz de Arruda, G., Rodrigues F. A., & Moreno, Y. (2016). *Multilayer networks: Metrics and spectral properties*. Available at https://cosnet.bifi. es/wp-content/uploads/2016/03/CFRM01.pdf

De Domenico, M., Solé-Ribalta, A., Cozzo, E., Kivelä, M., Moreno, Y., Porter, M. A., Gómez, S., & Arenas, A. (2013). Mathematical formulation of multilayer networks. *Physical Review X, 3*, 041022.

Degrande, T., Vannieuwenborg, F., Verbrugge, S., & Colle, D. (2018). Multi-sided platforms for the Internet of Things. In: B. Shishkov (Ed.), *Business Modeling and Software Design. BMSD 2018. Lecture notes in business information processing* (vol. 319). Cham: Springer.

de Reuven, M., Sørensen, C., & Basole, R. C. (2018). The digital platform: A research agenda. *Journal of Information Technology, 33,* 124–135.

Erdös, P., & Rényi, A. (1959). On Random Graphs I. *Publicationes Mathematicae Debrecen, 6,* 290–297.

Estrada, E., & Knight, P. A. (2015). *A first course in network theory.* Oxford: Oxford University Press.

Galvagno, M., & Dalli, D. (2014). Theory of value co-creation: A systematic literature review. *Managing Service Quality, 24*(6), 643–683.

Gander, J. (2015). *Designing digital business models.* Kingston: Kingston University.

Garcia, D. F., Garcia, R., Entrialgo, J., Garcia, J., & Garcia, M. (2008). *Experimental evaluation of horizontal and vertical scalability of cluster-based application servers for transactional workloads.* Paper presented at 8th WSEAS international conference on applied informatics and communications (AIC'08), Rhodes, Greece, August 20–22.

Gartner Research. (2022). *Emerging technologies: Critical insights on metaverse.* Available at https://www.gartner.com/en/documents/4010017

Gawer, A. (2014). Bridging differing perspectives on technological platforms: Toward an integrative framework. *Research Policy, 43*(7), 1239–1249.

Gneiser, M., Heidemann, J., Klier, M., Landherr, A., & Probst, F. (2012). Valuation of online social networks taking into account users's interconnectedness. *Information Systems and e-Business Management, 10,* 61–84.

Gupta, A., Christie, R., & Manjula, R. (2017). Scalability in internet of things: Features, techniques and research challenges. *International Journal of Computational Intelligence Research, 13*(7), 1617–1627.

Hoffman, R., & Yeh, C. (2018). *Blitzscaling.* New York: Crown Publishing Group.

Hyoung, Y., Arum Park, J., & Kyoung, J. L. (2020). Why are the largest social networking services sometimes unable to sustain themselves? *Sustainability, 12*(2), 502.

Ismail, S. (2014). *Exponential organizations.* New York: Singularity University Book.

Jackson, M. O. (2008). *Social and economic networks.* Princeton: Princeton University Press.

Jacobides, M. G., Cernamo, C., & Gawer, A. (2018). Towards a theory of ecosystems. *Strategic Management Journal, 39*(8), 2255–2276.

Jeong, H., Yi, Y., & Kim, D. (2022). An innovative e-commerce platform incorporating metaverse to live commerce. *International Journal of Innovative Computing Information and Control, 18*(1), 221–229.

Johnson, J. (2022). *Metaverse - statistics & facts*. Statista.

Jooyoung, K. (2021). Advertising in the metaverse: Research agenda. *Journal of Interactive Advertising, 21*(3), 141–144.

JP Morgan, O. (2022). *Opportunities in the metaverse. How businesses can explore the metaverse and navigate the hype vs. reality.* Available at https://www.jpmorgan.com/content/dam/jpm/treasury-services/documents/opportunities-in-the-metaverse.pdf

Kane, G. C., Alavi, M., Labianca, G., & Borgatti, S. P. (2014). What's different about social media networks? A framework and research agenda. *MIS Quarterly, 38*(1), 275–304.

Kenett, D., & Havlin, S. (2015). Network science: A useful tool in economics and finance. *Mind & Society: Cognitive Studies in Economics and Social Sciences*. Springer.

Kenney, M., & Zysman, J. (2016). The rise of the platform economy. *Issues in Science and Technology, XXXII*(3), 61.

Korpela, K., Hallikas, J., & Dahlberg, T. (2017). *Digital supply chain transformation toward blockchain integration*. Proceedings of the 50th Hawaii international conference on system sciences. Available at https://scholarspace.manoa.hawaii.edu/handle/10125/41666

Lee, K. M., Min, B., & Goh, K-I. (2015). Towards real-world complexity: An introduction to multiplex networks. *European Physical Journal B, 88*(2), 48.

Liu, Z., Ren, L., Xiao, C., Zhang, K., & Demian, P. (2022). Virtual reality aided therapy towards health 4.0: A two-decade bibliometric analysis. *International Journal of Environmental Research and Public Health, 19*(3), 1525.

Lòpez, L., Francisco, J., & Esteves, J. (2017). *Value in a digital world: How to assess business models and measure value in a digital world*. Cham: Palgrave Macmillan.

Moro Visconti, R., Larocca, A., & Marconi, M. (2017). *Big data-driven value chains and digital platforms: From Value co-creation to monetization*. In A. K. Somani & G. Deka G (Eds.), *Big data analytics: Tools, technology for effective planning*. Boca Raton: CRC Press.

Moro Visconti, R. (2019). Combining Network theory with corporate governance: converging models for connected stakeholders. *Corporate Ownership & Control, 17*(1), 125–139.

Murray, J. H. (2020). Virtual/reality: How to tell the difference. *Journal of Visual Culture, 19*(1), 11–27.

Mystiakidis, S. (2022). Metaverse. *Encyclopedia, 2*, 486–497.

Newman, M. E. J. (2010). *Networks: An introduction*. Oxford: Oxford University Press.

Odlyzko, A., & Tilly, B. (2005). *A refutation of Metcalfe's law and a better estimate for the value of networks and network interconnections.* Minneapolis: University of Minnesota.

Park, S. M., & Kim, Y. G. A. (2022). Metaverse: Taxonomy, components, applications, and open challenges. *IEEE Access, 10,* 4209–4251.

Pereira, D. (2021). *Multisided platform business model.* Available at https://businessmodelanalyst.com/multisided-platform-business-model/

Pesce, M. (2021). Mirror worlds the metaverse could help us better understand reality. *IEEE Spectrum, 58*(11), 25–25.

Radoff, J. (2021). *Network effects in the metaverse.* Available at https://medium.com/building-the-metaverse/network-effects-in-the-metaverse-5c39f9b94f5a

Reed, D. P. (2001, February). The law of the pack. *Harvard Business Review.*

Shen, B. Q., Tan, W.M., & Qin, P. (2021). How to promote user purchase in metaverse? A systematic literature review on consumer behavior research and virtual commerce application design. *Applied Sciences, 11*(23), 11087.

Spagnoletti, P., Resca, A., & Lee, G. (2015). A design theory for digital platforms supporting online communities: A multiple case study. *Journal of Information Technology, 30*(4), 364–380.

Tiwana, A., Konsynski, B., & Bush, A. A. (2010). Platform evolution: Coevolution of platform architecture, governance, and environmental dynamics. *Information Systems Research, 21*(4), 675–687.

Tsekeris, T. (2017). Global value chains: Building blocks and network dynamics. *Physica a: Statistical Mechanics and Its Applications, 488,* 187–204.

Van Steen, M. (2010). *Graph theory and complex networks. An introduction.* Maarten Van Steen.

Verma, A., & Nguyen, T. (2022). *Emerging technologies: Critical insights on metaverse.* Available at https://www.gartner.com/en/documents/4010017

Wang, D., & Zhou, X. (2017). Control energy and controllability of multilayer networks. *Advances in Complex Systems, 20*(04n05), 1750008.

Wang, F., Quin, R., Wang, X., & Hu, B. (2022). MetaSocieties in metaverse: MetaEconomics and MetaManagement for MetaEnterprises and MetaCities. *IEEE Transactions on Computational Social Systems, 9*(1).

Williams, L. G., & Smith, C. U. (2004). Web application scalability: A model-based approach. *Software Engineering Research and Performance Engineering Services.* Available at http://www.spe-ed.com/papers/scale04.pdf

Yang, Q., Zhao, Y., Huang, H., & Zheng, Z. (2022). *Fusing blockchain and AI with metaverse: A survey.* Available at https://arxiv.org/abs/2201.03201

CHAPTER 19

Cloud Storage Valuation

19.1 Introduction

Cloud computing is an outsourcing delivery of computing services—including servers, storage, databases, networking, software, analytics, and intelligence—over the Internet ("the cloud") to offer faster innovation, flexible resources, and economies of scale. The user typically pays only for cloud services you use, helping lower operating costs, run infrastructure more efficiently, and scale up as business needs change (https://micros oft.com/).

Current trends show that enterprises are increasingly embracing multi-cloud solutions, rising their cloud spending (https://www.flexera.com/blog/cloud/cloud-computing-trends-2021-state-of-the-cloud-report/).

The main features of cloud computing are synthesized in Fig. 19.1.

Numerous industries are implementing cloud computing as part of their business processes. Valuation patterns may so be concerned not only with public or private cloud but also with their impact on traditional businesses.

As-a-Service models represent a primary outsourcing option for end-users and may be synthesized in Fig. 19.2. They may also include Infrastructure as a Service (IaaS).

Cloud computing can be represented as a digital node that masters a virtual ecosystem, as shown in Fig. 19.3.

R. Moro-Visconti, *The Valuation of Digital Intangibles*, https://doi.org/10.1007/978-3-031-09237-4_19

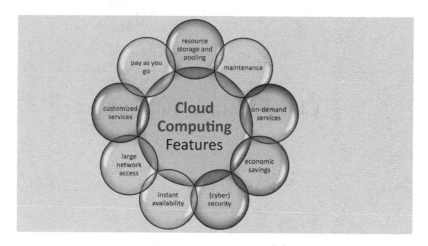

Fig. 19.1   Features of cloud computing

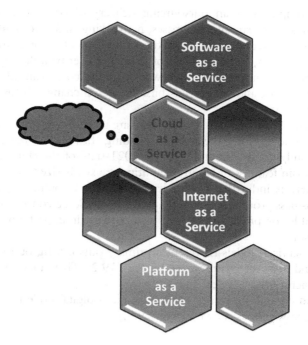

Fig. 19.2   As-a-service models

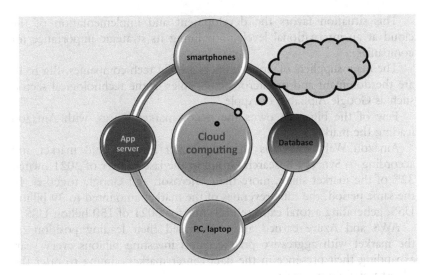

Fig. 19.3 Cloud computing ecosystem

19.2   THE MARKET

Big Techs rule this oligopolistic market that is currently presided by three main players (AWS/Amazon; Azure/Microsoft, and Google Cloud; public cloud adoption is, however, growing).

In 2021 the EU presented a document, the Digital Compass Target, for the sustainable digital development of businesses in the European Union. According to what has been published, the goal to be pursued is to have more than 75% of companies in the EU that rely on cloud computing services.

In 2020 the same data was recorded for cloud services with medium–high complexity levels and the percentage amounted to 26% of EU companies, with an increase of 15 percentage points compared to 2014. Most of the entities involved are large companies (48%), many of which operate in the consulting and computer programming sector (60% of 48%).

Among the territories most involved in the use, the Nordic countries stand out, Finland where more than 60% of companies use cloud services daily, followed by Sweden and Denmark.

This situation favors the development and implementation of the cloud at an international level, underlining its strategic importance for companies.

The main suppliers of cloud services are big tech companies. Big techs are the dominant and proliferous companies in the technological sector, such as Google Alphabet or Apple.

Few of the big tech owns the major market shares, with Amazon leading the market.

Amazon Web Service is an early comer in the cloud market and according to Synergy Research Group in the last quarter of 2021 owned 32% of the market share, more than Microsoft and Google together. In the same period, the total revenues of the market amounted to 39 billion US$, generating a total expected revenue for 2021 of 150 billion US$.

AWS and Azure earned and maintained their leading position on the market with aggressive practices and investing billions every year, expanding their presence in the data center market, aiming to offer the widest portfolio of services.

More than half of Amazon's operating profits come from cloud services and tools offered by AWS. Despite maintaining the market percentage unaltered, AWS profits are growing each quarter and Amazon is implementing the platform with new services every year.

Amazon managed to maintain its market share also relying on the efficiency of the business offers, competitors such as Google and Alibaba are not profitable yet.

Amazon and most of the companies involved in cloud computing are hiding the impacts of different services on the total revenue of the sector. It is estimated that around 50% of the revenues come from the renting of virtual operating power of computers in Amazon data centers (EC2).

EC2 is one of the first services provided by AWS and it seems to be covering a large part of gross profits.

In the years, AWS developed the first EC2 service launched in 2006, providing offers for different occasions of use. With the introduction of reserved instances, in which usage is subordinate to conditions such as the usage time, AWS claims to make companies reduce their cost by more than 70% compared to on-demand services. Today Amazon offers more than 300 instances based on chips from Intel, AMD, and NVIDIA.

This service is mainly offered to other businesses.

Other companies reported high margin returns thanks to computing storage and network services.

Space renting is the most known and diffused service through final customers, it allows the storage of files on the cloud to save space in personal devices.

Many B2C companies rely on S3 with single clients storing hundreds of petabytes (1 petabyte = 1 billiard of bytes). Many S3 users usually store unnecessary files on S3 resulting in a big waste of money.

Since the S3 market is very competitive, a platform such as AWS introduced exit prices in terms of millions of dollars per user just to move the stored data (this only applies to customers with huge quantities of data).

Some of the most diffused services of space renting among small users are iCloud from Apple and Dropbox.

Companies that deal with providing services in the Cloud must monitor various components for the system to function properly and to pay for their efforts as well as their resources, apply different pricing models.

The most used is pay-per-use, in which users pay a fixed price for each unit used based on space or time of use. Pay-per-use services are often used for single operations.

This model is widely used for extremely popular services, the distribution of which made it difficult to negotiate prices.

Similarly, a subscription model can be applied to the same products. In the model with subscribing, the user pays in advance for the use of a predetermined setup of service units for a certain time, usually longer than a month.

The prevalence of these models over the others could be given by their simplicity in use. Both have clear price levels and pre-established usage set-ups, avoiding cost overruns for excessive volumes.

Dynamic or variable pricing is a model in which the price of the chosen service is established based on supply and demand (e.g., auction or negotiation). This model is used for highly differentiated or high-value items.

Mechanisms that implement dynamic policies could ensure more cost-effective pricing of high-value differentiated services. To obtain higher revenues, providers should also apply customer selection processes to which to attribute the scarce resources of the sector.

These basic models can then be implemented based on the specifics of the service, or with the introduction of collateral utilities. Here are some examples.

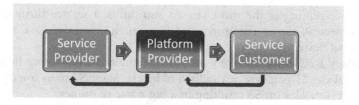

Fig. 19.4 Relations between providers and customers

In providing the end-user with the PaaS service, the service provider may have direct B2B relationships with a platform provider. In this relationship, the platform owner collects payments from the end-users.

Sometimes the result of the value chain may require the platform provider to pay interest to the service provider only after obtaining the consideration from the end customer (Fig. 19.4).

The value chain illustrated above shows the link between the final customer (end-user) and the service or platform provider that shapes the business model (Chang et al., 2010).

Another revenue add-on is the introduction of software upgrades, not necessarily under the payment of a fee but as customer attraction.

Cloud computing architecture refers to the components and subcomponents required for cloud computing. These components typically consist of a front-end platform (fat client, thin client, mobile), back-end platforms (servers, storage), a cloud-based delivery, and a network (Internet, Intranet, Intercloud). Combined, these components make up cloud computing architecture.[1]

The main infrastructure is composed of cloud clients. The clients are servers and mobile devices that users directly interact with to rely on the cloud. The connection with the cloud can happen through the web, virtual sessions, or mobile applications (Fig. 19.5).

Cloud brokers are entities dedicated to cloud use and performance weaving relationships between providers and end-users.

The presence of brokers makes it easier for customers to manage cloud services in usage by the companies. Relying on a broker can favor the synergic use of different cloud offerings, can choose, and change providers depending on different contexts, can offer some improvement to final customers by reporting cloud performances, enhancing security, or different support activities.

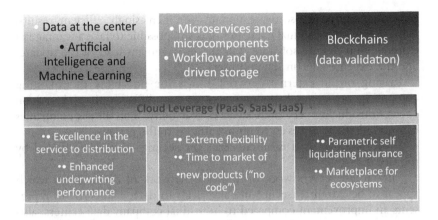

Fig. 19.5 Cloud architecture

Cloud brokers can also offer cost advantages due to the lower prices paid to providers for high levels of data stored in their databases.

It seems then convenient for relatively small users to rely on brokers, on the other hand, users may face compliance when dealing with brokers.

Cloud brokers could even potentially make the entire chain more complex by adding another layer. Users should also be aware of interests' conflict with brokers, when providing the service, they may avoid updated technologies to opt for a cheaper option at client expenses.

The applicability of cloud services is vast and constantly expanding. Every year, specialized supply companies develop new services and update software to meet customer needs.

Providers pursue economic balance and profit while respecting the interests of the customer by offering a series of advantages through their services, first cost reduction.

The direct effect of the adoption of cloud computing is the reduction of capital expenditure for the purchase of software and hardware, for electricity costs, in the case of private clouds also the cost of human capital for IT management.

Furthermore, relying on external structures that manage billions of data very often allows rapid execution of requests, offering extreme flexibility.

Improving performance involves more than just speed. Providers have among their interests to keep the level of service high, for this reason, they often introduce software updates for increasingly efficient results. With the use of individual databases, it is still possible to take advantage of extremely up-to-date software, but the management load of the updates and the expense falls on the end-user.

Relying on an external network allows the possibility of exploiting computing powers and storage memories at different times based on needs, introducing very high levels of scalability. This allows companies to respond efficiently even to high traffic or traffic peaks.

A very controversial issue concerns the security advantage offered by the cloud.

The largest servers work on a global network of data centers which appear to be extremely secure and always up-to-date. This certainly represents an improvement compared to individual company data centers, also in terms of costs, but the security offered is relative.

19.3   Digital Networks and Metcalfe's Law

Corporate and digital networks are particularly relevant for cloud computing and their fuelling (big) data. Any cloud computing service is strictly linked to the use of hardware and software resources distributed over the network.

Companies providing cloud services generate values for users through networks of devices remotely operating together for the same purposes.

The graphical representation of a network (consistent with the contents of Chapter 15) is depicted in Fig. 19.6.

Networks try to explain how a system of isolated elements can be transformed, through their interaction (using, for instance, digital platforms) into groups and communities. The implications may be relevant, even if largely unexplored. The value of a network can be estimated as the incremental value of the intangibles related to that network.

According to Metcalfe's law (examined in Chapter 3), the effect of a TLC network is proportional to the square of the number of connected users of the system (n^2). This generates a network effect that aggregates new members, with positive scalability (when revenues grow, fixed costs remain by definition unchanged, and variable costs slightly increase, improving EBITDA, EBIT, and other economic margins).

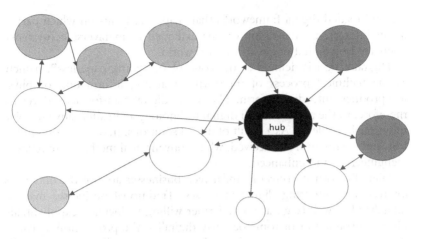

Fig. 19.6 Social networks

19.4   NETWORKING DIGITAL PLATFORMS

Digital platforms are at the basis of technology-enabled business models that facilitate exchanges between multiple groups—such as end-users and producers—who do not necessarily know each other. These platforms can be interpreted with network theory, considering each platform as a hub (mastering/connecting) node, characterized by intense Internet traffic of information (big data), and monetary transactions (relevant for valuation).

The continuous upgrade of the technological environment creates new possibilities and reshapes the value and supply chain of financial intermediation, disrupting the existing business models.

Whereas traditional firms create value within the boundaries of a company or a supply chain, digital platforms utilize an ecosystem of autonomous agents to co-create value (Hein et al., 2019). Stakeholders continuously interact (24/7) through the digital platform, shortening their supply chain (lesser and quicker passages, etc.), and increasing the overall value chains.

Digital platforms can be represented by cloud platforms, and they act as a bridging node that connects digital clients to traditional firms. Whenever platforms connect different layers (each representing a network sub-system), they can increase the overall systemic value. Digital platforms are multi-sided digital frameworks that shape the terms on which participants interact. Digitalization can be extended to metaverse ecosystems, connected by digital nodes to the real world.

Digitalization is defined as the concept of "going paperless", namely as the technical process of transforming analog information or physical products into digital form. The term "digital transformation" refers, therefore, to the application of digital technology as an alternative to solve traditional problems. As a result of digital solutions, new forms of innovation and creativity are conceived, while conventional methods are revised, reengineered, and enhanced.

Digitally born startups or similar tech businesses are not the only ones interested in adopting digital processes. Traditional businesses may be digitalized as well (e.g., a simple farmer willing to increase exponentially his/her production of tomatoes may digitalize the production activities through new systems or machines). In practice, with digitalization, traditional firms improve their crucial economic and financial parameters, as the EBITDA, which increases, while the WACC reduces, so improving the DCF and the overall enterprise value (EV), measured with DCF formulation, discounting the operating cash flow/FCFF with the WACC:

$$\frac{O_{CF} \uparrow}{WACC \downarrow} \cong \text{Enterprise Value} \uparrow\uparrow \tag{19.1}$$

In synthesis, digitalization brings speed and quality at a low cost, thus representing a crucial driver for scalability itself. Digitalization enables a business process re-engineering of traditional firms, which may presuppose an incremental production growth.

Figure 19.7 shows the link between digital transformation and scalability.

Digital platforms can be interpreted, as anticipated, in terms of network theory (see Barabási, 2016), the study of graphs as a representation of either symmetric or asymmetric relations between discrete objects. In computer science and network science, network theory is a part of graph theory: a network can be defined as a graph in which nodes and/or edges have attributes (e.g., names).

Digital platforms are intrinsically networked, and within networks, they represent a bridging node that connects users (stakeholders).

The properties of networked platforms are intrinsically consistent with the cloud ecosystem. Digital platform analysis can give an interpretation

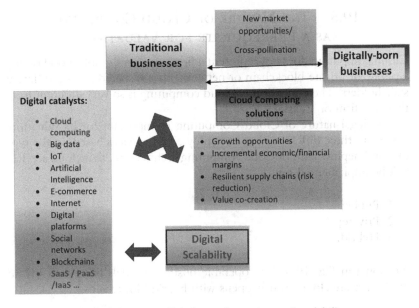

Fig. 19.7 The link between digital transformation and scalability

of the cloud ecosystem that considers from an unconventional perspective their properties and potential.

Cloud computing businesses are increasingly consistent with the Circular Economy patterns, and distant storage and outsourcing reduce the consumption of expensive and sharable technology.

A Circular Economy is an economic system aimed at eliminating waste and the continual use of resources. Circular systems employ reuse, sharing, repair, refurbishment, remanufacturing, and recycling to create a closed-loop system, minimizing the use of resource inputs and the creation of waste, pollution, and carbon emissions (Geissdoerfer et al., 2017).

The Circular Economy aims to keep products, equipment, and infrastructure in use for longer, thus improving the productivity of these resources.[2]

19.5   The Nature of Cloud Computing as a Prerequisite for Valuation

Cloud computing does not represent a firm but a semi-public good (being a public or private blockchain or network) that is shared among different stakeholders. The evaluation of cloud computing is so very different from that of a firm or an asset.

The legal nature of Cloud Computing is important for its valuation. There are three different ways to deploy cloud services based on the type of cloud deployment, or cloud computing architecture, that cloud services will be implemented on:

1. Public;
2. Private;
3. Hybrid.

As shown in Fig. 19.8. Interoperable business models bring to a hybrid public–private cloud, as it happens with hybrid blockchains.

The public cloud is defined as computing services offered by third-party providers over the public Internet, making them available to anyone who wants to use or purchase them. They may be free or sold on-demand, allowing customers to pay only per usage for the CPU cycles, storage, or bandwidth they consume. Public clouds can save companies from the

Fig. 19.8   Public, private, and hybrid cloud

expensive costs of having to purchase, manage, and maintain on-premises hardware and application infrastructure and can also be deployed faster than on-premises infrastructures and with an almost infinitely scalable platform. While security concerns have been raised over public cloud environments, when implemented correctly, the public cloud can be as secure as the most effectively managed private cloud implementation if the provider uses proper security methods, such as intrusion detection and prevention systems.[3]

To prevent unwanted access, providers offer two main tools: user encrypted private key and steganography. The encrypted key can be virtual or physical. The key automatically generates an access code every time the network detects an access attempt. Without the code, permission is denied.

Steganography is a technique used to hide information inside other file types such as images, audio, or video.

The only intrusion public clouds cannot avoid are intelligence and governate accesses.

The private cloud represents an on-demand cloud deployment model in which cloud computing services and infrastructure are hosted in a private environment and use proprietary resources. Typically, the management, maintenance, and operations of the private cloud are overseen by the company. While a private cloud offers a business greater control and security than a public cloud, managing it requires a higher level of IT skills. Conducting to management and controlling practices within the company, private clouds usually have high levels of costs and significantly reduce cost advantages. A private cloud can be offered both through the Internet or a private network and only to selected users (Table 19.1).

Private and public clouds can be combined to reach a double level of stored data and compose the hybrid cloud.

Hybrid clouds offer on-premises access for sensitive data and cloud archives for other less sensitive data. The infrastructure that supports the hybrid cloud typically includes a network, servers, and virtualization software. The servers host the data and view it remotely over the network. Virtualization software allows remote viewing of virtual resources (for example, desktops). Hybrid cloud involves a combination of both internal and third-party resources. These back-end components reside in two locations: on-premises in the corporate data center and at the third-party public cloud service provider.

Table 19.1 Pros and cons of private cloud

Pros	Cons
Exclusive access to data	Lack of data redundancy
Firewall access to specific IPS	Data security responsibility
Control and personalization	Need for trusted internal technical skills
	Unsafe reachability over time
	Poor physical and network security
	Slow scalability
	High management costs
	Non-proprietary management/sharing software
	Non-proprietary hardware

As cloud service providers support multiple tenants with various needs, they use advanced, high-density systems to host their cloud computing services. Virtualization software allows cloud service providers to host multiple operating systems on a single server, optimizing their resources. Furthermore, this network type allows companies to avoid excessive expenses for unneeded servers.

The double functionalities of hybrid clouds seem to guarantee a better level of data security. The network can rely on the private cloud's security measures and other features such as up-to-date software, cybersecurity, and disaster recovery (Table 19.2).

Providers offer different services for each cloud network, but the structure is not rigid, and each service could be applied to every model (Table 19.3).

In general, both users and cloud providers have their tasks.

Providers' core business is based on the back-office model, they manage physical infrastructures and security, they collect and free the

Table 19.2 Pros and cons of hybrid cloud

Pros	Cons
More control	Partial loss of confidentiality
High scalability	Non-proprietary hardware
Sharing solutions	Skills for configuration
Hardware management	
Physical, electrical safety	
Lower management costs	

Table 19.3 Cloud services taxonomy

Service	Description	Examples
Software as a Service (SaaS)	Software as a Service. This is the most used cloud computing function. The supplier provides an entire program that the customer can use	Typical examples of SaaS are email clients (such as Gmail) or tools that can be used online after subscription
Platform as a Service (PaaS)	Platform as a Service. For the development of a given program, the supplier takes care, entirely, of both the infrastructure and the basic software. In this way, the customer will have to focus solely on development. PaaS is a solution used by many software houses, which in this way can reduce the costs of purchasing, optimizing, and configuring hardware	Facebook allows his user to create applications for the platform
Infrastructure as a Service (IaaS)	The supplier provides the customer with the hardware infrastructure necessary for carrying out the activity. In many cases, this is hardware virtualization	The VPS, or virtual private server, can be considered an example of Infrastructure as a Service
Desktop as a Service (DaaS)	The supplier, usually via the web, provides the user/customer with the data or program that the latter requests. The user can use them as if they were present on the local disk of the device he is using. By its nature, this service is strongly integrated with SaaS	Street directories and file hosting or online storage services are all examples of DaaS

space to provide, they offer a technological tool needed for the practical functionality of cloud networks.

Users must take care of the cloud's setup, including system configuration, access management, adopting and taking care of encrypted keys, dispose of more mobile devices for safety purposes and Internet access, and more necessary or unnecessary steps and initiatives. Providers will never be able to manage users' tasks due to the intrinsic nature of these operations.

Table 19.4 User and provider tasks

User	Provider
Virtual private cloud configuration and security	Physical infrastructure
Firewall system	Physical security
Operating system	Storage
Application security	Network infrastructure
Service configuration	Virtualization layer
Architecture management	Service management
Service access policy	Management of Identity and Access Management services
Data encryption	
Resilience	
Disaster recovery	

For easier management of cloud services, end-users could rely on cloud brokers (Table 19.4).

The accountability of services ramification is not entirely entrusted to providers, the level of responsibility depends on the service. Considering the nature of the service, in the first place accessible from a private device, the responsibility is always shared at least for a small part of the process.

Users could avoid the use of cloud networks for many of the contingencies but at high costs and risks. Although adopting a cloud can be strategically helpful, companies choose whether to opt for private servers or clouds and which of the services are offered by providers.

19.6　The Accounting Background for Valuation

The evaluation is sensitive to forward-looking data that can be used to build up a sound business plan with a time horizon coherent with the average life cycle of the products and services of cloud computing.

A business plan is a formal accounting statement that numerically describes a set of business goals, the reasons why they are believed attainable, and the strategic plan and managerial steps for reaching those goals. Hypotheses and visionary ideas of game-changers must be transformed into numbers and need to be backed by reasonable and verifiable assumptions about future events and milestones (see Chapter 5).

The accounting background is composed of pro forma balance sheets (of some 3–5 years) and perspective income statements. The matching of these two documents produces expected cash flow statements. Economic and financial margins are the crucial accounting parameters for valuation that are represented by the EBITDA, the EBIT, the operating and Net Cash Flows, and the Net Financial Position, as it will be shown in the formulation of the appraisal approaches.

The appraisal methodology may conveniently start from a strategic interpretation of the business model (that derives from accounting data) to extract the key evaluation parameters to insert in the model, as shown in Figs. 19.9 and 19.10.

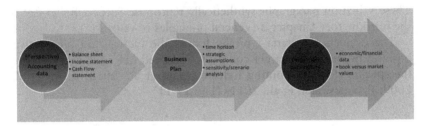

Fig. 19.9 Evaluation methodology

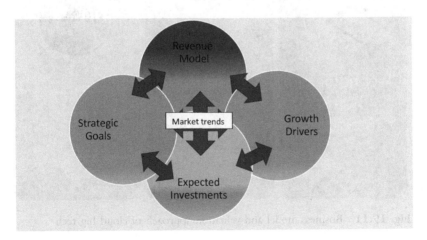

Fig. 19.10 Business model and value drivers

An analysis of the business model may conveniently consider:

(a) The revenue model;
(b) The strategic goals;
(c) The growth drivers;
(d) The expected investments;
(e) The market trends.

19.7   VALUATION METHODS

These valuation paragraphs synthetically repropose Sects. 2.8 and 2.9 of the introductory Chapter 2 (general principles of valuation).

The evaluation criteria typically follow the (actual and prospective) business model of the target company, and need fine-tuning considering the specific cloud computing industry (Kim et al., 2012; Klems et al., 2009; Parameswaran et al., 2011) (Fig. 19.11).

Fig. 19.11   Business model and valuation approach of cloud big tech

The value may be inferred even with differential income methodologies, traditionally used in the evaluation of intangible assets (within the income approaches).

According to the International Valuation Standard IVS 210, § 80:

> *80. Premium Profit Method or With-and-Without Method*
>
> *80.1 The premium profit method, sometimes referred to as the with-and-without method, indicates the value of an intangible asset by comparing two scenarios: one in which the business uses the subject intangible asset and one in which the business does not use the subject intangible asset (but all other factors are kept constant). (...).*
>
> *80.2 The comparison of the two scenarios can be done in two ways:*
>
> *a) calculating the value of the business under each scenario with the difference in the business values being the value of the subject intangible asset, and*
>
> *b) calculating for each future period the difference between the profits in the two scenarios. The present value of those amounts is then used to reach the value of the subject intangible asset.*

Among the main evaluation methodologies of cloud companies, the following are the most relevant:

1. Financial approach (Discounted Cash Flows—DCF);
2. Market comparables.

19.7.1 The Financial Approach

The financial approach, examined in Chapter 2, is based on the principle that the market value of the company is equal to the discounted value of the cash flows that the company can generate ("cash is king"). The determination of the cash flows is of primary importance in the application of the approach, as is the consistency of the discount rates adopted.

The doctrine (especially the Anglo-Saxon one) believes that the financial approach is the "ideal" solution for estimating the market value for limited periods. It is not possible to make reliable estimates of cash flows for longer periods. "*The conceptually correct methods are those based on cash flow discounting. I briefly comment on other methods since—even though they are conceptually incorrect—they continue to be used frequently*" (Fernandez, 2001).

This approach is of practical importance if the individual investor or company with high cash flows (leasing companies, retail trade, public and motorway services, financial trading, project financing SPVs, etc.) is valued.

Financial evaluation can be particularly appropriate when the company's ability to generate cash flow for investors is significantly different from its ability to generate income, and forecasts can be formulated with a sufficient degree of credibility and are demonstrable. The first parameter to be considered is represented by expected revenues (Kilcioglu & Maglaras, 2015) that are accounted in the first row of the income statement, presiding over the calculation of EBITDA and other valuation-sensitive parameters.

There are two complementary criteria for determining the cash flows:

a.1. The cash flow available to the company (Free cash flow to the firm – FCFF)

This configuration of expected flows is the one most used in the practice of company valuations, given its greater simplicity of application compared to the methodology based on flows to partners. It is a measure of cash flows independent of the financial structure of the company (unlevered cash flows) that is particularly suitable to evaluate companies with high levels of indebtedness, or that do not have a debt plan. In these cases, the calculation of the cash flow available to shareholders is more difficult because of the volatility resulting from the forecast of how to repay debts.

This methodology is based on the operating flows generated by the typical management of the company, based on the operating income available for the remuneration of own and third-party means net of the relative tax effect. Unlevered cash flows are determined by using operating income before taxes and finance charges.

Net operating income
− taxes on operating income
+ amortization/depreciation and provisions (non-monetary operating costs)
+ technical divestments (−investments)
+ divestments (−investments) in other assets

> + decrease (−increase) in operating net working capital
> = **Cash flow available to shareholders and lenders (operating cash flow − FCFF)**

The cash flow available to the company is, therefore, determined as the cash flow available to shareholders, plus financial charges after tax, plus loan repayments and equity repayments, minus new borrowings and flows arising from equity increases.

The difference between the two approaches is, therefore, given by the different meanings of cash flows associated with debt and equity repayments.

Cash flows from operating activities are discounted to present value at the weighted average cost of capital.

This configuration of flows offers an evaluation of the whole company, independently from its financial structure. The value of the debt must be subtracted from the value of the company to rejoin the value of the market value, obtained through the cash flows for the shareholders.

The relationship between the two concepts of cash flow is as follows:

cash flow available to the company = cash flow available to shareholders

+ financial charges(net of taxes) + loan repayments − new loans

$$(19.2)$$

a.2 The (residual) cash flow available to shareholders

This configuration considers the only expected flow available for members' remuneration. It is a measure of cash flow that considers the financial structure of the company (levered cash flow). It is the cash flow that remains after the payment of interest and the repayment of equity shares and after the coverage of equity expenditures necessary to maintain existing assets and to create the conditions for business growth.

In M&A operations, the Free Cash Flow to the Firm (operating cash flow) is normally calculated to estimate the Enterprise Value (comprehensive of debt). The residual Equity Value is then derived by subtracting the Net Financial Position.

The cash flow for the shareholders is determined, starting from the net profit:

Net profit (loss)
+ amortization/depreciation and provisions
+ divestments (−investments) in technical equipment
+ divestments (−investments) in other assets
+ decrease (−increase) in net operating working capital
+ increases (−decreases) in loans
+ equity increases (−decreases)
= **Cash flows available to shareholders (Free cash flow to equity - FCFE)**

The discounting of the free cash flow for the shareholders takes place at a rate equal to the cost of the shareholders' equity. This flow identifies the theoretical measure of the company's ability to distribute dividends, even if it does not coincide with the dividend paid.

Cash flow estimates can be applied to any type of asset. The differential element is represented by its duration. Many assets have a defined time horizon, while others assume a perpetual time horizon, such as shares.

Cash flows (CF) can, therefore, be estimated using a normalized projection of cash flows that it uses, alternatively:

- unlimited capitalization:

$$W1 = CF/i \tag{19.3}$$

- limited capitalization:

$$W2 = CF\,a\,n\neg i \tag{19.4}$$

where W_1 and W_2 represent the present value of future cash flows.

The discount rate to be applied to expected cash flows is determined as the sum of the cost of equity and the cost of debt, appropriately weighted according to the leverage of the company (the ratio between financial debt and equity). This produces the Weighted Average Cost of Capital (WACC):

$$\text{WACC} = k_i(1 - t)\frac{D}{D + E} + k_e\frac{E}{D + E} \tag{19.5}$$

where:

k_i = cost of debt;
t = corporate tax rate;
D = market value of debt;
E = market value of equity;
$D + E$ = raised capital;
k_e = cost of equity (to be estimated with the Capital Asset Pricing Model—CAPM or the Dividend Discount Model).

The cost of debt capital is easy to determine, as it can be inferred from the financial statements of the company. The cost of equity or share capital, which represents the minimum rate of return required by investors for equity investments, is instead more complex and may use the CAPM or the Dividend Discount Model (a method of valuing a company's stock price considering the sum of all its future dividend payments, discounted back to their present value. It is used to value stocks based on the Net Present Value of future dividends).

The formula of the CAPM is the following:

$$E(r)_{\text{Cloud Computing}} = r_{\text{free}} + \beta_{\text{Cloud Computing}}[(E(r)_{\text{market}} - r_{\text{free}}] \quad (19.6)$$

where:

$E(r)_{\text{FoodTech}}$ = expected return of the Cloud Computing listed stock
r_{free} = risk − free rate of return (e.g., of a long term Government bond)
β_{FoodTech} = sensitivity of the Cloud Computing stock to the market price
$E(r)_{\text{market}}$ = expected return of the (benchmark) Stock market

A central element is represented by the beta (β) of the cloud computing firm to be evaluated that consists of the ratio between the covariance of the cloud security with its stock market, divided by the variance of the market. Market betas, subdivided by industry, may be detected from the dataset of A. Damodaran.[4]

Once the present value of the cash flows has been determined, the calculation of the market value W of the company may correspond to:

(a) the unlevered cash flow approach:

$$W = \sum \frac{CF_0}{WACC} + VR - D \qquad (19.7)$$

(b) the levered cash flow approach:

$$W = \sum \frac{CF_n}{K_e} + VR \qquad (19.8)$$

where:

> $\sum CF_0/WACC$ = present value of operating cash flows (discounted FCFF)
> $\sum CF_n/K_e$ = present value of net cash flows (discounted FCFE)
> VR = terminal (residual) value
> D = initial net financial position (financial debt − liquidity)

The residual value is the result of discounting the value at the time n (before which the cash flows are estimated analytically). It is often the greatest component of the global value W (above all in intangible-intensive companies) and tends to zero if the time horizon of the capitalization is infinite ($VR/\infty = 0$).

The two variants (levered versus unlevered) give the same result if the value of the firm, determined through the cash flows available to the lenders, is deducted from the value of the net financial debts.

Operating cash flows (unlevered) and net cash flows for shareholders (levered) are determined by comparing the last two balance sheets (to dispose of changes in operating Net Working Capital, fixed assets, financial liabilities, and shareholders' equity) with the income statement of the last year.

The accounting derivation of the cash flow and its link to the cost of capital (to get DCF—Discounted Cash Flows) is illustrated in Table 19.5.

The net cash flow for the shareholders (FCFE) coincides with the free cash flow to equity and, therefore, with the dividends that can be paid out, once it has been verified that enough internal liquidity resources remain in the company. This feature, associated with the ability to raise equity from third parties and shareholders, is such as to allow the company to find adequate financial coverage for the investments deemed necessary to maintain the company's continuity and remain on the market in economic

Table 19.5   Cash flow statement and link with the cost of capital

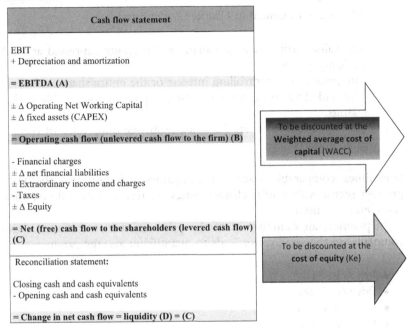

conditions (minimum objectives). They should allow for the creation of incremental value in favor of shareholders, who are the residual claimants (being, as subscribers of risky capital, the only beneficiaries of the variable net returns, which, as such, are residual and subordinate to the fixed remuneration of the other stakeholders).

The estimate of cash flows can be applied to any activity.

The differential element is service life. Many activities have a defined time horizon, while others assume a perpetual time horizon, such as company shares.

The discounted cash flow (DCF) approach can be complemented with real options (Náplava, 2016), that incorporate intangible-driven flexibility in the forecasts.

19.7.2   Empirical Approaches (Market Multipliers)

The market value examined in Chapter 2 identifies:

(a) The value attributable to a share of the equity expressed at stock exchange prices;
(b) The price of the controlling interest or the entire share equity;
(c) The traded value for the controlling equity of comparable undertakings;
(d) The value derived from the stock exchange quotations of comparable undertakings.

Sometimes comparable trades of companies belonging to the same product sector with similar characteristics (in terms of cash flows, sales, costs, etc.) are used.

In practice, an examination of the prices used in negotiations with companies in the same sector leads to quantifying average parameters:

• Price/EBIT
• Price/cash flow
• Price/book-value
• Price/earnings
• Price/dividend

These ratios seek to estimate the average rate to be applied to the company being assessed. However, there may be distorting effects of prices based on special interest rates, in a historical context, on difficulties of comparison, etc.

In financial market practice, the multiples methodology is frequently applied. Based on multiples, the company's value is derived from the market price profit referring to comparable listed companies, such as net profit, before tax or operating profit, cash flow, equity, or turnover.

The attractiveness of the multiples approach stems from its ease of use: multiples can be used to obtain quick but dirty estimates of the company's value and are useful when there are many comparable companies listed on the financial markets and the market sets correct prices for them on average.

Because of the simplicity of the calculation, these indicators are easily manipulated and susceptible to misuse, especially if they refer to companies that are not entirely similar. Since there are no identical companies in terms of entrepreneurial risk and growth rate, the assumption of multiples for the processing of the valuation can be misleading, bringing to "fake multipliers".

The use of multiples can be implemented through:

A. Use of fundamentals;
B. Use of comparable data:

    B.1. Comparable companies;
    B.2. Comparable transactions.

The first approach links multiples to the fundamentals of the company being assessed: profit growth and cash flow, dividend distribution ratio, and risk. It is equivalent to the use of cash flow discounting approaches.

For the second approach, it is necessary to distinguish whether it is a valuation of comparable companies or comparable transactions.

The comparability concerns different firms but is also related to their contents.

In the case of comparable companies, the approach estimates multiples by observing similar companies. The problem is to determine what is meant by similar companies. In theory, the analyst should check all the variables that influence the multiple.

In practice, companies should estimate the most likely price for a non-listed company, taking as a reference some listed companies, operating in the same sector, and considered homogeneous. Two companies can be defined as homogeneous when they present, for the same risk, similar characteristics, and expectations.

The calculation is:

– A company whose price is known (P_1),
– A variable closely related to its value (X_1)

the ratio $(P_1)/(X_1)$ is assumed to apply to the company to be valued, for which the size of the reference variable (X_2) is known.

Therefore:

$$(P_1)/(X_1) = (P_2)/(X_2) \qquad (19.9)$$

so that the desired value P_2 will be:

$$P_2 = X_2[(P_1)/(X_1)] \qquad (19.10)$$

According to widespread estimates, the main factors in establishing whether a company is comparable are:

- Size;
- Belonging to the same sector (see for instance the Statistical Classification of Economic Activities in the European Community, commonly referred to as NACE Rev 2);
- Financial risks (leverage);
- Historical trends and prospects for the development of results and markets;
- Geographical diversification;
- Degree of reputation and credibility;
- Management skills;
- Ability to pay dividends.

Founded on comparable transactions, the basis of valuation is information about actual negotiations (or mergers) of similar—i.e., comparable—companies.

The use of profitability parameters is usually considered to be the most representative of company dynamics.

Comparables may be looked for consulting databases like Orbis (https://www.bvdinfo.com/en-gb/our-products/data/international/orbis).

Among the empirical criteria, the approach of the multiplier of the EBITDA (Earnings Before Interest, Taxes, Depreciation, and Amortization) is widely diffused. The net financial position must be added algebraically to the EBITDA, to pass from the estimate of the enterprise value (total value of the company) to that of the equity value (value of the net assets). The formulation is as follows:

$W =$ average perspective EBITDA $*$ Enterprise Value/sector EBITDA

$\quad =$ Enterprise Value of the company $\qquad (19.11)$

And then:

$$\text{Equity Value} = \text{Enterprise Value} \pm \text{Net Financial Position} \qquad (19.12)$$

The DCF approach can be linked to the market approach since they both share as a starting parameter the EBITDA.

NOTES

1. https://en.wikipedia.org/wiki/Cloud_computing_architecture.
2. https://web.archive.org/web/20130110100128/, http://www.thecircul areconomy.org/.
3. https://microsoft.com/.
4. See, for instance, http://pages.stern.nyu.edu/~adamodar/New_Home_P age/datafile/Betas.html.

SELECTED REFERENCES

Barabási, A. (2016). *Network science*. Cambridge: Cambridge University Press.

Chang, V., Wills, W., & De Roure, D. (2010). A review of cloud business models and sustainability. In *2010 IEEE 3rd International Conference on Cloud Computing* (pp. 43–50).

Fernandez, P. (2001). *Valuation using multiples: How do analysts reach their conclusions?* IESE Business School. Available at https://www.researchgate. net/publication/4803035_Valuation_Using_Multiples_How_Do_Analysts_ Reach_their_Conclusions

Geissdoerfer, M., Savaget, P., Bocken, N. M. P., & Hultink, E. J. (2017). The circular economy – A new sustainability paradigm? *Journal of Cleaner Production, 143*, 757–768.

Hein, A., Schreieck, M., Riasanow, T., Setzke, M., Wiesche, M., Bohm, M., & Krcmar, H. (2019). Digital platform ecosystems. *Electronic Markets, 30*, 87–98.

Kilcioglu, C., & Maglaras, C. (2015). *Revenue maximization for cloud computing services*. Available at https://www0.gsb.columbia.edu/faculty/cmaglaras/pap ers/rm-cloud.pdf

Kim, J. M., Moon, J. K., & Hong, B. H. (2012). Research of virtualiza- tion services valuation for cloud computing environments. In J. Park, Y. S. Jeong, S. Park, & H. C. Chen (Eds.), *Embedded and multimedia computing technology and service*. Lecture Notes in Electrical Engineering, 181. Berlin: Springer.

Klems, M., Nimis, J., & Tai, S. (2009). Do clouds compute? A framework for estimating the value of cloud computing. In C. Weinhardt, S. Luckner, & J. Stößer (Eds.), *Designing e-business systems: Markets, Services, and networks*. Lecture Notes in Business Information Processing, 22. Berlin: Springer.

Náplava, P. (2016). Evaluation of cloud computing hidden benefits by using real options analysis. *Acta Informatica Pragensia, 2*, 162–179.

Parameswaran, S., Venkatesan, S., Gupta, M., Sharman, R., & Rao, H. R. (2011). Impact of cloud computing announcements on firm valuation. *AMCIS 2011 Proceedings*, 291.

CHAPTER 20

The Valuation of Digital Platforms and Virtual Marketplaces

20.1 Definition and Features

Digitalization is the process of transforming information or physical products into digital form, allowing businesses to "go paperless". Digitalization can be also interpreted as the process of converting data (not necessarily information) into a computer-readable format.

Thanks to digital solutions new forms of innovation and creativity are conceived while traditional business models are revised. Old-fashioned firms interact with digital startups, with a cross-pollination process that drives the analogic-to-digital transition. Digital links enable the real-time exchange of information or e-transactions (B2B2C), reducing information asymmetries and other frictions. Real-time interaction between stakeholders helps to minimize risk and enhance returns by win–win value co-creation paradigms.

Digital platforms are emerging as virtual stakeholder that bridges nodes among players inside and outside the firm. The platform, as well as firm interactions, may conveniently be interpreted with network theory, showing which are the links among the stakeholders and how they concretely work. Digitalization represents a bridge between the physical archetype and its IT representation, so merging complementary business models, adding value to the whole ecosystem.

Digital platforms are "software-based external platforms consisting of the extensible codebase of a software-based system that provides core

R. Moro-Visconti, *The Valuation of Digital Intangibles*, https://doi.org/10.1007/978-3-031-09237-4_20

functionality shared by the modules that interoperate with it and the interfaces through which they interoperate" (Tiwana et al., 2010). Software platforms are a technological meeting ground where application developers and end-users converge (Evans et al., 2006).

Platforms are facilitators of exchange (of goods, services, and information) between different types of stakeholders that could not otherwise interact with each other. Transactions are mediated through complementary players that share a network ecosystem (Armstrong, 2006; Rochet & Tirole, 2003). Due to their digital features, they have a global outreach that gives them the potential to scale.

A taxonomy of the platform typologies, following their architecture (Baldwin & Woodard, 2009) is recalled in Fig. 20.1.

Digital platforms are the basis of technology-enabled business models that facilitate exchanges between multiple groups—such as end-users and producers—who do not necessarily know each other. The generated value is proportional to the size of the community, with scalable network effects thanks to the Internet. Interaction within digital platforms follows innovative paradigms where stakeholders co-create and share value. Supply and value chains flatten and incorporate learning curves (economies of experience) that are fueled by real-time big data.

The digital platform consists of an IT infrastructure (hardware typically associated with one or more software) that provides technological services

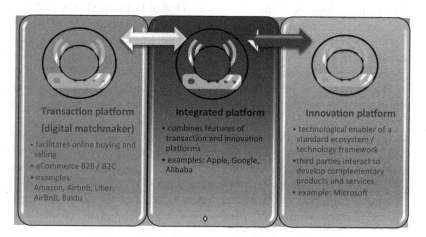

Fig. 20.1 Platform taxonomy

and tools, programs, and applications, for the distribution, management, and creation of free or paid digital content and services, including through the integration of multiple media (integrated digital platform) (Spagnoletti et al., 2015). The platform can be open source or commercial and can be structured, respectively, for public access or a limited target, after registration. It may include information, interactive, file sharing, downloading and uploading, streaming services as well as communication and sharing of multimedia material.

The use of online digital platforms is of primary importance for intermediation services and increasingly widespread applications such as e-commerce and payment services, Internet search engines, sharing economy, gig economy, e-learning, pay-TV and Video on-demand services, etc.

Digital businesses include transactions that are digitally mediated (often via m-apps) or that involve products or services that are used digitally by complementary users sharing a network (Kenney & Zysman, 2016).

Digital platforms consist of a complex set of software, hardware, information exchange operations (big data), or transactions and networks. Within digital platforms, the software, which oversees and manages its functions, is of particular importance. Software platforms are the technological place where application developers and end-users converge.

Digital platforms are the basis of innovative business models of highly profitable companies (such as Google or Facebook), thanks to the (presumed) gratuitousness of the services offered, typically offset by advertising revenues. Evaluation metrics take on relevance not only for the target companies but also to be able to enhance digital ecosystems that are increasingly pervasive and sophisticated in which users-consumers take on primary importance.

The monetary value of digital assets depends on parameters and value drivers that make it possible to overcome the traditional free access, with the hypothesis of indirect or mixed remuneration (freemium).

The sharing economy is the basis of an innovative economic system, based on the sharing of goods and services by a community of users, who operate through ad hoc digital platforms.

An innovative interpretation of digital platforms can be provided by network theory, in which digital platforms represent a virtual node that connects with other nodes manned by stakeholders, allowing the circulation of information, the execution of transactions, etc.

A further extension concerns the application of the paradigms of the sharing economy whose stakeholders interact through digital platforms.

Consistently to (Fig. 20.1), the main types of digital platforms are the following:

- e-commerce platforms (e.g., Amazon, Airbnb, eBay ...), which facilitate online B2B/B2C/C2C exchanges, etc.;
- integrated platforms (e.g., Google, Apple, Alibaba ...), which combine aspects of e-commerce platforms with innovative ones;
- innovative platforms (e.g., Microsoft), which allow third parties to develop complementary products and services, integrating proprietary business models with open-source extensions.

Digital platforms refer to a variety of complementary concepts that still need comprehensive systematization in the literature. A synthetic outlook of this recent research strand is important to make some critical remarks, consistent with the research question of this study.

A literature review on digital platforms is contained in Asadullah et al. (2018) and in Sutherland et al. (2018) that analyze sharing economy platforms. Spagnoletti et al. (2015, p. 364) define a digital platform as "a building block that provides an essential function to a technological system and serves as a foundation upon which complementary products, technologies, or services can be developed".

Digital businesses are those which carry out transactions that are digitally mediated or involve products or services that are experienced digitally (Weill & Woerner, 2013). Platforms are facilitators of exchange (of goods, services, and information). Transactions are mediated through complementary players that share a network ecosystem (Armstrong, 2006; Rochet & Tirole, 2003). This interpretation is consistent with the transaction cost theory that can be applied as a constructive stakeholder theory (Ketokivi & Mahoney, 2015).

Digital platforms are multi-sided digital frameworks that shape the terms on which participants interact. Digital platforms are also complex mixtures of software, hardware, operations, and networks (de Reuven et al., 2018; Gawer, 2014; Gawer & Cusumano, 2014). They provide a set of shared techniques, technologies, and interfaces to a broad set of users; social and economic interactions are mediated online, often by apps (Kenney & Zysman, 2016). Digital platforms are complementarily defined as "software-based external platforms consisting of the extensible codebase of a software-based system that provides core functionality shared by the modules that interoperate with it and the interfaces through which they interoperate" (Tiwana et al., 2010). Software platforms are a technological space where application developers and end-users converge (Evans et al., 2006).

Digital platforms have become a major mode for organizing a wide range of human activities, including economic, social, and political interactions (e.g., Kane et al., 2014; Tan et al., 2015). Platforms leverage networked technologies to facilitate economic exchange, transfer information, and connect people (Fenwick et al., 2019). Studies sharing this view focus on the technical developments and functions upon which complementary products and services can be developed, i.e., building on the top of the technical core that a platform owner offers and facilitates (Ceccagnoli et al., 2012; Ghazawneh & Henfridsson, 2015; Tiwana et al., 2010).

Other studies have conceptualized digital platforms based on a nontechnical view that presents platforms as a commercial network or market that enables transactions in the form of business-to-business (B2B), business-to-customer (B2C), or even customer-to-customer (C2C) exchanges (Pagani, 2013; Tan et al., 2015). Digital platforms may include crowdfunding and P2P stakeholders (Majchrzak & Malhotra, 2013) which are innovative ways of raising equity. Crowdfunding issues are a new frontier of corporate governance (Cumming et al., 2019).

An online marketplace (or online e-commerce marketplace) is a type of e-commerce website where product or service information is provided by multiple third parties. Online marketplaces are the primary type of eCommerce and can be a way to streamline the production process.

20.2 Legal Aspects

Digital services, as typically free, are sometimes assimilated into public goods. Typically these are so-called assets, not rivals, as their use by a consumer does not prevent the consumption of others, even at the same time. For example, while a sandwich is a typical rival good (it can only be consumed by one person), the enjoyment of a streaming film is open to a potentially unlimited number of consumers.

The fact that the (free) use of a digital service usually presupposes a user registration and profiling (generating data which is then subject to commercial exploitation, even surreptitiously, by the provider) places digital services between public goods and private.

Digital platforms can easily give rise to monopolistic rents that lead to antitrust problems. The large players, typically belonging to big tech have an infrastructure based on a capillary and scalable IT network, which can be adapted with relative simplicity to different geographical contexts, offering global services and content. This can lead to numerous behaviors potentially harmful to free competition.

Among the main assets subject to use that is not always transparent, there are big data, collected through systematic and capillary profiling of user information. Big data can feed baggage of information surreptitiously characterized by anti-competitive effects, creating barriers to entry into a market dominated by incumbents who can strengthen their dominant positions. In this context, the protection of transparency in the use of data must be combined with consumer protection.

Problems in the field of labor law can also be relevant. Digital platforms such as Google, Facebook, or Amazon, but also Foodora or Deliveroo are now an integral part of the daily life of billions of individuals. The gig economy is based on the organization of digital platforms, associated with dedicated mobile apps, which orchestrate the precarious interaction of freelancers with clients, as seen during the lockdown. Poor regulation facilitates the flexibility of a model which, moreover, lends itself to abuses that proliferate also thanks to the regulatory vacuum.

The recent phenomena linked to the Covid-19 pandemic constantly draw attention to the role of the major players of digital platforms, equipped with business models that are much more organized than others to implement agile working tools quickly and on a large scale (smart working).

20.3   NETWORKED GOVERNANCE AROUND DIGITAL PLATFORMS

The previous sections have proven how the firm, thanks to digitalization, can be considered as a network (Coasian nexus) of contracts. Some corporate governance implications have already been anticipated, consistently with the research question that is focused on the impact of digital platforms on the networking stakeholders. This section investigates in further detail how internal and external stakeholders interact around two bridging nodes: the networked firm and the digital platform.

Digital networks use a common platform as a pivoting (bridging) node which centralizes information sharing and transactions. Innovation is continuously proposing new paradigms for value creation, and reshaping governance interactions.

As described in (de Reuven et al., 2018), digital technologies imply homogenization (interoperability) of data, editability, re-programmability, distributedness, and self-referentiality (Yoo et al., 2010). Such features of digitality can lead to multiple inheritances in distributed settings, meaning there is no single owner of the platform core who dictates its design hierarchy (Henfridsson et al., 2014). This suggests that digital platforms, with their socio-technical features, may have "horizontal" features with interesting corporate governance implications in terms of value co-creation and sharing incentives. This feature is also consistent with the nature of distributed blockchains, where secured data are created and shared by cooperating stakeholders.

Internal stakeholders (mainly shareholders, managers, and employees) are the core part of the networked firm whereas external stakeholders are customers, suppliers, financial institutions (banks), and other players (P2P investors; competitors; partners, etc.). The firm may also be considered an "internal" platform (Gawer, 2014).

The digital platform is the bridging node between the firm and the external stakeholders (that may also have a direct link with the firm, bypassing the intermediating function of the platform) and it can be linked to a digital supply chain where suppliers interact with B2B transactions and e-Procurement. Value co-creation strategies (Beirão et al., 2017), are put in place by coordinated stakeholders.

Figure 20.2 (already introduced in Chapter 3) shows a case where players (stakeholders) are interacting nodes.

The two bridgings (hub) nodes shown in Fig. 20.2 are the networked firm and the digital platform. Internal stakeholders (shareholders, managers, employees, etc.) are a cohesive ecosystem within the firm that is linked to other external stakeholders (customers, suppliers, banks, interacting firms, etc.). These traditional internal and external stakeholders are complemented by the digital platform which is an innovative bridging node, linked also to P2P lenders, and digitized supply chains, following B2B or B2C transactional patterns.

The digital supply chain is a further bridging node between the digital platform, the traditional suppliers, and a further sub-network of e-suppliers that exchange information and trade in real-time

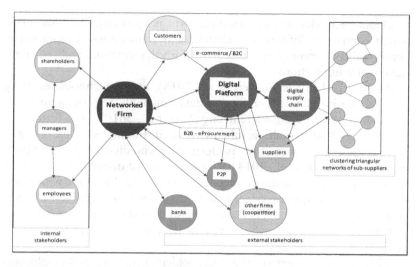

Fig. 20.2 Internal and external stakeholders linked to the firm and the digital platform

(24 hours/7 days a week). B2B2C stakeholders that make transactions through the platform exchange data and so fuel big data stored in the cloud. This information then feeds interoperable databases, with consequent artificial intelligence interpretation (and possible blockchain validation). The digital platform acts as an intermediating hub, increasing the number of nodes (vertices) as well as the quantity and quality of the links. For instance, any interaction between two agents that are mediated through the platform is digitally recorded.

A digital platform that mediates different groups of users (such as buyers and sellers) may be denoted as multi-sided. In two-sided markets, two distinct groups have a relationship where the value for one group increases as the number of participants from the other group increases (Evans et al., 2006). As platforms bring together multiple user groups, they create the so-called network effects or network externalities (de Reuver et al., 2018). This is consistent with Metcalfe's property of networks (examined in Chapter 3) and with the interpretation of platforms in networking terms. The added value of the eco-systemic network arises mainly from two synergistic features:

a. The "architectural" value of the network itself (depending on the outlay of the nodes and links), is measurable in numbers;

b. The functional value of the network (including the platform as a bridging node), depends on the intensity of the interactions among the different links (exchange of information; transactions, etc.). Architectural links are important to the extent that they incentive "traffic" among nodes (stakeholders).

Smart products in combination with innovative data-driven supply chain services help rethink supply chain management, leading to more self-organizing and self-optimizing systems. Digitization will play a growing role in global supply chains due to reasons such as the shift in values from the physical artifact to the data created by smart products, the emerging importance of services, the displacement of industry borders, the radical change of competitive structures, the transformation of business models, and more in general, the symptomatic creative destruction of established structures and behavior patterns (Pflaum et al., 2017).

20.4 Digital (Smart) Supply Chains

Digital supply (and value) chains are a further extension of the above considerations, consistently with the framework and aim of this study. Within a networked governance ecosystem, the information patterns and risk-return sharing of connected stakeholders are deeply affected by digitalization. This has an important impact on corporate governance.

A supply chain is a (physical) network between a company and its suppliers to produce and distribute a specific product to the final buyer. These links among the stakeholders shape their governance interactions and are re-engineered by digitalization. Network theory and its digital extension are consistent with the architectural framework of the supply chain. To the extent that the single steps ("rings") of the chain are affected by digitalization (e.g., thanks to a disintermediation process that shortens the chain), it can be inferred that the digitalization process produces savings—in the form of lower transactional costs—that improve the risk-return profile of the stakeholders that also benefit from the softening of information asymmetries.

What makes supply chains resilient is:

- A mix of complementary intangibles (e.g., big data and IoT that fuel patented processes and in-cloud artificial intelligence applications);
- A scalable network of expanding nodes and linking edges (consistent with network theory and its digital applications), incorporating growth real options, and B2B2C relationships;
- Digital platform services (cloud computing platforms where customers can develop, run, and manage applications without the requirement of building and maintaining the infrastructure typically needed when developing and launching an app) (Butler, 2013).

Network theory is mainly related to digital platforms, which are in turn catalyzers of scalable intangibles (that era intrinsically "networked", as it happens, for instance, with patent pools). The most powerful active platforms nowadays are Amazon, Alibaba, Apple, Google, and Facebook, together with other BigTechs that increasingly invest in the metaverse. Their common features are technologies not based on physical assets. They benefit from innovative ecosystems with core interactions between platform participants as consumers, producers, and third parties (Jacobides et al., 2018).

Korpela et al. (2017) show that digital supply chain integration is becoming increasingly dynamic. Access to customer demand needs to be shared effectively, and product and service deliveries must be tracked to provide visibility in the supply chain. Business process integration is based on standards and reference architectures that should offer end-to-end integration of product data. Companies operating in supply chains integrate processes and data through intermediating companies, who establish interoperability by mapping and integrating company-specific data for various organizations and systems. This practice has high integration costs, and adoption is still low. Business to business (B2B) integration within the supply chain refers to the exchange of electronic data over the Internet between business partners and value-added service providers.

The principal value drivers of digital supply chains are:

- Fast (just-in-time) end-to-end integration through digital enablers;
- Traceability and visibility of deliveries through smart logistics partners;
- Cost-effective cloud solutions provided by ICT partners;
- Sharing of real-time information in the cloud;

- Standardized transactions and collaboration through digital platforms accessed by supply chain members; and
- Networking with geolocalized e-commerce customers.

Digital (smart) supply and value chain technologies combine information, computing, communication, and connectivity innovation in applications or devices like Augmented reality; Big data; Cloud computing; Social media; Mobile, (cognitive) analytics or embedded devices; Cognitive technologies (machine learning, neural networks, robotic process automation, NPL, AI, etc.); IoT, wearables and Sensor technology; Nanotechnology; Omni-channel (to improve customer experience); Robotics; Self-Driving Vehicles and Unmanned Aerial Vehicles; and 3D printing.

The interactions among the networked firm, the digital platform, and the other external stakeholders can be examined with a value chain analysis that outlines its networked and digital features. The value chain is digitized by the devices/technologies reported above. An example is shown in Fig. 20.3.

Digital value chains tend to be flatter (more horizontal, more "democratic", and less hierarchical) than traditional value chains and the bridging platform acts as a coordinating hub, as shown in Fig. 20.3.

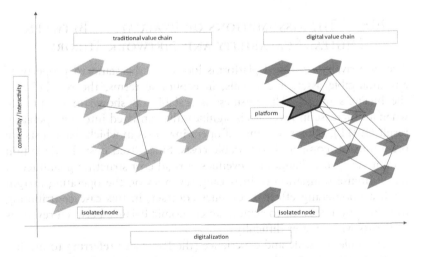

Fig. 20.3 From traditional to networked digital value chains

Blockchains preside over data validation, and can be considered a peculiar form of sequential digital platform. The digital network is intrinsically more valuable due to its highly interconnected architecture (higher number of links); value also depends on the increasing traffic of data or transactions among the linked nodes. This incremental value can be estimated using a with or without approach (consistent with the International Valuation Standard 210, examined in Chapter 2), according to which the value chain is estimated with-and-without its networked digital features, using the difference as a proxy for value.

Digital supply and value chains may be represented by two separated initially network ecosystems that eventually interact, within a multilayer network (Bianconi, 2018). This interpretation is consistent with the cloud manufacturing paradigm, an advanced form of networked manufacturing. This process is based on a combination of existing manufacturing systems and emerging technologies, such as cloud computing, virtual manufacturing, agile manufacturing, manufacturing grid, IoT, and service-oriented technologies (Akbaripour et al., 2015). Global supply chains (and related value chains) are becoming increasingly connected due to the increased globalization in terms of network size, strength, and connectivity, showing significant intertemporal changes, and higher clustering (Tsekeris, 2017).

20.5   THE ASSUMPTIONS OF EVALUATION BETWEEN DIGITAL SCALABILITY AND NETWORK THEORY

The non-rivalry of digital platforms looks like the standard property of any intangible asset, and entails, in economic terms, the scalability of the business model. The business is scalable, as shown in Chapter 3, when an increase in revenues is significantly translated into the operating result (EBIT), thanks to a mix of operating costs in which fixed costs are predominant, compared to variable costs. Since fixed costs by definition do not vary with changes in revenues, a rigid cost structure guarantees a more intense translation of increasing revenues on the operating margin (with a boomerang effect if revenues contract, in this case contributing to increasing losses. or to achieve an economic balance between revenues and costs with greater difficulty).

Economies of scale and experience (the latter also referring to mechanisms of interaction with customers, who with their feedback participate in the creation of value) represent a fundamental strategic lever for interpreting innovative value drivers.

Scalability can be greatly increased in the presence of digital platforms that mediate between stakeholders in real-time (24/7) and everywhere, guaranteeing dissemination and comparability of information.

The proactive role of digital platforms can be better understood by considering their interactive properties in terms of network theory.

A network represents, in its most basic formulation, a set of points (vertices or nodes) connected by lines (sides or edges). Social networks take on particular importance, which rely on digital platforms (such as Facebook or LinkedIn) as a point of interchange (so-called "bridge node"—"bridge ring") between different individuals. The network theory assumes economic and legal importance also in the interpretation of corporate governance issues, where the stakeholders are considered to be interconnected nodes, also thanks to the intermediation of "bridge nodes" such as digital platforms that represent a new stakeholder intangible.

20.6   A Theoretical Background for the Economic Valuation

The economic evaluation profiles depend above all on the type of platform being estimated (e.g., open-source or commercial). A further prerequisite is represented by the subject who relates to the platform to be evaluated: the owner, the consumer-user, the intermediary (who provides hosting services or available M-App, etc.).

While the evaluation of the proprietary platform involves a relatively small number of subjects, the extension to consumers concerns a much wider audience of potentially interested parties. In this context, it is not the value of the platform itself, but rather the added value that it generates on the user's activity (net of intermediation costs for the use of the third-party platform).

If the economic evaluation refers to an asset (or business unit) that can be independently identified and susceptible to economic exploitation and consequent estimate in terms of value, no particular methodological findings emerge.

On the other hand, the estimate of the value for non-owners (such as consumers-users) is more complex. Profiles of co-creation of value emerge that enrich the traditional valuation landscape, inserting new stakeholders such as consumers, who, although not co-owners of the good or service being valued, participate (sometimes even with surreptitious strategies to which they are unwittingly subjected), with the release of personal information (habits and customs then profiled for vertical marketing strategies; feedback that feeds big data, etc.) that create a still strongly underestimated value.

The same characteristic of the "good" being valued—the digital platform—and its nature above all from the point of view of legal ownership (public, private, or consortium good?). Contributes to fueling a debate also of an "ontological" nature on the rationale and objectives of the estimate. Analogously, a reference to blockchains can be hypothesized, which can also be of public, private, or consortium nature and which present significant intersections, especially in perspective, with digital platforms, being able to preside over a certification/authentication of digitized information, that pass through the platform.

The interrelationships between digital platforms and other intangible assets can also be relevant, such as patents or know-how (with platforms that incorporate inventions), already mentioned intangibles such as software (which represents the essential IT infrastructure of digital platforms), blockchains, big data (which feed the platforms, leaving them enriched, with a surplus to be evaluated also economically), (social) networks, mobile apps (which represent an "IT shortcut" to access platforms). They also detect additional intangibles that process information intermediated by platforms, using algorithms orchestrated by artificial intelligence, which processes information data stored in the cloud in interoperable databases. Furthermore, brands should not be forgotten, even in their digital branding extensions, and platforms with high visibility are often referable to as Big Techs.

From an evaluation point of view, the examination of the business model of the platform is aimed at identifying and estimating the value drivers that emanate from it. In this context, the following levers of value creation, first of all, stand out:

- Internet traffic conveyed by the platform, instrumental to economic use of data and information, atomistically considered as "small data" but then aggregated at a "big data" level; and
- the volumes of transactions conveyed by e-commerce platforms, with B2B/B2C profiling depending on the counterpart of the business operator, which can be another company or a consumer.

The digital platform and its virtual showcase function allow, thanks to the use of the web, to overcome space–time barriers, operating in a space–time context so-called "24/7" and allowing to pursue digital scalability strategies, also through a co-creation of value between providers and users.

20.7   Open-Source Platforms

The evaluation of open-source digital platforms has clear similarities with open-source software, in which the source codes are freely available by developers who contribute, equally free of charge, to improve their characteristics and performance.

In this context, the co-creation of value strategies is implemented, susceptible to an autonomous enhancement by the individual subjects participating in the initiative.

The estimate can be oriented, singularly, first of all by the analysis of cost savings and efficiency recoveries that the user can personally derive from the use of free software.

The evaluation of the usefulness of the use of open-source platforms can be estimated, consistently with the premises mentioned above, for example through a "with or without" approach, which estimates the value of the good or service or company, respectively, before and after the intermediation of the platform.

The "with or without" approach, examined in Chapter 2, is traditionally used in the estimation of intangible assets and is explicitly recalled also by the International Valuation Standard 210, in the context of income approaches (because it considers, at a differential level, the increase in income made possible by use of the intangible asset being valued), comparing the valuation that incorporates the use of the platform ("with") with that without ("without") the platform.

20.8   Proprietary (Commercial) Platforms

The proprietary platforms can implement e-commerce or data collection services (typically, big data, also powered by sensors—IoT). The services provided by the platform can also be used by non-owners, who "rent" them by paying fees (subject to economic evaluation and similar to royalties).

There can be models of Platform as a Service (PaaS), an economic activity that consists of the service of making available processing platforms (Computing platforms). The elements of PaaS allow you to develop, test, implement, and manage business applications without the costs and complexity associated with purchasing, configuring, optimizing, and managing basic hardware and software. Elements of PaaS can be used for application development and application services such as team collaboration, web integration, database integration, security, and health management. These services can be used as an integrated solution on the web.

Complementary, there are as-a-Service services in the fields of software, the Internet, or other applications.

The proprietary platforms are used by operators who carry out online transactions mainly compared to the use of outsourced digital shops.

20.9   ADAPTATION OF THE GENERAL VALUATION APPROACHES

For the specific evaluation of digital platforms, it should first of all be noted that they are not—in their essence—easily identifiable by the rest of the companies that contain them (unless they constitute the corporate purpose). From this, it follows that, for their estimate, in most cases, it is necessary to refer to the evaluation of the entire company, the owner of the digital platform.

For evaluation purposes, first of all, the placement between the subject intended for the estimate is noted: the owner of the platform or the user (belonging to a much more heterogeneous category) or any intermediaries, the value chain (supply/value chain).

Taking up the approaches described for the valuation of intangible assets described in par. 5, a brief critical examination of their applicability to the present case is possible.

The cost approach can only be used on a residual and orientative basis, as:

- the costs incurred for the development of the platform are not always clearly and autonomously identifiable and others can be separated; and

– the historicity of costs is weakly correlated with the prospective value of the platform, which depends on scenarios and expectations based on expected market dynamics, rather than on costs incurred.

The income-financial approach is based, first of all, on the estimate of expected cash flows, to be discounted to represent the current value of the investment/firm. Determining the size of these FCFF or FCFE flows is of primary importance in applying the method and so is the consistency of the discount rates adopted.

Where the digital platform represents a business branch, its value can be estimated, incrementally, with the aforementioned differential income with or without approach. The differential (incremental) income also represents a useful investigation tool for estimating the surplus value induced by the platform for the consumer.

The use of a differential method can also be useful for estimating the so-called profit of the infringer, often used in disputes relating to trademarks or patents, also considering the benefits achieved by the perpetrator of the violation.

The incremental value for the user can be estimated first of all by considering the scalability of revenues. Scalability is typical of non-rival intangible assets (that is, they can be used simultaneously by several subjects) and allows to increase operating revenues exponentially and quickly, minimizing variable extra costs, thus giving the business model plasticity that enhances the key value drivers. Scalability is typical of digital applications and can also affect traditional sectors, even within its application limits (think of an e-commerce platform that allows the sale of local wine on a global scale).

The time horizon for discounting income or financial flows must consider the expected useful life of the platform, which depends on the persistence of its intrinsically ephemeral competitive advantage. The estimate of this horizon is one of the most critical parameters, considering the volatility of the reference markets and the related business models, in a highly competitive context, in which constant innovation implies elements of discontinuity that cannot be easily estimated.

Another methodology—also traditionally used in the estimation of intangible assets—is that of presumed royalties, based on the hypothetical fee that the company would pay if it were to obtain the license to use a platform owned by a third party.

The market approach is based on the assumption of being able to identify comparable transactions (of digital platforms or similar companies), from which to derive reliable benchmarks for evaluation.

The estimate of the market value is based on the screening of comparable transactions involving intangible assets, by way of sale or license, using the international databases now available on the web can provide useful clues about their value (also in terms of price comparison).

Still, in the context of the empirical approach, a further method of enhancement of so-called "Quick and dirty" digital platforms could concern, in partial analogy with the estimate of the value of Internet sites, their diffusion (number of users), or the number of transactions and the volumes of traffic generated by them. This is information that feeds big data and, as such, can be subject to further enhancement (think of the profiling of customers' tastes and habits).

The taxonomy of the aforementioned approaches (cost, income, and market) intersects with the most frequently used methodologies for estimating companies tout court, based on discounted cash flows (which represent a subset of the income-financial approach) or on the stock market multipliers (Enterprise Value/EBITDA, etc.) of comparable companies, attributable to the market approach.

Both the accounting cash flows and the income parameter to which the multiplier is applied are, respectively, derived from or represented by the GOP/EBITDA, where GOP stands for Gross Operating Profit A fortiori, the importance of EBITDA derives from its fungibility, being the only parameter that simultaneously has the characteristics of an economic and financial margin, suitable for expressing the liquidity generated (or absorbed, if the algebraic sign is negative) in the context of typical or characteristic economic management (operational management, before debt service, taxes, and extraordinary operations). EBITDA is calculated by subtracting monetary operating costs (OPEX – purchases, salaries, etc.) from operating monetary revenues (essentially, sales). The application of the differential income to the EBITDA makes it possible to estimate the incremental/differential impact, also for the consumer (by how much has the EBITDA increased thanks to the use of the digital platform?).

Big data, typically stored in the cloud, are included in the evaluation as assets with increasing market value. They feed the interoperable databases with information input data from which data can be extracted to be interpreted also with the aid of artificial intelligence. Artificial intelligence amplifies the potential of the digital world and helps make it more autonomous and self-referential, distancing it, and abstracting it from its empirical substrate.

In evaluating digital platforms, the apps generally related to them and the Internet sites themselves must also be considered.

Transactions of packages comprising multiple assets or multiple intangibles make the valuation of stand-alone intangibles more complicated based on an empirical method. These difficulties are even more evident taking into account that, from an accounting point of view, according to IAS 38 there is no active market for intangibles, which tend to be unaccounted for, and their fair value appears difficult to estimate.

The evaluation criteria are accompanied by those, no less insidious, of sharing the value among the stakeholders, who face traditional problems of negotiation asymmetry, such as monopoly rents (typical of the dominant platforms operated by big techs).

In more general terms, the broad theme of the enhancement of digital platforms cannot fail to intersect, at least at the level of interdisciplinary connection, with aspects of a sociological and psychological nature. This is because consumers' perceptions, attitudes, and expectations influence increasingly globalized choices and lifestyles, with evident economic impacts, which are also relevant in the context of evaluation metrics.

A still largely unexplored aspect concerns the link between the "physicality" of empirical reality and the parallel virtual world, which develops into ever more abstract digital platforms. The ancient link between immanent reality and the transcendent dimension intersects with a technological innovation destined to have profound socio-economic implications. The legal aspects and evaluation metrics are based on the analysis of an underlying reality whose boundaries, largely unexplored, must be the subject of constant interdisciplinary examination.

Technological evolution is bringing great progress in many fields of human life but also has a dangerous impact on his behavior. The smartphones on which we spend most of our time are today real prostheses of body and mind and are leading to a division between two brains: ours and the one we "carry in our pockets".

The "virtual splitting" of the user-consumer, which inspires innovative business models but at the same time surreptitiously suffers the consequences, re-proposes ancient themes. In this context, the hermeneutics of Plato's cave myth helps. The virtual shadows projected from the outside and viewed by the prisoners can well exemplify the ever closer link between the real world and virtual reality, whose dangerous relationships manifest a hierarchical order that is not always defined.

SELECTED REFERENCES

Akbaripour, H., Houshmand, M., & Valilai, O. F. (2015). Cloud-based global supply chain: A conceptual model and multilayer architecture. *Journal of Manufacturing Science Engineering, 137*(4), 040913.

Armstrong, M. (2006). Competition in two-sided markets. *Rand Journal of Economics, 37*(3), 668–691.

Asadullah, A., Faik, I., & Kankanhalli, A. (2018). *Digital platforms: A review and future directions*. Twenty-second Pacific Asia Conference on Information Systems, Japan.

Baldwin, C. Y., & Woodard, C. J. (2009). The architecture of platforms: A unified view. In A. Gawer (Ed.) *Platforms, markets and innovation*. Cheltenham: Edward Elgar.

Beirão, G., Patrício, L., & Fisk, R. P. (2017). Value co-creation in service ecosystems. *Journal of Service Management, 28*(2), 227–249.

Bianconi, G. (2018). *Multilayer networks*.Oxford: Oxford University Press.

Butler, B. (2013). PaaS primer: What is platform as a service and why does it matter? *Network World*, February 11.

Ceccagnoli, M., Forman, C., Huang, P., & Wu, D. J. (2012). Co-creation of value in a platform ecosystem: The case of enterprise software. *MIS Quarterly, 36*(1), 263–290.

Cumming, D. J., Vanacker, T., & Zahra, S. A. (2019). Equity crowdfunding and governance: Toward an integrative model and research agenda. *Academy of Management Perspectives, 35*(1), 69–95.

de Reuven, M., Sørensen, C., & Basole, R. C. (2018). The digital platform: A research agenda. *Journal of Information Technology, 33,* 124–135.

Evans, D. S., Hagiu, A., & Schmalensee, R. (2006). *Invisible engines: How software platforms drive innovation and transform industries*. Cambridge: MIT University Press.

Fenwick, M., McCahery, J. A., & Vermeulen, E. P. M. (2019). The end of 'corporate' governance: Hello 'platform' governance. *European Business Organization Law Review, 20*(1), 171–199.

Gawer, A. (2014). Bridging differing perspectives on technological platforms: Toward an integrative framework. *Research Policy, 43*(7), 1239–1249.

Gawer, A., & Cusumano, M. A. (2014). Industry platforms and ecosystem innovation. *The Journal of Product Innovation Management, 31*(3).

Ghazawneh, A., & Henfridsson, O. (2015). A paradigmatic analysis of digital application marketplaces. *Journal of Information Technology, 30*(3), 198–208.

Henfridsson, O., Mathiassen, L., & Svahn, F. (2014). Managing technological change in the digital age: The role of architectural frames. *Journal of Information Technology, 29,* 27–43.

Jacobides, M. G., Cernamo, C., & Gawer, A. (2018). Towards a theory of ecosystems. *Strategic Management Journal, 39*(8).

Kane, G. C., Alavi, M., Labianca, G., & Borgatti, S. P. (2014). What's different about social media networks? A framework and research agenda. *MIS Quarterly, 38*(1), 275–304.

Kenney, M., & Zysman, J. (2016). The rise of the platform economy. *Issues in Science and Technology, 32*(3).

Ketokivi, M., & Mahoney, J. T. (2015). Transaction cost economics as a constructive stakeholder theory. *Academy of Management Learning & Education, 15*(1).

Korpela, K., Hallikas, J., & Dahlberg, T. (2017). *Digital supply chain transformation toward blockchain integration.* Proceedings of the 50th Hawaii International Conference on System Sciences. Available at https://scholarsp ace.manoa.hawaii.edu/handle/10125/41666

Majchrzak, A., & Malhotra, A. (2013). Towards an information systems perspective and research agenda on crowdsourcing for innovation. *Journal of Strategic Information Systems, 22*(4), 257–268.

Pagani, M. (2013). Digital business strategy and value creation: Framing the dynamic cycle of control points. *MIS Quarterly, 37*(2), 617–632.

Pflaum, A., Bodendorf, F., Prockl, G., & Chen, H. (2017). *The digital supply chain of the future: Technologies, applications and business models minitrack.* Hawaii International Conference on System Sciences. Available at https:// scholarspace.manoa.hawaii.edu/handle/10125/42513

Rochet, J. C., & Tirole, J. (2003). Platform competition in two-sided markets. *Journal of the European Economic Association, 1*(4), 990–1029.

Spagnoletti, P., Resca, A., & Lee, G. (2015). A design theory for digital platforms supporting online communities: A multiple case study. *Journal of Information Technology, 30*(4), 364–380.

Sutherland, W., & Jarrahi, M. H. (2018). The sharing economy and digital platforms: A review and research agenda. *International Journal of Information Management, 43,* 328–341.

Tan, B., Pan, S. L., Lu, X., & Huang, L. (2015). The role of IS capabilities in the development of multi-sided platforms: The digital ecosystem strategy of Alibaba.com. *Journal of the Association for Information Systems, 16*(4), 248–280.

Tiwana, A., Konsynsky, B., & Bush, A. A. (2010). Platform evolution: Coevolution of platform architecture, governance, and environmental dynamics. *Information Systems Research, 21*(4), 675–687.

Tsekeris, T. (2017). Global value chains: Building blocks and network dynamics. *Physica A: Statistical Mechanics and Its Applications, 488*, 187–204.

Yoo, Y., Henfridsson, O., & Lyytinen, K. (2010). The new organizing logic of digital innovation: An agenda for information systems research. *Information Systems Research, 21*(4), 724–735.

Weill, P., & Woerner, S. L. (2013). Optimizing your digital business model. *MIT Sloan Management Review*, March.

PART V

Residual Goodwill, Bundled Intangibles, and Bankability Issues

CHAPTER 21

Digital Goodwill Valuation

21.1 The Controversial Concept of Goodwill

IVS 210 § 20.6. indicates that "Goodwill is any future economic benefit arising from a business, an interest in a business or from the use of a group of assets which has not been separately recognized in another asset. In general terms, the value of goodwill is the residual amount remaining after the values of all identifiable tangible, intangible and monetary assets, adjusted for actual or potential liabilities, have been deducted from the value of a business. It is typically represented as the excess of the price paid in a real or hypothetical acquisition of a company over the value of the company's other identified assets and liabilities".

According to OECD (2017) "Depending on the context, the term goodwill can be used to refer to several different concepts. In some accounting and business valuation contexts, goodwill reflects the difference between the aggregate value of an operating business and the sum of the values of all separately identifiable tangible and intangible assets. Alternatively, goodwill is sometimes described as a representation of the future economic benefits associated with business assets that are not individually identified and separately recognized. In still other contexts goodwill is referred to as the expectation of future trade from existing customers. The term ongoing concern value is sometimes referred to as the value of the assembled assets of an operating business over and above the sum of the separate values of the individual assets. It is generally recognized that

R. Moro-Visconti, *The Valuation of Digital Intangibles*, https://doi.org/10.1007/978-3-031-09237-4_21

615

goodwill and ongoing concern value cannot be segregated or transferred separately from other business assets" (par. 6.27).

Goodwill indicates the ability of a company or one of its branches to generate an extra profit (new incremental wealth or excess capital), that is the concrete attitude to produce profits higher than the average of the reference sector; this is represented by a typically indistinct set of intangible conditions (the image and the prestige of the company, the clientele, the organization, the management, the quality of the products, the commercial network, etc.) that express the competitive capacity of the company on the market.

Goodwill is related to commercial viability: "*as a general rule, intangibles relating to products with established commercial viability will be more valuable than otherwise comparable intangibles relating to products whose commercial viability is yet to be established*" (OECD, par. 6.124).

On the controversial and multi-faceted concept of goodwill, jurists and businessmen have intervened for years. Before them, the topic was addressed, in terms of differential rent, by classical economists like Malthus or Ricardo.

The concept then evolved, acquiring a more articulated economic-strategic meaning, which finds its genesis in competitive advantages of price or differentiation, based on which the extra income finds justification and rationality either in the ability to sell goods and services at a lower cost than customers, or making them distinguish and prefer for their qualitative or merchandise characteristics. These features differentiate them from the competition and legitimate a premium price. Goodwill is frequently associated with registered trademarks or, sometimes, with patent protection. Trademarks and goodwill are concepts that often tend to overlap and sometimes improperly merge.

Goodwill derives from specific factors which, although positively contributing to the production of income and having formed over time in a burdensome manner, do not have an autonomous value. It may also originate from synergistic increases in value that company assets acquire concerning the sum of individual assets, under the organization of assets in an efficient and suitable system to produce profits. Digital goodwill represents the last frontier, incorporating its most abstract features (complete immateriality), while deploying its full adaptability to any possible context (also considering the bridging features of "brick & mortar" businesses that are, at least partially, converted to the digital playground).

21.1.1 Accounting

IFRS 3 (2008) on Business Combinations aims at improving the relevance, reliability, and comparability of information provided about business combinations (M&A) and their effects. It sets out the principles for the recognition and measurement of acquired assets and liabilities, the determination of goodwill, and its disclosure.

The functional coordination of company assets (movable and fixed, fungible and non-fungible, tangible and intangible), as a nexus of organized assets, determines an increase in their bundled value (the synergistic whole is worth more than the individual parts). A coordinated value in use that exceeds the exchange value generates implicit goodwill.

Goodwill accounting must consider the competitive arena that may be represented by imperfect competition, monopolistic rents, oligopoly, etc. Size and characteristics of the market matter.

The term "goodwill" commonly means the ability of a company to generate an extra profit (new incremental wealth) that is the concrete attitude to produce gains higher than the average of the reference sector. The creation of incremental wealth is fully consistent with the with-or-without approach illustrated in the IVS 210, as it shows the difference between a firm that incorporates the digital goodwill, versus a comparable company that does not. Appropriate benchmarking is anyway necessary for the estimation.

Goodwill is represented by a typically indistinct set of intangible conditions (the image and prestige of the company, customers, organization, management, product quality, the sales network, etc.) that qualify the competitive position of the company in the market. Network theory interpretations add value to this classic framework, as they consider the wider digital ecosystem where the firm is positioned, interacting with other firms and stakeholders to fully deploy its unexpressed value. It should not, however, be forgotten that even goodwill is an ephemeral concept, and that there is no magic in digitalization, as it just represents a double-edged sword, able to catalyze success and scalability, but also to incorporate sudden value destruction. Full-scale comparability, eased by digitalization, minimizes information asymmetries, to the benefit of scaling up firms, counterbalanced by the pitfalls of declining companies, whose weakness becomes immediately evident. When goodwill goes digital, these features are enhanced, and the party becomes hardly everlasting.

Digitalization also impacts know-how, a basic prerequisite of internally generated goodwill (that cannot be recorded, but can be evaluated). Digitalized know-how is easier to record, compare, and use, but also likelier to be transferred and possibly stolen. A further impact of digitalization concerns trademarks—digital branding—that are closely linked, once again, to goodwill.

21.1.2   Useful Life, Limited Period of Use, and Impairment Test

The useful life of an intangible asset coincides with the period, expressed in years, between its acquisition and the time when it has no longer utility and, therefore, is no longer able to bring economic benefits to the company.

The estimate of the useful life of the goodwill is delegated to the directors, which will be able to use approved business plans or fairness opinions of independent evaluators.

Budgets and updated business plans are useful tools for estimating the evolution of the company, and the persistence of its goodwill across time.

According to IAS 22 (now repealed), paragraph 48, the main factors that can influence the estimate of the useful life of goodwill are:

a) Nature and foreseeable economic life of the acquired activity;
b) The stability and foreseeable economic life of the sector to which the goodwill refers;
c) Public information on the characteristics of goodwill in similar industries or companies and the life cycles characteristic of similar activities;
d) The effects of product obsolescence, changes in demand, and other economic factors on the business acquired;
e) Expectations about the permanence in service of (key) employees and whether the activity acquired can be efficiently operated by another management group;
f) The level of maintenance costs or the level of funds required to obtain future economic benefits expected from the activity acquired and the capacity and intention of the company to reach this level;
g) The strategies envisaged by current or potential competitors;
h) The period in which control over the activity acquired is exercised and the legal or contractual clauses that influence the useful life of the asset.

The estimate of the useful life is a prerequisite to the impairment test, introduced by IAS 36.

21.2 BADWILL

In some cases, goodwill can be negative. Badwill generally occurs when, on the acquisition of a company, the overall price is lower than the equity book value (the difference between assets and liabilities). This happens when the acquired company is expected to generate economic losses, a typical event of a crisis or turnaround. Badwill can also be the result of digitally-driven B2B2C competition that, once again, represents a double-edged sword.

The purchase of a business unit at a price lower than its book value of equity may be justified by a price discount and by the ability of the acquirer to restructure the business, even spin-offing some of its divisions, creating long-term value that can eventually offset the negative outlook.

As with goodwill, badwill can be purchased or generated internally. The argument does not appear to have been specifically considered by accounting standards. The internally generated badwill, unlike goodwill, must be recorded in the financial statements, in compliance with the principle of prudence. The accounting can take place directly, by devaluing individual assets (through the impairment test or the allocation of permanent losses of value to specific fixed assets).

The valuation of goodwill, corresponding to a potential intangible even in the presence of historical losses, foreseeing a growth rate or a terminal value of the investment is not infrequent, even if the most recent past experiences (as the deflation of the speculative Internet bubble in 2000–2001 or the worldwide financial crisis of 2008–2009) have somewhat reduced this practice.

In companies characterized by a unit in crisis and another healthy, the separation of the non-profitable branch, which is associated with a badwill, if timely and free of revocatory actions, joint liability, etc., can allow the protection of goodwill in the healthy branch, avoiding value-destroying contagion.

21.3 AN INTRODUCTION TO VALUATION

The estimation of goodwill has unavoidable elements of subjectivity and is influenced by the human psyche, megalomania, and the sense of immortality, which leads many to overestimate its entity and consider it perpetual. Any competitive advantage is, however, intrinsically ephemeral, capable of producing extra returns that inevitably corrupt over time, and are subject to competitive attacks, more intense when the perceived value is higher, or to antitrust pressures, against monopolistic rents that damage consumers.

The most common valuation approach for independent estimation of goodwill (positive or negative), is the mixed capital-income approach.[1] The valuation is determined starting from the adjusted net equity (capital), calculated based on the simple or complex balance sheet-based approach, and to the value of the goodwill (excess economic margin) that the company can produce outperforming its competing companies. If the excess income is negative (excess-loss), there is a badwill. Any (positive or negative) excess income can be compared to the with-or-without incremental/differential approach.

As previously noted, the IAS/IFRS international accounting standards provide for the use of financial approaches for the goodwill impairment test.

21.4   The Estimate of Goodwill: Fair Value, Value of Use, Impairment Test, and Firm Valuation

IAS 36 "Impairment of assets" shows in the definitions that "fair value less sale costs is equal to the amount obtainable from the sale of an asset or cash flow generating unit in a free transaction between knowledgeable and available parties, less the disposal costs".

The impairment test estimates the recoverable amount, which IAS 36, paragraph 6, defines as the amount "greater than its fair value, less the costs to sell and it's use-value". If the book value exceeds the recoverable value, goodwill must be written down, recognizing an impairment loss.

Use value means the present value of future cash flows which are supposed to derive from the permanent use and disposal of the asset at the end of its useful life (realization price).

Figure 21.1 contains a schematic example of the comparison between the book and the recoverable value underlying the impairment test.

Market prices represent a less subjective reference parameter than estimates based on analytical approaches (capital, income, mixed, financial, etc.), especially if they refer to the ideal case of binding sales agreements in free competition. Analytical approaches, also examined in Chapter 2,

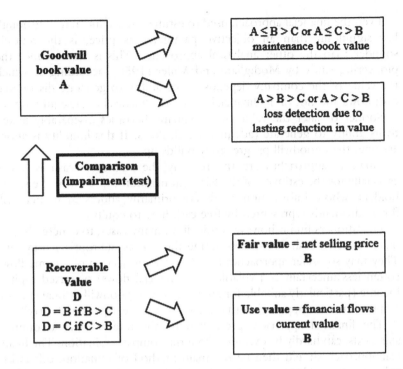

Fig. 21.1 Impairment test: comparison between book value and recoverable value

may provide a subjective estimate to arrive at the determination of an (objective) market price.

The issues, in terms of harmonization between accounting principles and company valuation approaches, are not negligible.

From a theoretical point of view, the market price approach may be considered as the main valuation parameter (the only one, in the fair value assessment).

This parameter is referred to as "prices established for sales agreements" or "recent and comparable transactions" preferably "binding" within an "active market". These characteristics make it rarely readily available. IAS 36 acknowledges these circumstances and regulates the absence of a binding sales agreement or an active market (a typical characteristic of intangibles).

Even the financial approach used to estimate the value in use, although less significant than an objective parameter as price, is theoretically sounder than the other analytical approaches. This is known since the pioneering study by Modigliani and Miller (1958), according to which the value of the company depends on its ability to generate discounted cash flows and not on its financial structure (financial debt/equity ratio).

Sooner or later the value of a company becomes inseparably linked to its ability to generate (adequate) cash flows. If this liquidity is above average, then goodwill progressively builds up.

Financial approaches are theoretically the soundest (cash is king), especially for the estimate of the fair remuneration expected by the shareholders, whose information needs are primarily addressed to net cash flows (dividends represented by free cash flow to equity).

Practitioners find it however difficult, in many cases, to concretely estimate expected cash flows, discounting them at an appropriate risky rate. They may so prefer approaches based on the projection of income flows (often less uncertain and volatile than financial flows) or mixed capital-income (particularly suitable for an independent goodwill estimate) or on empirical market approaches that are known to be "quick and dirty".

The financial approach, prescribed by the international accounting standards, can hardly be excluded from the company valuation. The financial approach should then be the main method of valuation, otherwise, subsequent problematic applicability of the impairment test should be considered.

21.5   COMPETITIVE ADVANTAGE PERIOD AND MONOPOLISTIC RENTS

The Competitive Advantage Period (CAP) considers the time frame during which the company is expected to be able to achieve returns on invested capital higher than the weighted average cost of capital (ROIC > WACC) and so represents positive goodwill. The implicit surplus value in the CAP is conveyed into the strategic components of the company (competitive advantages, linked to product differentiation or cost advantages; technological, marketing, and organizational resources and skills; industry attractiveness, etc.) and in the economic and financial aspects (first of all, the incremental EBITDA margin).

The CAP, according to the resource-based approach, is based on purely intangible characteristics such as rarity or inimitability, uniqueness, distinctive and integration capabilities, resource-picking, and capability-building mechanisms, at the base of competitive differentiation from other firms.

The CAP can depend on economies of scale and/or experience and on monopolistic rents, typical of operators who have market power deriving from uniqueness (for example, a natural monopoly or a patented invention) and allow the holder to set the price freely, taking advantage of the lack of free competition.

Rents, as well as monopolistic (or oligopolistic), can be:

- Ricardian (resource-based), deriving from the limited intangible resources that guarantee a competitive advantage;
- Schumpeterian, if based on innovative products or services that allow an economic marginality (largely) higher than the production costs;
- Paretian, if based on the difference between better use and lower use of resources. In all cases, the intangible components play a major role.

Above-average performance, in the absence of monopolistic rents that are increasingly contrasted by antitrust provisions, inevitably decreases over the years, due to external competitive pressures or the introduction of new standards, inventions, or models that make the initial competitive advantage obsolete. This should be considered in the estimation procedures, which may be biased if they overestimate the capacity of the goodwill to persist indefinitely. The high growth rate, intangible-driven and typical of many startups, usually converges toward a stable and more realistic sustainable growth rate in the medium–long term.

The creditworthiness (borrowing capacity) of companies with positive economic rents and CAP is generally sound, although it must be subject to constant monitoring (through periodical impairment testing) to assess its residual useful life and current entity. Valuation concerns may address the sustainability, regeneration, and defensibility of the competitive advantage of the incumbents, considering the entry barriers of the sector that limit the competition (attracted by the competitive advantages of incumbent rentiers).

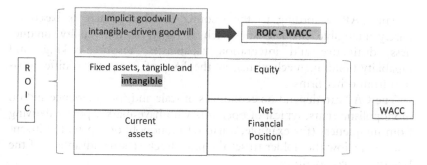

Fig. 21.2 Goodwill as a positive differential between the yield and the cost of invested capital

The intensity and duration of the CAP are at the base of the valuation models of the surplus value (implicit goodwill), driven by the intangible sources of the expected competitive advantages, which allow reinvestments at a rate of return on invested capital higher than the weighted average cost of capital (ROIC > WACC).

The sustainable enterprise value corresponds to the valorization of the existing assets, added to the (typically intangible) value of growth opportunities (Fig. 21.2).

21.6   Economic and Market Value-Added

The CAP is consistent with the notion of goodwill, in its meaning of excess return concerning the industry average. The concept is connected to the Economic Value Added and, in a multi-year cumulated perspective, to the Market Value Added.

The Economic Value Added (EVA) expresses the difference between the return and the cost of the invested capital (expressed in market terms). The Market Value Added (MVA) represents the present value of a stream of future EVA.

EVA is a performance measure devised by Bennet Stewart (1991), based on the difference between the return and the cost of capital. It is obtained by subtracting the cost of capital employed from the operating result (= EBIT) normalized and after taxes (NOPAT):

$$EVA = NOPAT - WACC * Ic \qquad (21.1)$$

or:

$$EVA = (r - WACC) * Ic \qquad (21.2)$$

where:

- NOPAT = normalized operating income after taxes;
- Ic = [adjusted] invested capital (shareholders' equity + financial debts + equity equivalents);
- r = NOPAT/Ic = ROIC = return on invested capital;
- WACC = weighted average cost of capital.

Being EVA expressed in terms of WACC, it is independent of the financial structure (unless the latter has an impact on the WACC)[2] and therefore does not discriminate between levered and unlevered companies.

In any case, if a company is not indebted (D = 0), the invested capital corresponds to the net assets and the NOPAT $\approx$ net profit; so, NOPAT/Ci = Return on Equity (ROE) and WACC = k_e(cost of equity). Since both the NOPAT and the invested capital are expressed at market value (thanks to the adjustments made with the Equity Equivalents), then NOPAT/Ic $\approx$ WACC = k_e and consequently EVA $\approx$ 0.

Based on EVA, a company:

- Creates wealth (EVA > 0) when the return on capital (r = ROIC) is higher than the weighted average cost of capital (WACC);
- Destroys wealth in the opposite case (r = ROIC < WACC).

The original EVA calculation method prescribes some adjustments to the "raw" NOPAT and invested capital book values. These adjustments (equity equivalents)[3] are necessary to express a correct measure of both the capital invested by the corporate lenders and the income available for the latter.

Market Value Added (MVA) is the difference between the market value and the invested capital, equivalent to the sum of the discounted future EVA:

MVA = market value − invested capital

    = present value of all future EVA = $EVA_1/(WACC - g)$

    = (economic profit of existing assets and growth opportunities)/WACC   (21.3)

The MVA is the measure of the value that a company has created in excess (goodwill) compared to the resources already bound to the company. This relates, in particular, to the measure of the excess market value (referring to the value of the current and fixed assets, including intangible assets) concerning the book value of the capital raised (or invested), which is an expression of the accounting liabilities (shareholders' equity + financial debts = current assets + fixed assets + equity equivalents).

The MVA estimate can be broken down using a mixed capital-income valuation approach.

Since EVA is positive when $r>$WACC, a company has an MVA > 0 when it is expected that in the future $r/$WACC >1.

Intangible assets typically have a significant role in the formation of EVA and MVA, as shown in Figs. 21.3. Fig. 21.4. shows the progressive formation of operating and then financial Operating Profit (NOPAT) that adds value to the stakeholders that have underwritten the raised capital (financial debtholders, ultimately followed by shareholders).

The acquisition of resources (funding sources or collected capital) is preparatory to their use (invested capital), even in intangibles that generate a positive economic and financial margin/flow (and a NOPAT)

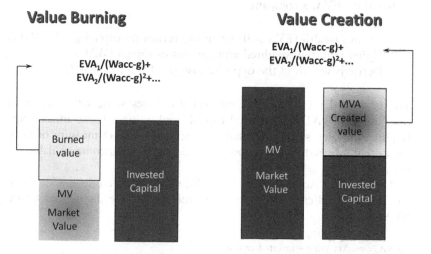

Fig. 21.3 Relations between Economic Value Added and Market Value Added

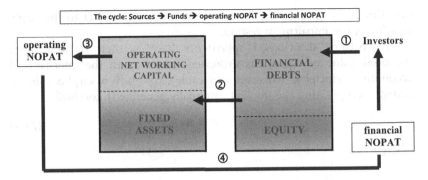

Fig. 21.4 Acquisition of financing sources and creation of economic-financial value

at the operational level. This positive economic margin assumes a financial connotation (through the EBITDA incorporated in the EBIT and then in the NOPAT), creating cash flows primarily allocated to debt service (operating cash flows) and, residually, to the remuneration of the shareholders (free cash flow to equity).

1. Capital underwritten by equity holders and debtholders (raised capital)
2. Investment (of raised capital) in operating (commercial) net working capital and fixed assets (invested capital) that include intangibles
3. Generation of operating Net Operating Profit After Taxes—NOPAT (economic marginality due to digital scalability and other strategic factors)
4. Operating NOPAT generates operating cash flows for investors (debtholders and, residually, shareholders) that are so remunerated for their investment (raised capital, see point 1).

21.7 A COCKTAIL OF APPROACHES FOR AN INTEGRATED ASSESSMENT

The classification, and the estimation of the goodwill from complementary sides, enable us to better appreciate its changing characteristics. Any estimate, however, incorporates elements of subjectivity and is variable over time, raising sustainability concerns, which are subject to the yearly scrutiny of the impairment testing.

The balance sheet-based approaches have as their starting point the book value of equity (as expressed according to the international accounting principles, wherever applicable), to which a surplus value is added, incorporating the implicit (internally generated) goodwill:

$$W_E = K + W_{INT} \tag{21.4}$$

where:

> W_E = market value of equity;
> K = book value of equity;
> W_{INT} = surplus value of the intangibles (already recorded in the balance sheet, if acquired, or internally generated), residually represented by the goodwill.

The market value of equity is a function of the economic projection of income or financial flows or mixed capital-income weighting or empirical (market) approaches, based on comparable multipliers.

In the income approach, goodwill is incorporated in the normalized (extra) income (operating, pre-tax, or net) to be discounted at a risky rate.

If the capitalization period is unlimited:

$$W_R\infty = (\text{average normal income} + \text{sustainable goodwill}) \tag{21.5}$$

If the capitalization is limited:

$$W_R n = (\text{average normal income} + \text{sustainable goodwill}) a_n \neg I \tag{21.6}$$

The stratification of differential income (excess earnings) over time generates an incremental wealth, which expresses the difference between the market value and the book value of the company. Whenever the market value (proxied by the price, P) exceeds the book value, P/BV > 1; this formula is also known as the Tobin Q, and is routinely used for listed firms. The usual distinction between Enterprise Value and Equity Value applies, and so the former value includes financial debt whereas the latter is referred to as residual shareholders (net equity); in both cases, the goodwill matters.

This formula represents a complementary way to express the surplus value of the intangible assets that are typically underrepresented (or absent) in the book value of the assets, as they are not recorded within the CAPEX, for prudentiality rules.

The limited capitalization of the average profit, used to estimate the goodwill, is determined as the difference between the average prospective (extra) income of the company and the expected "normal" income of the capital invested in comparable firms (with a similar risk profile). This difference is then discounted for a specific number of years at a "normal" interest rate consistent with the type of investment under evaluation.

Formula [21.7] is recalled here:

$$W = K + an\neg i^{*}(R - iK) \tag{21.7}$$

In the context of market indicators, the Price/Cash Flow may also be used. The ratio is given by dividing the market price per share and the cash flow per share generated by the listed company. This payback multiple expresses the time necessary for the invested capital in shares to return to the investor in the form of cash flow.

The incremental equity attributable to the internal goodwill can be estimated through the aforementioned Tobin Q index. This indicator corresponds to the ratio between the market value of the company and the replacement cost of its tangible assets (P/BV=Q); if $Q>1$, the company is worth more than its tangible assets and this surplus expresses the proxy value of the intangible assets (residually, the implicit goodwill).

The Tobin Q expresses the comparison between the market value and the book value of equity, highlighting an "unbooked" surplus value if $Q>1$. The indicator is simple, reliable (being based on an objective market price and net equity deduced from the balance sheet), and easily available, but it mainly applies only to listed companies.

The surplus value that expresses the goodwill derives from a combination of specific strategic value drivers connected with the valuation approaches.

21.8 VALUATION OF TURNAROUND COMPANIES

The valuation of turnaround companies needs to adapt the previous considerations to their delicate context considering the following aspects:

- The investment horizon is typically shorter: this circumstance is relevant for the calculation of the discount rate ($a_{n \neg i}$) and concerns the income, mixed, and financial approaches;
- Goodwill is reduced to zero, and a badwill typically occurs: this is especially true in income approaches with an independent estimate of the goodwill;
- Higher-than-average risk (compared to going concern companies) increases the WACC, used as a discount rate for the DCF relevant for the estimate of the Enterprise Value;
- Market multiples are lower: this is relevant to empirical approaches that typically consider other distressed companies or apply a discount to healthy firms;
- The fair value of the securities cannot be easily estimated, and the market price can be significantly lower than the intrinsic value;
- Intangible assets may have permanent and significant losses in value;
- Banks could request the immediate repayment of the loans, up to the point of endangering the survival of the firm;
- The financial squeeze out reduces leveraged acquisitions and financial flexibility (capacity to use debt to back profitable investments).

The valuation must be conveniently preceded by an estimate of the actual and prospective existence of the business continuity (going concern).

In such difficult contexts, it is appropriate to carry out sensitivity analysis, to quantify different risk scenarios in investment decisions.

Sensitivity analysis identifies the single impact of different strategic options and managerial choices, i.e., the factors for which a small change from the basic hypothesis determines a change in the performance of a project.

Together with the sensitivity analysis, it is generally advisable to carry out scenario analyses, which allow—with an increasing degree of complexity—to estimate the combined effects of several parameters that simultaneously change, reconstructing different alternative scenarios, in respect of some basic assumptions and hypotheses.

The erosion of goodwill is periodically recorded through the impairment test but may undergo important amortization (impairment losses) in a crisis context.

The representation is reported in Fig. 21.5.

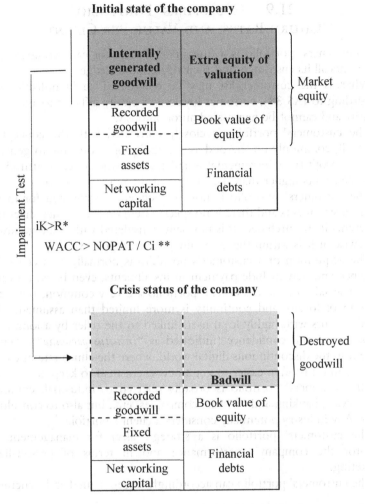

Initial state of the company

iK>R*

WACC > NOPAT / Ci **

Crisis status of the company

Impairment Test

* The average industry return on capital is higher than the company's return.

** The operating return of the company capital is lower than its cost of capital (weighted average).

Fig. 21.5 Erosion of goodwill

21.9   CUSTOMERS' PORTFOLIO, CHURN RATES, AND VALUE PER CLIENT

The customers' portfolio is a fundamental asset for each company and represents all its customers and their related knowledge.

Whereas the customer list may be considered an identifiable asset (according to IAS 38), customer loyalty is typically difficult to assess and identify and cannot be negotiated autonomously.

The customers' portfolio is closely correlated with the concept of goodwill, commonly understood as the ability of a company to generate an extra profit (new incremental wealth), that is the concrete attitude to produce profits higher than the average of the reference sector.

The customers' portfolio is not independently accounted for in the financial statements and there is no specific item on the balance sheet that represents it. If purchased, it is normally considered within the goodwill, otherwise, it falls within the internally generated goodwill.

The acquisition of a customer's portfolio is normally subject to due diligence and may include payment in installments, even based on earn-outs. The sales of the customers' portfolio are very common, but often the rate of loyalty and continuity is more limited than assumed. This mainly occurs with highly loyal users linked to the seller by a long-term acquaintance and confidence (indicated as *"intuitus personae"*). This is evident in the discontinuous digital world, where the churn rate of clients is high, and it is often easier to get a new client than to keep her.

The customers' portfolio is broadly referred to industrial, commercial, service, banking and financial companies, etc., but also to consulting firms. Any industry potentially considers a client's portfolio.

The customers' portfolio is a strategic asset for management, to monitor the company's performance and in terms of personalized marketing.

The customers' portfolio can accordingly be segmented and structured by:

- Sales channel (consumer, industry, other);
- Type of customer (B2B or B2C);
- Supply methods;
- Type of the outlet market (wholesalers or retailers, distributors or dealers or customers operating on the domestic market or foreign customers).

This may allow to carry out strategic analyses in terms of:

- Sales trend (which is relevant for estimating lost profits in the event of disputes);
- Contribution margin[4];
- Collection days;
- Service level;
- Comparison with the budget;
- Comparison with the previous year.

The customers' portfolio is included in the broader concept of goodwill and can have, in a synergistic portfolio, correlations with other intangibles, first of all, the trademarks and, sometimes, the patents and know-how, if the sales (and the corresponding customers, more or less loyal) are linked to a marketing and technological surplus value, showing a comparative advantage.

The customers' equity (client assets) represents the economic value of customer relationships, in an overall stratification of the value of the customers' portfolio that is discounted over time.

The strategic drivers of the customers' equity are represented by:

- Equity value (value attributed by the customer to the goods or services produced/supplied by the company);
- Brand equity[5] (value of the brand);
- Retention equity (brand loyalty even when it involves an incremental price compared to other comparable products or services).

In marketing, the term "retention" generally refers to the ability of a company to preserve its customers. The retention rate consists of a loyalty indicator that expresses the percentage of loyal customers over time. Digitalization is a strong disrupting force, with deep marketing consequences.

An increase in the retention rate may correspond to a more than proportional increase in turnover.

Traditional valuation approaches can be usefully combined with specific methodologies that describe the metrics and typical parameters of the customers' portfolios. The complementarity between traditional and specific approaches can be found by estimating traditional parameters (as

EBITDA or operating cash flows) through specific metrics, such as the average advertising revenue per customer.

More sophisticated models (Estrella-Ramon et al., 2013) for estimating the customers' value (Customer Lifetime Value—CLV) consider future flows generated by each customer and the retention rate (loyalty).

The CLV represents the value per client and can be defined as the current value of all the cash flows generated by each user, dividing all the present and future consumers into different groups.

The calculation of the Customer Lifetime Value (CLV) is complex, but it can be approximated considering the current value of the constant customer in the future:

$$CLV = A \times S \times G \qquad (21.8)$$

where:

- A = duration, in years, of the relationship between customer and company;
- S = average cost of a customer per year;
- G = percentage gain.

The main drivers of the CLV are:

- The abandonment (churn) rate;
- The average number of purchases during the year;
- The frequency of purchases during the year;
- The costs of acquiring a new customer;
- Marketing costs for development and retention activities.

Starting from the assumption that a buyer is not valued according to what he/she has just bought, but for all the potential purchases that he/she will be able to make in the future, the CLV allows to classify customers in different segments and to implement more targeted marketing actions.

Alongside the traditional methodologies for evaluating companies (mixed capital-income approach with an independent assessment of goodwill), for the valuation of the customers' portfolio, there are specific approaches proposed by appraisal practitioners (Customer Lifetime Value—CLV).

Concerning the customers' portfolio, the valuation metrics should take into consideration the following specific aspects:

- The cost of reconstruction/replacement;
- The aging (schedule);
- The incremental EBITDA;
- The additional cash flows.

These considerations need to be adapted to a digital world where scalability is enhanced by the market base, mainly represented by an increasing number of loyal clients. Ephemeral retention rates need however to be properly considered, in a volatile scenario where higher opportunities are mitigated by a correspondingly higher risk profile.

Scalability-driven higher expected cash flows are discounted at higher rates. DCF metrics incorporate both in its formulation.

21.10 BANKABILITY ISSUES

Goodwill can be recorded in the financial statements only if purchased; this leads to a lack of accounting for internally generated goodwill, which is considered only in the valuation phase (see Fig. 21.1).

The bankability issues of the acquired (paid) goodwill reflects its residual importance and its merely potential collateral value, ontologically connected to the entire company, to be evaluated in a context of continuity (going concern). In some cases, goodwill can be acquired with a branch of the company.

A feature of the goodwill is that it represents if one considers its systematic amortization due to impairment losses, a non-monetary cost that does not burn liquidity and therefore does not affect the service of the debt and the EBITDA. Bankability concerns also matter in the distinction between Enterprise and Equity Value.

Given these characteristics, some banks base their rating on conservative criteria, deducting from the book value of equity the recorded goodwill (and other intangibles), to express, as a residual guarantee, the tangible net equity, as shown in Fig. 21.6.

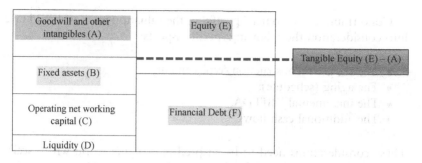

Fig. 21.6 From book to tangible equity

21.11   Digital Goodwill

Digitalization is a powerful catalyzer of added value and goodwill, due to its scalability properties, shown in Chapter 3. Real options and blitzscaling boost revenues, with a positive spillover impact on key valuation parameters (EBITDA, EBIT, net profit, FCFF, FCFE, etc.). Digitalization also impacts on OPEX, possibly reducing both fixed and variable operating costs, thanks to a more resilient and efficient supply chain.

The nature of digital goodwill is, however, intrinsically volatile, so increasing the risk component embedded in the discount formula of DCF, or the projections of revenue streams. The DCF metrics is, once again, referred to either the Enterprise Value (discounting the FCFF/operating cash flow at the WACC) or the Equity Value (if the FCFE/net cash flow is discounted at the cost of equity).

This is reflected, for instance, in the volubility of the clients' preferences, amplified by real-time digital comparability.

As an example, we may consider the media entertainment industry, where customers frequently swap from Netflix to Disney Channel, Apple TV, Amazon Prime Video, etc. Subscription and fees comparisons, as well as contents, are easily available online, and web surfers continuously adapt their preferences, so making goodwill unstable.

Churn rates consist of the annual percentage rate at which customers stop subscribing to a service or employees leave a job. A high churn rate means that clients are not loyal to the brand. TLC firms are a classic example of high churn rates, sometimes exceeding 25%. The importance of this indicator is the fact that retaining a customer is much cheaper than attracting a new one. Churn rates are typically high in the digital ecosystem and represent a strong softening factor against goodwill accumulation. Churn rates are even known as customer attrition and are calculated by dividing the number of clients who unsubscribe in the period by the number of customers at the start of the same period.

Other features of digital goodwill are represented by complementary technological characteristics, whose capricious interactions are uneasy to assess. For instance, the intangible bundling of brands, know-how, and patents with IoT, big data, artificial intelligence, blockchains, etc., can have several outcomes, mastered by evolving digital network ecosystems. These "shanghai" patterns producing domino effect can be forecasted and recorded with probabilistic estimates (deterministic or stochastic) and reflected in real-time in the "augmented" business planning (see Moro Visconti, 2022, Chapter 5).

The accounting and economic impact on goodwill are potentially remarkable but discontinuous, so requiring timely fine-tuning and periodical impairment testing.

NOTES

1. See paragraph 2.5.
2. This is never the case in an "ideal" Modigliani & Miller world, where the financial leverage does not impact on the firm's vale that only depends on its DCF.
3. Adjustments to the accounting parameters, to make them compliant with market values.
4. It expresses the incremental money generated for each product/unit sold after deducting the variable portion of the firm's costs.
5. See paragraph 9.7.

SELECTED REFERENCES

De Franca, J. (2018). Valuation of impairment of non-monetary assets in business management: Analytical proposal for IAS 36. *International Journal of Development Research, 8,* 23794–23800.

Estrella-Ramon, A. M., Sánchez-Pérez, M., Swinnen, G., & VanHoof, K. (2013). A marketing view of the customer value: Customer lifetime value and customer equity. *South African Journal of Business Management, 44*(4), 47–64.

Feldman, S. J. (2004, April). A primer on calculating goodwill impairment. *Business Valuation Review.*

Ferr, S., Fiorentino, R., & Garzella, S. (2018). Goodwill and value creation: Insights from Italian pioneers. *International Journal of Critical Accounting, 9,* 329.

Guler, L. (2016, November 12). Has SFAS 142 improved the usefulness of goodwill impairment loss and goodwill balances for investors? *Review of Managerial Science, 3,* 559–592.

Hamberg, M., & Beisland, L. A. (2014). Changes in the value relevance of goodwill accounting following the adoption of IFRS 3. *Journal of International Accounting, Auditing and Taxation, 23*(2), 59.

Hellman, N., Andersson, P., & Froberg, E. (2016). The impact of IFRS goodwill reporting on financial analysts' equity valuation judgements: Some experimental evidence. *Accounting and Finance, 1,* 113–157.

IFRS 3. (2008). *Business combinations.* Available at https://www.iasplus.com/en/standards/ifrs/ifrs3.

Jackson, A. (2016). The impact of IFRS goodwill reporting on financial analysts' equity valuation judgements: Some experimental evidence (Digest summary): N. Hellman, P. Andersson & E. Froberg. *Accounting & Finance, 56*(1), 113–157.

Jarret, J. E. (2018). *Intellectual property valuation and accounting. Top 5 Contributions on social & political sciences.* Avid Science. Available at http://www.avidscience.com/book/top-5-contributions-on-social-political-sciences/.

Johansson, S. E., Hielstrom, T., & Hellman, N. (2016). Accounting for goodwill under IFRS: A critical analysis. *Journal of International Accounting, Auditing and Taxation, 27,* 13–25.

Kimbro, M. B., & Xu, D. (2016). The accounting treatment of goodwill idiosyncratic risk and market pricing. *Journal of Accounting, Auditing & Finance, 31,* 365–387.

Knauer, T., & Wohrmann, A. (2015, April). Market reaction to goodwill impairments. *European Accounting Review, 25*(3), 421–449.

Kurakova, O., & Orlova, A. (2019). *Methodical and practical approaches to goodwill valuation.* Advances in Economics, Business and Management Research.

Kwon, S. H., & Wang, G. (2019). *Market responses to private and public targets: The role of goodwill valuation.* Available at SSRN: https://ssrn.com/abstract=3318705 or https://doi.org/10.2139/ssrn.3318705.

Leliuc Cosmulese, C., Grosu, V., & Hlaciuc, E. (2017). Definitions attributed to goodwill in the economic literature and conceptual delimitations regarding the way of valuation and exposure of this patrimonial component in the balance sheet. *Ecoforum, 6*(3), 1–6.

Li, K. K., & Sloan, G. (2017). Has goodwill accounting gone bad? *Review of Accounting Studies, 2,* 964–1003.

Li, S. (2016). Managerial ability and goodwill impairment. *Advances in Accounting, 32,* 42–51.

Lohrey, P. L., Di Gabriele, J. A., & Nicholson, J. (2017). A risk assessment of intangible asset valuation: The Post-Hoc association between goodwill impairments and risk hazards in mergers and acquisitions. *American Journal of Management,* 17 (1). Available at SSRN: https://ssrn.com/abstract=305 7794.

Modigliani, F., Merton, H., & Miller, M. H. (1958). The cost of capital, corporation finance and the theory of investment. *The American Economic Review, 48*(3), 261–297.

Moro Visconti, R (2022). *Augmented corporate valuation: From digital networking to ESG compliance.* Cham: Palgrave Macmillan.

Neri, L., Russo, A., Coronella, A., & Risaliti, G. (2017). *Accounting for goodwill: The pioneering thought of Gino Zappa (1910).* University of Greenwich.

OECD. (2017). *Transfer pricing guidelines for multinational enterprises and tax administrations.* Available at https://www.oecd.org/tax/oecd-transferp ricing-guidelines-for-multinational-enterprises-and-tax-administrations-207 69717.htm.

OIC/EFRAG/ASBJ. (2014). *Should goodwill still not be amortized? Accounting and disclosure for goodwill.* Available at http://www.fondazioneoic.eu/wpc ontent/uploads/downloads/2014/07/140722_Should_goodwill_still_not_ be_amortised_Research_Group_paper.pdf.

Ratiu, V. R., & Tiron Tudor, A. (2013). The theoretical foundation of goodwill—A chronological overview. *Procedia—Social and Behavioural Sciences, 92,* 784–788.

Reilly, R. F., & Schweihs, R. P. (2014). *Guide to intangible asset valuation* (Vol. 1). New York: Wiley.

Schatt, A., Doukakis, L., Bessieux Ollier, C., & Walliser, E. (2016). Do goodwill impairments by European firms provide useful information to investors? *Accounting in Europe, 13,* 307–327.

Shi, H. (2018). *Goodwill asset, ultimate ownership, management power and cost of equity capital: A theoretical review.* Paper presented at International Conference on Geo-Spatial Knowledge and Intelligence 2017.

Shimada, N., & Homma, T. (2015). *Analysis of the impact of goodwill impairment information on corporate value.* Available at https://ideas.repec.org/p/ sek/iacpro/3105400.html.

Wen, H. J., & Moehrle, S. R. (2015). *Accounting for goodwill: A literature review and analysis.* Available at https://papers.ssrn.com/sol3/papers.cfm?abstract_ id=2685922.

Wen, H., & Moehrle, S. R. (2016). Accounting for goodwill: An academic literature review and analysis to inform the debate. *Research in Accounting Regulation, 28,* 11–21.

CHAPTER 22

Portfolio of Intangibles, Smart Infrastructural Investments, and Royalty Companies

22.1 THE PORTFOLIO OF INTANGIBLE ASSETS

Intangible assets may be considered atomistically or—in many cases—within a bundled portfolio. Input information to correctly classify the intangibles is often difficult to get.

According to OECD (2017):

- *"The enhancement to a value that may arise from the complementary nature of a collection of intangibles when exploited together is not always reflected on the balance sheet"* (par. 6.7).
- *"Intangibles (including limited rights in intangibles) may be transferred individually or in combination with other intangibles"* (par. 6.92).
- *"It may be the case that some intangibles are more valuable in combination with other intangibles than would be the case if the intangibles were considered separately"* (par. 6.93).
- *"In some situations, intangibles or rights in intangibles may be transferred in combination with tangible business assets, or in combination with services"* (par. 6.98).

The patent pool is a consortium or joint venture of two or more companies that agree to exchange patent licenses relating to a specific technology. Patent pooling is consistent with the digital nature of many

R. Moro-Visconti, *The Valuation of Digital Intangibles*, https://doi.org/10.1007/978-3-031-09237-4_22

intangibles that are nowadays much easier to integrate and jointly consider.

As Colangelo (2008) points out, *"technological collaboration represents, from this point of view, a moment of mediation between the need to reward creative activity and at the same time guarantee the dissemination of knowledge: a step that is more relevant if we consider that the balance between incentives and access is achieved in full compliance with the basic principles of both intellectual property and competition law, without sacrificing the prerogatives of some on the altar of the objectives pursued by others. This is an important organizational innovation: a growing number of companies is involved in increasingly systematic cooperation activities, in the form of consortia, joint ventures, research communities, technology clubs"*.

More generally, the portfolio of intangible assets includes all the intangibles, sometimes within the scope of a specific royalty company, which are often the object of synergistic exploitation (supply chain inventions; trademarks associated with patents; digital trademarks associated with web domains, etc.).

Intangible portfolios between several companies may occur more frequently and intensively in joint ventures or consortia or business networks or specialized industrial districts.

The total value of intangible assets can be usefully divided into several components, which separately highlight the most significant intangibles, based on their taxonomy.

Simon and Sullivan (1993) distinguish between the value of brand equity, intangible assets linked to technology, and the value of immateriality based on the attractiveness of the sector. Extending this taxonomy, the overall value can be broken down into the main categories of intangible assets (related to marketing, technology, the Internet world, or, residually, goodwill) in the following elements:

$$
\begin{aligned}
\text{Value of intangible assets } =\ & \text{Value of assets related to marketing} \\
& + \text{ Value of technological assets} \\
& + \text{ Value of Internet assets} \\
& + \text{ Goodwill and synergies} \qquad (22.1)
\end{aligned}
$$

Table 22.1. includes a list of the main intangible assets linked to each subset.

Table 22.1 Taxonomy of intangible assets

Intangible assets
1. Marketing-related goods
1.1. Trademarks, logos, digital branding
1.2. Newspaper headings
2. Technology-related goods
2.1. Patents, industrial designs, ornamental models
2.2. Know-how, process, and product innovations
2.3. Technological startup
3. Internet-related goods
3.1. Software and database
3.2. Internet domains and websites
3.3. Mobile App
3.4. Big Data
3.5. Internet of things
3.6. Internet companies and social networks
3.7. Digital branding
3.8. Metaverse/NFT
3.9. Blockchains
4. Goodwill
4.1. Goodwill and customer portfolio

Intangible assets are subdivided into three main categories (marketing, technology, and Internet). Possible overlaps and capital gains fall, residually, in goodwill which includes digitally-driven synergies.

Other intangibles or processes like blockchains or artificial intelligence overlap contiguous subsets (for instance, technology and the Internet) (Fig. 22.1).

Networked intangibles enhance scalability and bring systemic valuation patterns, as shown in Fig. 22.2.

22.2 SMART CITIES AND SMART HOSPITALS

A portfolio of intangible assets is present in complex infrastructure projects, such as smart cities or smart hospitals, functionally connected with the industry 4.0. The hyperconnected digital revolution is at the base of systemic innovation, based primarily on sensors linked to the Internet of things for smart remote management of buildings (smart facility management) and complex systems such as cities or hospitals.

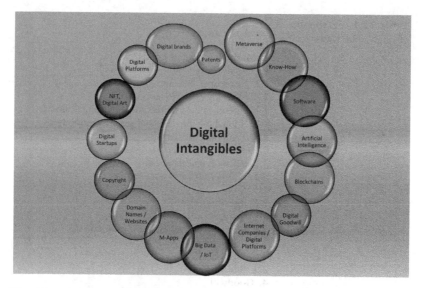

Fig. 22.1   Interaction between intangible assets

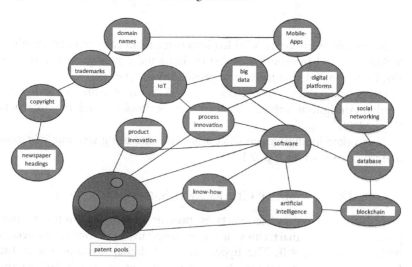

Fig. 22.2   Systemic valuation of networked intangibles

Smart cities consist of a set of urban planning strategies aimed at optimizing and innovating public services to relate the physical infrastructure of cities to the human, intellectual, and social capital of those who live there. This is possible thanks to the widespread use of new communication technologies, mobility, the environment, and energy efficiency, to improve the quality of life and meet the needs of citizens, businesses, and institutions.

The underlying technologies of smart cities are based on a systemic interaction of intangible assets along a coordinated and digital supply chain, within which different stakeholders coexist.

Smart projects have different areas of application, including mobility, lighting, environmental sustainability, etc.

Smart hospitals are based on optimized and automated processes built around a computerized environment of interconnected assets, based on the Internet of Things (Dimitrov, 2016), to improve patient care procedures and introduce new healthcare processes.

Electronic instruments and sensors connect patients with doctors in real-time, improving clinical information systems. Healthcare facilities are increasingly digitalized and connected through integrated sensors, establishing real-time connections that link the machines with patients, through computer platforms that store data in the cloud and then populate the database to obtain information (healthcare big data; see Moro Visconti & Morea, 2019).

The networks between patients, doctors, nurses, and IT operators along the healthcare supply chain are constantly reintegrated through interconnected smart sensors that govern new procedures and innovative storage systems (such as computerized medical records populated by sensitive big data and available on IT platforms in real-time). Interaction between stakeholders is a primary source of value co-creation focused on the patient (Moro Visconti & Martiniello, 2019).

The issues summarized above in terms of smart cities or smart hospitals offer delicate interpretations for an overall enhancement or spread over the individual links in the value chain. The synergic value of the described applications is relevant, the immaterial component assumes a prominent weight.

The bankability issues[1] related to investments (largely intangible) can be tackled with the use of rewarding performance-based financing mechanisms, in which remuneration is linked to results.

22.3   DIGITAL INFRASTRUCTURAL INVESTMENTS WITH PUBLIC–PRIVATE PARTNERSHIPS

Infrastructural smart investments are increasingly digitized, and their complex architecture is mastered by technological and Internet-related intangibles, ranging from know-how and patents to process innovation patterns that rotate around artificial intelligence and blockchains and are fueled by big data and IoT sensors. What characterizes infrastructural investments is their size and complexity.

Most infrastructural investments have a public interest that exploits the expertise of private investors, typically with Public–Private Partnerships that are often backed by Project Financing (PF) schemes. Digitalization is a powerful catalyzer of infrastructural projects, whose intrinsic rigidity can be substantially softened.

Infrastructures are typically public goods, due to their universal utility and the consequent need to be protected from private monopolistic rents. Public authorities are, however, often unable to exploit these infrastructures on their own, lacking the expertise to build and manage smart projects where the intangible components are relevant. Hence the necessity to involve private firms that can share their knowledge, participating to value co-creating schemes.

Usually, a PF structure involves several equity investors, known as sponsors, as well as a syndicate of banks that provide loans to the operation. The loans are most commonly non-recourse, paid entirely from project cash flow, rather than from the general assets or creditworthiness of the project sponsors.

A Special Purpose Vehicle (SPV) is a legally independent project company created for each project by the concessionaire, thereby shielding other assets owned by its sponsors from the detrimental effects of a project failure. Being an SPV, the project company has no assets other than the project. Capital contribution commitments (limited recourse) by the owners of the project company are sometimes necessary to ensure that the project is financially sound. No recourse, no personal risk for the SPV shareholders.

Project finance is typically more complicated than alternative financing methods (standard corporate lending).

Risk transfer and sharing from the public to the private part is a key element in PF: a principal/agent optimal risk allocation and co-parenting are the core philosophy of project finance. Risk transfer is deeply involved with the allocation of risks associated with the operation of a PFI contract according to the principle that it should lie with the party best able to manage it.

Value for Money[2] for the public part must consider not only an economic and financial comparison with alternative financial packages and instruments but parameters such as:

- project efficiency (optimal use of assets—facilities during the concession life ...) and (financial and economic) sustainability;
- multi-benefit considerations (level of tangible and intangible social benefits to the end-users and the collectivity ...);
- effective risk transfers to the private counterpart (considering the real value of the construction risk transfer, often underestimated).

As Robinson and Scott (2009) point out, "value for money" in a PFI project crucially depends on performance monitoring to provide incentives for improvement and to ensure that service delivery is under the output specification. However, the effectiveness of performance monitoring and output specification cannot be fully assessed until PFI projects become operational. There is a need to examine the role of the performance monitoring mechanism in ensuring that "value for money" is achieved throughout the delivery of services.

A comprehensive private SPV performs all the main business activities of the project financing investment scheme (project, build, finance, operate, and transfer), according to the PBOT scheme which can be replaced by many other variants, following a well-known Alphabet soup—a metaphor for an abundance of abbreviations or acronyms:

- BDOT: Build-Design-Operate-Transfer
- BLT: Build-Lease-Transfer
- BOO: Build-Own-Operate
- BOOS: Build-Own-Operate-Sell
- BOOT: Build-Own-Operate-Transfer
- BOT: Build-Own-Transfer
- BTO: Build-Transfer-Operate
- BRT: Build-Rent-Transfer

Many of these activities can be digitized, particularly during the management phase, where information, for instance, is collected, stored in the cloud, processed, and shared with value-adding artificial intelligence patterns.

Digitization may conveniently concern the construction phase where the private investors have an incentive to pursue quality due to the future savings and efficiency gains that start with operations during the management phase.

22.3.1   The Risk Matrix

The risk is a concept that identifies and—possibly—measures the expected probability of specific eventualities (possible states of the world). Technically, the notion of risk is independent of the notion of value and, as such, eventualities may have both beneficial (upside risk) and adverse (downside risk) consequences. Lenders intrinsically have downside sensitivity.

However, in general usage, the convention is to focus only on the potential negative impact of some characteristic of value that may arise from a future event.

Risk can conveniently be measured if compared to the desired outcome for the public part, mainly identifiable in output (contractually) based specification and consequently to the probability that the effective ex-post outcomes are different (lower) than the envisaged ones. Pricing risk is often more difficult than expected and unforeseen events are an additional and unpredictable source of risk (Fig. 22.3).

Even if many of the risks of a project financing scheme are similar to those of a standard long-term investment with multiple stakeholders pivoting around it, some characteristics are typical of the PF structure, such as risk segregation of the SPV's shareholders, due to the ring-fence and no (little) recourse finance. The very fact that the property of the infrastructural investment belongs from the beginning to the public entity increases the no-recourse paradigm since creditors of the SPV are unable to grasp neither the personal assets of the SPV's shareholders (ring-fence protection) nor the real estate property, built using the money that mainly privileged debtholders have lent to the SPV.

The main risks can interact within the risk matrix, with many possible outcomes often difficult to model and forecast; in many cases, the interaction follows a sort of shanghai model, according to which each stick can randomly hit the others, causing a chain effect with unforeseen results.

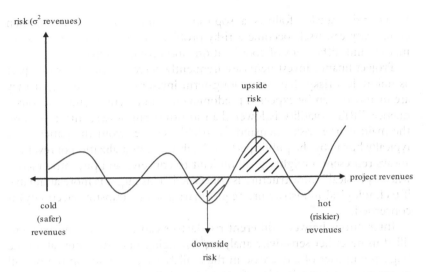

Fig. 22.3 Upside and downside risk, due to the project revenues' volatility

The impact of risk on the public or the private part (represented by the SPV and its stakeholders) is highly asymmetric and while some risks are shared (e.g., bad project design; contractual risk; *force majeure*; inflation ...), most of them are borne either by the public part (first of all, the demand for health services) or by the private SPV (construction risk; bankability; and liquidity ...).

To the extent that the SPV transfers its risk to its shareholders and, in a broader sense, stakeholders, there can be a mitigation effect, not only as a consequence of the intrinsic diversification and spreading, but because professional stakeholders might undertake the specific risk that they can conveniently handle. For example, a construction company can undertake the building risk, while a financial shareholder can monitor the cash flow statements and a professional manager the operations during the management phase.

Pass-through (back to back) agreements, according to which the SPV delegates and contracts out some functions (e.g., laundry; surveillance ...), are highly frequent and can bring substantial risk transfers, leaving few if any residual risks within the SPV—good news for its lenders, not so for the lenders of the subcontractors if the risk is both diversified and reduced, to the extent that is professionally managed.

If the risk transfer follows a sophisticated number of passages, then complexity can itself become a risky problem, hiding information asymmetries and difficulties of coordination, and problem detection.

Project finance investments are frequently perceived by the private part as mildly less risky than other long-term investments,[3] especially if they are mainly driven by expected predominant cold revenues and as a consequence EBIT volatility is lower than in other businesses; this is because the main market risk—demand for health services from the patients—is typically borne by the public part. Scalability and digitalization of revenues always represent a mighty goal, difficult to conceive and put into practice when "physical" infrastructure is concerned. This target is more attainable if technological infrastructure (e.g., smart grids to transmit electricity) is concerned.

Interactions between different risk factors can take place and be identified using either sensitivity analyses,[4] changing one parameter at a time (e.g., the impact of a decrease in the availability payment[5] on the overall economic and financial plan, from sustainability to bankability and profitability ...) or more complex what-if scenario analyses, where different parameters change simultaneously, producing possible future events by considering alternative outcomes.[6]

Risk mitigation is a key issue that makes everybody happy, both from the public and the private side; the problem is that it is much easier to say than to do. Among the main devices, the following are the most used and effective:

- specialization of the agent (public or private) who professionally deals with a specific risk;
- risk sharing among different subjects (e.g., multiple shareholders of the SPV);
- insurance, somewhat expensive and in many cases not possible (examples include construction risk but not market risks, traditionally not insurable);
- putting quality first; good construction, maintenance, and management can substantially decrease risks and related costs.

22.3.2 A Synthetic Financial Measure of Risk: WACC

The weighted average cost of capital (WACC), used in the denominator of the DCF formula to estimate the Enterprise Value of the firm, is the rate that a company is expected to pay to debtholders, and, residually, shareholders, to finance its assets with adequate raised capital. WACC is the minimum return that a company must earn on existing assets to satisfy its creditors, owners, and other providers of sources of capital, consisting of a calculation of a firm's cost of capital in which each category of capital (ordinary or preferred shares, etc.) is proportionately weighted.

The market value of the firm's equity and debt is difficult to assess if the SPV is not listed—this being the standard case. Should this be the case, the value of equity may consider as proxy market capitalization, while the value of debt could be represented by listed bonds; in standard SPVs, capital market benchmarks can be conveniently used only in countries or industries where there is a significant number of listed and comparable companies. The very fact that each project is unique represents an obstacle to comparisons.

The WACC is a key discount parameter in project financing (intrinsically linked to DCF metrics), strongly connected with other key financial ratios, as it is shown in Table 22.2.

The WACC level can be a—rough—measure of the risks effectively transferred from the public to the private part. And the financial structure of the SPV (initial and subsequent, along with the whole life of the project) is another complementary indicator of the risk borne by the private part, up to the limit (absolute and relative debt, measured by leverage) accepted by the financial sponsor.

A leverage simulation—with a break-even point (floor)/disaster case scenario—may be helpful in detecting which is the maximum bearable debt.

The relationship between the NPV of the project and its IRR can be represented in the following graph, well-known to any corporate finance practitioner. According to the graph—and the formulas of NPV and IRR—when WACC grows, the discounted cash flows of the project get smaller, approaching zero; actually, the Internal Rate of Return represents the point at which NPV is equal to zero.

Sensitivity analyses, aiming at finding the break-even point under stress tests where each variable at a time changes, are particularly useful (Fig. 22.4).

Table 22.2 Interactions between WACC and other key financial ratios

Ratio	Formula	Links and interactions with WACC
WACC	$WACC = k_e \frac{E}{D_f + E} + k_d (1 - t) \frac{D_f}{D_f + E}$ where: D_f = Financial debts E = Equity K_e = Cost of equity K_d = Cost of debt t = Corporate tax rate	–
$IRR_{project}$	$NPV_{project} = \frac{CFO_1}{1 + IRR_{project}} + \frac{CFO_2}{(1 + IRR_{project})^2} + \cdots + \frac{CFO_n}{(1 + IRR_{project})^n} - CF_0 = 0$ where: CFO = Operating Cash Flow CF_0 = initial investment	If WACC $> IRR_{project}$, $NPV_{project} < 0$; then it's possible that CF_0 (which strongly depends on the cost of collected capital) $> \sum_{t=1}^{n} \frac{CFO_n}{(1 + IRR_{project})^t}$ If WACC $= IRR_{project}$, $NPV_{project} = 0$ and $CF_0 = \sum_{t=1}^{n} \frac{CFO_n}{(1 + IRR_{project})^t}$ If WACC $< IRR_{project}$, $NPV_{project} > 0$ and $CF_0 < \sum_{t=1}^{n} \frac{CFO_n}{(1 + IRR_{project})^t}$

Ratio	Formula	Links and interactions with WACC
IRR_{equity}	$NPV_{equity} = \frac{CFN_1}{1+IRR_{equity}} + \frac{CFN_2}{(1+IRR_{equity})^2} + \dots + \frac{CFN_n}{(1+IRR_{equity})^n} - CF_0 = 0$ where: CFN = Net Cash Flow CF_0 = Initial investment	If WACC $> IRR_{equity}$, $NPV_{equity} < 0$; then it's possible that CF_0 (which strongly depends on the cost of collected capital) $> \sum_{t=1}^{n} \frac{CFN_n}{(1+IRR_{equity})^t}$ If WACC $= IRR_{equity}$, $NPV_{equity} = 0$ and $CF_0 = \sum_{t=1}^{n} \frac{CFN_n}{(1+IRR_{equity})^t}$ If WACC $< IRR_{equity}$, $NPV_{equity} > 0$ and $CF_0 < \sum_{t=1}^{n} \frac{CFN_n}{(1+IRR_{equity})^t}$
$NPV_{project}$	$NPV_{project} = \sum_{t=1}^{n} \frac{CFO_t}{(1+WACC)^t} - CF_0$ where: CFO = Operating Cash Flow t = time CF_0 = initial investment	If K_d or K_e grows, WACC increases; $NPV_{project}$ decreases If K_d or K_e reduces, WACC decreases; $NPV_{project}$ increases
NPV_{equity}	$NPV_{equity} = \sum_{t=1}^{n} \frac{CFN_t}{(1+K_e)^t} - CF_0$ where: CFN = Net Cash Flow t = time CF_0 = initial investment	If K_e grows, WACC increases and NPV_{equity} decreases. If K_e reduces, WACC decreases and NPV_{equity} increases. K_d changes might influence WACC, but not NPV_{equity}

(continued)

Table 22.2 (continued)

Ratio	Formula	Links and interactions with WACC
APV$_{equity}$ (Adjusted Present Value)	NPV$_{equity}$ + Present Value of Tax Benefit	Like NPV$_{equity}$, considering the fiscal benefit of debt. Higher leverage increases APV, provided that there is a positive taxable base and that increasing probabilities of default do not prevent debt raising
Average Debt Service Cover Ratio (ADSCR)[7]	$ADSCR = \dfrac{\sum_{t=1}^{n} \frac{CFO_t}{D_{f_t} + I_t}}{n}$ where: CFO = Operating Cash Flow D_f = Financial Debts I = Interests t = time from 1 to n years	If K_d increases, financial charges (interests) increase too. In this case, ADSCR decreases, while WACC might increase (to the extent that riskier debt is not counterbalanced by safer equity) If K_d decreases, interests decrease too. ADSCR increases, while WACC might decrease
LEVERAGE	$\dfrac{D_f}{E}$ where: D_f = Financial Debts E = Equity	If D_f grows, K_d increases and K_e decreases If D_f is reduced, K_d decreases and K_e increases WACC might be unaffected

Ratio	Formula	Links and interactions with WACC
$NPV_{project}/EBITDA$	$NPV_{project}/EBITDA =$ $$\left(\sum_{t=1}^{n} \frac{CFO_t}{(1 + WACC)^t} - CF_0 \right) / EBITDA_{AVERAGE}$$	This standardized indicator expresses in relative, rather than in absolute terms, the multiplier of a project's value times the $EBITDA$,[8] allowing for market comparisons. If the average $EBITDA$ grows, even CFO increases, normally at a lower rate,[9] a higher $EBITDA$ may lower the cost of capital, with a positive impact on the $WACC$ since the overall risk for both equity and debtholders is reduced by a higher cash generation, provided that the CFO grows
Discounted Project Payback Period	$$\sum_{t=0}^{n} \frac{CFO_t}{(1 + WACC)^t} = 0$$ where: CFO = Operating Cash Flow t = time from 1 to n years	If CFO decreases or $WACC$ grows, payback period increases If CFO grows or $WACC$ decreases, payback period shortens
Discounted Equity Payback Period	$$\sum_{t=0}^{n} \frac{CFN_t}{(1 + K_e)^t} = 0$$ where: CFN = Net Cash Flow t = time	If CFN decreases or K_e grows, payback period increases If CFN grows or K_e decreases, payback period shortens. K_e is part of $WACC$, but its changes may have no effects on $WACC$, to the extent that cost of debt (K_d) symmetrically adjusts

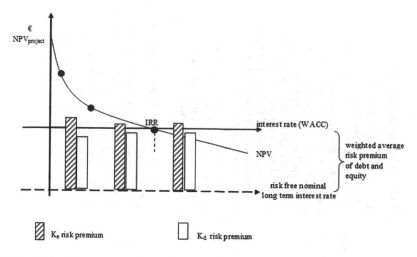

Fig. 22.4 Net present value and internal rate of return of a project

Banks often consider both but are bound only to the formal plan, the only that legally matters.

Project evaluations using NPV suffer from a lack of flexibility. The use of real options allows considering in the model the possibility to differ, expand, suspend, abandon, and terminate a project. Since PF is a long-term project, many different states of the world occur during its different phases (project/construction, and then management), and that is why standard NPV metrics may appear too rigid. Business plan refreshing, incorporating real options, network externalities or timely bottom-up evidence, also contributes to forecast improvements.

During the tender, NPV is driven down by competitive bidders, but not to the point of making the project unbankable (no lent money, no party).

If the winner has a low NPV—even approaching zero—one might wonder why the project is still profitable and bankable. The only possible explanation is that revenues are underestimated and/or costs are overstated and there can be (significant) savings. Even in this case, digitalization matters. In some detrimental cases, informal commercial, as well as building activities, may bring inappropriate—fiscal savings, and unofficial money can fuel corruption and fraud.

The risk matrix has a strong impact on the cost of capital (cost of equity and quasi-equity, including subordinated debt; the cost of senior debt; WACC to estimate the Enterprise Value, discounting the FCFF), especially if we consider the financial aspects of risk, mainly depending on:

- Time span/duration (of the project)
- Financing unavailability (capital rationing)
- Bankability
- Liquidity
- Degree of maturity (of the loans)
- Availability of institutional investors and other qualified sources of funds
- Currency and interest rate risk, sometimes bringing to an Assets & Liability mismatch (of the SPV)
- The amount and cash timing of the grant, the availability payment, and other revenues.

Financial risk is important since this shows how risk is priced by capital providers. Periodical market evaluation of the SPV, wherever possible, should embody its overall risk assessment and scoring. But two big problems make this theoretically sound reasoning hardly work: the very fact that SPVs are typically not listed (PF is not a conventional asset class) and, even if they would, capital markets imperfections and malfunctioning in risk pricing.

Figure 22.5. shows that financial leverage (D_f/E) reaches its peak at the end of the construction phase and the nit starts decreasing, allowing for the payment of dividends during the management phase.

The main risks of the SPV are the operating risk and the financial risk. The operating leverage[10] is a measure of how revenue growth translates into growth (Δ Sales) in operating income (ΔEBIT). It is a measure of how risky (volatile) a company's operating income is:

$$\text{Operating} - \text{Leverage} = \frac{\Delta EBIT}{\Delta SALES}$$
$$= \frac{\Delta(\text{EBITDA} + \text{Depreciation/provisions})}{\Delta SALES}$$

$$(22.1)$$

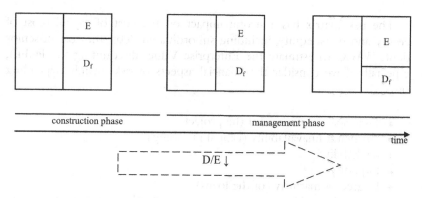

Fig. 22.5 Leverage decreases from the construction to the management phase

The factors that influence the operating revenue are:

- revenue volumes and margins;
- variable costs;
- fixed costs (Fig. 22.3).

A comparison between standard corporate debt investments and corporate finance, useful to assess Value for Money, bankability issues, and profitability, is synthesized in Table 22.4.

22.4 ROYALTY COMPANIES

The royalty companies are corporations whose main or exclusive activity is the possession of intangible assets and their subsequent licensing to other subjects, belonging or not to the same group, generally under license and against payment of periodic fees known as royalties (originally intended as sovereign income). Even digital intangibles can be concentrated in a specific firm that deals them together with other immaterial assets.

The centralization—at an international level—of the management of brands and patents can lead to synergies and economies of scale and experience, concentrating resources and professionalism in a dedicated company and allowing for the autonomous valorization of intangible assets, separated from the production or commercial structures that so become independently negotiable.

Table 22.3 Links between the operating leverage and key financial ratios

Items	Formula	Links with operating leverage
OPERATING REVENUES	Operating (monetary) revenues − monetary and operating fixed costs − monetary and operating variable costs	Growing operating revenues generate an increase in EBIT, depending on the fixed/variable costs mix
EBITDA EBIT	**= EBITDA** = operating revenues − monetary OPEX - amortization, depreciation and provisions **= EBIT** +/− Δ Capital Expenditure (CAPEX) +/− Δ Operating Net Working Capital **= OPERATING CASH FLOW = O**$_{CF}$	EBITDA, given by the difference between operating revenues and (monetary) operating costs, influences Operating Cash Flow. The same happens with EBIT, which additionally considers non-monetary operating costs (depreciation, amortization, provisions)
OPERATING CASH FLOW		Increases in operating revenues increase EBITDA, EBIT, and Commercial Net Working Capital, normally pushing up Operating Cash Flow

(continued)

Table 22.3 (continued)

Items	Formula	Links with operating leverage
WACC	$\text{WACC} = k_e \dfrac{E}{D_f + E} + k_d (1-t) \dfrac{D_f}{D_f + E}$	If operating revenues grow, EBIT and consequently net profit should increase, with an induced Equity growth; if equity grows, ceteris paribus leverage decreases and there is a transfer of risk from debtholders to equity-holders; to the extent that this risk transfer is symmetric, WACC should be unaffected
NPV$_{\text{project}}$	$\text{NPV}_{\text{project}} = \sum\limits_{t=1}^{n} \dfrac{\text{CFO}_t}{(1+\text{WACC})^t} - \text{CF}_0$	If EBITDA grows, Operating Cash Flow (CFO) increases, with a positive impact on NPV, especially if WACC decreases
IRR$_{\text{project}}$	$\text{NPV}_{\text{project}} = \dfrac{\text{CFO}_1}{1+\text{IRR}_{\text{project}}} + \dfrac{\text{CFO}_2}{(1+\text{IRR}_{\text{project}})^2} + \cdots + \dfrac{\text{CFO}_n}{(1+\text{IRR}_{\text{project}})^n} - \text{CF}_0 = 0$	If Operating Cash Flow grows, NPV might increase, then IRR grows, increasing the financial break-even point; the project is more easily bankable

Items	Formula	Links with operating leverage
Average Debt Service Cover Ratio	$$\text{ADSCR} = \frac{\sum_{t=1}^{n} \frac{\text{CFO}_t}{D_{ft}+I_t}}{n}$$	The Operating Leverage is strictly connected with average debt service cover ratio—a typical debt metric—which strongly depends on Operating Cash Flow. If cumulated CFOs grow, then the financial debt may be reduced
(FINANCIAL) LEVERAGE[11]	$k_e =$ $[\text{WACC} + (\text{WACC} - k_d) * D_f/E]\, \text{NR}/\text{PT}$ where: NR = Net Result PT = Pre-tax Profit	If the difference $(\text{WACC} - k_d)$ between the weighted average cost (return) of capital and the cost of debt is positive, then leverage above unity (where $D_f > E$) enhances this positive difference, with a consequential positive effect on the cost (return) of equity

(continued)

Table 22.3 (continued)

Items	Formula	Links with operating leverage
EBITDA/financial charges	EBITDA/financial charges	EBITDA should be consistent enough to cover financial charges and other monetary costs; this parameter deeply changes across time, being negative in the construction phase and sometimes even at the beginning of the management phase; higher financial charges, embodied in the cost of debt and in the WACC, decrease the margin multiplier (EBITDA should be at least 5–6 times the financial charges, depending on the amount of the other monetary costs), with a direct impact on cover ratio and leverage

Table 22.4 To lend or not to lend? Comparison between corporate debt and project finance

Parameter/situation	Corporate debt finance	Project finance
Guarantees	Asset-based projects bear physical guarantees and, to the extent that they are not sufficient, personal covenants from the shareholders	The guarantee is given by the cash flows of the project. Limited or no-recourse models make SPV's shareholders mildly or not responsible
Leverage	The (optimal) amount of leverage is a consequence of the guarantees and many other parameters (bankability; conflicts of interests and information asymmetries ...)	Typically, higher than in standard corporate investments, with a profile more similar to LBOs. Lower risks, described in many parameters in this table, make this possible, to the extent that has to be decided and monitored case by case
Adverse selection	Adverse selection is a typical problem in money lending since banks—not knowing who is who—cannot easily discriminate between good and risky borrowers, who should deserve higher interest rate charges	The track record and reputation of borrowers are less easily identifiable in project finance since the SPV typically has several shareholders, but—to the extent that the borrower is the new SPV and that the investment project is highly detailed, adverse selection problems are not so important in project finance
Moral hazard	Moral hazard is a classical "take the money and run problem" since borrowers might try to abscond with the bank's money or try not to fully engage them in the project for which they have been financed	Cash flow channeling through the lending bank makes money hiding extremely difficult

(continued)

Table 22.4 (continued)

Parameter/situation	Corporate debt finance	Project finance
Information asymmetries	In economics and contract theory, information asymmetry is present when one party to a transaction has more or better information than the other party	Moral hazard, adverse selection, and assets substitution are much less harmful in project financing and cash flows pass through the lending institutions and are easier to forecast and monitor, leading to a consistent reduction in information asymmetries, considering that there is just one well-known (albeit complex) investment to monitor
Strategic bankruptcy	Strategic bankruptcy is false information that the borrower gives about the outcome of his financed investment, stating that it has failed even if it's not true only not to give back the borrowed money The lender's right to liquidate is central to forcing the borrower to repay its debt	Less probable with verifiable cash flows
Probability of default	Should the financed corporation go bankrupt, the residual value becomes important and companies with a high level of intangibles, mainly valuable in a going concern context, are typically penalized while asking for money Debtholders may threat to file for bankruptcy, to force repayments. This threat is effective to the extent that there is an expected value from asset liquidation[12]	A project company SPV is separated and bankruptcy remote from the investing firm sponsors that create it. The project company relies extensively on debt capital provided by creditors to fund project operations. Creditors provide more (less) debt as a percentage of overall project capital when there is less (more) risk of project failure and non-repayment

Parameter/situation	Corporate debt finance	Project finance
Asset substitution	A company's exchange of lower risk investments for higher risk investments. Firms may use asset substitution as a form of financing, or as a move to please shareholders. It can be detrimental to the company's bondholders as it increases the possibility of default without any corresponding benefit because bonds have a fixed interest rate. On the other hand, asset substitution can benefit shareholders as it carries the possibility of higher returns This risk makes the debt more difficult and expensive	This risk is unlikely in project finance, where investments are contractually fixed and observable by financing institutions
Level of legal protection of debtholders	Asset-based, often with guarantees	Cash flow based, with little if any guarantee (limited or no recourse)
Cash flow volatility	The volatility of the business model and, in particular, the fact that the demand risk is entirely borne by the company, typically makes cash flows highly volatile and hardly predictable—bad news for lenders	Even in project finance cash flows are volatile, but normally consistently less than in other businesses, especially if cold revenues and cash flows are predominant, leaving core demand risk to the public part
Cash flow segregation	Difficult with multiple projects; would be a (potentially harmful) impediment to managerial discretion. The lender's right to claim money back is central to force the borrower to repay, limiting strategic default temptations	Contractually envisaged in the agreements between the SPV and its lenders, it allows avoiding most conflicts between equity and debtholders

(continued)

Table 22.4 (continued)

Parameter/situation	Corporate debt finance	Project finance
Cash flow verifiability	Strictly dependent on the business and market model, normally consistently harder than that of project financing	When cash flows are more verifiable, the entire distribution of cash flows available to all fixed and residual claimants shifts to the right
Upside potential	Reward and excess return of the investment, typically belonging only to the shareholders. Should the risk/return profile be unbalanced, peculiar sources of funds, more suitable to follow the assets' profile, may be issued (convertible bonds or other hybrid securities …)[13]	Upside potential is limited, due to the limited presence of hot revenues and to contractual caps (market testing …) on other revenues. As a consequence, there is little if any need to issue hybrid securities
Evaluation	Cash flow evaluations are difficult, to the extent that this parameter is hardly predictable. Market comparisons are possible and make sense if there is a sufficiently wide and similar database of other transactions	The evaluation[14] has to consider the following peculiarities: • no terminal value since the SPV is typically dissolved once the concession has expired, its terminal value is zero; • less volatile (more predictable); • precise (contractual) duration of useful life; • market comparisons are hindered by the project's uniqueness

Parameter/situation	Corporate debt finance	Project finance
Change in the business model(Mission drift)	Possible and even frequent, especially from a substantial point of view, trying to adapt the business to a wildly changing market. Unperceived changes increase information asymmetries and assets substitution chances	There is no risk of a change in the business model, due to little competitive threats and binding contractual agreements
Time extension of the investment	Normally consistently shorter than in project finance, often uneasy to be contractually bound, often overlapping with other investments having different amounts and maturities. As a consequence, even short-term financing has a rollover implicit option	Long-term investment, typically exceeding 20 years, is an intrinsic risk
Residual value	Infrastructural investments typically have a residual value, representing a worthy guarantee if the debt is by then still outstanding	Little is any residual value if the project is abandoned. In any case, with a free transfer of the infrastructure to the public part, the residual value of the SPV is typically zero

As a corporation, the royalty company is a set of assets (the portfolio of intangible assets) destined for marketing (license). The business branch represents a coherent subset, sometimes coinciding with a single intangible asset.

The ontological ratio that is at the base of the convenience of the company in general—and of the royalty company in particular—is consistent with the Coase theory of the firm (considered as a nexus or network of contracts),[15] based on the efficiency of transaction costs that the legal nature of the firm minimizes.

The model assumes that the costs deriving from market transactions lead to organizational innovations (the birth of companies) which allow these costs to be reduced and internalized. The rationality of companies is based on the existence of costs for the management of the company that is lower than the market transaction costs in the absence of companies. The centralization of contractual relationships within the royalty company can allow significant efficiency gains, especially considering the legal nature of the various intangible assets (whether registered or not) and the growing need for their protection. Digitalization can bring in further savings (lower OPEX, etc.), reinforcing this theoretical background.

The ownership and management of trademarks, patents, and other intangibles, which in many corporate objects of companies is an ancillary activity, becomes the main one, overturning the contents of the corporate mission and typically providing limited boundary activities.

The royalty company is rarely set up with a portfolio of intangible assets contextually created (whose initial value is typically negligible, unless they arise from intangible assets already valued). In most cases, it acquires them through partial demergers (in which the original company, industrial or commercial, lists its patents or trademarks in favor of the beneficiary royalty company), sale of intangible assets (or of a company branch that includes them), contribution in kind (the royalty company is owned by the company that assigns the intangibles).

The royalty company can be a direct (even partial) user or—more frequently—a licensor; it can be a monad (stand-alone) firm or—more often—inserted in a group context, often articulated at the international level, especially in the presence of well-known and globalized intangibles.

The assets may be represented by trademarks, patents, copyright, and know-how. Reference is, however, typically made to trademarks, patents, and copyrights, while know-how, industrial secrets (...) represent innovations often in an embryonic stage, whose licensing, outside the group, can involve problems of protection of the invention. Other digital assets can be included in the portfolio, together with the aforementioned "classic" intangibles.

Royalties may relate to non-renewable resources (rights to exploit oil wells...) or classic intangible assets including copyrights in publishing or music, software licenses, etc.). Digital assets, like NFTs, can also generate royalties.

Royalty charges must consider the transfer pricing problems and triangulation opportunities that exploit possible arbitration between the various treaties against double taxation (treaty shopping). An intangible may be subject to indirect sales (from A to B, and from B to C) if these two passages reduce overall taxation.

Various types of royalty companies can be identified, depending on whether the possession of intangible assets and the perception of royalties constitutes their exclusive activity or not.

There are pure royalty companies, which exclusively carry out the activities, and mixed royalty companies, which perform other activities, such as financial or managerial coordination.

22.5 CENTRALIZATION OF THE INTANGIBLE ASSETS WITH A ROYALTY CONDUIT COMPANY

The royalty conduit companies are particularly widespread in the Netherlands, Ireland (especially for trademarks), Cyprus, or Malta (especially for patents), and in other systems that have favorable double taxation agreements regarding intellectual property.

The exploitation of a trademark can occur mainly through different schemes exemplified in the following cases:

a) A US holding company licenses the trademark to a royalty company that develops the brand and sublicenses it to other companies of the group or third parties.

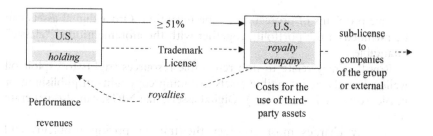

b) A US holding company licenses the trademark to a foreign royalty company, part of the group;

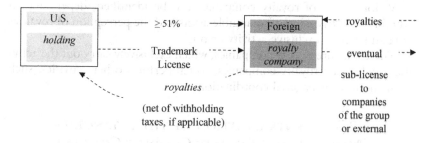

c) A foreign holding grants the trademark to a US royalty company;

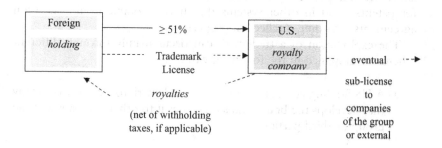

According to OECD (2017) *"The geographic scope of the intangibles or rights in intangibles will be an important comparability consideration. A global grant of rights to intangibles may be more valuable than a grant limited to one or a few countries, depending on the nature of the product,*

the nature of the intangible, and the nature of the markets in question" (par. 6.120).

22.6 ROYALTIES CHARGED TO THE LICENSEE

The charge of the royalties to the other companies of the group is based on contractual agreements (founded on market criteria between independent companies, according to the arm's length principle, not to generate transfer pricing problems) defined before, which often determine the cost based on the percentages of the revenues that are achieved through the intangible asset. Typically, it goes from percentages of 1–2% (for weak intangibles, which give a limited competitive advantage), up to values that can exceed 10% (if the intangible is particularly strong, for example in the field of fashion or for blockbuster inventions).

If the royalty company develops the intangible asset internally, incurring costs that increase its value, it is entitled to charge the companies that use it.

The problems of transfer pricing must be carefully considered and remain controversial. These issues are sensitive to valuation, even concerning hard-to-assess digital intangibles.

In the technological field, the license is the contract with which the holder of a patent right (the licensor) alienates a third party (the licensee), for remuneration, the right to use the patented invention, without definitively undressing it (unlike what happens with the fire sale of the patent). Upon conclusion of the license, the licensor and the licensee normally agree to decide whether to affix an exclusivity clause whereby the licensor agrees not to grant others a license for the same patent. In the case of a license with an exclusive clause, the licensor, although no longer in possession of the right to exploit the invention for profit, retains residual powers, such as the right to use the conventional priority for deposits abroad, or the right to counterfeit.

The commercial license of a trademark is a contract by which the owner assigns to the licensee the temporary right to exploit it in the production of goods or provision of services, in compliance with certain conditions decided by the parties. The license can be total, and in that case, there is the full transfer of the brand, in the (inter)national territory and for all the products for which it was registered. If, on the other hand, the license is partial, the holder of the trademark grants it only for certain products or locations, but always with exclusive rights over them, such as to prevent the licensor from producing those products by affixing that trademark to them.

The classification of the license agreements and their actual operation cannot ignore relevant and absorbing tax considerations.

To fight tax havens, the tax authorities pay growing attention to the fees applied by the royalty company to the licensee companies, especially if they are levied at the group level and in an international context.

Any fair judgment of the royalties paid rotates around their normal (fair) value.

Reference is to the average remuneration for similar goods and services under free competition (arm's length). The assets are represented by the intangible assets subject to the license and the services (which incorporate these assets) from the license itself. It is, therefore, a question of making a comparison between the licensed services and other similar comparable services, provided under free competition.

At an international level, OECD (2017), paragraph 3.25, detect that the comparisons between controlled (not independent) transactions of the taxpayer and other external transactions but always controlled, and therefore intragroup, are not relevant in the application of the arm's length principle since they may be biased.

The congruity of the intercompany royalties applied by the licensor to the (foreign) licensee must be corroborated by a comparison with similar royalties, external to the group and ongoing between independent counterparties, namely located outside the group.

There are two essential prerequisites for effective comparability: the similarity between comparable royalties—which cannot be separated from their object, represented by the specific intangible license—and the circumstance that the royalty (which concerns the taxpayer, licensor, and specular licensee) is intragroup (otherwise the transfer pricing issue would not be applicable). The external comparison must refer to a company outside the taxpayer's group because otherwise the OECD principle that the comparable transaction cannot be controlled would be violated.

The second requirement (comparison with the uncontrolled external group) derives from the first (identification of similar royalty, as regards the object and function) so that their contemporary existence reduces the sample of comparable situations. Whenever the two comparisons are possible, their significance should be carefully investigated. Digitalization and professional storage of information eases comparisons, even for transfer pricing purposes.

For convenience, the discussion is limited to trademarks and patents, the most well-known of the licensed intangibles, with the warning that should it be extended to other intangibles, less coded or non-recordable (as know-how, goodwill, IoT, blockchains, other digital assets, etc.), the difficulties would exponentially increase.

Trademarks and patents are by their intrinsic nature hardly comparable, especially when such comparison had actual importance, in the presence of blockbuster brands and superstar patents.

The conclusions that can be drawn end up in a paradox: the (absolute) market value of trademarks and patents is the higher the more they are exclusive and therefore the less they are comparable with other intangible assets. The more the brands and patents are valuable (as unique), the less they are comparable: the normal (fair) value, therefore, seems applicable to residual and poor cases, less interesting for the tax authorities.

Comparing the tax legislation with the legal nature of trademarks and patents, trenchant conclusions are reached: if the brands are not original and do not constitute true distinctive signs, they can hardly be registered, as well as the absence of intrinsic novelty and originality is one of the impediments to patenting.

The concept of normal (fair) value relevant for tax purposes must be compared with the legal characteristics of trademarks and patents and their implications in terms of economic valuation.

A first comparison of the various cases of normal (fair) value, applied to trademarks and patents, is carried out in Table 22.5.

An invention, by definition, is patentable if it is original (and therefore different); the trademark can be registered only if it is unique and so unlikely to be confused: these assumptions are enough to understand that the comparison is ontologically hampered by the very nature of these intangibles, which incorporate expectations of uniqueness and exclusivity.

International accounting standards confirm this interpretation; IAS 38, paragraph 78 explicitly excludes the application of fair value for trademarks and patents, under the uniqueness of this asset and therefore its difficult comparability with similar elements. The uniqueness can give rise to well-known monopoly rents, especially in the patent field; this case is much less frequent and intense in the trademarks, but potentially less ephemeral since trademarks have a potentially indefinite useful life, which contrasts with the limited, typically twenty-year life of the patents.

If the normal (fair) value of the trademarks and patents is uneasy to determine, it follows that the royalties are not easily assessable.

Table 22.5 The normal value of trademarks and patents

Tax concept of normal (fair) value	Legal aspects	Economic valuation: assumptions
Average price or compensation for goods or services of the same or similar type ...	The goods are of the same species or similar, they tend to refer to unrecordable trademarks (as they lack the distinctive function of identification and can be confused with other trademarks) or to non-patentable inventions (if they are like others, they cannot be new)	The methods of economic evaluation based on the comparables presuppose real and effective comparability with similar companies and substitute products, difficult for the trademarks and impossible for patents; the difficulties of the comparison grow with the increase in the specificity of trademarks and patents, to which a greater value is typically connected
... in conditions of free competition ...	The registration of the trademark and the patenting of industrial inventions are aimed at obtaining exclusive and exclusive rights	The economic objective and the advantage of investments in trademarks and patents consist first in the research for monopoly rents and differentiation strategies, aimed at excluding or limiting free competition as much as possible

Tax concept of normal (fair) value	Legal aspects	Economic valuation: assumptions
... at the same marketing stage ...	For comparisons at the same marketing stage, keep in mind that trademarks are finished products, and patents; the problem is further complicated by dependent patents, which greatly hinder comparisons, typically very complex, and at different marketing stages	There are semi-finished products such as know-how or industrial secrets, already and not yet concerning finished products patents; patents can be related to inventions that are not yet commercialized or that never will be; the trademarks of products being launched or already established .... Considering these differentiating factors, which are economically significant, the already narrow spaces of comparison are further reduced
... in the time in which the operation was carried out or in the nearest time ...	Patents, unlike trademarks, have a deadline that can hinder or prevent temporal comparisons	The homogeneity of the temporal comparison is complex under the economic profile and the timing is often a fundamental parameter, especially in the presence of fickle markets (in particular for trademarks, which are affected by the fashion effect) or innovative (in which patents can become rapidly obsolete)

(continued)

Table 22.5 (continued)

Tax concept of normal (fair) value	Legal aspects	Economic valuation: assumptions
… in the place where the operation was carried out or in the nearest place …	The territorial extension of trademarks and patents can be limited already during the registration phase (to limit costs), hindering analogical geographical and territorial comparisons	Failure to cover certain areas hinders already difficult comparisons and may constitute a bridgehead for counterfeiters, always lurking; the markets can be very different, due to different consumer tastes (for trademarks) or different technological standards (for patents); globalization is a powerful factor of homologation, which leads to the convergence of lifestyles and standards
… with reference, as far as possible, to the price lists or tariffs of the person who supplied the goods or services and, in the absence of these, to the price lists of the chambers of commerce and professional rates, considering the discounts on use	Price lists and tariffs are applied first to sales in a series of standard products, all the opposite of trademarks and patents The residual reference to price lists of chambers of commerce and professional rates does not seem relevant to trademarks and patents	Commercially, price lists and formally standard rates provide for exceptions, discounts, and more and more extensive and frequent detailed treatments, hindering comparisons
For goods and services subject to price regulation, reference is made to the provisions in force	The case in point is not normally applicable to trademarks and concerns only special cases of patents (pharmaceuticals …)	Price regulation is a regressive phenomenon in economically more developed countries and is viewed with suspicion, being a phenomenon of leadership, which often hinders free competition, ending up damaging consumers instead of protecting them

The comparison with the trademark and patent license made by third-party companies that are not part of a group is used as a benchmark. Assuming that there are comparable companies, with trademarks or similar patents, it emerges that royalty companies (pure or mixed) license their intangible assets mostly at the intercompany level, being rare the cases in which the licensor and the licensee are not bound by a participatory constraint, thus being able to express a reporting value at arm's length level.

The comparison, imposed by the OECD principles, between intercompany transactions and similar transactions outside the group, to be carried out to validate the adequacy of the former, involves application problems which, in the minefield of intangible assets, often become insurmountable. Therefore, an unavoidable discretion remains, from which it is much more dangerous to counter the risk of a forced parameterization with false comparables.

It is relatively easy in transfer pricing to compare interest rates, referring to similar basic nominal rates, and discriminating only for the different risk premia (and those at the intercompany level are typically reduced since information asymmetries and counterparty risk is lower within parent companies). For intangibles, the matter is different, since they are hardly comparable to standardizable commodities.

The use of international databases of other transactions concerning the application of royalties can, however, be useful, at least as a guideline, not only to have a reference range of the applicable royalties.

The identification of risks and their dynamic monitoring represents a need that is increasingly felt in the legal field, not only to assess the going concern of the company but to better map the contractual clauses that regulate the relations between the royalty company and its licensees. These clauses should clearly define the contractual scope and the responsibilities of the licensor and licensee, concerning the risks held or transmitted.

For example, the licensing contract typically identifies the party that bears the costs of promotion and advertising, taking the related risks, and—above all—provides, although indirectly, an indication of who bears the market risk, where it provides a determination of the royalties that can follow different criteria (alternative or mixed/complementary), such as:

- Presence of a guaranteed minimum: the higher it is, the more the market risk is transferred to the licensee;
- Payment of a pre-established royalty, by way of lump sum: the risk is transferred to the licensee, proportionally to the entity of the fee above, and the likelihood that the licensee will be able to operate profitably, exceeding the break-even point between costs and revenues.

If the license is intercompany, the transfer of risk is compensated within the group and its accounting representation is offset in the consolidated financial statements.

22.7   THE CAPITAL STRUCTURE OF THE ROYALTY COMPANY AND ITS BORROWING CAPACITY

The capital structure of the royalty company highlights the arrangement of its assets and the composition of the sources of financing, as usually represented by equity and debts. The structure of the company and its contractual obligations follow a Coasian interpretation of the firm as a nexus (network) of contracts and must adapt to the specific cases that occur. These concern, above all, the fact that the royalty company belongs or not to a group (since the first case is the most frequent) and the gradation (exclusive, as it often happens in groups, or prevalent) with which it deals with the possession and management of intangible assets.

If the royalty company is inserted in a group, typically international (especially if the size of the group and its intangible assets are relevant), its portfolio of assets and liabilities must be analyzed:

- from a stand-alone perspective (regarding the individual company, its perimeter of assets, and its specific nexus of contracts);
- from a consolidated perspective, given that the contractual relationships are reabsorbed in a group logic (for example the guarantees and the group debt rating).

The case of stand-alone royalty companies is different, less frequent, more specialized, and often significantly smaller than those included in a group context.

The asset portfolio is typically dominated by intangibles, especially if the royalty company is pure and this is reflected in the composition of liabilities.

The existence of intangible assets, especially if they are not recorded in the balance sheet (or accounted for with symbolic amounts), limits the company's borrowing capacity, due to the difficulty of establishing a guarantee on them and their uncertain market value. The intuition based on which the capacity for indebtedness grows in the presence of tangible assets with a collateral value on which a guarantee can be established is confirmed by numerous studies, among which are those of Jensen and Meckling (1976) or Long and Malitz (1985).[16]

The market value of intangible assets significantly differs from their book value, due to the amortization procedures that entail a rapid write-off from the balance sheet. This generates information asymmetries between managers and external debtholders: while the former tend to be aware of the real value of intangible assets, external lenders have incomplete information that normally leads to an underestimation of intangible assets. This sounds like bad news for everybody, as it brings to sub-optimal investing. Digitalization and IT may, once again, contribute to reducing information asymmetries.

The presence of intangible assets in the balance sheet tends to limit the borrowing capacity if this effect can be mitigated by belonging to a group or by the mere presence of license agreements that ensure a predictable flow of fees to the royalty company.

22.8   Valuation of the Royalty Companies: Intangible Synergies and Holding Discount

The valuation of the royalty company is a function of the portfolio of its assets and of the economic and financial flows that can be drawn from their exploitation. Intangible assets can be valued on a stand-alone basis, if they are autonomously tradable, or—preferably—in a synergistic portfolio.

Although the methodologies and valuation criteria can be defined according to the individual cases, considering their specificity, some common characteristics can be identified, as the synergistic interaction (2 + 2 > 4) between different intangible assets (e.g., a trademark associated with a patent, or a portfolio of different trademarks or patents).

The assessment is strongly influenced by the scenario concerning the company (in the case of business continuity or liquidation or insolvency); in the second case, the estimate must be aimed at identifying the recoverable value. There are frequent cases of assessment to estimate the damages deriving from unfair competition or counterfeiting.

The royalty companies represent the safe box in which trademarks, patents, and other intangibles are kept. The separation of intangible assets from other assets, made possible by the existence of royalty companies, normally pure, allows to better appreciate their functions and characteristics and can constitute a valid economic reason for extraordinary transactions (demergers, transfers, exchanges, etc.) fiscally non-evasive.

The growing importance of intangible elements in shaping and preserving the strategic value of companies derives from the fact that—according to the now-classic Porter (1998) theory—competitive advantage derives from either cost leadership (which now mainly belongs to emerging economies) or from product differentiation.

Given their growing strategic importance, intangible values tend to progressively emerge, like the tip of an iceberg that increasingly needs to be explored in its entirety. And royalty companies are naturally destined to be a preferred target for investigation.

In this competitive scenario, the role of royalty companies represents an effective tool for the packaging of intangible resources.

A further valuation topic emerges when the royalty company takes the form of a mixed holding, being the holder of intangible assets (typically referring to the same investee companies) and of stakes in participated entities.

The value of a holding (or sub-holding) company is given by the sum of the intrinsic value of the holding company, without considering the holdings it owns (the value of the mere shell) and the value of the sole holdings (the value of the mere content, regardless of the shell, it is possible to make a comparison with an oyster that holds a pearl). The value of the shell is obtained by the difference between the market value of the holding (expressed by its market capitalization) and the Net Asset Value, represented by the market value of the subsidiaries. If the differential is negative, a holding discount emerges.

In formulae:

$$W_H = W_{\text{book equity}} + \left[W_{\text{market value}} - W_{\text{book equity}} \right] (1 - t) \qquad (22.1)$$

where:

W_H = Market value of the holding company;
$W_{book\ equity}$ = Book Value of Equity of the holding company;
$W_{market\ value}$ = Market Value of Equity of the holding company;
t = corporate tax rate.

The higher this holding discount, the bigger the incentive to liquidate the holding company, rather than keep it alive (as the break-up value is higher than the going concern value). This opportunity is rarely exploited by the majority shareholders, who normally defend their status locking down control and erecting barriers that hinder hostile takeovers.

22.9 THE CREDITWORTHINESS OF THE INTANGIBLE PORTFOLIO AND ROYALTY COMPANIES

The portfolio of intangible assets shows some criticalities in terms of bankability. This mainly turns out when considering the identifiability of the portfolio, especially if it is represented by heterogeneous intangibles that are not always easily identifiable (as the know-how).

In an intangible portfolio its synergistic characteristics, which cannot be easily subdivided, are the first to be assessed and valued, if this operation would in many cases be useless, given that it is precisely the joint combination of intangibles that adds value compared to the sum of its parts.

The inventions, even patented, make up the portfolio and characterize it from a technological point of view, normally associated with tangible assets (machinery or other) in a product and process innovation pattern that generates surplus value and makes the company more difficult to imitate by external competitors.

Information on intangibles, at the level of synergic portfolios, can influence the rating processes primarily from a qualitative point of view.

NOTES

1. See Chapter 24.
2. See http://www.hm-treasury.gov.uk/d/vfm_assessmentguidance061006 opt.pdf.
3. In project finance longer maturity loans are not necessarily perceived by lenders as being riskier than shorter-term credits. This contrasts with other types of debt, where credit risk is found instead to increase with maturity ceteris paribus. We emphasize a number of peculiar features of project finance structures that might underlie this finding, such as high leverage, non-recourse debt, long-term political risk guarantees, and the timing of project cash flows.
4. Sensitivity analysis is a means of gauging the impact of individual risks on a financing. Key risks can occur in three time periods:—Feasibility, engineering and construction phase;—Startup phase (usually through completion);—Operating phase (post completion).
5. Payments to cover construction, building maintenance, lifecycle repair and renewal and project financing should conveniently be made on an availability and performance basis, so as to stimulate the concessionaire to maintain a high-quality profile along all the useful life of the project.
6. Given the uncertainty inherent in project forecasting and valuation, analysts will wish to assess the sensitivity of project NPV to the various inputs (i.e., assumptions) to the Discounted Cash Flow (DCF) model. In a typical sensitivity analysis the analyst will vary one key factor while holding all other inputs constant, ceteris paribus. The sensitivity of NPV to a change in that factor is then observed (calculated as Δ NPV/Δ factor).
7. Other cover ratio measures include Loan Life Cover Ratio, defined as: Net Present Value of Cash flow Available for Debt Service/Outstanding Debt in the period.
8. Alternatively, EBIT may be used instead of EBITDA.
9. being EBITDA $\pm \Delta$ operating net working capital $\pm \Delta$ capital expenditure $=$ CF$_O$, any increase in EBITDA is typically accompanied by an increase in Operating Net Working Capital (a higher inventory and a bigger credit exposure are normally linked to a growing operating economic margin) and in capital expenditure (more investments are typically needed for an EBITDA increase). So, if EBITDA grows, its positive marginality on CFO is normally lowered by an increase in Operating Net Working Capital and capital expenditure, which burns out some of the extra cash created by the EBITDA's increase.
10. See Chapter 3.
11. This is the standard Modigliani & Miller proposition II, adjusted for taxes. The M&M theorem states that, in a perfect market, how a firm is financed is irrelevant to its value.

12. See Hart (1995).
13. See Smith Warner (1979).
14. The valuation can be assets side $\approx \text{NPV}_{project}$ or equity side $\approx \text{NPV}_{equity}$.
15. See paragraph 15.5.
16. See Chapter 24.

SELECTED REFERENCES

Bredillet, C., Tywoniak, S., & Tootoonchy, M. (2017). Exploring the dynamics of project management office and portfolio management co-evolution: A routine lens. *International Journal of Project Management, 36*, 27–42.

Cohen, J. A. (2011). *Intangible assets: Valuation and economic benefit.* Hoboken, NJ: Wiley.

Colangelo, G. (2008). *Gli accordi di patent pooling.* Milano: Giuffrè.

Dimitrov, D. V. (2016, July). Medical Internet of Things and big data in healthcare. *Health Informatics Research, 22*, 156–163.

Hall, N. G., Long, Z., Qi, J., & Sim, M. (2014). Managing underperformance risk in project portfolio selection. *Operations Research, 63*, 489–749.

Hart, O. (1995). Corporate governance: Some theory and implications. *The Economic Journal, 105*, 678–698.

Heipertz, J., Renciere, R., & Valla, N. (2019). Domestic and external sectoral portfolios: Network structure and balance-sheet contagion. *Journal of International Money and Finance, 94*, 206–226.

Huang, X. (2010). *Portfolio analysis: From probabilistic to credibilistic and uncertain approaches.* Berlin: Springer.

Jensen, M., & Meckling, W. (1976). Theory of the firm: Managerial behavior, agency costs and ownership structure. *Journal of Financial Economics, 3*, 305–360.

Juranek, S., Schndler, D., & Schjelderup, G. (2017). Transfer pricing regulation and taxation of royalty payments. *Journal of Public Economic Theory, 20*, 67–84.

Kaiser, G. M., Michael, G., El Arbi, F., & Ahlemann, F. (2014). Successful portfolio management beyond project selection techniquest: Understanding the role of structural alignment. *International Journal of Project Management, 33*, 126–139.

Killen, K. P. (2017). Managing portfolio interdependencies: The effects of visual data representations on project portfolio decision making. *International Journal of Managing Project in Business, 10*, 856–879.

Long, M., & Malitz, I. (1985). Investment patterns and financial leverage. In B. M. Friedman (Ed.), *Corporate capital structure in the United States.* Chicago: University of Chicago Press.

Moro Visconti, R., & Martiniello, L. (2019). Smart hospitals and patient-centered governance. *Corporate Ownership & Control, 16*(2), 83–96.

Moro Visconti, R., & Morea, D. (2019). Big data for the sustainability of healthcare project financing. *Sustainability, 11,* 3748.

OECD. (2017). *Transfer pricing guidelines for multinational enterprises and tax administrations.* https://www.oecd.org/tax/oecd-transfer-pricingguidelines-for-multinational-enterprises-and-tax-administrations-20769717.htm.

Ovais Ahmad, M., Lwakatare, L.E., Kuvaja, P., Oivo, M., & Markkula, J. (2016). An empirical study of portfolio management and Kanban in agile and lean software companies. *Journal of Software: Evolution and Process, 29,* e1834.

Parchomovsky, G., & Wagner, R. P. (2004). *Patent portfolios* (Paper 51). Scholarship at Penn Law, University of Pennsylvania Law School.

Porter, M. E. (1998). *Competitive advantage: Creating and sustaining superior performance.* New York: The Free Press.

Reitzig, M. (2006). Valuing patents and patent portfolios from a corporate perspective: Theoretical considerations, applied needs and future challenges. In D. L. Bosworth & E. Webster (Eds.), *The management intellectual property* (Chapter 15). Cheltenham, UK: Edward Elgar.

Robinson, H. S., & Scott, J. (2009, February). Service delivery and performance monitoring, PFI/PPP projects. *Construction Management & Economics, 27* (2), 181–197.

Sandner, P. (2010). *The valuation of intangible assets: An exploration of patent and trademark.* Berlin: Springer.

Smith, C. W., & Warner, J. B. (1979). On financial contracting: An analysis of bond covenants. *Journal of Financial Economics, 7*(2), 117–161.

CHAPTER 23

Digitalization and ESG-Driven Valuation

23.1 Introduction

In economics, capital consists of assets used to produce goods and services. A typical example is a machinery used in factories. Adam Smith defined capital as "part of man's stock which he expects to afford him revenue". In economic models, capital is an input in the production function. The total physical capital at any given moment in time is referred to as the capital stock (not to be confused with the capital stock of a business entity). Capital goods, real capital, or capital assets are already-produced, durable goods, or any non-financial asset that is used in the production of goods or services. In Marxian economics, capital is money used to buy something only to sell it again to realize a profit. Capital is extracted from the workers by the capitalist class, and the worker is left without any capital despite producing more value compared to their employers. For Marx, capital only exists within the process of the economic circuit and formed the basis of the economic system of capitalism. In more contemporary schools of economics, this form of capital is generally referred to as "financial capital" and is distinguished from "capital goods".[1]

Capital is a broad term that can describe anything that confers value or benefit to its owners, such as a factory and its machinery, intellectual property like patents, or the financial assets of a business or an individual.

R. Moro-Visconti, *The Valuation of Digital Intangibles*, https://doi.org/10.1007/978-3-031-09237-4_23

While money itself may be construed as capital, capital is more often associated with cash that is being put to work for productive or investment purposes.[2]

Capital accumulation is related to economic growth and is a major topic of investigation for economists (Piketty, 2013). Piketty's central thesis is that inequality is not an accident but rather a feature of capitalism that can be reversed only through state intervention. ESG targets are consistent with some state aid and may consider inequality reduction as a sustainable goal.

According to the Financial Times,[3] ESG is a term commonly used by investors to assess corporate activities related to environmental, social, and governance areas. ESG factors are also considered non-financial performance indicators and are used to identify issues related to business ethics, corporate social responsibility, and corporate governance. Digitalization, with its paperless features, positively impacts on sustainability, and so represents an ESG-compliant instrument.

According to Cornell and Damodaran (2020), "The argument that corporate managers should replace their singular focus on shareholders with a broader vision, where they also serve other stakeholders, including customers, employees, and society, has found a receptive audience with corporate CEOs and institutional investors. The pitch that companies should focus on 'doing good' is sweetened with the promise that it will also be good for their bottom line and shareholders. In this paper, we build a framework for the value that will allow us to examine how being socially responsible can manifest in the tangible ingredients of value and look at the evidence for whether being socially responsible is creating value for companies and investors".

Cornell and Shapiro (2021) front a core cost–benefit issue: "in addition to explicit contracts, corporations issue their stakeholders' implicit claims, including fair treatment of employees and the promise of continuing service to customers. Corporate value is created by selling these implicit claims for more than it costs to honor them. Recently, a new class of non-investor stakeholders, related to environmental, social, and governance (ESG) issues, has arisen. Although many ESG advocates stress their role in creating shareholder value, they do not explain how this value creation occurs".

The world we live in is characterized by growing complexity and disruptive events, starting from climatic changes. ESG protocols tackle these issues, even if their effectiveness is still questionable.

According to Milton Friedman, the main responsibility of a company is the maximization of the shareholders' returns. For decades, environmental, social, and governance (ESG) responsibilities were not considered relevant by most of the companies that have been focusing on profit maximization. Not only were ESG responsibilities believed to merely have no incidence on financial performance, but they were also perceived as a potential burden to the latter, being related to cost increases. Nevertheless, in the last twenty years, environmental, social, and governance issues revealed their influence not only on the profitability but also on the financial viability of several firms. As a natural consequence, the process of asset allocation started evolving. Furthermore, a raising environmental, social, and governance consciousness has been observed worldwide (Billio et al., 2021).

23.2   The Big Accounting and Market Picture

A comprehensive accounting picture of the three main statements—balance sheet, income statement, and cash flow statement—shows which are the main parameters (CAPEX, OPEX, Net Working Capital, liquidity, equity, financial debt, sales, EBITDA, EBIT, pre-tax profit, net profit, operating cash flow, net cash flow ...) that can be forecast to build up the business plan. These parameters can also be integrated with macroeconomic indicators (interest rates, inflation, exchange rates, etc.) to get discounted cash flows (DCF) and other input factors for firm evaluation, considering either the Enterprise or the Equity Value.

This classic representation represents the starting point for a sustainable integration, where ESG parameters complement the accounting and market picture.

Figure 23.1 shows the integrated balance sheet—economic-financial—empirical and market valuation, consistent with the contents of Chapter 2.

23.3   From Book to Market Value of Equity

Net equity is represented, in accounting terms, by the sum of the share capital (fully paid up, should we consider its real financial consistency), the reserves, and the net profit of the year.

Considering a synchronized asset and liability management structure, it becomes important to assess which is the accounting counterpart, in the

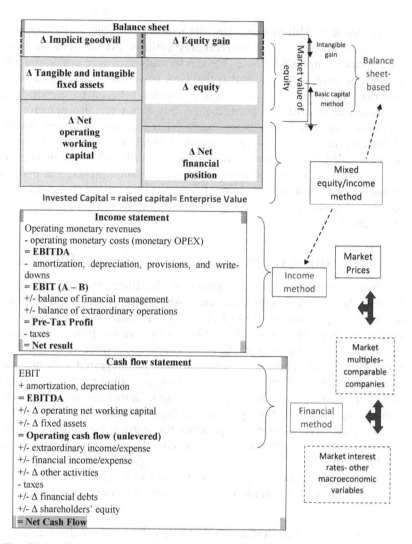

Fig. 23.1 The integrated balance sheet—economic-financial—empirical and market valuation

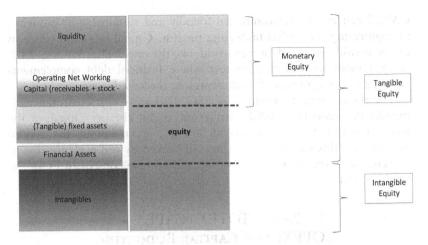

Fig. 23.2 Book, monetary, tangible and intangible equity in a debt-free context

assets, of the book value of equity. A synthetic representation is depicted in Fig. 23.2.

Monetary equity has a temporal dimension, and it may be subdivided in:

- "Immediate" monetary equity, considering in the assets only the liquidity;
- Short-term ("net working") monetary equity, including the liquidity that is going to be generated (and absorbed) by the evolution of the operating net working capital (cashed in receivables, paid out payables, etc.).

The concept of monetary equity allows bypassing the controversial accounting treatment of intangibles that include capitalized costs (CAPEX versus OPEX, recorded in the income statement). What really matters is TOTEX = CAPEX + OPEX.

This traditional accounting representation has important corporate finance consequences, concerning for instance the financial leverage (ratio between the financial debt and the equity, in market terms).

ESG capital may conveniently start from these premises, integrating the basic outlook with sustainability extensions. It will be shown that "green"

CAPEX can embed environmental-friendly and sustainable investments, re-engineering the capital budgeting process. Capital rationing concerns can be considered in a debt-free world, like the one depicted in Fig. 23.2, or in a more sophisticated context where financial debt complements equity, and both sources of funds represent the raised capital.

The thesis—long proclaimed by ESG advocates—that environmental-friendly investments (CAPEX) attract more and cheaper capital, in the form of equity and/or financial debt (e.g., green bonds) has a deep influence on this scenario, producing—if backed by real evidence that is, however, still controversial—important and positive consequences for the firm's goodwill.

23.4   TOTEX (CAPEX + OPEX) and Capital Budgeting

A consequential step of the accounting and financial approach considers equity resources and the synchronization between liabilities (that include the equity) and assets. Capital/equity is the accounting difference between assets and liabilities. The corresponding asset component of equity is important to assess its nature and consistency.

CAPEX with its OPEX yearly extensions—and so, TOTEX—represents the bulk of capital budgeting techniques, where invested capital is covered by raised capital, so proving adequate sources for long-term investments.

"Social" capital is properly identified not only by its sourcing under-writers (shareholders) but also by its effective destination to sustainable targets.

Capital expenditures (CAPEX) and operating expenses (OPEX) represent two complementary categories of business expenses, deriving from the capital and operating budgets that are created by companies to support growth.

Capital budgets cover capital expenses, which are capitalized and appear as long-term assets on the balance sheet. CAPEX corresponds to the amounts that companies use to purchase long-term assets as major physical goods or services that will be used for more than one year. These assets may be physical (plant, equipment, property, vehicles, etc.) or represented by intangibles that are not directly expensed in the income statement. As these long-term assets depreciate over their useful lives, the depreciation for a given year shows up on the income statement as a non-monetary expense in that year. Therefore, CAPEX is subject to depreciation (with a linear methodology in constant installments over the useful life or with an impairment test, whenever applicable).

OPEX refers instead to the ordinary costs for a company to run its daily business operations (purchases; salaries; rents; sales, general, and administrative expenses; property taxes, etc.). OPEX can be divided into monetary OPEX + depreciation/amortization.

Intangibles are a major source of sustainable value and directly impact monetary OPEX and CAPEX (when intangible investments are capitalized, and their annual quota is amortized). Amortization is, therefore, a part of non-monetary OPEX. Only monetary OPEX affects the EBITDA.

Since the fixed or intangible asset recorded in the balance sheet is part of normal business operations, depreciation is considered in this case an operating expense (non monetary, since it neither creates nor absorbs liquidity).

Scalability is an intangible characteristic of the digital business that can quickly boost volumes of sales, up to blitzscaling, as shown in Chapter 3.

Intangibles can, however, have a complementary impact on the business model (and consequent value creation), and they can have a joint impact on both, OPEX and CAPEX. What mostly matters is their intrinsic nature, and interdependence.

For what concerns OPEX, intangibles can ignite productivity gains where input costs to reach a target output are minimized. If OPEX is reduced, economic margins such as EBITDA, EBIT, pre-tax profit, or net profit improve, and so does valuation.

Capitalization of intangible assets (into CAPEX) instead of accounting within monetary OPEX does not change Operating Cash Flows (O_{CF}) that include these items anyway since:

$$\text{Enterprise Value} = \sum \frac{(sales - monetary\,OPEX) = EBITDA \mp \Delta NWC \mp \Delta CAPEX}{(1 + WACC)^i}$$

$$= \sum \frac{Operating\,Cash\,Flow}{(1 + WACC)^i} \tag{23.1}$$

where ΔNWC indicates the differential Net Working Capital (concerning the previous year).

While DCF (expressed by $\sum O_{CF}/WACC$) is invariant to the accounting treatment of intangibles (i.e., to the fact that they are capitalized or not), this is not true in the other valuation method. Should the Enterprise Value be proxied by the average EBITDA times a market multiplier of a comparable firm, then the EBITDA is influenced by the capitalization of intangibles. More precisely, capitalized intangibles (as development expenses) that become part of the CAPEX (and are never part of monetary OPEX) increase the EBITDA, and so the Enterprise Value is estimated with market comparables. DCF can also be residually calculated to express the net financial returns to shareholders (Equity Value): in this case, the FCFE (net cash flow) is discounted at the cost of equity. Even with this metric, digitalization matters, as it can maximize the FCFE, and reduce the risk component embodied in the cost of equity.

Operating costs are divided into variable and fixed costs, to better understand the impact of scalability on operating leverage (EBIT increase due to an increase in sales).

Scalability directly boosts sales but has an impact also on the EBIT that is given not only by increased revenues but also by the presence of fixed costs in the OPEX mix. Since fixed costs are—by definition—invariant to sales, the higher their proportion within the OPEX, the better the impact on the EBIT increase due to growing scalable sales. The opposite happens when sales decrease: in that case, fixed costs are a burden that can produce an operating loss, if the firm is unable to reach its economic break-even.

Intangibles may have a positive impact even on CAPEX, should they contribute to improving productivity, so decreasing the amount of CAPEX needed to run the business and to generate economic and financial positive margins (EBITDA; EBIT; operating and net cash flows, etc.).

There is so a positive impact attributable to scalable intangibles improving the market value of the firm, due to the higher economic and financial marginality.

Higher operating cash flows improve the discounted cash flows (O_{CF}/WACC) and a better EBITDA boosts the economic value complemented by market multipliers that are also based on the average EBITDA.

Accounting distortions may impact the dichotomy between OPEX and CAPEX, due to the slippery qualification of the intangibles and the caution that often prevents their capitalization. There may so be, in practice, some difficulty in discriminating about the impact of intangibles on either OPEX or CAPEX, where the impact on CAPEX may be underestimated due to accounting prudentialism.

Sustainable capital budgeting should conveniently embody ESG considerations within the metrics of Net Present Value, Internal Rates of Return, or the (discounted) Payback period that represents a financial break-even.

The key financial ratios used in the capital budgeting process, recalled in Table 23.1, are linked to the sales/revenues of the firm and the EBITDA/EBIT margins. The ratio between a change in the sales and a corresponding impact in the EBIT is represented by the operating leverage, with its scalability consequences. Scalability, as it will be shown later, matters even for long-term sustainability.

ESG's impact on these metrics is important, albeit under-investigated, especially for sustainable business planning and firm continuity plans.

The relationship between the NPV of the project and its IRR can be represented in the following graph, well-known to any corporate finance practitioner. According to Fig. 23.3—and the formulas of NPV and IRR—when WACC grows, the discounted cash flows of the project get smaller, approaching zero; actually, the Internal Rate of Return represents the point at which NPV is equal to zero.

Sensitivity analyses, aiming at finding the break-even point under stress tests where each variable at a time changes, are particularly useful. ESG-compliant projects reshape the OPEX and CAPEX following sustainable patterns. Sensitivity is consistent with business planning using different scenarios, in a deterministic or stochastic framework, where—once again—digitalization matters.

Figure 23.3 shows the interaction between the NPV of the project and its corresponding IRR, indicating the cost of equity (K_e risk premium) and the cost of debt (k_i risk premium) over the nominal rate of interest (real rate of interest + expected long-term inflation).

Any investment with a positive NPV has an IRR>WACC, meaning that the threshold rate of return is higher than the cost of collecting capital. ESG investments impact this traditional scenario, and they may worsen initial payoffs (if the initial investments for starting up the ESG project are higher than the traditional ones), even if in the long-run sustainable investments may compensate for higher profitability.

The payback of ESG investments may be longer, at least till when economies of experience can be incorporated into ecological projects, but this should not worry investors if the subsequent payoffs—after the break-even cut-off rate—are higher than those of traditional investments.

23.5 SUSTAINABLE BUSINESS PLANNING

Business planning is a core pillar of dynamic sustainability, as it represents a formal document that envisages long-term economic and financial

Table 23.1 Links between the operating leverage and key financial ratios

Items	Formula	Links with operating leverage
	Operating revenues − monetary and operating fixed costs − monetary and operating variable costs = **EBITDA** − amortization, depreciation, and provisions = **EBIT** + / − Δ Capital Expenditure (CAPEX) + / − Δ Commercial Net Working Capital = **OPERATING CASH FLOW** = **CFO**	
Operating revenues		Growing operating revenues generate an increase in EBIT, depending on the fixed/variable costs mix
EBITDA EBIT		EBITDA, given by the difference between operating revenues and (monetary) operating costs, influences Operating Cash Flow. The same happens with EBIT, which additionally considers non-monetary operating costs (depreciations, amortizations, provisions)

Items	Formula	Links with operating leverage
Operating cash flow		Increases in operating revenues increase EBITDA, EBIT, and Commercial Net Working Capital, normally pushing up Operating Cash Flow
WACC	$WACC = k_e \frac{E}{D_f + E} + k_d(1-t)\frac{D_f}{D_f + E}$	If operating revenues grow, EBIT and consequently net profit should increase, with an induced Equity growth; if equity grows, ceteris paribus leverage decreases and there is a transfer of risk from debtholders to equity-holders; to the extent that this risk transfer is symmetric, WACC should be unaffected

(continued)

Table 23.1 (continued)

Items	Formula	Links with operating leverage
NPV$_{project}$	$$NPV_{project} = \sum_{t=1}^{n} \frac{CFO_t}{(1+WACC)^t} - CF_0$$	If EBITDA grows, Operating Cash Flow (CFO) increases, with a positive impact on NPV, especially if WACC decreases
IRR$_{project}$	$$NPV_{project} = \frac{CFO_1}{1+IRR_{project}}$$ $$+ \frac{CFO_2}{(1+IRR_{project})^2} + \cdots + \frac{CFO_n}{(1+IRR_{project})^n}$$ $$- CF_0 = 0$$	If Operating Cash Flow grows, NPV might increase, then also IRR grows, increasing the financial break-even point; the project is more easily bankable
Average debt service cover ratio	$$ADSCR = \frac{\sum_{t=1}^{n} \frac{CFO_t}{D_{ft}+I_t}}{n}$$	The Operating Leverage is strictly connected with the average debt service cover ratio—a typical debt metric—which strongly depends on Operating Cash Flow. If cumulated CFOs grow, then the financial debt may be reduced
(Financial) Leverage	$K_e = [\text{WACC} + (\text{WACC} - k_d) * D_f/E] \, NR/PT$ where: NR = Net Result PT = Pre-tax result	If the difference (WACC—k_d) between the weighted average cost (return) of capital and the cost of debt is positive, then leverage above unity (where $D_f > E$) enhances this positive difference, with a consequential positive effect on the cost (return) of equity

Items	Formula	Links with operating leverage
EBITDA/financial charges	EBITDA/financial charges	EBITDA should be consistent enough to cover financial charges and other monetary costs; this parameter deeply changes across time, being negative in the construction phase and sometimes even at the beginning of the management phase; higher financial charges, embodied in the cost of debt and the WACC, decrease the margin multiplier (EBITDA should be at least 5–6 times the financial charges, depending on the amount of the other monetary costs), with a direct impact on cover ratio and leverage

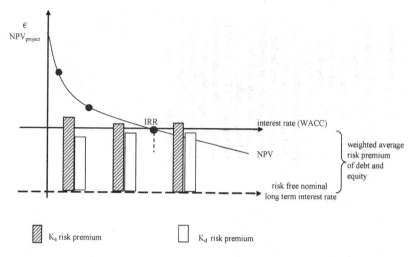

Fig. 23.3 Net Present Value and Internal Rate of Return of a project

perspectives (Moro Visconti, 2020b). Appropriate business planning, with continuous fine-tuning, backs sustainability strategies, and so fosters ESG compliance. ESG targets may well be embodied in business planning key factors, for instance envisaging:

a. A periodical check-up of the business continuity (capacity for the firm to keep a going concern for at least the next 6–12 months);
b. A consequential consideration of the perspective of economic and financial equilibrium (capacity of the firm to generate positive economic and financial margins, respectively, represented by EBITDA, EBIT, pre-tax/net profit, or operating and net cash flows).
c. A sensitivity analysis, conducted with a deterministic or stochastic approach that embodies stress tests, to assess the break-even point, with appropriate strategies to avoid or bypass a disaster case;
d. A continuous re-engineering (similar to an "F5" keyboard refreshing) and reformulation of the business plan hypotheses, exploiting bottom-up evidence from the external market and customers;
e. A prompt reaction to equity or cashflow burnouts, should these criticalities occur.

Business planning is a well-known tool for strategic formulations and execution (Lasher, 2010; Sahlman, 1997). The value of planning is driven by the possibility of evaluating alternative actions and being able to improve strategies. Before market entry, the main purpose of the evaluation is to pursue good and terminate bad business ideas (Chwolka & Raith, 2012). Planning is beneficial for performance (Brinckmann et al., 2010). Decision-making, however, remains a challenging task in the current age of forecasting (Asaduzzaman et al., 2015). As Razgaitis (2003) shows, prognosticators apply Monte Carlo Analysis to determine the likelihood and significance of a complete range of future outcomes; Real Options Analysis can then be employed to develop pricing structures, or options, for such outcomes. The forecasting effectiveness of traditional financial risk measures can be improved by integrating financial risk with an ESG risk measure that considers the ESG entropy (Ielasi et al., 2021).

Designing and creating a business model is crucial for a successful firm's operation in today's market in a complex and changing environment. A business model is a factor that differentiates one firm from another—it defines the distinctions of the firm, how the firm deals with the competition, the firm's partnerships, and customer relations (Koprivnjak & Peterka, 2020). Business modeling is increasingly focused on sustainability orientation, extended value creation, systemic thinking, and stakeholder integration (Breuer et al., 2018). In this process, digitalization matters.

Business planning follows a typical managerial top-down approach where management-prepared forecasts and projections are conceived within the firm and occasionally compared with market returns. The increasing availability of timely big data, sometimes fueled by the Internet of Things (IoT) devices, allows receiving continuous feedback that can be conveniently used to refresh assumptions and forecasts, using a complementary bottom-up approach. Top-down and bottom-up are both strategies for information processing and knowledge ordering.

Forecasting accuracy can be substantially improved by incorporating timely empirical evidence, with a consequent reduction of both information asymmetries and the risk of facing unexpected events, concerning the magnitude of their impact. Since risk is represented by the difference between expected and real events, if occurrences are timely incorporated into expectations, this differential is minimized. This intuitive concept is well-known, but its practical implications are amplified by the unprecedented presence of big data.

Valuation criteria of the project or investment are typically linked to business planning metrics, especially if they are based on Discounted Cash Flows (DCF). DCF forecasting can be greatly improved by timely big data feedback that positively affects the numerator, represented by growing cash flows (that incorporate real option flexibility), and decreasing discount rates (cost of capital) that reflect reduced risk. Value-adding strategies can conveniently reshape supply and value chains that embed information-driven resilience.

Network theory may constitute a further interpretation tool, considering the interaction of nodes represented by IoT and big data, mastering digital platforms, and physical stakeholders (shareholders, managers, clients, suppliers, lenders, etc.). Artificial intelligence, database interoperability, and blockchain applications are consistent with the networking interpretation of the interaction of physical and virtual nodes.

The interaction of big data with traditional budgeting patterns creates flexible (real) options nurtured by a networked digital ecosystem, eventually bringing to augmented business planning (Moro Visconti, 2020b).

23.6   DCF and Cost of Capital Metrics

This valuation paragraph synthetically repurposes paragraph 2.23 of the introductory Chapter 2 (general principles of valuation).

The main capital budgeting appraisal approach is probably represented by Net Present Value. TOTEX (= CAPEX + OPEX) is the target of the estimate and projected cash flows deriving from the investment are discounted at a risk factor that incorporates the cost of collecting capital. Within an ESG dimension, both the cost of capital (in the denominator of the discount formula [23.1]) and the cash flows (in the numerator) reflect the sustainability issues that go beyond standard corporate finance considerations. Market value maximization for the shareholders is a traditional target for the firm that is reconsidered in a wider context, including not only the other direct stakeholders (employees, debtholders, suppliers, customers, etc.) but also the external "civil society".

DCF analysis represents the cornerstone of the financial approach to corporate valuation.

The financial approach is based on the principle that the market value of the company is equal to the discounted value of the cash flows that the company can generate ("cash is king"). The determination of the cash flows is of primary importance in the application of the approach, as is the consistency of the discount rates adopted. The discount rate expresses the firm's cost of capital that represents the minimum acceptable rate of return that any investment must yield and is regarded as a long-term opportunity cost of the financing employed by the firm (Fernandes, 2014).

The doctrine (especially the Anglo-Saxon one) believes that the financial approach is the "ideal" solution for estimating the market value for limited periods. It is not possible to make reliable estimates of cash flows for longer periods. "The conceptually correct methods are those based on cash flow discounting. I briefly comment on other methods since - even though they are conceptually incorrect - they continue to be used frequently" (Fernandez, 2017).

This approach is of practical importance if the individual investor or company with high cash flows (leasing companies, retail trade, public and motorway services, financial trading, project financing SPVs, etc.) is valued.

Financial evaluation can be particularly appropriate when the company's ability to generate cash flow for investors is significantly different from its ability to generate income and forecasts can be formulated with a sufficient degree of credibility and are demonstrable.

Discounted cash flow (DCF) analysis is a method of valuing security, project, firm, or asset using the time value of money. All future cash flows are estimated and discounted by using the cost of capital to express their present values. Cash flows in the numerator of the formula need to keep an intrinsic consistency with the cost of capital in the denominator that incorporates risk factors. That is why FCFF is discounted using the WACC, and FCFE is discounted at the cost of equity.

This well-known framework reflects the forecast business model of the firm that incorporates trendy issues like Environmental, Social, and Governance (ESG) drivers, and other sustainability patterns, ranging from corporate social responsibility (CSR) concerns to Circular Economy issues. The digital dimension (Moro Visconti, 2020a) also contributes to reshaping the DCF metrics, easing the circulation of big data that softens information asymmetries. Intangible-driven scalability potential reflects in higher economic and financial marginality, proxied by the EBITDA or other parameters, and fostered by B2B2C-enabling digital platforms.

The impact of social responsibility and ESG compliance on the creation of market value for firms and investors is still questioned. Further research is so needed to analyze this interdisciplinary issue.

DCF can be expressed both in unlevered and levered terms. Unlevered DCF expresses the operating cash flow before debt service (Free Cash Flow to the Firm—FCFF). In the latter case, debt is deducted from the liquidity and what is left corresponds to the Free Cash Flow to Equity (FCFE).

The discount factor, represented by the opportunity cost of capital, needs to be consistent with the cash flow reported in the numerator of the formula, and so corresponds to the WACC to discount the CFFF or the cost of equity to discount the FCFE.

There are two criteria for determining cash flows:

a. The cash flow residually available to shareholders (FCFE)

The first configuration considers the only flow available for members' remuneration. It is a measure of cash flow that considers the financial structure of the company (levered cash flow). It is the cash flow that remains after the payment of interest and the repayment of equity shares and after the coverage of equity expenditures necessary to maintain existing assets and to create the conditions for business growth.

In M&A operations, the Free Cash Flow to the Firm (operating cash flow) is normally calculated, to estimate the Enterprise Value (comprehensive of debt). The residual Equity Value is then derived by subtracting the Net Financial Position.

The cash flow for the shareholders is determined, starting from the net profit:

Net profit (loss)
+ amortization/depreciation and provisions
+ divestments (− investments) in technical equipment
+ divestments (− investments) in other assets
+ decrease (− increase) in net operating working capital
+ increases (− decreases) in loans
+ equity increases (− decreases)
= **Cash flows available to shareholders (Free cash flow to equity—FCFE)**

The discounting of the free cash flow for the shareholders takes place at a rate equal to the cost of the shareholders' equity. This flow identifies the theoretical measure of the company's ability to distribute dividends, even if it does not coincide with the dividend paid.

b. The operating cash flow available to the company (Free cash flow to the firm)

The second configuration of flows is the one most used in the practice of company valuations to estimate the Enterprise Value (comprehensive of financial debt), given its greater simplicity of application compared to the methodology based on flows to partners. Enterprise converges towards Equity Value if the (negative) Net Financial Position is subtracted.

FCFF (discounted at the WACC) is a measure of cash flows independent of the financial structure of the company (unlevered cash flows) that is particularly suitable to evaluate companies with high levels of indebtedness, or that do not have a debt plan. In these cases, the calculation of the cash flow available to shareholders is more difficult because of the volatility resulting from the forecast of how to repay debts.

This methodology is based on the operating flows (FCFF) generated by the typical management of the company, based on the operating income available for the remuneration of own and third-party means net of the relative tax effect.

Unlevered cash flows are determined by using operating income before taxes and finance charges.

Net operating income
- taxes on operating income
+ amortization/depreciation and provisions (non-monetary operating costs)
+ technical divestments (− investments)
+ divestments (− investments) in other assets
+ decrease (− increase) in operating net working capital
= **Cash flow available to shareholders and financial lenders (operating cash flow – FCFF)**

The cash flow available to the company (FCFF) is, therefore, determined as the cash flow available to shareholders FCFE), plus financial charges after tax, plus loan repayments and equity repayments, minus new borrowings and flows arising from equity increases. An example is given in Fig. 23.4.

The difference between the two approaches is, therefore, given by the different meanings of cash flows associated with debt and equity repayments.

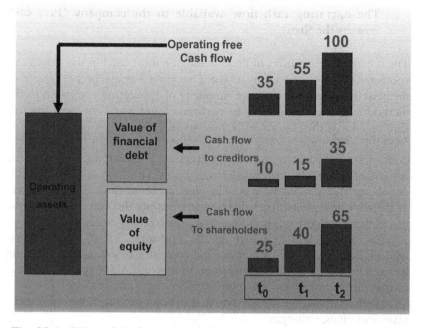

Fig. 23.4 Value of the firm and cash flows

Cash flows from operating activities are discounted to present value at the weighted average cost of capital.

This configuration of flows offers an evaluation of the whole company, independently from its financial structure. The value of the debt must be subtracted from the value of the company to rejoin the value of the market value, obtained through the cash flows for the shareholders.

The relationship between the two concepts of cash flow is as follows:

cash flow available to the company = cash flow available to shareholders

$$+ \text{ financial charges (net of taxes)}$$
$$+ \text{ loan repayments } - \text{ new loans}$$

$$(23.2)$$

Cash flow estimates can be applied to any type of asset. The differential element is represented by its duration. Many assets have a defined time horizon, while others assume a perpetual time horizon such as shares.

Cash flows (CF) can, therefore, be estimated using a normalized projection of cash flows that it uses, alternatively:

$$\text{unlimited capitalization:} \quad W_1 = CF/i \qquad (23.3)$$

$$\text{limited capitalization:} \quad W_2 = CF \, a \, n\neg i \qquad (23.4)$$

where W_1 and W_2 represent the present value of future cash flows.

The discount rate to be applied to expected cash flows is determined as the sum of the cost of equity and the cost of debt, appropriately weighted according to the leverage of the company (the ratio between financial debt and equity). This produces the Weighted Average Cost of Capital (WACC):

$$WACC = k_i(1-t)\frac{D}{D+E} + k_e\frac{E}{D+E} \qquad (23.5)$$

where:

k_i = cost of debt = real interest rate + expected inflation + spread (specific risk premium for the firm);
t = corporate tax rate;
D = market value of debt;
E = market value of equity;
$D+E$ = raised capital;
k_e = cost of equity (to be estimated with the Capital Asset Pricing Model—CAPM or the Dividend Discount Model—DDM).

The cost of debt capital is less controversial to calculate than the cost of equity capital. Due to the debt tax shield and its lower risk profile (being debt privileged over equity), the cost of debt capital is generally lower than that of equity capital.

The cost of debt capital is easy to determine, as it can be inferred from the financial statements of the company. The cost of equity or share capital, which represents the minimum rate of return required by investors for equity investments, is instead more complex and may use the Capital Asset Pricing Model or the Dividend Discount Model.

The WACC formulation shows that in the estimate of the cost of capital there is an internal and an external (systematic) component, both in the cost of debt and in the cost of equity:

- In the cost of debt, the market interest rate (risk-free nominal interest rate = real interest rate + expected inflation) represents the systematic component, whereas the spread is the firm-specific parameter;
- In the cost of equity, the systematic component is represented by the market premium (stock market return compared to the risk-free nominal interest rate), whereas the specific parameter is proxied by the firm's Beta (β):

$$ER_i = R_f + \beta_i \left(ER_m - R_f \right) \tag{23.6}$$

where:

ER_i = expected return of investment
R_f = risk-free rate
β_i = beta of the investment (sensitivity of the firm toward the stock market) = cov (i, market)/σ^2 market
$(ER_m - R_f)$ = market risk premium
if the cost of equity is proxied by the Dividend Discount Model (see formula 23.10), the discount rate r incorporates both the standard market discount rate and the specific firm risk.

Once the present value of the cash flows has been determined, the calculation of the market value W of the company may correspond to:

a. The unlevered cash flow approach:

$$W = \sum \frac{CF_0}{WACC} + VR - D \tag{23.7}$$

b. The levered cash flow approach:

$$W = \sum \frac{CF_n}{K_e} + VR \tag{23.8}$$

where:

$\sum CF_0 / WACC$ = present value of operating cash flows

$\sum CF_n/K_e$ = present value of net cash flows
VR = terminal (residual) value
D = initial net financial position (financial debt − liquidity)

The residual value is the result of discounting the value at the time n (before which the cash flows are estimated analytically). It is often the greatest component of the global value W (above all in intangible-intensive companies) and tends to zero if the time horizon of the capitalization is infinite ($VR / \infty = 0$).

The two variants (levered versus unlevered) give the same result if the value of the firm, determined through the cash flows available to the lenders, is deducted from the value of the net financial debts.

Operating cash flows (unlevered) and net cash flows for shareholders (levered) are determined by comparing the last two balance sheets (to dispose of changes in operating Net Working Capital, fixed assets, financial liabilities, and shareholders' equity) with the income statement of the last year, as can be seen in Table 23.2 that shows the accounting scheme of the cash flow statement.

The net cash flow for the shareholders coincides with the free cash flow to equity and, therefore, with the dividends that can be paid out, once it has been verified that enough internal liquidity resources remain in the company. This feature, associated with the ability to raise equity from third parties and shareholders, allows the company to find adequate financial coverage for the investments deemed necessary to maintain the company's continuity and remain on the market in economic conditions (minimum objectives). They should allow for the creation of incremental value in favor of shareholders, who are the residual claimants (being, as subscribers of risky capital, the only beneficiaries of the variable net returns, which, as such, are residual and subordinate to the fixed remuneration of the other stakeholders).

The estimate of cash flows can be applied to any activity. The differential element is service life. Many activities have a defined time horizon, while others assume a perpetual time horizon such as company shares.

The discounted cash flow (DCF) approach can be complemented with real options that incorporate intangible-driven flexibility in the forecasts.

DCF is ubiquitous in financial valuation and constitutes the cornerstone of contemporary valuation theory (Singh, 2013). The robustness of the model, as well as its compatibility with the conventional two-dimensional risk-return structure of investment appraisal, makes it suited

Table 23.2   Cash flow statement and the link with the cost of capital

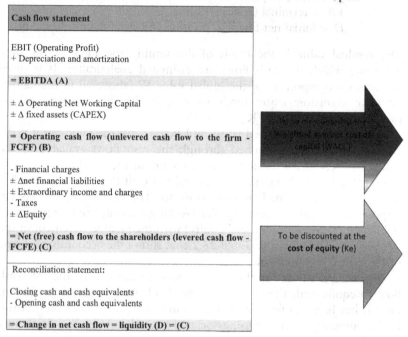

Cash flow statement
EBIT (Operating Profit) + Depreciation and amortization
= EBITDA (A)
± Δ Operating Net Working Capital ± Δ fixed assets (CAPEX)
= Operating cash flow (unlevered cash flow to the firm - FCFF) (B)
- Financial charges ± Δnet financial liabilities ± Extraordinary income and charges - Taxes ± ΔEquity
= Net (free) cash flow to the shareholders (levered cash flow - FCFE) (C)
Reconciliation statement:
Closing cash and cash equivalents - Opening cash and cash equivalents
= Change in net cash flow = liquidity (D) = (C)

To be discounted at the Weighted average cost of capital (WACC)

To be discounted at the cost of equity (Ke)

to a multitude of valuations. Accounting standards across the globe recognize the efficacy of this model and advocate its use, wherever practicable. FAS 141 and 142 of the United States and IAS 39 that relate to the accounting of intangible assets recommend the use of DCF methodology for attributing a value to such assets.

All these traditional valuation metrics need, once again, to be adapted to the "augmented" ESG dimension.

23.6.1   *The Cost of Collecting Capital: A Comparison Between Traditional and ESG-Firms*

The cost of capital for a firm represents the economic-financial expenditure to collect equity and financial debt from shareholders or, respectively, debtholders. Whereas traditional—often "polluting"—firms collect ordinary capital/equity from shareholders and issue standard debt (underwritten by banks, bondholders, etc.), ESG-compliant firms issue capital for targeted equity-holders and green bonds or other sustainable debt.

A comparison is represented in Fig. 23.5.

Giese et al. (2019) show that companies' ESG information is transmitted to their valuation and performance, both through their systematic risk profile (lower costs of capital and higher valuations) and their idiosyncratic risk profile (higher profitability and lower exposures to tail risk).

The cost of capital represents, as shown above, the denominator of the DCF, since the cost of equity is used to discount net cash flows, and the WACC to discount operating (unlevered) cash flows.

ESG factors can contribute to changing DCF in two ways—modifying either the cash flows in the numerator and/or the corresponding cost of capital in the denominator. The standard DCF formula is:

$$DCF\ operating = \sum_{i=1}^{n} \frac{CF_1 + CF_2 + \ldots + CF_n}{(1 + WACC)} \qquad (23.9)$$

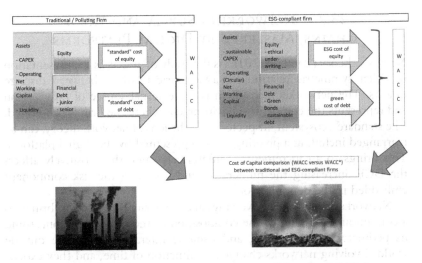

Fig. 23.5 Cost of capital: comparison between traditional and ESG-firms

where *CF* is the operating cash flow and *WACC* is the weighted average cost of capital.

Should ESG parameters have a positive impact on both cash flows and WACC, the formula would be:

$$DCF\, operating* \uparrow\uparrow = \sum_{i=1}^{n} \frac{CF1 \uparrow + CF2 \uparrow + \ldots + CFn \uparrow}{(1 + WACC) \downarrow}$$

(23.9bis)

The rationale behind this multiplying improvement that affects both the numerator and the denominator, boosting the DCF*, may be found in the ability to improve cash flows, thanks to savings or revenue increases, and to minimize the risk embedded in the WACC, lowering the cost for collecting sustainable capital. This proves an uneasy but highly rewarding target.

Should the cost of capital increase and/or the cash flows decrease, stakeholders (both debtholders and shareholders, if operating cash flow is the selected parameter) would face a deteriorating situation. This may be the case in the first years of the environmental investment when the payoff is still far and the startup costs increase.

23.7 Networking Supply and Value Chains, Mastered by Digital Platforms

Network theory (Barabási, 2016) is the study of graphs as a representation of either symmetric relations or asymmetric relations between discrete objects. The networked ecosystem is the external source of information and represents the competitive environment where the firm is positioned. The standard ecosystem, inspected with the lens of network theory, can be rearranged including a pivoting node represented by the digital platform. This brings to an incremental (differential) value that positively affects the DCF, increasing the numerator, and softening the risk component embedded in the denominator.

Networks are, however, evolving, and their kinetic evolution brings to a continuous reshaping of the composition of the ecosystem, concerning its perimeter, internal links, and osmotic interaction with the outside world. Evolving networks change as a function of time, and they experiment with growth patterns since are added to the network over time and are more likely to link to other nodes with high distributions (like digital platforms that maximize the number of connections to other nodes). Nodes that dynamically increase their degree (number of edges connected to the node) intermediate more "traffic", from information (big data) to economic transactions, improving the overall value of the ecosystem.

Networks connect discrete objects or intangible assets with relations that establish an edging link among otherwise dispersed nodes. Physical networks may be used to explain traditional supply and value chains that can become "smart" following innovation patterns and other industry 4.0 applications, as exemplified in Fig. 23.6.

A comprehensive picture of the evolving network ecosystem, consistent with Fig. 23.4, is shown in Fig. 23.7.

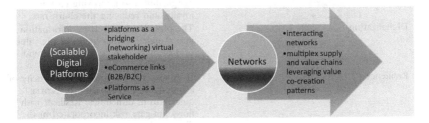

Fig. 23.6 From digital platforms to networks

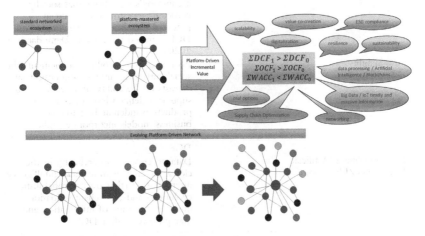

Fig. 23.7 Platform-driven evolving networks

The strategic drivers that impact the DCF formulation are recalled in Table 23.3.

Table 23.3 Impact of the strategic drivers on the discounted cash flows

Strategic driver	Impact on the discounted cash flows
Scalability	A scalable firm can improve profit margins while sales volume increases. This positively affects the EBITDA and the operating and net cash flow
Value co-creation	The joint creation of value by the firm and the customer with her feedback positively impacts economic and financial marginality, also improving customer loyalty, and reducing the churn rate
Digitalization	The process of converting information into a digital format increases the value of data making them accountable and manageable
Resilience	It expresses the toughness or elasticity of a system, and its capacity to recover quickly from difficulties. Resilient cash flows mitigate risk incorporated in the discount factor
ESG compliance	Environmental, social, and governance (ESG) criteria are a set of standards for a company's operations that socially conscious investors use to screen potential investments. Their impact on DCF is mixed (Cornell & Damodaran, 2020)
Sustainability	Economic sustainability complements the social and environmental dimensions and consists of the ability of an economy to support a defined level of economic production indefinitely. Sustainable business models incorporate resilience and scalability, with a positive impact on DCF
Data processing/Artificial Intelligence/Blockchains	Data processing and archiving in the cloud, together with artificial intelligence interpretation (that tracks probabilistic evolution) and blockchain validation, improve the value of information and may positively affect DCF

(continued)

Table 23.3 (continued)

Strategic driver	Impact on the discounted cash flows
Big Data/IoT	Big data and IoT nurture the business planning input factors with massive and timely information, improving the expected cash flows, and reducing their riskiness
Networking	Networking, especially if mastered by digital platforms, is a scalability catalyzer that impacts DCF
Supply chain optimization	Digital supply chains reduce intermediation costs, and improve resilience, with positive effects on cash flows
Real options	Real options increase the resilience and scalability of forecasted cash flows

The network interacts with business planning through digital and physical connections, and transactions. The sequential impact is dynamic and subject to continuous adjustments, due also to the feedback that fuels value co-creation, reshaping the supply and value chain. A representation is reported in Fig. 23.8.

Firm networks are increasingly digitally mastered, as platforms (e-commerce hubs, etc.) act as facilitators of exchange, intermediating money, and information (from small to big data). This systemic interconnection also concerns financial and sustainable capital, shaping a new paradigm where connectivity—for the bad or the worse—is levered by digitalization.

23.8 The Financial Value of Growth: Multi-Stage Cash Flows and Dividends

Growth, with its economic and financial implications, is the engine behind sustainability, value (co)creation, and sharing. Future cash flows are a natural consequence of growth, and they remunerate financial debt and, residually, equity. Sustainability issues emerge as a by-product, remembering that economic (and financial) sustainability is preliminary to environmental or social aspects, incorporated in the ESG metrics. No money, no party.

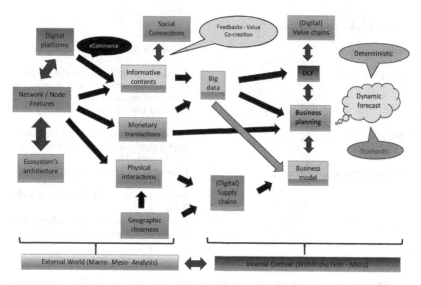

Fig. 23.8 From interacting networks to business model and planning

Within this broad context, standard corporate finance considerations apply, also relating to the remuneration of shareholders, mainly in the form of dividends. Equity remuneration follows the absolute priority rule where financial creditors have a priority over shareholders. The dividend payment may so be considered good news for all the stakeholders since shareholders are the last recipients. Whereas these are classic corporate finance considerations, the reality is more complex, and there is emerging evidence that some "silent" stakeholders may be biased by this mechanical "pie sharing". They are represented, in general terms, by the Environment, the Civil Society and the Institutions, the communities surrounding the firm, etc.

Some classic finance considerations will precede a wider debate about these unassuming stakeholders.

Multi-stage Dividend Discount Model (DDM) is a technique used to calculate the intrinsic value of a stock by identifying different growth phases of a stock; projecting dividends per share for each period in the high growth phase and discounting them to the valuation date, finding terminal value at the start of the stable growth phase using the

Gordon growth model, discounting it back to the valuation date and adding it to the present value of the high growth phase dividends.

The basic concept behind the multi-stage Dividend Discount Model is the same as the constant-growth model, i.e., it bases intrinsic value on the present value of expected future cash flows of a stock. The difference is that instead of assuming a constant dividend growth rate for all periods in the future, the present value calculation is broken down into different phases.

Figure 23.9 shows the growth rates of dividends in a three-stage timesheet. The cost of equity should ideally be decreasing across time, as initial high growth rates coincide with the startup phase where equity risk is higher (also due to the lower level of leverage that normally characterizes this phase).

The Dividend Discount Model (DDM) is a method of valuing a company's stock price based on the theory that its stock is worth the sum of all of its future dividend payments, discounted back to its present value. In other words, it is used to value stocks based on the Net Present Value of future dividends. The equation most widely used is called the Gordon growth model.

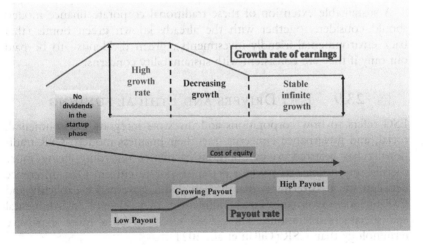

Fig. 23.9 Multi-stage dividend growth

The formula is:

$$P_0 = \frac{\overbrace{D_0(1+g)}^{\text{Next dividend}}}{\underbrace{r-g}_{\text{Discount rate}}} = \frac{D_1}{r-g}$$

Next dividend

Discount rate

Growing at (growth)

(23.10)

where:

P_0 is the current stock price
g is the constant growth rate in perpetuity expected for the dividends.
r is the constant cost of equity capital for that company.
D_1 is the value of the next year's dividends.

This model embeds constant growth that is a theoretical oversimplification of the real world.

A sustainable extension of these traditional corporate finance models should consider, together with the already known green bonds (that back environmental-friendly investments), green dividends—to be paid out only if they are consistent with sustainability concerns.

23.9   ESG DRIVERS AND ETHICAL FUNDING

ESG refers to how corporations and investors integrate environmental, social, and governance concerns into their business models. CSR traditionally has referred to corporations' activities regarding being more socially responsible, to being a better corporate citizen. One difference between the two terms is that ESG includes governance explicitly and CSR includes governance issues indirectly as they relate to environmental and social considerations. Thus, ESG tends to be a more expansive terminology than CSR (Gillan et al., 2021).

The key ESG issues are recalled in Table 23.4.[4]

Key ESG issues like those recalled in Table 23.4 could be conveniently matched with corporate finance issues, with the following caveats:

Table 23.4 Key ESG issues

Environmental	Social	Governance
Carbon emissions	Financial inclusion	Corporate governance
The carbon footprint from products	Healthcare universal coverage	Gender parity
Raw material insourcing	Schooling/instruction	Monopolistic/anti-competitive strategies
Cutting toxic emissions and waste	Health/nutrition improvements	Corruption and money laundering
Energy efficiency/waste reduction	Labour/HR management	Financial system instability concerns
Packaging biodiversity	Human Capital development	Stakeholders' discrimination
Climate change risk insurance	Supply Chain Labor improvements	Business ethics and fraud
Electronic waste	ICT access	Racial/gender discrimination
Water sources distress	Controversial sourcing	
CleanTech/ClimateTech opportunities	Copying with demographic risk	
Green Building opportunities	Health and safety issues	
Threat to biodiversity	Financial products compliance	
Threat to sustainable land use	Product safety and quality control	
Use of renewables	Chemical safety	
Financing environmental upgrades (green bonds, etc.)	Insuring health	
	Privacy/Data security	
	Responsible social impact investing	

a. Discrimination between Environment, Social, and Governance is essential, firstly within different industries, since many issues are not applicable everywhere (e.g., carbon emissions). Governance aspects normally have broader applications;

b. ESG parameters may impact two key parameters: (unlevered) cash flows and the cost of capital (WACC); in an ideal situation, ESG should increase cash flows (thanks to scalability real options that embed new opportunities and better resilience), and decrease risk (incorporated in the WACC);

c. E + S + G issues may be interacting and self-fulfilling; for example, environmental compliance implies positive social and governance externalities.

Ignoring ESG aspects exposes firms to risks that diminish value, shrink returns, and even lead to failure. Firms considering ESG aspects are perceived as less risky by capital providers. Such capital suppliers accept lower returns and lending rates when providing capital to firms with superior ESG practices and disclosure (Johnson, 2020).

Both the EBITDA and the cost of capital are sensitive to ESG parameters. The growing relevance of sustainability suggests that managerial decisions that improve corporate environmental footprint and risks might be priced by investors, thus reducing the cost of capital for global companies (Gianfrate et al., 2018).

Clark et al. (2015) show that corporate sustainability standards can be a crucial factor in lowering the cost of capital, which comprises the cost of debt (i.e., credit score/risk) and the cost of equity.

ESG refers to the three central factors in measuring the sustainability and societal impact of an investment in a company or business. These criteria help to better determine the future financial performance of companies (return and risk).

From a consumer perspective, firms that behave responsibly provide goods and services that protect the environment, satisfy needs, protect the consumer, and do so at a reasonable price; from an investor perspective, socially responsible firms create value while minimizing risk. However, the identification of socially responsible firms is difficult ex-ante due to information asymmetries (Minutolo et al., 2019).

Some studies analyze the relationship between corporate social performance and market returns. Preliminary results found no extra returns in Italy (Landi & Sciarelli, 2019). The impact of ESG compliance on cash flows and the cost of capital is still controversial; whether there is a hope of a positive impact on (higher) cash flows and (lower) cost of capital, the evidence is still mixed.

The ESG scores developed by Bloomberg are one mechanism that signals to the market the level of transparency and disclosure by the firm and an indicator of overall social responsibility. Scores such as Bloomberg's ESG have become an important measure for many investors because it conveys a level of risk (Huber & Comstock, 2017).

ESG parameters may impact both the numerator and the denominator of DCF metrics, so affecting corporate valuation. The impact of ESG parameters on the estimated cash flows reported in the numerator, the discounting cost of capital in the denominator, and the overall market estimate represented by the sum of the DCF are asymmetric if $E1 \neq E2 \neq E3$, $S1 \neq S2 \neq S3$, and finally, $G1 \neq G2 \neq G3$.

This means that the same parameters have a different impact on the cash flows, the cost of capital, and their discounted sum (DCF). This may well be the case because cash flows are an internal parameter (calculated within the firm), whereas the cost of capital reflects the discount risk of the cash flows but also incorporates external factors (the risk-free market interest rates, the market equity premium, etc.). The impact of ESG factors must be interpreted dynamically, as it changes across time.

Figure 23.10 shows the impact on DCF according to this asymmetric interpretation.

Ethical funding may concern corporate bond issues that are the main component of the cost of debt. According to Koelbel and Busch (2013), there is a significant effect of stakeholder pressure regarding ESG issues on corporate bond spreads.

23.10 SUSTAINABILITY PATTERNS

The forecast of future cash flows is possibly the main criticality of DCF metrics, and the risk that effective cash flows may (greatly) differ from expected ones needs to be incorporated into the cost of capital. This well-known consideration is difficult to put into practice, especially when projections are long-termed or when they concern volatile businesses, such as startups or technological industries.

Sustainability concerns so affect estimates, and the cost of capital discount factor may conveniently incorporate heterogeneous functions that refer to:

a. Circular economy patterns;
b. Sharing economy;
c. The resilience of supply and value chains;
d. Digital platforms and networks;
e. Intangible-driven scalability potential and real options.

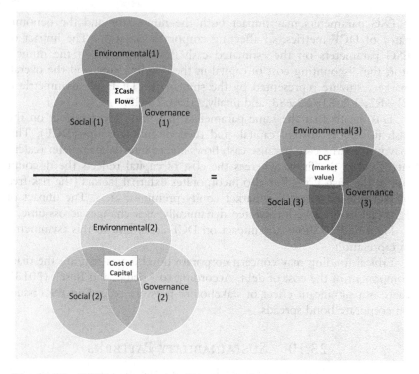

Fig. 23.10   ESG impact on cash flows, cost of capital, and DCF value

Sustainability factors are expected to lower the cost of capital, improving the occurrence and stability of expected cash flows. Both costs of debt and cost of equity are lower for firms that disclose sustainability performance information when compared to firms that do not disclose similar information (Ng & Rezaee, 2012).

Sustainability so impacts the firm's value, expected cash flows, and systematic risk of an overall market portfolio. Figure 23.11 recalls the main sustainability patterns.

Sustainability patterns may affect both the systematic and the specific cost of capital components of a firm. As anticipated, the systematic component relates to the market (risk-free interest rates, then summed up with the firm-specific spread to determine the cost of debt; firm's beta, to

Fig. 23.11 Sustainability patterns

express its sensitivity toward the stock market premium, as a proxy of the cost of equity).

Sustainability strategies impact both the ecosystem and the individual firm. The ecosystem, eventually related to the stock markets, benefits from the impact of sustainability factors, especially if they are coordinated and synergistic, and is sensitive to ESG achievements that improve the overall wealth. At the firm level, a better ecosystem may lower the overall cost of capital, making the capital markets more efficient and resilient.

Digital platforms improve the architectural frame-working of the ecosystems and catalyze its functioning, operating as an orchestra director that coordinates and fine-tunes the market players.

Scalability is both market- and firm-driven, as it benefits from an overall ecosystem functioning that creates the market conditions for individual firm achievements.

Jiménez and Grima (2020) point out that the link between the cost of equity and sustainability is extremely timely as it can have great potential in reinforcing good practices regarding sustainable engagement among listed companies, which can also be regarded as trendsetters by other types of companies and institutions.

23.10.1   Circular Economy

A Circular Economy is an economic system aimed at eliminating waste and the continual use of resources.

The impact of the Circular Economy model on the cost of capital is still largely undetected. Initial green investments may have long-term payback but should eventually become sustainable. The cost of capital of these investments may so increase in the first years but then gradually decrease, especially if there are incentives to carry on green investments (and restrictions for polluting ones). What matters is, more than the individual cost of capital (within each firm), the overall collective cost (of capital) borne by a comprehensive ecosystem.

Circular systems employ reuse, sharing, repair, refurbishment, remanufacturing, and recycling to create a closed-loop system, minimizing the use of resource inputs and the creation of waste, pollution, and carbon emissions.

Combining sustainable consumption with the Circular Economy concept could help tackle challenges, such as resource scarcity and climate change by reducing resource throughput and increasing the cycling of products and materials within the economic system, thereby reducing emissions and virgin material use (Tunn et al., 2019).

According to the Center for Economic Development & Social Change, global economic growth is facing increasing challenges in terms of sustainability. Under this assumption, the new model of Circular Economy takes place: it promises economic growth with low or zero costs in terms of materials, energy, and environmental impact. As the Industrial Revolution promised benefits from an excess availability of resources, the Circular Economy takes advantage of resource constraints. Increasing efficiency means improving the ratio between input (environmental impact) and output (return) through behavior, technology, and planning. The reasons to achieve better efficiency are many: the scarcity of resources, the increasing environmental impact, and the promised economic return. The challenges are also many. First, incentives are low. That is because of the low cost of some resources, too low to encourage recycling and efficiency. Moreover, investments in efficiency require pay-back periods longer than the industrial standard, beyond a large financial capital.

Figure 23.12 shows an example of a Circular Economy flowchart.

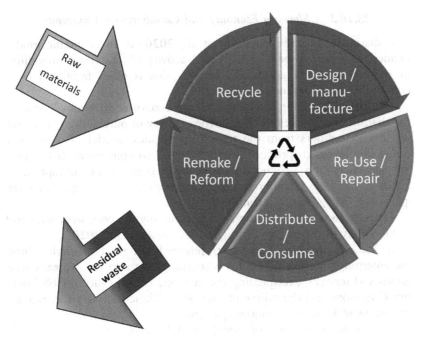

Fig. 23.12   Circular economy flowchart

23.10.2   Resilient Supply and Value Chains

Supply and value chains are becoming more resilient, thanks to digitalization and networking. This impacts the cost of capital, softening overall risk. Resilience is also embedded in real options and may be estimated with a differential approach, comparing a standard (and somewhat rigid) supply chain with a resilient one (which is the added value?).

Resilient networks (e.g., digital supply chains) are elastic to external shocks, for instance, given by a node deletion (what happens if a physical or digital bridging node is deleted? Railway systems are more vulnerable than aviation systems since it is easier to replace a missing airport than a central station. Node deletion is, however, useful during pandemics).

Upson and Wei (2019) examine the impact of supply chain concentration on a firm's financing costs, showing that purchasing firms engaging in multiple supplier relationships are subject to higher firm risk and cost of equity.

23.10.3   Sharing Economy and Collaborative Commons

The sharing economy (Mallinson et al., 2020) is an economic model defined as a peer-to-peer (P2P) based activity of acquiring, providing, or sharing access to goods and services that is often facilitated by a community-based online platform.

The capitalist sharing economy is a socio-economic system built around the sharing of resources. It often involves a way of purchasing goods and services that differs from the traditional business model of companies hiring employees to produce products to sell to consumers. It includes the shared creation, production, distribution, trade, and consumption of goods and services by different people and organizations (https://en.wik ipedia.org/wiki/Sharing_economy).

The key assumptions of the sharing economy are consistent with the sustainability of the supply chain (Banaszyk & Łupicka, 2020).

In *The Zero Marginal Cost Society*, Jeremy Rifkin (2014) describes how the emerging Internet of Things is speeding us to an era of nearly free goods and services, precipitating the meteoric rise of a global Collaborative Commons and the eclipse of capitalism. These visionary theories are consistent with sharing economy patterns.

The impact on the cost of capital is still debated.

23.10.4   Scalability and Real Options

Scalability positively impacts the expected cash flows, sometimes to a great extent. It may also have an impact on the cost of capital that is, however, more difficult to ascertain. Scalable cash flows reported in the numerator of the DCF formulation may be more volatile than normal ones, so demanding a higher discount rate. On the other side, scalability may have a positive impact on resilience and sustainability.

Scalability first impacts the EBIT and sterilizes the impact of non-monetary operating costs (depreciation and amortization), on the EBITDA representing the real engine behind value creation and economic-financial growth.

Based on these premises, further consideration concerns the impact of the intangible investments on the EBITDA's components, represented by the difference between the operating (monetary) revenues and the (monetary) OPEX.

The representation may be synthesized in Fig. 23.13.

Flexibility (resilience) represents a key characteristic of scalability and can be enhanced using real options, concerned with the right—but not

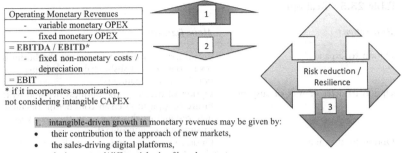

1. intangible-driven growth in monetary revenues may be given by:
   - their contribution to the approach of new markets,
   - the sales-driving digital platforms,
   - the incremental/differential role of brands, patents
   - revenue and market share protection, with entry barriers
   - digital scalability, driven by Metcalfe or Moore law externalities
   - real options (to expand, contract out …)

2. intangible-driven savings in monetary OPEX may be given by:
   - productivity and efficiency gains
   - (digital) supply chain savings

3. Risk reduction:
   - Affects the denominator of DCF (discount factor incorporating the cost of capital)
   - Reduces the difference between expected and real outcomes, even thanks to timely re-engineering of the business planning incorporating big data (Moro Visconti, Montesi & Papiro, 2018)
   - Improves the resilience and flexibility of the supply and value chain.

Fig. 23.13 The impact of the intangible investments on the EBITDA

the obligation—to undertake certain business initiatives. In particular, the options available can concern the expansion, the deferral, or the abandonment of a capital investment project, such as described in Table 23.5.

Real options create the right, but not the obligation, to purchase the underlying asset at a defined exercise price. A case of real options application is the use of patents; in fact, patents allow their owners to choose between exclusively commercializing the patented invention sometimes during the patent term or foregoing commercialization altogether. So, real options affect the valuation of potential investments and may be incorporated in discount models as the Net Present Value, in the sense that when investments or assets, like patents, are evaluated through NPV techniques, real options can be used to make forecasts more flexible (Iazzolino & Migliano, 2015).

ESG features that embed real options (e.g., to expand an environmental-friendly business, or to suspend and reconvert a polluting

Table 23.5 Real options

Real option	Main features
Option to expand	To undertake a project to expand the business operations (e.g., a sushi chain considering opening new restaurants)
Option to defer or wait or suspend	Option of deferring the business decision to the future (e.g., a food chain considering opening new restaurants this year or in the next year) or to suspend an unprofitable activity
Option to abandon	Option to cease a project to realize its scrap value (e.g., a manufacturing company decides to sell old equipment)

activity) can improve the resilience of capital budgeting forecasts, potentially adding value. The extent of this gain is, however, still largely undetected, as is the cost of capital savings.

23.11   Beyond Market Value Maximization: Toward a New Theory of the Firm?

Market value maximization is still considered the main target for shareholders. According to the classic study of Grossmann and Stiglitz (1977) there exist shareholders' meetings, the right to vote at these shareholders' meetings often has a market value (market prices for voting and non-voting shares often differ); disagreements occasionally arise at these meetings; takeover bids are not uncommon, and takeovers are often disputed. The modern corporation is an economic institution in which there is always a potential political (i.e., voting) aspect. Thus, Grossmann and Stiglitz model the firm as if the action it takes were determined by a majority vote of its shareholders. The shareholder's meeting is the top decisional center of the firm, since it appoints the directors (and, indirectly, the managers), approves the balance sheet, and so has an ultimate "voice" over the company.

The idea of maximizing market value is related to the idea of maximizing shareholder value, as market value is the price at which an asset would trade in a competitive auction setting; for example, returning value to the shareholders if they decide to sell shares or if the firm decides to sell. There are many different models of corporate governance around the world. These differ according to the variety of capitalism in which they are embedded. The Anglo-American (US and UK) "model" tends to emphasize the interests of shareholders. The sole concentration on shareholder value has been widely criticized, particularly after the late 2000s financial crisis, where attention has risen to the concern that a management decision can maximize shareholder value while lowering the welfare of other stakeholders. Additionally, short-term focus on shareholder value can be detrimental to long-term shareholder value (https://courses.lumenlear ning.com/boundless-finance/chapter/goals-of-financial-management/).

The theory of the firm intersects the relationships among the stakeholders and consists of some economic theories that explain and predict the nature of the firm, company, or corporation, including its existence, behavior, structure, and relationship to the market (Spulber, 2009).

According to Coase (1937), people begin to organize their production in firms when the transaction cost of coordinating production through the market exchange, given imperfect information, is greater than within the firm.

Coase set out his transaction cost theory of the firm in 1937, making it one of the first (neo-classical) attempts to define the firm theoretically concerning the market.

In the 1960s, the neo-classical theory of the firm was seriously challenged by alternatives such as managerial and behavioral theories. Managerial theories of the firm (Chirat, 2020), as developed by Baumol (1959), Marris (1964) (for a historical review, see Williamson, 2010), suggest that managers would seek to maximize their utility and consider the implications of this for firm behavior in contrast to the profit-maximizing case. (Baumol suggested that managers' interests are best served by maximizing sales after achieving a minimum level of profit that satisfies shareholders.)

Baumol (1959) raised serious questions on the validity of profit maximization as an objective of the firm. He stressed that in competitive markets, firms would rather aim at maximizing revenue, through maximization of sales. According to him, sales volumes, and not profit volumes, determine market leadership in competition. He further stressed that in large organizations, management is separate from owners. Hence there would always be a dichotomy between managers' goals and owners' goals. Manager's salary and other benefits are largely linked with sales volumes, rather than profits.

A question that arises in this context is whether ESG issues have an impact on sales. Are consumers prone to buy mainly ESG-compliant products? To which extent is the government going to restrict polluting or harmful goods?

Baumol also hypothesized that managers often attach their prestige to the company's revenue or sales; therefore, they would rather attempt to maximize the firm's total revenue, instead of profits. Moreover, sales volumes are a better indicator of a firm's position in the market, and growing sales strengthen the competitive spirit of the firm. Since operations of the firm are in the hands of managers, and managers' performance is measured in terms of achieving sales targets, therefore it follows that management is more interested in maximizing sales, with a constraint of minimum profit. Hence the objective is not to maximize profit, but to maximize sales revenue, along with which, firms need to maintain a minimum level of profit to keep shareholders satisfied. This minimum level of profit is regarded as the profit constraint.

Sales are the igniting factor of business planning dynamics since budgets over years are revenue-driven. Costs follow the dynamics of sales, and their difference produces operating margins. ESG compliance is, eventually, a strategy that pays off for the managers.

The managerial theory has developed into a contractual "principal–agent" analysis that models a typical corporate governance case where, due to the presence of information asymmetries, a principal (a shareholder or firm for example) cannot costless infer how an agent (a manager or supplier, say) is behaving. This may arise either because the agent (e.g., a manager) has greater expertise or knowledge than the principal, or because the principal cannot directly observe the agent's actions; it is asymmetric information that leads to a problem of moral hazard. This means that to an extent managers can pursue their interests. Traditional managerial models typically assume that managers, instead of maximizing profit, maximize a simple objective utility function (this may include salary, perks, security, power, prestige) subject to an arbitrarily given profit constraint (profit satisficing).

Principal–agent criticalities are evident even in an ESG context.

Figure 23.14 shows the interaction between the shareholder and stakeholder view versus the theory of the firm and its ESG extensions.

ESG operations impact on transaction costs: from one side, expenses may increase since green investments may require an extra burden; from the other, long-term sustainability can be rewarding and produce savings.

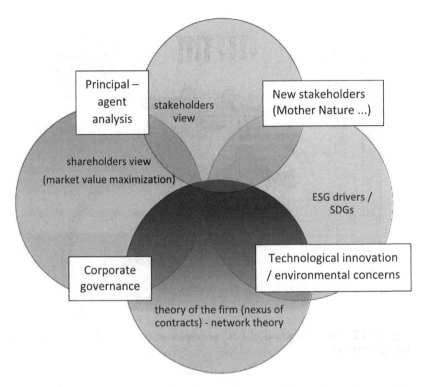

Fig. 23.14 Shareholder and stakeholder view, the theory of the firm, and the ESG extensions

The impact of transaction cost theory may be conveniently assessed along with the whole supply and value chain since all the intermediation passages need to be ESG-compliant.

23.12 Corporate Governance Implications

In an ESG world, stakeholders go beyond the traditional corporate finance and corporate governance boundaries, as they include also external players, such as the civil society or—mother nature.

Both corporate finance and corporate governance's main principles are re-engineered by ESG considerations, as shown in Fig. 23.15.

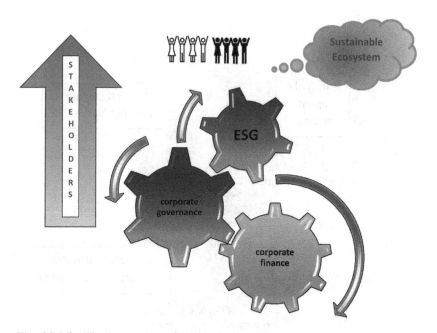

Fig. 23.15 The interaction of ESG principles in corporate finance and corporate governance

The "augmented" boundaries of the firm's ecosystem reshape the interaction between the stakeholders. These interactions are increasingly mastered by digital platforms and follow the network theory patterns. An analysis of these extensions and interactions is preceded by a short resume of the main corporate governance classic propositions and concerns.

According to the survey of Shleifer et al. (1997) "corporate governance deals with how suppliers of finance to corporations assure themselves of getting a return on their investment. How do the suppliers of finance get managers to return some of the profits to them? How do they make sure that managers do not steal the capital they supply or invest it in bad projects? How do suppliers of finance control managers? At first glance, it is not entirely obvious why the suppliers of capital get anything back. After all, they part with their money and have little to contribute to the enterprise afterward. The professional managers or entrepreneurs who run the firms might as well abscond with the money. Although they sometimes do, usually they do not. (...). The subject of corporate governance is of enormous practical importance".

And again "people who sink the capital need to be assured that they get back the return on this capital. The corporate governance mechanisms provide this assurance".

The very first concern, a core point within standard companies, deals with managerial discretion (investment in bad projects; improper retention or diversion of cash ...), a well-known agency problem (being the manager the agent of the principal's money deriving from equity-holders and debtholders).

A core issue of corporate governance is concerned with the agency problem, sometimes referred to as the separation of ownership from control, within firms that can be interpreted as a Coasian nexus of contracts among different resource holders.

Agency relationships arise whenever an individual, called a principal, delegates other individuals, called agents, to perform some service; the two main relationships are:

- The principal-stockholders and the agents-managers, which are delegated to invest shareholders' capital;
- The principal-debtholders and the agents-stockholders, where the former provide funds to the firm, underwriting debt, and these funds are managed by stockholders and their ultimate agents, represented by managers, following the aforementioned relationship.

Since these relationships are not necessarily harmonious, conflicts of interests may easily arise and so agency theory is primarily concerned with the binding mechanisms and incentives that principals may use with agents to get their money back, possibly with a fair and risk-adjusted gain.

In an ideal world where managers already own all the money they need for investments, principals would coincide with agents and no agency conflict would arise; the problem surges whenever specialized managers lack the money they need for investments, but also when financiers need the managers' expertise and professional skills to properly manage their money: mutual convenience is the natural glue behind any agreement.

According to agency theory, in imperfect labor and capital markets, managers will inevitably seek to maximize their utility at the expense of shareholders. Agents-managers can operate in their conflicting self-interests rather than in the best interests of the firm. This happens because of asymmetric inside information (since they know better than shareholders whether they can meet the shareholders' objectives) and physiological uncertainty (since myriad factors contribute to outcomes, it may so not be evident whether the agent directly caused a given outcome, positive or negative).

The legal protection system of creditors in project finance is represented by a complex nexus of loan contracts, together with monitoring powers—and duties—from the debtholders' side. Loan contracts are the legal backbone behind financial and economic bankability and their binding nature intrinsically minimizes managerial discretion.

According again to Shleifer et al. (1997) "the agency problem in this context refers to the difficulties financiers have in assuring that their funds are not expropriated or wasted on unattractive projects. The trouble is, most future contingencies are hard to describe and foresee, and as a result, complete contracts are technologically infeasible". And again: "When contracts are incomplete and managers possess more expertise than shareholders, managers typically end up with the residual rights of control, giving them enormous latitude for self-interested behavior".

The utopia of complete contracts, ideally able to cover with their legal provisions all the possible states of the world, must realistically face an imperfect context, where unforeseen and risky events are always possible and likely to occur. To minimize problems and fallacies within necessarily incomplete contracts, two different approaches may be used and confronted, each with its advantages and pitfalls:

- Detailed contractual provisions, trying to regulate with analytical clauses any possible situation and state of the world, targeting "complete" contracting goals;
- Extensive referral to existing laws and codes, following general principles, as far as possible.

The dichotomy between long/detailed versus short/generalized contracts is also influenced by the general legal system of the country where investments are located; civil law countries, particularly concentrated in Continental Europe, make the reference to codified laws easier and more systematic, whereas common law countries, following analogical court cases, are more diffused in Anglo-Saxon countries and typically bring to more detailed contractual provisions, within a less codified general framework.

Since contracts are ontologically incomplete, legal protection may be insufficient for shareholders, in their potential conflicts with managers, and especially for debtholders, in their conflicting interests with shareholders. Conflicts may arise also between managers and debtholders, for example, if the former illegally extract money for personal abuses, threatening proper debt service and breaching their duty of loyalty, even though they are typically intermediated by shareholders, who appoint the managers. Bank loans are typically contracted by the managers with the lending institutions but even here there might be a role for shareholders, who may smooth the relationship with their reputational standing or with personal guarantees.

Another typical conflict of interests between managers and investors is concerned with managerial discretionary investment decisions, which may typically reflect the personal interests of the former. According to the free cash flow theory, managers are inclined to reinvest the free cash in the company rather than return it to investors; this over-investment problem, opposed to the under-investment problem where the conflicts of interest are between shareholders and debtholders, is however quite unlikely within the project finance industry, also because investments are notoriously not so discretionary and free cash flow may form only after many years, when high initial leverage reaches a much lower level; also dividends, that cash out free liquidity, are typically foreseen since inception and, to the extent that they can be paid, it is uneasy not to fulfill this commitment toward thirsty shareholders.

Agency problems may undermine the reputation of agents acting in their self-interest and, from the other side, reputation-building, so useful for managers seeking employment, but also for shareholders attempting to collect the debt, is a common explanation for why people respect their commitments even if they cannot (always) be forced to do so.

Within the capital structure theoretical models, there is an important paper by Myers and Majluf (1984) regarding information asymmetries and raised capital. Since managers have inside superior information, these asymmetries increase the cost of collecting external capital. This cost may be minimized by raising at first funds that are weakly sensitive to asymmetric information, i.e., for example, secured debt; equity may be collected only at a premium that properly discounts these asymmetries;

in this however in the self-interest of managers to voluntarily minimize information asymmetries, with self-imposed monitoring and transparency, to ease the equity placement, so decreasing its cost.

Traditional corporate governance patterns are based on the interaction among composite stakeholders and the various forms of separation between ownership and control. Stakeholders cooperate around the Coasian firm, represented by a nexus of increasingly complex contracts. These well-known occurrences have been deeply investigated by growing literature and nurtured by composite empirical evidence.

Apparently unrelated network theory is concerned with the study of graphs as a representation of (a)symmetric relations between discrete objects (nodes connected by links). Network theory is highly interdisciplinary, and its versatile nature is fully consistent with the complex interactions of (networked) stakeholders, even in terms of game-theoretic patterns.

The connection between traditional corporate governance issues and network theory properties is, however, still under-investigated (Moro Visconti, 2019). Hence the importance of an innovative reinterpretation that brings to "network governance". Innovation may, for instance, concern the principal–agent networked relationships and their conflicts of interest or the risk contagion and value drivers—three core governance issues. Networks and their applications (like blockchains, P2P platforms, game-theoretic interactions, or digital supply chains) foster unmediated decentralization. In decentralized digital platforms, stakeholders inclusively interact, promoting cooperation and sustainability. To the extent that network properties can be mathematically measured, governance issues may be quantified and traced with recursive patterns of expected occurrences.

ESG implications reshape the boundaries and interactions of the "augmented" stakeholders:

1. The mission of the firm changes and market value maximization for the shareholders is not anymore, the only goal; advocates of this theory claim that if equity-holders are satisfied, all the other stakeholders should be happy, but this assumption does not consider that some new stakeholders are hardly visible and have limited "voice". Mother Nature has traditionally been suffocated by Father Profit …;

2. Digitally mastered networking reshapes in real-time the interactions among composite stakeholders, and traditional loopholes as information asymmetries are mitigated by big data sourcing, storage, and treatment (increasingly using artificial intelligence with blockchain validation);
3. Sustainability, in its largest sense, emerges as the new ultimate mission.

All these considerations contribute to reshaping both corporate finance and corporate governance boundaries and patterns.

23.12.1 Beyond Fake News and Greenwashing: Data Validation with Blockchains

To evaluate the sustainability level, environmental, social, and governance (ESG) reporting is widely adopted especially for the listed companies. However, due to the lack of data authentication, consistency, and transparency, the ESG-based sustainability evaluation is still inadequate (Liu et al., 2021).

Improving supply chain sustainability is an essential part of achieving the UN's sustainable goals. Digitalization, such as blockchain technology, shows the potential to reshape supply chain management. Using distributed ledger technology, the blockchain platform provides a digital system and database to record the transactions along the supply chain. This decentralized database of transactions brings transparency, reliability, traceability, and efficiency to supply chain management (Park & Li, 2021).

Fintech and blockchain facilitate access to new sources of finance and investment, from a larger investor base—especially from private investors. In addition, they operate in decentralized systems, bypassing traditional intermediaries such as banks or other financial institutions, decreasing costs and inefficiencies. Blockchain technology further enables effective monitoring, reporting, and verification, increases transparency and accountability, and reduces the risk of greenwashing. However, uniform standards and definitions for green finance as well as adequate legal and regulatory frameworks are still required.

Within this framework, blockchain technology can ease the application of ESG strategies validating data, and so preventing circumventive behaviors such as greenwashing.

Information asymmetries occur when one party in a transaction has more information than the other. This situation occurs in any firm and represents a main corporate governance concern, igniting conflicts of interest among the stakeholders.

ESG-compliance is becoming an industry standard in most sectors, even if sustainable and green investments may prove expensive or hardly feasible, either within the firm or considering, in wider terms, its supply chain.

Greenwashing is the process of conveying a false impression or providing misleading information about how a company's products are more environmentally sound. Greenwashing is considered an unsubstantiated claim to deceive consumers into believing that a company's products are environmentally friendly. For example, companies involved in greenwashing behavior might claim that their products are from recycled materials or have energy-saving benefits. Although some of the environmental claims might be partly true, companies engaged in greenwashing typically exaggerate their claims or the benefits to mislead consumers.[5]

Fake news is particularly difficult to detect in sophisticated environments where the supply chain is dispersed and products or services are sophisticated—and so difficult to compare, incorporating information asymmetries.

Blockchains may be conveniently used to validate data, especially along the whole supply chain. A potential danger, however, lies within the very first data that are validated, producing a chain effect on subsequent ones: should there be any manipulation, it would be trespassed to following data, pretending that they are all valid.

According to OECD (https://www.oecd.org/finance/Blockchain-tec hnologies-as-a-digital-enabler-for-sustainable-infrastructure-key-findings. pdf), blockchain technology:

1. Could unlock new sources of financing and mobilize existing industry pledges to carbon reduction through establishing new financing platforms. A clear objective is to lower the cost of capital for infrastructure projects, along with improved liquidity, transparency, and expanded access to finance.
2. The technology could bring visibility to alignment with sustainability goals by enabling countries and stakeholders to track data and information on infrastructure projects. Blockchain-enabled platforms are a way to standardize data, assess asset performance, and

enhance compliance (such as to sustainability or ESG standards), which may be further augmented when they are integrated with remote sensors (Internet of things), or linked to deep analytics like artificial intelligence applications.

3. It can enhance awareness and access by acting as a transaction-enabling infrastructure of new market models. This can incentivize and increase institutions and consumers' willingness to build long-term sustainability, driving also changes within industries to adapt to the shifting demands of consumers.

23.13 ESG Reporting and Investment Management Process

Van Duuren et al. (2016) investigate how asset managers integrate ESG factors in their investment practice. ESG investing focuses on different non-financial dimensions of a stock's performance. It specifically relates to the impact of the company on the environment, a social dimension, and governance. For each dimension, a lot of information on the firm's practices and policies is being collected and analyzed. The analysis is used by a portfolio manager to construct a diversified portfolio. This usually is structured to meet minimum standards concerning the three dimensions.

The main ESG strategies are:

- Negative screening (i.e., excluding particular firms or industries);
- Positive screening (i.e., concentrating on particular industries);
- Best-in-class investing (i.e., selecting the best 33 or 25% regarding ESG); activism (filing petitions and voting on annual general meetings of shareholders);
- Engagement (meeting with the board of the corporate and trying to convince them to perform better on ESG).

Mervelskemper and Streit (2017) show that ESG performance is valued more strongly and in the (desired) positive direction when firms publish an ESG report, irrespective of its type (stand-alone or integrated). Furthermore, integrated reporting is associated with superior outcomes compared with a stand-alone report for composite ESG and corporate governance performance.

Buallay (2019) analyzes the banking industry and shows that there is a significant positive impact of ESG on performance. However, the relationship between ESG disclosures changes if measured individually; the environmental disclosure positively affects the Return on Assets (ROA) and Tobin Q. However, corporate social responsibility disclosure negatively affects the three models. The corporate governance disclosure found negatively affects the ROA, and ROE and positively affects Tobin's Q.

23.14   ESG-Compliant Investment Ratios

The investment ratios are represented by key financials, derived from the accounting statements (balance sheet, income, and cash flow statement), and macroeconomic or market input data (e.g., interest rates, market cap, etc.). These ratios are, more or less, ESG-sensitive, even if the causality impact is not always straightforward or clear-cut.

The main investment ratios that rotate around the EBITDA (a key investment parameter, as it simultaneously represents economic and financial marginality) are the following:

EV/EBITDA

Enterprise Value (EV) is the sum of a company's equity value or market capitalization plus its debt-less cash. EV is typically used when evaluating a company for a potential buyout or takeover. The EV/EBITDA ratio is calculated by dividing EV by EBITDA to achieve an earnings multiple.

Improved intangible-driven scalability reflects on the Enterprise Value/EBITDA (EV/EBITDA) multiplier that compares a firm's market value (inclusive of debt), to its overall economic-financial profitability.

Financial analysts use the EV/EBITDA ratio to measure a company's value over its earnings. The metric is better than the P/E ratio because it considers the enterprise value irrespectively of the company's capital structure. For instance, if a company raises additional capital through equity financing, the company's P/E ratio will be higher because the price will rise.

EBITDA may impact either the market capitalization or/and the net financial position. An intangible-driven improved EBITDA creates additional liquidity, so increasing the net financial position, and may be reflected in higher market prices. The impact of the higher denominator EBITDA on the numerator EV may, however, change.

The multiplier is:

$$\frac{EV}{EBITDA} = \frac{Market\ Value\ of\ Equity + Market\ Value\ of\ Debt}{EBITDA}$$

(23.11)

EV/FCFF

Enterprise Value (EV) to Free Cash Flow to Firm (FCFF) compares the total valuation of the company with its ability to generate operating cash flows.

Investments in intangibles may have an impact on the FCFF, both in terms of economic margin (EBITDA) and CAPEX.

$$\frac{EV}{FCFF} = \frac{Market\ Value\ of\ Equity + Market\ Value\ of\ Debt}{\begin{array}{c}Operating\ (debt - free)\ Cash\ Flow = EBITDA \\ \pm\ \Delta Operating\ Net\ Working\ Capital \pm \Delta CAPEX\end{array}}$$

(23.12)

FCFF corresponds to Operating (unlevered or debt-free) Cash Flows that are used for the calculation of Discounted Cash Flows.

P/FCFE

This multiplier Price (P) to free cash flow is an equity valuation metric used to compare a company's per-share market price (P) to its per-share amount of Free Cash Flow to Equity (FCFE). This metric is very similar to the valuation metric of price to cash flow but is considered a more exact measure, since it uses free cash flow, which subtracts capital expenditures (CAPEX) from a company's total operating cash flow, thereby reflecting the actual cash flow available to fund non-asset-related growth.

Because the price to free cash flow is a value metric, lower numbers generally indicate that a company is undervalued, and its stock is relatively cheap concerning its free cash flow.

Also, in this case, investments in intangibles may have an impact on the FCFE, in terms of economic margin (EBITDA), CAPEX, and (eventually) financial charges.

$$\frac{P}{FCFE} = \frac{Market\ Price}{EBITDA \pm \Delta Operating\ Net\ Working\ Capital \pm \Delta CAPEX}$$
$$= FCFF - negative\ interests \pm \Delta financial\ debt \pm \Delta equity$$

(23.13)

Price to earnings (P/E)

The price-earnings, also known as the P/E ratio, P/E, is the ratio of a company's share (stock) price to the company's earnings per share. The ratio is used for valuing companies and to find out whether they are overvalued or undervalued.

The price/earnings ratio is the most widely used method for determining whether shares are "correctly" valued concerning one another. But the PER does not in itself indicate whether the share is a bargain. The P/E depends on the market's perception of the risk and future growth in earnings.

Intangibles may impact earnings, contributing to the growth of the net profit.

$$\frac{Price}{Earnings} = \frac{Market\ Price}{Net\ Result = EBITDA - deprecitation - negative\ interests - taxes \ldots} \tag{23.14}$$

Price to operating profit (P/OP)

The price (P) to operating profit (OP) is the ratio of a company's share (stock) price to the company's operating profit per share.

Operating profit is strictly correlated to the EBITDA and may be affected by intangibles.

$$\frac{Price}{Operating\ Profit} = \frac{Market\ Price}{EBITDA - depreciation = EBIT} \tag{23.15}$$

Price to sales (P/S)

The price to sales (P/S) is a valuation ratio that compares a company's stock price to its revenues. It is an indicator of the value placed on each dollar of a company's sales or revenues.

The P/S ratio can be calculated either by dividing the company's market capitalization by its total sales over a designated period—usually twelve months, or on a per-share basis by dividing the stock price by sales per share.

$$\frac{Price}{Sales} = \frac{Market\ Price}{EBITDA + monetary\ OPEX} \tag{23.16}$$

The P/S ratio is also known as "sales multiple" or "revenue multiple"; as stated before, intangibles may impact sales.

Price to book value (P/BV)

Analysts use the price to book (P/BV) ratio to compare a firm's market capitalization to its book value. It is calculated by dividing the company's stock price per share by its book value per share. An asset's book value is equal to its carrying value on the balance sheet, and companies calculate it by netting the asset against its accumulated depreciation.

Intangible assets impact the company's book value, contributing to the growth of the net profit that is then stored in the book value of equity (unless paid out as a dividend).

$$\frac{Price}{Book\ Value} = \frac{Market\ Price}{Book\ Value}$$

$$(incorporating\ EBITDA - driven\ retained\ earnings)$$

$$(23.17)$$

Net Financial Position/EBITDA

This multiplier is often used as a debt covenant, and it expresses the ratio between the outstanding financial debt (net of the liquidity) and the EBITDA. The net debt-to-EBITDA ratio is a payback ratio that shows how many years it would take for a company to pay back its debt if net debt and EBITDA are held constant. Being EBITDA, a measure of the liquidity generated (absorbed) within the income statement, the ratio shows the contribution of internal resources to debt service:

$$\frac{Net\ Financial\ Position}{EBITDA} \qquad (23.18)$$

23.15 THE RELATIONSHIP BETWEEN THE ESG DRIVERS AND THE INVESTMENT PARAMETERS

The main corporate finance implications of ESG drivers can be detected considering the causal relationship between the ESG metrics (input) and the main financials (output), as shown in Fig. 23.16.

More specifically, the ESG parameters interact with the risk & return metrics of the firm that is embedded in the DCF formulation. The key value driver is represented by sales (revenues) and by their volatility.

As shown before, sales are accounted for within the income statement and ignite value creation. The difference between sales (monetary operating revenues) and monetary OPEX produces the EBITDA that brings

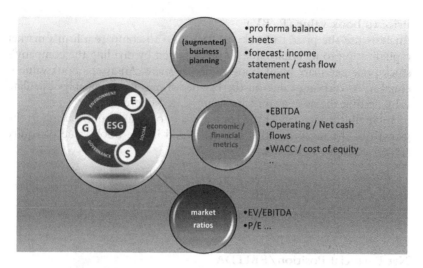

Fig. 23.16   The interaction of ESG drivers with the investment parameters

to the operating cash flow (incorporating both net working capital and CAPEX variations). The discount factors of the operating and net cash flows (represented, respectively, by the WACC and the cost of equity) reflect the volatility of the numerator of the DCF formula and may be influenced by the ESG parameters. The challenge, as already seen, is to improve the cash flows by reducing their risk level.

A graphical representation is synthesized in Fig. 23.17.

23.16   Facing the Green Swan: Climate Value at Risk (VaR)

According to MSCI (https://www.msci.com/our-solutions/esg-inv esting/climate-solutions/climate-data-metrics), Climate Value-at-Risk (Climate VaR) is an innovative and pioneering climate risk metric, designed to provide a forward-looking and return-based valuation assessment to measure climate-related risks and opportunities in an investment portfolio. The fully quantitative model offers deep insights into how the physical and transition risks and opportunities of climate change could affect company valuations.

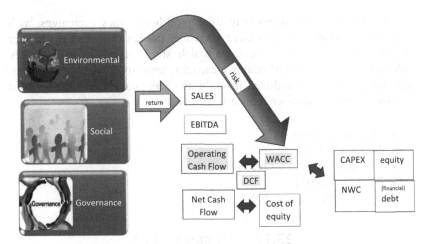

Fig. 23.17 ESG Impact on the risk and return profile of sustainable investments

According to the Economist (2021), in recent years regulators have begun warning about the threat that climate change poses to the stability of the financial system.

Climate change can affect the financial system in three ways:

1. The first is through what regulators describe as "transition risks". These are most likely to arise if governments pursue tougher climate policies. If they do, the economy restructures capital moves away from dirty sectors and toward cleaner ones. Companies in polluting industries may default on loans or bonds; their share prices may collapse.
2. The second channel is financial firms' exposure to the hazards of rising temperatures. The financial system could also be exposed to any wider economic damage caused by climate change, say if it triggered swings in asset prices.
3. the third concerns a worst-case scenario for the financial system where transition risks crystallize very suddenly and cause wider economic damage (Minsky moment).

The systemic ecological risk may affect worldwide stock exchanges, with a selective incidence. The extent to which markets respond to disaster onsets depends on the extent to which stock prices incorporate key information on the firms' adaptive capacity, amid increasingly calamitous disaster patterns and reduced insurability (Seetharam, 2017). The most known ecological disasters concern for instance:

- Chernobyl 1986
- Tsunami 2004
- Southern Asia Pollution Haze 2009
- Fukushima 2011
- Diesel Gate Scandal 2015.

23.17   GREEN CAPEX

Capital expenditures (CAPEX) and operating expenses (OPEX) represent two complementary categories of business expenses, deriving from the capital and operating budgets that are created by companies to support growth and adjust resources. CAPEX is increasingly driven by environmental considerations, and frequently concerns intangible investments that are intrinsically less polluting than material ones.

Capital budgets cover capital expenses, which are capitalized and appear as long-term assets on the balance sheet. CAPEX corresponds to the amounts that companies use to purchase long-term assets as major physical goods or services that will be used for more than one year. These assets may be physical (plant, equipment, property, vehicles, etc.) or represented by intangibles that are not directly expensed in the income statement. As these long-term assets depreciate over their useful lives, the depreciation for a given year shows up on the income statement as a non-monetary expense in that year. Therefore, CAPEX is subject to depreciation (with a linear methodology in constant installments over the useful life or with an impairment test, whenever applicable).

OPEX refers instead to the ordinary costs for a company to run its daily business operations (purchases; salaries; rents; sales, general, & administrative expenses; property taxes, etc.). OPEX can be divided into monetary OPEX + depreciation/amortization.

Intangibles impact directly on monetary OPEX and CAPEX (when intangible investments are capitalized, and their annual quota is amortized). Amortization is, therefore, a part of non-monetary OPEX. Only monetary OPEX affects the EBITDA.

Since the fixed or intangible asset recorded in the balance sheet is part of normal business operations, depreciation is considered in this case an operating expense.

Scalability is an intangible characteristic of the business that can quickly boost volumes of sales, up to blitzscaling.

For what concerns OPEX, intangibles can ignite productivity gains where input costs to reach a target output are minimized. If OPEX is reduced, economic margins such as EBITDA, EBIT, pre-tax profit, or net profit improve.

Capitalization of intangible assets (into CAPEX) instead of accounting within monetary OPEX does not change Operating Cash Flows (O_{CF}) that include these items anyway since:

$$\begin{aligned} \text{Enterprise Value} &= \sum \frac{(sales - monetary\ OPEX) = EBITDA \mp \Delta NWC \mp \Delta CAPEX}{(1 + WACC)^i} \\ &= \sum \frac{Opearting\ Cash\ Flow}{(1 + WACC)^i} \end{aligned} \tag{23.19}$$

where ΔNWC indicates the differential Net Working Capital (concerning the previous year).

While DCF (expressed by $\sum O_{CF}/WACC$) is invariant to the accounting treatment of intangibles (i.e., to the fact that they are capitalized or not), this is not true in the other valuation method. Should the Enterprise Value be proxied by the average EBITDA times a market multiplier of a comparable firm, then the EBITDA is influenced by the capitalization of intangibles. More precisely, capitalized intangibles (as development expenses) that become part of the CAPEX (and are never part of monetary OPEX) increase the EBITDA, and so the Enterprise Value is estimated with market comparables.

Operating costs are divided into variable and fixed costs, to better understand the impact of scalability on operating leverage (EBIT increase due to an increase in sales).

Scalability directly boosts sales but has an impact also on the EBIT that is given not only by increased revenues but also by the presence of fixed costs in the OPEX mix. Since fixed costs are—by definition—invariant to sales, the higher their proportion within the OPEX, the better the impact on the EBIT increase due to growing scalable sales. The opposite happens when sales decrease: in that case, fixed costs are a burden.

Intangibles may have a positive impact even on CAPEX, should they contribute to improving productivity, so decreasing the amount of CAPEX needed to run the business and to generate economic and financial positive margins (EBITDA; EBIT; operating and net cash flows, etc.).

There is so a positive impact attributable to scalable intangibles improving the market value of the firm, due to the higher economic and financial marginality.

Higher operating cash flows improve the discounted cash flows (O_{CF}/WACC) and a better EBITDA boosts the economic value complemented by market multipliers.

Accounting distortions may impact the dichotomy between OPEX and CAPEX, due to the slippery qualification of the intangibles and the caution that often prevents their capitalization. There may so be, in practice, some difficulty in discriminating about the impact of intangibles on either OPEX or CAPEX, where the impact on CAPEX may be underestimated due to accounting prudentialism.

Scalable intangibles impact on the composition of raised capital (equity + financial debt):

> Any profitability gain improves, ceteris paribus, the net profit and so the equity; if dividends are paid out, then the benefit eventually accrues to the shareholders;
>
> Improvements in the EBITDA (that represents the contribution of the income statement to the generation of liquidity) may be used to pay back debt (so decreasing the financial leverage, expressed by the debt over equity ratio), or to fuel new investments without increasing outstanding debt or asking additional money to the shareholders. This may have a positive impact on the Weighted Average Cost of Capital (WACC) that is used to discount the Operating Cash Flow in the DCF formulation; any decrease in the WACC improves the market value of the firm, being value $\approx O_{CF}$/WACC.

Any improvement in the EBITDA backs the pecking order theory, according to which internally generated liquidity (proxied by the EBITDA) precedes the issue of risky debt and then equity.

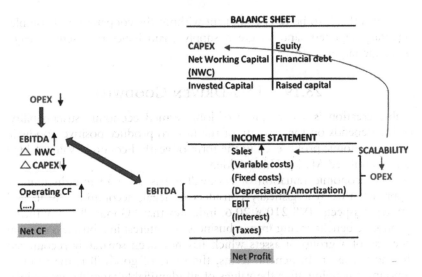

Fig. 23.18 Impact of scalable intangibles on OPEX and CAPEX

These considerations are valid not only for digital-native firms but also for traditional corporations that increasingly use new intangibles, becoming tech-enabled.

Should intangibles improve the flexibility of the supply chain where the firm is strategically positioned, then the business model may become more resilient to downturns and volatile market conditions. This reduces the difference between dreamy expectations and hard reality, so decreasing risk and the cost of collecting capital (WACC), and contributes to the reduction of the DCF formula denominator.

Figure 23.18 depicts the impact of scalable intangibles on OPEX, CAPEX, and the economic and financial margins.

23.18 THE OPEX DILEMMA: INSIDE THE GREEN SUPPLY CHAIN

OPEX is complementary to CAPEX, as shown before, but is also highly sensitive, like returns, to the supply chain interactions that link the firm with its suppliers and clients, within its industry ecosystem.

It is difficult to be ESG-compliant without the cooperation of complementary suppliers, and so green supply chain issues represent a major strategic target.

23.19   ESG-Driven Goodwill

Value creation is a core pillar of long-termed economic sustainability. Value depends on the capacity of the firm to produce positive goodwill, or an economic profit, even in the form of yearly Economic Value Added and cumulated Market Value Added.

The economic valuation of goodwill is based on an interdisciplinary approach that synergistically considers its legal, accounting, fiscal, and strategic aspects. IVS 210 § 20.6. indicates that "Goodwill is any future economic benefit arising from a business, an interest in a business or from the use of a group of assets which has not been separately recognized in another asset. In general terms, the value of goodwill is the residual amount remaining after the values of all identifiable tangible, intangible, and monetary assets, adjusted for actual or potential liabilities, have been deducted from the value of a business. It is typically represented as the excess of the price paid in a real or hypothetical acquisition of a company over the value of the company's other identified assets and liabilities".

According to OECD (2017) "*Depending on the context, the term goodwill can be used to refer to several different concepts. In some accounting and business valuation contexts, goodwill reflects the difference between the aggregate value of an operating business and the sum of the values of all separately identifiable tangible and intangible assets. Alternatively, goodwill is sometimes described as a representation of the future economic benefits associated with business assets that are not individually identified and separately recognized. In still other contexts goodwill is referred to as the expectation of future trade from existing customers. The term ongoing concern value is sometimes referred to as the value of the assembled assets of an operating business over and above the sum of the separate values of the individual assets. It is generally recognized that goodwill and ongoing concern value cannot be segregated or transferred separately from other business assets*" (par. 6.27).

Goodwill, already examined in Chapter 21, indicates the ability of a company or one of its branches to generate an extra profit (new incremental wealth), that is the concrete attitude to produce profits higher than the average of the reference sector; this is represented by a typically indistinct set of intangible conditions (the image and the prestige of the company, the clientele, the organization, the management, the quality of the products, the commercial network, etc.) that express the competitive capacity of the company on the market.

Goodwill is related to commercial viability: *"as a general rule, intangibles relating to products with established commercial viability will be more valuable than otherwise comparable intangibles relating to products whose commercial viability is yet to be established"* (OECD, par. 6.124).

The Competitive Advantage Period (CAP) considers the time frame during which the company is expected to be able to achieve returns on invested capital higher than the weighted average cost of capital (ROIC > WACC) and so represents positive goodwill. The implicit surplus value in the CAP is conveyed into the strategic components of the company (competitive advantages, linked to product differentiation or cost advantages; technological, marketing, and organizational resources and skills; industry attractiveness, etc.) and in the economic and financial aspects (first, the incremental EBITDA margin).

The CAP, according to the resource-based approach, is based on purely intangible characteristics such as rarity or inimitability, distinctive and integration capabilities, resource-picking, and capability-building mechanisms, at the base of competitive differentiation.

The CAP can depend on economies of scale and/or experience and on monopolistic rents, typical of operators who have market power deriving from uniqueness (for example, a natural monopoly or an invention) and allow the holder to set the price freely, taking advantage of the lack of free competition.

Rents, as well as monopolistic (or oligopolistic), can be:

- Ricardian (resource-based), deriving from the limited intangible resources that guarantee a competitive advantage;
- Schumpeterian, based on innovative products or services that allow an economic marginality (largely) higher than the production costs;
- Paretian, based on the difference between better use and lower use of resources. In all cases, the intangible components play a major role.

Above-average performance, in the absence of monopolistic rents that are increasingly contrasted by antitrust provisions, inevitably decreases over the years, due to external competitive pressures or the introduction of new standards, inventions, or models that make the initial competitive advantage obsolete. This should be considered in the estimation procedures, which may be biased if they overestimate the capacity of the goodwill to persist indefinitely. The high growth rate, intangible-driven and typical of many startups, usually converges toward a stable and more realistic sustainable growth rate in the medium–long term.

The creditworthiness (borrowing capacity) of companies with positive economic rents and CAP is generally sound, although it must be subject to constant monitoring (through periodical impairment testing) to assess its residual useful life and current entity. Valuation concerns may address the sustainability, regeneration, and defensibility of the competitive advantage of the incumbents, considering the entry barriers of the sector that limit the competition (attracted by the competitive advantages of incumbent rentiers).

The intensity and duration of the CAP are at the base of the valuation models of the surplus value (implicit goodwill), driven by the intangible sources of the expected competitive advantages, which allow reinvestments at a rate of return on invested capital higher than the weighted average cost of capital (ROIC > WACC).

The sustainable enterprise value corresponds to the valorization of the existing assets, added to the (typically intangible) value of growth opportunities (Fig. 23.19).

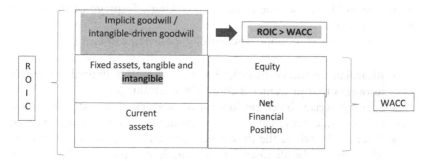

Fig. 23.19 Goodwill as a positive differential between the yield and the cost of invested capital

23.20 ESG-Related Bonds

From a corporate finance perspective, the issue of bonds is a major source of external funds, especially for listed firms. Bonds increase the financial leverage and their issue has an economic and financial impact on the firm that depends on the cost of debt. Bonds may be quoted and exchanged in the market, or privately issued. Smaller firms often issue mini-bonds. ESG-related bonds add up sustainability targets and features.

The Green Bond Principles are reported in https://www.icmagr oup.org/sustainable-finance/the-principles-guidelines-and-handbooks/green-bond-principles-gbp/.

a. **Climate (green) bonds**

Climate bonds (also known as green bonds) are fixed-income financial instruments (bonds) that have positive environmental and/or climate benefits.

They differ from sustainability bonds in that the latter also needs to have a positive social outcome, besides simply having a positive impact on the environment.

b. **Social bonds**

the Social Bond Principles https://www.icmagroup.org/sus tainable-finance/the-principles-guidelines-and-handbooks/social-bond-principles-sbp/.

c. **Sustainability bonds**

The main principles can be found in:

- Sustainability Bond Guidelines (SBG) https://www.icmagr oup.org/sustainable-finance/the-principles-guidelines-and-handbooks/sustainability-bond-guidelines-sbg/.
- and the Sustainability-Linked Bond Principles (SLBP) https://www.icmagroup.org/sustainable-finance/the-principles-guidel ines-and-handbooks/sustainability-linked-bond-principles-slbp/.

23.21 Smart Capital Structure and ESG-Compliant Pecking Order

The capital structure is determined by several factors and there are different theories regarding why a company chooses a specific type of

financing. One of these is the Pecking Order Theory which emphasizes that capital structure decisions are dependent on the concept of
asymmetric information, referring to the fact that managers know more
about their companies than investors do. According to the Pecking Order
Theory, this makes the managers first turn to internal funds, primarily
reinvested funds, followed by new issues of debt and as a last resort, new
equity (Brealey et al., 2017, pp. 479–480). This could be because the
issuance of new equity might signal that the firm's stock is overvalued or
that the firm is facing financial difficulties. The firm also tries to avoid
sudden changes in dividend payouts since this could give investors the
impression that the company is in trouble (Brealey et al., 2017, p. 481).

The Pecking Order Theory emphasizes that capital structure decisions
are dependent on the concept of asymmetric information, referring to
the fact that managers know more about their companies than investors
do. According to the Pecking Order Theory, this makes the managers
first turn to internal funds, primarily reinvested funds (retained earnings),
followed by new issues of debt (safe, and then risky) and as a last resort
new equity (Brealey et al., 2017, pp. 479–480).

This ranking also depends on the implicit costs of the funding: whereas
internal funds (fueled by EBITDA and then considering other economic
and financial margins) are free of charge, as they already belong to
the firm, the issue of debt and then equity faces an increasing cost of
capital (due to the marginal risk increase that is incorporated in equity,
so commanding a return premium). Within this standard context, the
main question that arises is about the ESG impact on hierarchical choices
concerning the optimal funding for the firm.

ESG metrics impact:

1. On internally generated funds (EBITDA, EBIT, pre-tax and net
   profit; operating and net cash flows, etc.) through their value drivers
   that may foster revenues, and minimize OPEX;
2. On the cost of collected debt that may be sensitive to sustainability
   concerns, easing green funding;
3. On the cost of equity, underwritten by sensitive stakeholders.

The provision of ESG rating mitigates information asymmetry. Current
leverage ratios are not altered significantly for ESG-rated firms, but these
firms redistribute their financing sources from public debt (bonds debt)

to private debt (bank loans). This substitution effect is mainly driven by environmental and social factors and is more pronounced for firms with high financial pressure, low growth opportunities, and specialized assets. Debt restructuring remains valid under various robustness and endogeneity tests. These results are consistent with the trade-off and pecking order theories of capital structure (Asimakopoulos et al., 2021).

23.22 ESG Behavioral Finance

"Green" is symbolic of products and services that are environment-friendly or cause minimum ecological and environmental damage. What about Green Finance? Then logically it should be financing activities that promoted this ecological and environmental growth. But the question is: How? Well, it simply implies that fund needs to be collected from people who care about Green and be deployed to the companies who care about Green. Is it so simple? Going Green needs a long-term commitment on the part of the top management, requires a thorough set of practices that incorporate sustainability within its framework, and of course, a huge amount of outlay is required. To channel funds for Green Commitment, returns and risk are the two important issues that need to be taken care of (Panja & Das, 2020).

Behavioral finance, a subfield of behavioral economics, proposes that psychological influences and biases affect the financial behaviors of investors and financial practitioners. Moreover, influences and biases can be the source for the explanation of all types of market anomalies and specifically market anomalies in the stock market, such as severe rises or falls in stock price. Within this framework, ESG targets influence investors, managers, and other stakeholders.

23.23 From ESG to PESTLE Considerations

PESTLE and SWOT analyses provide a systematic and comprehensive reflection of the external and internal operational environment. PESTLE considerations represent a dashboard that intersects the ESG framework (Table 23.6).

PESTLE considerations, being essentially external, somewhat tend to precede SWOT analyses: while the former shape the analytical framework of the investment, the latter resume environmental analysis (scanning the

Table 23.6 Interaction of PESTLE and SWOT analysis

Variable	Definition	Interaction with other variables
PESTLE	Strategic methodology comprehensively using Political, Economic, Social, Technological, Legal, and Environmental trendy analysis for reviewing the macro environment, with its external forces that impact the ability to plan	PESTLE analysis is a preliminary overlook of the strategic environment, often anticipating other surveys. Typically combined with SWOT analysis
SWOT	Structured planning method used to evaluate the Strengths, Weaknesses, Opportunities, and Threats involved in a project, to consider if the objective is attainable and, if so, how	Its discriminating functions (Strengths/Opportunities vs. Weaknesses/Threats) ease strategic comparisons

business environment for Threats and Opportunities), with a subsequent internal focus on organizational issues (Strengths and Weaknesses).

PESTLE acronyms include Environmental and Social concerns, with an overlap with ES(+G), as shown in Fig. 23.20.

Fig. 23.20 ESG and PESTLE

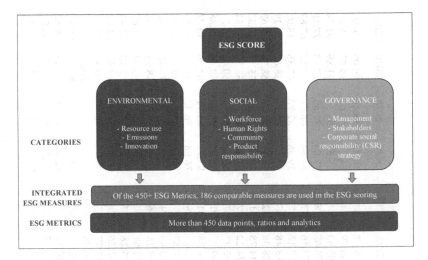

Fig. 23.21 ESG score

23.24 An Empirical Analysis

ESG scoring according to the database Refinitiv—Datastream follows the taxonomy reproduced in Fig. 23.21.

The ESG Combined Scores provide a rounded and comprehensive scoring of a company's ESG performance based on the reported information in the ESG pillars.

A numerical representation of the ESG Score concerning a subset of Italian listed companies (for which all the data since 2011 are available) is contained in Table 23.7. Data show, on average, a trendy improvement in the scoring.

23.25 Concluding Remarks

Financial capital—i.e., monetary equity conferred by the shareholders in a business entity—has traditionally been a scarce and expensive resource, being embedded in the risky cost of equity.

Whereas liquidity is increasingly abundant, thanks to the loose monetary policy still in place after the big financial crisis of 2008, the patience of Mother Nature is exhausting, after decades of wild exploitation of the

Table 23.7 ESG score of the main Italian listed companies

ESG Score	2011	2012	2013	2014	2015	2016	2017	2018	2019	2020
A2A	61.91	61.78	58.47	61.01	58.73	63.48	70.28	66.46	80.08	76.9
ARNOLDO MONDADORI ED	65.45	64.23	61.86	53.92	48.79	44.29	54.2	60.67	59.07	58.57
ASSICURAZIONI GENERALI	92.31	91.44	89.49	90.28	85.63	84.54	85.58	91.35	91.89	91.74
ATLANTIA	66.98	64.79	62.47	65.3	76.67	78.87	77.03	77.55	83.53	77.15
AUTOGRILL	66.18	65.02	68.73	73.41	73.56	72.3	67.54	68.57	72.67	67.87
AZIMUT HOLDING	5.72	3.25	7.2	15.55	12.13	17.27	19.38	32.73	42.85	43.02
BANCA MEDIOLANUM	39.3	48.48	50.67	42.51	53.48	53.98	58.47	62.13	58.63	70.19
BPER BANCA	19.09	24.82	26.32	24.13	28.38	32.84	45.14	51.72	68.72	67.69
BUZZI UNICEM	53.45	52.18	45.67	44.83	44.78	51.26	42.67	50.39	55.11	54.32
CAMPARI	7.99	16.04	22.42	24.68	24.22	27.34	37.87	43.72	53.18	61.51
EDISON RSP	66.92	71.5	71.33	66.36	65.8	67.56	65.4	67.14	60.63	55.7
ENEL	84.97	81.24	85.07	87.17	89.77	91.1	89.77	90.03	88.62	90.38
ENI	87.07	78.12	78.46	78.77	80.58	81.45	83.9	84.91	84.86	80.72
HERA	74.95	75.4	78.47	71.56	75.25	79.28	76.58	76.37	81.18	89.16
INTESA SANPAOLO	77.41	65.72	69.88	75.42	77.87	77.65	74.62	77.3	72.51	78.94
LEONARDO	67.8	66.41	65.18	70.26	72.86	74.8	71.97	76.92	76.45	82.16
MEDIASET	43.5	50.34	48.02	52.58	53.18	56.07	55.63	58.83	58.95	65.64
MEDIOBANCA	29.74	27.86	22.3	36.56	42.69	40.53	46.55	61.86	55.32	52.67
PIRELLI & C	73.87	82.62	84.67	79.06	75.28	63.19	73.15	72.52	73.13	74.43
PRYSMIAN	49.68	57.71	59.55	58.34	57.36	61.21	59.33	64.67	69.53	72.62
SAIPEM	89.47	82.45	85.29	84.83	85.37	85.68	86.08	90.89	90.46	88.65
SARAS	63.14	62.42	51.79	43.9	50.68	53.16	51.72	55.23	50.8	48.26
SNAM	83.08	81.71	80.23	81.13	78.5	81.98	84.6	90.38	84	88.22
CATTOLICA ASSICURAZIONI	17.02	17.08	19.19	20.21	20.52	24.49	35.63	40.44	50.44	48.52
TELECOM ITALIA	72.97	72.01	77.36	69.3	80.27	77.25	88.26	84.12	82.71	86.01
TERNA RETE ELETTRICA NAZ	67.4	62.98	61.58	65.67	64.72	66.41	66.79	72.77	72.22	77.51

ESG Score	2011	2012	2013	2014	2015	2016	2017	2018	2019	2020
TOD'S	22.13	19.13	17.65	20.01	18.42	25.8	40.02	40.87	55.27	56.63
UNICREDIT	84.68	83.79	84.18	81.43	84.18	80.63	77.96	87.24	87.12	84.8
UNIPOL	49.81	46.08	46.82	55.21	53.76	61.94	67.18	68.07	64.22	60.2
Mean	**40.50**	**38.80**	**39.07**	**43.42**	**42.99**	**45.19**	**50.96**	**50.63**	**55.52**	**63.42**

Source Refinitiv Datastream

environment. ESG capital so emerges as a natural bridge between the patient money of capitalism and the growing sustainability concerns.

The ESG paradigm proposes to use environmental, social, and governance factors to evaluate companies on how far advanced they are with sustainability. In recent years, stock market investors have become concerned regarding ESG issues of the companies involved, because ESG combines sustainable returns and risk reduction, with accountability toward the environment and society (Casañ et al., 2021). Consistently, Steen et al. (2020) show that there is a financial reward from tilting investments toward European companies with high ESG ratings or in general investing in companies with a low ESG rating and, as an active owner, contribute to an improvement of the fund's rating.

The impact of ESG parameters on the cost of (collecting and remunerating) capital remains, however, a challenging issue. Common wisdom suggests that ESG-compliant firms should reduce their cost of capital, but empirical evidence is still largely missing or contradictory. The relationship between corporate social performance and corporate financial performance is analyzed in Dorfleitner et al. (2020). Evidence from Chouaibi and Chouaibi (2021) reveals a significant positive relationship between societal and ethical practices and businesses' market valuation. Indahl and Jacobsen (2019) wonder to what extent "externalities", such as the social costs associated with climate change and rising levels of inequality, affect corporate financial performance and value, showing that the evidence so far is ambiguous.

Disclosure of ESG-compliant policies reduces the information asymmetries, potentially decreasing the cost of capital. Recent findings provide evidence that companies highly rated in terms of ESG score report higher excess returns and lower volatility, this being supported by the assumption that ESG factors are considered, by market agents, as a good proxy for firms' financial soundness (La Torre et al., 2020). ESG factors positively affect corporate profitability and credit rating (Kim & Li, 2021). ESG strengths increase firm value (Fatemi et al., 2018).

ESG rating agencies represent a fundamental player in widespread ESG compliance. They have integrated new criteria into their assessment models to measure corporate performance more accurately and robustly to respond to new global challenges. However, a deep analysis of the criteria also shows that ESG rating agencies do not fully integrate sustainability principles into the corporate sustainability assessment process (Escrig Olmedo et al., 2019).

Literature and empirical evidence show that the cost of capital is sensitive even to other factors. For instance, cybersecurity investments should reduce the firm's cost of capital (Havakhor et al., 2020).

An innovative interpretation of the cost of capital may consider its systemic (market-related) and firm-specific components. Both are affected by ESG indicators that influence the ecosystem and the firm itself.

ESG certification lowers a firm's cost of capital, while Tobin's Q increases significantly. These findings, while consistent with existing studies in developed economies, demonstrate the value enhancement of corporate social responsibility disclosure by firms in emerging and developing nations. Overall, the study confirms the benefits to stakeholders from firms pursuing an ESG agenda (Wong et al., 2021).

Corporate finance is undergoing a paradigm shift, and the traditional target of the firm—wealth maximization for its shareholders—is being adapted to a wider context, where other stakeholders are considered, embracing unrelated players such as the environment and its long-lasting governance.

ESG consciousness goes beyond the empty promise of never-ending growth that is embedded in old-style capitalism. Environmental-friendly innovation, levered by digitalization and other intangibles, shapes a new paradigm around sustainable capital. As Alan Eddison warns, modern technology owes ecology an apology.

Notes

1. https://en.wikipedia.org/wiki/Capital.
2. https://www.investopedia.com/terms/c/capital.asp.
3. http://lexicon.ft.com/Term?term=ESG.
4. Adapted from MSCI (2014). MSCI ESG Intangible Value Assessment, https://www.msci.com/documents/10199/25a39052-0b0e-4a10-bef8-e78dbc854168.
5. https://www.investopedia.com/terms/g/greenwashing.asp.

Selected References

Asaduzzaman, M., Shahjahan, M., & Murase, K. (2015). Real-time decision-making forecasting using data mining and decision tree. *International Journal on Information, 18*(7), 3027–3047.

Asimakopoulos, S., Asimakopoulos, P., & Xinyu, L. (2021). *The role of environmental, social, and governance rating on corporate debt structure.* Available at https://ssrn.com/abstract=3889307

Banaszyk, P., & Łupicka, A. (2020). Sustainable supply chain management in the perspective of sharing economy. In K. Grzybowska, A. Awasthi, & R. Sawhney (Eds.), *Sustainable logistics and production in Industry 4.0. EcoProduction* (Environmental Issues in Logistics and Manufacturing). Springer: Berlin.

Barabási, A. (2016). *Network science.* Cambridge: Cambridge University Press.

Baumol, W. J. (1959). *Business behavior, value and growth.* London: The Macmillan Company.

Billio, M., Costola, M., Hristova, I., Latino, C., & Pelizzon, L. (2021). Inside the ESG ratings: (Dis)agreement and performance. *Corporate Social Responsibility and Environmental Management, 28*(5), 1426–1445.

Brealey, R. A., Myers, S. C., & Allen, F. (2017). *Principles of corporate finance.* New York: McGraw-Hill Education.

Breuer, H., Fichter, K., Lüdeke-Freund, F., & Tiemann, I. (2018). Sustainability-oriented business model development: Principles, criteria and tools. *International Journal of Entrepreneurial Venturing, 10*(2), 256–286.

Brinckmann, J., Grichnik, D., & Kapsa, D. (2010). Should entrepreneurs plan or just storm the castle? A meta-analysis on contextual factors impacting the business planning–performance relationship in small firms. *Journal of Business Venturing, 25*(1), 24–40.

Buallay, A. (2019). Is sustainability reporting (ESG) associated with performance? Evidence from the European banking sector. *Management of Environmental Quality, 30*(1), 98–115.

Casañ, M. J., Alier, M., & Llorens, A. (2021). A collaborative learning activity to analyze the sustainability of an innovation using PESTLE. *Sustainability, 13*, 8756.

Chirat, A. (2020). *The correspondence between Baumol and Galbraith (1957–1958). An unsuspected source of managerial theories of the firm.* Available at https://halshs.archives-ouvertes.fr/halshs-02981270/document

Chouaibi, S., & Chouaibi, J. (2021). Social and ethical practices and firm value: The moderating effect of green innovation: Evidence from international ESG data. *International Journal of Ethics and Systems, 37*(3), 442–465.

Chwolka, A., & Raith, M. A. (2012). The value of business planning before start-up—A decision-theoretical perspective. *Journal of Business Venturing, 27*(3), 385–399.

Clark, G. L., Feiner, A., & Viehs, M. (2015). *From the stockholder to the stakeholder: How sustainability can drive financial outperformance.* Oxford: Smith School of Enterprise and the Environment.

Coase, R. H. (1937). The nature of the firm. *Economica, 4*(16), 386–405.

Cornell, B., & Damodaran, A. (2020). *Valuing ESG: Doing good or sounding good?* New York: NYU Stern School of Business. Available at https://ssrn.com/abstract=3557432

Cornell, B., & Shapiro, A. C. (2021). Corporate stakeholders, corporate valuation and ESG. *European Financial Management, 27*(2), 196–207.

Dorfleitner, G., Kreuzer, C., & Sparrer, C. (2020). ESG controversies and controversial ESG: About silent saints and small sinners. *Journal of Asset Management, 21*, 393–412.

Economist. (2021). *Could climate change trigger a financial crisis?* Available at https://www.economist.com/finance-and-economics/2021/09/04/could-climate-change-trigger-a-financial-crisis?frsc=dg%7Ce

Escrig-Olmedo, E., Fernández-Izquierdo, M. Á., Ferrero-Ferrero, I., Rivera-Lirio, J. M., & Muñoz-Torres, M. J. (2019). Rating the raters: Evaluating how ESG rating agencies integrate sustainability principles. *Sustainability, 11*(3), 915.

Fatemi, A., Glaum, M., & Kaiser, S. (2018). ESG performance and firm value: The moderating role of disclosure. *Global Finance Journal, 38*, 45–64.

Fernandes, N. (2014). *Finance for executives.* New York: NPV Publishing.

Fernandez, P. (2017). *Company valuation methods.* Available at https://ssrn.com/abstract=274973 or http://dx.doi.org/10.2139/ssrn.274973

Gianfrate, G., Schoenmaker, D., & Wasama, S. (2018). *Cost of capital, and sustainability: A literature review.* Rotterdam School of Management. Available at https://www.rsm.nl/fileadmin/Images_NEW/Erasmus_Platform_for_Sustainable_Value_Creation/11_04_Cost_of_Capital.pdf

Giese, G., Lee, L., Melas, D., Nagy, Z., & Nishikawa, L. (2019). Foundations of ESG investing: How ESG affects equity valuation, risk, and performance. *The Journal of Portfolio Management, 45*(5), 69–83.

Gillan, S. L., Koch, A., & Starks, L. T. (2021). Firms and social responsibility: A review of ESG and CSR research in corporate finance. *Journal of Corporate Finance, 66*.

Grossman, S. J., & Stiglitz, J. E. (1977). On value maximization and alternative objectives of the firm. *The Journal of Finance, 32*(2), 389–402.

Havakhor, T., Rahman, M. S., & Zhang, T. (2020). *Cybersecurity investments and the cost of capital.* Available at https://ssrn.com/abstract=3553470

Huber, B. M., & Comstock, M. (2017). ESG reports and ratings: What they are, why they matter? *The Corporate Governance Advisor, 25*(5), 1–12.

Iazzolino, G, & Migliano, G. (2015). The valuation of a patent through the real options approach: a tutorial. *Journal of Business Valuation and Economic Loss Analysis, 10*(1), 99–116.

Ielasi, F., Capelli, P., & Russo, A. (2021). Forecasting volatility by integrating financial risk with environmental, social, and governance risk. *Corporate Social Responsibility and Environmental Management, 28*(5), 1483–1495.

Indahl, R., & Jacobsen, H. G. (2019). Private equity 4.0: Using ESG to create more value with less risk. *Journal of Applied Corporate Finance, 31*(2).

Jiménez, R. G., & Grima, A. Z. (2020). Corporate social responsibility and cost of equity: Literature review and suggestions for future research. *Journal of Business, Accounting and Finance Perspectives, 2*(3), 15.

Johnson, R. (2020). The link between environmental, social and corporate governance disclosure and the cost of capital in South Africa. *Journal of Economic and Financial Sciences, 13*(1).

Kim, S., & Li, Z. F. (2021). Understanding the impact of ESG practices in corporate finance. *Sustainability, 13*, 3746.

Koelbel, J., & Busch, T. (2013). Does stakeholder pressure on ESG issues affect firm risk? Evidence from an international sample. *Academy of Management Annual Meeting Proceedings, 2013*(1), 15874–15874.

Koprivnjak, T., & Peterka, S. O. (2020). Business model as a base for building firms' competitiveness. *Sustainability, 12*(21), 1–18.

La Torre, M., Mango, F., Cafaro, A., & Leo, S. (2020). Does the ESG index affect stock return? Evidence from the eurostoxx50. *Sustainability, 12*(16), 6387.

Landi, G., & Sciarelli, M. (2019). Towards a more ethical market: The impact of ESG rating on corporate financial performance. *Social Responsibility Journal, 15*(1), 11–27.

Lasher, W. (2010). *The perfect business plan made simple: The best guide to writing a plan that will secure financial backing for your business.* New York: Broadway Books.

Liu, X., Wu, H., Wu, W., Fu, Y., & Huang, G. Q. (2021). Blockchain-enabled ESG reporting framework for sustainable supply chain. In S. G. Scholz, R. J. Howlett, & R. Setchi (Eds.), *Sustainable design and manufacturing 2020.* Smart Innovation, Systems and Technologies, 200. Berlin: Springer.

Mallinson, D. J., Morçöl, G., Yoo, E., Azim, S. F., Levine, E., & Shafi, S. (2020). Sharing economy: A systematic thematic analysis of the literature. *Information Polity, 25*(2), 143–158.

Marris, R. (1964). *The economic theory of managerial capitalism.* London: Macmillan.

Mervelskemper, L., & Streit, D. (2017). Enhancing market valuation of ESG performance: Is integrated reporting keeping its promise? *Business Strategy and the Environment, 26*(4), 536–549.

Minutolo, M. C., Kristjanpoller, W. D., & Stakeley, J. (2019). Exploring environmental, social, and governance disclosure effects on the S&P 500 financial performance. *Business Strategy & the Environment, 28*(6), 1083–1095.

Moro Visconti, R. (2019). Combining network theory with corporate governance: Converging models for connected stakeholders. *Corporate Ownership & Control, 17*(1).

Moro Visconti, R. (2020a). *The valuation of digital intangibles. technology, marketing and internet.* Cham: Palgrave Macmillan.

Moro Visconti, R. (2020b). *The interaction of big data, flexible options, and networked ecosystems in augmented business planning.* Available at https://www.researchgate.net/publication/346442792_THE_INTERACTION_OF_BIG_DATA_FLEXIBLE_OPTIONS_AND_NETWORKED_ECOSYS TEMS_IN_AUGMENTED_BUSINESS_PLANNING

Myers, S. C., & Majluf, N. S. (1984). Corporate financing and investment decisions when firms have information that investors do not have. *Journal of Financial Economics, 13*(2), 187–221.

Ng, A. C., & Rezaee, Z. (2012). *Sustainability disclosures and cost of capital.* Available at https://ssrn.com/abstract=2038654

OECD. (2017). *Transfer pricing guidelines for multinational enterprises and tax administrations.* Paris.

Panja, S., & Das, A. R. (2020). Exploring green investment on the dynamics of behavioral finance and stock performance. In M. Datta, R. Mahajan, & M. Bose (Eds.), *Business, economics and sustainable development.* New York: Bloomsbury.

Park, A., & Li, H. (2021). The effect of blockchain technology on supply chain sustainability performances. *Sustainability, 13*, 1726.

Piketty, T. (2013). *Capital in the 21st century.* Cambridge, MA.

Razgaitis, R. (2003). Dealmaking using real options and Monte Carlo analysis. Hoboken: Wiley Finance.

Rifkin, J. (2014). *The zero marginal cost society: The internet of things, the collaborative commons, and the eclipse of capitalism.* Cham: Palgrave Macmillan.

Sahlman, W. A. (1997). How to write a great business plan. *Harvard Business Review, 75*(4), 98–109.

Seetharam, I. (2017). *Environmental disasters and stock market performance.* Stanford: Stanford University. Available at https://web.stanford.edu/~ish uwar/Disasters_Stocks_Current.pdf

Shleifer, A., & Vishny, R. W. (1997). A survey of corporate governance. *Journal of Finance, 52*(2), 737–783.

Singh, J. P. (2013). On the intricacies of cash flow corporate valuation. *Advances in Management, 6*(3), 15–22.

Spulber, D. F. (2009). *The theory of the firm: Microeconomics with endogenous entrepreneurs, firms, markets, and organizations.* Cambridge: Cambridge University Press.

Steen, M., Moussawi, J. T., & Gjolberg, O. (2020). Is there a relationship between Morningstar's ESG ratings and mutual fund performance? *Journal of Sustainable Finance & Investment, 10*(4), 349–370.

Tunn, V. S. C., Bocken, N. M. P., van den Hende, E. A., & Schoormans, J. P. L. (2019). Business models for sustainable consumption in the circular economy: An expert study. *Journal of Cleaner Production, 212,* 324–333.

Upson, J., & Wei, C. (2019). *Supply chain concentration and cost of capital.* Available at https://ssrn.com/abstract=3532089

van Duuren, E., Plantinga, A., & Scholtens, B. (2016). ESG Integration and the investment management process: Fundamental investing reinvented. *Journal of Business Ethics, 138,* 525–533.

Williamson, O. E. (2010). Transaction cost economics: The natural progression. *The American Economic Review, 100*(3, June), 673–690.

Wong, W. C., Batten, C. A., Ahmad, A. H., et al. (2021). Does ESG certification add firm value? *Finance Research Letters, 39*(C).

CHAPTER 24

Corporate Governance Concerns and Bankability Issues of the Digital Assets: More Guarantees with Less Collateral?

24.1 Leveraging Intangible Assets

The evaluation of the intangibles as an "asset" (being part of the invested capital) should always be conducted considering also their financial coverage, represented by the raised capital (equity + financial debt).

This chapter considers the issue in general terms, and then must be adapted to the specific intangible to be appraised. Whereas some intangibles like trademarks (as shown in Sect. 9.6) or patents keep some residual value even when the firm passes from a going concern to a breakup scenario, other less (legally) protected intangibles (e.g., know-how) lose most of their value.

When the appraisal concerns the enterprise value (market value of equity + financial debt) of an intangible-driven firm, the intangible assets always must be considered together with their backing sources.

These issues have long been debated in the scientific literature, as it will be shown in the next paragraphs, even if the "new" intangibles like IoT, big data, blockchains, etc., have hardly been considered.

The borrowing capacity is an essential characteristic of the corporate governance concerns that will be synthetically analyzed in the last paragraph. Corporate governance and its inherent conflicts of interest among composite stakeholders strongly affect the evaluation process. For example, whenever the conflicts of interest grow, they are immediately

R. Moro-Visconti, *The Valuation of Digital Intangibles*, https://doi.org/10.1007/978-3-031-09237-4_24

reflected in a higher cost of capital, so reducing the Discounted Cash Flows that are currently used in the valuation process.

The very existence of intangible assets, especially if not recorded as CAPEX in the balance sheet, traditionally limits the company's borrowing capacity, due to the difficulty of establishing security on them and their uncertain or non-existent market value.

The growing importance that intangible assets have in contributing to the competitive advantage of companies, however, should induce to reveal the value of intangible assets externally, to finance economically convenient investments. For external lenders, the increase in profitability deriving from the use of intangible assets should be more important than the presence of collateral assets. In this context, it may be possible to exploit the autonomous market value of some intangibles, such as trademarks and patents.

Alongside the traditional information asymmetries, the fiscal treatment matters, deriving from the possibility of expensing some costs in the income statement (especially R&D and advertising). Companies with the best profitability—which are naturally associated with a greater debt capacity—tend to be those with lower recorded intangibles. Consequently, the companies with the highest profitability are those that have more difficulties in communicating externally the value—at least in accounting terms—of their intangibles.

The preparation of a balance sheet not distorted by the tax rules on business income may allow mitigating the effect of these asymmetries. A more incisive contribution to the asymmetries deriving from the insufficient representation in the balance sheet of intangible assets can come from the preparation, by the company in need of financing, of an additional prospectus. This document should contain a valuation of intangible assets which enables us to appreciate both the incremental profitability deriving from their use in a going concern context and their possible independent market value, which is relevant in a context of liquidation or insolvency.

Investment in intangible assets may be backed by hybrid debt instruments, such as convertible bonds, complementary to traditional bank loans, based on innovative clauses that should reflect the information about the real value of intangible assets.

The tendency to borrow is advantageous for a firm due to the tax shield connected to the deductibility of debt service charges, while the existence of agency costs limits the debt convenience. The composition of the assets and the presence of intangibles impact this trade-off, which represents an extension of the original model of Modigliani and Miller (1958).

The capacity for indebtedness grows in the presence of tangible assets with a collateral value on which a guarantee can be established, as confirmed by numerous classic studies (Bradley et al., 1984; Jensen & Meckling, 1976; Long & Malitz, 1985). Accordingly, Titman and Wessels (1988) note that if the debt can be collateralized, the borrower is forced to use it for a specific project. Since no guarantees can be created on non-collateralizable projects, creditors demand higher interest rates, inducing companies to resort to equity raising rather than debt issues.

The contrary thesis of Grossman and Hart (1982) is based on the existence of a conflict of interest between shareholders, managers, and financiers. Shareholders must monitor the behavior of managers, avoiding expropriation. The need to go for debt to mitigate the agency costs between shareholders and managers is stronger in the presence of intangibles, whose value is more difficult to control: debt is associated with a control function that is carried out by the lenders and in this case occurs for the benefit of the shareholders. This happens in public companies where ownership and control are separated.

The original model of Black and Scholes (1973) for the valuation of the options provides an interpretation that supports the thesis of the lower capacity to borrow in the presence of risky assets (like the intangibles). Assuming that the financial structure is represented exclusively from bonds and shares, equity can be considered as a European call option on bonds, since it gives shareholders the right to repurchase the entire company from the bondholders, on the maturity date of the bond loan and at an exercise price corresponding to the nominal repayment of the loan.

If at the maturity of the bond the value of the company (V) is higher than the nominal value of the bonds (D), the shareholders will exercise the call option paying the nominal value and cashing in the difference $V - D$. If $V < D$, the shareholders will not honor the debt and will not exercise the option. Therefore, at the maturity of the loan, the shareholder wealth (S) is like that of a European call option: $S = \max [0, V - D]$, while the bondholder wealth (B) corresponds to $B = \min [V, D]$.

From this asymmetry it results that the shareholders have the convenience to accept risky investments, which will increase the market value of equity, making the bonds riskier. According to the Black and Scholes model (1973), the value of a call option increases with the increase in the volatility of the underlying security (in this case, the bond).

The disincentive to externally communicate investments in risky assets (in intangibles) derives from the fact that if the shareholders realize that the investments are not profitable and that the shares are overvalued, they can sell them before the market incorporates this information in the price (Myers & Majluf, 1984).

Investments in intangibles allow shareholders to increase business risk without the debtholders becoming aware of it quickly (for example, by investing R&D in projects with a low probability of high profits). Following this approach, the shareholders have the advantage of maintaining the information asymmetries that prevent the disclosure of the value of the intangible assets, provided that the internal resources of the company (self-financing or equity increase) are sufficient to finance all the investment projects with positive Net Present Value, otherwise an adverse selection problem arises. From this trade-off, a debate arises on whether the book and market value of intangible assets should be revealed to the outside world.

24.2   Unsecured Intangible-Driven Growth

Debt service is guaranteed by the capacity of the firm to generate adequate future cash flows to pay it back. The primary component of generated liquidity is represented by revenue growth, and its marginal by-products (EBITDA, operating and net cash flow, etc.).

The impact of scalable (digital) intangibles on growth has been extensively examined in Chapter 3. What is worth recalling is the volatile nature of intangible-driven growth and its potential inconsistency with the rigidity of debt payback schemes. Hence the natural caution of lenders to give credit to unsecured growth, whose volatility may produce insufficient liquidity for debt payback.

The graphical representation shows a two-sided forecast of sales growth and operating cash flow that in the worst-case are insufficient for debt repayment (Fig. 24.1).

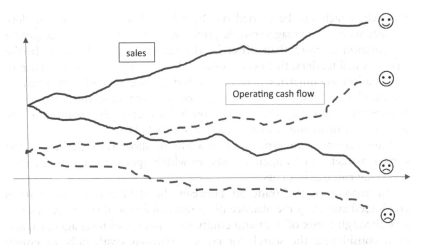

Fig. 24.1 Volatility of sales and operating cash flow

24.3 Information Asymmetries and the Signaling Effects of Intangible Assets

The market value of the intangible assets significantly differs from their book value, due to the amortization process, and entails a rapid write-off from the balance sheet. This generates information asymmetries between managers and external lenders, which are significantly reduced, although not eliminated, with the publication of the balance sheet. While the former tend to be aware of the real value of the intangible assets, external lenders have access to incomplete information, normally a source of underestimation of intangible assets; in the case of listed companies, the stock exchange prices may not entirely reflect these latent values.

According to Brennan (1990), the existence of latent values (not only linked to intangible components) can lead the company to sell them off, when they are positive, through M&A operations that allow the alienation of the entire company or one of its branches, or to defer the sale, if negative.

The existence of a liquid market of firms facilitates the spread of intangible assets' value. Digitalization fosters comparability, and could reduce information asymmetries.

In the absence of intangible assets operations, there remains an interest on the part of the lenders to gather information on their value. This research, which can be carried out by minor shareholders, not in close contact with the management, is profitable only if the cost of acquiring information is more than offset by the value attributable to it. In the case of small lenders, this occurs only with grouping. The permanence of information asymmetries may be justified by the cost of disseminating information or the lack of convenience to encourage third parties to finance the company, which may already have enough resources in the form of self-financing (through cumulated EBITDA).

Information asymmetries lead to a loss of allocative efficiency in the capital market and to agency costs, in which agent-managers may suboptimally run the business.

An analysis of the trade-off between the debt and equity costs is conducted assuming the absence of an optimal financial structure, achievable through a mix of debt and equity that minimizes total agency costs, even considering the search for corner solutions (with debt or equity alternately equal to zero) (Fig. 24.2).

The debt agency costs are influenced by the existence of intangibles financed through the debt:

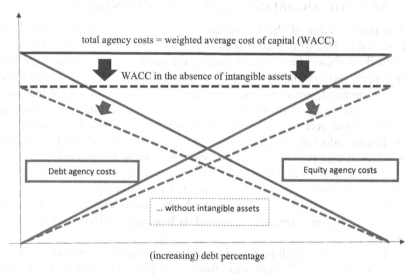

Fig. 24.2 Trade-off between agency costs of debt and equity in the presence and in the absence of intangibles

- insolvency costs must consider intangible assets without independent market value (e.g., know-how, instead of patents);
- the costs of the incentive to accept investments with a positive Net Present Value may relate to investments in intangibles;
- the costs of the incentive to accept risky investments may involve investments in intangibles.

Even the agency costs of the equity decrease in the absence of intangibles: the equity tends to coincide with the tangible equity, reducing the existence of information asymmetries that can generate conflicts of interest (between old and new shareholders), involving other stakeholders.

24.4 TYPES OF DEBT AND SUPPORT GUARANTEES

The choice of the forms of debt suitable to finance the company's investments (in particular those in intangibles) represents an essential moment in the strategic management of the company, as it must optimize the following constraints:

1. lending must be enough to finance the investments deemed profitable, to avoid adverse selection problems;
2. the cost of debt (i) must be minimized, to keep the differential (ROIC $-$ i), on which financial leverage operates, always positive[1];
3. the composition of the debt and the financial leverage expressing the debt/equity ratio must guarantee the financial balance of the company, maintaining a positive structural margin (equity > fixed assets, including capitalized intangibles).

The financing choices can be considered a communication tool that, assuming that the propositions of Modigliani and Miller (1958), about the irrelevance of the financial structure are valid. Changes in corporate financing policy are, nevertheless, an essential signal of the real prospects of the company.

The bank–company relationships must consider information asymmetries that prevent the optimal financing of investments in intangibles, going beyond the original Modigliani and Miller model. Their mitigation can be sought with complex financial contracts that allow third-party lenders to be protected while minimizing the cost of capital for the company (WACC) that is used to discount the FCFF, to get the Enterprise Value.

The conflict of interest between shareholders and creditors can be reduced with covenants that prevent abuses from the shareholders as the distribution of reserves or dividends, the issue of new secured debt, the disposal of safe assets (e.g., liquidity, but not intangibles), and the execution of sub-optimal or risky investments (Smith & Warner, 1979). There are therefore restrictions affecting the composition of both assets, liabilities, and equity. An overall picture is represented in Fig. 24.3.

Financial contracts that can be used to allow investments in intangibles, reducing agency costs, are represented by hybrid instruments (quasi-equity), such as convertible bonds or bonds cum warrant, or subordinated shareholders loans. The existence of a put option incorporated in the security issued by the company allows to overcome the debtors' disincentive to finance risky investments: this is described in the Black and

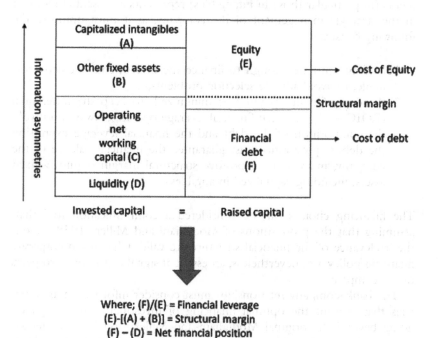

Fig. 24.3 Balance sheet and capital structure

Scholes model (1973). In more general terms, hybrid instruments allow a better synchronization of outgoing cash flows (for debt service) with the incoming ones, reducing the cost of capital of the firm. Positive liquidity reduces debt and leverage. In a riskless Modigliani and Miller (1958) world, the value of the firm is unaffected by the change in debt. If the debt becomes risky, its reduction may positively affect (reduce) the cost of capital.

Third parties may be induced to agree to finance risky investments in intangibles if they receive an adequate risk premium (which can sometimes be too burdensome for the company, making the difference between return and investment cost negative) or being able to participate in profits from investments.

If the issue of convertible bonds is used to finance investments in intangibles with an uncertain outcome (R&D), bondholders can enjoy an income that is independent of the degree of the investment success. This success is associated with the possibility to share the rewards of the investment, if it proves profitable, through conversion into shares at a pre-established exercise price. The fact that the exercise price is pre-established allows bondholders to participate in the results of the investment even if the conversion takes place after the profitability that comes from it unless the shareholders decide to pay high dividends before the conversion, to cash in all the profits from the investment (to avoid this, specific bond covenants can be envisaged).

24.5 THE FINANCIAL HIERARCHY IN THE USE OF EXTERNAL CAPITAL

Among the objectives of sound financial management, a relevant concern is represented by the need to minimize the issuance of risky debt, due to higher costs (in terms of guarantees and/or higher financial charges).

Based on the theory of financial hierarchy or the pecking order hypothesis, companies resort to self-financing (EBITDA creation) and, if they need external financing, firms first draw on less risky debt, then on hybrid forms, and lastly on the issue of shares. The cost of capital accordingly grows, and is maximized when riskier funds (equity) are collected. Digitalization, with its mild reduction of information asymmetries, may help softening these difficulties.

Since the issuance of unsecured or subordinated debt often precedes secured (privileged or senior) debt, there is a natural disincentive for unsecured creditors to allow the company to make additional risky investments financed by new preferred debt. If the company has issued subordinated debt (D_s) and privileged debt (D_p) with the same maturity, there may be three different cases, depending on the capacity of the company (V) to meet all or only a part of its obligations:

Result	Privileged debt	Subordinated debt	Equity
$V > D_p + D_s$	D_p	D_s	$V - D_p - D_s$
$D_p + D_s \geq V > D_p$	D_p	$V - D_s$	0
$D_p \geq V$	V	0	0

24.6   PROFITABILITY AND BORROWING CAPACITY IN A GOING CONCERN CONTEXT

The borrowing capacity is a function of the company's profitability: when considering a going concern company, the contribution of intangible assets to profitability can be measured by the differential income approach (consistent with IVS 210 prescriptions). This approach assumes that the value of the intangible asset is intimately linked to the contribution it makes to the corporate profitability, allowing to achieve positive price and/or volume differentials (and therefore, economic margins).

The question this approach tries to answer is the following: what is the additional income deriving from the exploitation of the intangible? (or how much would the income decrease if the intangibles were not used?).

The application of the approach presupposes the discounting of the expected differential income, as the differential of the sale price (premium price approach) or as a source of cost savings. Assuming a company aimed at the exclusive exploitation of the intangible, its value can be given by:

$$W = R\, a_{n\neg i} \tag{24.1}$$

where W is the value of the intangible asset, R is the expected average income, n is the number of years considered and i is the discount rate (if $n \to \infty$, we have: $W = R/i$).

As an alternative to the income approach (with limited or unlimited capitalization if $n \rightarrow \infty$,), a mixed capital-income approach can be used, for example, that of the autonomous estimate of goodwill with a limited capitalization of the average profit.[2] In this case:

$$W = K + a_{n\neg i}(R - iK) \qquad (24.2)$$

where K is the adjusted equity, R is the expected average normal income, n the (limited) number of years, i the interest rate deemed appropriate concerning the type of investment considered, i' the discount rate of the excess income (goodwill), given by the difference $(R - iK)$.

The income that can be associated with the exclusive use of the intangible asset can be determined directly, through the fees expected in the event of a transfer of the rights to exploit the intangible. An indirect way to evaluate the intangible assets consists in attributing higher value to the tangible assets to which they are associated (e.g., patent $+$ machinery): this enhances the function of intangible assets as a link between capital and labor.

The presence of intangible assets often has a significant impact on profitability ratios (ROS, ROE, ROIC, ROA, etc.), which must be adjusted to consider intangibles: in the absence of such adjustments, there would be an overestimation of the profitability indicators (deriving from an underestimation of their denominator, where assets, equity, etc., are considered, without any recording of the intangibles).

The economic profitability is connected to the ability to generate positive cash flows, primarily through the EBITDA: the profitability of intangible assets must so be seen by the cash flows emanating from them. From a differential perspective, a comparison must be made between the company's cash flows with or without intangibles, following an approach like the one just described.

24.7 MARKET VALUE AS COLLATERAL IN AN INSOLVENCY SCENARIO

The transition from a going concern to a break-up scenario implies the loss of the company's income expectations: in this perspective, it only detects the market value of the individual assets (including the intangibles) that make up the company. In the event of liquidation or insolvency, information asymmetries decrease drastically, since the need to liquidate assets to pay creditors requires a fair game, and risky investments slow down.

Intangibles are normally not collateralizable, even if some of them—as registered trademarks and patents—may be compared to physical assets (like real estate) and can, therefore be pledged as such. Digital intangibles, especially if representing an extension of classical ones (e.g., digital brands; domain names associated with trademarks, etc.) could also incorporate some collateral value, especially in a going concern scenario.

The market value of most intangibles is normally well below the going concern value and sometimes even below the book value (as is the case for intangible assets without market value): using the concept introduced by Adam Smith, this is due to the prevalence of the exchange-value over the use value.

The presence of highly specialized assets (firm-specific) increases the difference between use- and exchange-value and if it makes these assets more difficult to sell, it reduces the agency costs between shareholders and creditors, since the former will find it more difficult to make substitutions with other assets, making their collateralization more complicated—but less necessary (Smith & Warner, 1979). Intangibles are, in most cases, firm-specific, even if digitalization could (slightly) increase their comparability and diffusion.

The market value of an intangible asset essentially depends on its ability to produce income even in a context different from the original one. Therefore, the determination of the market value is connected to the measurement of profitability. In both settings, the differential income approach and the relief-from-royalties, and the cost of reconstruction or replacement will be applicable with different degrees of intensity. In the first case, the question is how many royalties should be paid by the company if it uses an intangible (trademark, patent, etc.) owned by third parties, while in the second reference is made to costs (at current and not historical values) that the company should incur to reconstitute its assets.

The market value of an intangible asset implies that its ability to generate income is transferable to third parties. In the event of liquidation or insolvency, it is necessary to estimate how much of the value gets lost, bearing in mind that many investments in intangibles are irreversible (if they are abandoned, have a null value) and perishable (they must be exploited, otherwise they soon lose value). To determine the possible market value of intangible assets, it is necessary to distinguish between:

(a) intangibles that have an independent market value;
(b) intangibles without autonomous individuality, having a market value only if negotiated together with other assets;
(c) intangibles that have a potential market value (autonomous or integrated);
(d) intangibles without any market value.

Table 24.1 provides some indications regarding the negotiability of the intangibles.

Table 24.1 mainly refers to classic intangibles. Trendy digital intangibles are even harder to evaluate and typically have a lower if any autonomous market value.

Table 24.1 Negotiability of the various types of intangibles

Intangible	Negotiability
Setting and expansion costs	Normally, no
Research and development costs (R&S)	Potential, usually subject to patenting
Know-how, industrial secrets	If the search stage is not complete, additional costs incur
Industrial patents	Yes, autonomously; sometimes together with technical fixed assets or other patents on which they depend
Patterns and ornamental designs	Not autonomously
Advertising costs	Potential, subject to trademark registration
Trademarks	Yes, autonomously; sometimes together with other general or special trademarks
Customer portfolio and product sales networks	In some cases, together with other assets (credits)
Concessions	Yes, if transferable to third parties
Licenses	Yes
Rights to use intellectual property (copyright)	Yes
Goodwill	No; eventual market value in the context of the sale of a business branch
Fixed assets in progress and advance payments	Potential, subject to completion and sometimes associated with other fixed assets
Other capitalized multiannual costs	No

The market value of an intangible asset (as well as of a tangible asset) depends, in large part, on the existence of a consolidated secondary market. The secondary market thins out when the intangible good turns out to be specific (Titman & Wessels, 1988), even if it is normally endowed with greater added value in going concern scenarios. Experience shows that companies with many intangibles are those that have the most to lose in the event of insolvency, not only because of their lower collateralization potential.

A correct analysis of the liquidation or insolvency costs (which do not necessarily coincide) must consider both the statistical probability that the unwanted event occurs and the loss of value that the event generates.

24.8   Intangible Assets, Rating, and Borrowing Capacity

The supervisory bank rating expresses the reliability of the indebted company and is closely connected with the legal requirements of the supervisory capital of the banks. Loans to the riskiest companies entail the need for the bank to set aside more supervisory capital that needs to be remunerated at higher rates.

The Basel agreements, applicable to European banks, provide for valuation systems by choosing between two alternative methods:

1. standard method with the use of external ratings by specialized agencies;
2. method based on internal, basic, or advanced ratings (established internally by the bank).

The risk factors considered in assigning internal ratings are:

(a) the probability of default (PD) of the debtor, which expresses the possibility that within a year there will be a negative event that will lead the entrusted company to no longer be able to repay in whole or in part the debt (interest and capital);
(b) the expected loss in the event of insolvency (loss given default, LGD), expressed by the extent of the portion of the credit that the bank considers at risk of failure to return in the event of insolvency;

(c) the exposure at the time of insolvency (exposure at default, EAD), corresponding to the estimated exposure of the bank at the time the insolvency of the entrusted company occurs;

(d) the residual life (maturity) of the debt.

The capital provision contributes to influencing the financial conditions of the loan (spread), considering the expected loss (PD × LGD) and the unexpected loss cost.

The assignment of the rating by the bank is based on quantitative information (accounting documentation, data of credits drawn from the Central Credit Register or other sources, etc.) and qualitative (legal and corporate structure, governance system, internal control systems, quality of management, industrial plans, commercial strategies, competitive capacity, etc.).

The quantitative accounting information includes parameters and indicators such as the degree of indebtedness (leverage), the level of liquidity, profitability, etc.

The credit risk can be mitigated with real or personal guarantees of the entrusted company or group companies or other specialized intermediaries.

These are, in a nutshell, the standard aspects of the rating, in continuous evolution, with limitations foreseen in the use of internal (especially advanced) risk assessment models.

Intangibles influence the rating in various complementary areas, which affect both the quantitative components and the qualitative aspects. Some banks subtract the CAPEX from the equity of the target firm, so considering the Net Tangible Equity as a benchmark for true collateral.

The probability of insolvency and the guarantees are for example influenced by the intangibles. On the one hand, intangibles tend to reduce the insolvency probability, producing incremental economic and financial margins, but on the other, they are characterized, especially if the company abandons a business continuity scenario, by higher risk. In the latter case, the residual collateral value is limited if any (with differences, between intangibles with an autonomous market value and other intangible assets, such as goodwill or know-how or digital intangibles, much more difficult to exploit in the transition phase from the going concern to the break-up).

Intangible-driven information is hard to collect and process in the bank loans procedures. This operation can be attempted by comparing the company with or without intangibles (as indicated by the IVS 210 examined in Chapter 2), to estimate their contribution to the production of income and incremental financial flows and their impact on indicators present in the models for estimating insolvencies, such as the well-known Altman Z-Score.[3] From a qualitative point of view, there is a wide range of soft information that the company can provide to the banking analyst to express the characteristics of its intangible portfolio.

24.9   COVER RATIOS AND OTHER BANKABILITY PARAMETERS

Bankability is the characteristic of a project or proposal with enough collateral, future cash flow, and a high probability of success, to be acceptable to institutional lenders for financing.

The bankability, therefore, indicates the feasibility, in financial terms, of a given project, and the firm's capacity to serve its financial debt, fully paying it back.

The bankability of an investment project entails the absence of capital rationing problems, which arise if the investment does not find adequate financial coverage.

In theory, every investment project characterized by a positive Net Present Value should always be bankable. This, however, does not always occur, due both to credit rationing problems and inadequate financial marketing, linked to the inability to make potential lenders understand the validity and sustainability of the project.

Bankability is becoming increasingly important for applying the Basel parameters set for European banks, or complementary creditworthiness criteria.

In the preliminary assessment to undertake an investment or not, bankability is one of the fundamental aspects. If a project is not bankable, it cannot be committed, unless fully backed by equity (as it happens to many startups).

Bankability expresses a complex concept, subject to change over time and dependent on numerous elements (reference sector, type of project), primarily based on the perception that each lender has its specific risks.

The term bankability is used to define the acceptability, for the banking sector, of the overall structure of a project for its financing.

In the calculation of bankability, it is necessary to consider some specific indicators, including, first, the Debt Service Cover Ratio (DSCR) and the Loan Life Cover Ratio (LLCR).

The debt service cover ratio (DSCR) is equal to the ratio, calculated for each given period of the forecast time horizon for the duration of the loans, between the operating cash flow generated by the project and the debt service including the principal and the interests:

$$DSCR = \frac{O_{CF}}{D_F + I_T} \tag{24.3}$$

where:

O_{CF} = operating cash flow for the t-th year;

Df_t = principal amount of financial debt to be repaid when it expires;

I_t = interests to be paid (financial charges) when it expires.

The meaning of this indicator is easy: a value equal to or greater than the unit represents the capacity of the investment to produce enough liquidity to cover the debt installments. The minimum value of the ratio, to be acceptable, cannot, however, be equal to one since in this case the possibility of paying out dividends would be compromised, until the total repayment of the debt. Moreover, the debt underwriters likely require an adequate margin of guarantee.

However, there is no standard level that allows comparing the debt coverage ratios, the limit considered admissible will be negotiated from time to time concerning the riskiness of the project, the guarantees provided, and the contractual strength of the parties.

The Debt Service Cover Ratio is an annual debt index: it, therefore, expresses an instantaneous index, as it verifies the project's ability to repay the debt installment for the current year.

Calculating the average of the individual Debt Service Cover Ratio along the amortization period (n) the Average Debt Service Cover Ratio (ADSCR) is obtained:

$$ADSCR = \frac{\sum_{t=1}^{n} \frac{FCO_t}{Df_t + I_t}}{n} \tag{24.4}$$

The following example is based on a forward-looking cash flow statement. The combination of the proforma balance sheet variations with the forecast income statements for the years T1 to T4 (that are not reported in this synthetic example) gives the expected cash flow statement. The operating cash flow indicates the liquidity that is created if the parameter is positive (years T2 and T4) or destroyed (years T1 and T3) from the ordinary business. Whatever is left after appropriate debt service belongs to the shareholders (net cash flow).

Whenever the cover ratio is higher than unity, the firm generates enough liquidity to pay back financial debt. Intangibles are likely to play a key role in this process, as a cash-generating catalyzer (Table 24.2).

The Loan Life Cover Ratio (LLCR) is defined as the ratio between the discounted sum of the available cash flows for the Debt Service, between the moment of valuation and the last year foreseen for the repayment of the loans, and the residual debt considered at the same moment of valuation.

The cash flow to consider here is the cash flow available for debt service.

The numerator of the ratio, therefore, represents the (current) value of the flows generated by the project on which the lenders rely for the future repayment of the outstanding debt (expressed in the denominator).

The more the coverage ratio exceeds the unit (equilibrium point), the better the financial solidity of the investment and the guarantee of the repayment.

The Loan Life Cover Ratio is a dynamic index, which considers the operating cash flows trend available for debt service, for the entire residual duration of the debt.

In formulae:

$$LLCR = \frac{\sum_{t=s}^{s+n} \frac{FCO_t}{(1+i)^t} + D}{O_t} \qquad (24.5)$$

where:

s = moment of valuation;
$s + n$ = last year for which the repayment of the debt is envisaged;
D = available debt (debt reserve);
O = residual debt.

Table 24.2 Cash flow statement and debt service cover ratio

Cash Flow Statement	T1	T2	T3	T4
Monetary operating revenues	5,446,200	11,090,970	3,270,575	10,280,375
Other monetary operating costs	5,504,212	10,913,982	3,353,587	9,571,587
Cash flow from the operating area	**(58,012)**	**176,988**	**(83,012)**	**708,788**
Net working capital variation	(2,880,847)	1,044,097	14,192	578,367
Fixed assets variation	(17,166)	0	0	0
Operating cash flow – FCFF	**(2,956,025)**	**1,221,085**	**(68,820)**	**1,287,155**
Financial charges	(80,000)	(105,000)	(97,000)	(89,000)
Equity variation	(95,217)	146,820	146,820	146,820
Financial debt variation	133,939	(255,989)	(61,025)	(61,025)
Other	0	0	0	0
Taxes	(10,000)	(10,000)	(10,000)	(31,608)
Shareholders net cash flow – FCFE	**(3,007,303)**	**996,916**	**(90,025)**	**1,252,342**
Initial liquidity	(1,074,697)	(4,082,000)	(3,085,084)	(3,175,109)
Final liquidity	(4,082,000)	(3,085,084)	(3,175,109)	(1,922,767)
Cash flow variation	**(3,007,303)**	**996,916**	**(90,025)**	**1,252,342**
Debt Service Cover Ratio	**T1**	**T2**	**T3**	**T4**
Operating cash flow (FCO) – FCFF	(2,956,025)	1,221,085	(68,820)	1,287,155
Financial debt (Df)	10,844,264	11,243,800	9,393,575	4,827,075
Net financial burden (Of)	(80,000)	(105,000)	(97,000)	(89,000)
Debt Service Cover Ratio (FCO/Df + Of)	**−27.46%**	**10.96%**	**−0.74%**	**27.17%**
Average Debt Service Cover Ratio	**2.48%**			

In the following example, it is assumed that the last year for the repayment of loans is T4 and that the discount rate is 5% (Table 24.3).

If we discount the operating cash flows for the entire duration of the investment project, even after the possible repayment of the debt, we have the so-called Project Cover Ratio (PRC). The Project Cover Ratio is a dynamic index, as it considers the operating cash flows (FCFF) available for debt service, throughout the project (concession, investment).

For the calculation of the Debt Service Cover Ratio, the unlevered cash flow (FCFF) is considered in the numerator, while the denominator shows all the forms of financing (debt installments and interests).

The other bankability indexes include leverage (debt/equity ratio), and the ratio between EBITDA and financial charges. This last indicator represents the EBITDA multiplier (economic and financial flow, which expresses the margins generated at the operational level) concerning the financial charges serving the debt. A reasonable multiple is necessary to cover other monetary costs (salaries, purchases, taxes, etc.).

Banks that finance companies propose a variable spread (concerning a fixed rate of remuneration for debt, anchored—for example—to the EURIBOR). An example of variable spread (in basis points), depending on the performance of the borrowing company, is (Table 24.4).

Table 24.3 Simulation of loan life cover ratio

	T1	T2	T3	T4
Operating cash flows	150.000	240.000	200.000	357.000
Sum of discounted cash flows	868.367	754.286	540.000	
Debt reserve	15.000	15.000	15.000	
Residual debt	240.000	160.000	80.000	–
Loan Life Cover Ratio	**3.68**	**4.81**	**6.94**	

Table 24.4 Example of a rating

Parameter	Financially sound company	Company in financial equilibrium	Company close to financial disequilibrium	Company close to insolvency or bankruptcy
Debt/equity (D/E) (financial leverage)	D/E < 2	2 < D/E < 3.25	2.5 < D/E < 3.25	>3.25
EBITDA/net negative interests (E/OFN)	E/OF > 5	3 < E/OF < 4	3 < E/OF < 4	<3
Spread	+175	+200	+225	Withdrawal of the financing

Investments in intangible assets influence the EBITDA/OFN (where OFN = net negative interest rate) ratio, above all at the numerator level, increasing it thanks to incremental income flows (that could be digitally-driven). The net financial charges may increase, only if the purchase or internal creation of the intangible resources is financed by the bank debt.

A possible increase in debt affects the numerator of financial leverage, while the equity in the denominator is influenced by intangible-driven incremental profitability if the increase of net profit is stored in the equity.

24.10 IMPACT OF INTANGIBLE ASSETS ON BORROWING CAPACITY

Within the vast literature on the theory of optimal financial structure, some models deal with the causal link between intangible assets and the leverage of the company. Table 24.5 summarizes the results of the most relevant models.

Between the intangible assets and the leverage, there is normally an inverse proportionality, which limits the borrowing capacity of the companies, since the intangibles are normally without collateral value and considered risky assets. This setting does not consider some important circumstances:

1. the contribution of intangible assets to the profitability of the company—on which the ability to repay debt depends, not less than the existence of asset-backed guarantees—becomes increasingly essential;
2. intangible assets are often difficult to observe, primarily due to the criteria for their recognition in the balance sheet (within the CAPEX), where they are traditionally underestimated for prudentiality reasons;
3. the possibility, from a legal point of view, to establish a pledge on marketable intangibles as trademarks or patents.

The contribution of the intangibles to corporate profitability is a key factor of competitive advantage, which is increasingly essential in many sectors. The same market value of collateralized tangible assets is often increased by the presence of intangibles (as plants associated with patents).

The appreciation of the value of the intangibles is hindered by informational asymmetries that naturally arise, because of the accounting of these

Table 24.5 Effect of intangible assets on borrowing capacity

Model description	Relationship between intangibles and debt capacity	Bibliographical references
The ability to borrow increases in the presence of tangible assets with collateral value	Inversely proportional	Galai and Masulis (1976) Jensen and Meckling (1976) Myers (1977) Myers and Majluf (1984) Bradley et al. (1984) Long and Malitz (1985) Titman and Wessels (1988)
Leverage increases if the liquidation value increases (which depends on intangibles with market value)	Inversely proportional	Harris and Raviv (1990)
Leverage increases if investigative costs decrease (and therefore assets that are difficult to observe like intangibles)	Inversely proportional	Harris and Raviv (1990) Brennan (1990)
Investments in very risky assets (as some intangibles) favor shareholders to the detriment of third-party creditors	inversely proportional	Black and Scholes (1973)
The propensity to borrow to mitigate the agency costs between shareholders and managers, leaving creditors part of the control over them, grows in the presence of assets that are difficult to observe, like the intangibles	Directly proportional	Grossman and Hart (1982)
Companies with high tax deductions, such as investments in intangibles that are rapidly depreciable or directly recorded s an expense in the income statement, have tax advantages like debt and therefore reduce the use of leverage	Inversely proportional	Titman and Wessels (1988)

(continued)

Table 24.5 (continued)

Model description	Relationship between intangibles and debt capacity	Bibliographical references
The high investments in intangibles (especially R&D) increase the specificity of the company, decreasing the market value and the negotiability of the assets This results in lower collateral value and greater tax shields other than debt, decreasing the company's borrowing capacity	Inversely proportional	Titman and Wessels (1988)
The borrowing capacity to finance investments in intangibles is growing in the presence of hybrid securities, which reduce agency costs	Directly proportional	Jensen and Meckling (1976) Smith and Warner (1979) Green (1984)
The trades, in which the buyer pays a market price (with a differential represented by goodwill) generate an increase in the percentage weight of intangible assets and therefore decrease the capacity for debt	Inversely proportional	Titman and Wessels (1988)

items—and due to tax interferences—which suggest their rapid write-off from the balance sheet, if the firm is profitable and shows a positive taxable income. The phenomenon is particularly noticeable in companies with higher profitability, encouraged to pursue more rapid depreciation policies, for which a curious paradox emerges: their competitive advantage is increasingly due to the presence of intangibles, which are moreover subject to a growing unobservability, as they are quickly written-off.

The costs of an inappropriate valuation of the intangibles fall both on companies, burdened with a higher cost of capital, and on third-party financiers, which sub-optimally allocate their financial resources. This paradox is exacerbated by international accounting standards, according to which prudence prevails over substance.

Some possible solutions for the mitigation of information asymmetries can be sought in the preparation, by the company, of a management information prospectus, complementary to the balance sheet, with analytical indications of the costs of intangibles (effective intangible CAPEX), and their residual life, expected profitability, and the estimated market value. If the company is unable to carry out a marketing operation, by communicating the real value of the intangibles externally, it risks not having the necessary funds to finance profitable investments.

From the outside, greater attention should be paid from the banks to the income aspects of the company and the contribution of intangible assets to the economic and financial results.

24.11 INFORMATION ASYMMETRIES AND DEBT RATIONING

Information asymmetries have a paradoxical impact on intangibles, since, in many cases, they are necessary to discourage imitation, as it happens with know-how and, to a lesser extent, with patents, while they cause communication problems that could damage the trademarks and the external perception of the company image.

Information asymmetries are intrinsically related to intangible assets, whose value is not easily perceivable and communicable externally. The missing bookkeeping in the financial statements of internally developed intangible assets increases information asymmetries, hindering comparability.

The valuation and dissemination of the market value of the company can thus be misrepresented, causing incorrect market behavior, in the form of adverse selection, moral hazard, or other governance criticalities.

Since intangibles are not easily estimated, their value can lead to market failures that involve investors (shareholders or creditors), who may be discouraged.

The capacity of the debt grows in the presence of tangible assets with a potential collateral value, supported by the guarantees applicable to them, as confirmed by Jensen and Meckling (1976), whose theory is based on agency problems created by the coexistence between creditors and managers.

Intangible assets intrinsically incorporate information asymmetries (Aboody & Lev, 2000), and managers control information on the value and prospects of the company, concerning outsiders. Information asymmetries lead to sub-optimal decisions and can reduce the collection of equity or debt, causing debt rationing problems that could block the financing of profitable projects, bringing to sub-optimal underinvestment decisions.

The corporate governance concerns and conflicts of interest among the stakeholders are exacerbated by the problematic monitoring of debt and control rights in the presence of undetected intangible assets. The creditors' guarantees, including the collateral assets, and the (theoretical) right to liquidate the business, are weakened by the presence of intangible assets with reduced fungibility.

Information asymmetries are constantly fed by imperfections, and cause uncertainty and inefficiencies, in contrast to the correct information. These imperfections translate into an increase in costs and volatility, through distorted estimates, which hinder profitable choices, essential to assess the real impact of intangibles. Because of their fragile boundaries and their intangible, hardly measurable form, immaterial assets are difficult to evaluate and their differential impact on economic and financial flows is uneasy to estimate and identify, as well as their potential replacement cost. IVS 210 and other best practices could help, but are uneasy to implement.

Investments in intangible assets raise problems of replacing assets, to the extent that companies can trade their low-risk assets for riskier investments. Since creditors have a fixed remuneration, the higher risk attributed to the assets is not offset by higher interests and, consequently, there is a transfer of risk from the shareholders to the creditors.

These well-known corporate governance problems must be managed correctly, bringing the interests of internal subjects closer to those of external stakeholders, through monitoring and responsibility.

The progressive evolution from the industrial era to the information age (and industry 4.0) subverts traditional value chains, with an impact on conventional financing forms, with a transition from loans secured with tangible assets to intangible assets, difficult to be negotiated but able to increase the company's value.

Comparability is appreciated when companies must be evaluated through market comparisons, while it is difficult to apply in the case of intangibles with characteristics of uniqueness or exclusivity. Hence the paradox between intangible assets and information asymmetries.

The imitation of legally unprotected intangible assets reduces information asymmetries but compresses their value. Violations are increasingly common in a technological environment where information is easier to obtain, store, and transfer in real-time, to make it publicly available through the web.

The consequences of this paradox, even in terms of bankability, are relevant.

Some strategies can mitigate information asymmetries:

- since the presence of intangible assets increases corporate profitability, attributable only to shareholders, the issue of convertible debt could mitigate the asymmetry between risk and return (Smith & Warner, 1979); if the investment is eventually profitable, bond underwriters can convert the invested sums into equity, so benefiting from the value increase of the firm;
- the voluntary disclosure of the intangible value can fill the information gaps, reducing the asymmetries, reducing the opportunism of the managers, and facilitating value sharing;
- introduction of debt covenants (Smith & Warner, 1979): for example, dividends are limited in the presence of significant intangible assets (as happens with startups);
- reduction of debt extension: the operating debt, which supports intangible investments, is typically short-lived and frequently renegotiated, with an implicit repayment option for creditors, reducing managers' discretion, facilitating monitoring, and mitigating the information asymmetries;
- use of the pecking order hypothesis, in which self-financing (supported by EBITDA, up to the undistributed net profits) fully reflects the contribution of intangible assets, being hierarchically preferred to (riskier) debt and, finally, to new equity;
- protection of intangible assets can be transferred without constraints by the managers (often with shareholders' complicity); if this happens, the creditors can be damaged;
- correct accounting representation of the differential income of intangibles in the income statement, which could mitigate the information asymmetries, traditionally present in the balance sheet, in which intangibles are underestimated.

If companies struggle to survive without developing ever more sophisticated intangible assets, lending banks are challenged by radical changes in their clients' strategies.

For this reason, the valuation of intangible assets is essential also for credit institutions. The lack of soft loans related to intangibles can cause a biased credit allocation, with consequent market inefficiencies.

The main theoretical aspects can be summarized as follows:

1. market and income approaches and, to a lesser extent, cost approaches, consistent with IVS 210 prescriptions, are closely related to accounting parameters, for example, EBITDA;
2. the EBITDA linked to the intangibles is correlated with the operating leverage and digital scalability and has an impact on the operating cash flows (FCFF) serving the debt;
3. the problems of replacing assets can increase corporate risk, but investments in intangible assets, even if without collateral value, can increase economic and financial margins, with a positive impact on debt service;
4. the enterprise value relating to intangibles is positively correlated with bankability and debt coverage;
5. in the event of default, the intellectual capital tends to be worthless, but its presence in going concern situations makes the probability of default more remote.

More research is needed, considering the still obscure relationship between value and assets composition, closely related to debt service, in the presence of intangible assets.

The hierarchy and the composition of funding sources represent another fundamental aspect, which needs further investigation: according to the Pecking Order Hypothesis elaborated by Myers and Majluf (1984), the cost of indebtedness increases in the presence of information asymmetries and intangibles. Among the sources of funding, companies give priority to self-financing and, after cheap borrowing, to equity.

Since intangible assets represent a driver of operating margins (EBITDA), their strategic presence is consistent with the pecking order. Accordingly, when investments in intangibles are significant, as is the case for growth and digitally-oriented companies, and the ability to borrow is limited, companies mostly rely on their equity, so being self-financed by the shareholders, and by the internally generated cash (EBITDA).

In-depth analyses and research are required for this critical value driver issue, especially in recessionary situations.

The IAS compliant financial valuation, although recognized as the preferable one for the valuation of the intangibles, still represents an uphill road, which needs further improvements.

The differential impact of intangible assets on value, starting from Porter's (1998) theory on competitive advantage, represents a well-known cornerstone in terms of independent assessment of the intangible assets, but its correct application is still uneasy, especially due to the accounting issues related to internally generated intangibles. Identifying and estimating the hidden value of intangibles remains a daunting task.

Information asymmetries preserve, while keeping hidden, the value of intangibles, with a double-edged impact on bankability.

The value of the intangibles grows, as they represent the main strategic driver at the base of differentiation, with economic and financial marginal improvements on value.

24.12   CORPORATE GOVERNANCE CONCERNS IN A DIGITAL SCENARIO

According to the survey of Shleifer and Vishny (1997) "corporate governance deals the ways in which suppliers of finance to corporations assure themselves of getting a return on their investment. How do the suppliers of finance get managers to return some of the profits to them? How do they make sure that managers do not steal the capital they supply or invest it in bad projects? How do suppliers of finance control managers? At first glance, it is not entirely obvious why the suppliers of capital get anything back. After all, they part with their money and have little to contribute to the enterprise afterward. The professional managers or entrepreneurs who run the firms might as well abscond with the money. Although they sometimes do, usually they do not (…). In fact, the subject of corporate governance is of enormous practical importance".

And again "people who sink the capital need to be assured that they get back the return on this capital. The corporate governance mechanisms provide this assurance".

The very first concern, a core point within standard companies, deals with managerial discretion (investment in bad projects; improper retention or diversion of cash …), a well-known agency problem (being the manager the agent of the principal's money deriving from equity holders and debtholders).

A core issue of corporate governance is concerned with the agency problem, sometimes referred to as the separation of ownership from control, within firms that can be interpreted as a Coasian nexus of contracts among different resource holders.

Agency relationships arise whenever an individual, called a principal, delegates other individuals, called agents, to perform some service; the two main relationships are:

- the principal-stockholders and the agents-managers, which are delegated to invest shareholders' capital;
- the principal-debtholders and the agents-stockholders, where the former provide funds to the firm, underwriting debt, and these funds are managed by stockholders and their ultimate agents, represented by managers, following the aforementioned relationship.

Since these relationships are not necessarily harmonious, conflicts of interests may easily arise and so agency theory is primarily concerned with the binding mechanisms and incentives that principals may use with agents to get their money back, possibly with a fair and risk-adjusted gain.

In an ideal world where managers already own all the money they need for investments, principals would coincide with agents and no agency conflict would arise; the problem surges whenever specialized managers lack the money they need for investments, but also when financiers need the managers' expertise and professional skills to properly manage their money: mutual convenience is the natural glue behind any agreement.

According to agency theory, in imperfect labor and capital markets, managers will inevitably seek to maximize their utility at the expense of shareholders. Agents-managers can operate in their conflicting self-interests rather than in the best interests of the firm. This happens as a consequence of asymmetric inside information (since they know better than shareholders whether they are capable of meeting the shareholders' objectives) and physiological uncertainty (since myriad factors contribute to outcomes, it may so not be evident whether the agent directly caused a given outcome, positive or negative).

The legal protection system of creditors in project finance is represented by a complex nexus of loan contracts, together with monitoring powers—and duties—from the debtholders' side. Loan contracts are the legal backbone behind financial and economic bankability and their binding nature intrinsically minimizes managerial discretion.

According again to Shleifer and Vishny (1997) "the agency problem in this context refers to the difficulties financiers have in assuring that their funds are not expropriated or wasted on unattractive projects. The trouble is, most future contingencies are hard to describe and foresee, and as a result, complete contracts are technologically infeasible". And again: "When contracts are incomplete and managers possess more expertise than shareholders, managers typically end up with the residual rights of control, giving them enormous latitude for self-interested behavior".

The utopia of complete contracts, ideally able to cover with their legal provisions all the possible states of the world, has to realistically face an imperfect context, where unforeseen and risky events are always possible and likely to occur. To minimize problems and fallacies within necessarily incomplete contracts, two different approaches may be used and confronted, each with its advantages and pitfalls:

- detailed contractual provisions, trying to regulate with analytical clauses any possible situation and state of the world, targeting "complete" contracting goals;
- extensive referral to existing laws and codes, following general principles, as far as possible.

The dichotomy between long/detailed versus short/generalized contracts is also influenced by the general legal system of the country where investments are located; civil law countries, particularly concentrated in Continental Europe, make the reference to codified laws easier and more systematic, whereas common law countries, following analogical court cases, are more diffused in Anglo-Saxon countries and typically bring to more detailed contractual provisions, within a less codified general framework.

Since contracts are ontologically incomplete, legal protection may be insufficient for shareholders, in their potential conflicts with managers, and especially for debtholders, in their conflicting interests with shareholders. Conflicts may arise also between managers and debtholders, for example, if the former illegally extract money for personal abuses, threatening proper debt service and breaching their duty of loyalty, even though they are typically intermediated by shareholders, who appoint the managers. Bank loans are typically contracted by the managers with the lending institutions but even here there might be a role for shareholders, who may smooth the relationship with their reputational standing or with personal guarantees.

Another typical conflict of interests between managers and investors is concerned with managerial discretionary investment decisions, which may typically reflect the personal interests of the former. According to the free cash flow theory elaborated by Jensen (1986), managers are inclined to reinvest the free cash in the company rather than return it to investors; this over-investment problem, is opposed to the under-investment problem where the conflicts of interest are between shareholders and debtholders, is however quite unlikely within the project finance industry, also because investments are notoriously not so discretionary and free cash flow may form only after many years, when high initial leverage reaches a much lower level; also dividends, that cash out free liquidity, are typically foreseen since inception and, to the extent that they can be paid, it is uneasy not to fulfill this commitment toward thirsty shareholders.

Agency problems may undermine the reputation of agents acting in their self-interest and, from the other side, reputation-building, so useful for managers seeking employment, but also for shareholders attempting to collect the debt, is a common explanation for why people respect their commitments even if they cannot (always) be forced to do so.

Within the capital structure theoretical models, there is an important paper by Myers and Majluf (1984) regarding information asymmetries and raised capital. Since managers have inside superior information, these asymmetries increase the cost of collecting external capital. This cost may be minimized by raising at first funds that are weakly sensitive to asymmetric information, i.e., for example secured debt; equity may be collected only at a premium that properly discounts these asymmetries; in this however in the self-interest of managers to voluntarily minimize information asymmetries, with self-imposed monitoring and transparency, to ease the equity placement, so decreasing its cost.

Intangible assets have a deep influence on most of the corporate governance issues that have been synthetically recalled here. A better understanding of how these issues might be interpreted may shed new light on the way intangible-driven firms are appraised. And corporate governance concerns may be explained with network theory applications, as shown in Moro Visconti (2019).

NOTES

1. This is consistent with Modigliani and Miller (1958) proposition II, according to which the differential (ROIC − i) between Return on Investment Capital and the cost of debt (i) is multiplied by the financial leverage (debt/equity).
2. See Sect. 2.4.
3. The Altman Z-score is the output of a credit-strength algorithm that forecasts firm's likelihood of bankruptcy. It is based on five financial ratios that calculate from data found on a firm's annual reports. It uses profitability, leverage, liquidity, solvency, and activity to predict whether a firm has high probability of being insolvent.

SELECTED REFERENCES

Abell, M. (2009). Mixed know-how and patent licensing agreement. In D. Campbell & R. Proksch (Eds.), *International business transactions* (pp. 5–20). Alphen aan den Rijn, The Netherlands: Kluwer Law International.

Aboody, D., & Lev, B. (2000). Information asymmetry, R&D, and insider gains. *Journal of Finance, 55*(6), 2747–2766.

Al-Najjar, B., & Elgammal, M. M. (2013). Innovation and credit ratings, does it matter? UK evidence. *Applied Economics Letters, 20*(5), 428–431.

Andriessen, D. (2004). IC valuation and measurement: Classifying the state of the art. *Journal of Intellectual Capital, 5*(2), 230–242.

Arvidsson, S. (2011). Disclosure of non-financial information in the annual report: A management-team perspective. *Journal of Intellectual Capital, 12*(2), 277–300.

Baeyens, K., & Manigart, S. (2006). *Who gets private equity? The role of debt capacity, growth and intangible assets* (Vlerick Leuven Gent Management School Working Paper Series 2006-24). Available at http://ideas.repec.org/p/vlg/vlgwps/2006-24.html

Ballester, M., Garcia-Ayuso, M., & Livnat, J. (2003). The economic value of the R&D intangible asset. *European Accounting Review, 12*(4), 605–633. Available at http://3ws-contabilidad.ua.es/trabajos/2024.pdf

Black, F. (1986). Noise. *Journal of Finance, 41*(3), 529–543.

Black, F., & Scholes, M. (1973). The pricing of options and corporate liabilities. *The Journal of Political Economy, 81*(3, May–June), 637–654.

Boujelben, S., & Fedhila, H. (2011). The effects of intangible investments on future OCF. *Journal of Intellectual Capital, 12*(4), 480–494.

Bradley, M., Jarrel, G. A., & Kim, E. H. (1984). On the existence of optimal capital structure: Theory and evidence. *Journal of Finance, 39*, 857–880.

Brennan, M. J. (1990). Latent assets. *The Journal of Finance, 45*(3, July), 709–730.

Chen, M. C., Cheng, S. J., & Hwang, Y. (2005). An empirical investigation of the relationship between intellectual capital and firms' market value and financial performance. *Journal of Intellectual Capital, 6*(2), 159–176.

Corcoles, Y. R. (2010). Towards the convergence of accounting treatment for intangible assets. *Intangible Capital, 6*(2), 185–201.

Degryse, H., De Goeij, P., & Kappert, P. (2012). The impact of firm and industry characteristics on small firm's capital structure. *Small Business Economics, 38*(4), 431–447.

Galai, D., & Masulis, R. W. (1976). The option pricing model and the risk factor of stock. *Journal of Financial Economics, 3*(1–2), 53–81.

Garcia-Meca, M., Parra, I., Larran, M., & Martinez, I. (2005). The explanatory factors of intellectual capital disclosure to financial analysts. *European Accounting Review, 14*(1), 63–94.

Garcia-Parra, M., Simo, P., Sallan, J. M., & Mundet, J. (2009). Intangible liabilities: Beyond models of intellectual assets. *Management Decision, 47*(5), 819–830.

Giuliani, M. (2013). Not all sunshine and roses: Discovering intellectual liabilities "in action." *Journal of Intellectual Capital, 14*(1), 127–144.

Giuliani, M., & Marasca, M. (2011). Construction and valuation of intellectual capital: A case study. *Journal of Intellectual Capital, 12*(3), 377–391.

Green, R. C. (1984). Investment incentives, debt, and warrants. *Journal of Financial Economics, 13*, 115–136.

Grossman, S. J., & Hart, O. D. (1982). Corporate financial structure and managerial incentives. In J. J. McCall (Ed.), *The economics of information and uncertainty*. University of Chicago Press.

Harris, M., & Raviv, A. (1990). Capital structure and the informational role of debt. *The Journal of Finance, 45*(2), 321–349.

Jensen, M. (1986). Agency cost of free cash flow, corporate finance, and takeovers. *American Economic Review, 76*(2), 323–329.

Jensen, M., & Meckling, W. (1976). Theory of the firm: Managerial behaviour, agency costs and ownership structure. *Journal of Financial Economics, 3*(4), 305–306. Available at http://www.sfu.ca/~wainwrig/Econ400/jensenmeckling

Kristandl, G., & Bontis, N. (2007). The impact of voluntary disclosure on cost of equity capital estimates in a temporal setting. *Journal of Intellectual Capital, 8*(4), 577–594.

Lagrost, C., Martin, D., Dubois, C., & Quazzotti, S. (2010). Intellectual property valuation: How to approach the selection of an appropriate valuation method. *Journal of Intellectual Capital, 11*(4), 481–503.

Leland, H., & Pyle, D. (1977). Informational asymmetries, financial structure, and financial intermediation. *Journal of Finance, 32*(2), 371–387.

Lim, S., Macia, A. J., & Moeller, T. (2018, June 4). *Intangible assets and capital structure*. Available at SSRN: https://ssrn.com/abstract=2514551

Long, M. S., & Malitz, E. B. (1985). Investment patterns and financial leverage. In B. Freidman (Ed.), *Corporate capital structures in the United States*. Chicago: University of Chicago Press.

Maditinos, D., Chatzoudes, D., Tsairidis, C., & Theriou, G. (2011). The impact of intellectual capital on firms' market value and financial performance. *Journal of Intellectual Capital, 12*(1), 132–151.

Metha, A. D., & Madhani, P. M. (2008). Intangible assets—An introduction. *The Accounting World, 8*(9), 11–19.

Modigliani, F., & Miller, M. (1958). The cost of capital, corporation finance and the theory of investment. *American Economic Review, 48*(3), 261–297.

Moro Visconti, R. (2012). Exclusive patents and trademarks and subsequent uneasy transaction comparability: Some transfer pricing implications. *Intertax, 40*(3), 212–219.

Moro Visconti, R. (2013). Evaluating know-how for transfer price benchmarking. *Journal of Finance and Accounting, 1*(1), 27–38.

Moro Visconti, R. (2019). Combining network theory with corporate governance: Converging models for connected stakeholders. *Corporate Ownership & Control, 17*(1), 125–139.

Mouritsen, J., Bukh, P. N., & Marr, B. (2004). Reporting on intellectual capital: Why, what and how? *Measuring Business Excellence, 8*(1), 46–54.

Myers, S. C. (1977). Determinants of corporate borrowing. *Journal of Financial Economics, 5*, 147–175.

Myers, S. C., & Majluf, N. S. (1984). Corporate financing and investment decisions when firms have information that investors do not have. *Journal of Financial Economics, 13*(2), 187–221. Available at http://www.nber.org/papers/w1396.pdf?new_window=1

Oestreicher, A. (2011). Valuation issues in transfer pricing of intangibles: Comments on the scoping of an OECD project. *Intertax, 39*(3), 126–131.

Porter, M. E. (1998). *Competitive advantage: Creating and sustaining superior performance*. New York: Free Press.

Roslender, R., & Fincham, R. (2001). Thinking critically about intellectual capital accounting. *Accounting, Auditing and Accountability Journal, 14*(4), 383–399.

Shleifer, A., & Vishny, R. W. (1997). A survey of corporate governance. *Journal of Finance, 52*(2), 737–783.

Singh, J. P. (2013). On the intricacies of cash flow corporate valuation. *Advances in Management, 6*(3), 15–22.

Singh, S., & Kansal, M. (2011). Voluntary disclosures of intellectual capital: An empirical analysis. *Journal of Intellectual Capital, 12*(2), 301–318.

Smith, C. W., & Warner, J. (1979). On financial contracting: An analysis of bond covenants. *Journal of Financial Economics, 7*(2), 117–161.

Titman, S., & Wessels, R. (1988). The determinants of capital structure choice. *The Journal of Finance, 43*, 1–19.

Valladares Soler, L. E., & Cuello De Oro, C. D. J. (2007). Evaluating the scope of IC in firms' value. *Journal of Intellectual Capital, 8*(3), 470–493.

Vanacker, T. R., & Manigart, S. (2010). Pecking order and debt capacity considerations for high-growth companies seeking financing. *Small Business Economics, 35*(1), 53–69.

Wu, X., & Yeung, C. K. A. (2012). Firm growth type and capital structure persistence. *Journal of Banking & Finance, 36*(12), 3427–3443.

INDEX

A

actuators, 257, 279, 427, 428, 432

adjacency matrix, 443, 444, 547

advertising, 4, 55, 57, 64, 90, 114, 117, 144, 180, 243, 251, 261, 288, 289, 298, 311, 312, 317, 322, 323, 326–329, 333–336, 339, 341, 352, 355–360, 362, 366, 371, 377, 384, 386, 389, 399, 449, 450, 456, 457, 459, 460, 473, 494, 500, 505, 525, 537, 541, 542, 593, 634, 677, 766

agency costs of debt, 770

algorithm, 3–5, 17, 74, 87, 144, 219, 220, 237, 255, 267, 268, 270, 272, 274, 323, 326–330, 351, 354, 357, 362, 364, 366, 377, 385, 389, 394, 406–408, 414, 418, 430, 432, 450, 460, 519, 604

Analytics as a Service (AaaS), 407

Android, 238, 385, 386, 394

Application Service Provider (ASP), 252, 428

application software, 239, 355, 384, 389, 395

App store, 243, 386

artificial intelligence (AI), 1–3, 5, 16, 17, 74, 115, 120, 123, 124, 129, 131, 134, 157, 183, 184, 219, 221–223, 255, 265–268, 270, 272–277, 279, 280, 313, 403, 408, 414, 417, 419, 429, 455, 456, 471, 484, 506, 512, 530, 538, 544, 598, 600, 604, 608, 637, 643, 646, 648, 700, 712, 737

artwork, 342, 491, 496, 503, 542

augmented reality (AR), 16, 267–269, 275, 313, 515, 530, 540, 601

Avatar, 515–517, 532–534, 536, 542, 543, 545, 548, 549, 553, 554

Average Revenue per User (ARPU), 436, 451, 459